AF521873

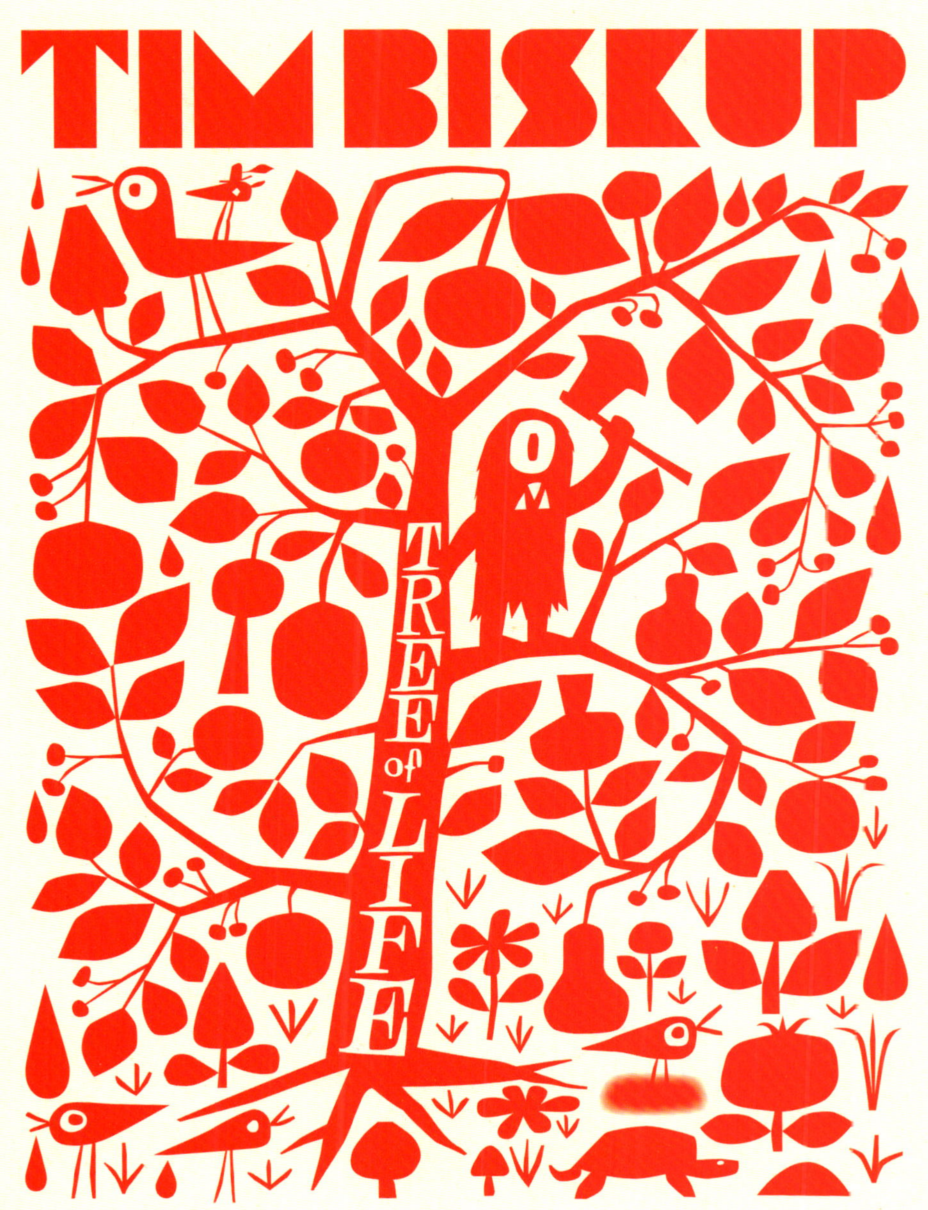

CHRONICLE CHROMA

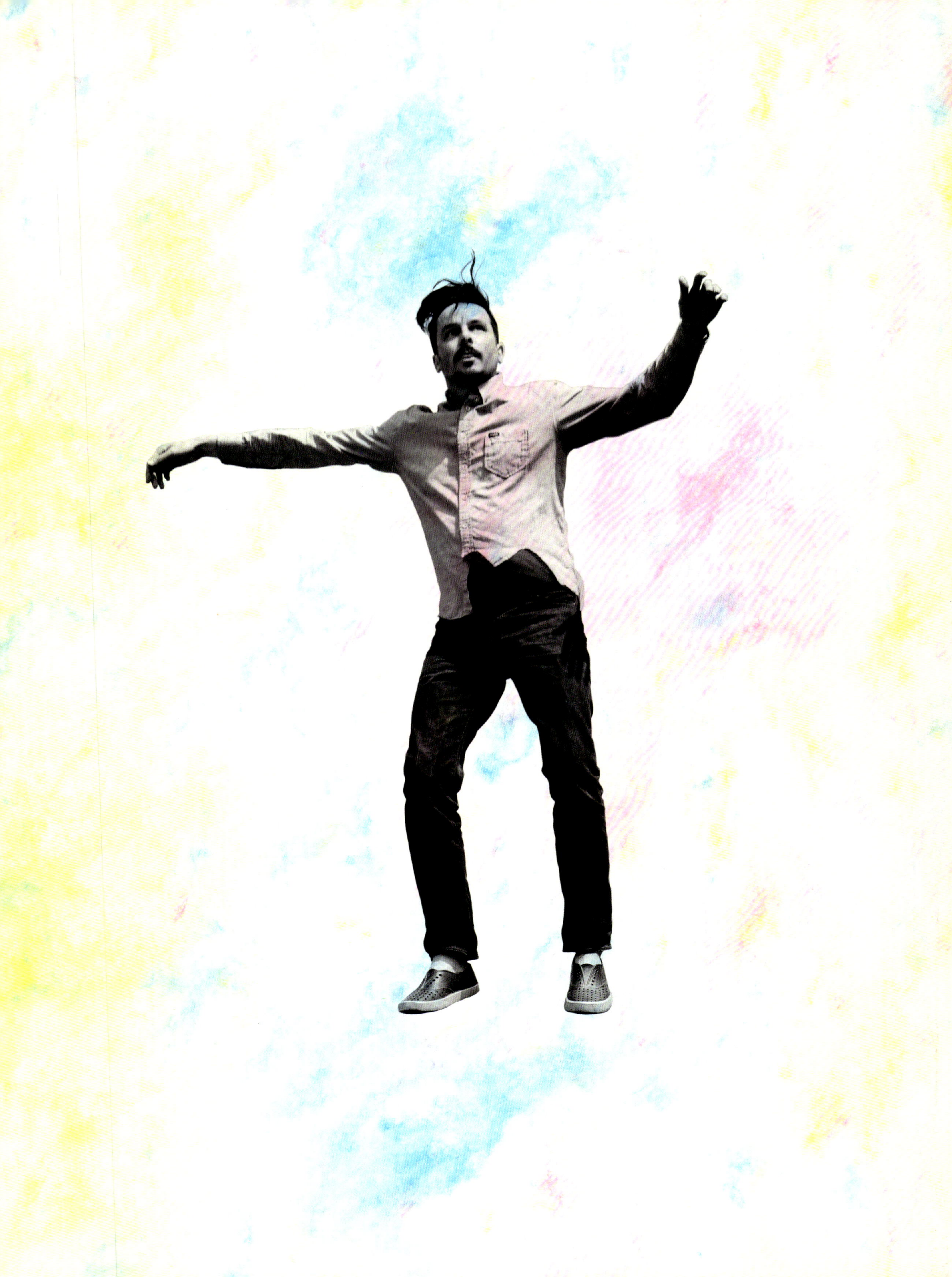

I always thought that being a good artist was about finding the perfect balance of chaos and strategy. When there was too much chaos I felt like a crazy person wallowing in nonsense that only I could understand. If I applied too much strategy I felt like a salesman hawking a product and missing my soul. This book shows some of what I made over the past few decades in my search for that balance. In the process I found that if I simply trust my intuition and work hard, balance (and happiness) comes naturally.

I have taken a break from showing my art in galleries and opened my own venue called Face Guts where I can present my work in all of its many forms. If you find yourself in Los Angeles, come say hello.

Thank you,
Tim

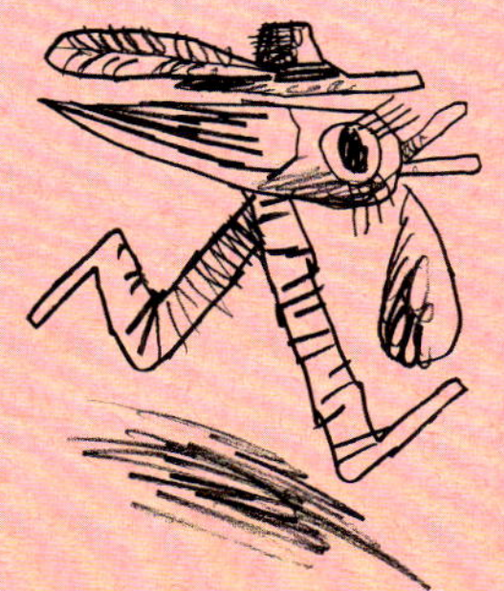

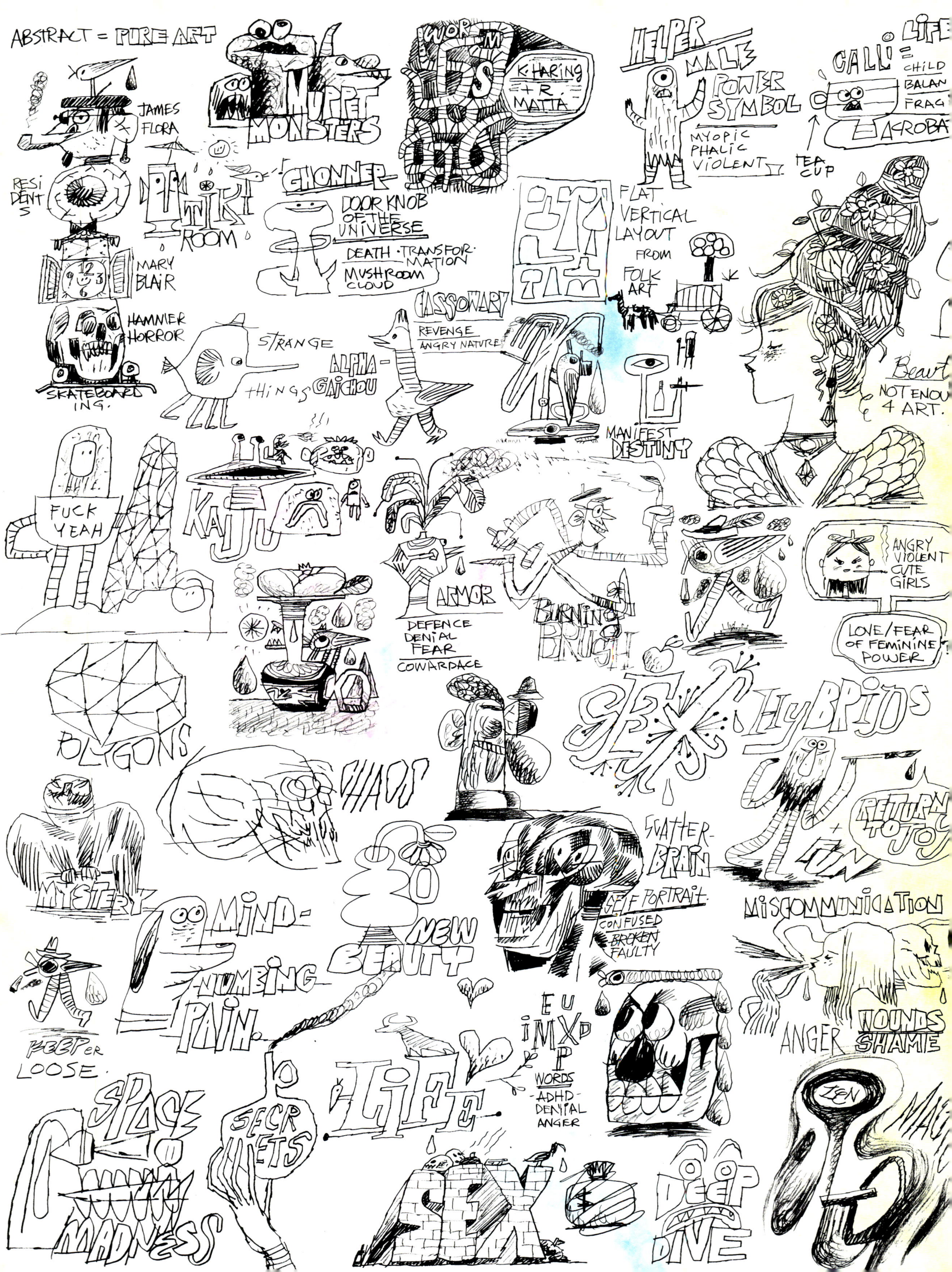

ABSTRACT = PURE ART
MUPPET MONSTERS
K. HARING + R. MATTA
HELPER
MALE POWER SYMBOL
MYOPIC PHALIC VIOLENT
TEA CUP
CALLI = LIFE
CHILD
BALAN
FRAG
ACROBA
JAMES FLORA
RESIDENTS
TIKI ROOM
GHONNER
DOOR KNOB OF THE UNIVERSE
DEATH TRANSFORMATION
MUSHROOM CLOUD
FLAT VERTICAL LAYOUT FROM FOLK ART
MARY BLAIR
HAMMER HORROR
SKATEBOARDING.
STRANGE THINGS
ALPHA-GAICHOU
CASSOWARY
REVENGE
ANGRY NATURE
MANIFEST DESTINY
NOT ENOU
4 ART.
FUCK YEAH
KAIJU
ARMOR
DEFENCE DENIAL FEAR
COWARDACE
BURNING BRUSH
ANGRY VIOLENT CUTE GIRLS
LOVE/FEAR OF FEMININE POWER
POLYGONS
SEX
HYBRIDS
CHAOS
RETURN TO JOY
SCATTER-BRAIN
MYSTERY
MIND-NUMBING PAIN
NEW BEAUTY
SELF PORTRAIT
CONFUSED BROKEN FAULTY
MISCOMMUNICATION
ANGER
WOUNDS SHAME
KEEPER LOOSE
MIXED UP WORDS
- ADHD - DENIAL ANGER
SPACE MADNESS
SECRETS
LIFE
SEX
DEEP DIVE
ZEN

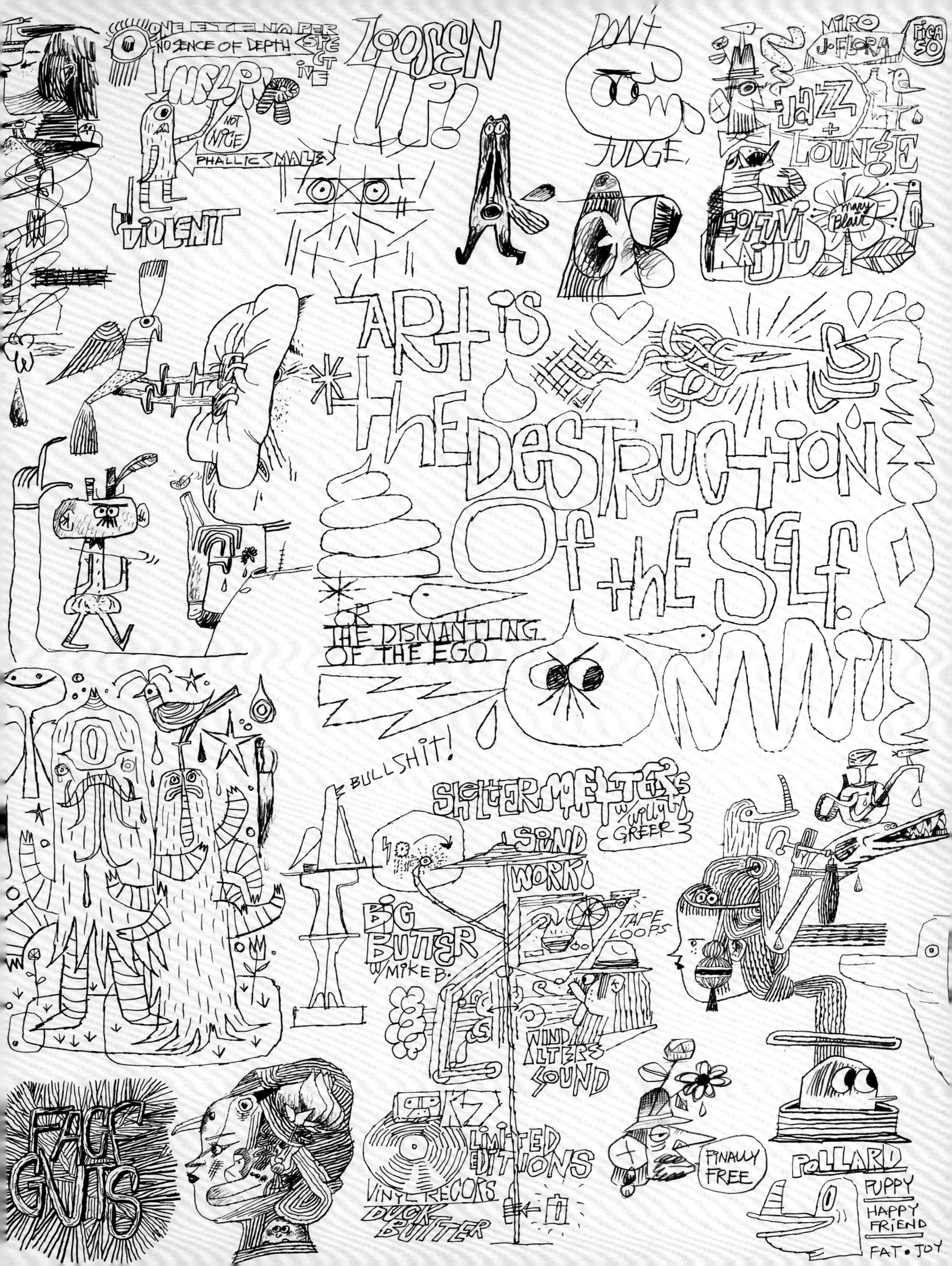

NO SENCE OF DEPTH
NOT NICE
PHALLIC MALE
VIOLENT
LOOSEN UP!
DON'T JUDGE.
MIRO
J. FLORA
PICASSO
JAZZ + LOUNGE
Mary Blair
KAIJU
ART IS THE DESTRUCTION OF THE SELF.
OR THE DISMANTLING OF THE EGO
BULLSHIT!
SHELTER MELTERS
w/ WILLY GREER
SOUND WORK
TAPE LOOPS
BIG BUTTER w/ MIKE B.
WIND ALTERS SOUND
LIMITED EDITIONS
VINYL RECORDS
DUCK BUTTER
FACE GUTS
FINALLY FREE
POLLARD
PUPPY
HAPPY FRIEND
FAT • JOY

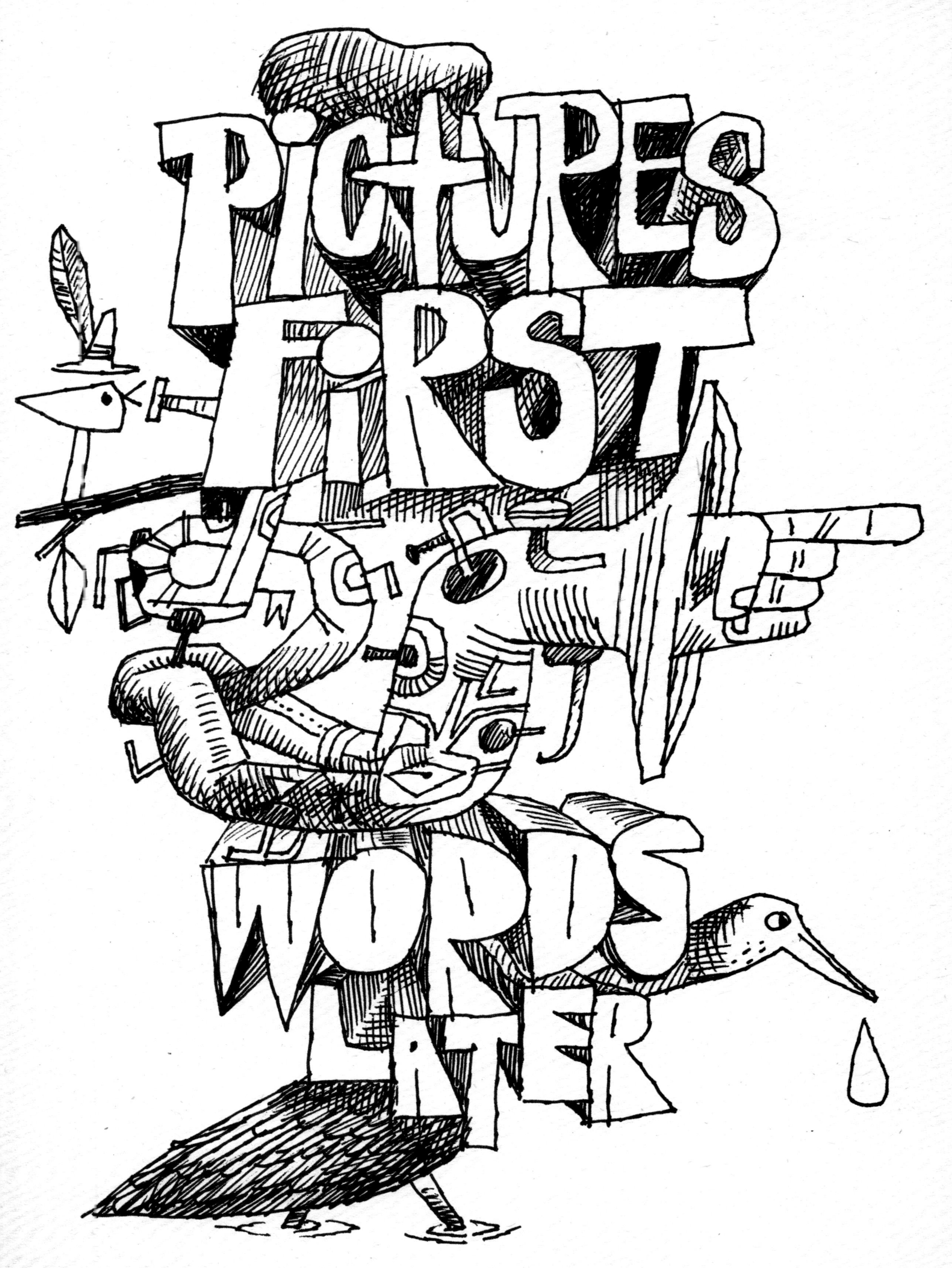
PICTURES
FIRST
WORDS
LATER

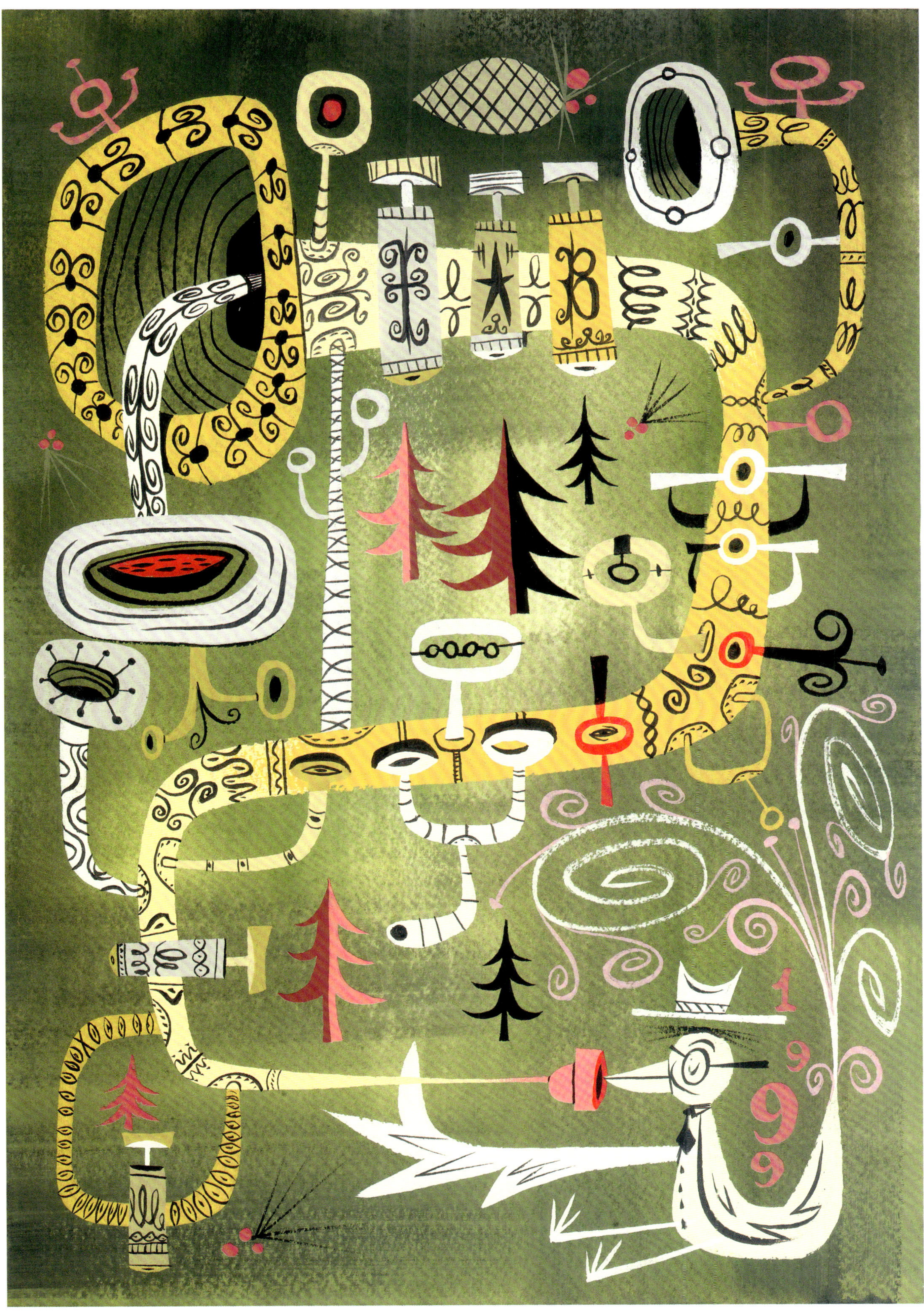

Blow, Bird, Blow
1999. Gouache on Paper. 9" x 7"

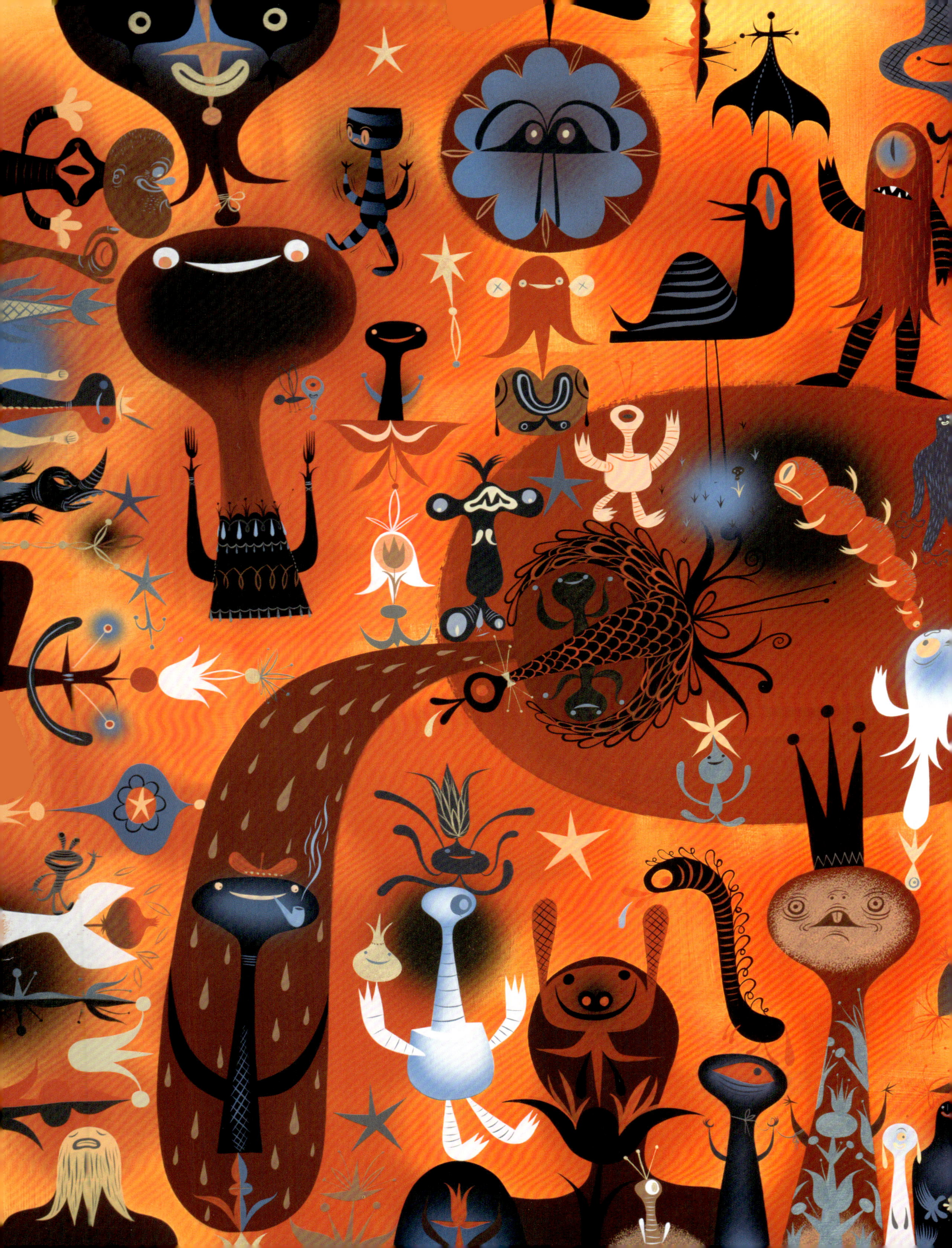

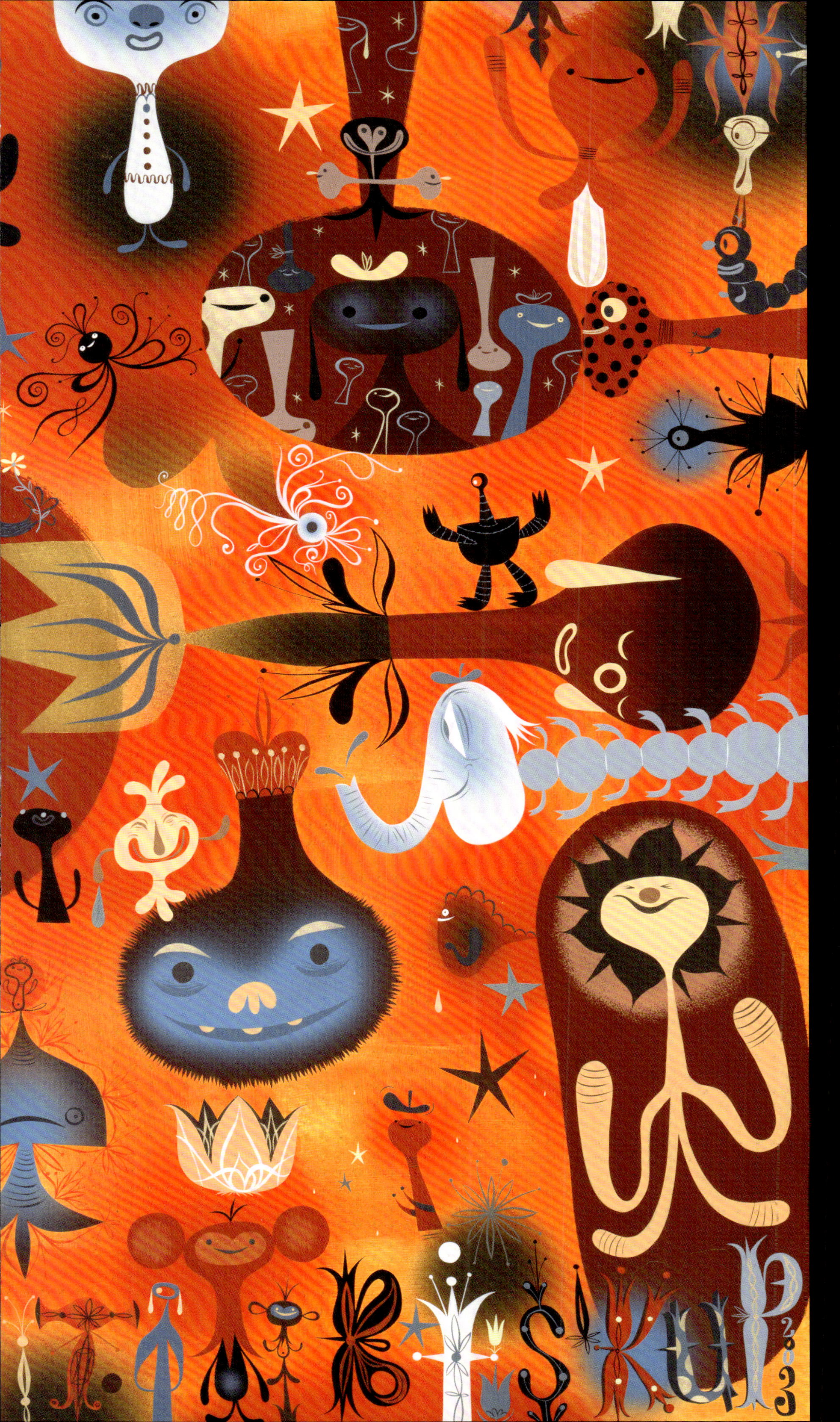

The Doorknob of the Universe
2003. Gouache on Panel. 36" x 48

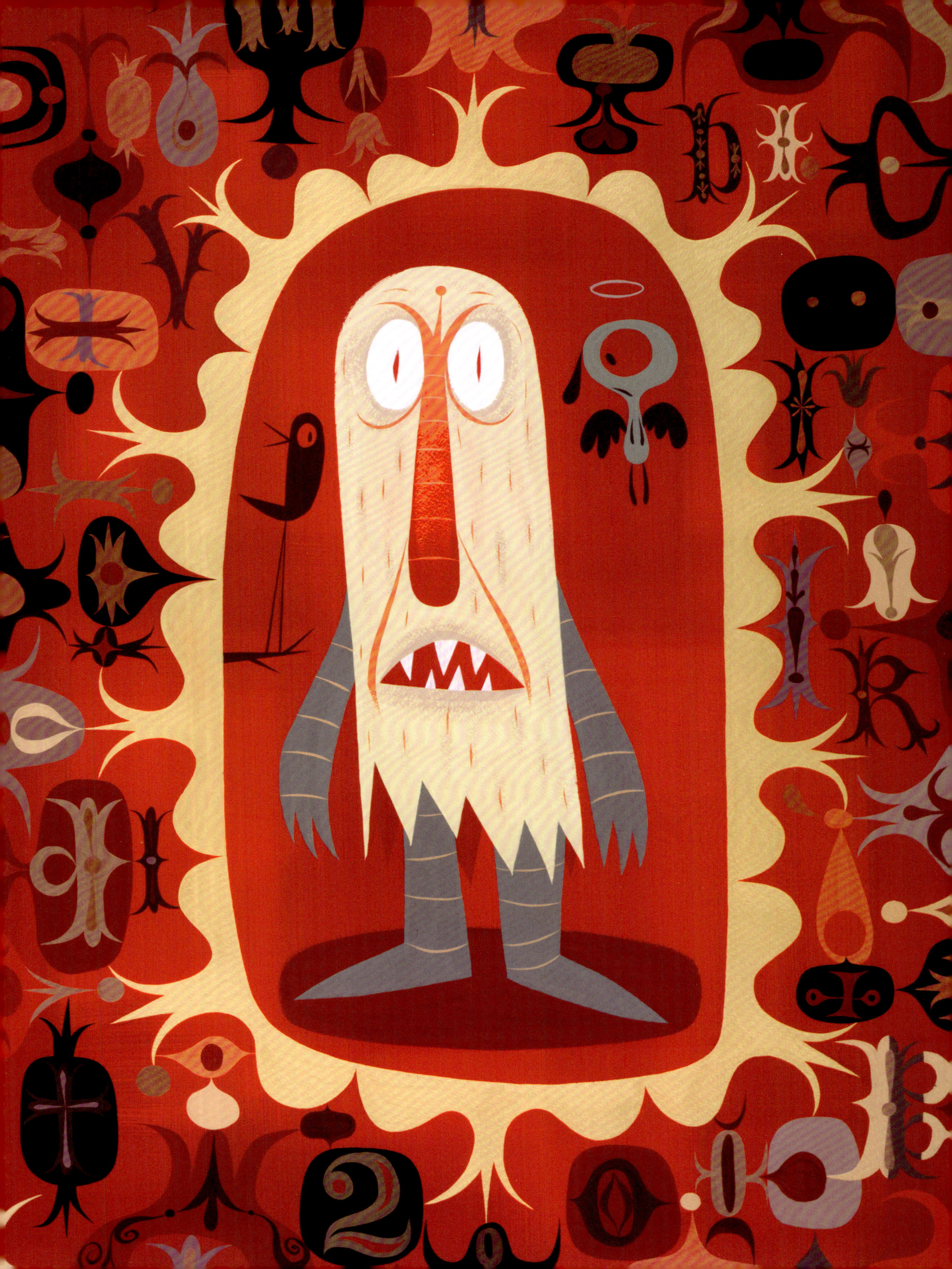

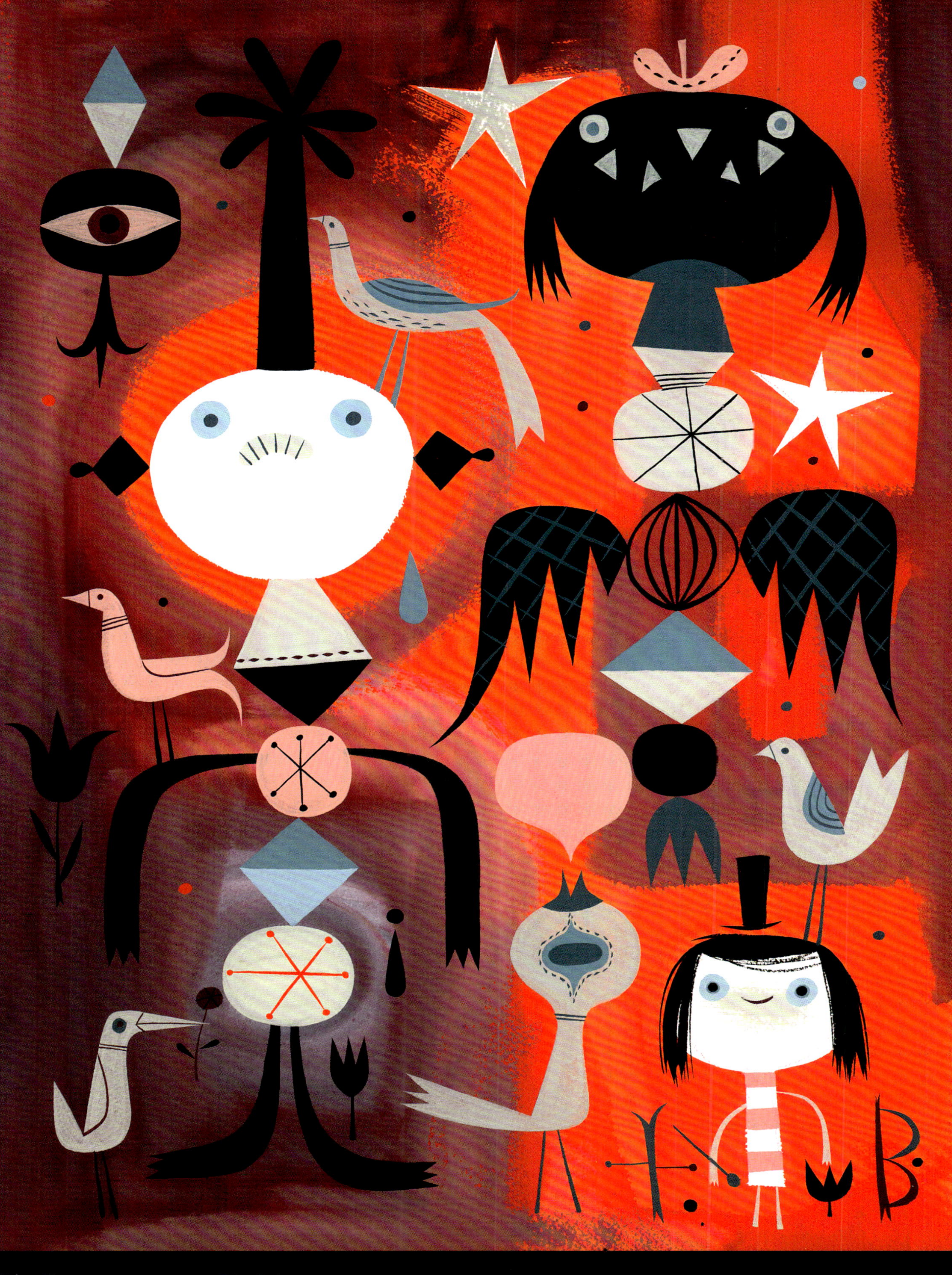

Helper: Blur
2002. Gouache on Paper. 29" x 20"

Totem Park
2005. Acrylic on Paper. 24" x 18"

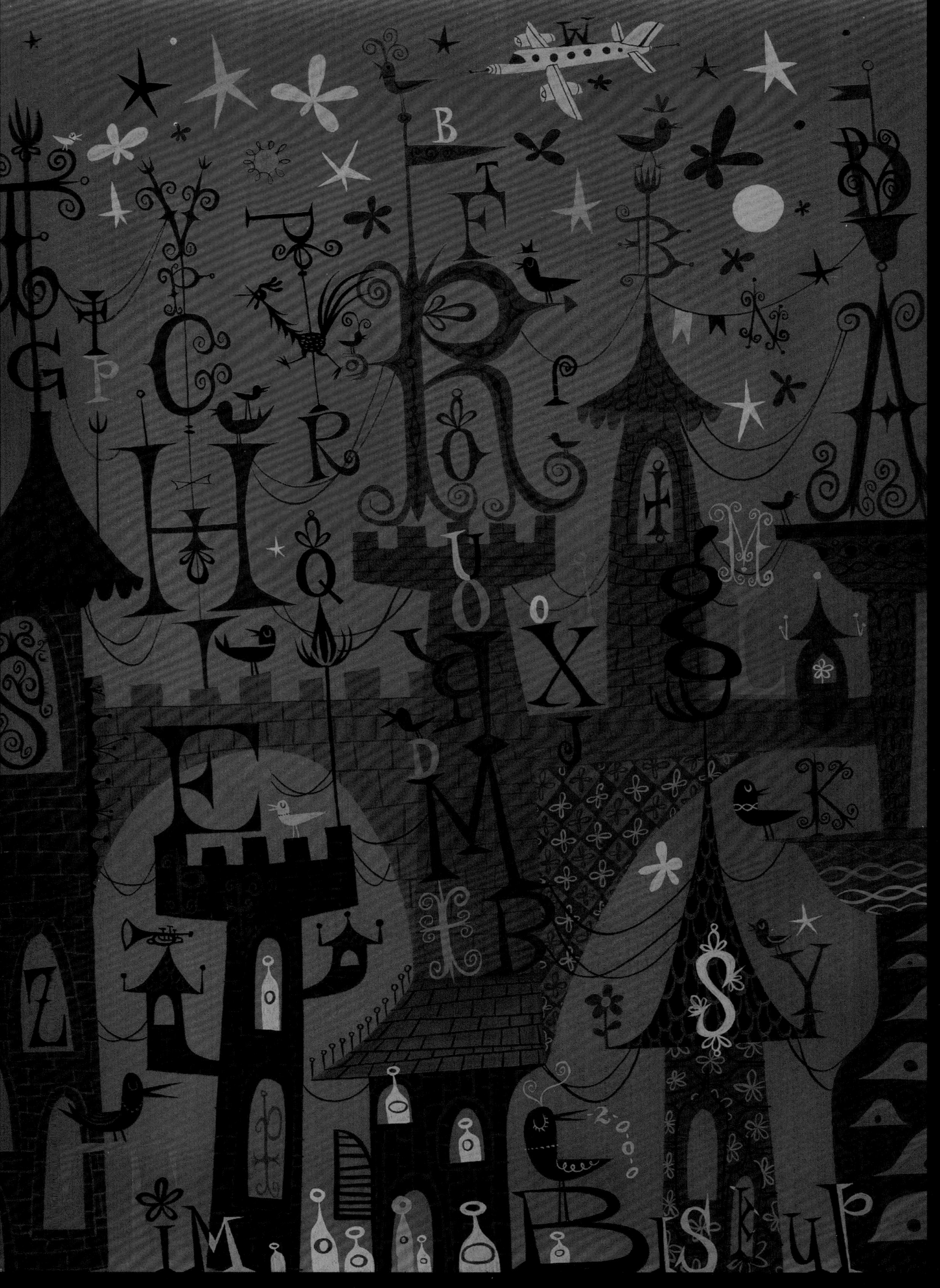
BISKUP

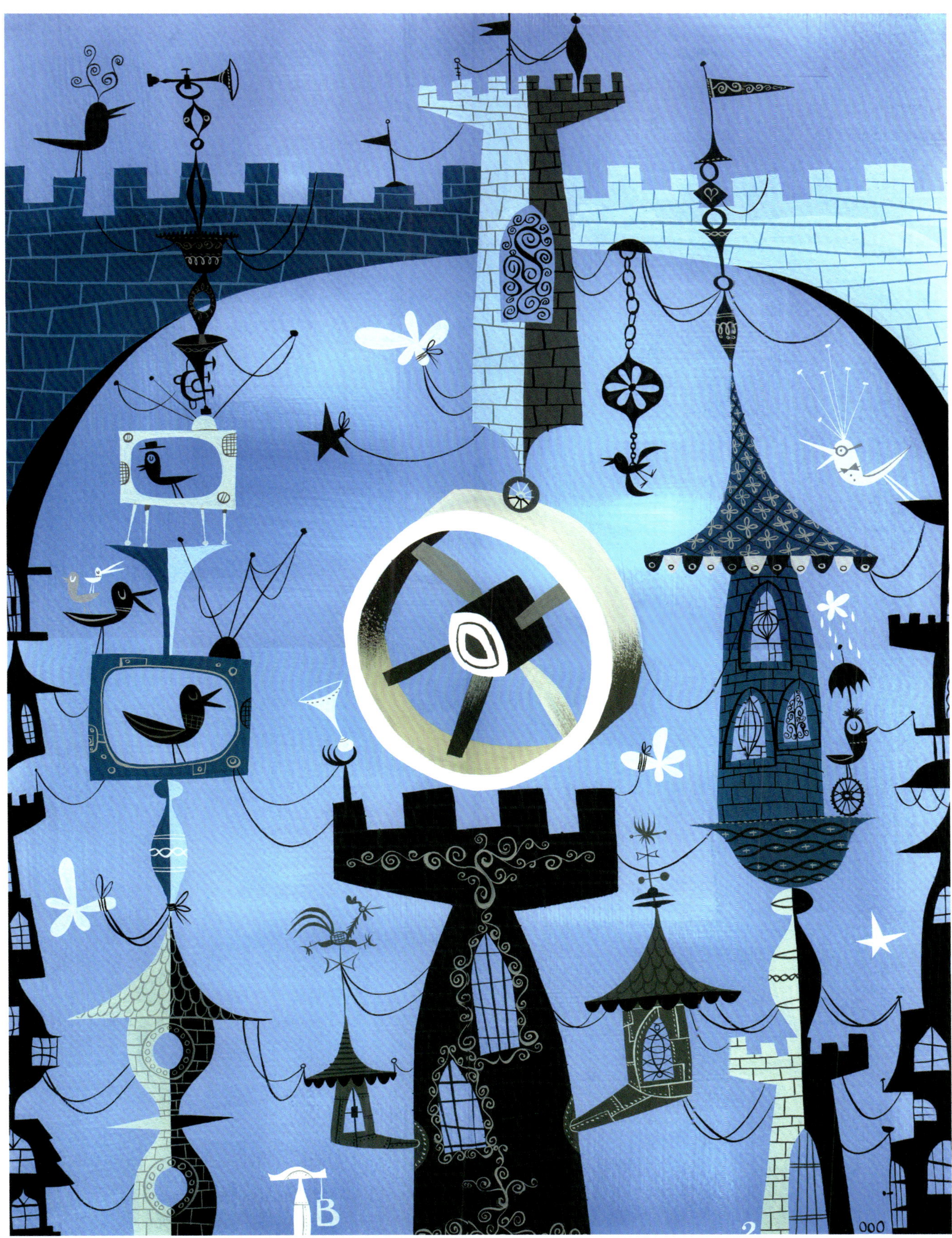

Alphabet Castle
2000. Gouache on Paper. 20" x 16"

Blue Castle Wheel
2002. Gouache on Paper. 20" x 16"

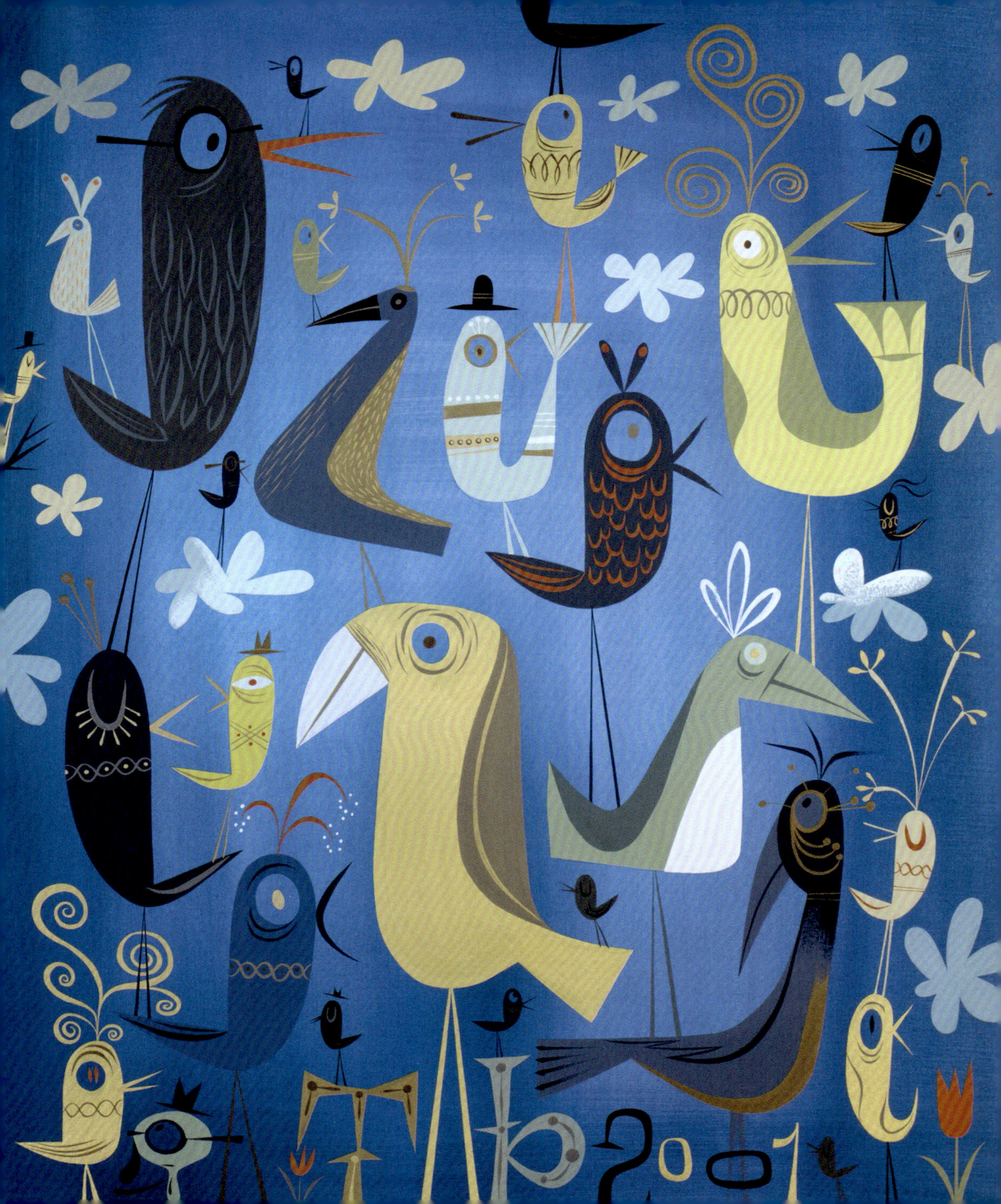
2001

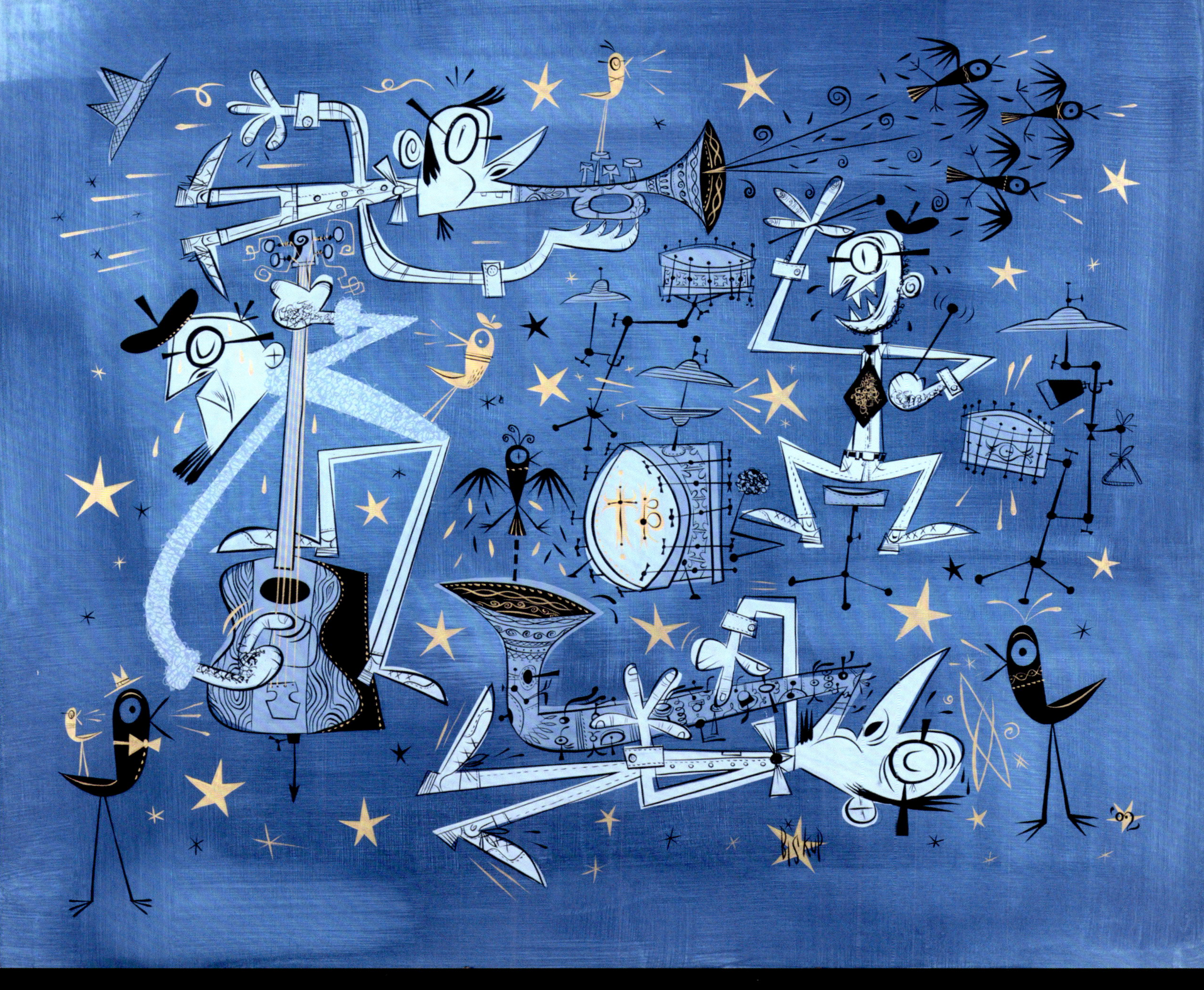

Bluebird Band
2002. Gouache on Panel. 25" x 30"

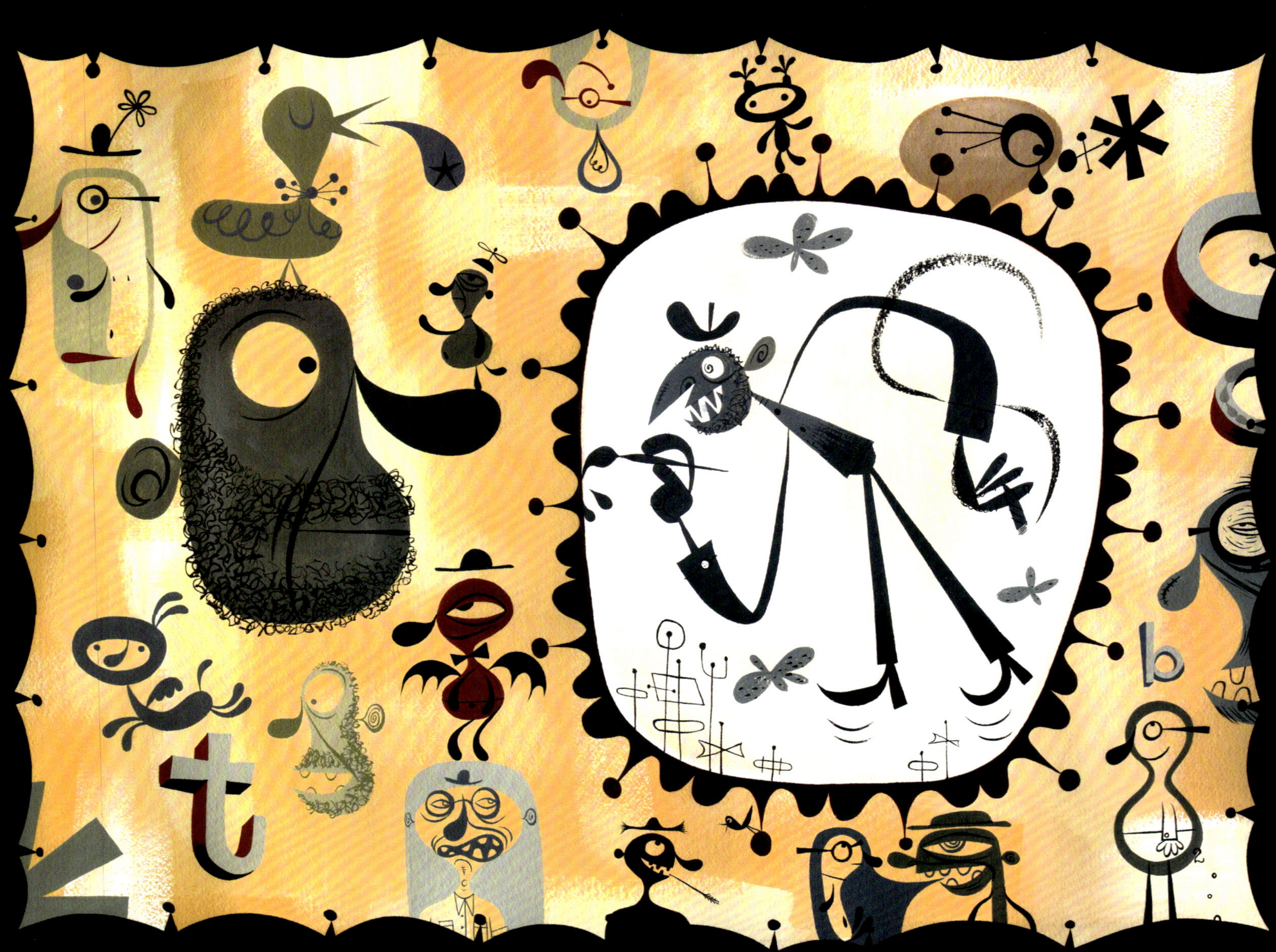

The Demon Painter
2000. Gouache on Paper. 18" x 24"

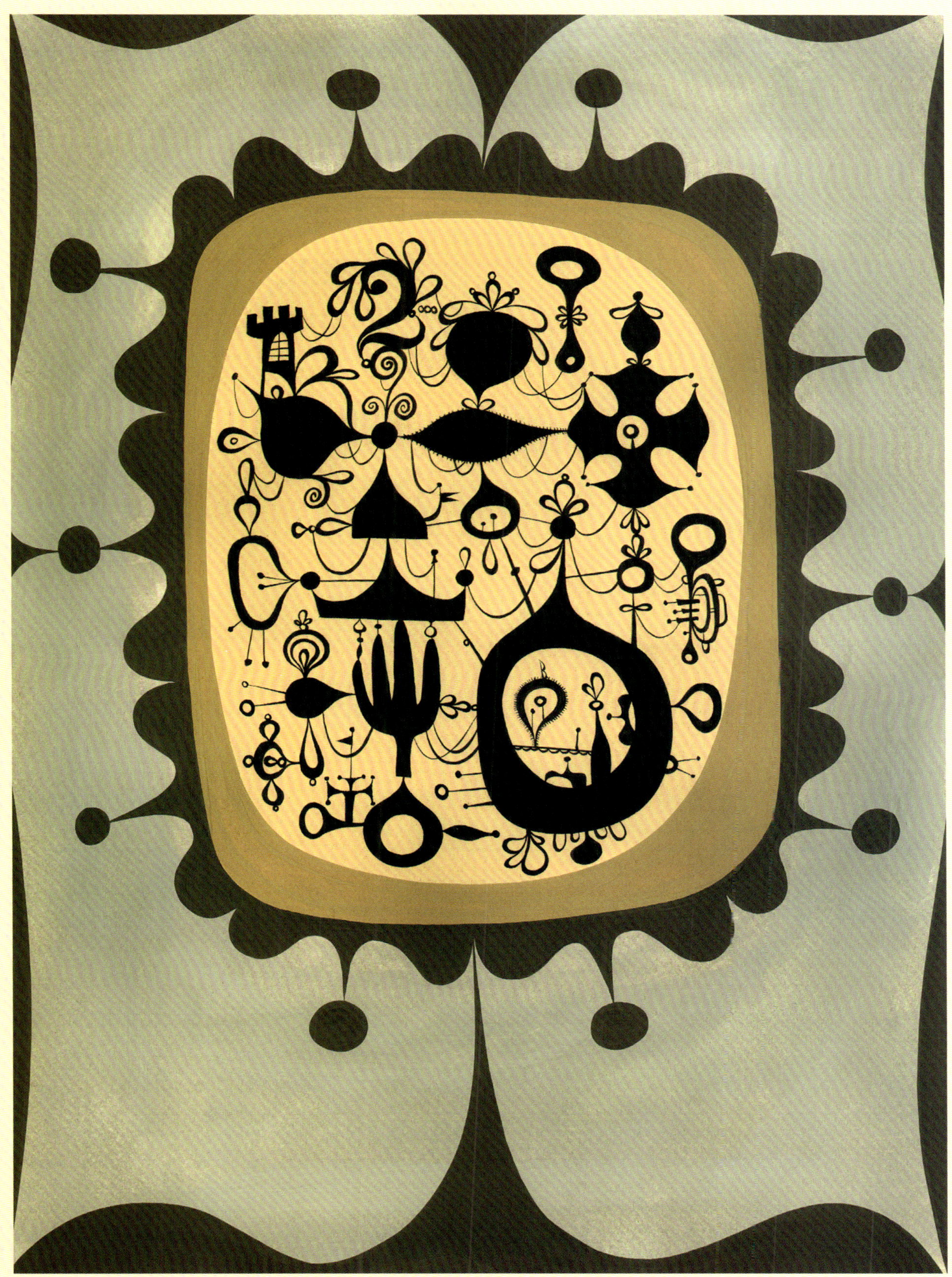

Sunflower
2000. Gouache on Paper. 14" x 11"

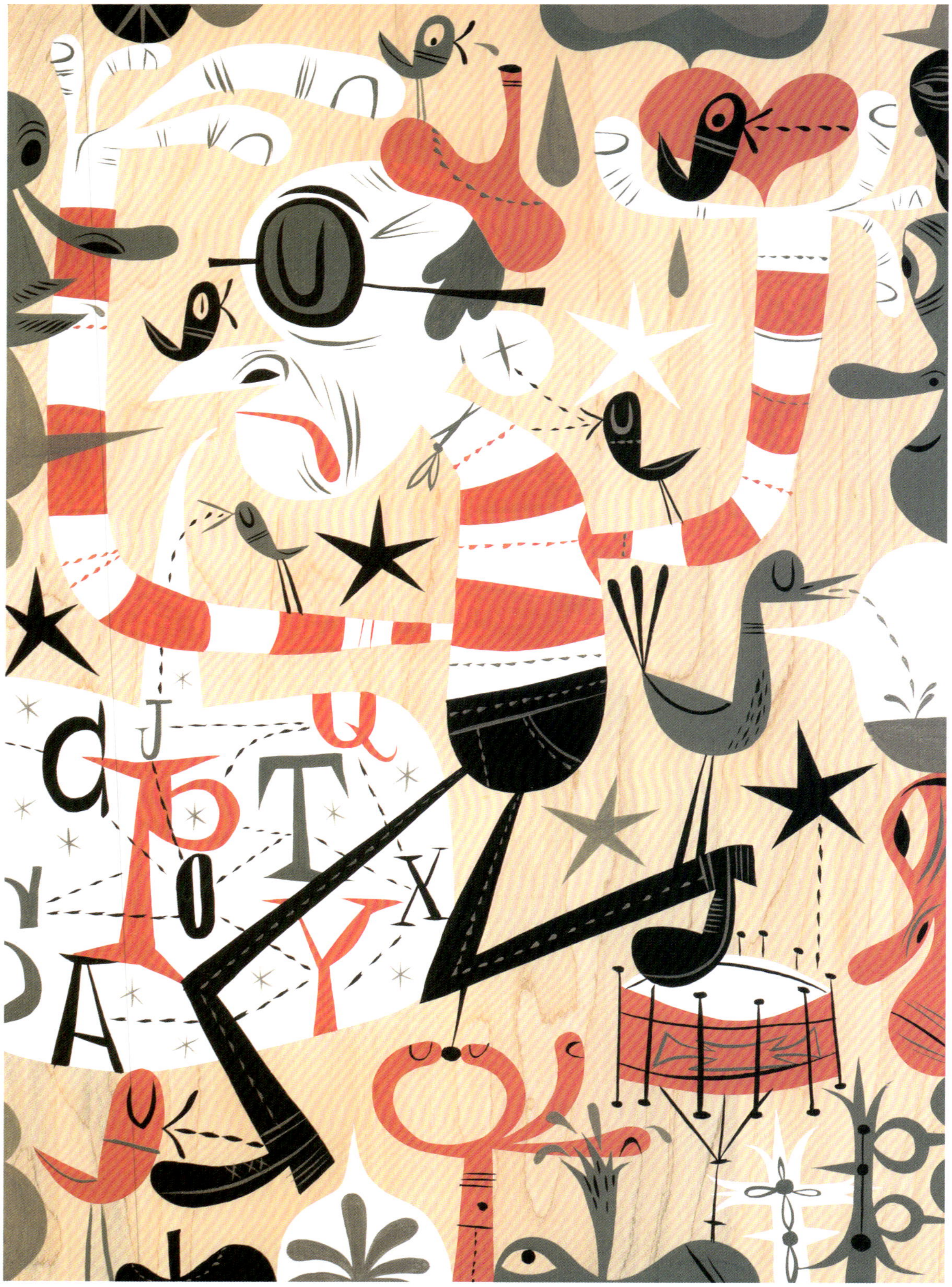

Beat Blabber
2005. Acrylic on Panel. 14" x 11"

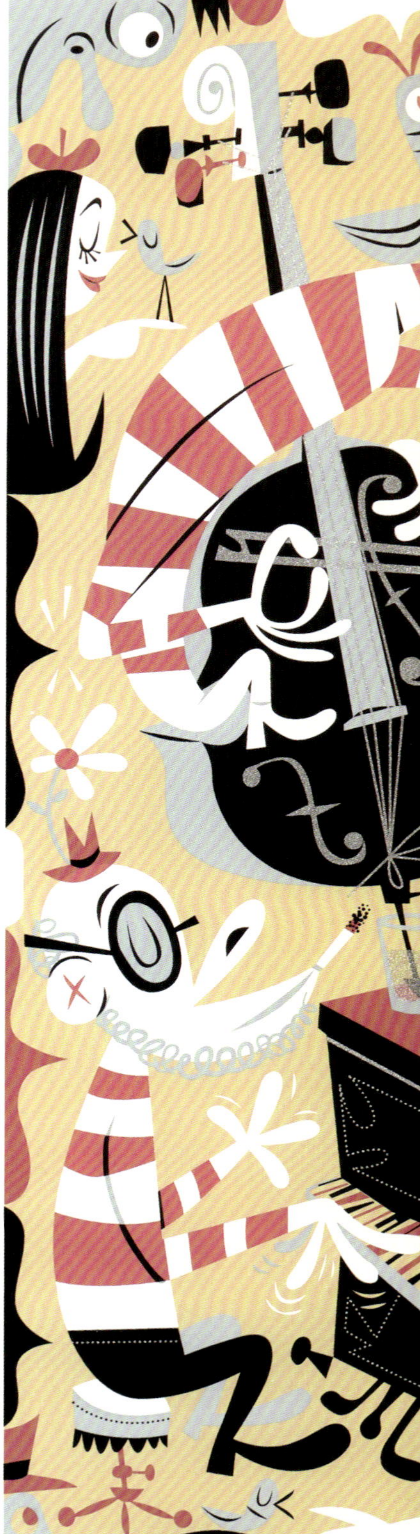

Beatnik Band
2003. 4-Color Serigraph on Paper. 23" x 28"

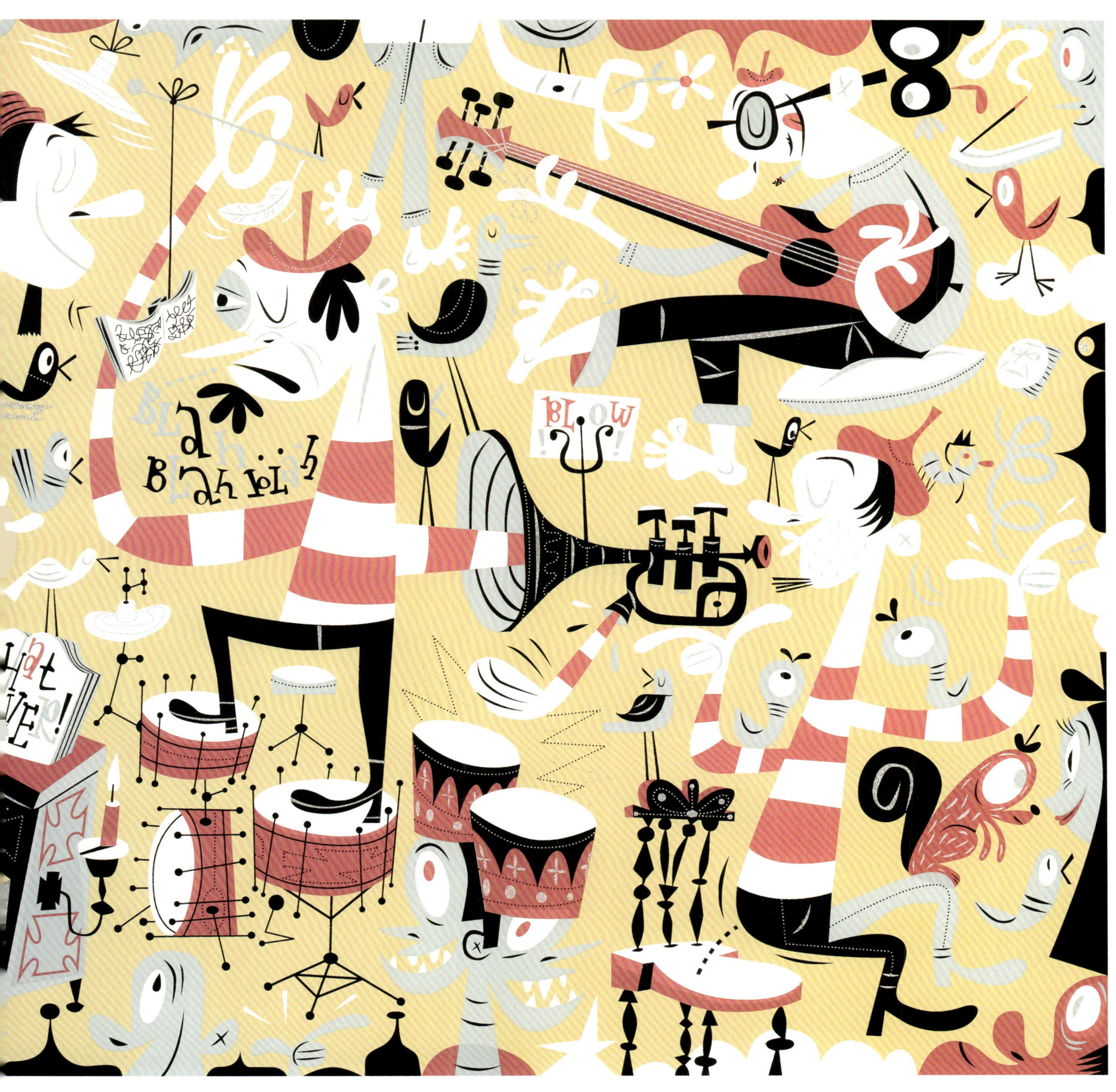
BLOW

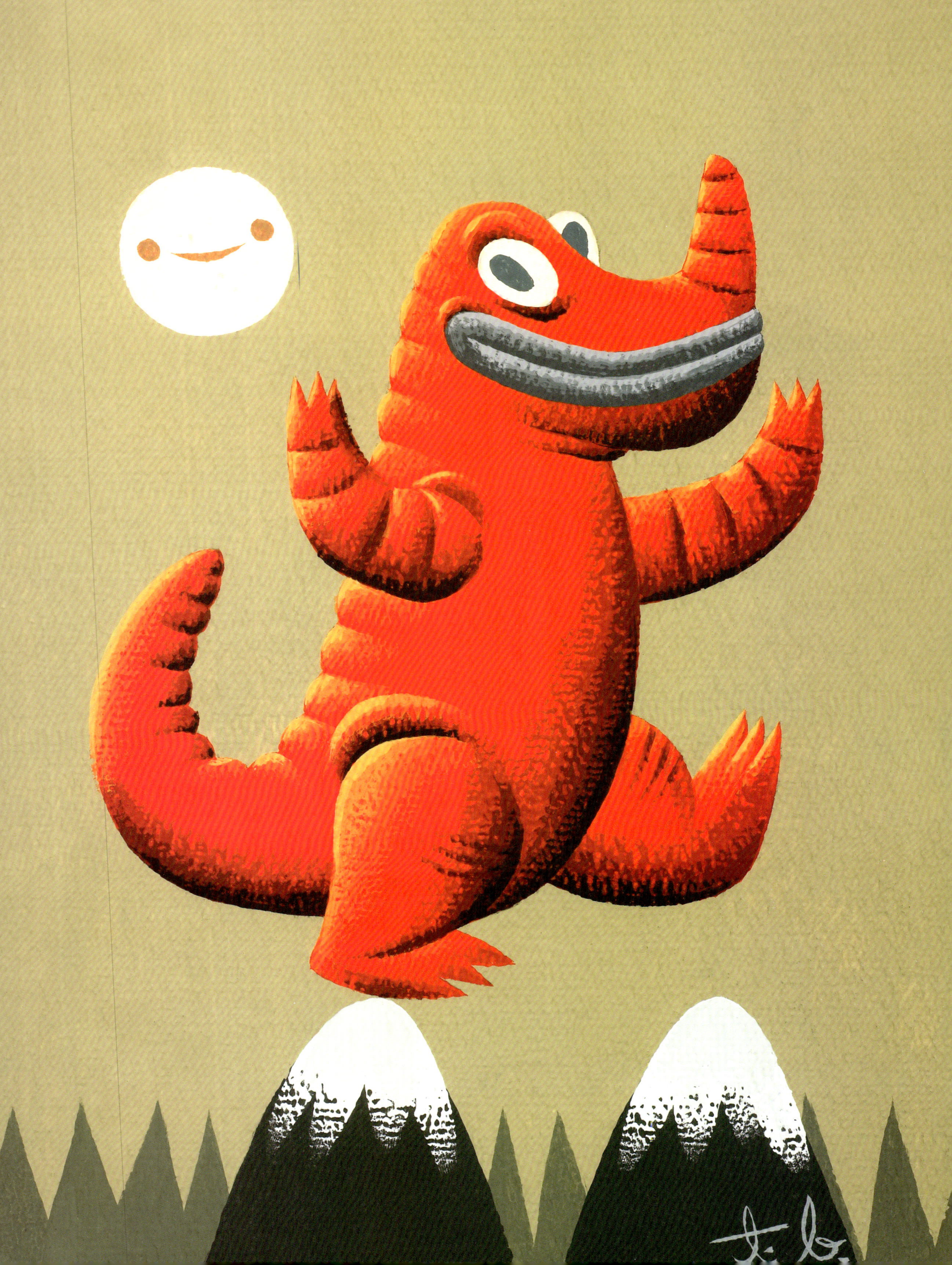

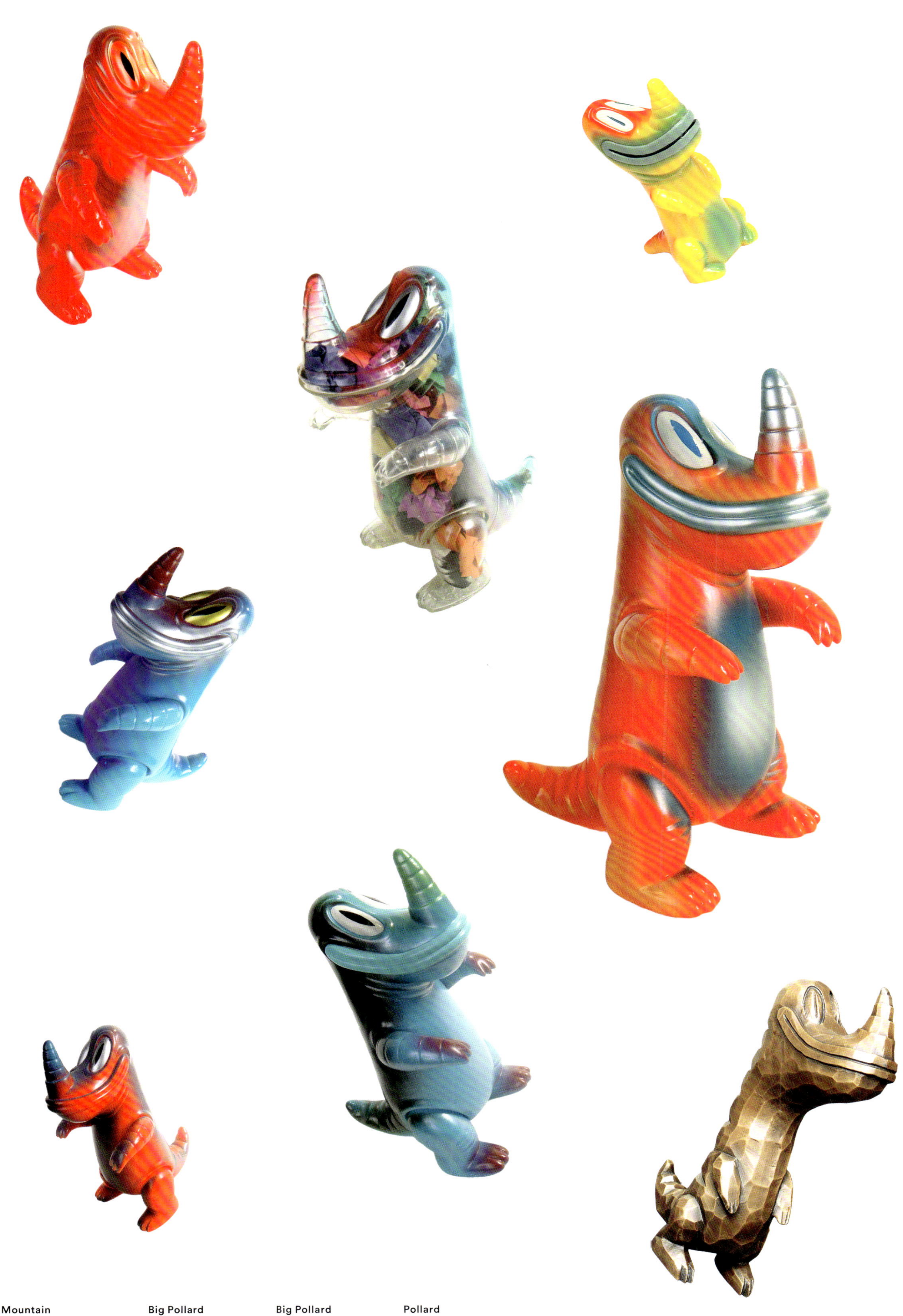

Pollard Mountain
2006. Acrylic on Paper. 14" x 11"

Big Pollard
2006. Vinyl. 9" tall

Big Pollard
2003. Vinyl. 4" tall

Pollard
2009. Bronze. 7" tall

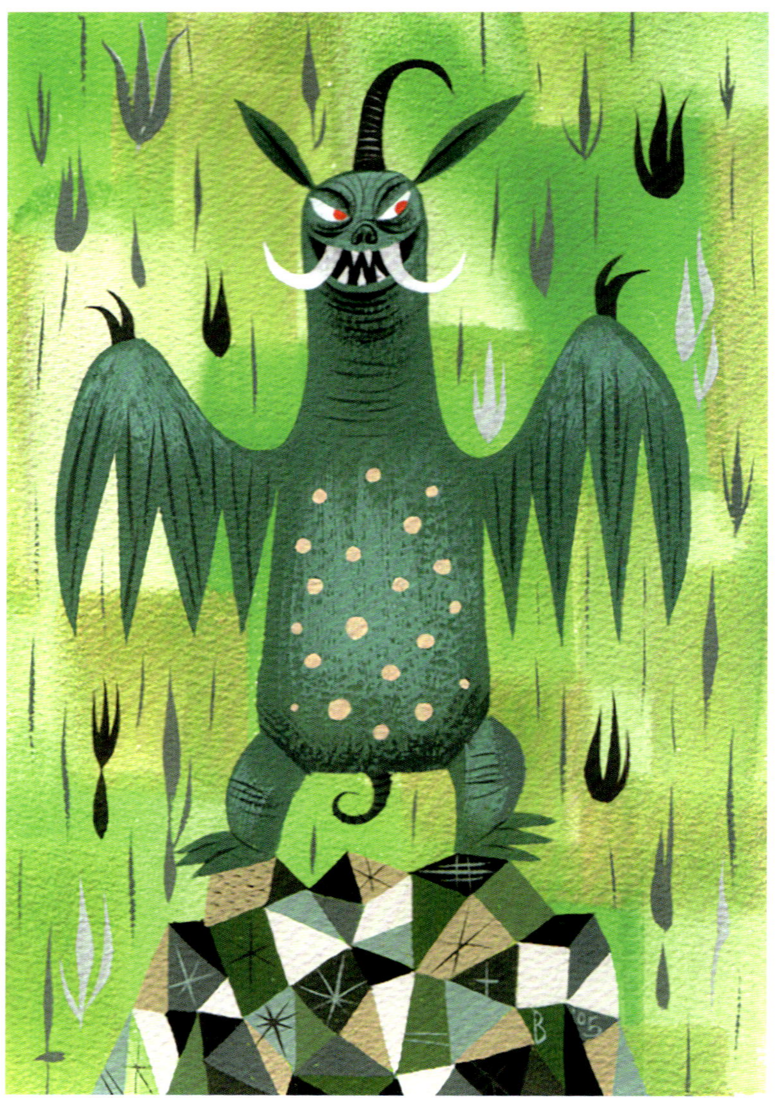

Peguira
2005. Gouache on Paper. 7" x 5"

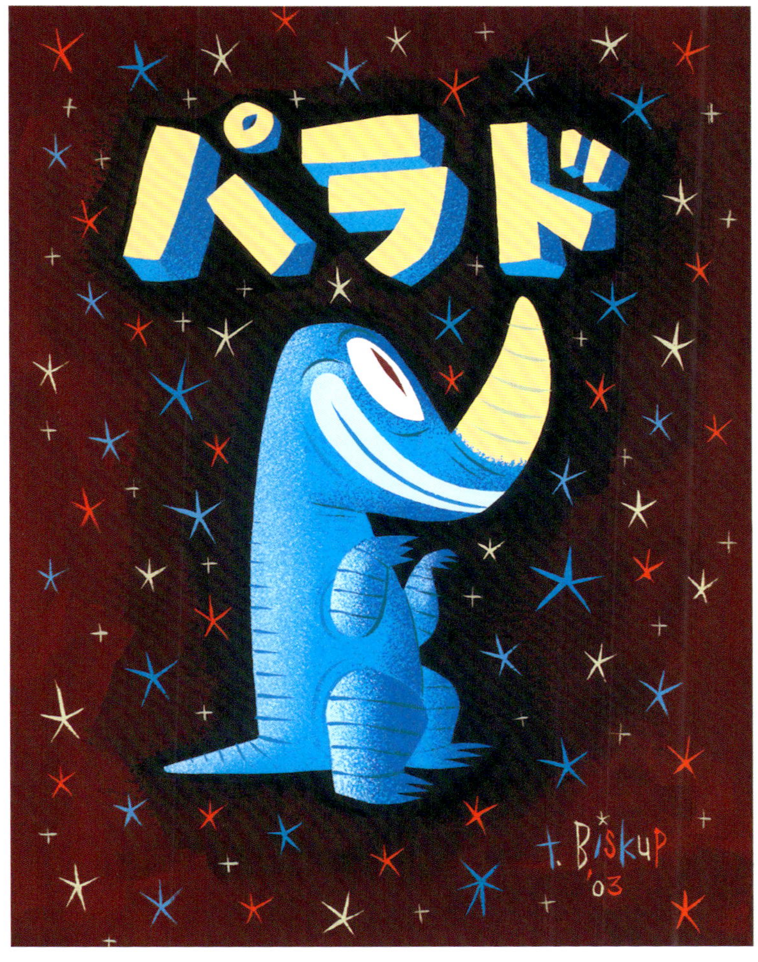

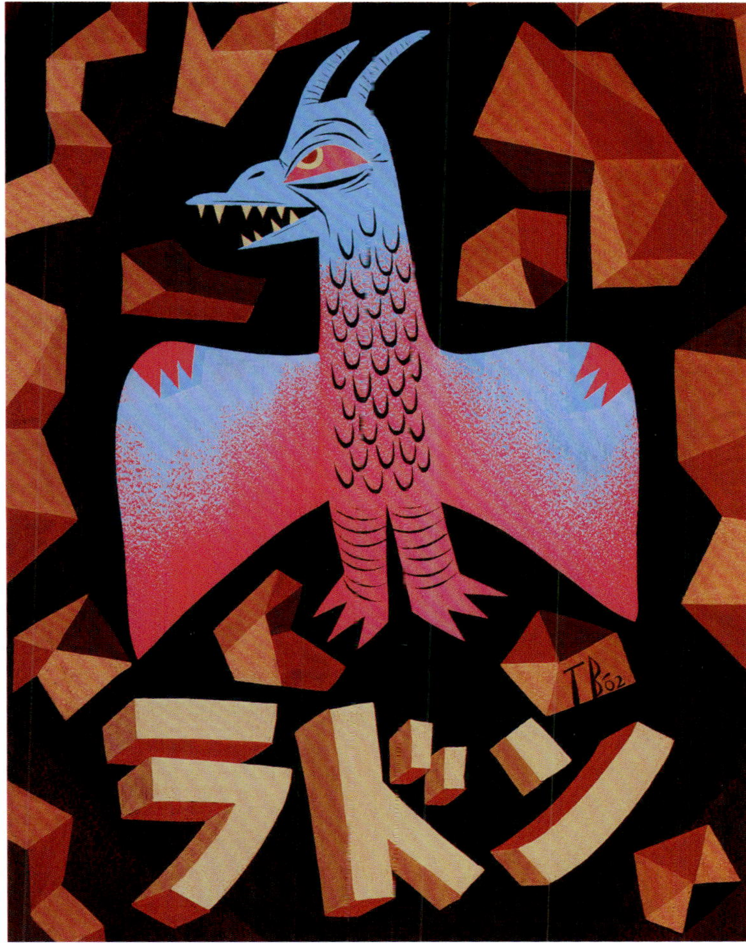

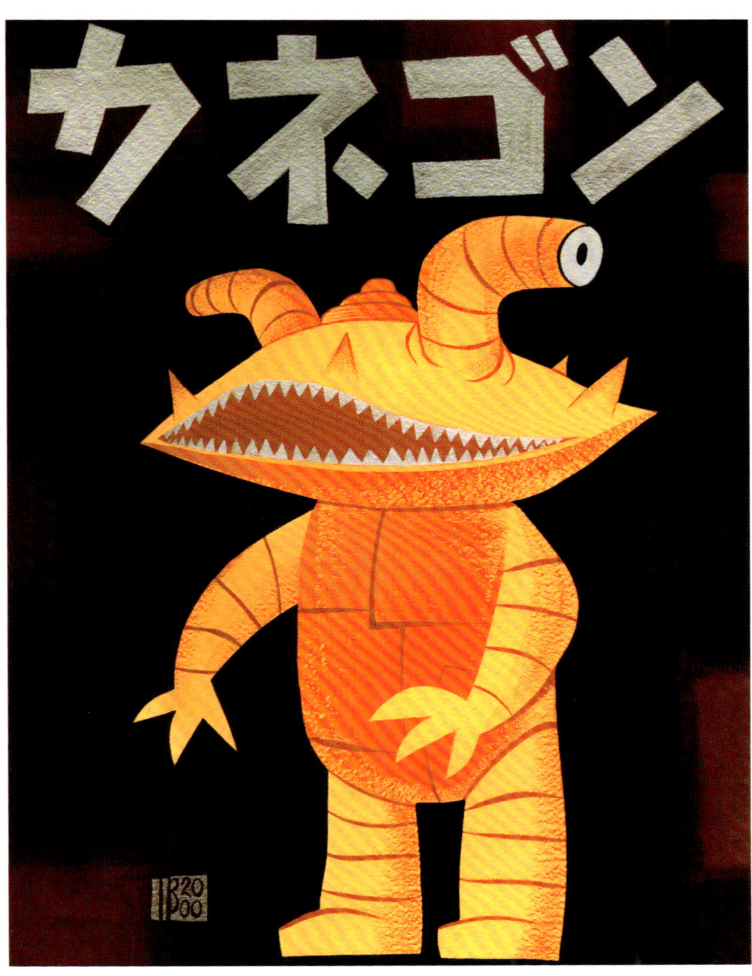

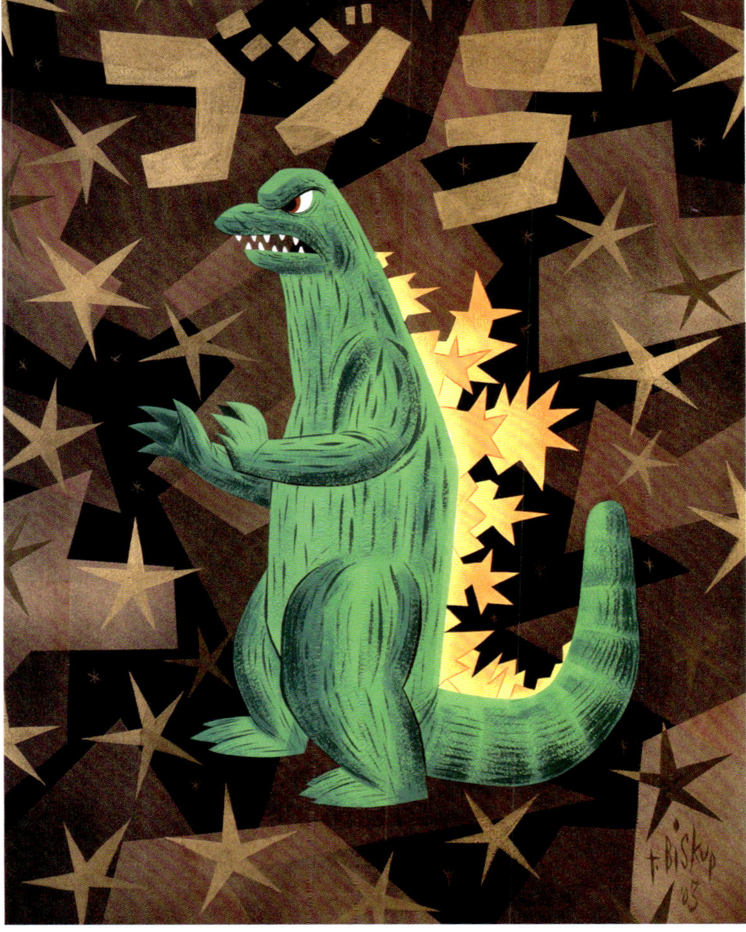

Pollard
2003. Gouache on Paper. 10" x 8"

Kanegon
2000. Gouache on Paper. 14" x 11"

Radon
2002. Gouache on Paper. 14" x 11"

Gojira
2003. Gouache on Paper. 24" x '8"

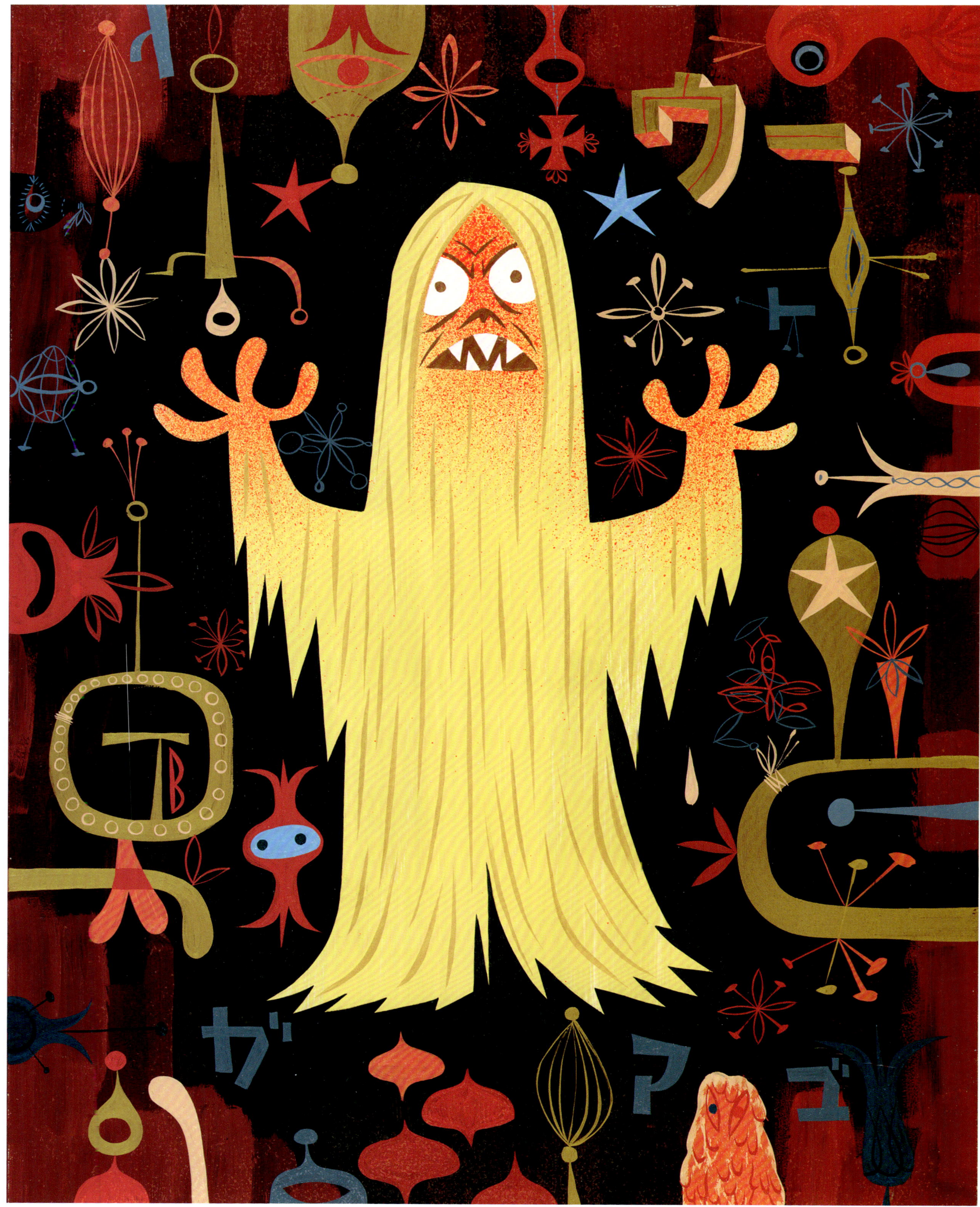

Woo
2002. Gouache on Panel. 14" x 11"

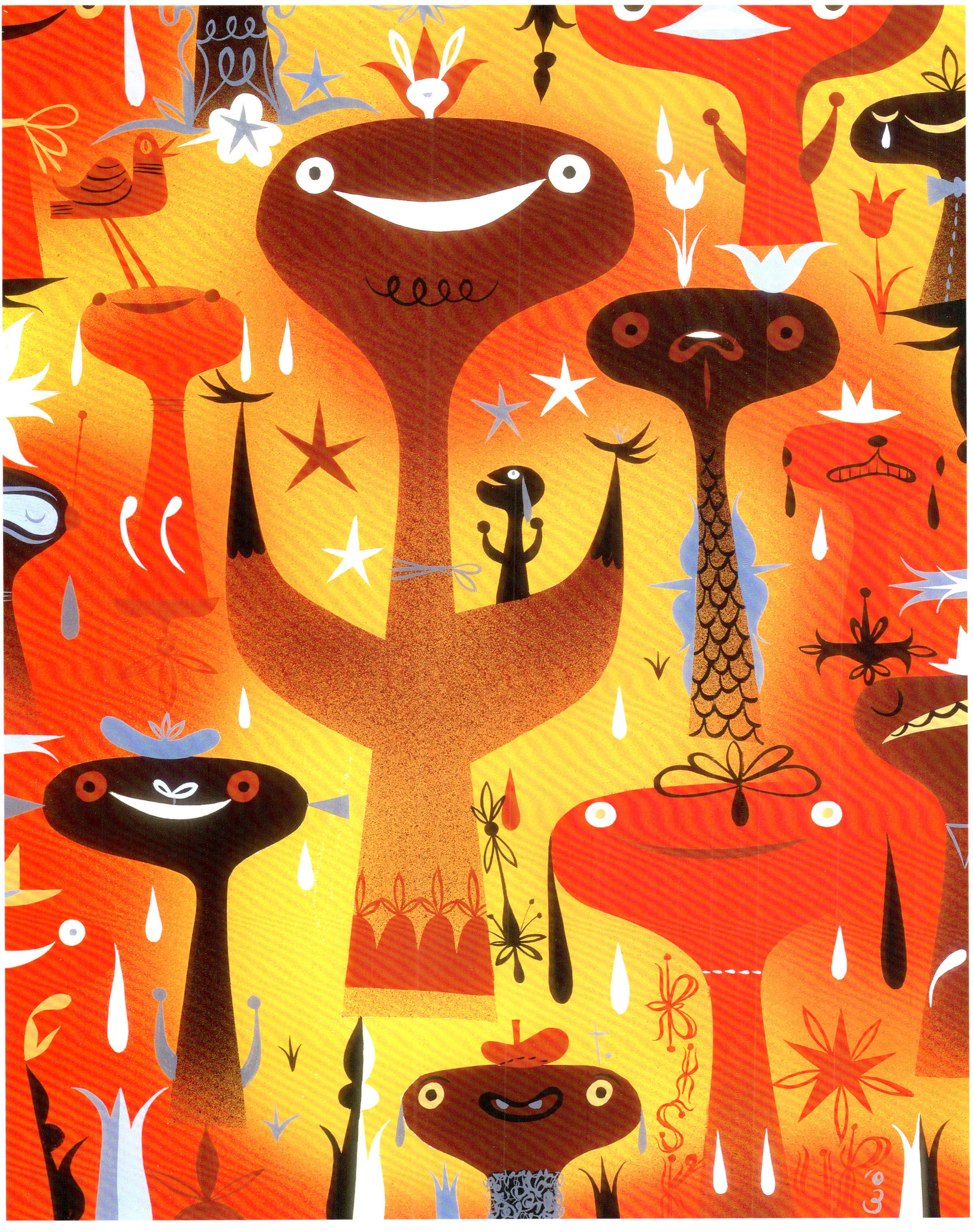

Ghonner Group
2003. Acrylic on Panel. 11" x 8.5"

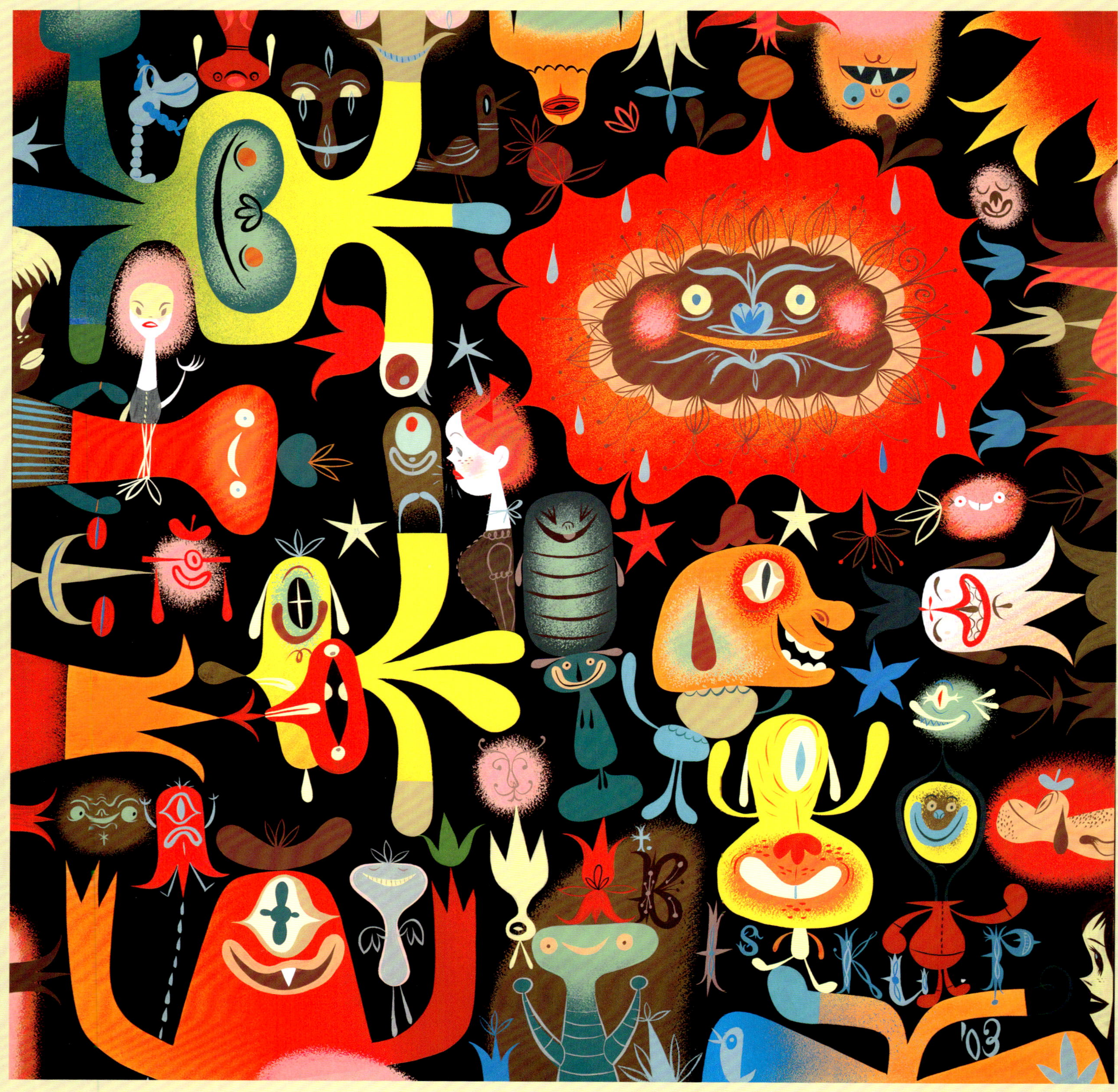

Darkride: Hot
2003. Acrylic on Panel. 24" x 24"

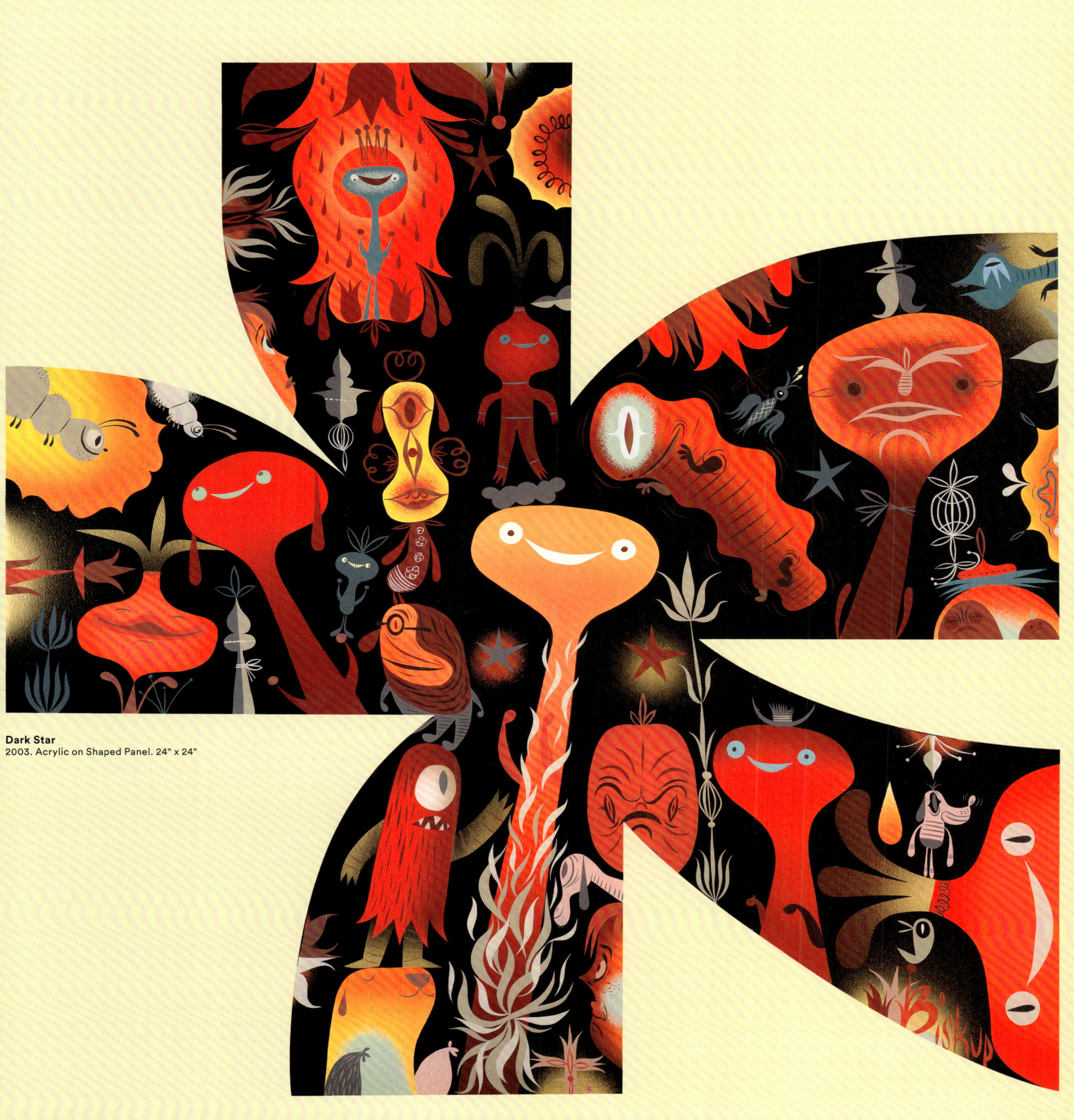

Dark Star
2003. Acrylic on Shaped Panel. 24" x 24"

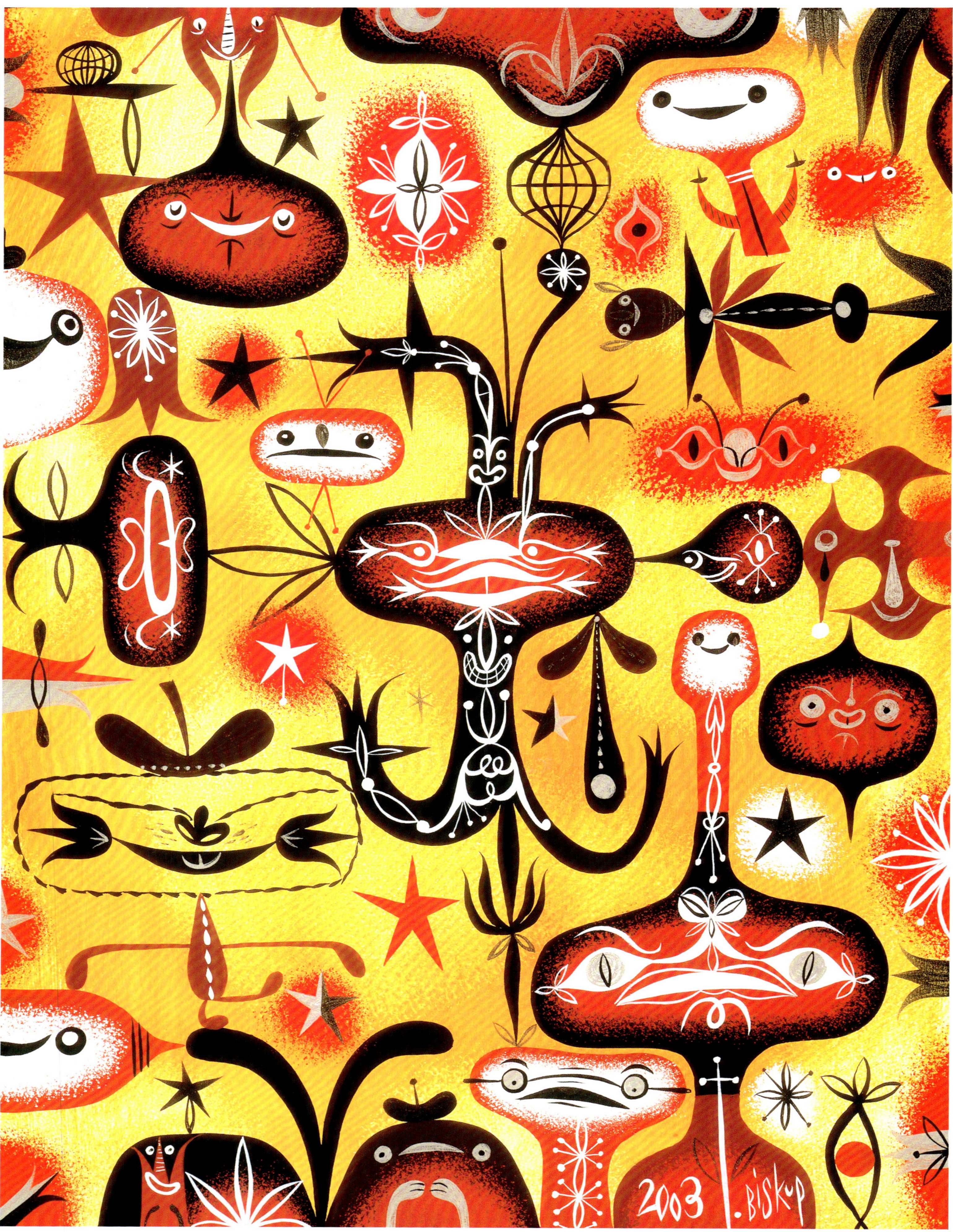

Flaming Ghost Blossom
2003. Acrylic on Panel. 13" x 10"

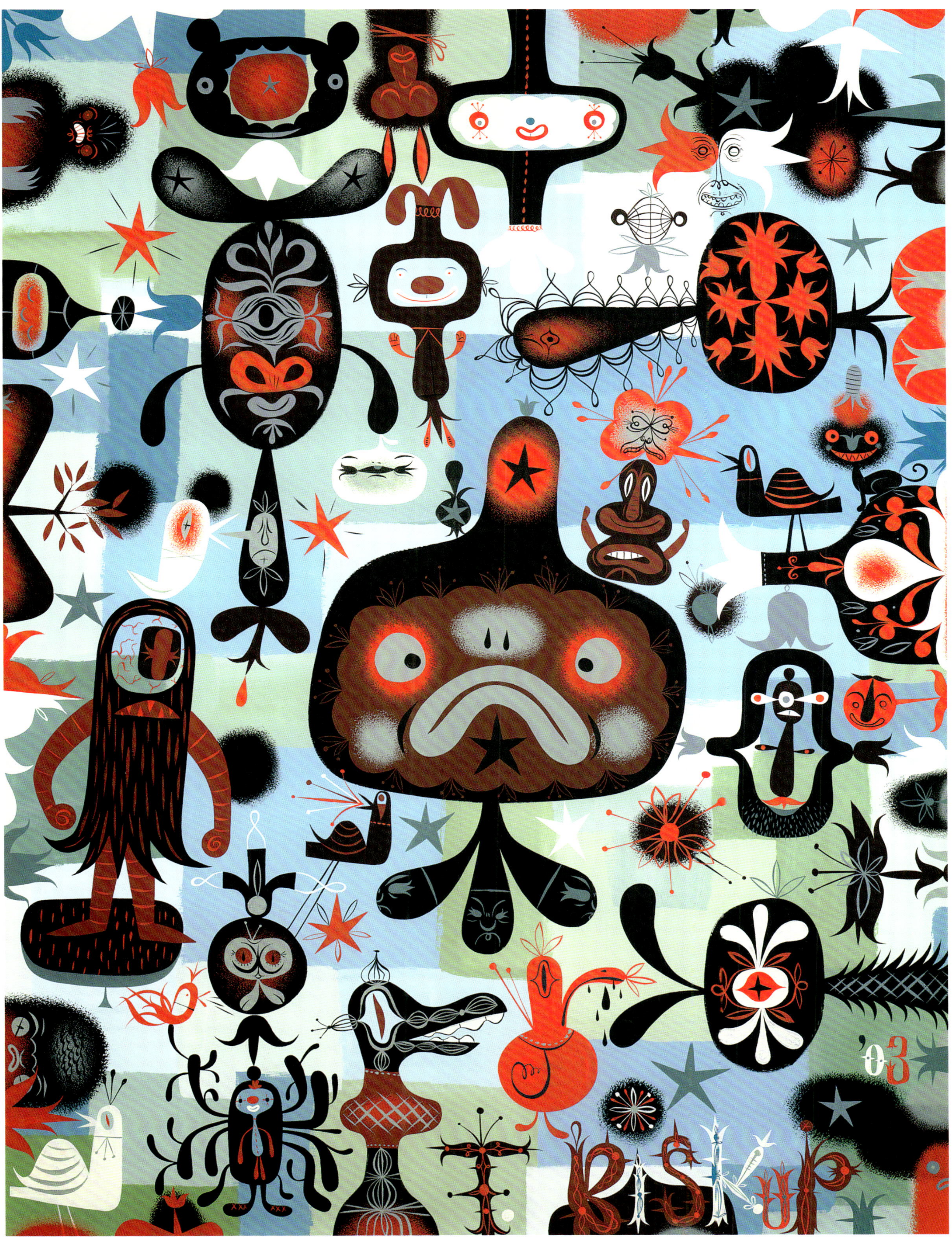

Black Patriot District
2003. Acrylic on Panel. 40" x 30"

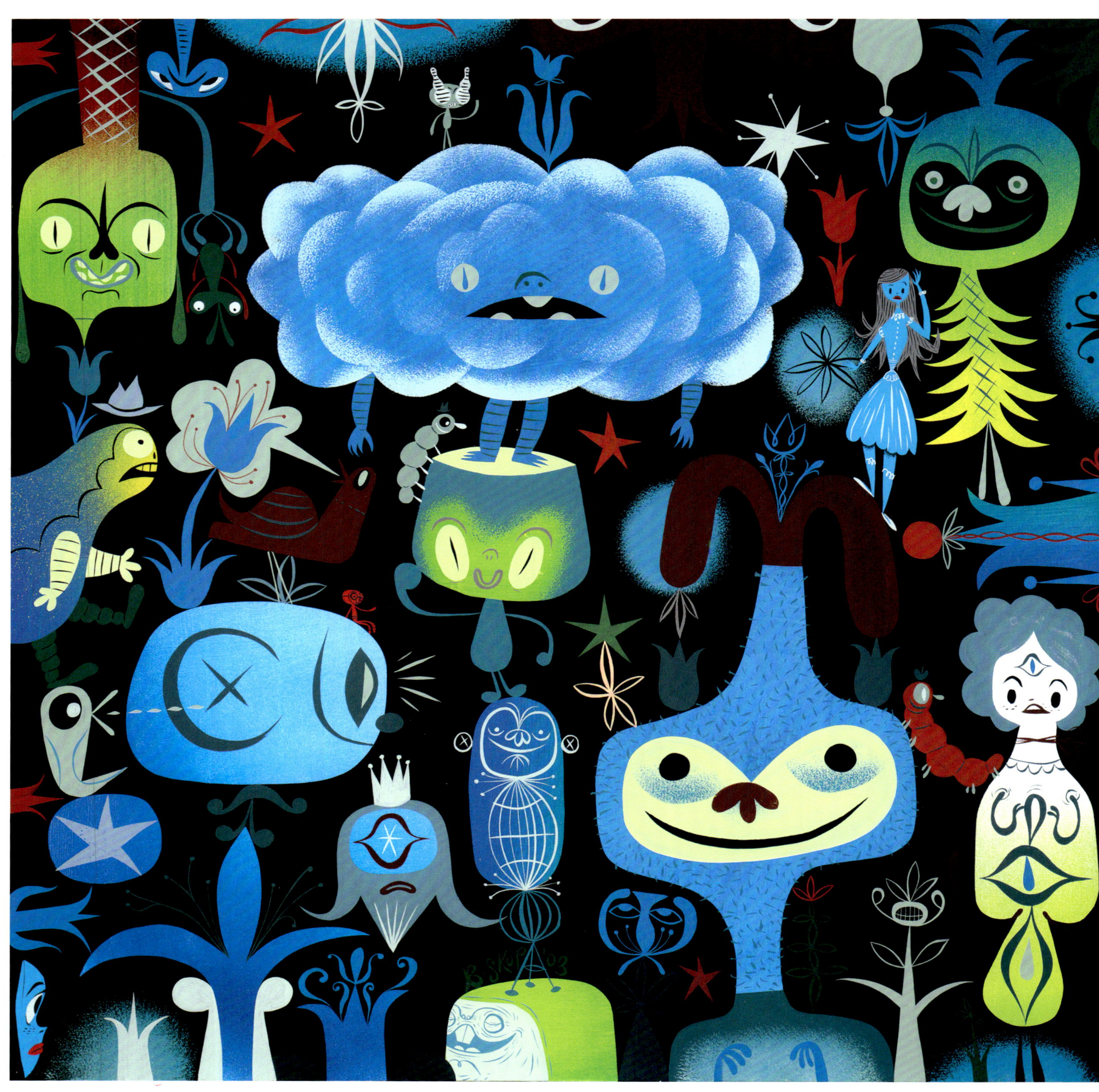

Darkride: Cold
2003. Acrylic on Panel. 24" x 24"

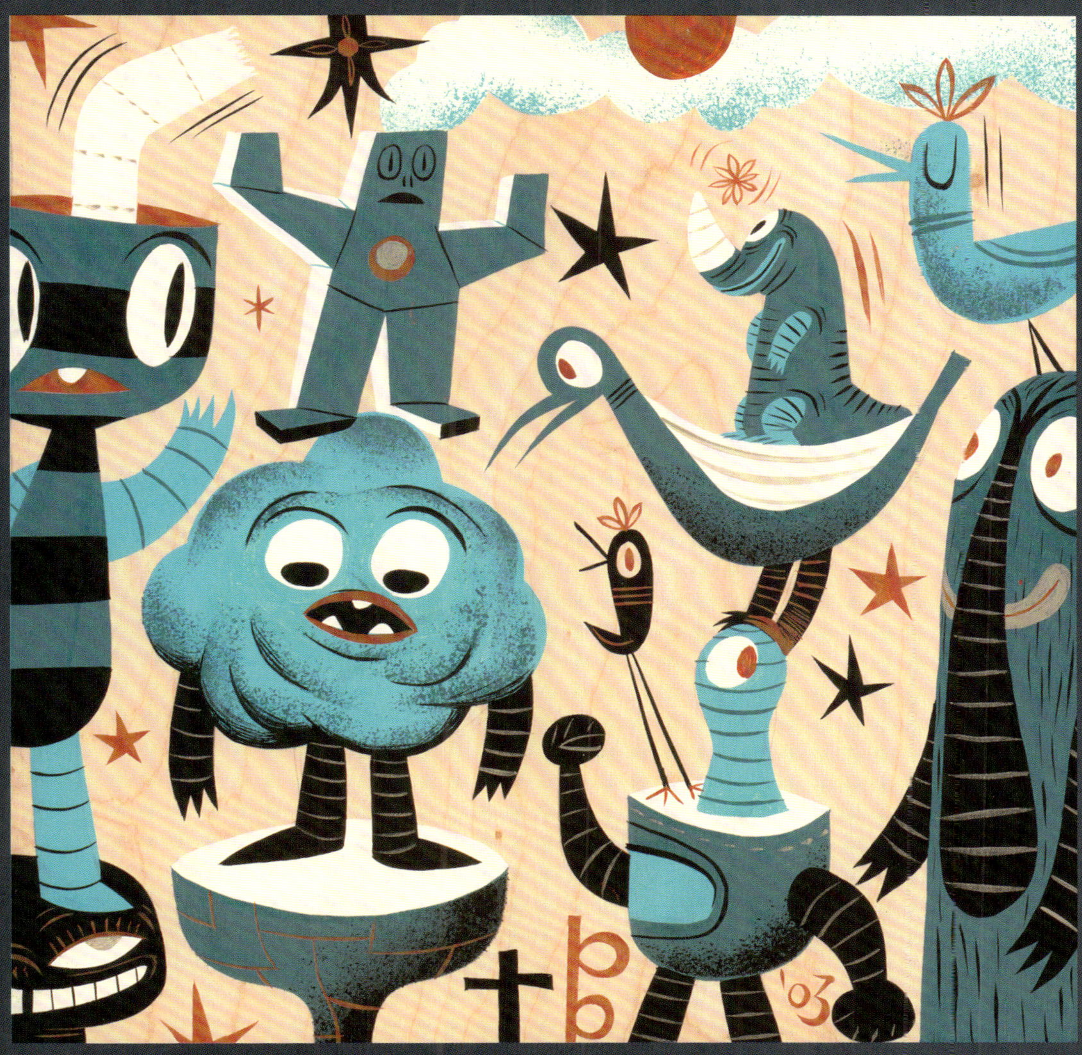

Alphabeastiary
2003. Acrylic on Panel. 8" x 8"

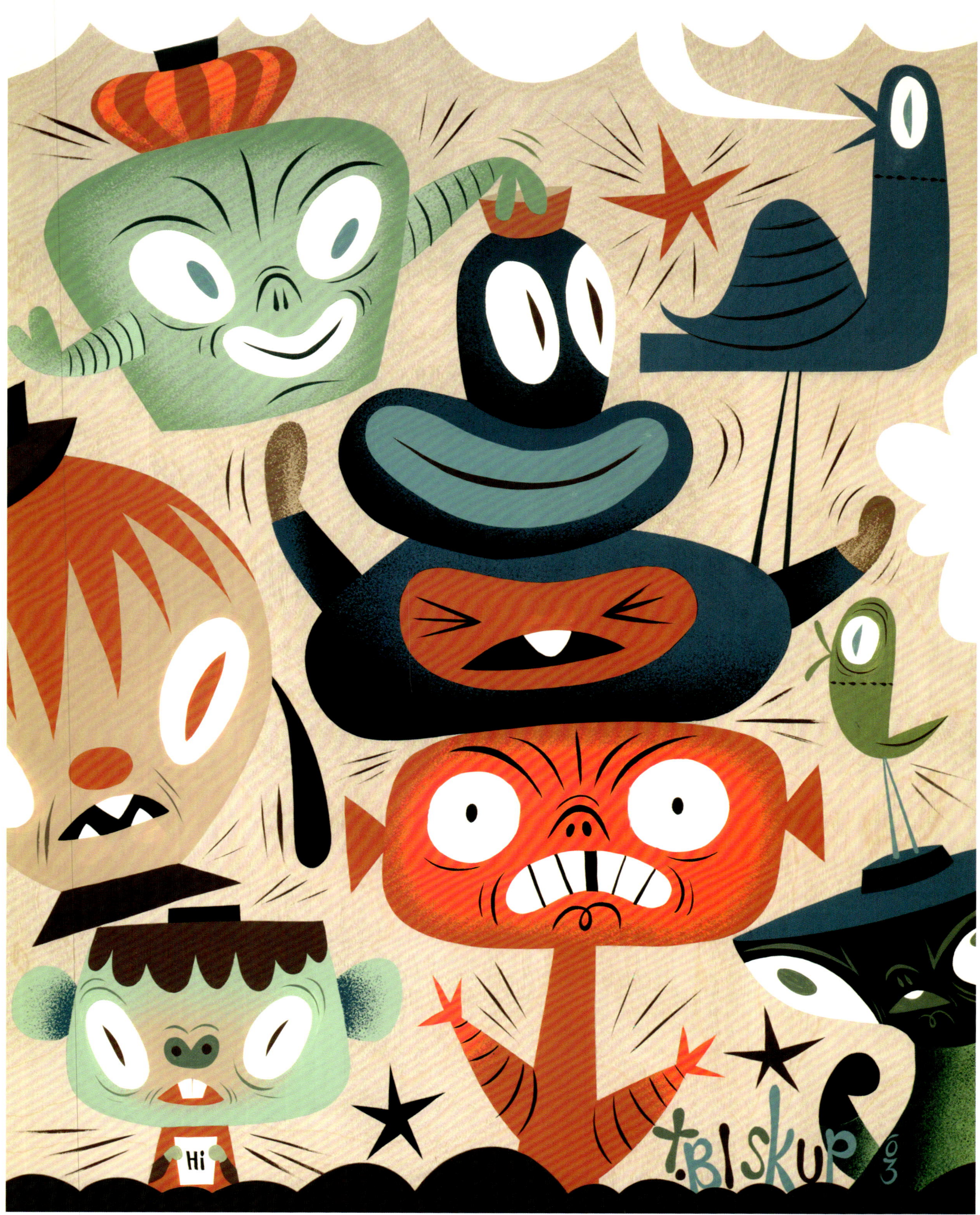

Stack Pack Group
2003. Acrylic on Panel. 20" x 16"

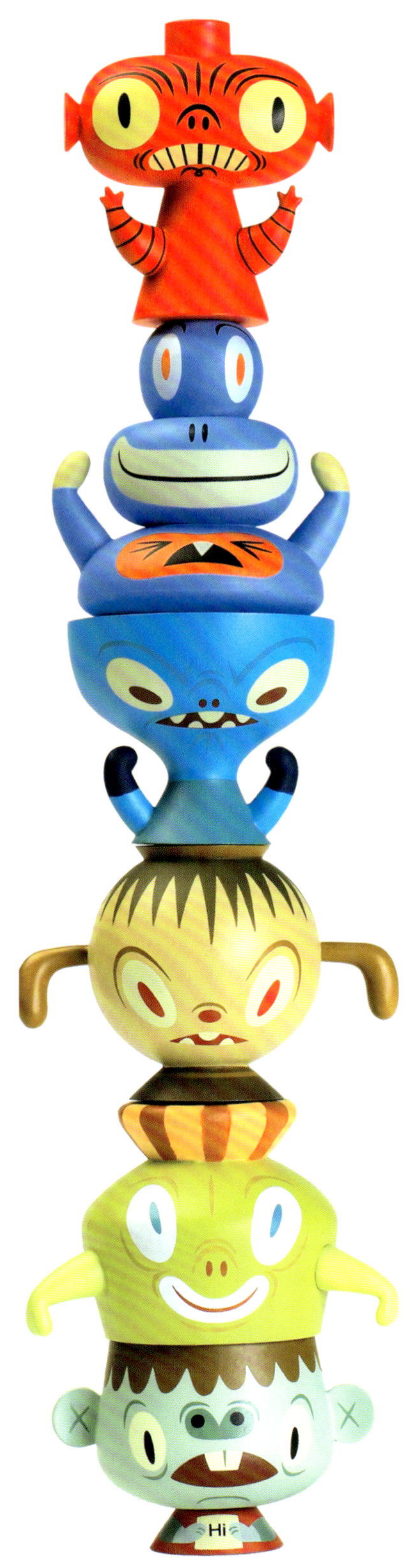

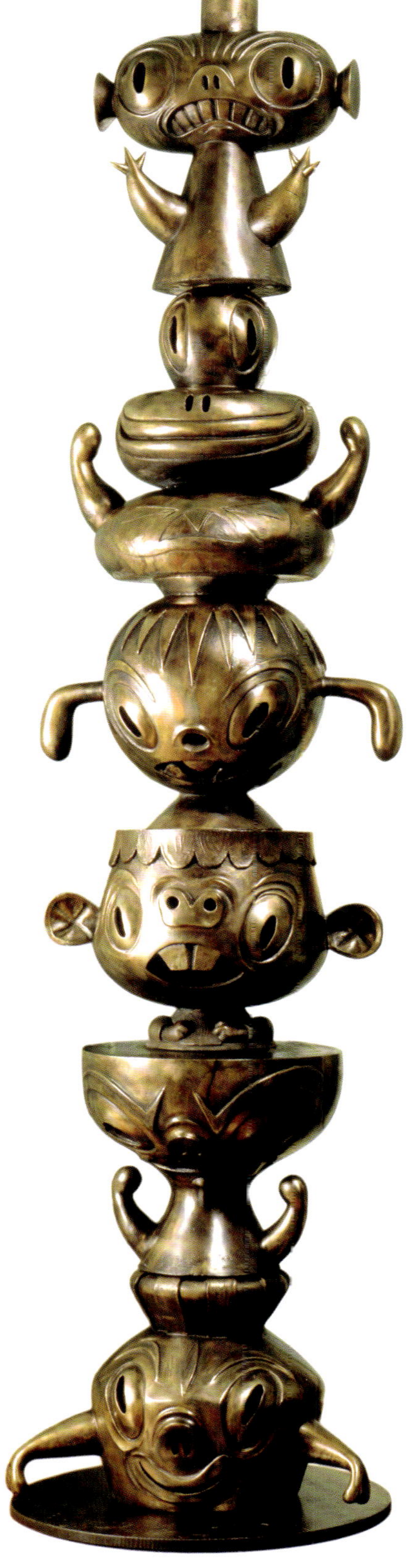

Stack Pack
2004. PVC. Apx 8" tall

Stack Pack
2005. Bronze. 72" tall

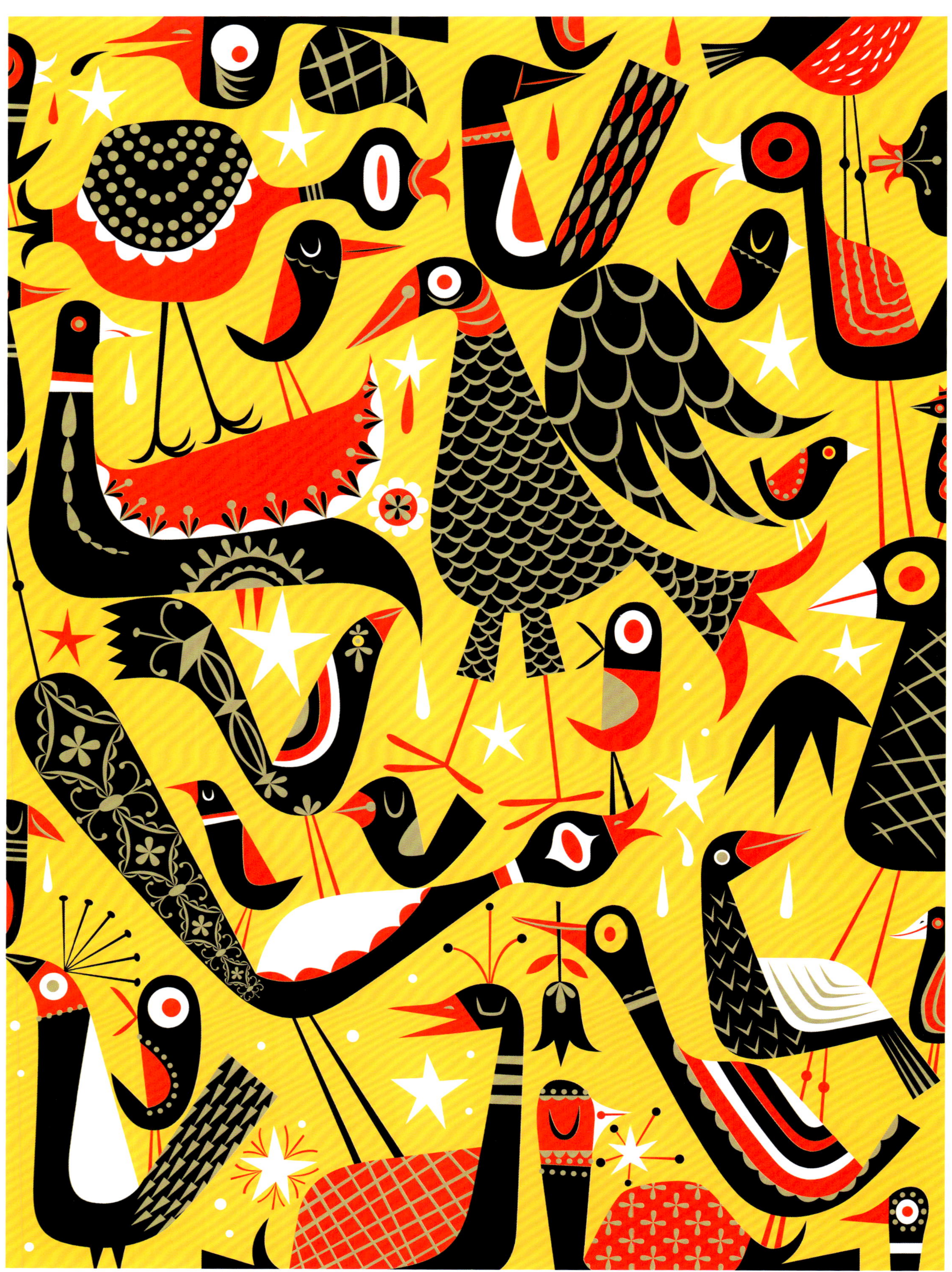

Bird Virus
2004. 4-Color Serigraph on Paper. 24" x 18"

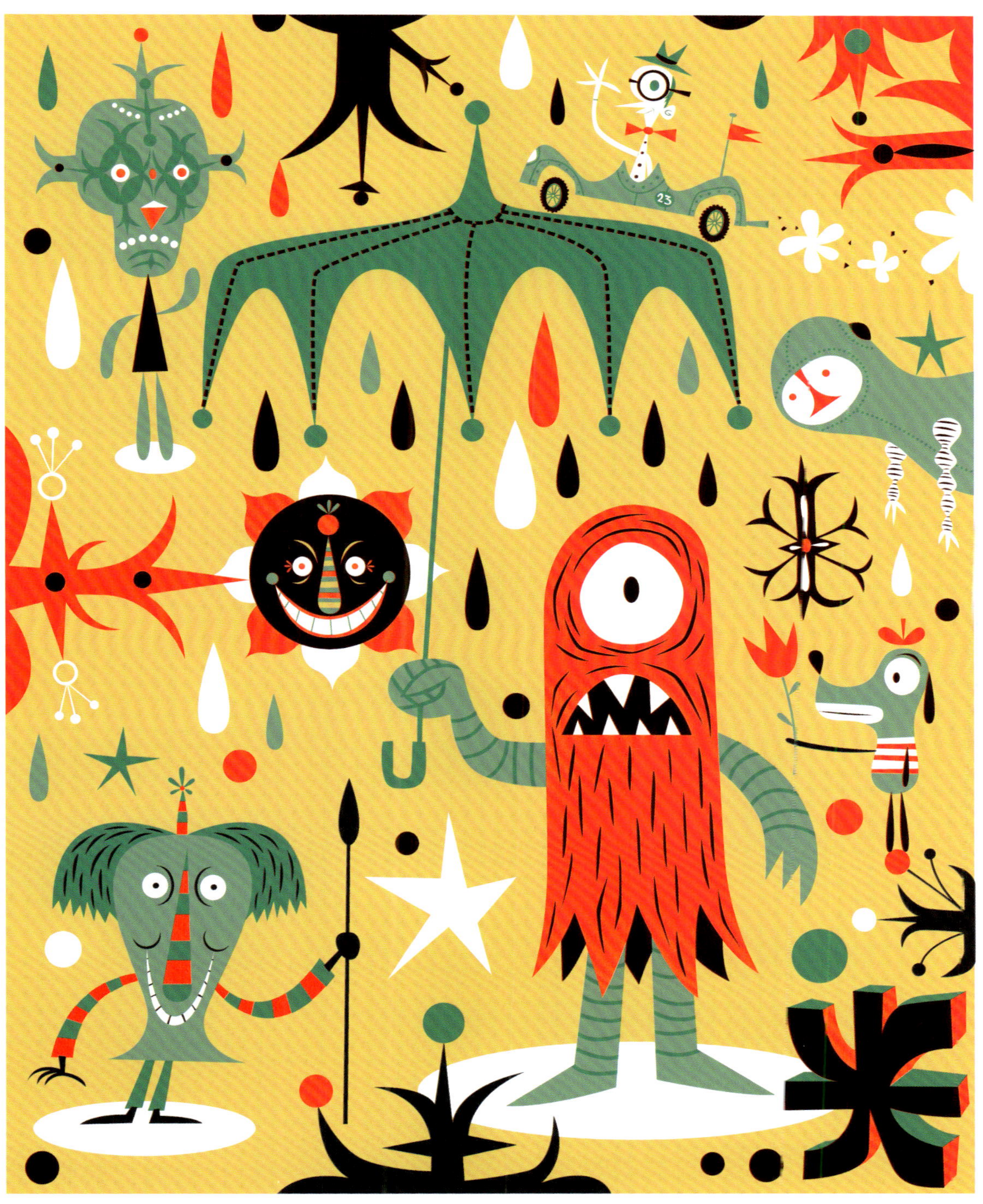

Chaos Family
2003. Giclée Print on Paper. 12" x 9"

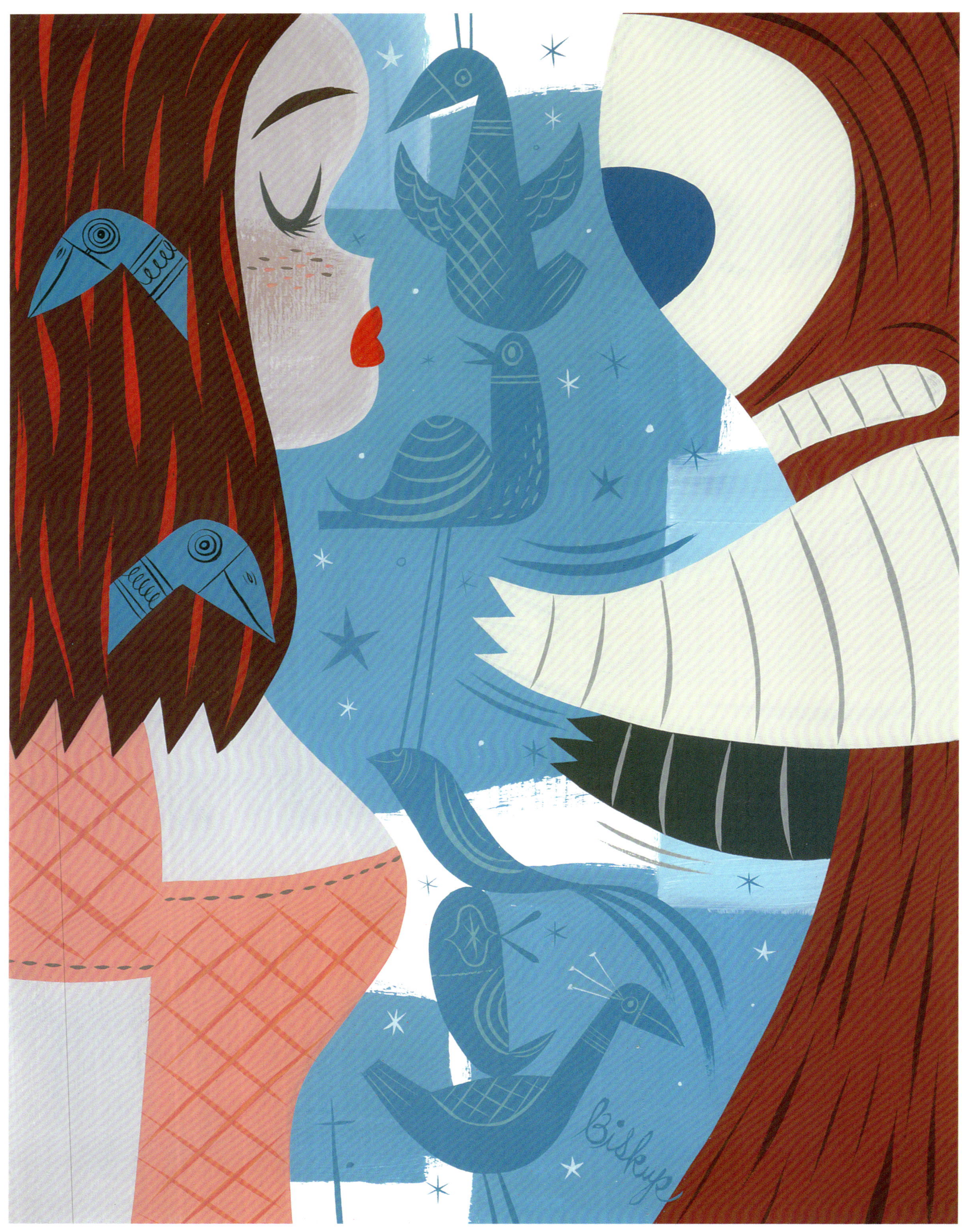

The Fondler
2004. Acrylic on Panel. 14" x 11"

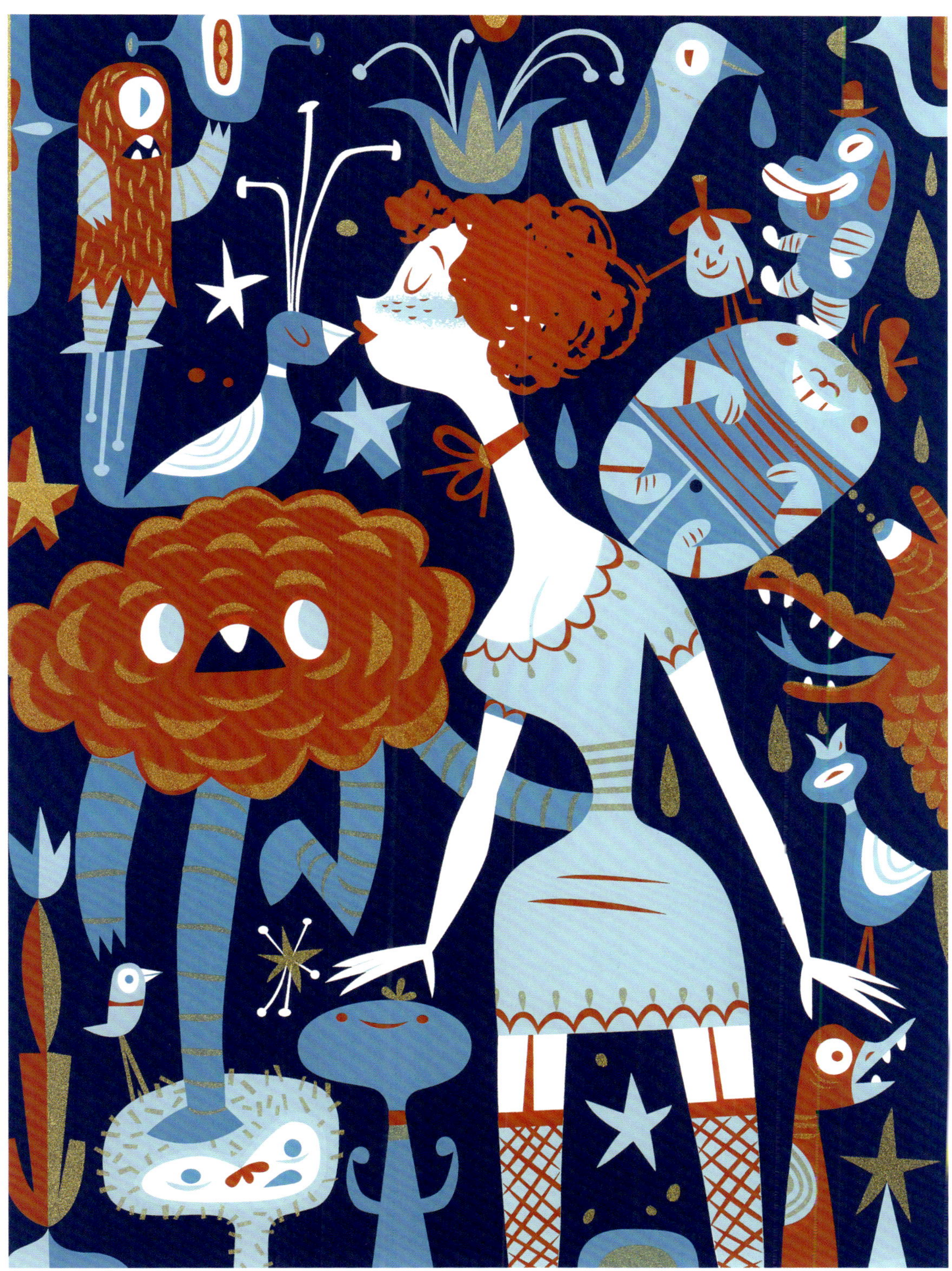

Red Pheasant Queen
2003. 4-Color Serigraph on Paper. 24" x 18"

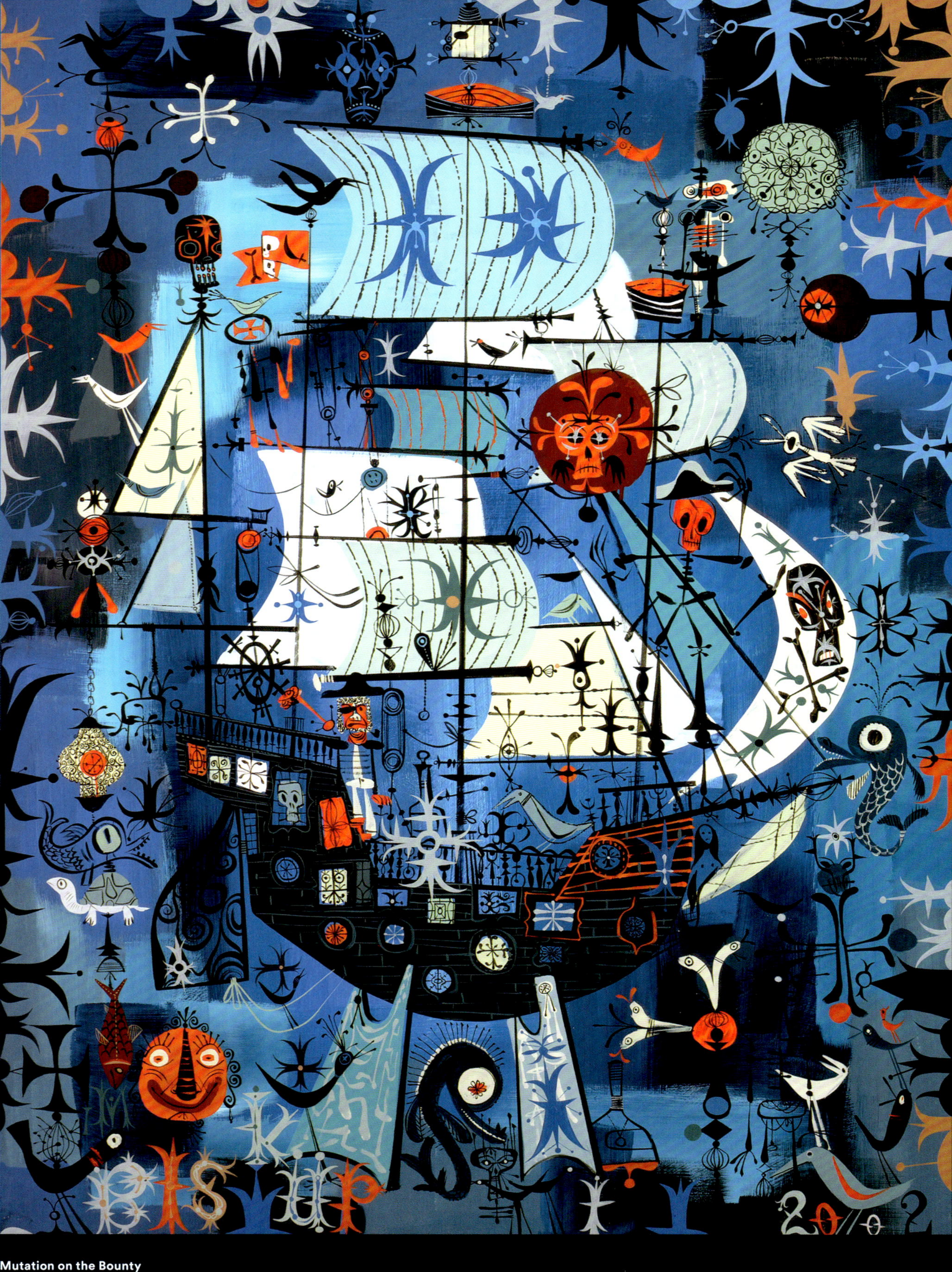

Mutation on the Bounty
2002. Acrylic on Panel. 40" x 30"

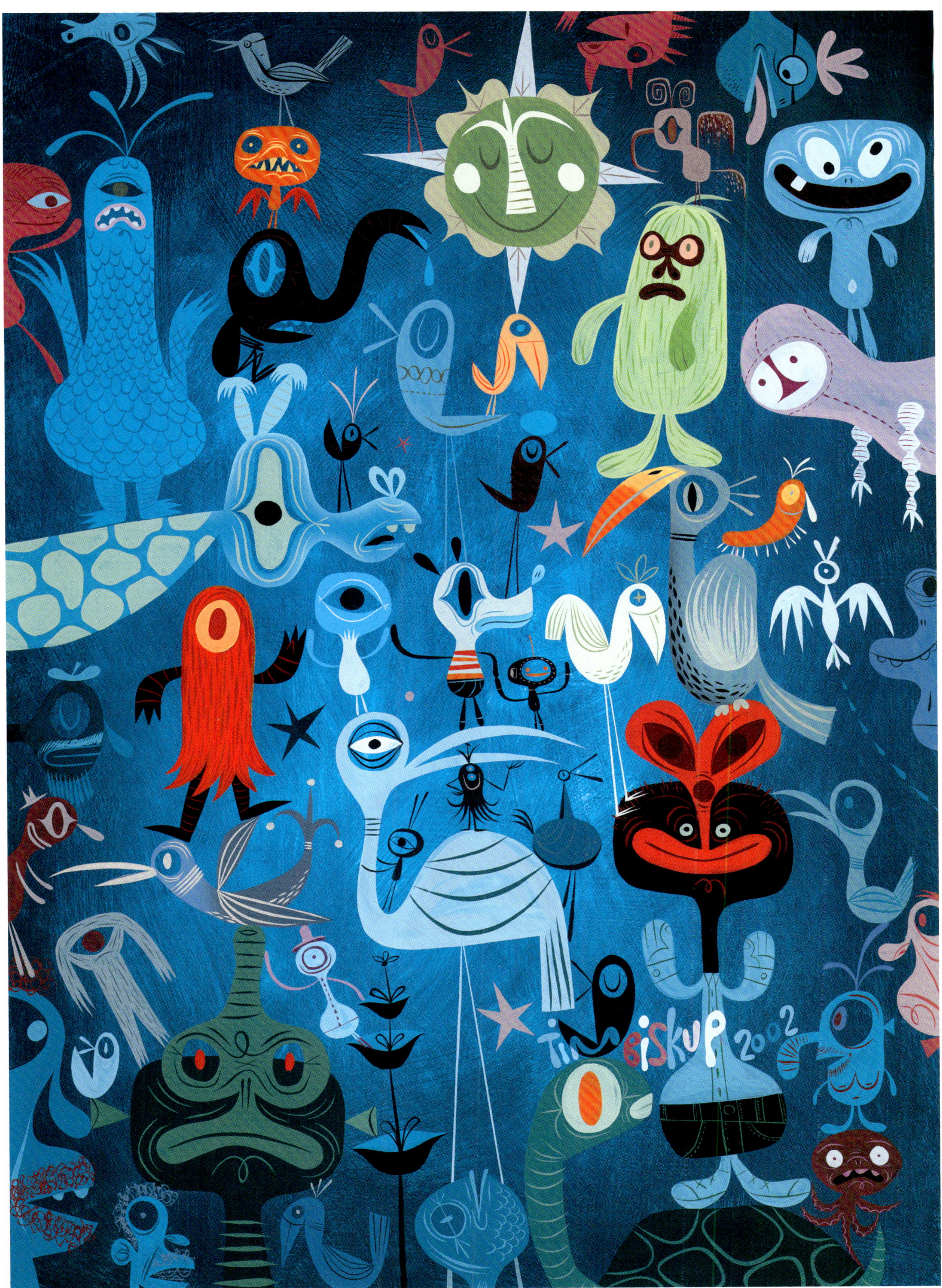

Birds and Beasts
2002. Gouache on Panel. 26" x 18"

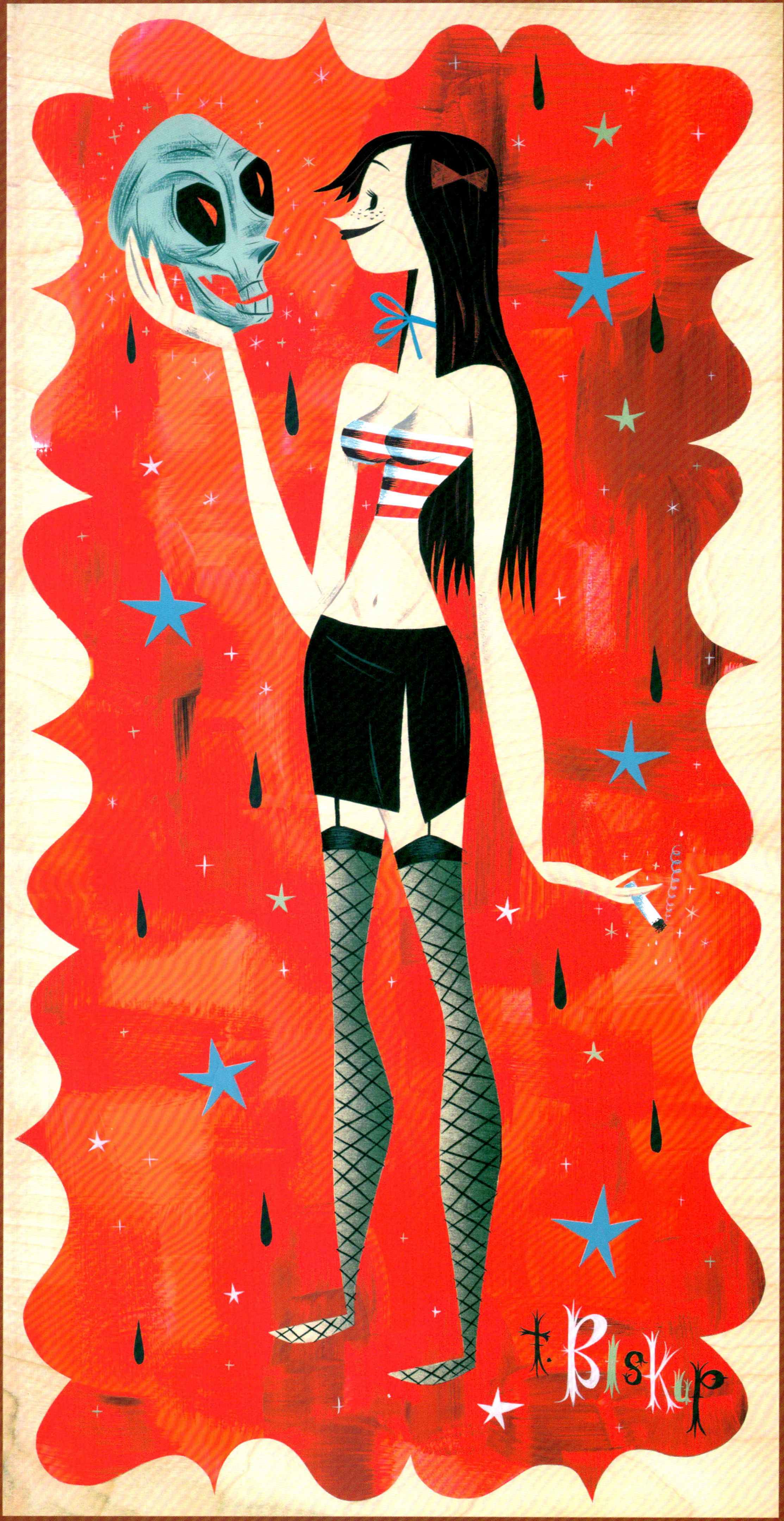

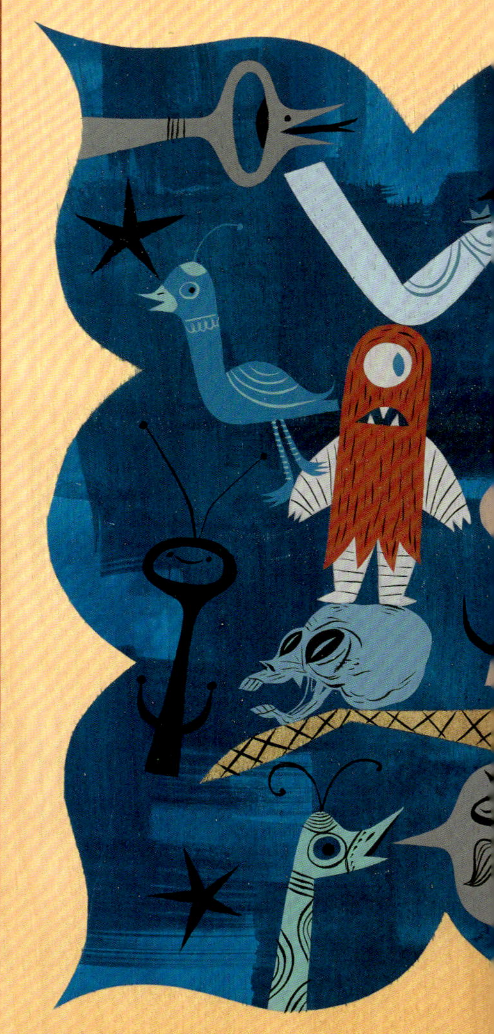

Hamlet
2003. Gouache on Panel. 24" x 12"

Night Light
2003. Gouache on Panel. 12" x 24"

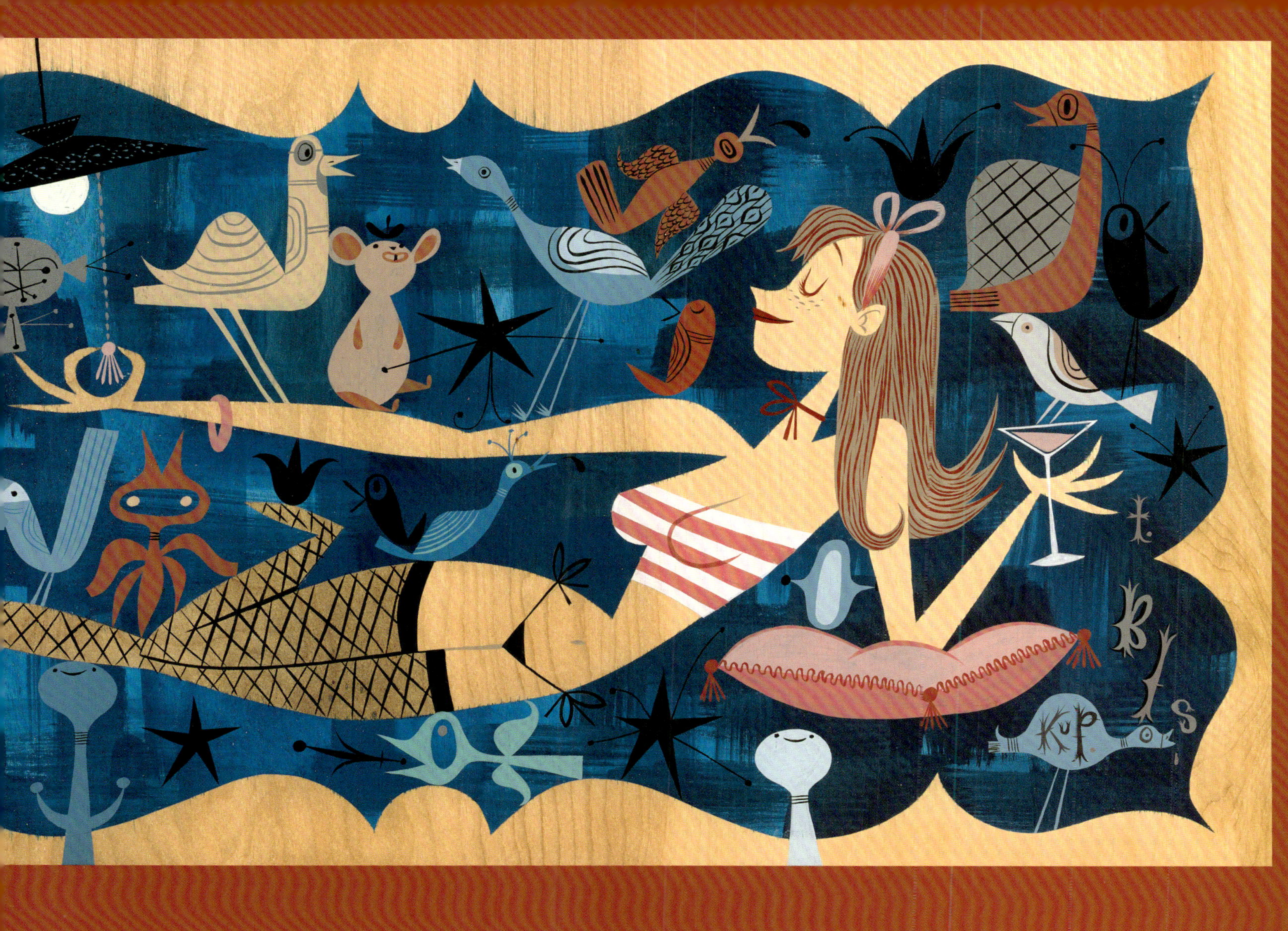

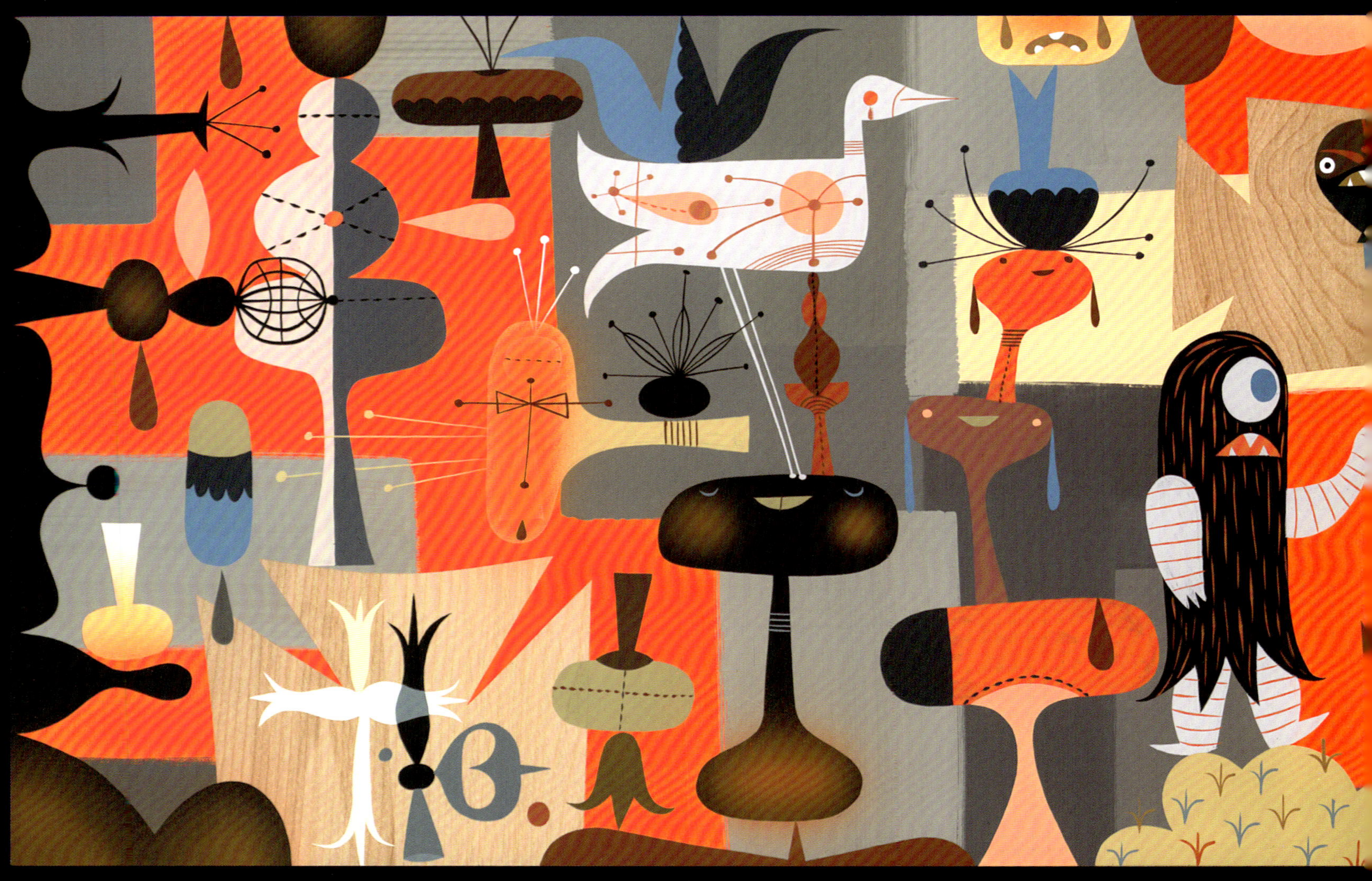

Black Helium
2004. Acrylic on Panel. 12" x 38"

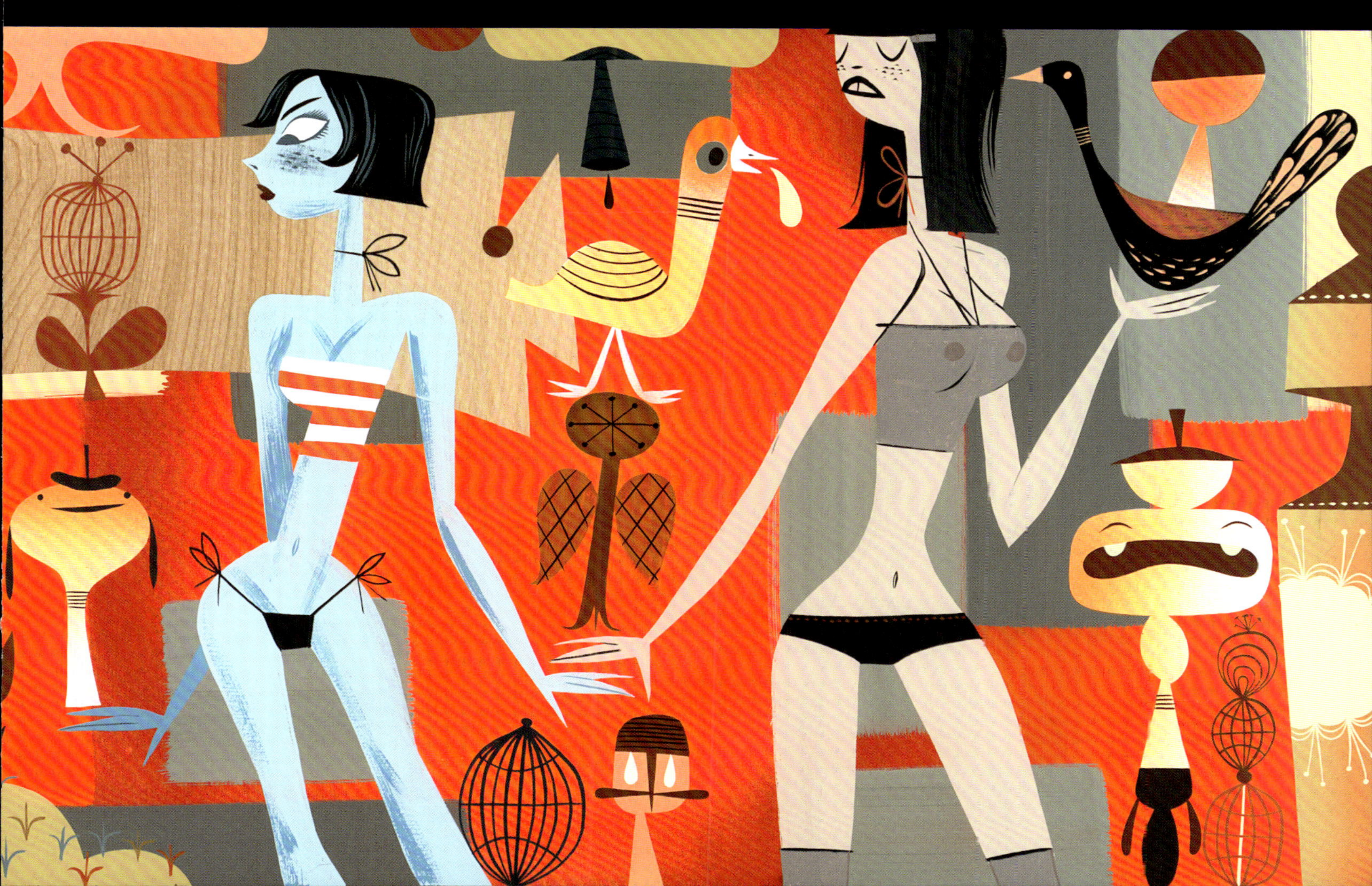

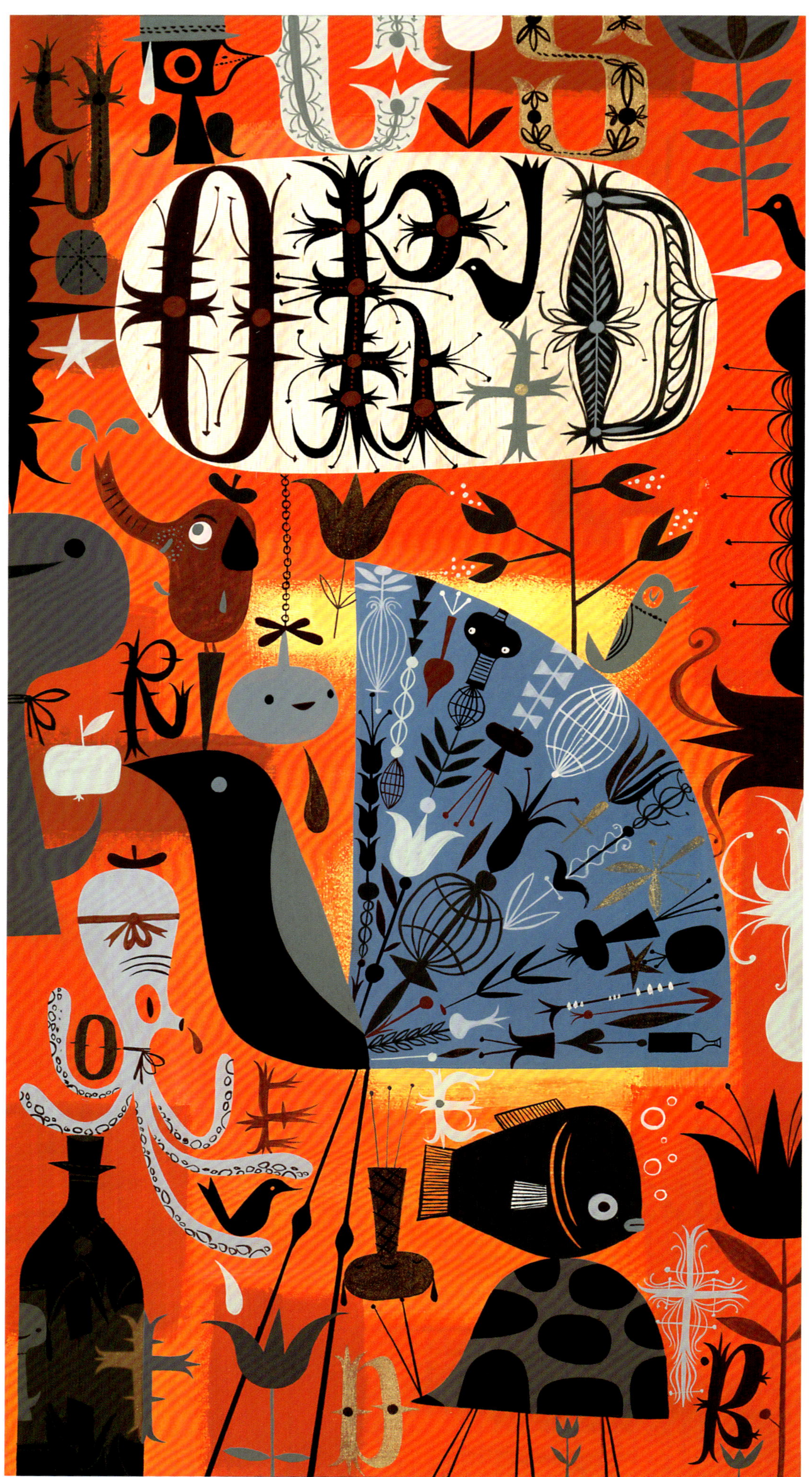

Deco-Virus Peacock
2004. Acrylic on Panel. 20" x 10"

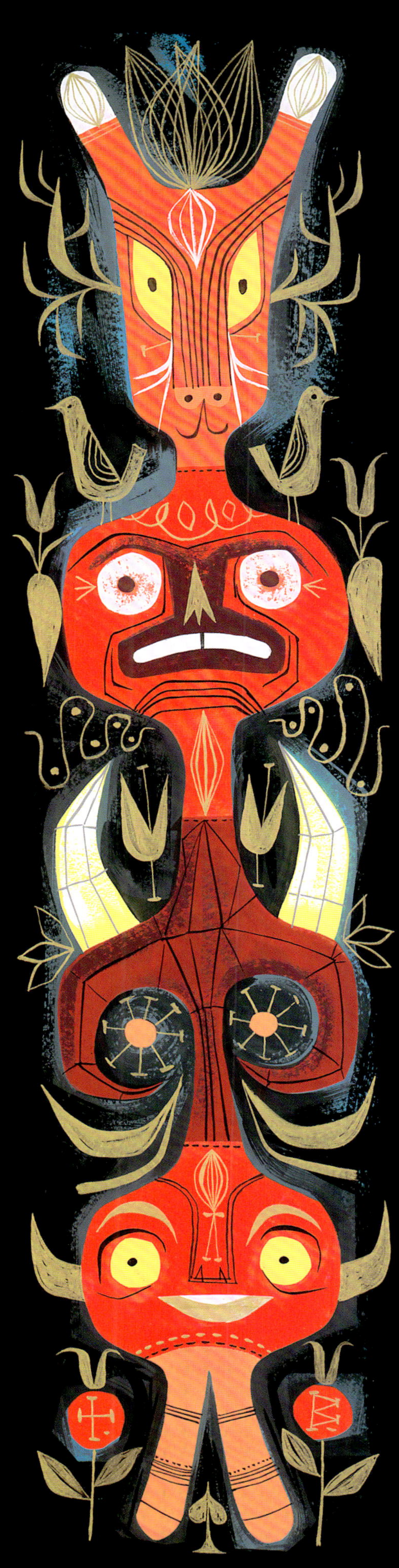

Paranoia Totem
2006. Acrylic on Paper. 22" x 7"

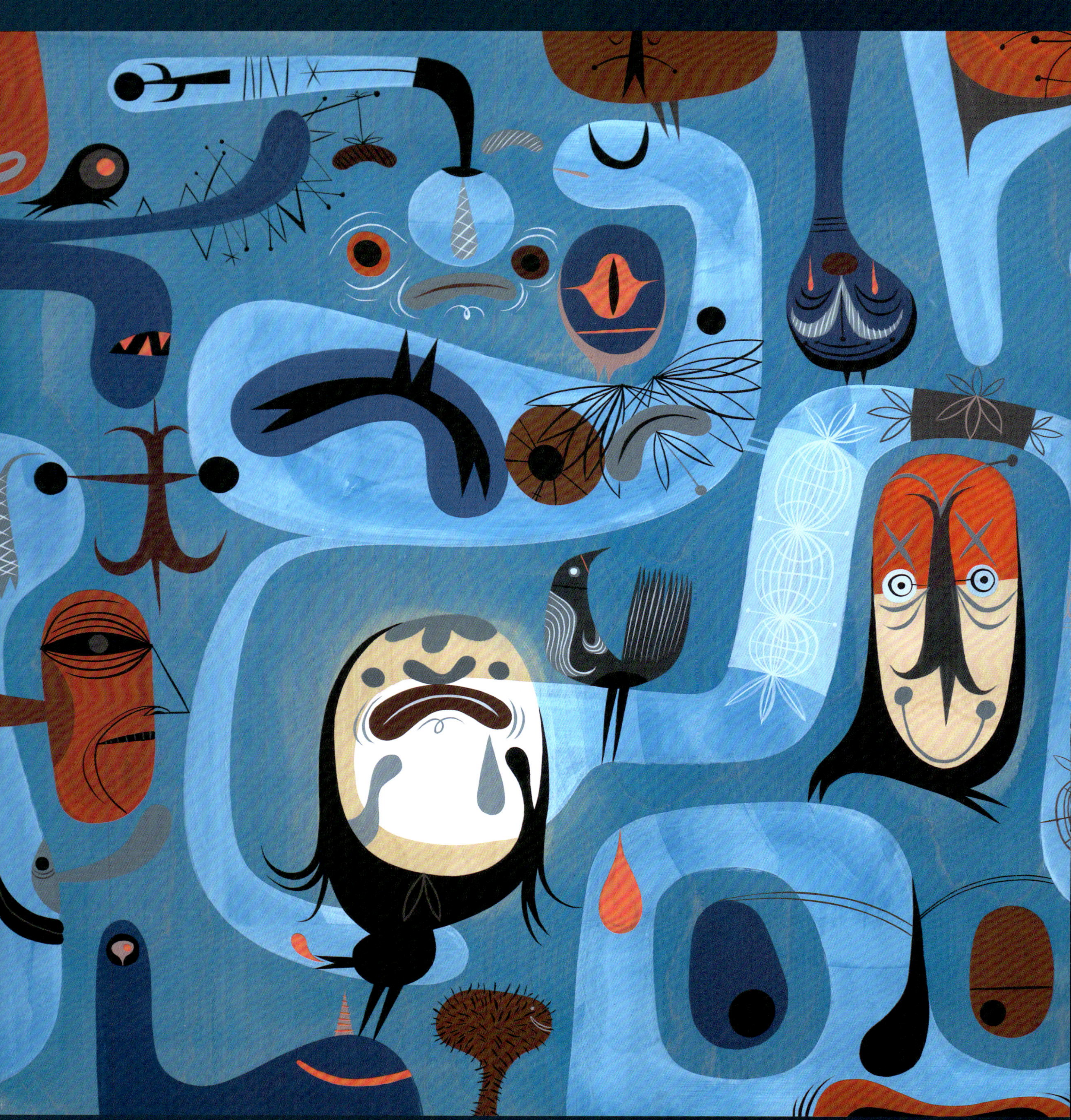

Savage Sectional
2006. Acrylic on Panel. 12" x 24"

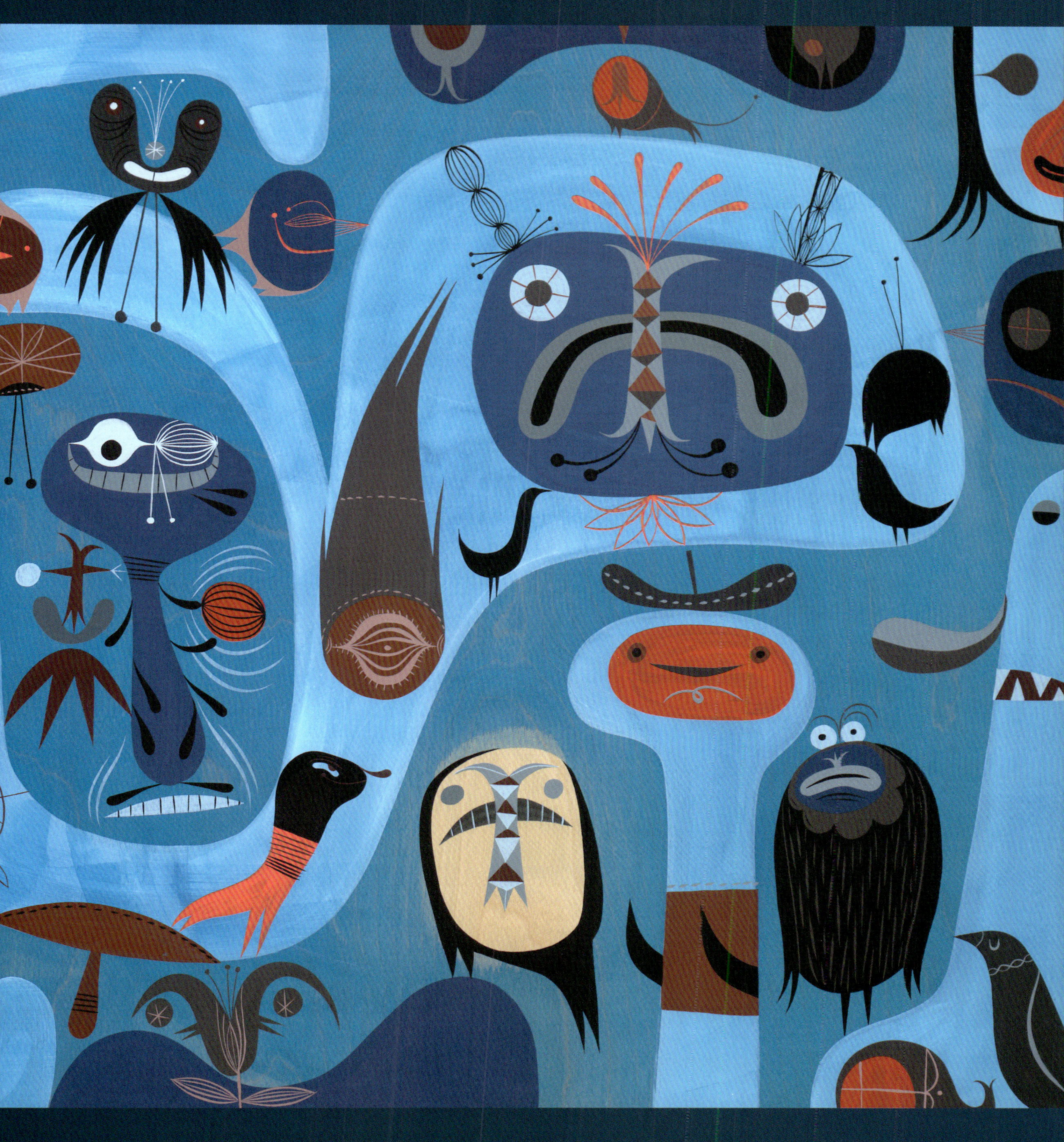

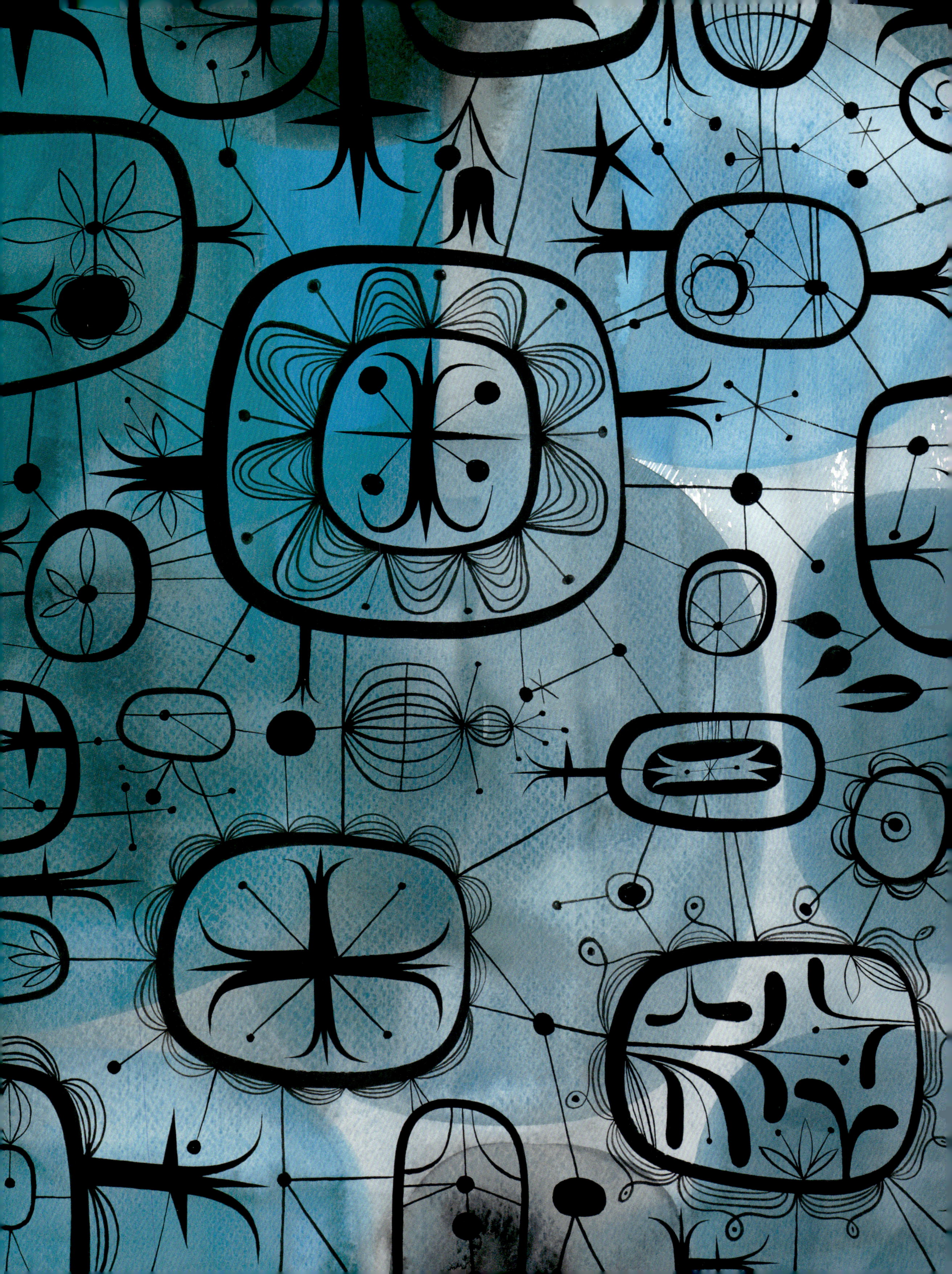

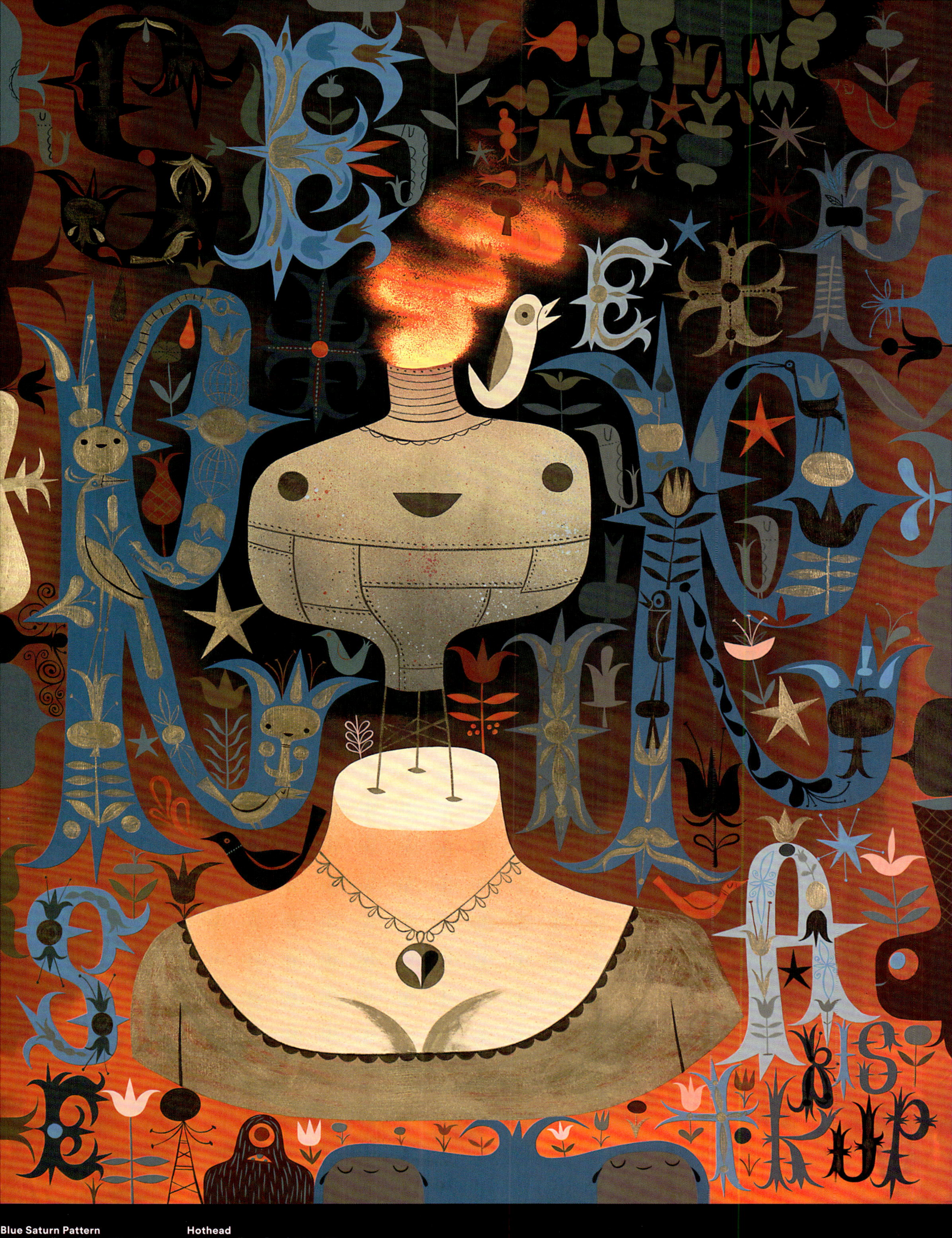

Blue Saturn Pattern
2005. Acrylic on Paper. 14" x 11"

Hothead
2004. Acrylic on Panel. 30" x 20"

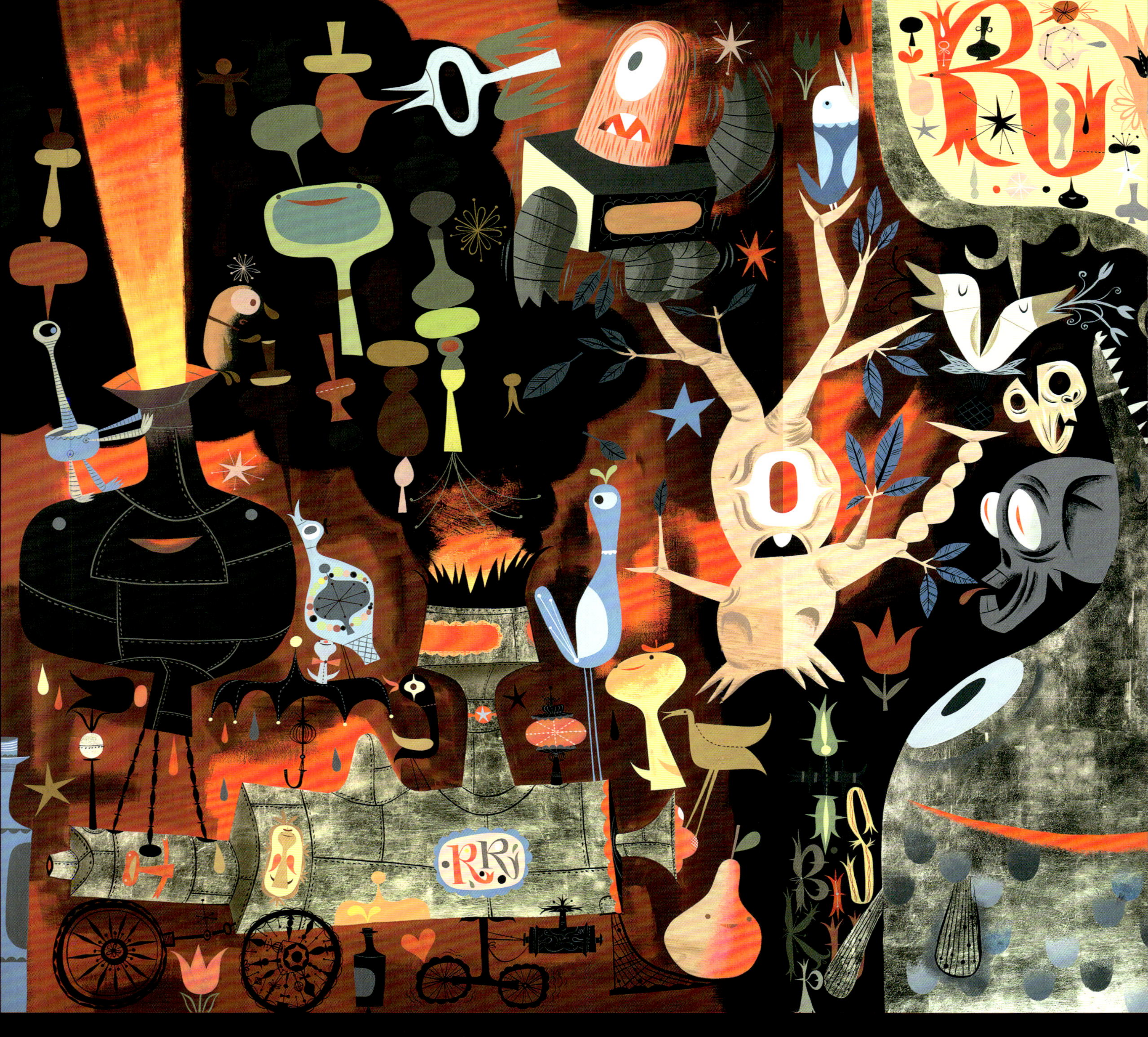

The Golden Plague
2004. Acrylic, Gold Leaf and Spray Paint on Panel. 48" x 108"

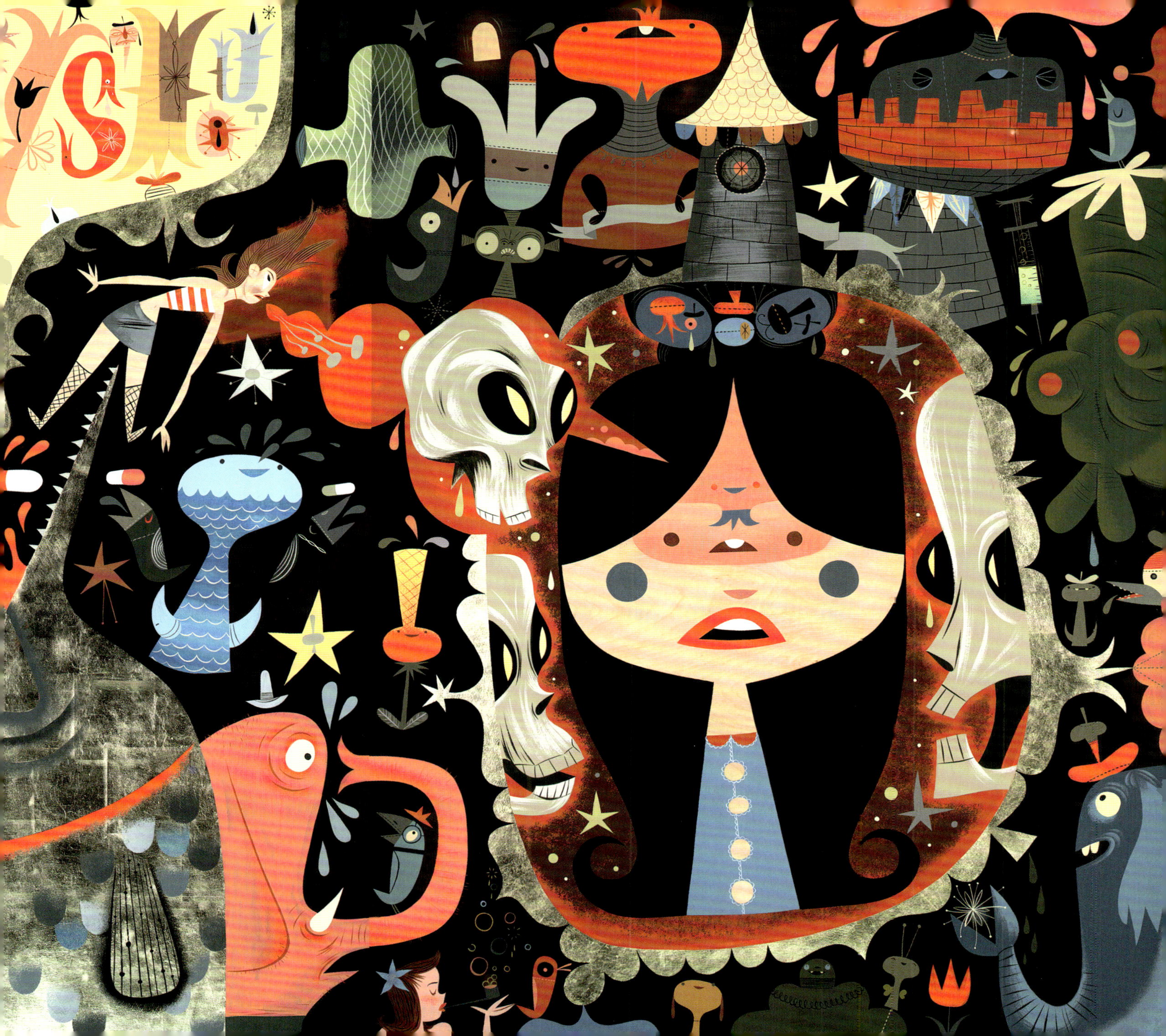

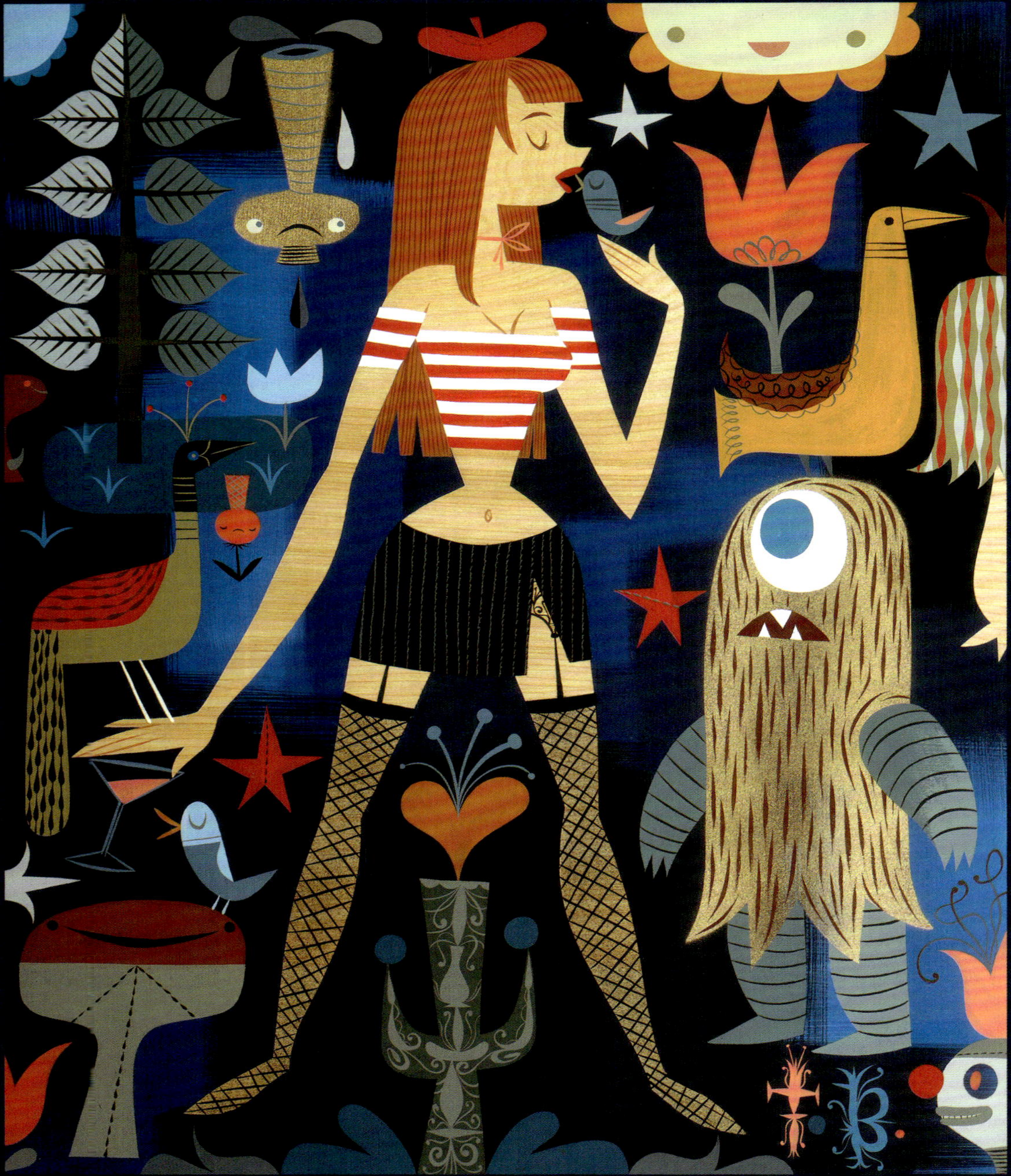

The Pink Drink
2004. Acrylic and Spray Paint on Panel. 30" x 20"

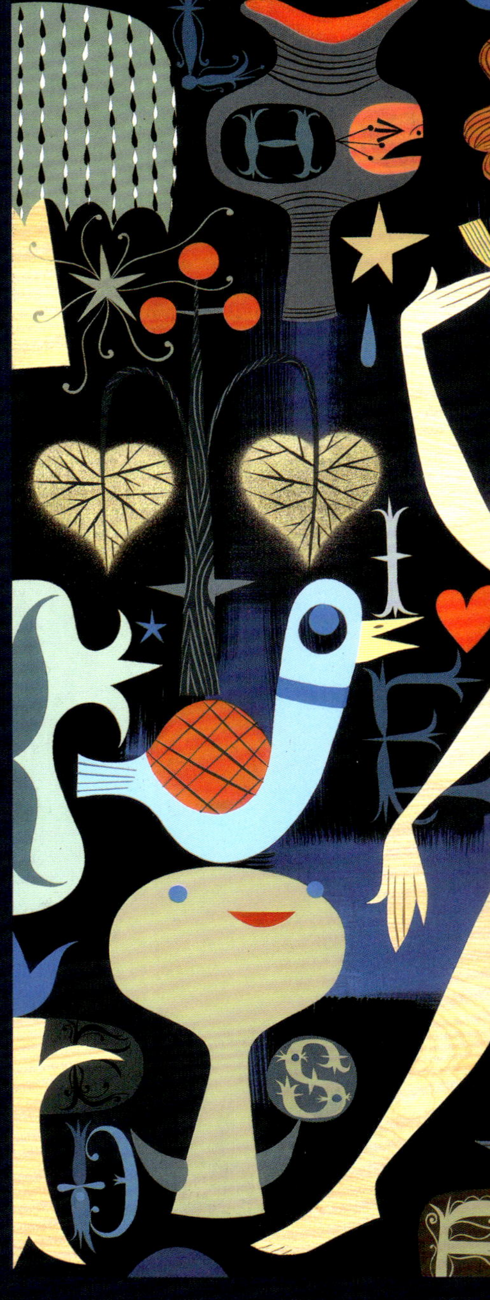

Hazel's Field
2004. Acrylic and Spray Paint on Panel. 30" x 20"

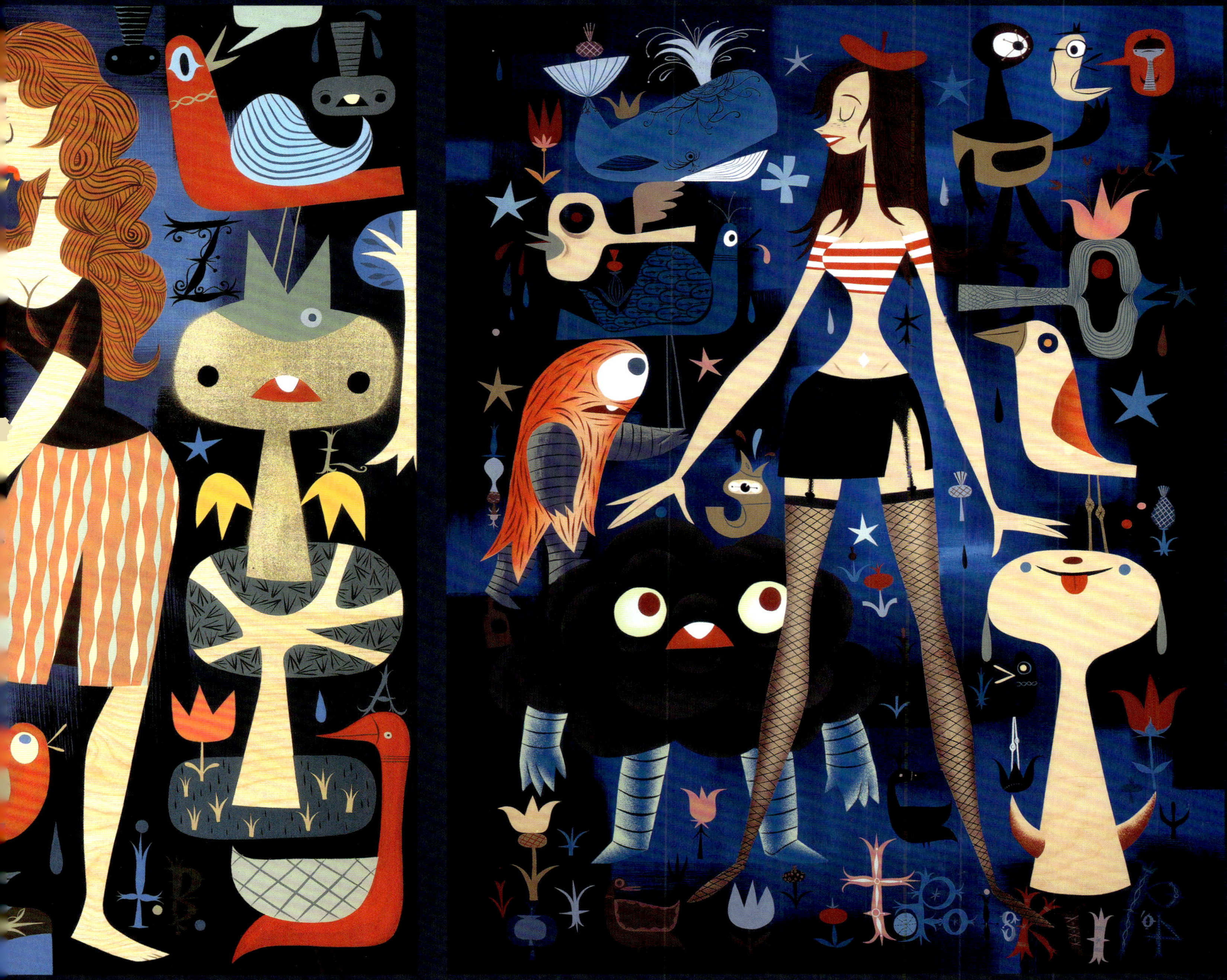

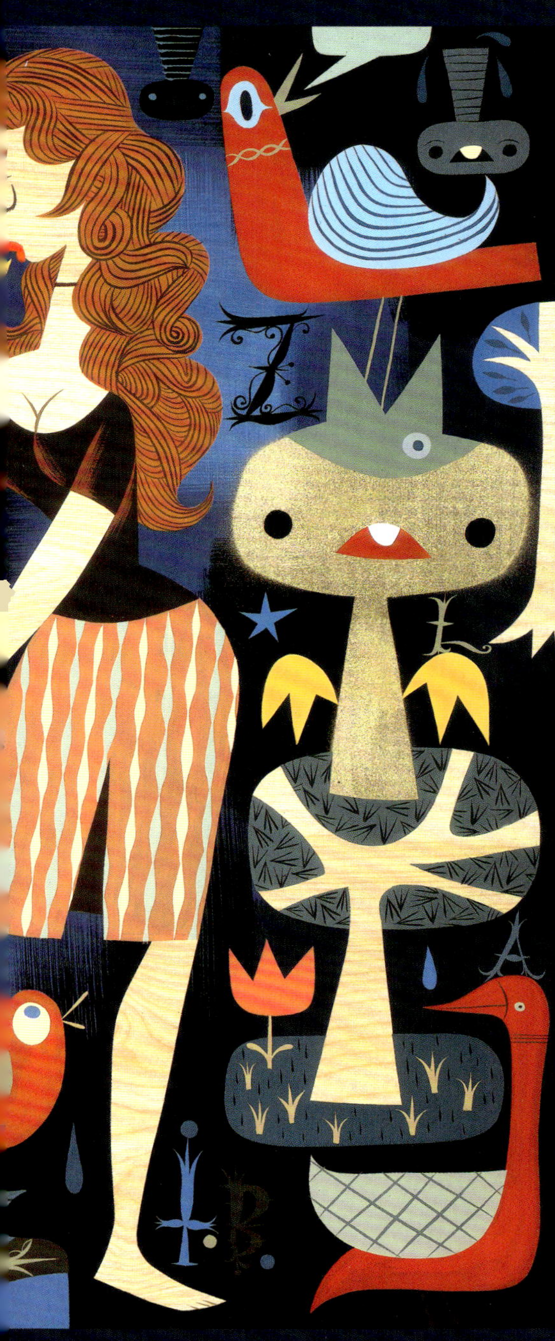

Channeler
2004. Acrylic on Panel. 30" x 20"

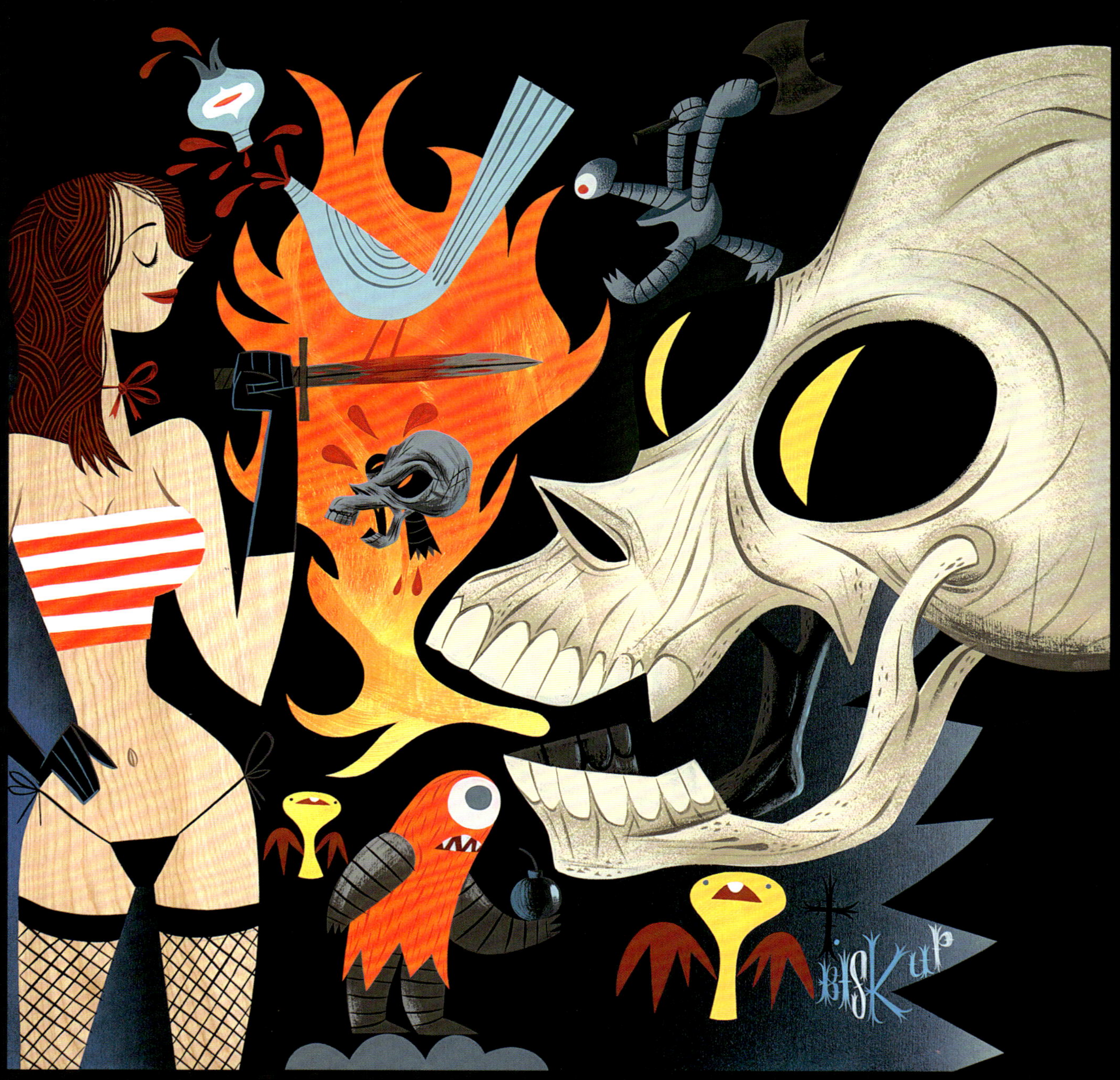

Broken Beak
2004. Acrylic on Panel. 18" x 18"

The Furnace
2004. Acrylic on Panel. 36" x 24"

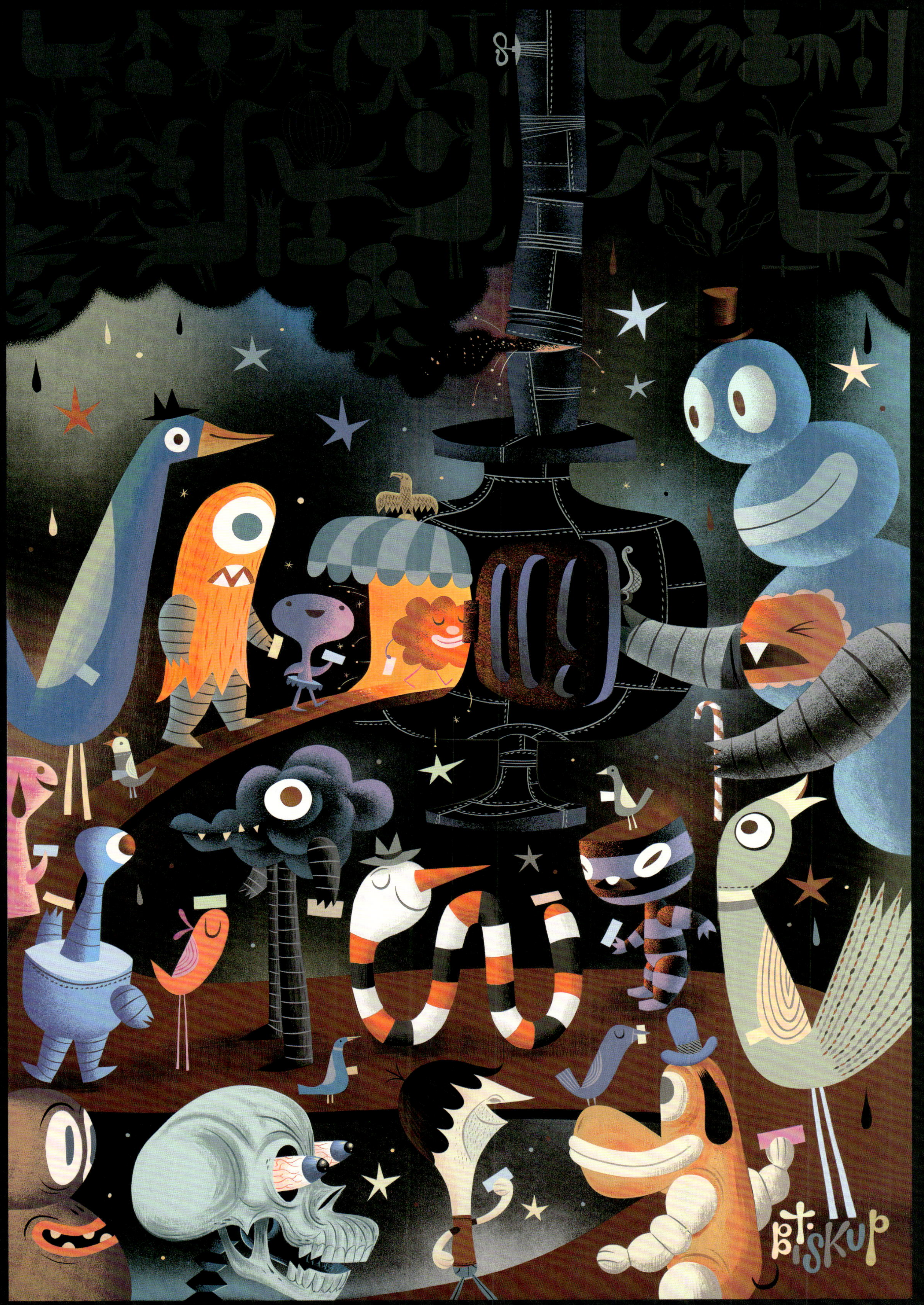
pt. piskup

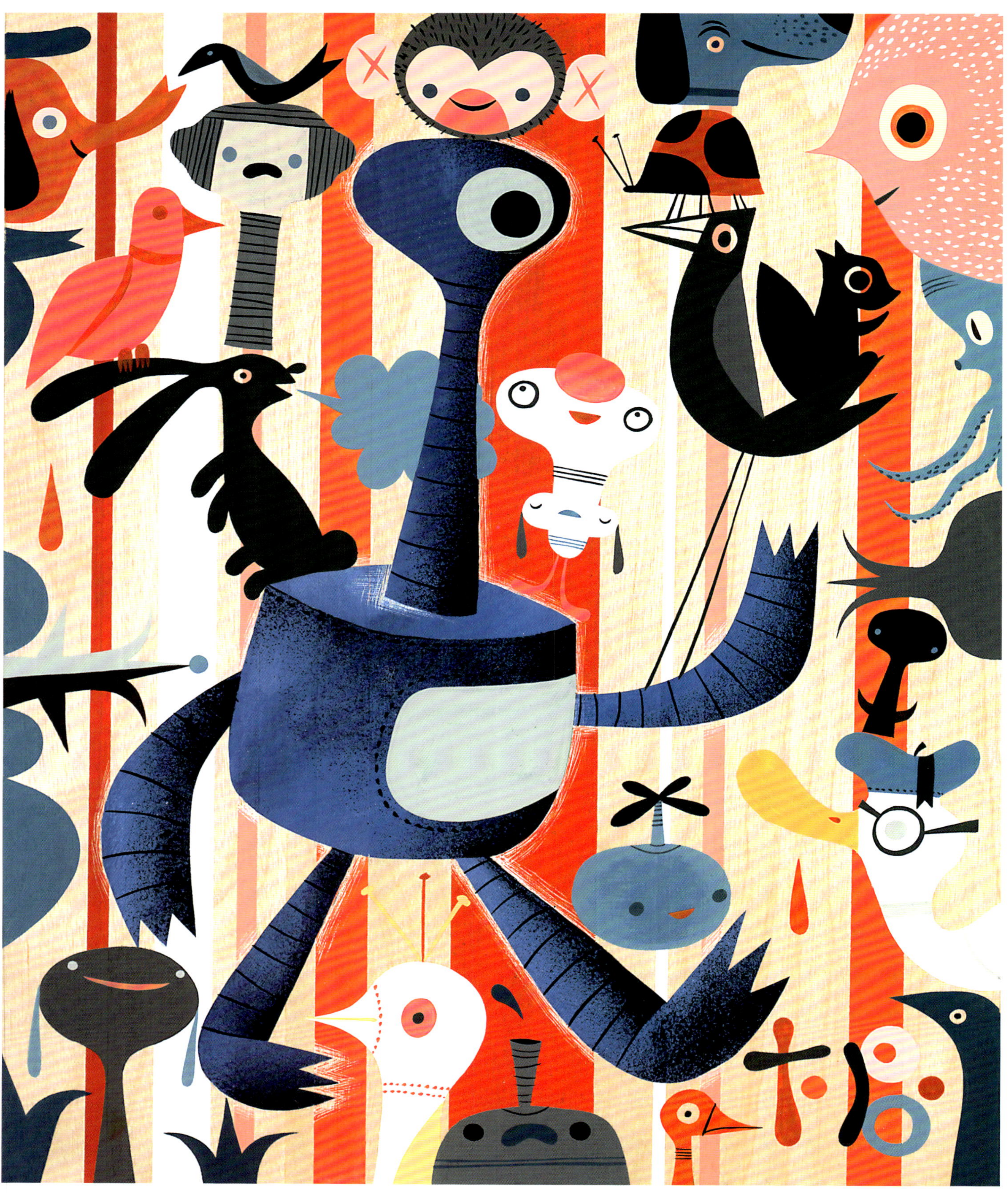

Robotic Magnetism
2004. Acrylic on Panel. 14" x 11"

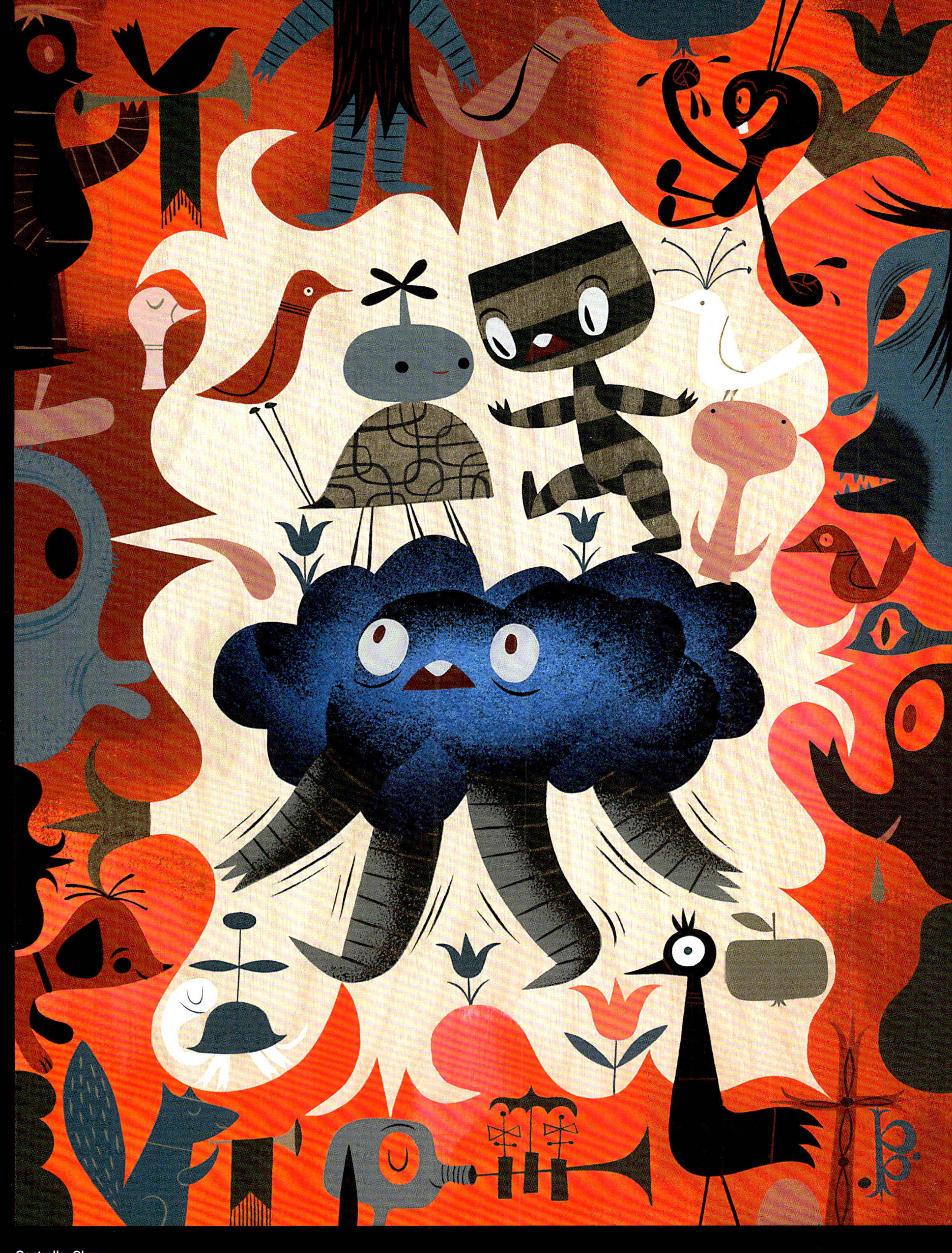

Controller Clump
2004. Acrylic on Panel. 14" x 11"

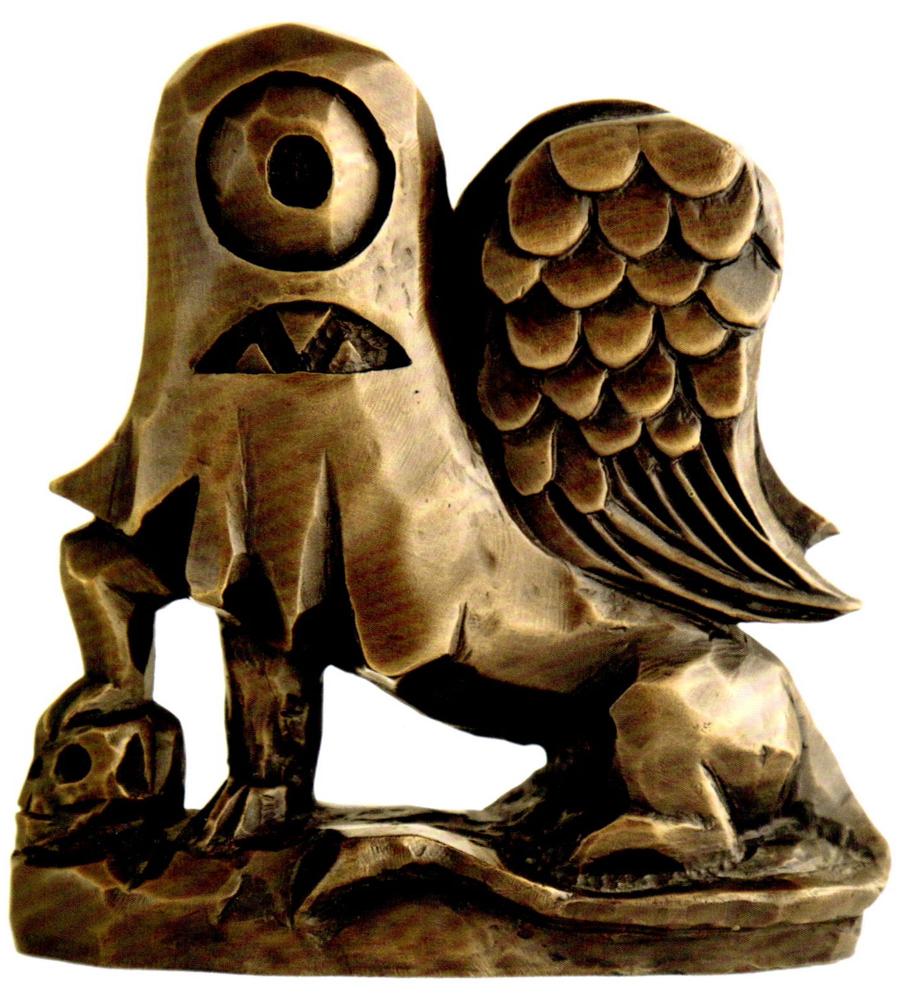

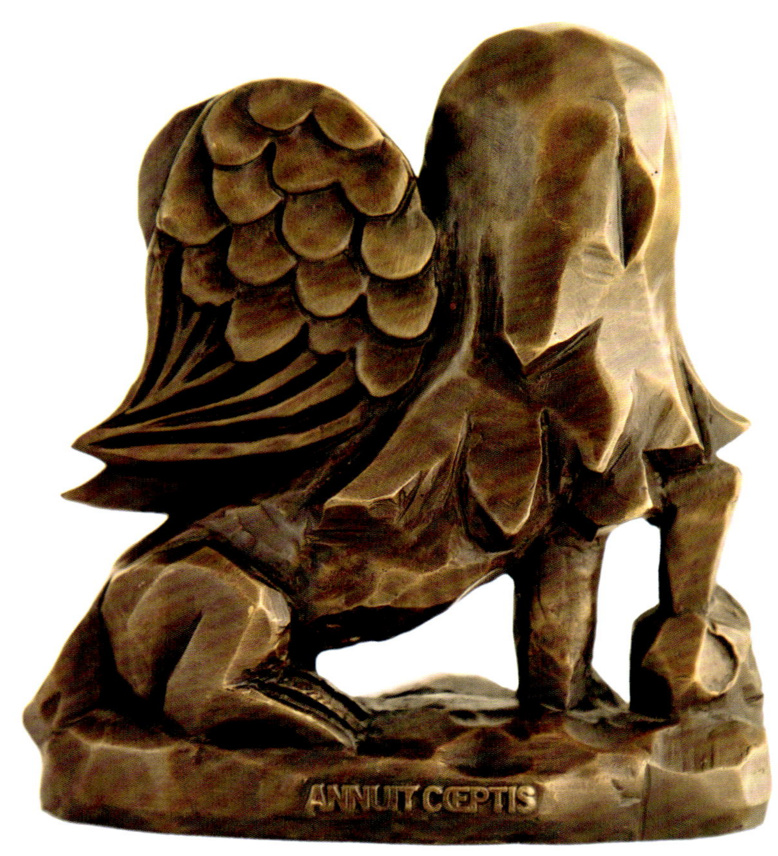

Helper Dragon
2009. Bronze. 6" tall

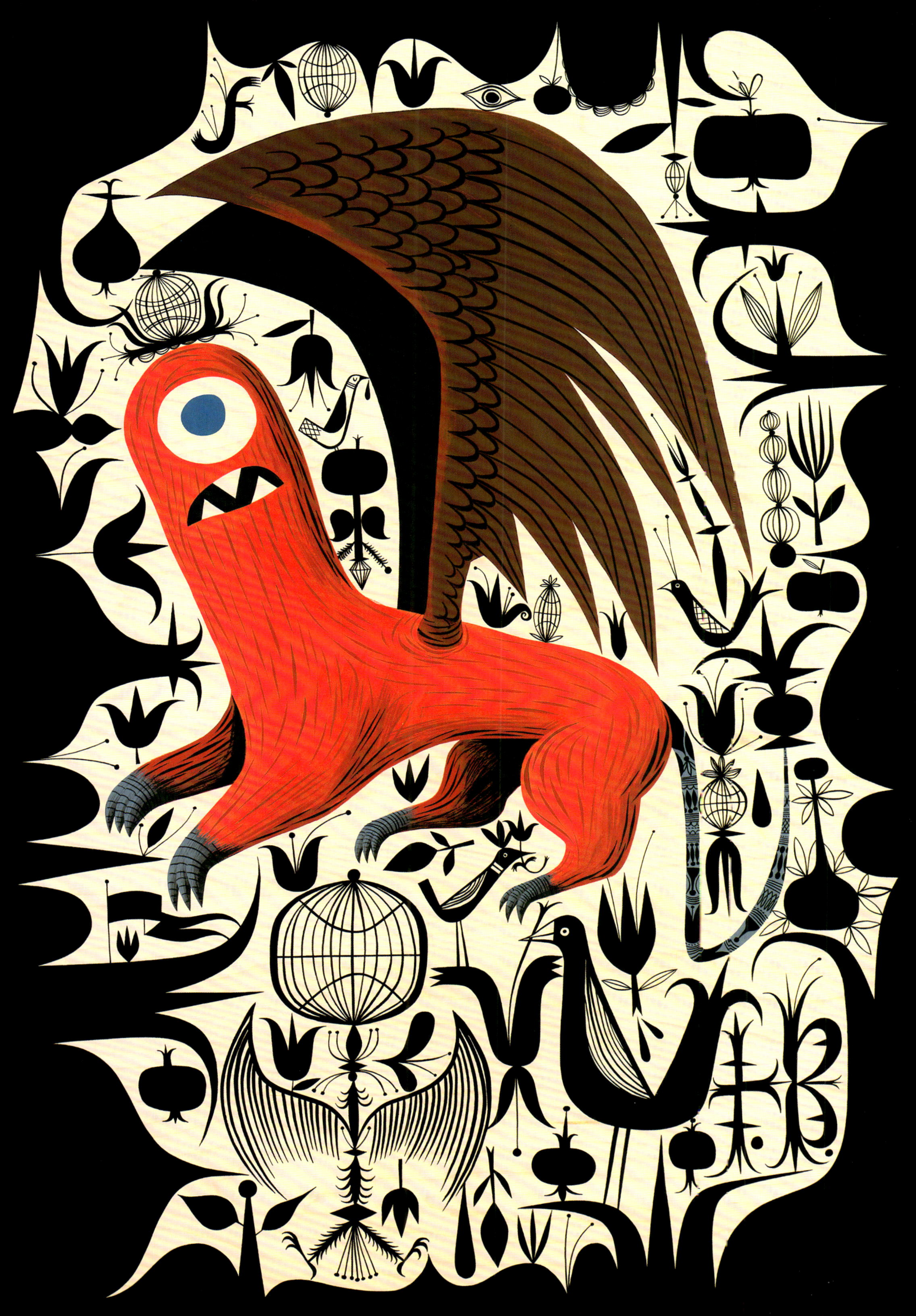

Helper Dragon
2005. Acrylic on Panel. 36" x 24"

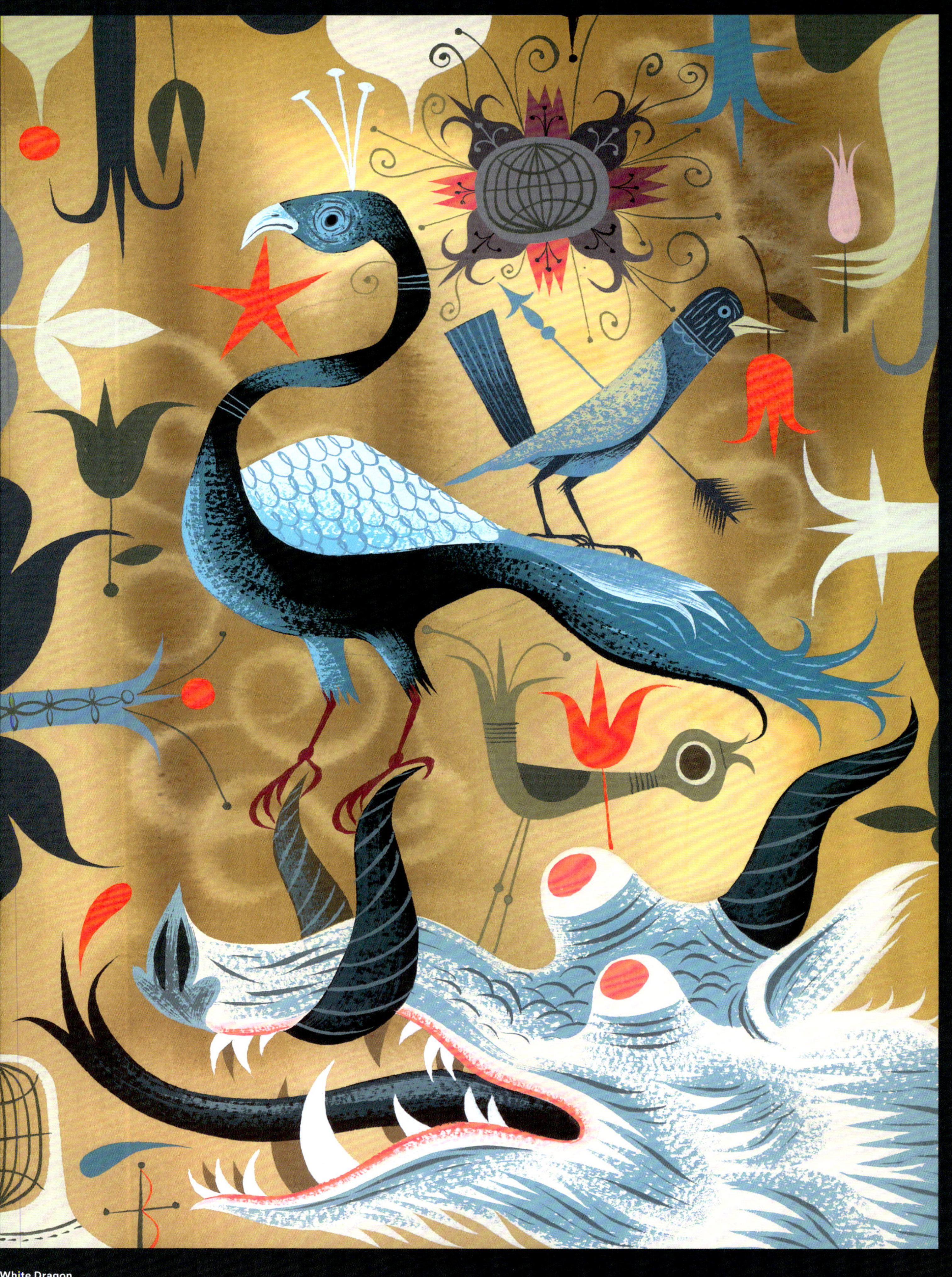

White Dragon
2005. Gouache on Paper. 12" x 9"

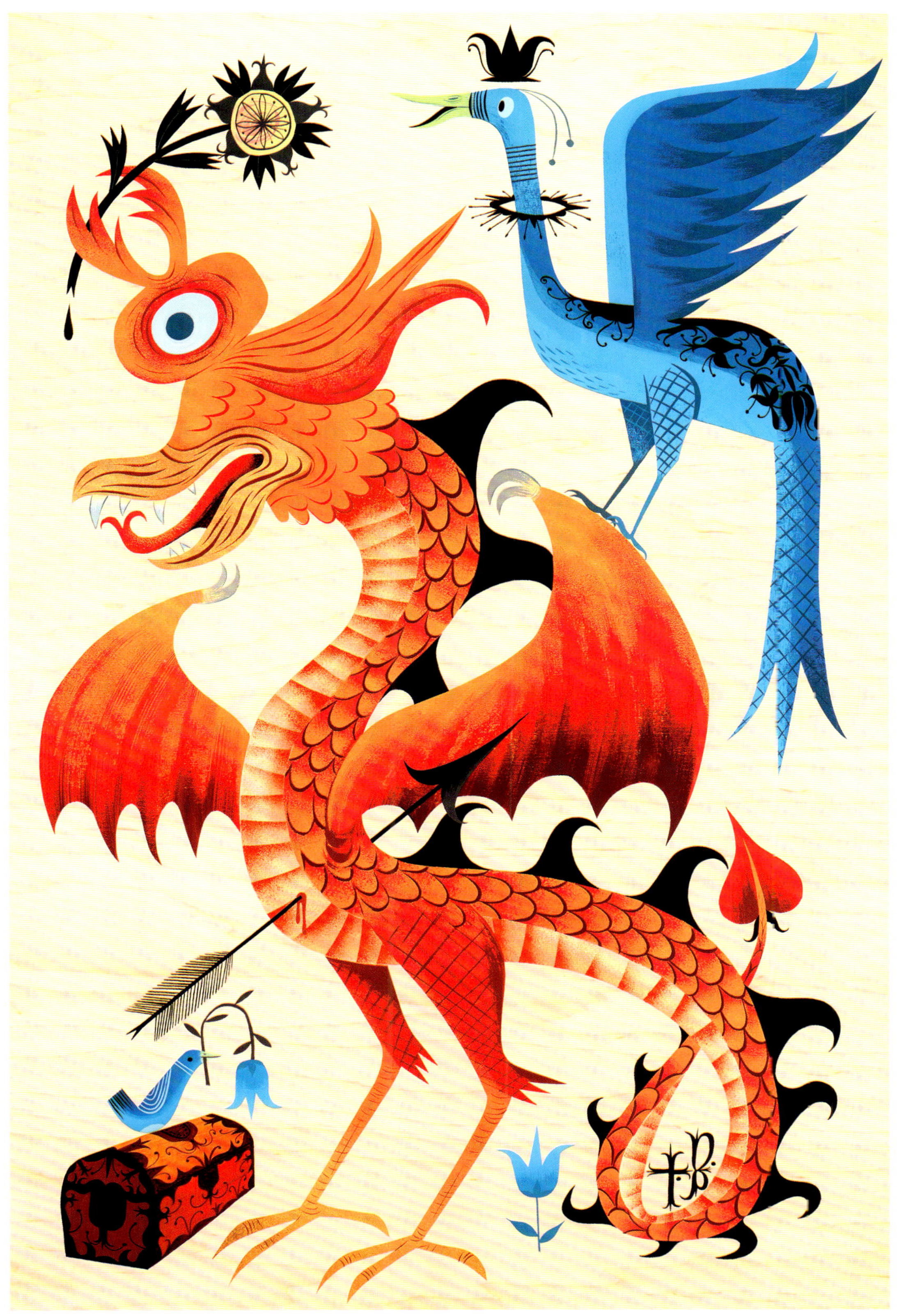

Red Dragon
2005. Acrylic on Panel. 36" x 24"

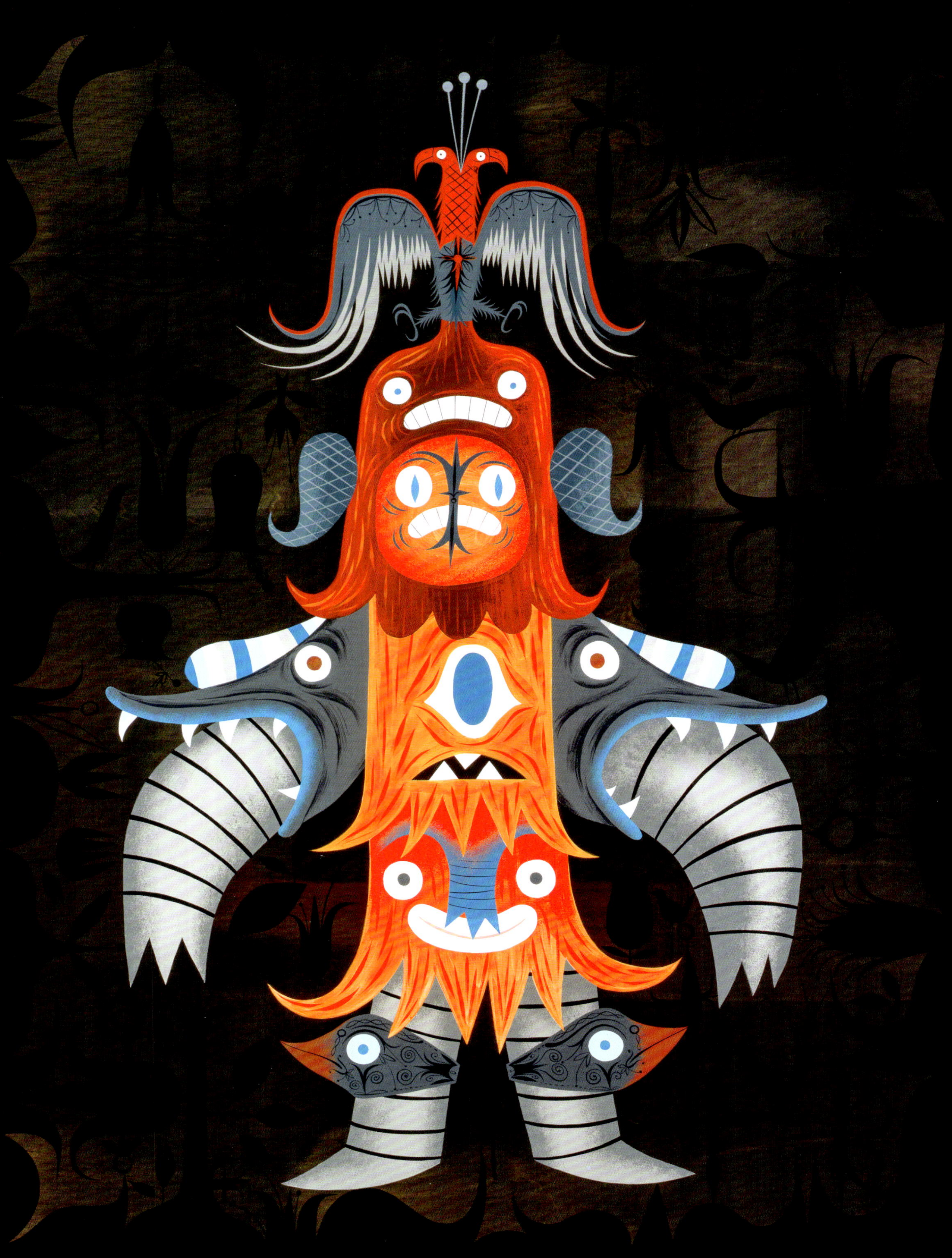

Armor Totem
2005. Acrylic on Panel. 48" x 36"

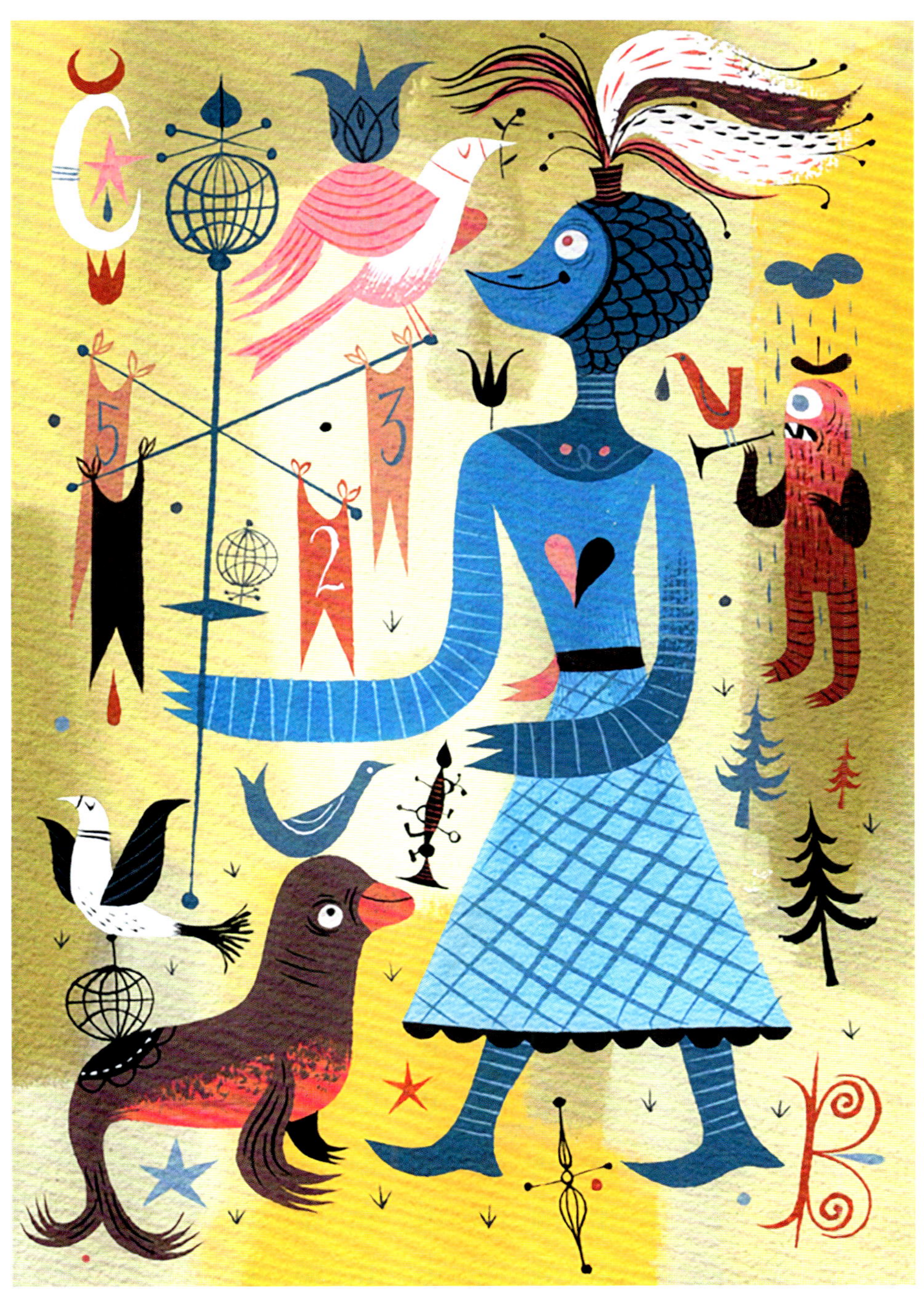

The Push Over
2005. Gouache on Paper. 10" x 7"

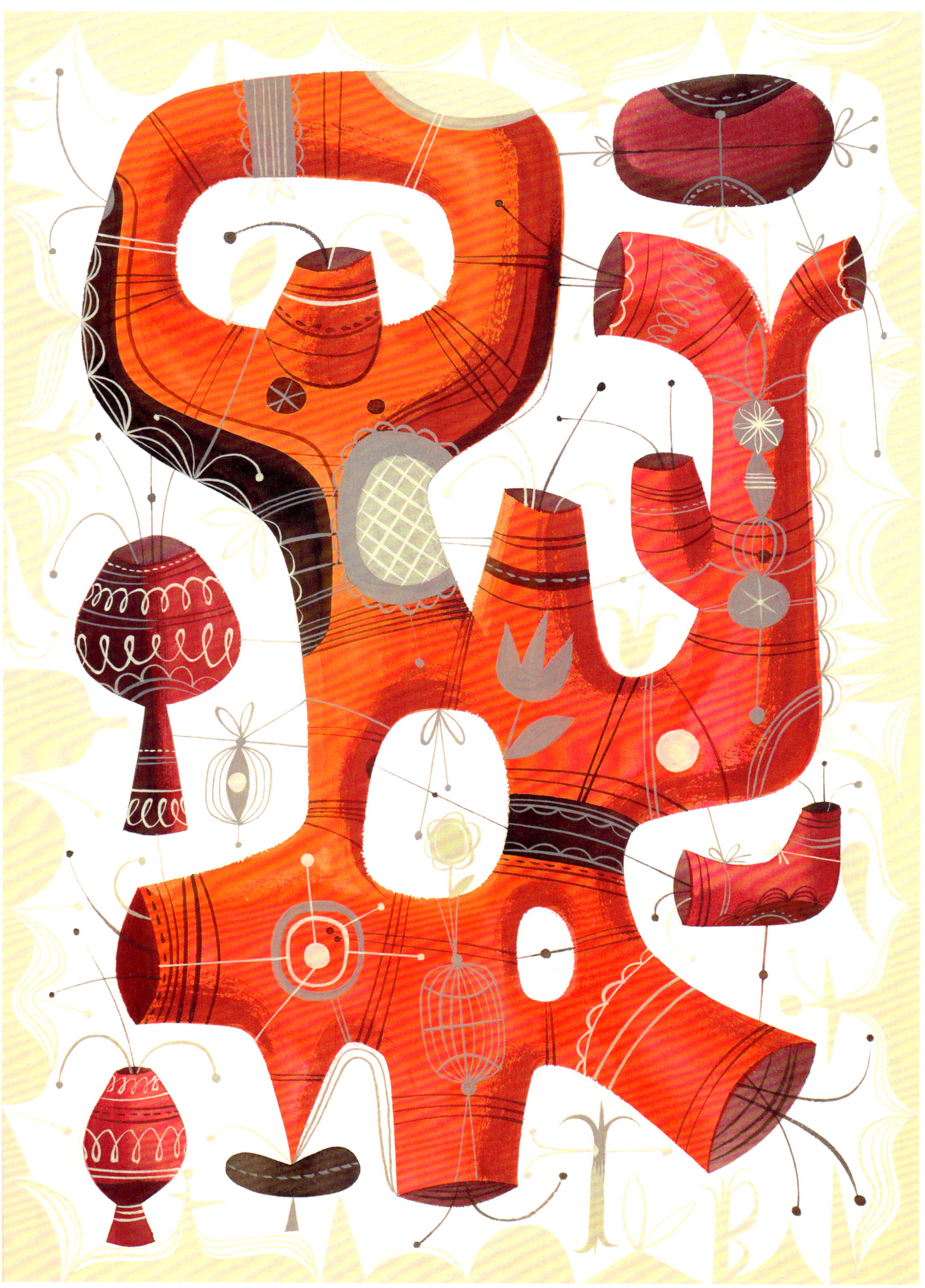

The Strangler
2005. Gouache on Paper. 20" x 16"

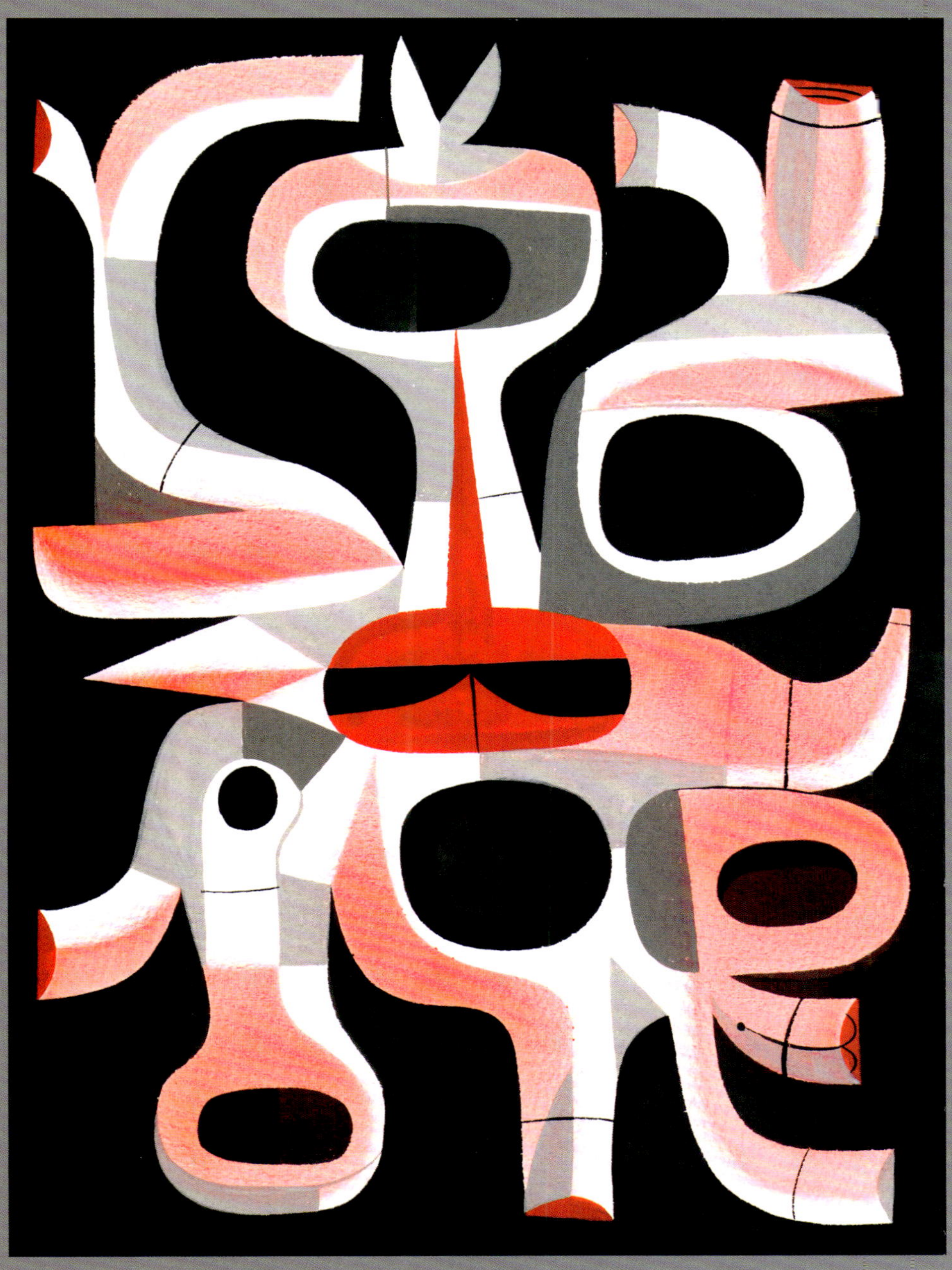

Sniper Kit
2005. Gouache on Paper. 14" x 11"

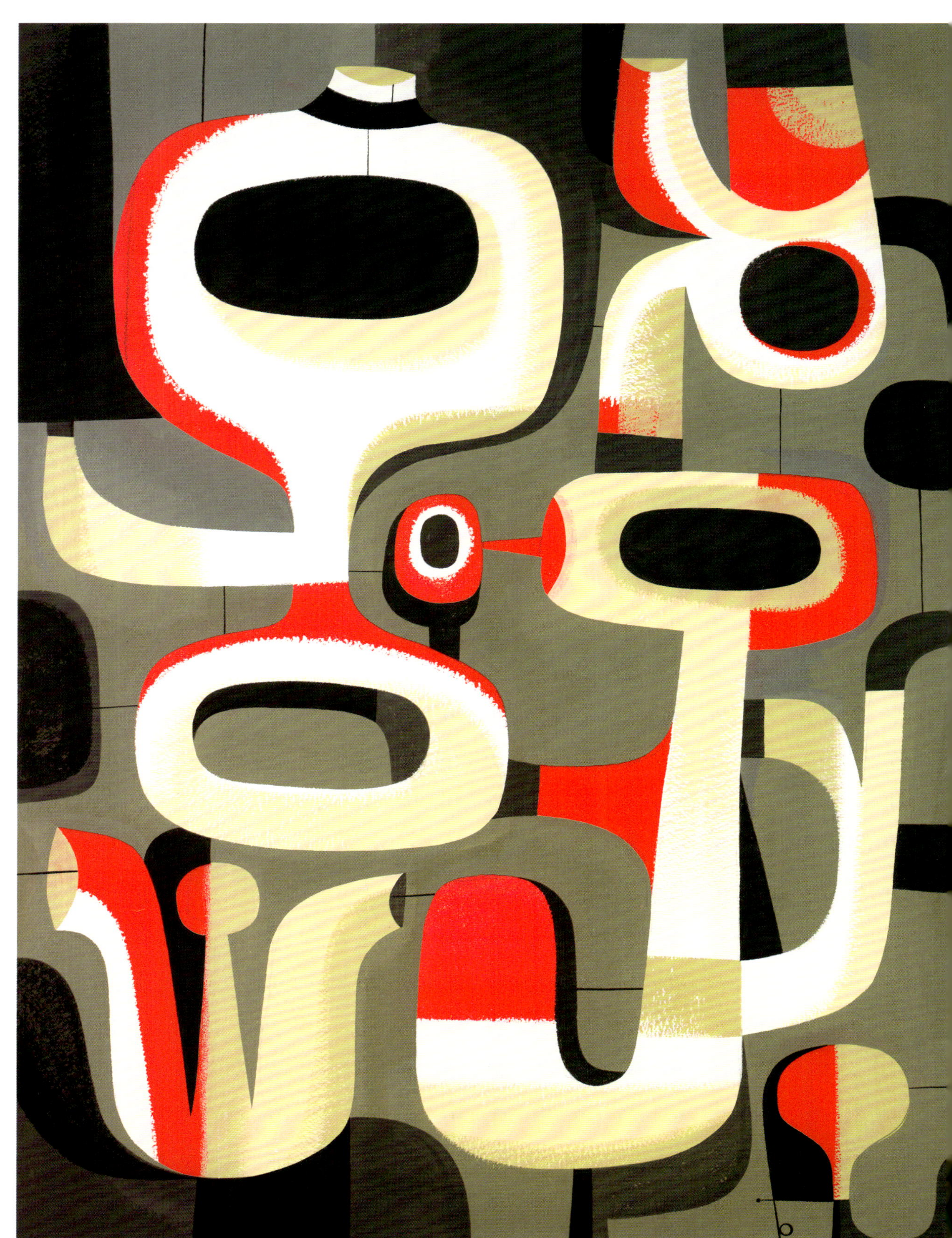

Vacant Pangolin
2005. Gouache on Paper. 29" x 20"

Golden Cannibal
2005. Gouache on Paper. 14" x 11"

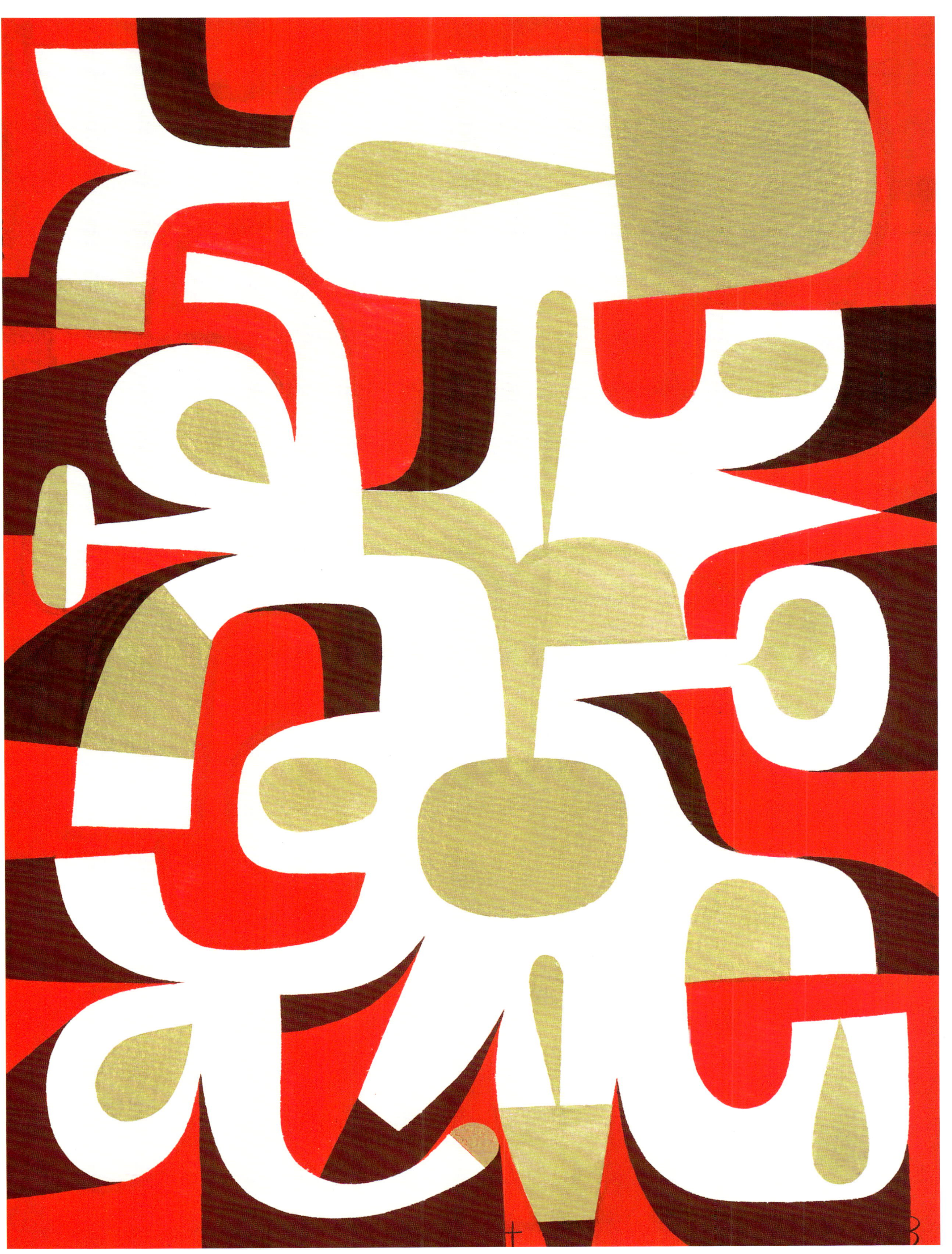

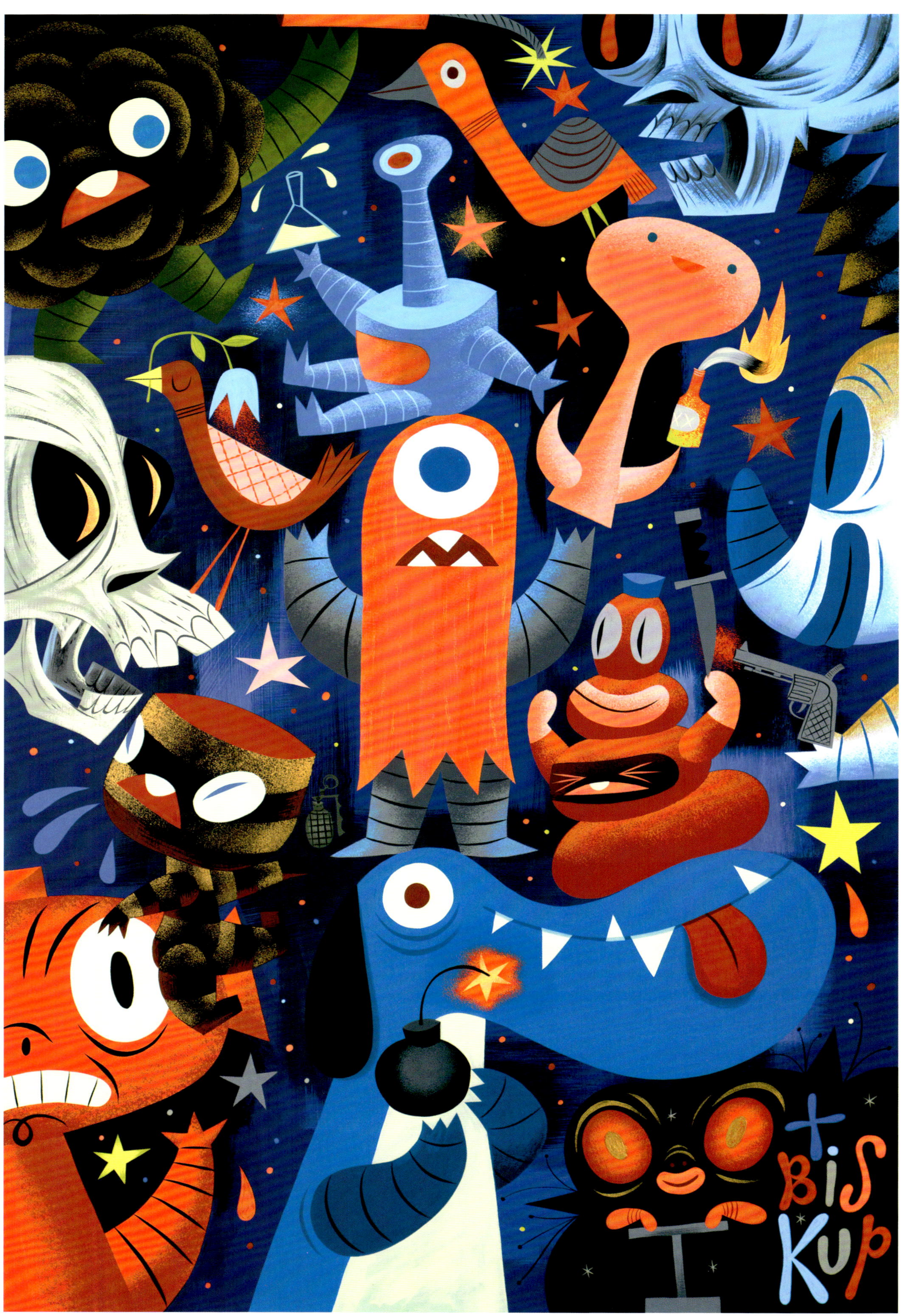

Helper Power No 2
2004. Acrylic on Panel. 30" x 20"

Helper Power No 1
2004. Acrylic on Panel. 30" x 20"

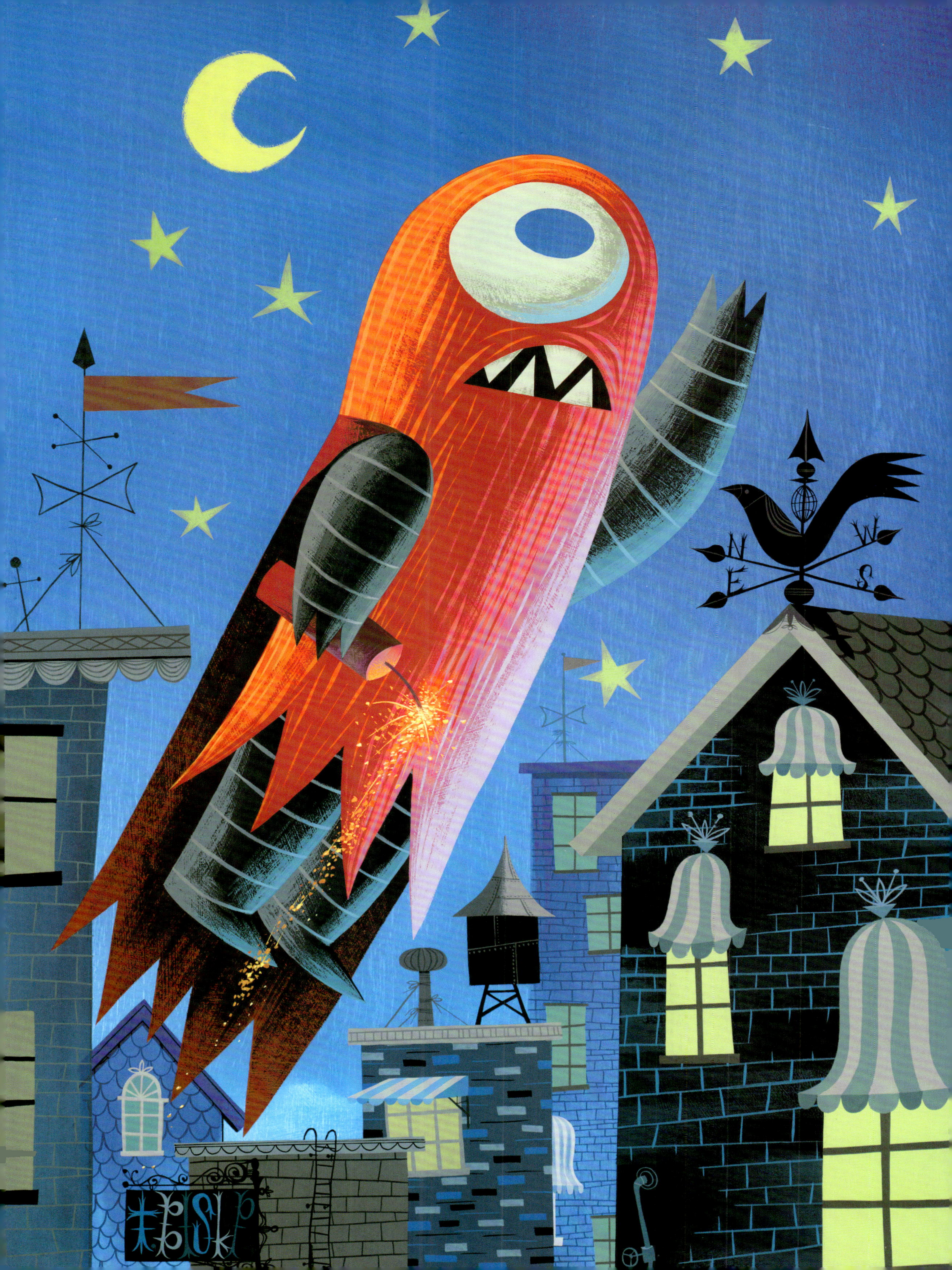

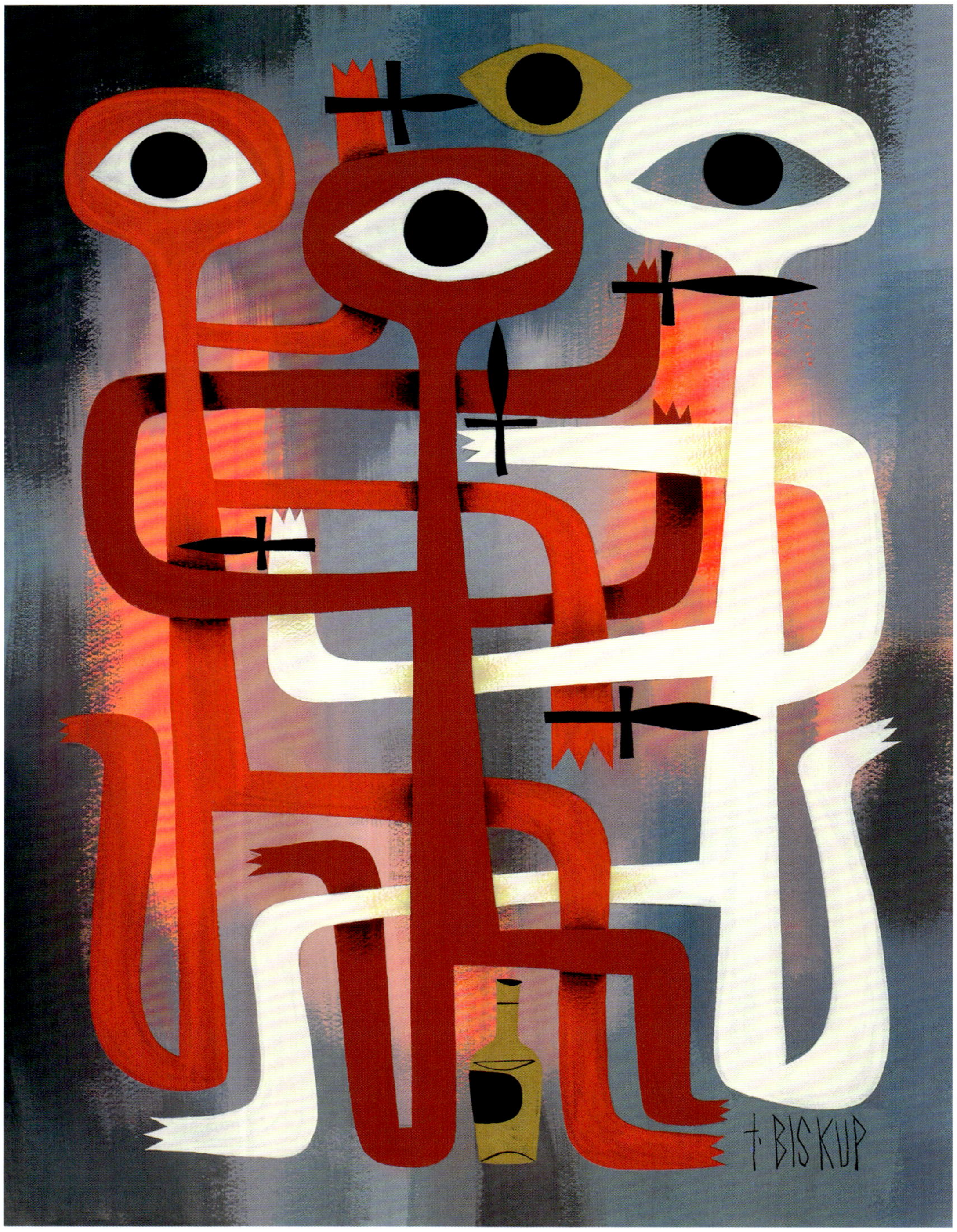

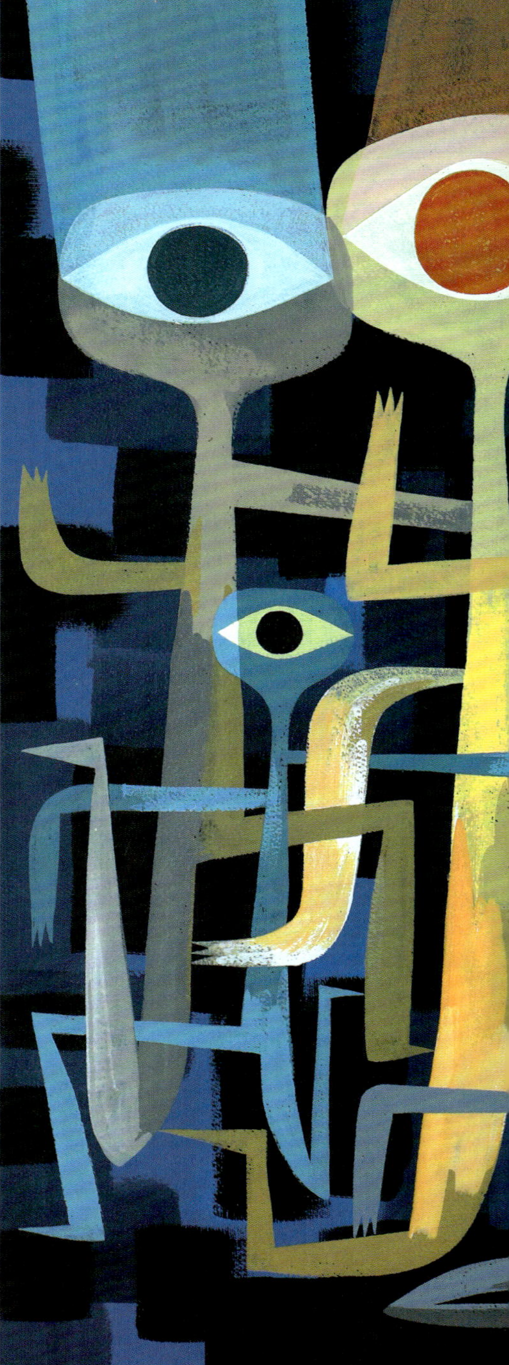

Wise Men
2006. Acrylic on Paper. 20" x 16"

Vision No 1
2006. Acrylic on Paper. 24" x 18"

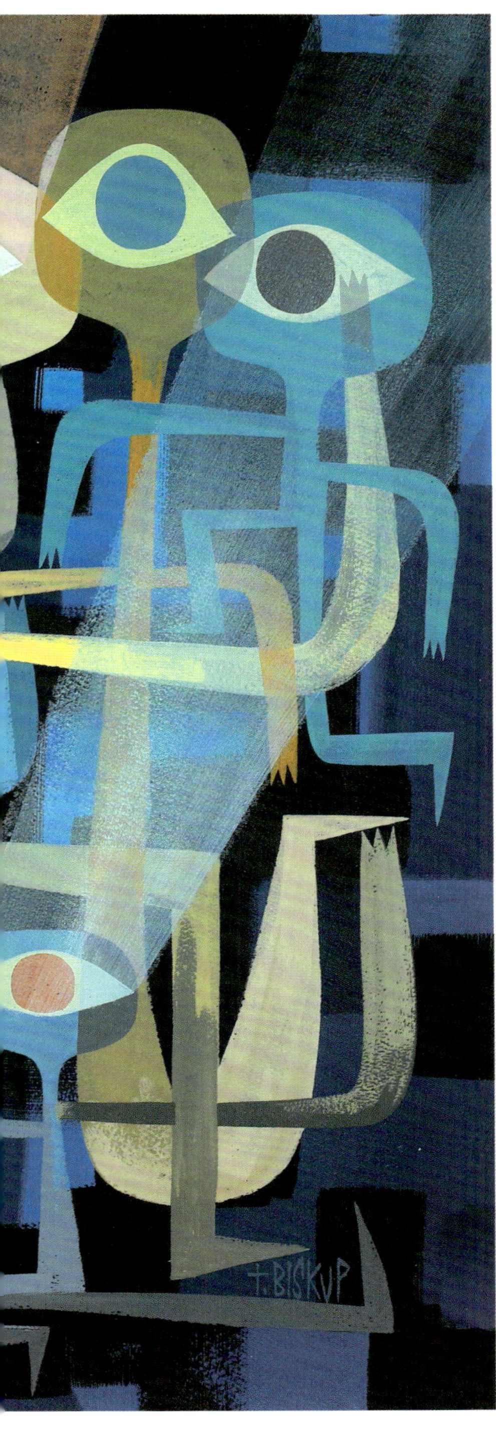

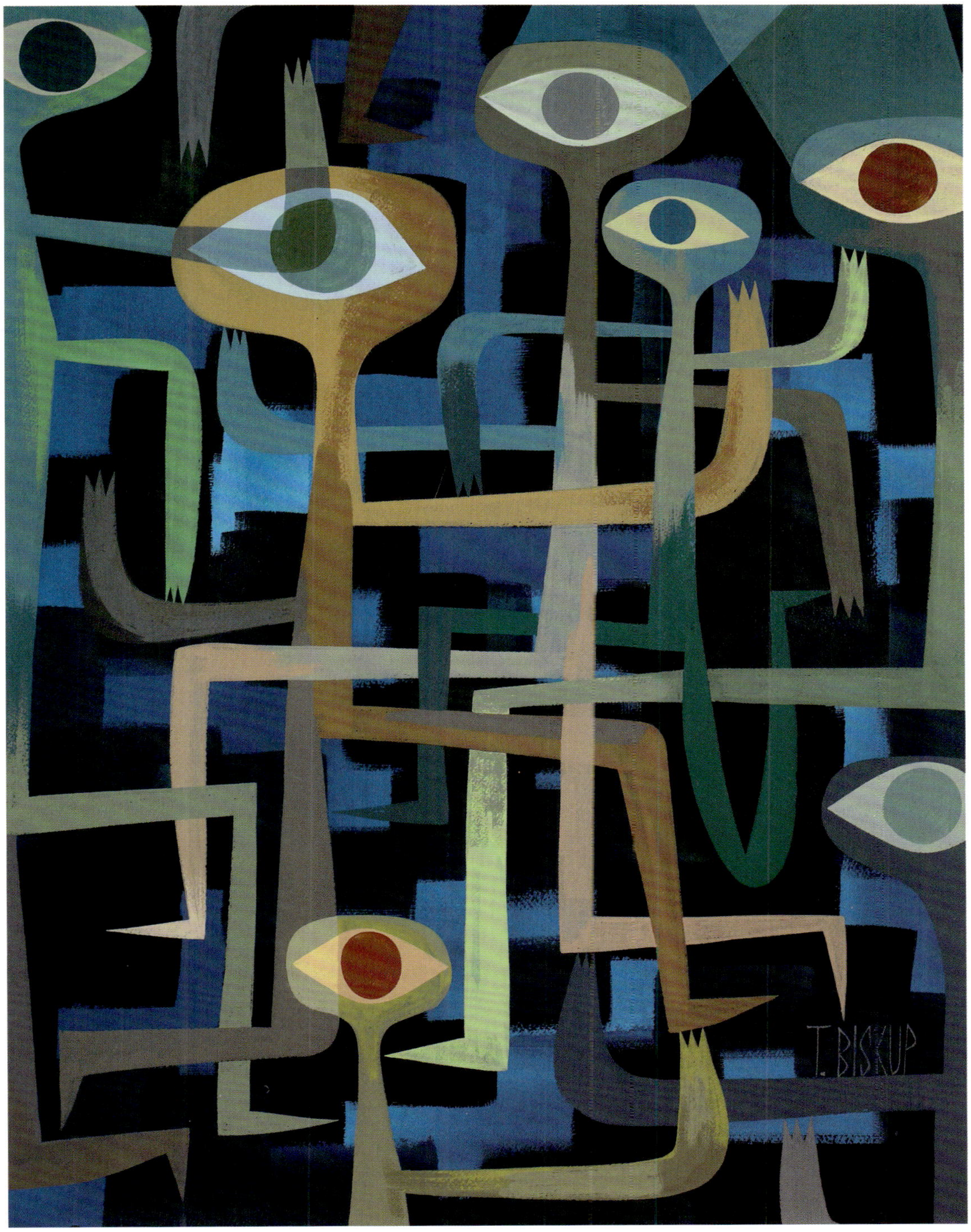

Vision No 2
2006. Acrylic on Paper. 24" x 18"

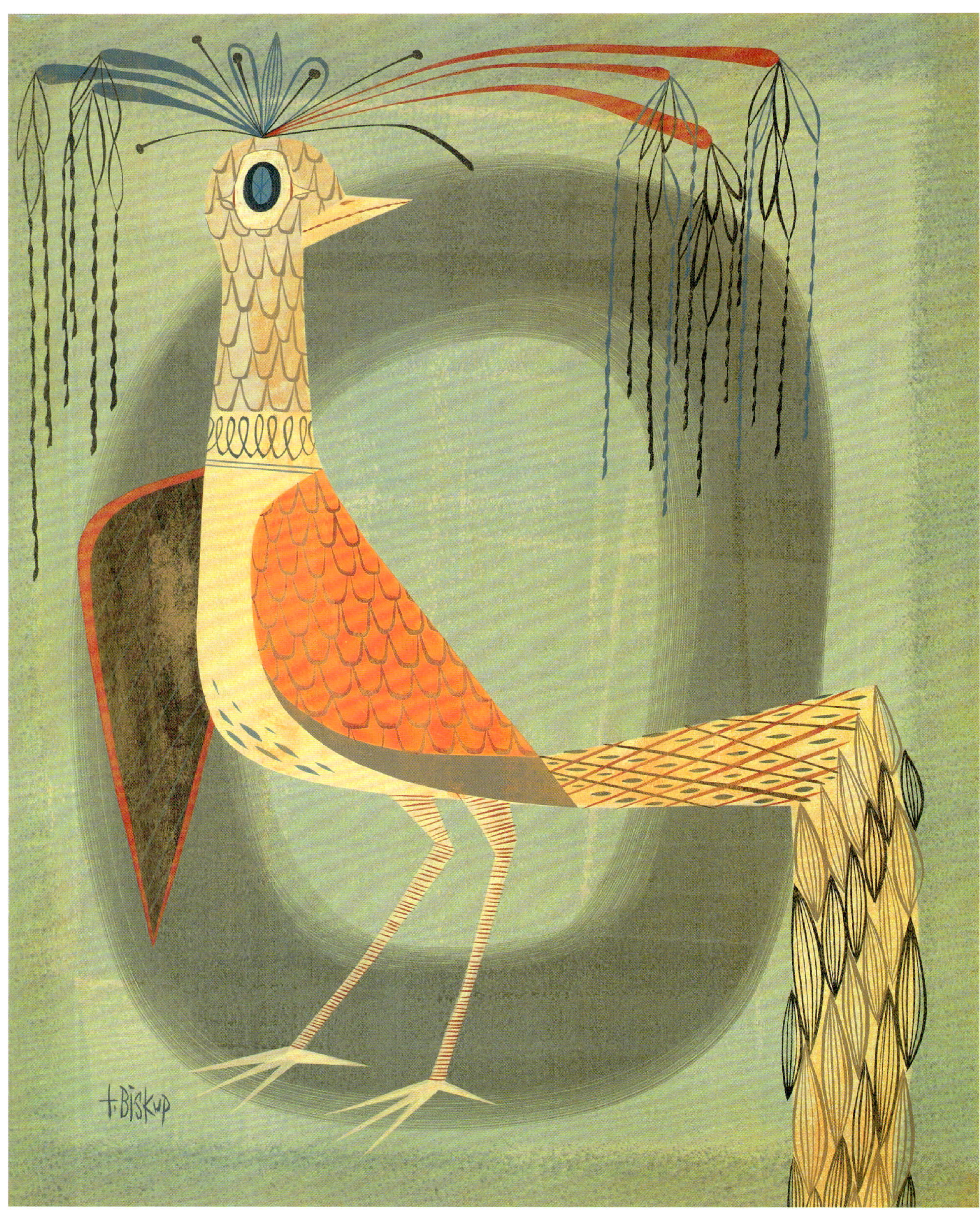

Magic Bird
2008. Acrylic on Panel. 20" x 16"

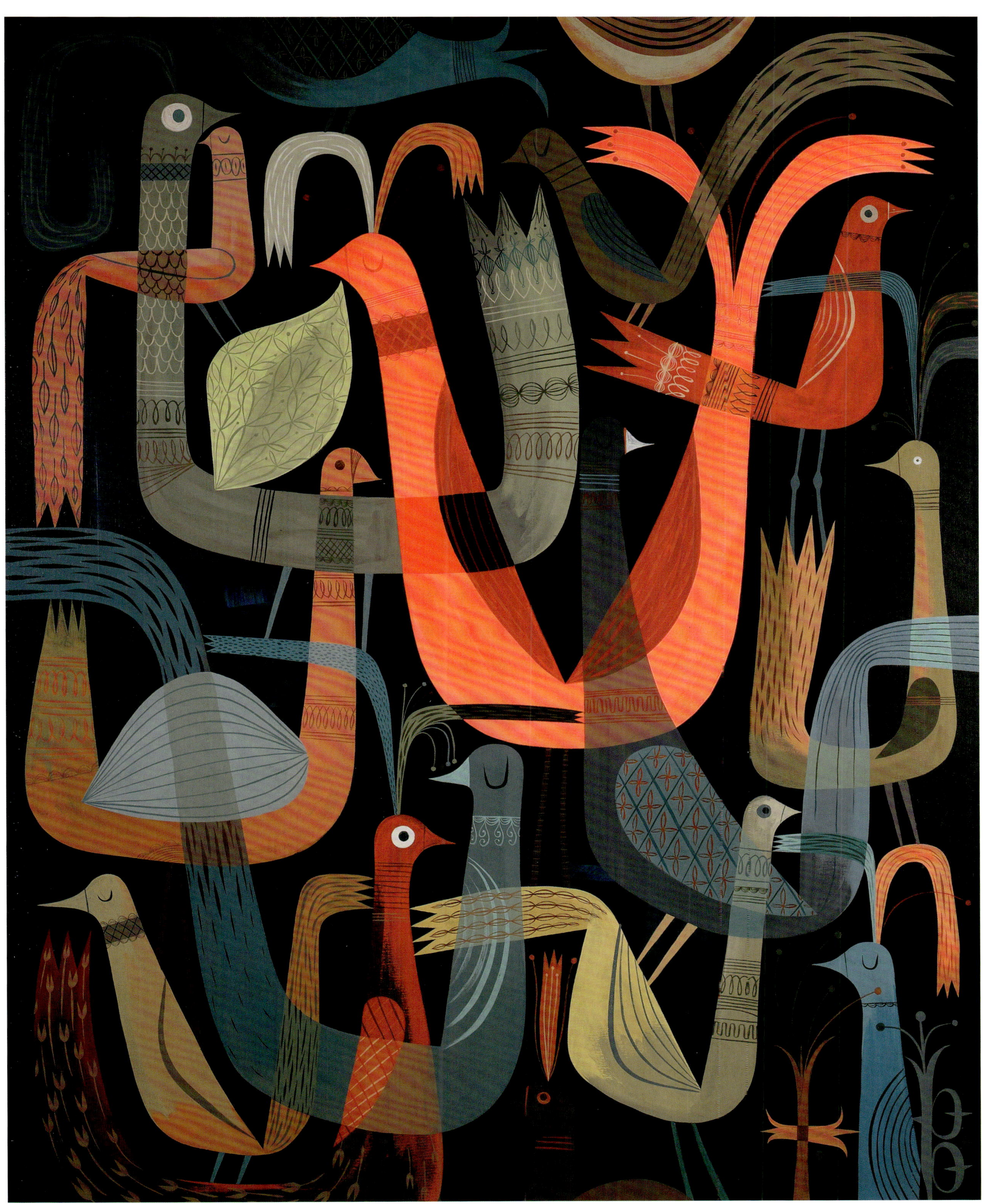

Bird School
2006. Acrylic on Canvas. 48" x 36"

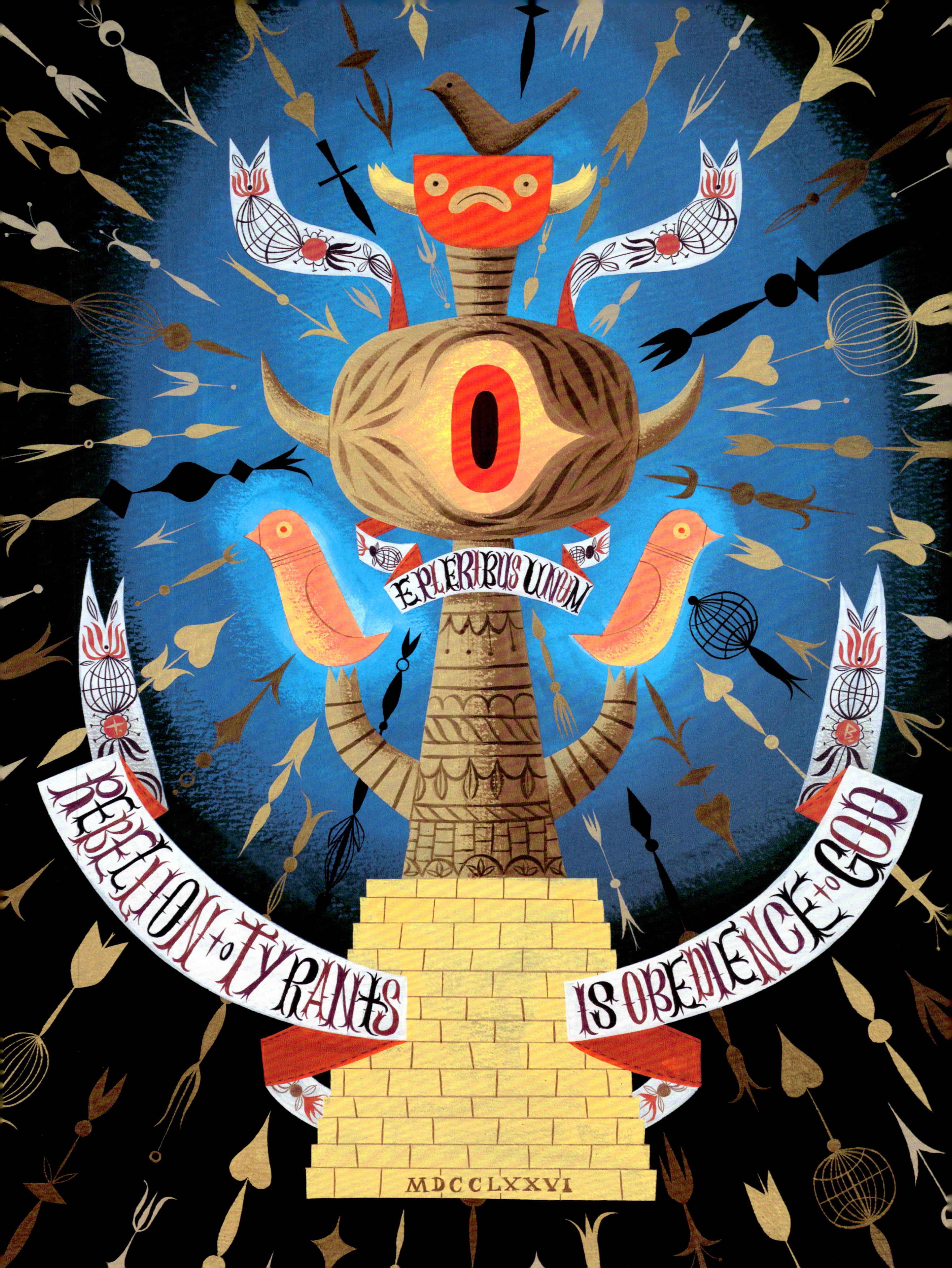
E PLURIBUS UNUM
REBELLION TO TYRANTS IS OBEDIENCE TO GOD
MDCCLXXVI

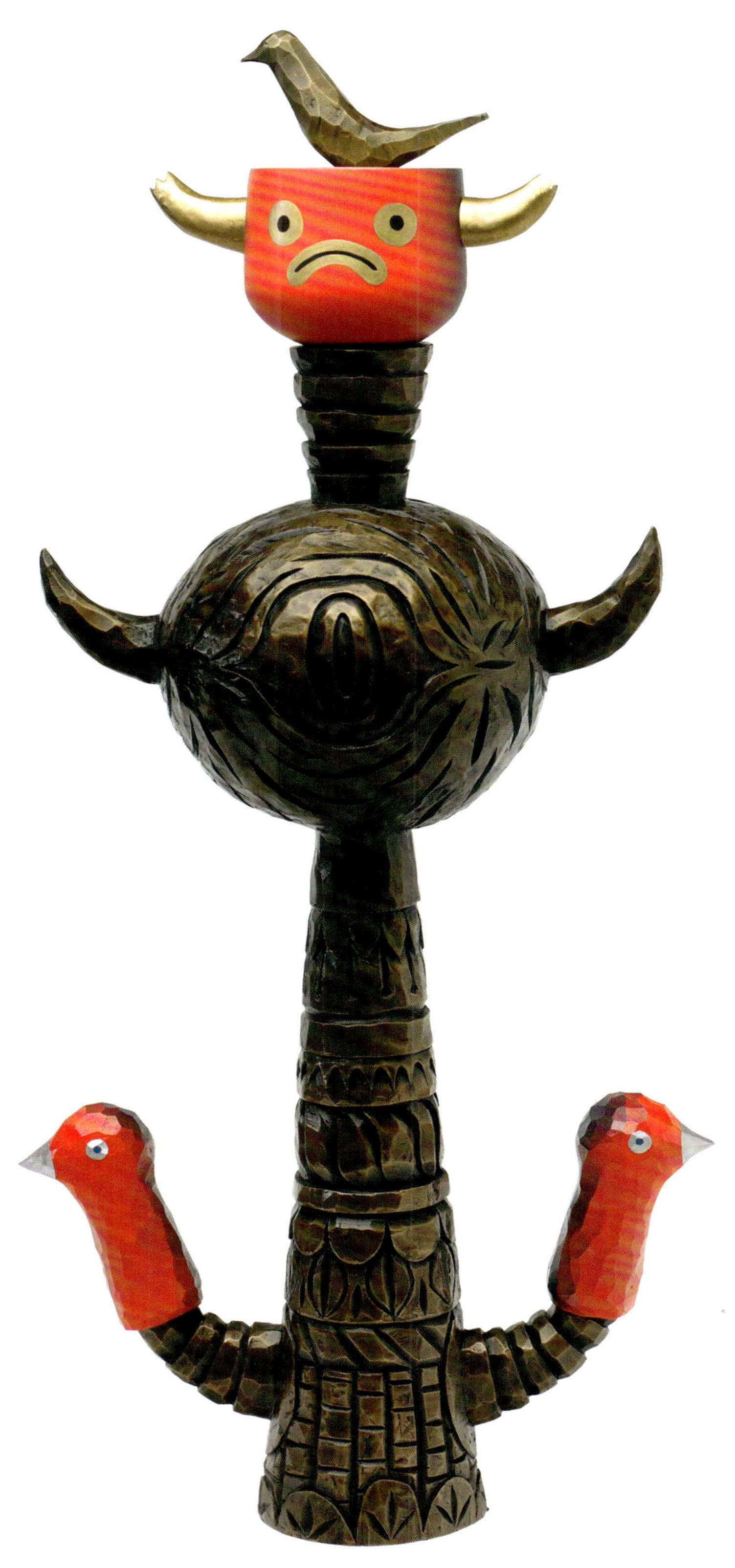

Cyclops Totem
2006. Acrylic on Paper. 29" x 20"

Cyclops Totem
2006. Bronze, Vinyl and Resin. 25.5" x 11.5" x 6"

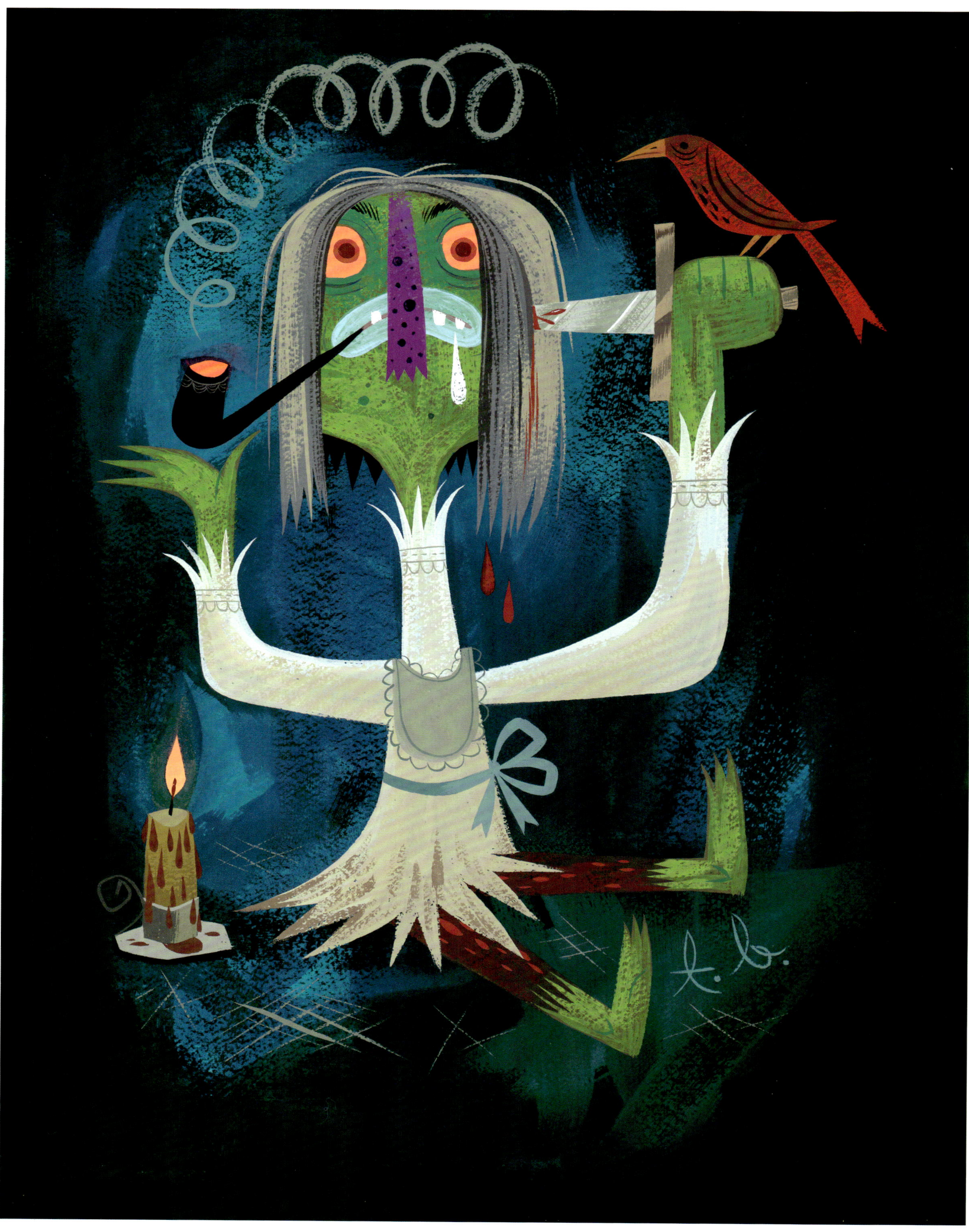

Sarah
2006. Gouache on Paper. 14" x 11"

Calli Garden
2006. Gouache on Paper. 24" x 18"

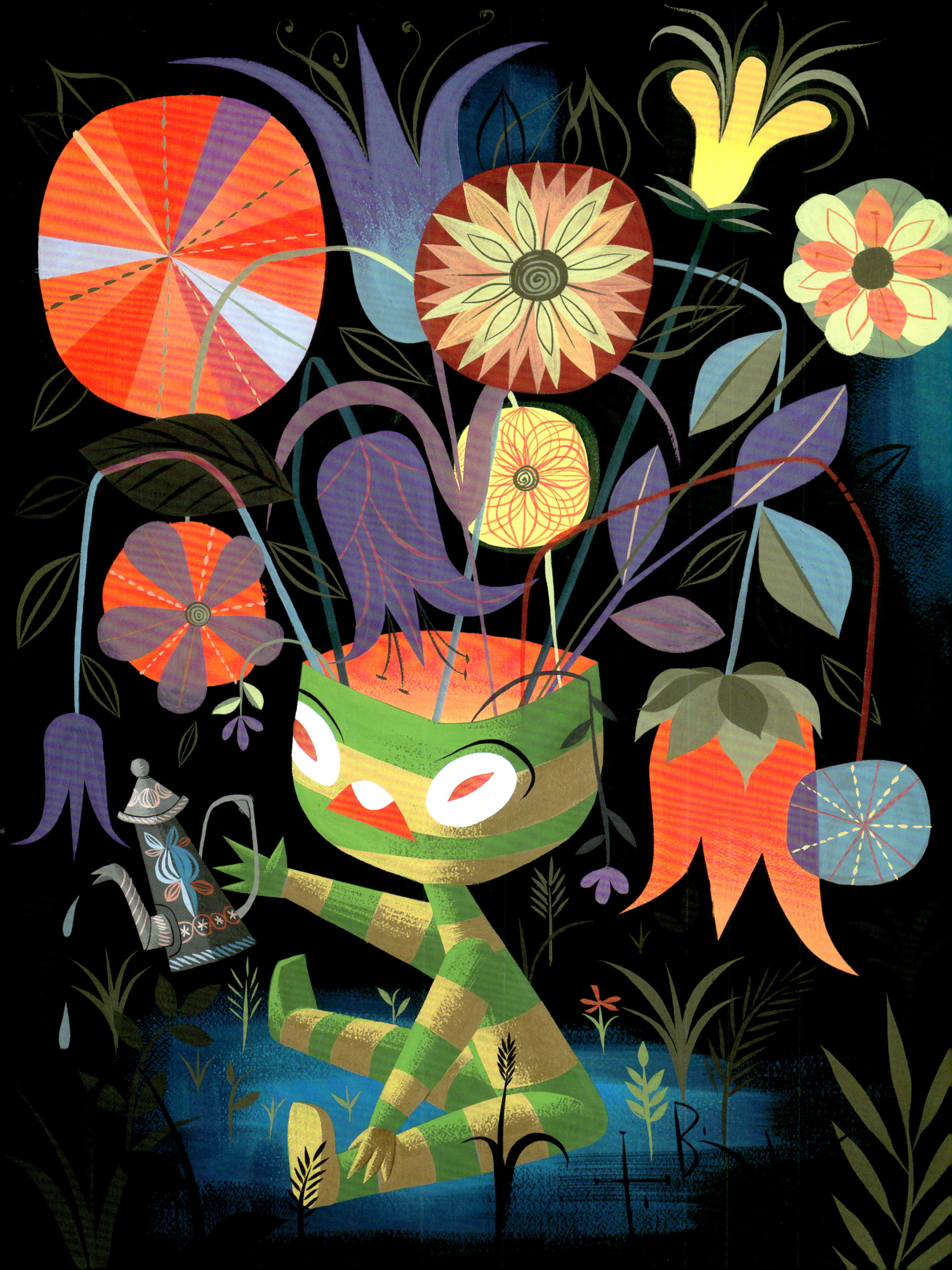

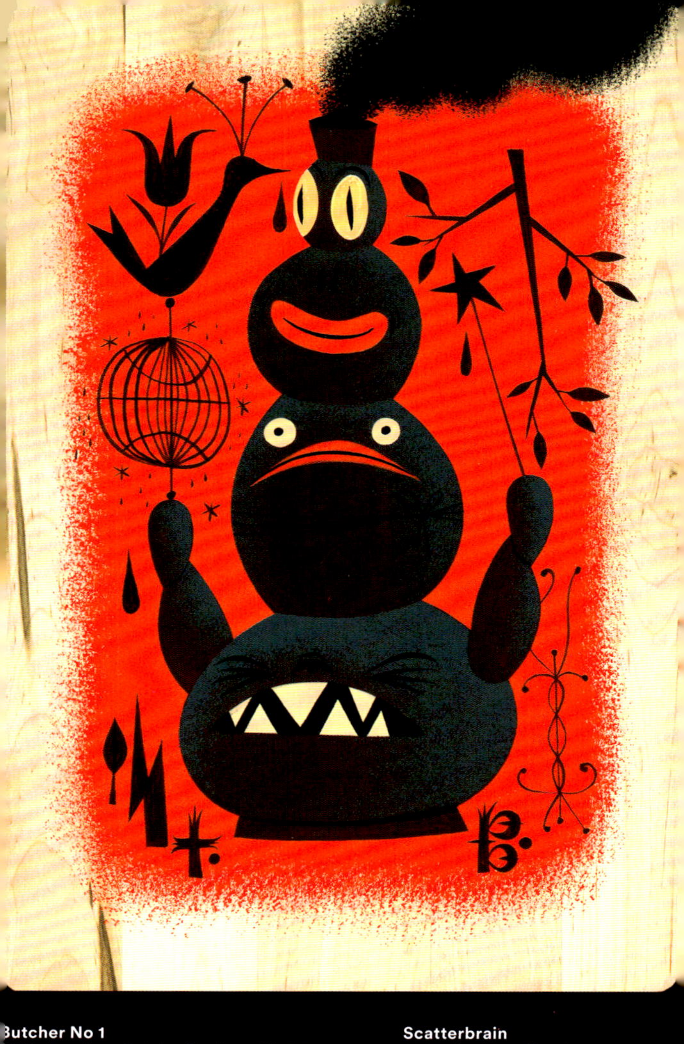

Butcher No 1
2004, Acrylic on Butcher Block, 11.75" x 7.75"

Scatterbrain
2006, Acrylic on Panel, 12" x 9"

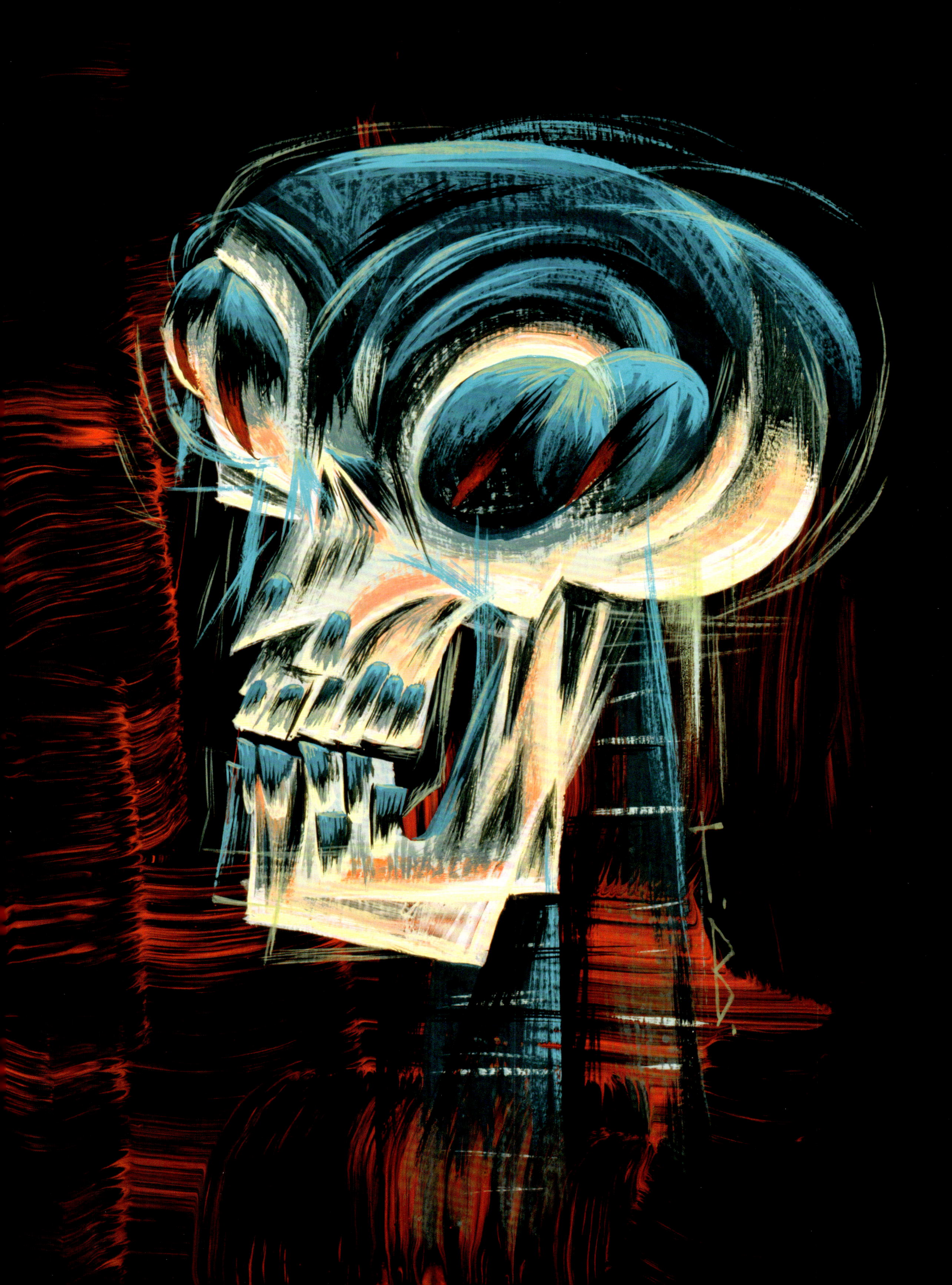

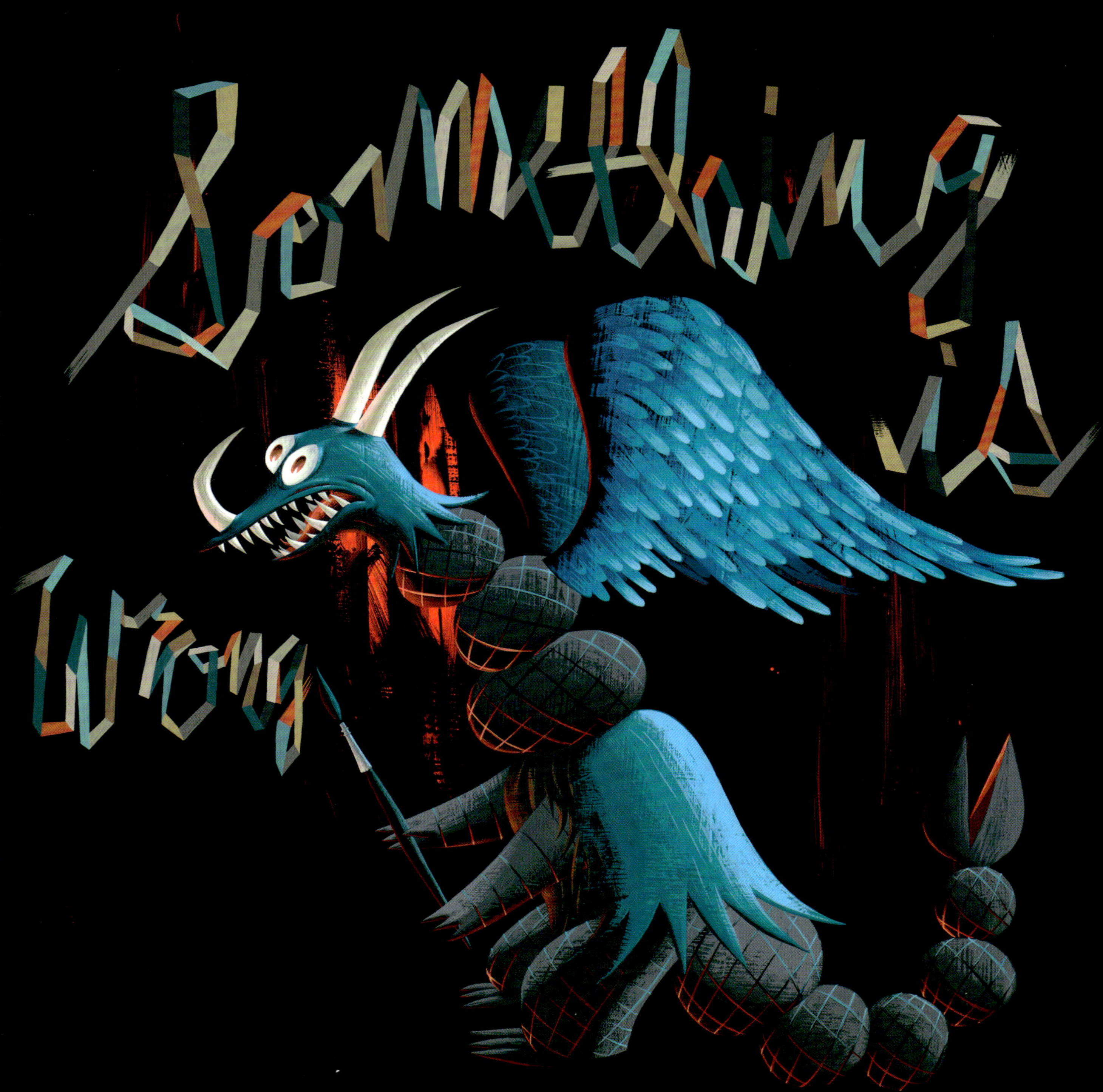

Wrong
2006. Acrylic on Panel. 24" x 24"

Passing
2006. Acrylic on Paper. 16" x 12"

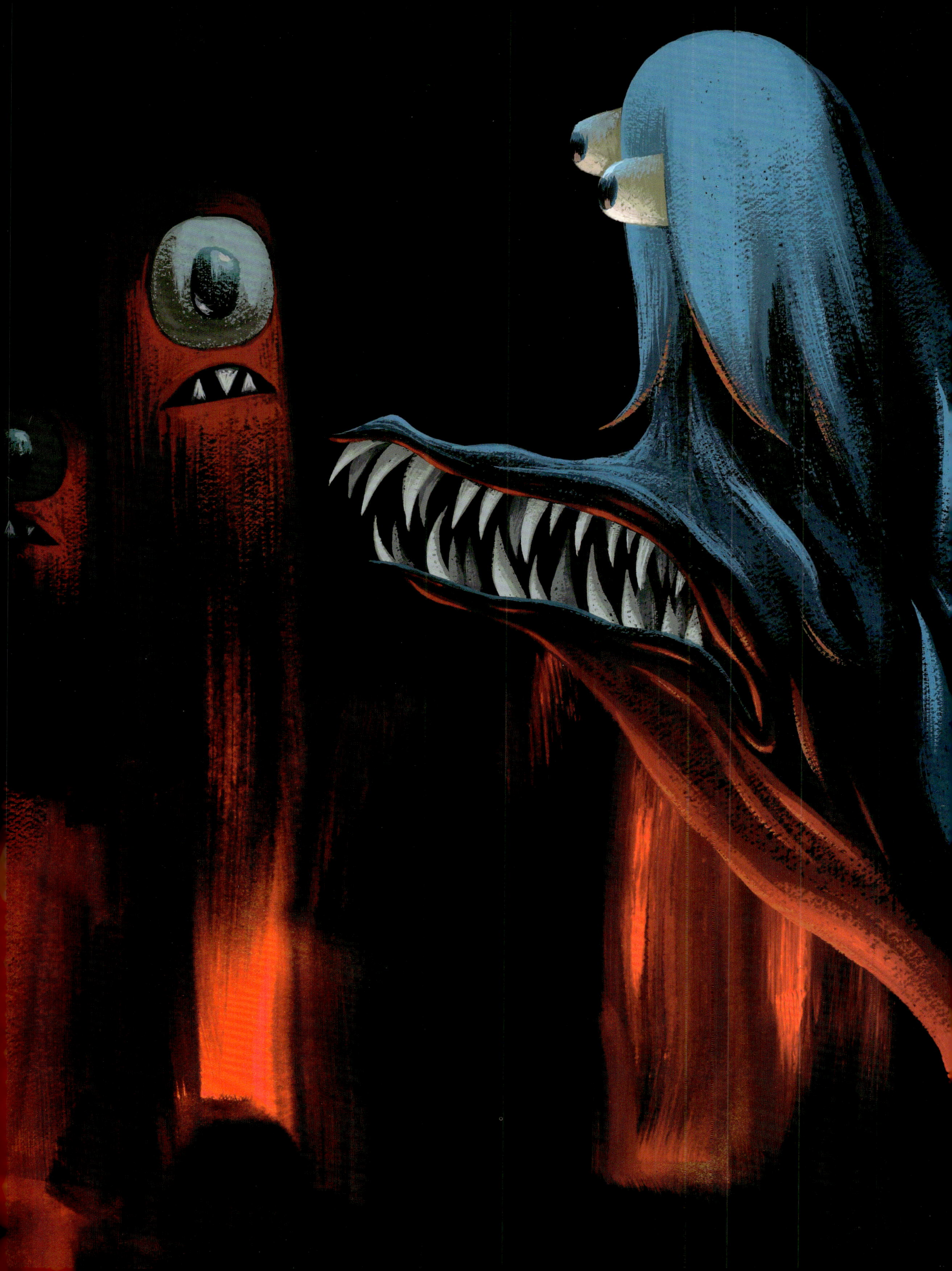

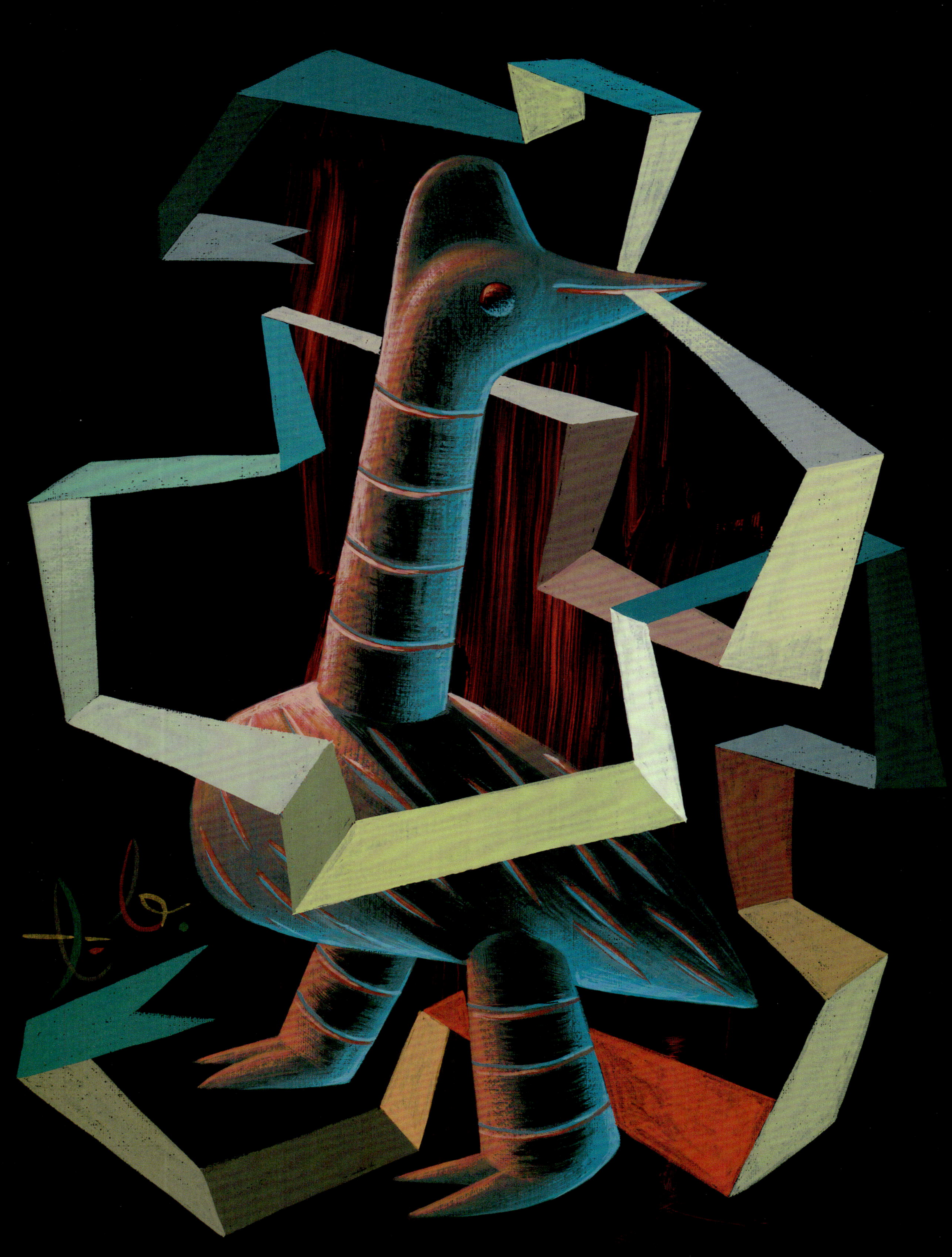

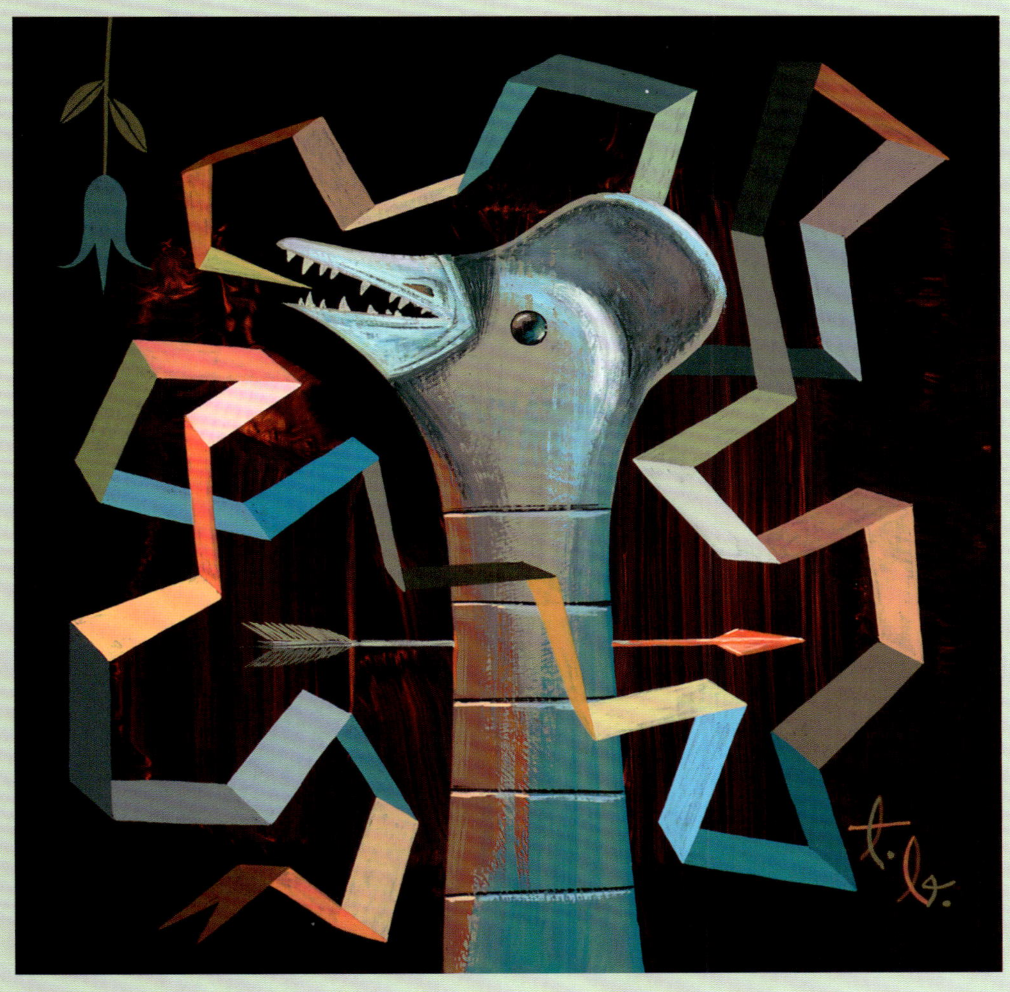

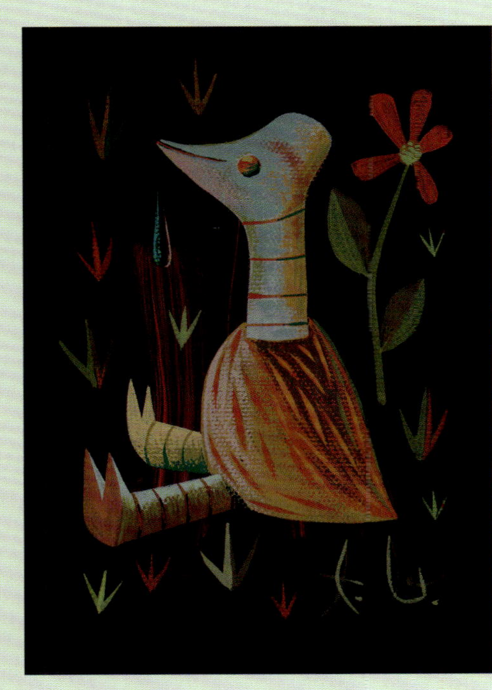

Alpha-Gaichou
2006. Acrylic on Paper. 12" x 9"

Birdsong
2006. Acrylic on Panel. 10" x 10"

Pest
2006. Acrylic on Canvas. 3" x 2"

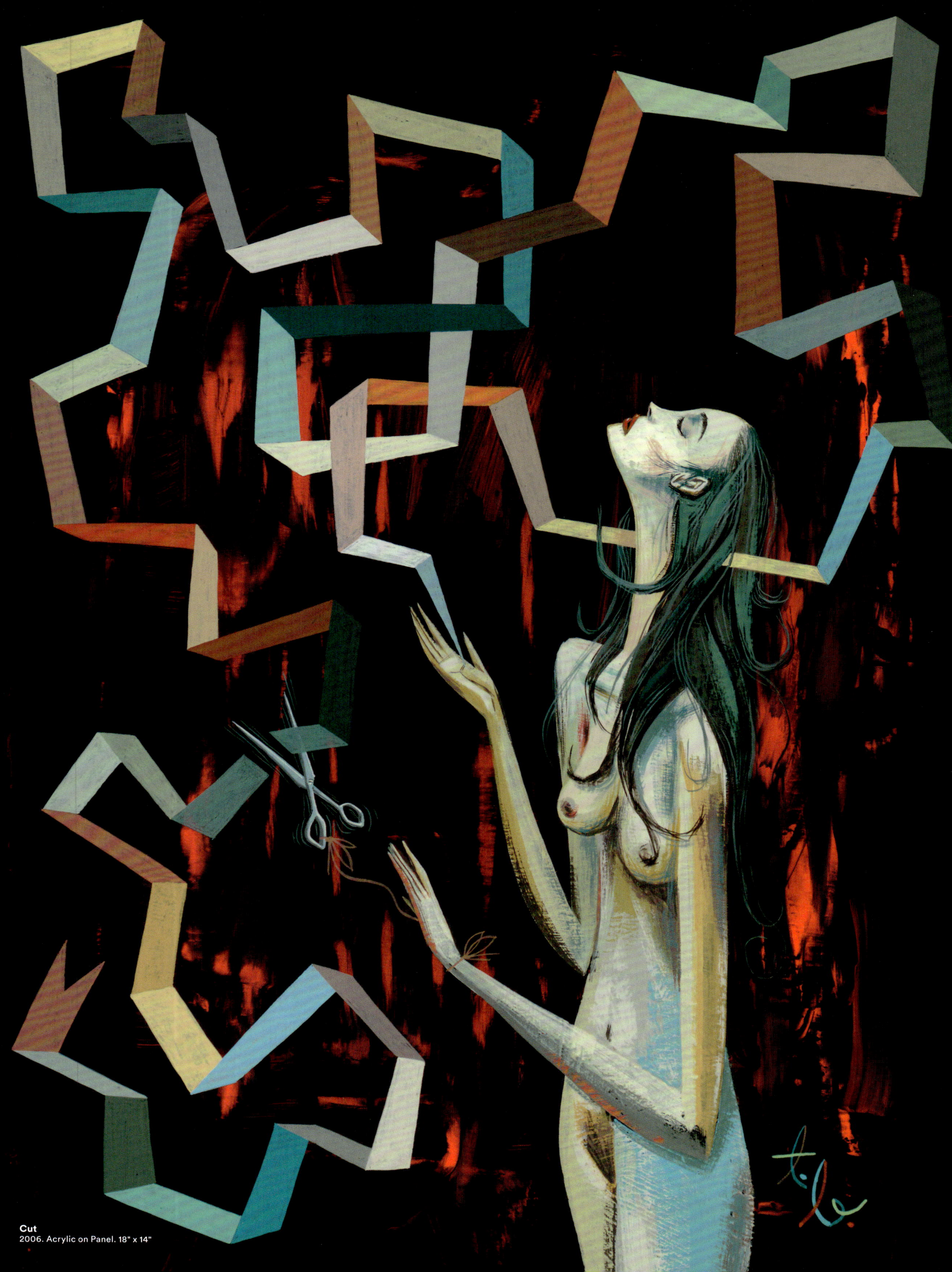

Cut
2006. Acrylic on Panel. 18" x 14"

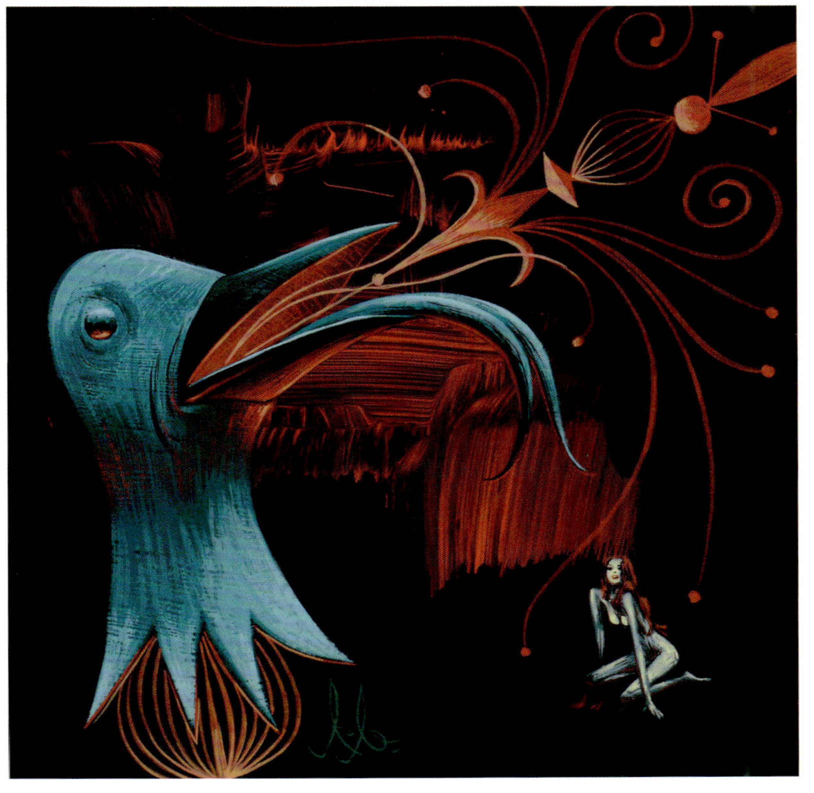

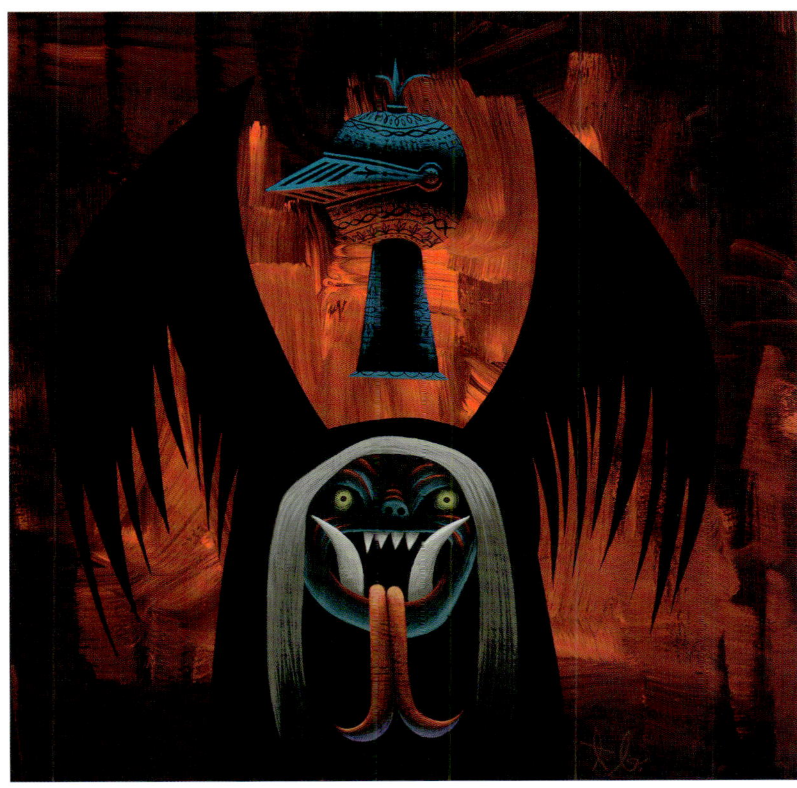

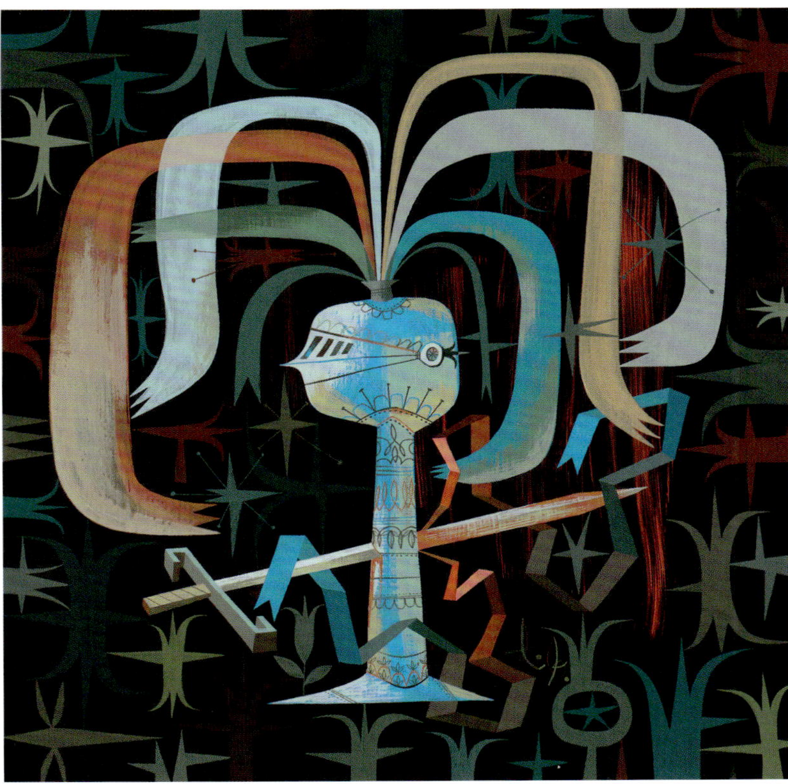

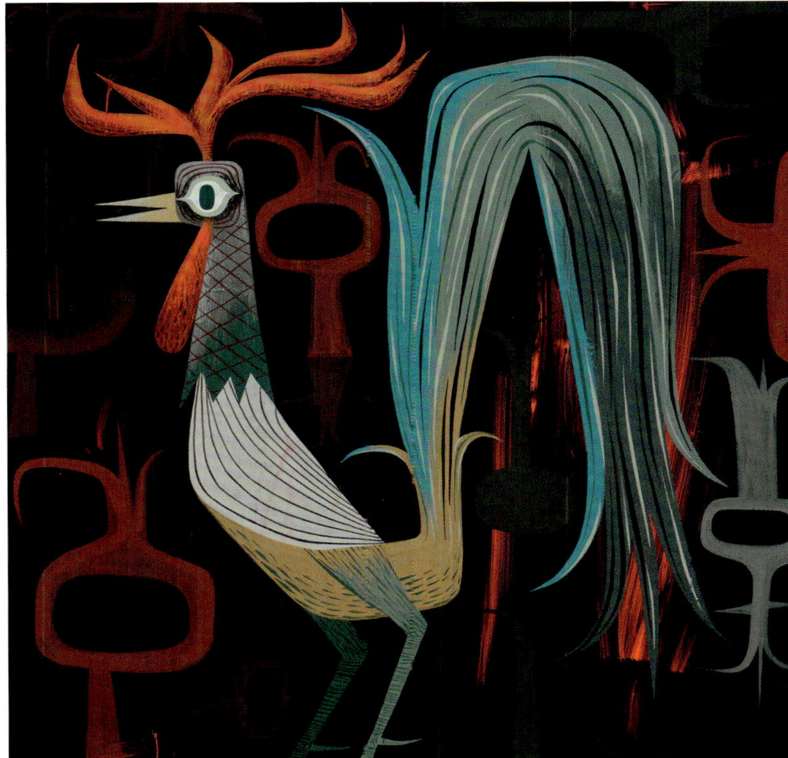

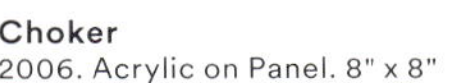

Choker
2006. Acrylic on Panel. 8" x 8"

Witness
2006. Acrylic on Panel. 16" x 16"

Failure
2006. Acrylic on Panel. 20" x 20"

Poison Rooster
2006. Acrylic on Panel. 20" x 20"

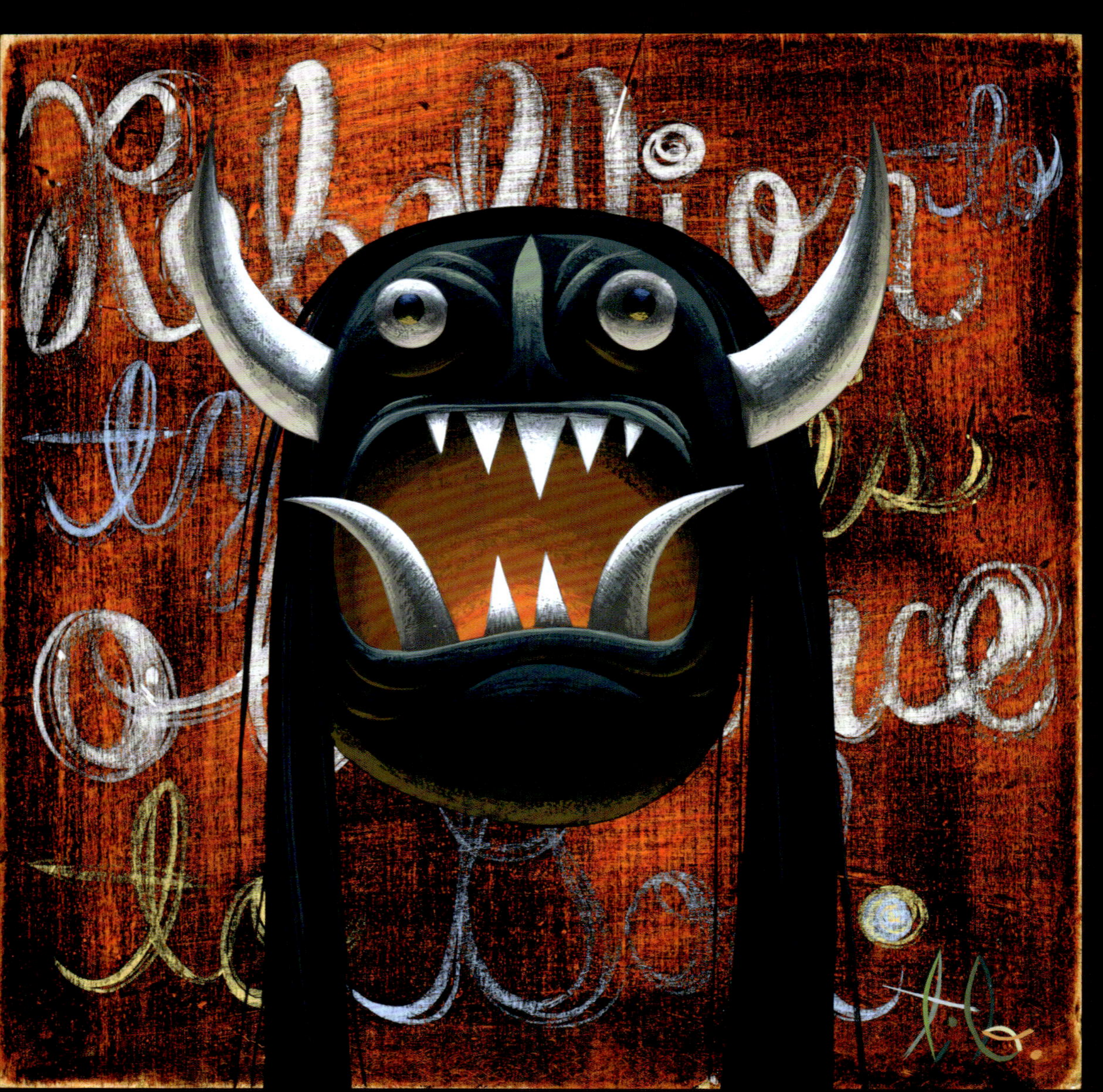

Slayer
2006. Acrylic on Panel. 24" x 24"

Tyrant
2006. Acrylic on Panel. 10" x 10"

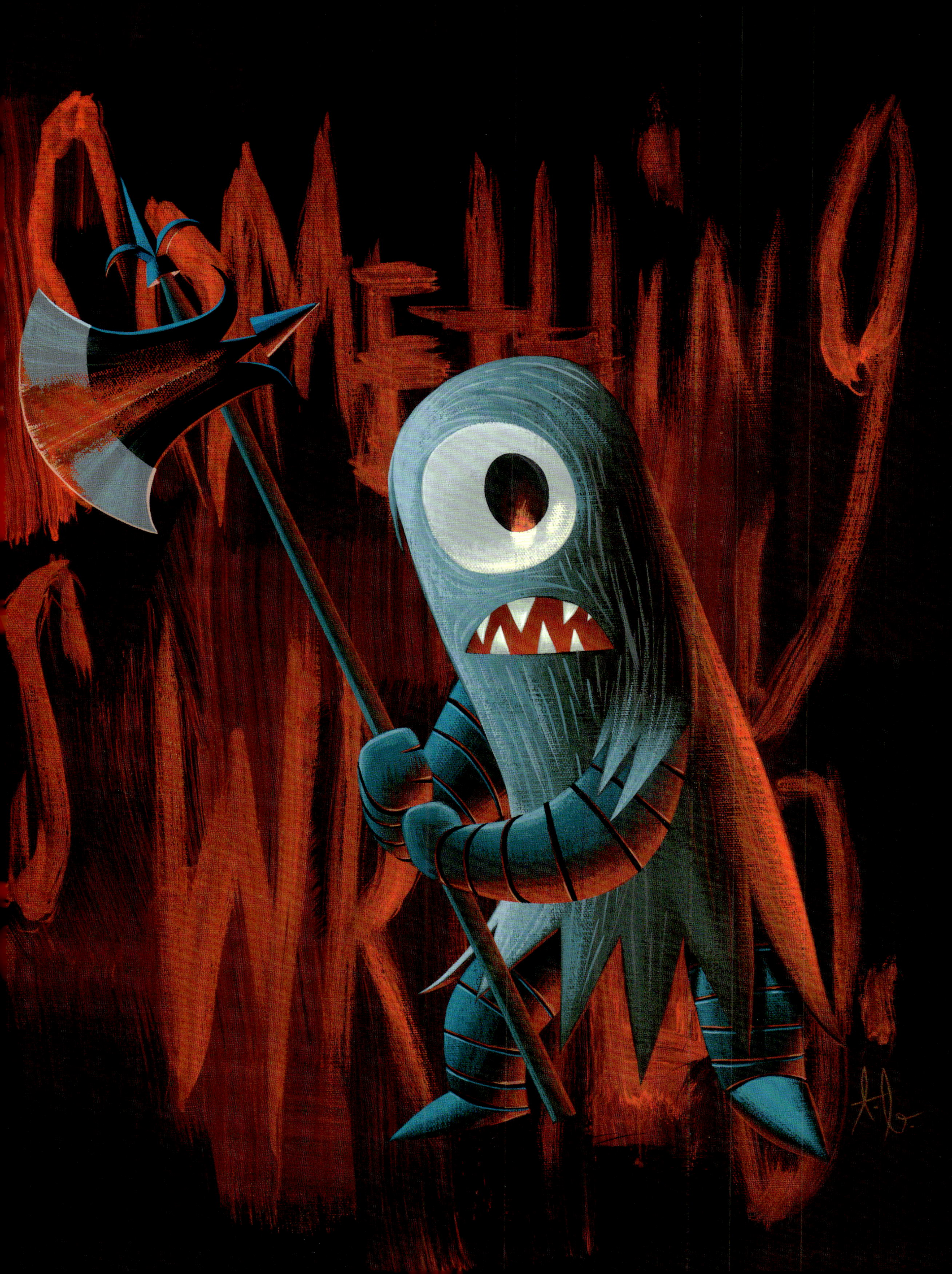

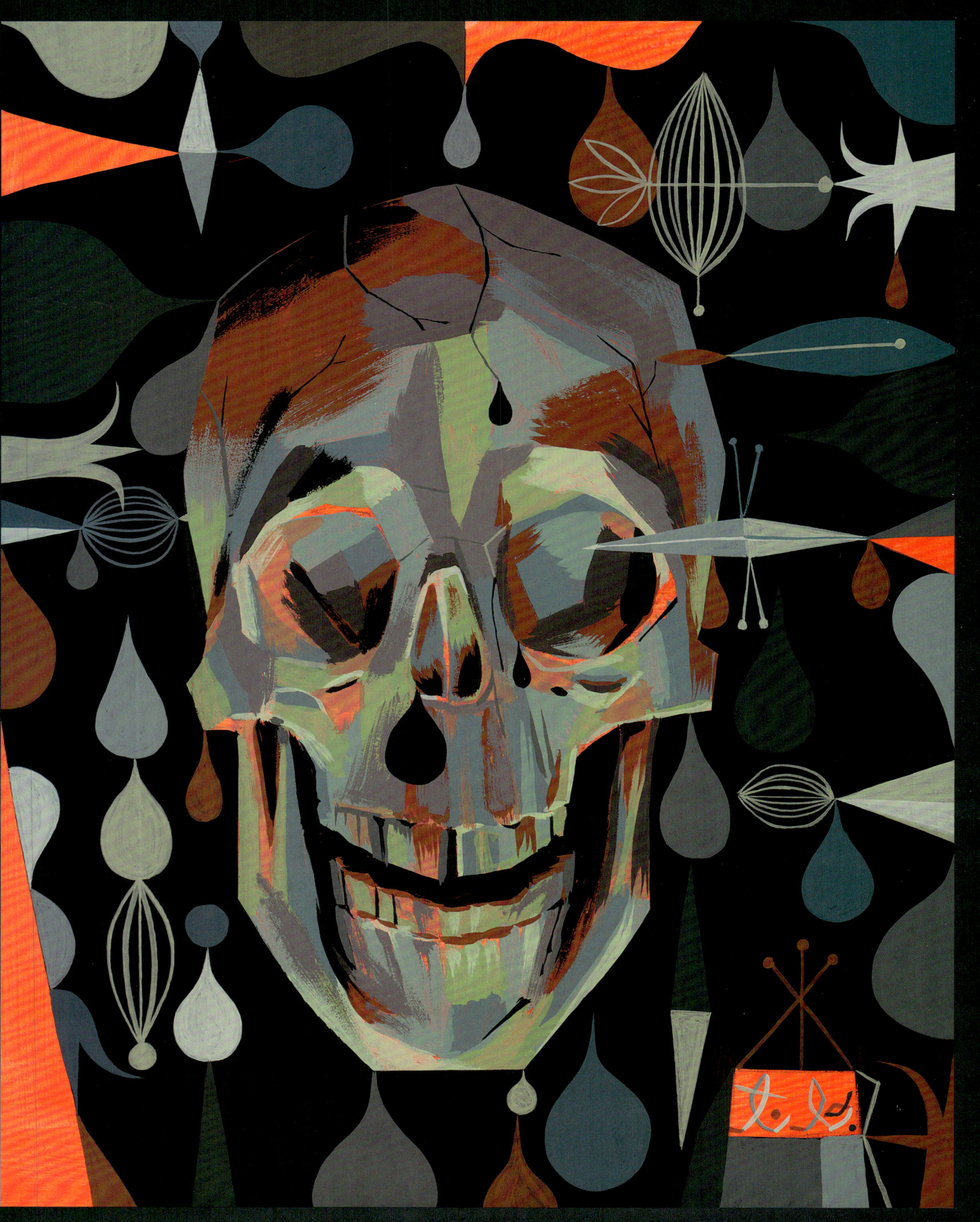

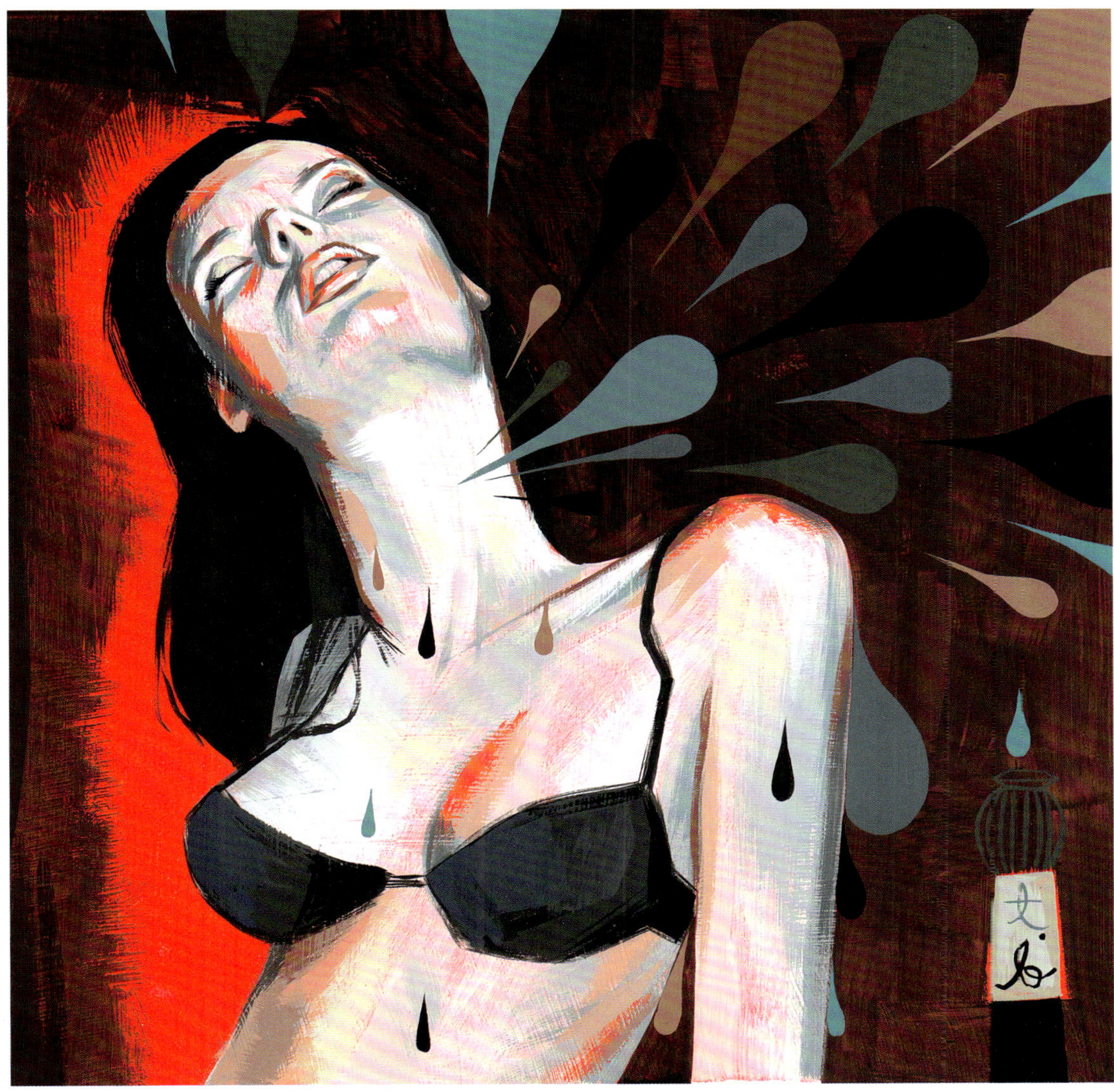

Monitor
2007. Acrylic on Panel. 14" x 10"

Stem
2007. Acrylic on Panel. 12" x 12"

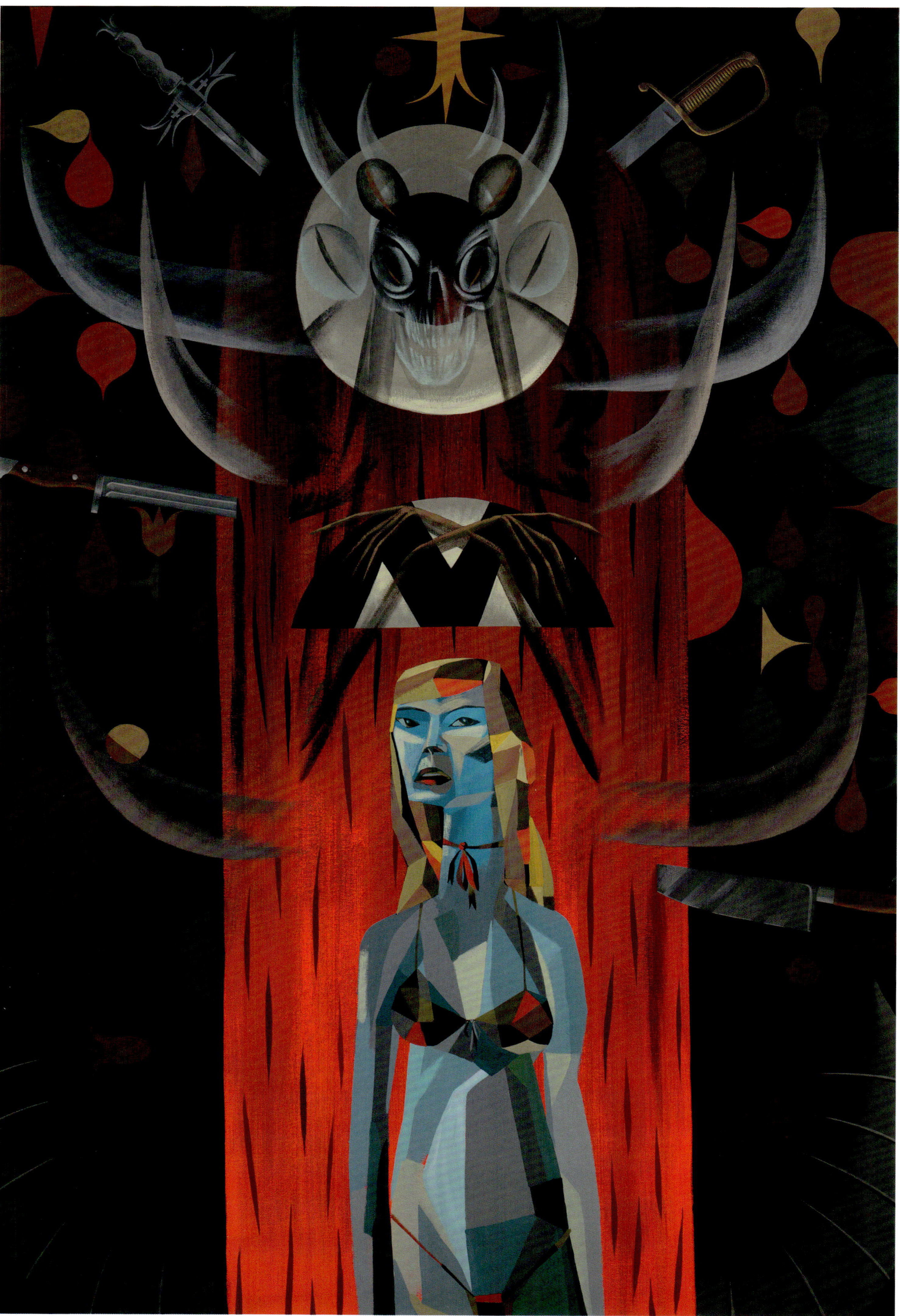

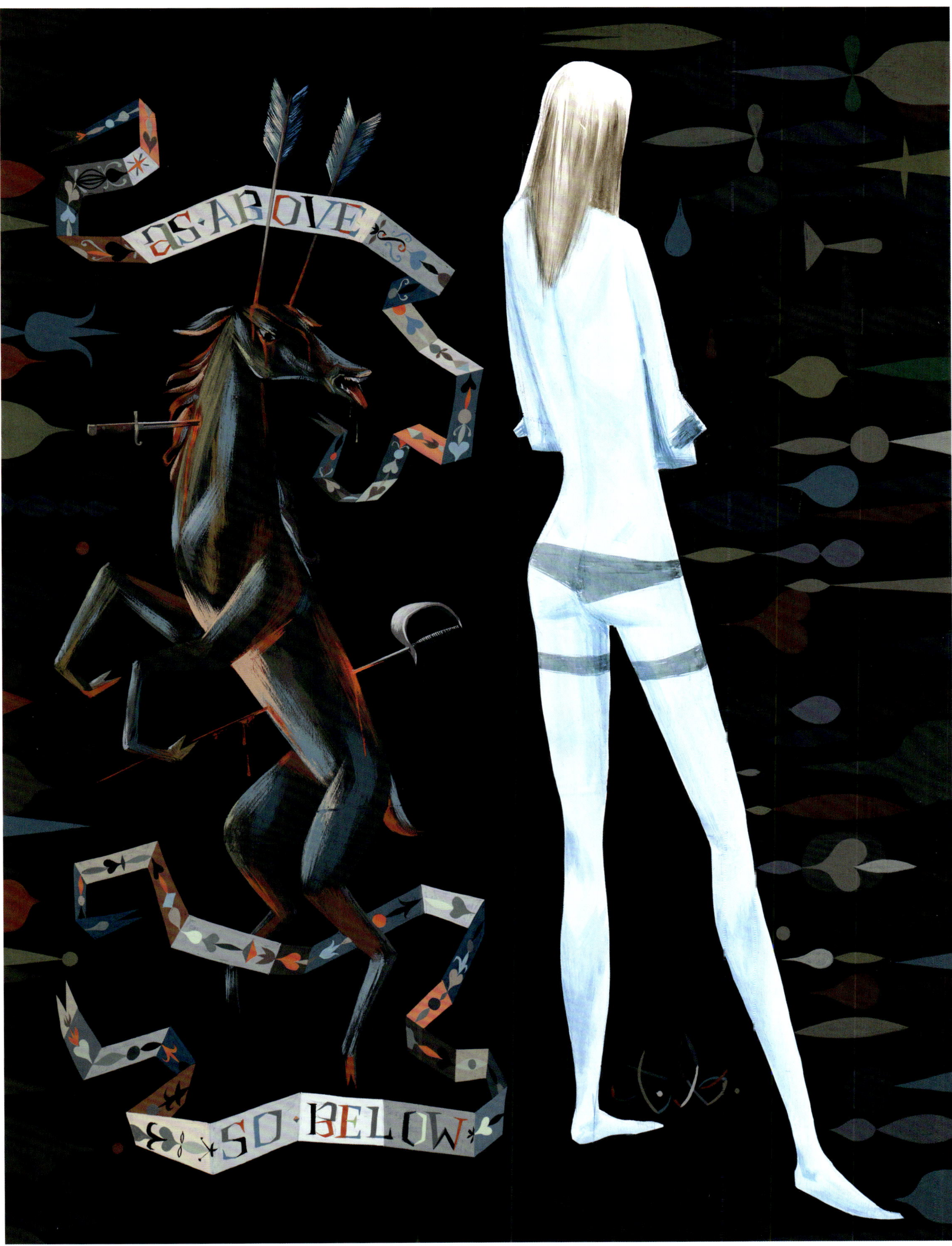

Dominator
2007. Acrylic on Canvas. 72" x 48"

As Above, So Below
2007. Acrylic on Panel. 24" x 18"

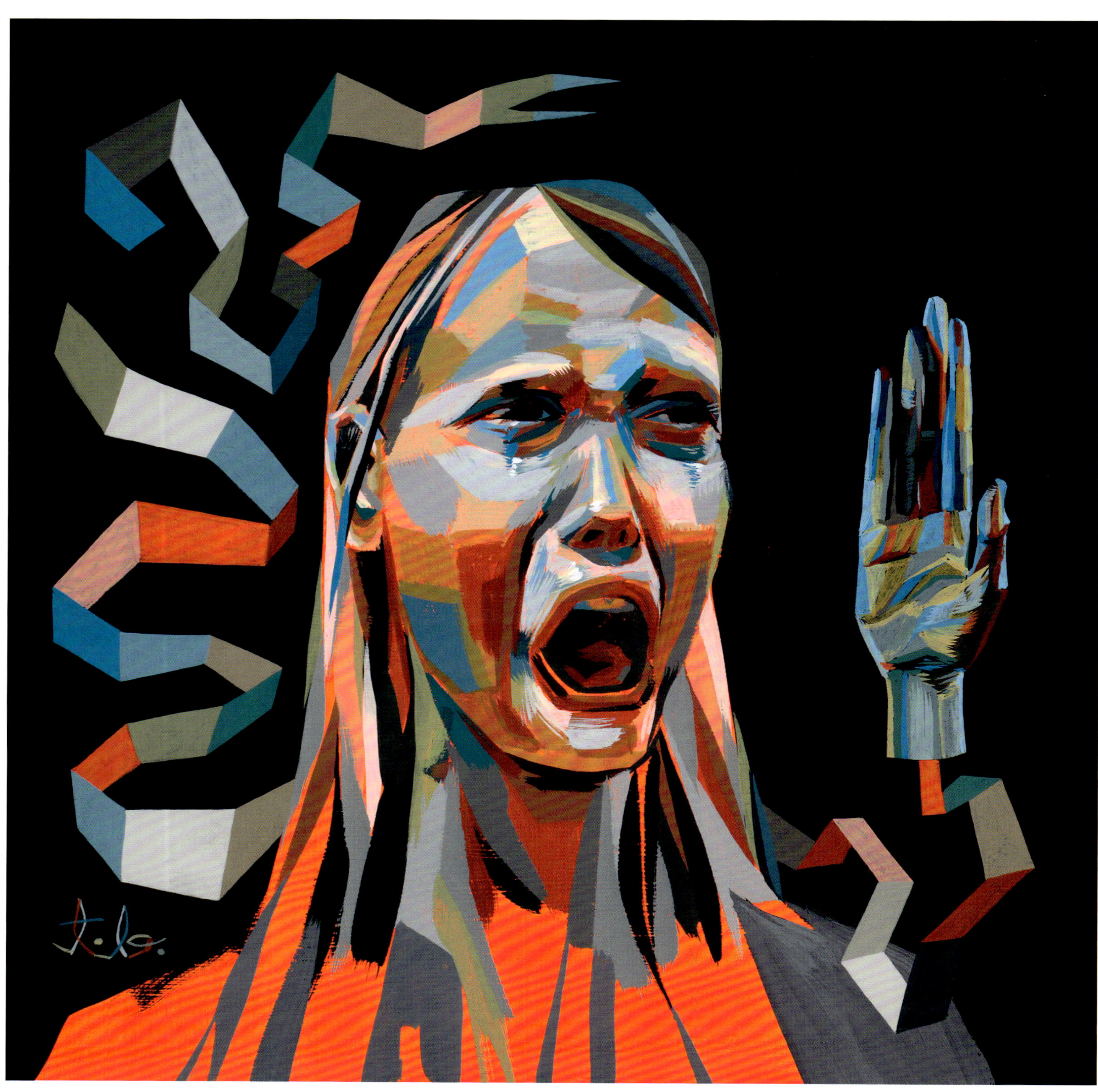

Right Hand
2007. Acrylic on Panel. 12" x 12"

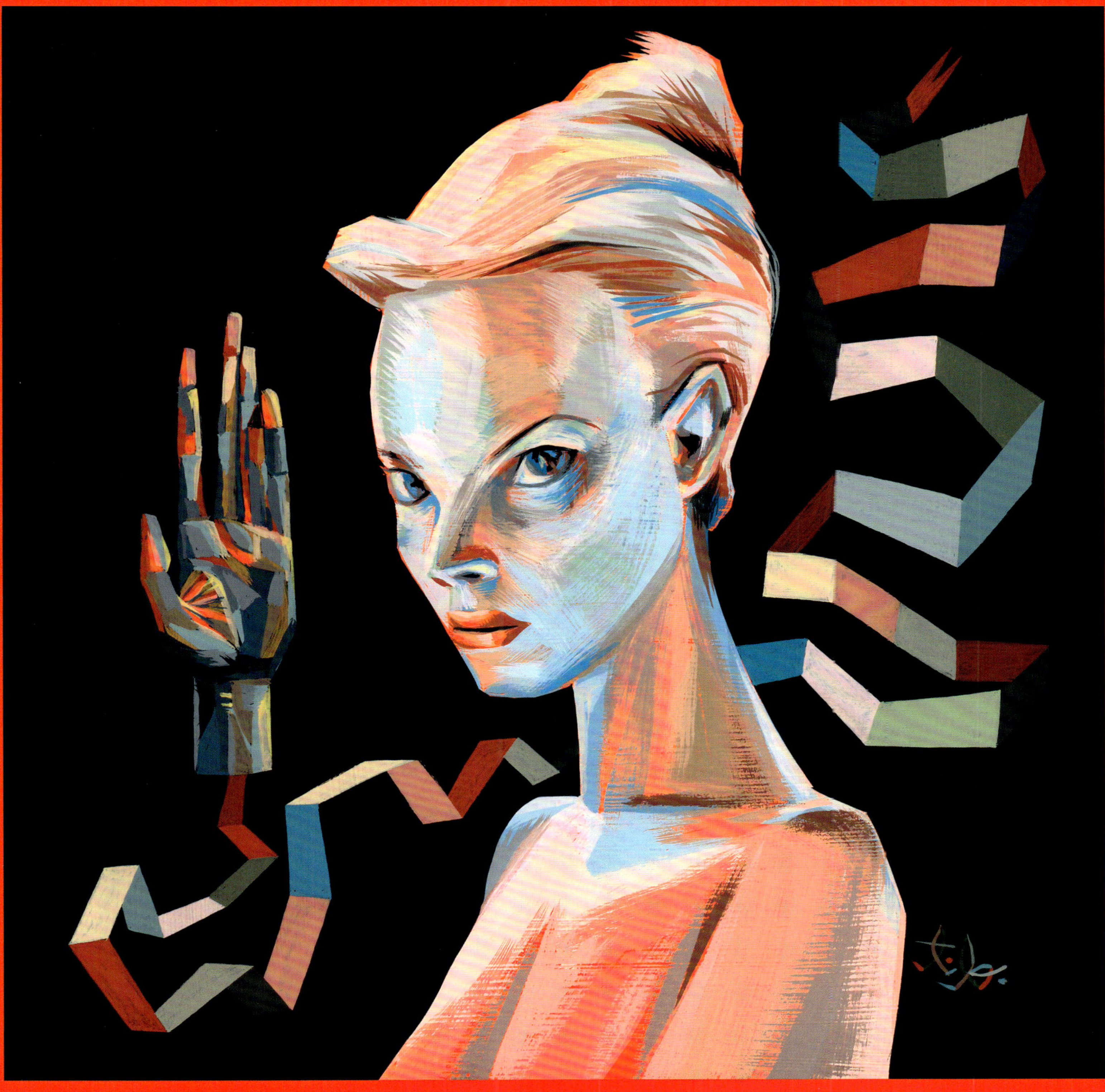

Left Hand
2007. Acrylic on Panel. 12" x 12"

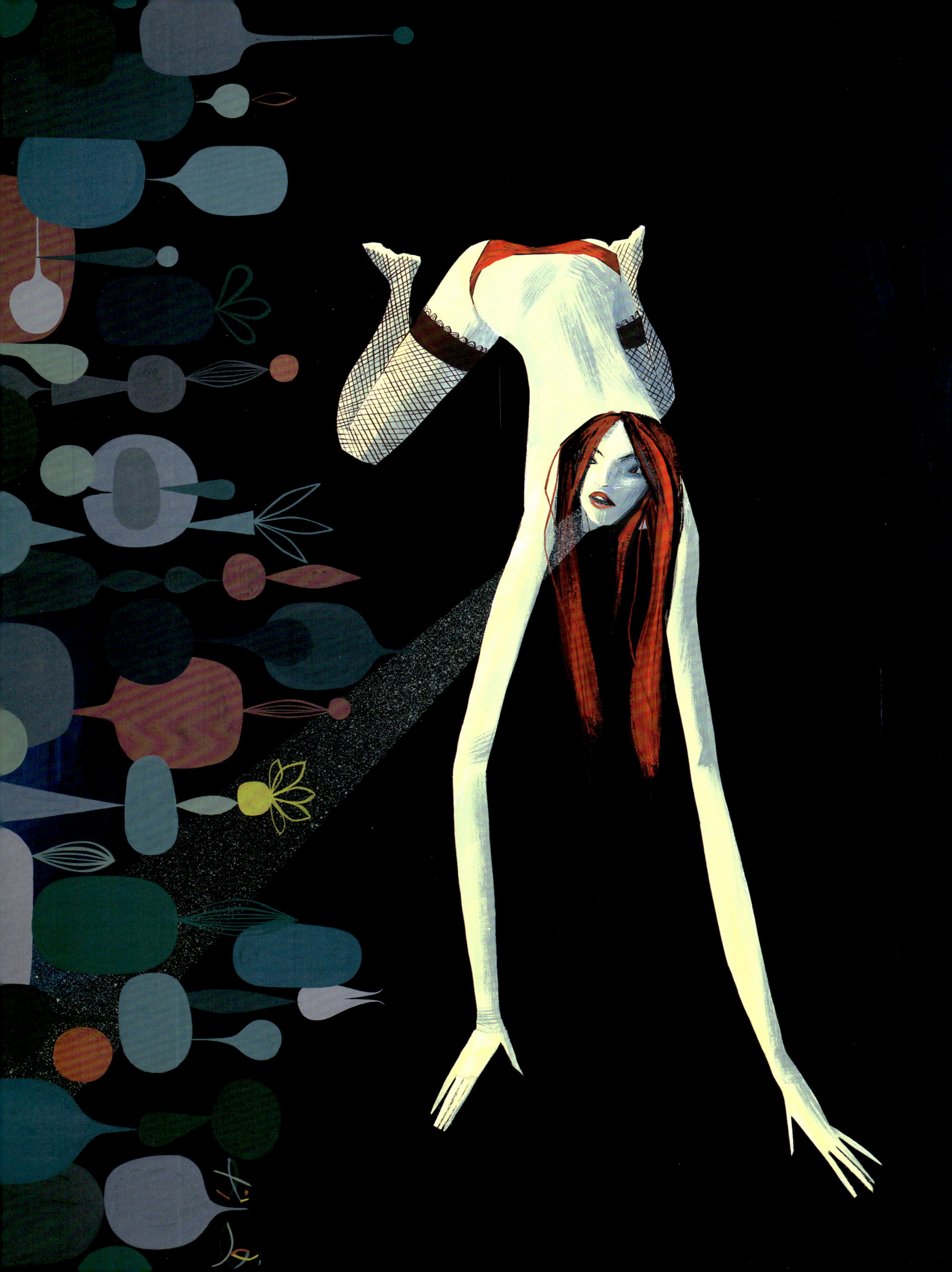

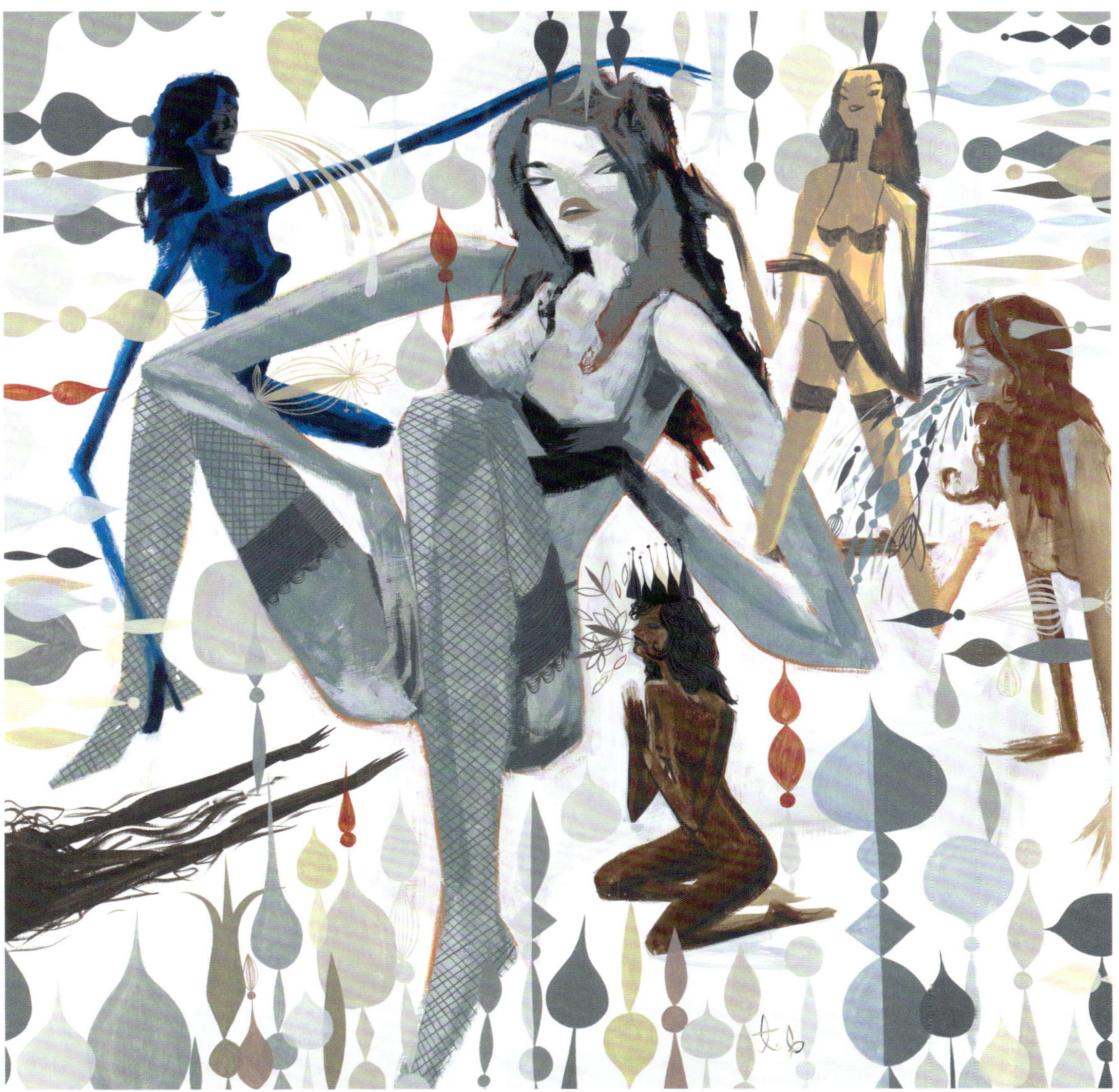

Injected
2007. Acrylic on Panel. 24" x 18"

Conversion
2007. Acrylic on Panel. 36" x 36"

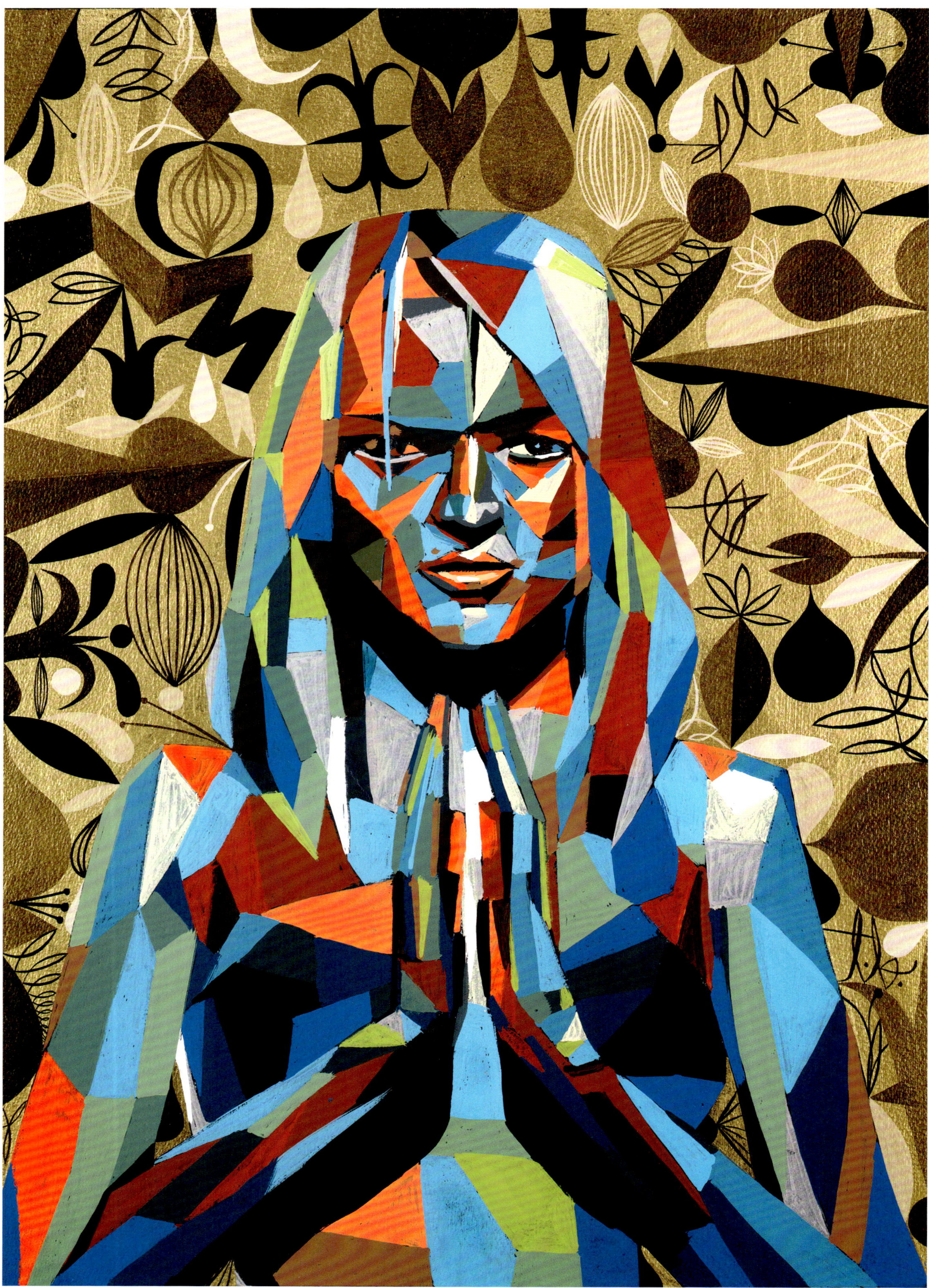

Conviction
2008. Acrylic on Paper. 20" x 16"

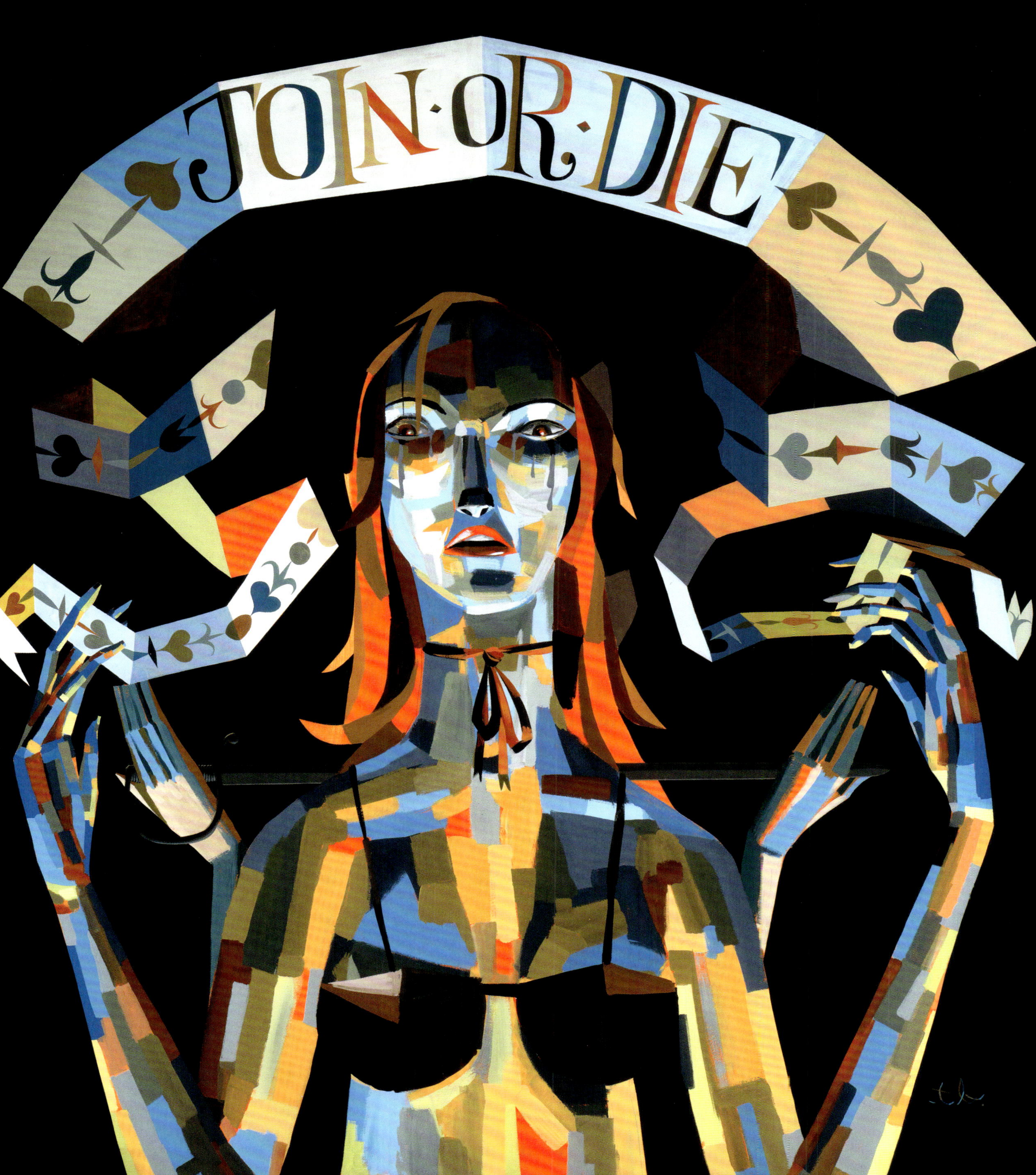

oin or Die
007. Acrylic on Canvas. 70" x 70"

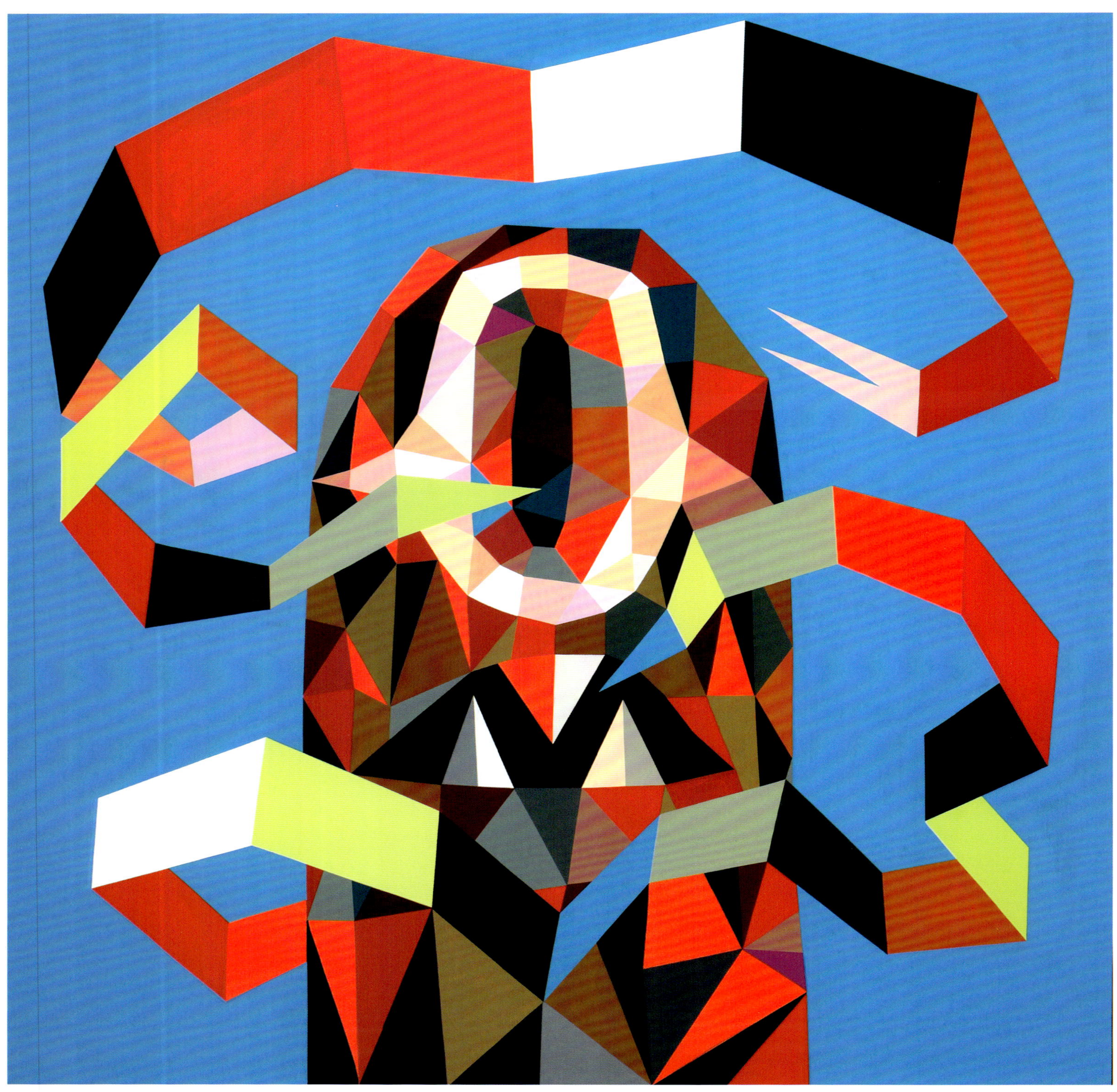

No God But God
2008. Acrylic on Panel. 36" x 36"

Doom Loop No 2
2008. Acrylic on Panel. 14" x 10"

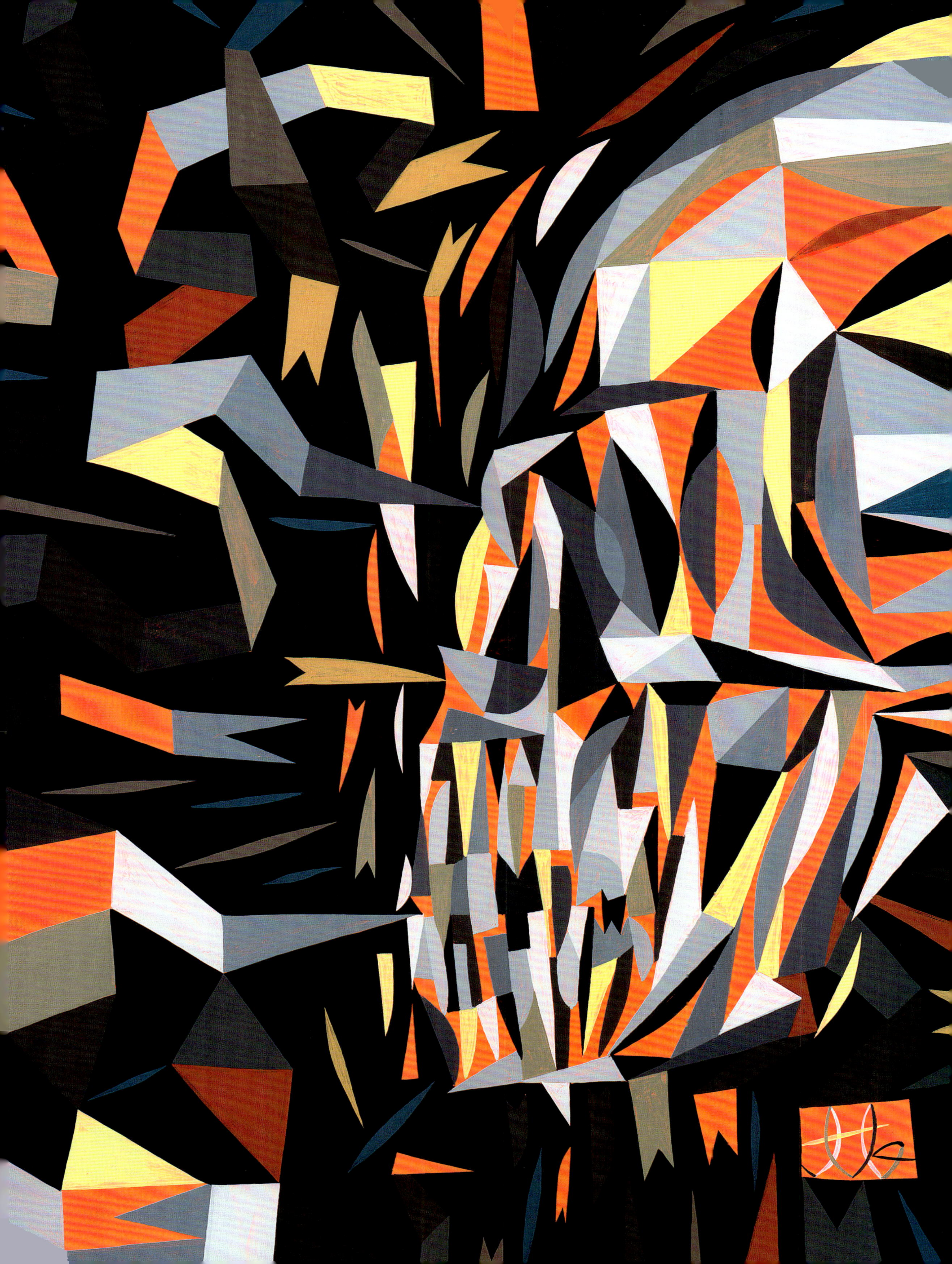

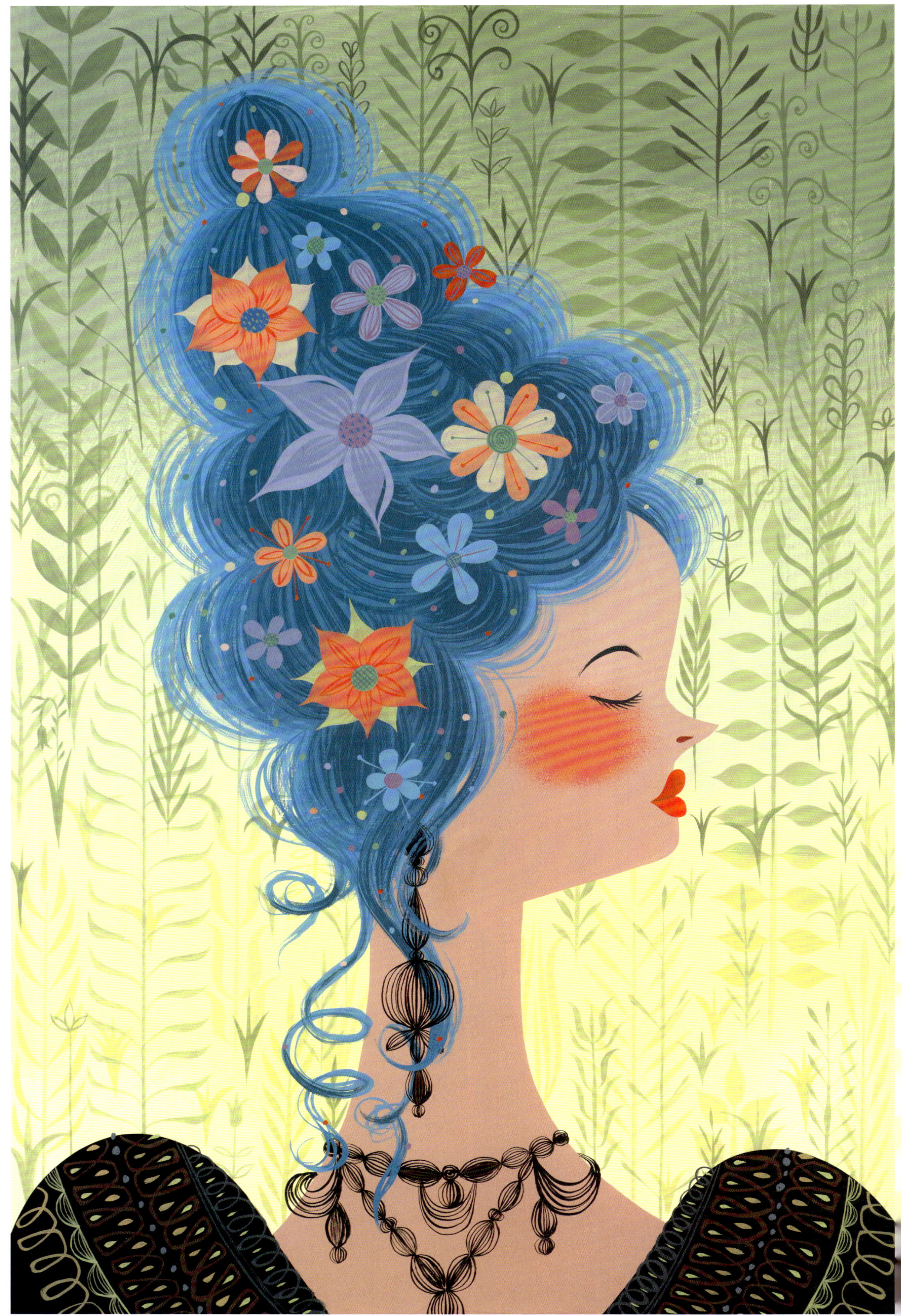

Asylum
2008. Acrylic on Panel. 36" x 24"

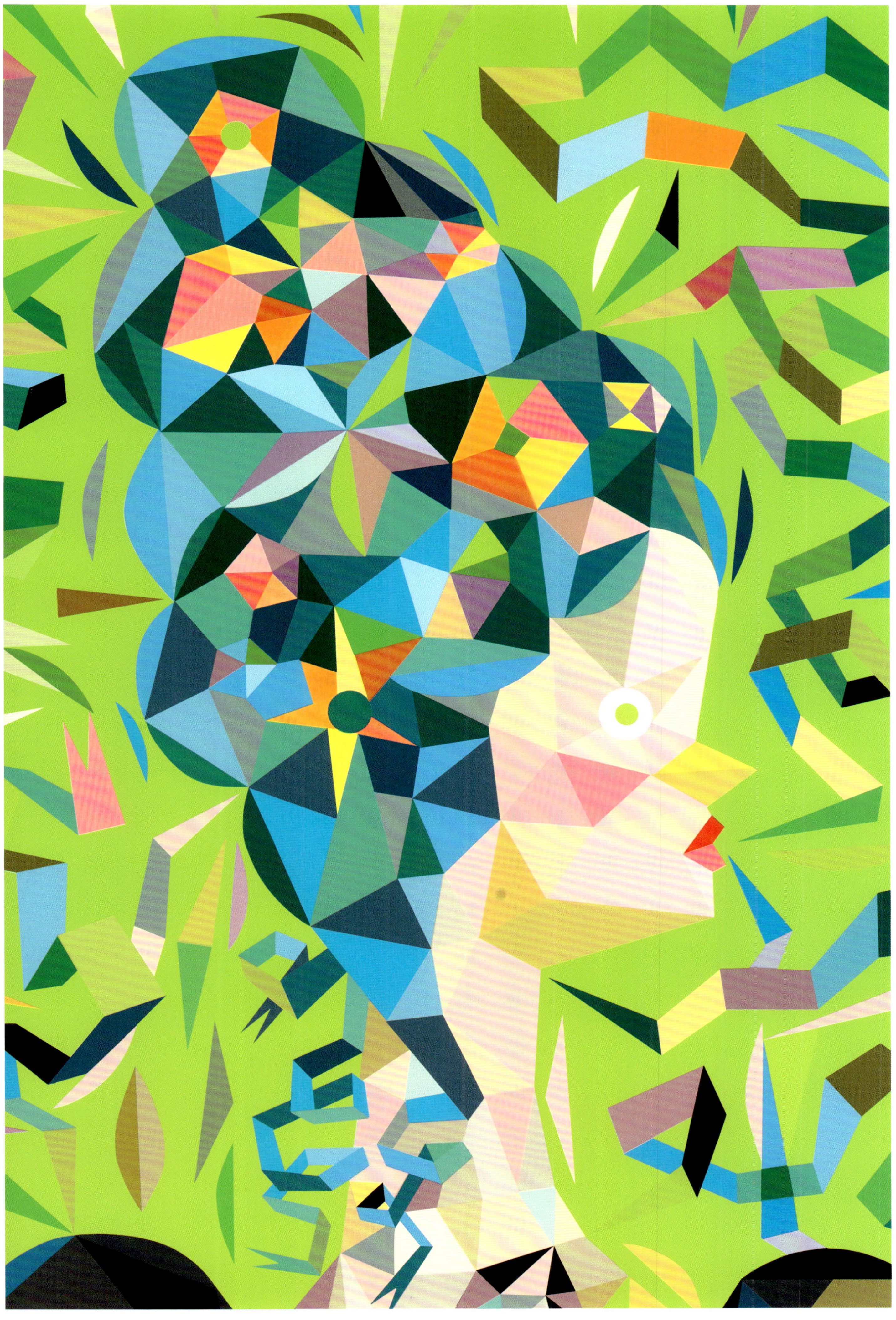

Asylum No 4
2008. Acrylic on Panel. 36" x 24"

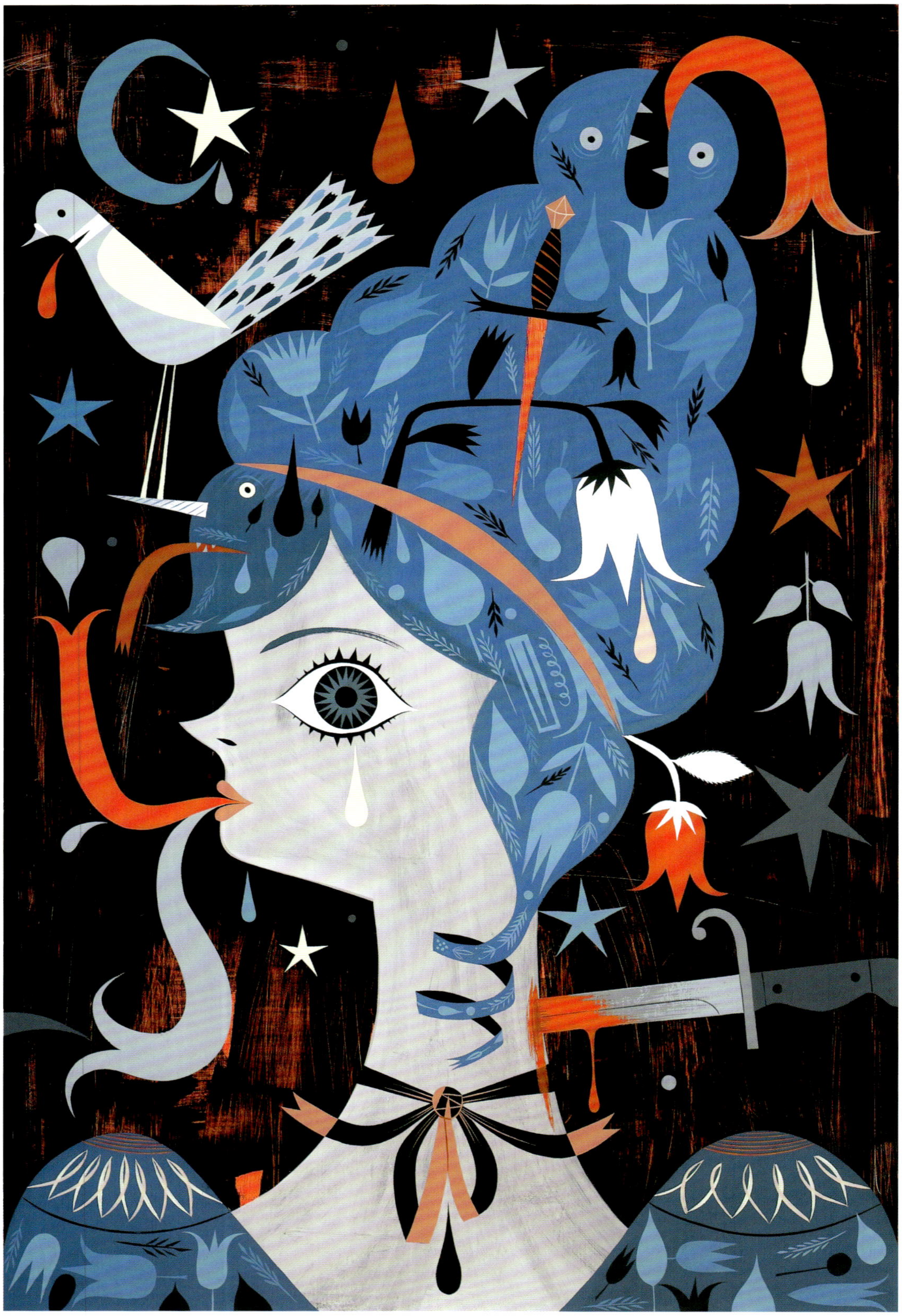

Asylum No 5
2008. Acrylic on Panel. 36" x 24"

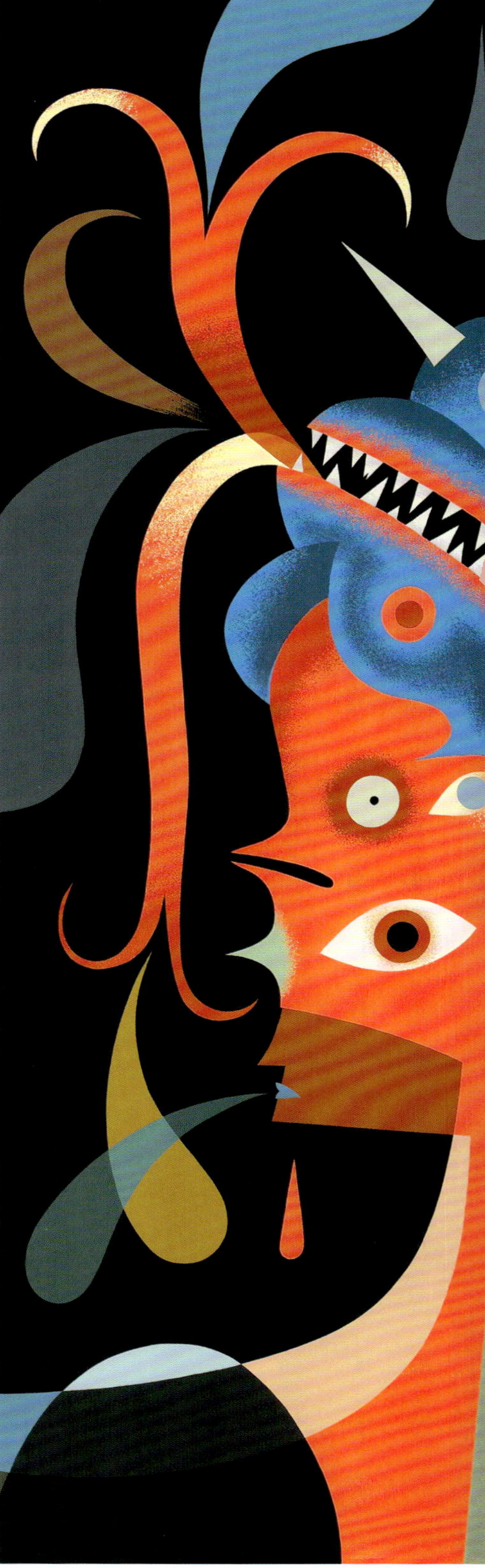

Asylum No 2
2008. Acrylic on Panel. 36" x 24"

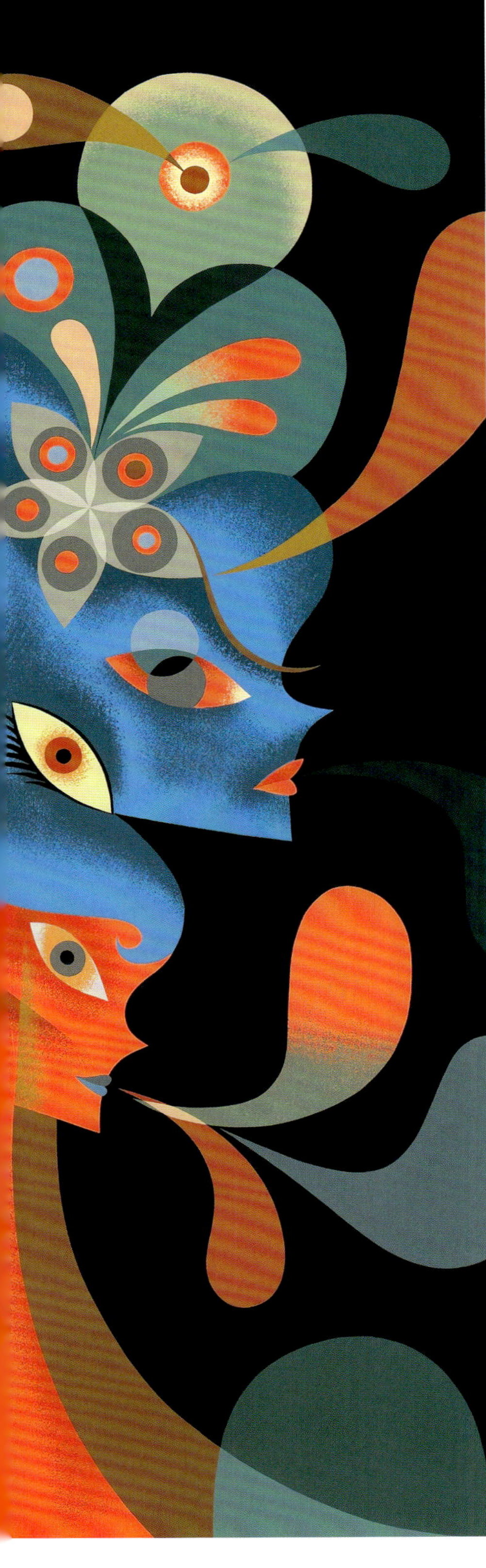

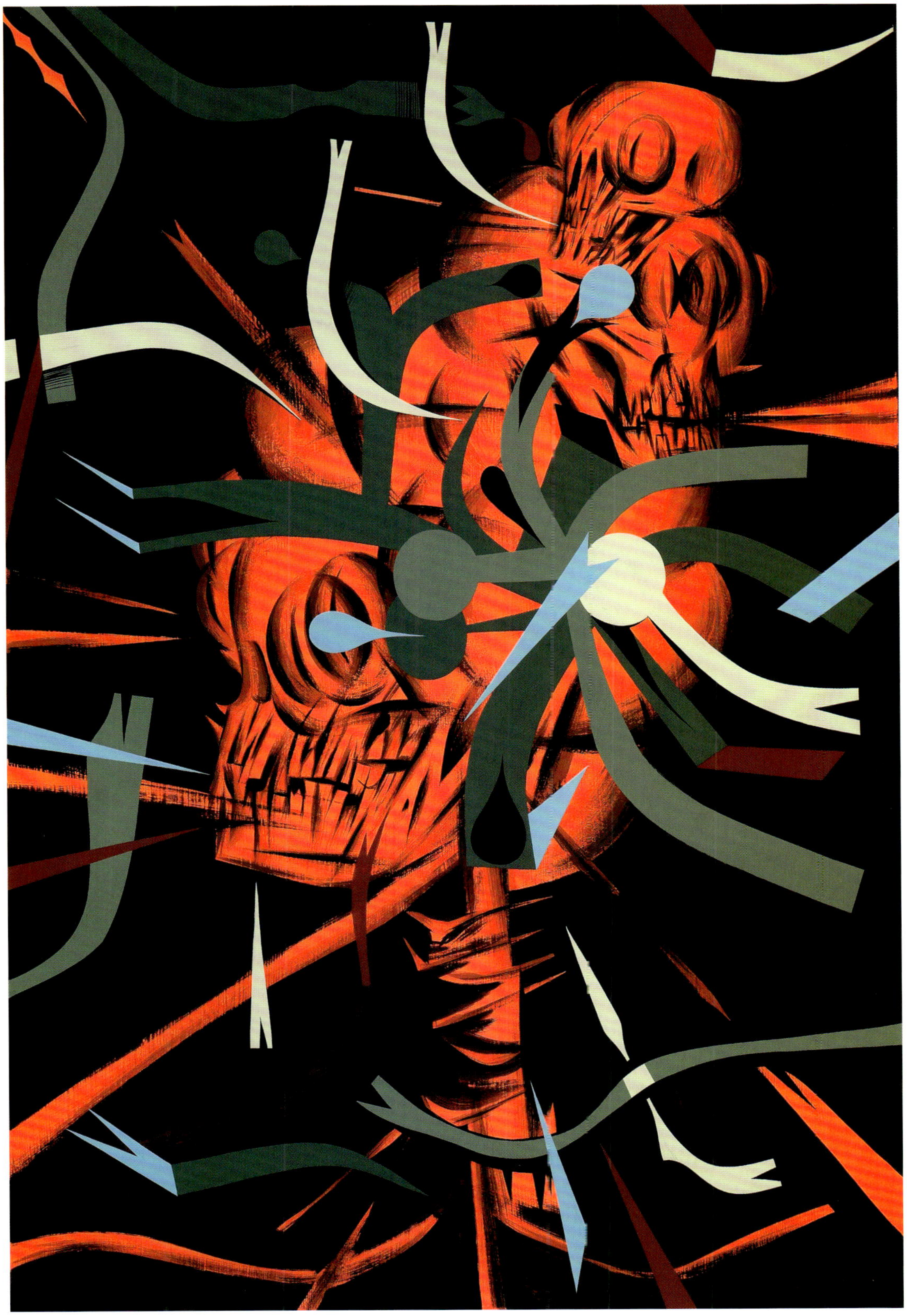

Asylum No 3
2008. Acrylic on Panel. 36" x 24"

Following page:

Minotaur No 2
2007. Acrylic on Panel. 14" x 11"

Minotaur No 1
2007. Acrylic on Panel. 14" x 11"

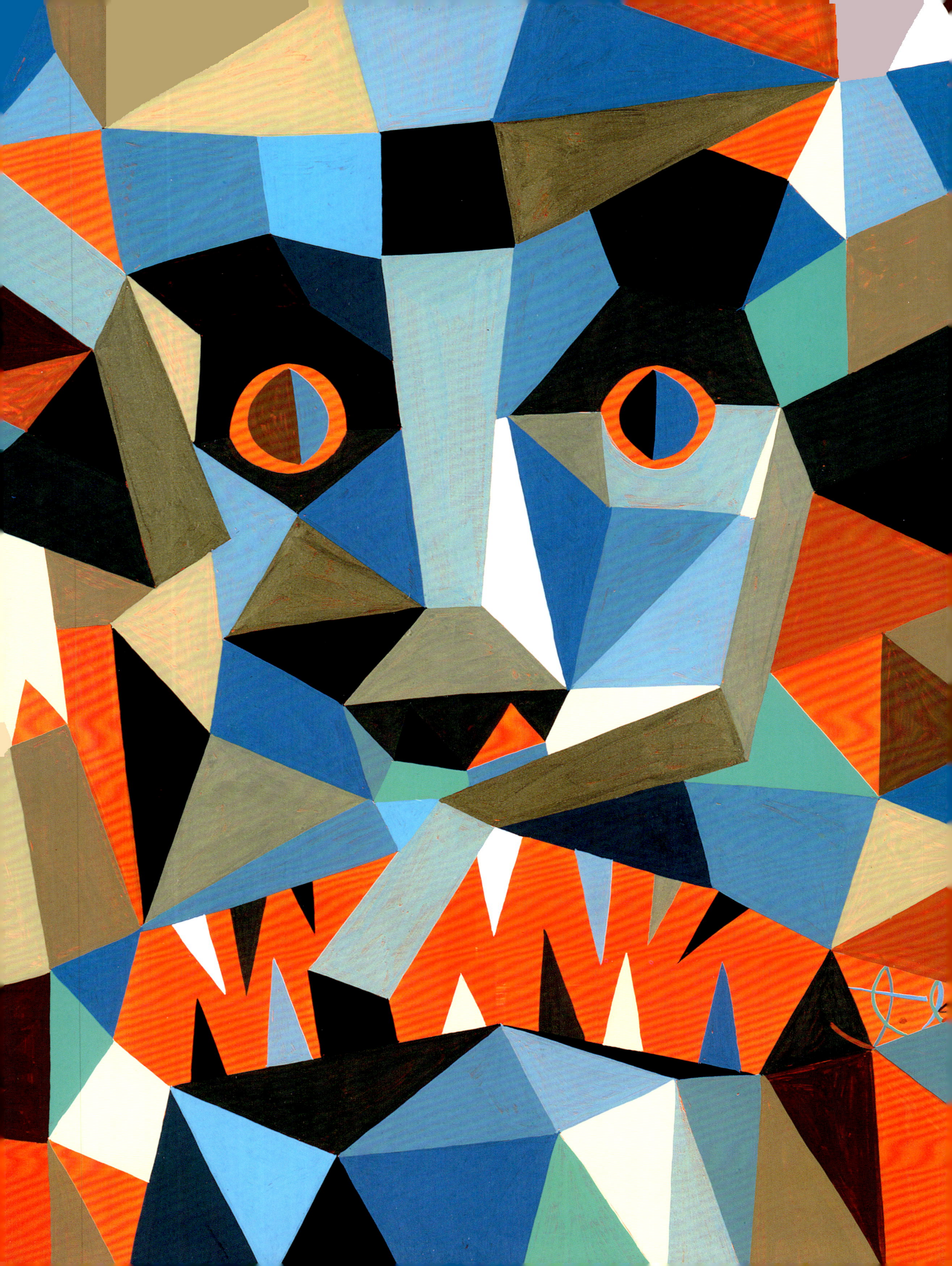

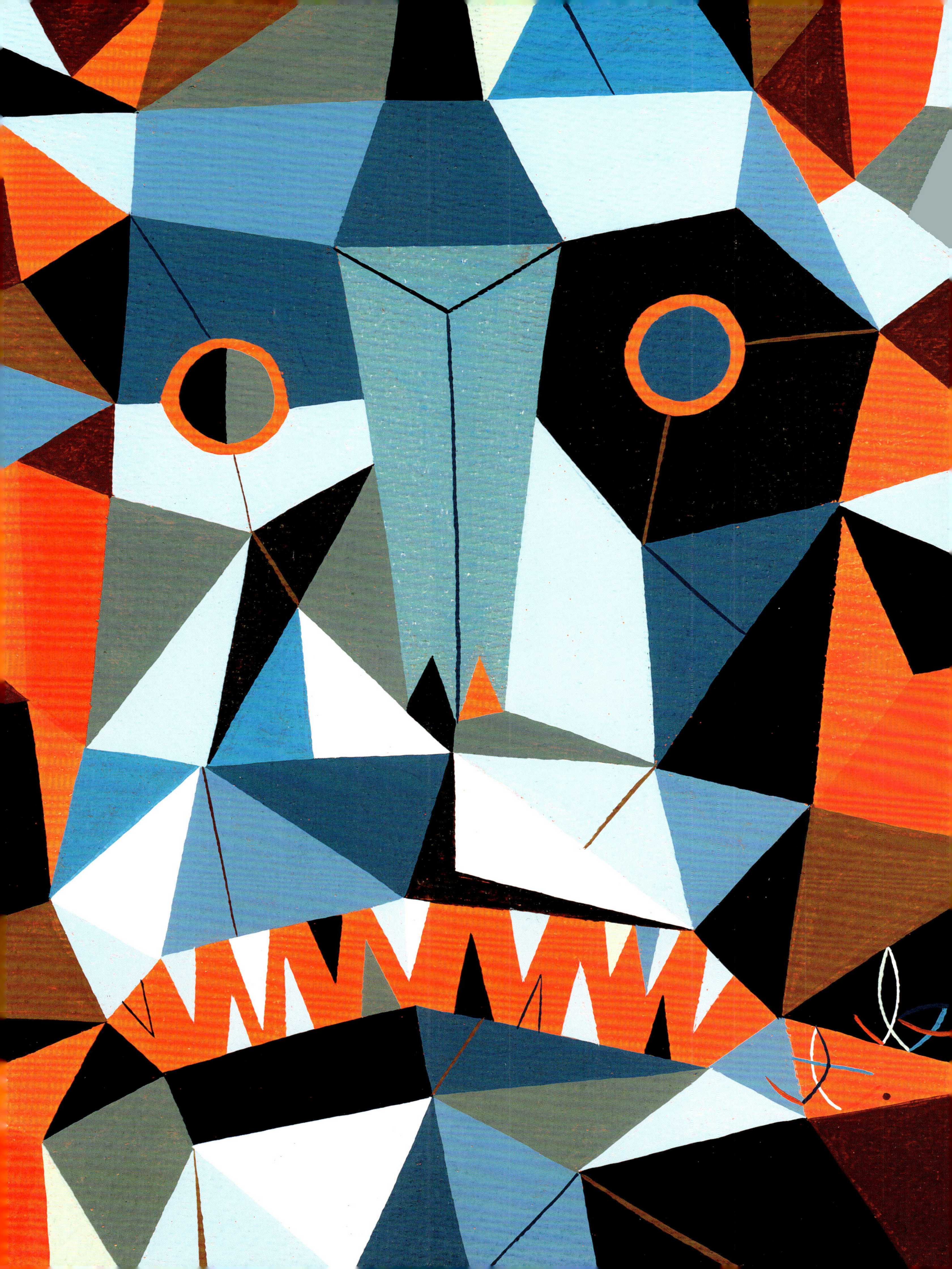

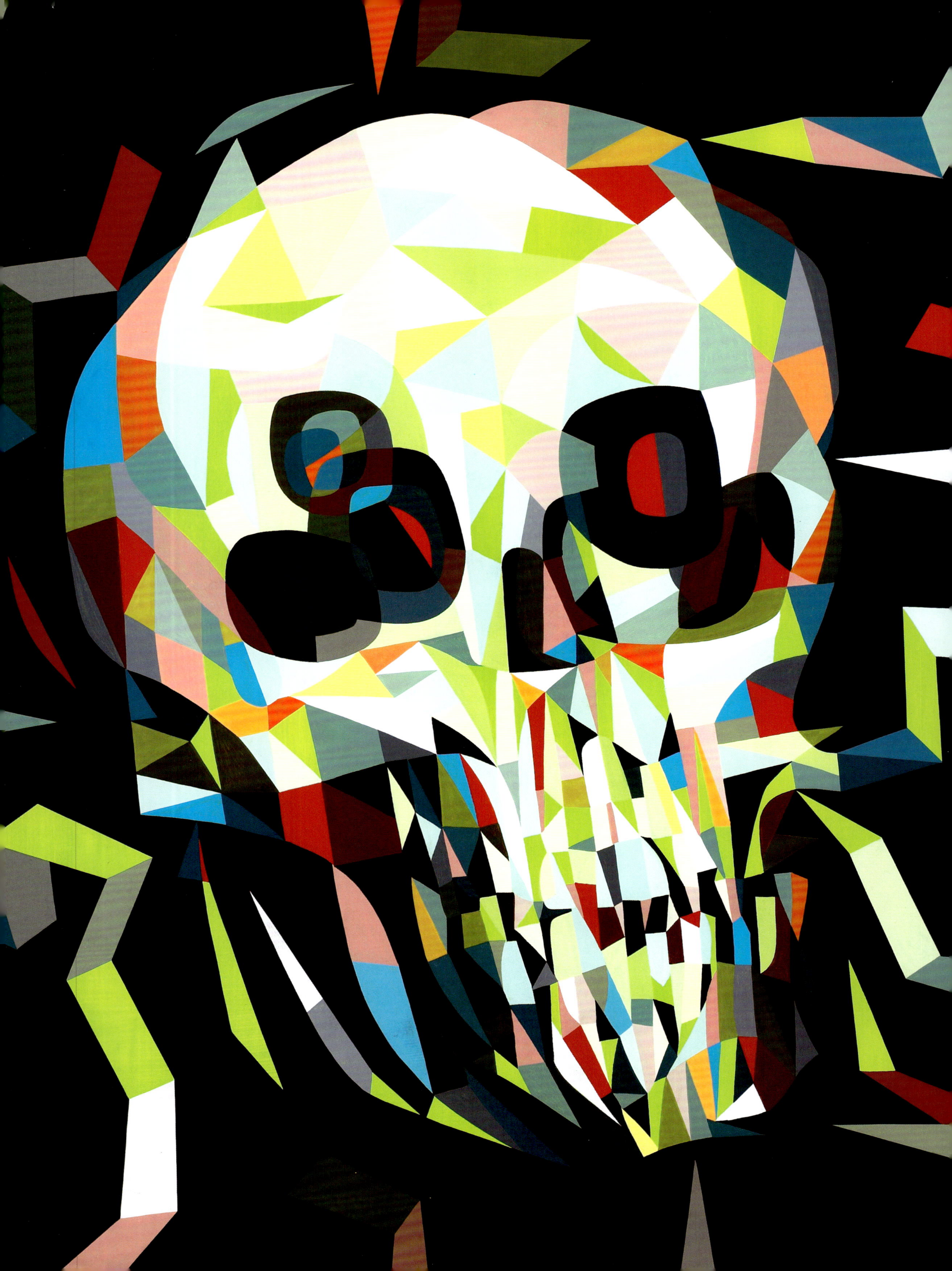

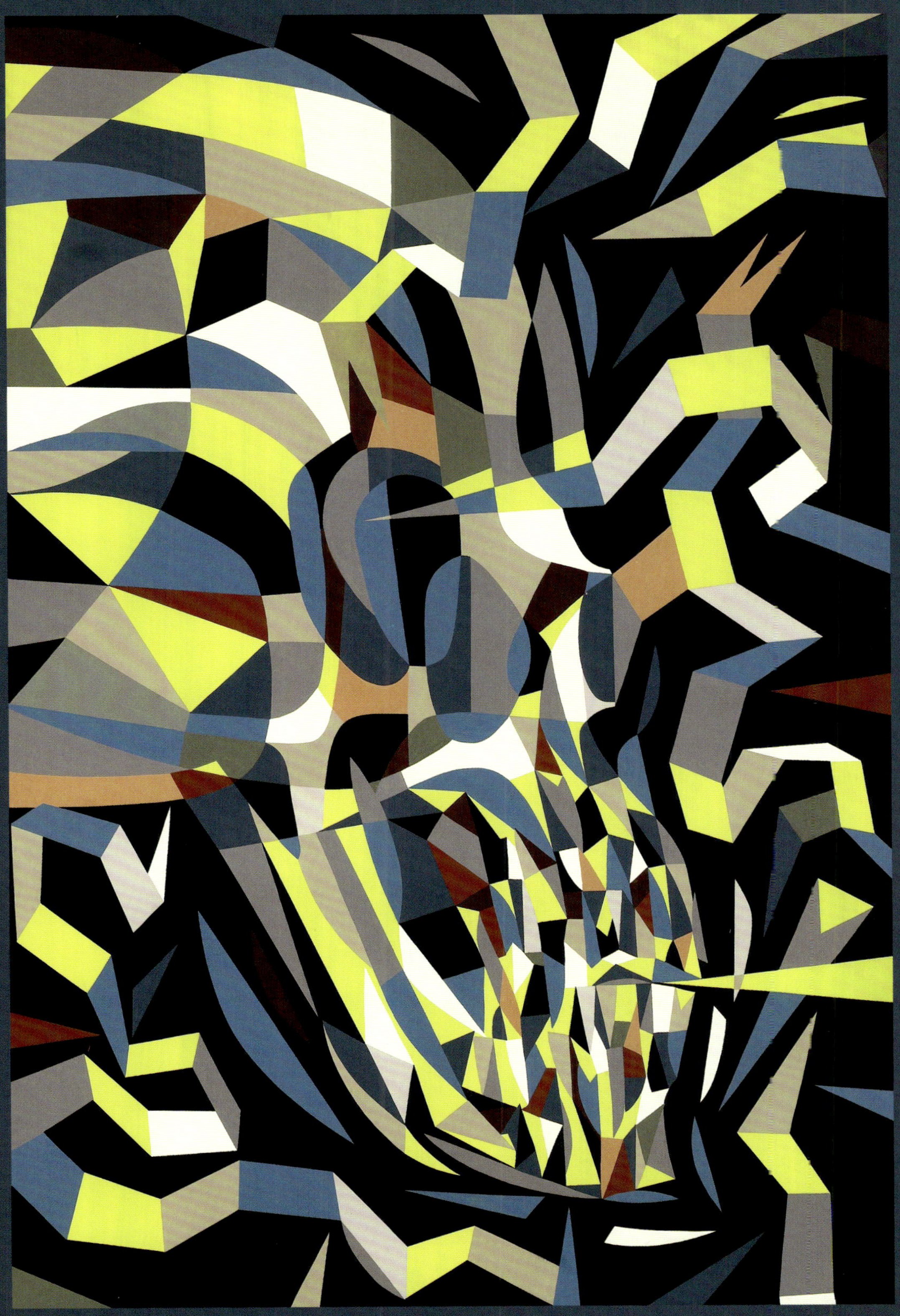

Doom Loop No 6
2008. Acrylic on Paper. 24" x 18"

Doom Loop No 4
2008. Acrylic on Panel. 36" x 24"

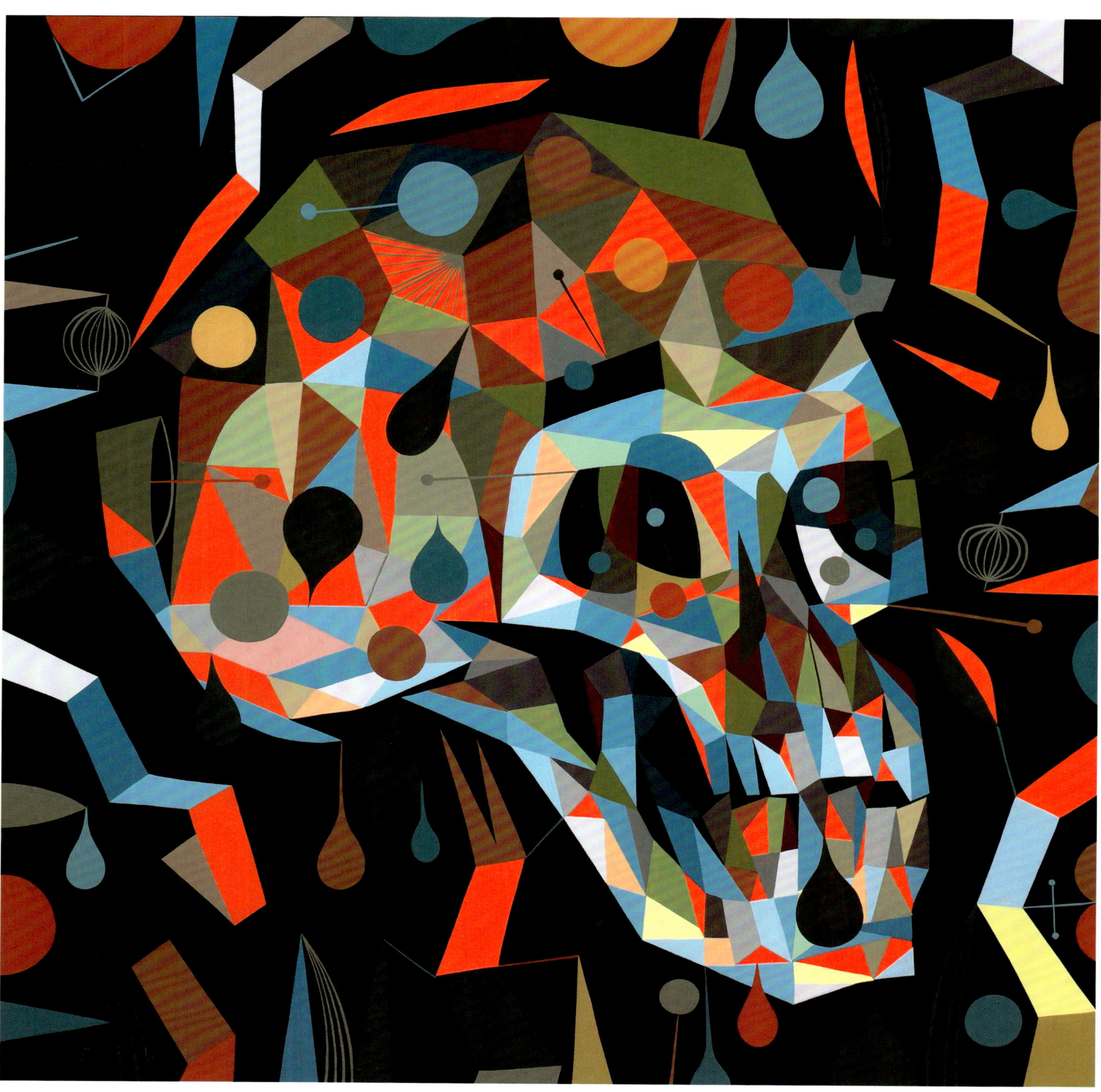

Doom Loop with Sprinkles
2008. Acrylic on Panel. 18" x 18"

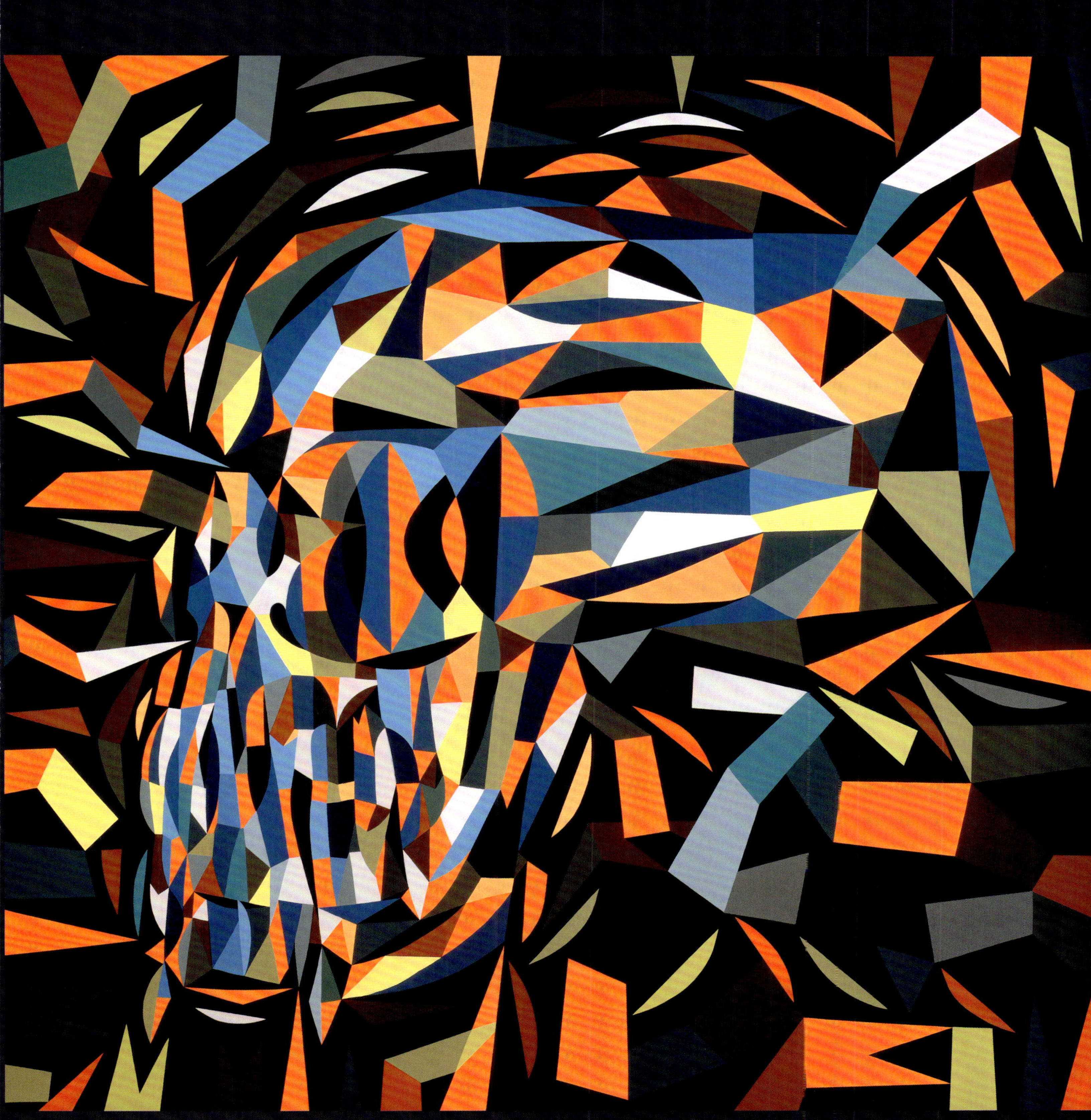

Doom Loop No 1
2008. Acrylic on Canvas. 78" x 78"

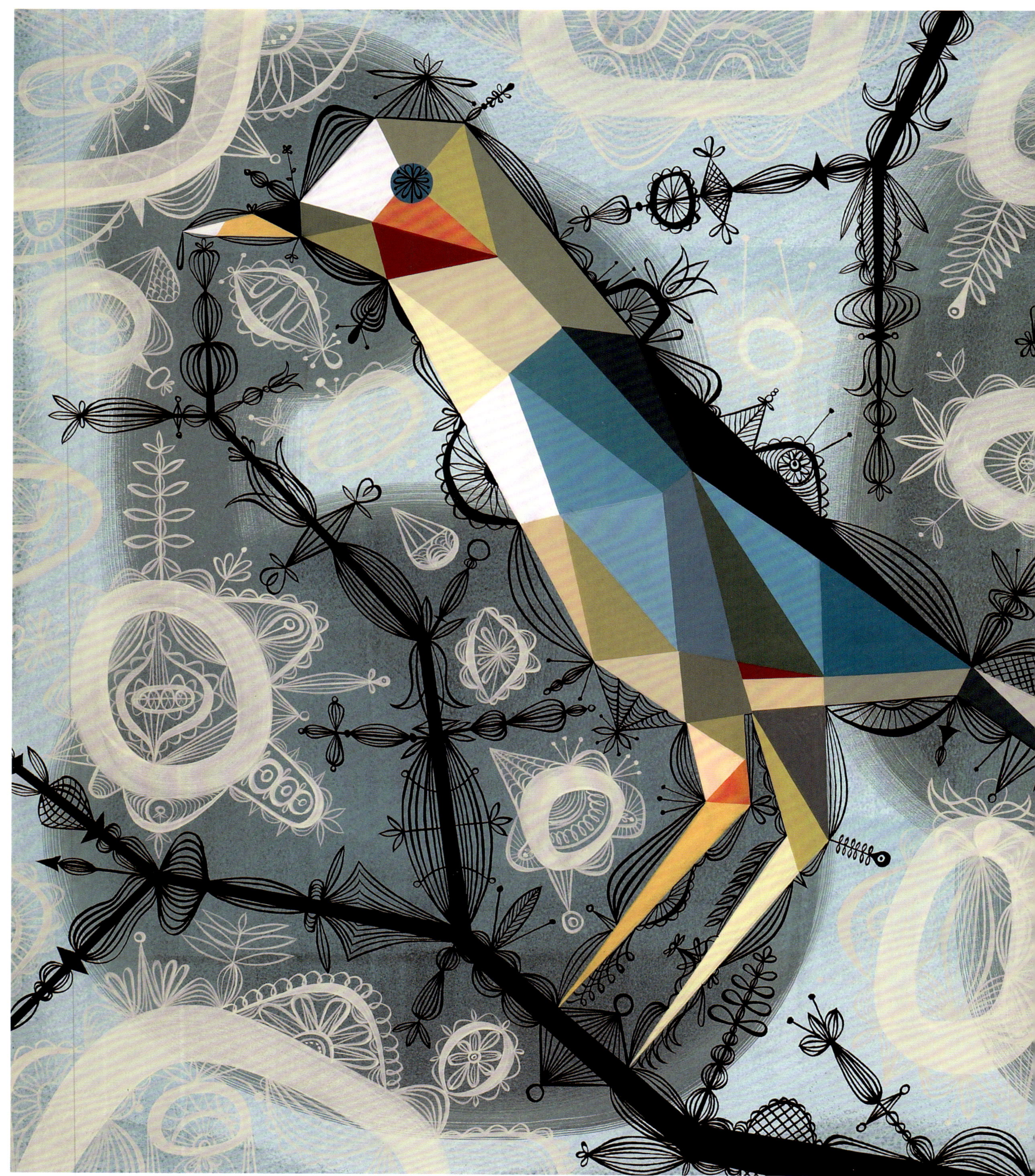

Painting from System No 9
2008. Acrylic on Panel. 18" x 24"

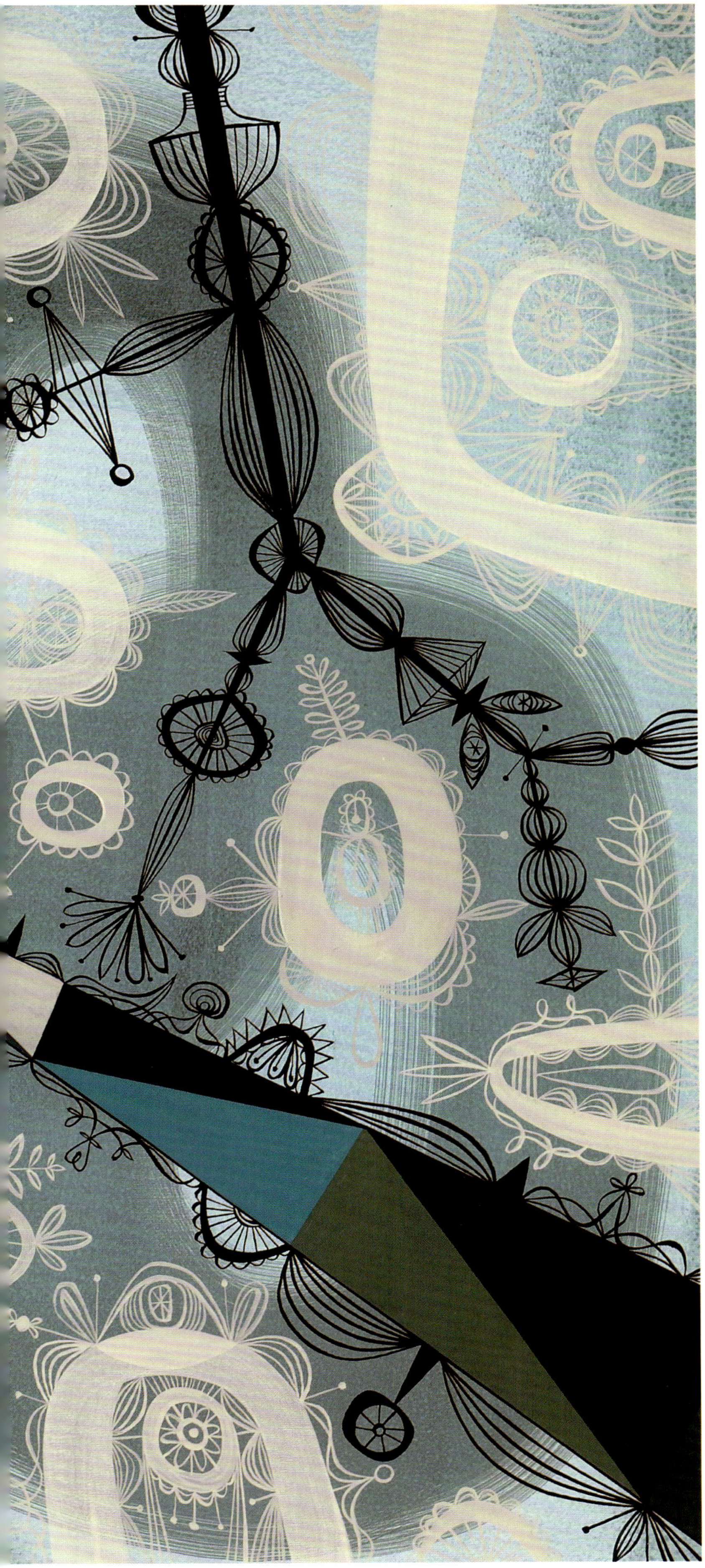

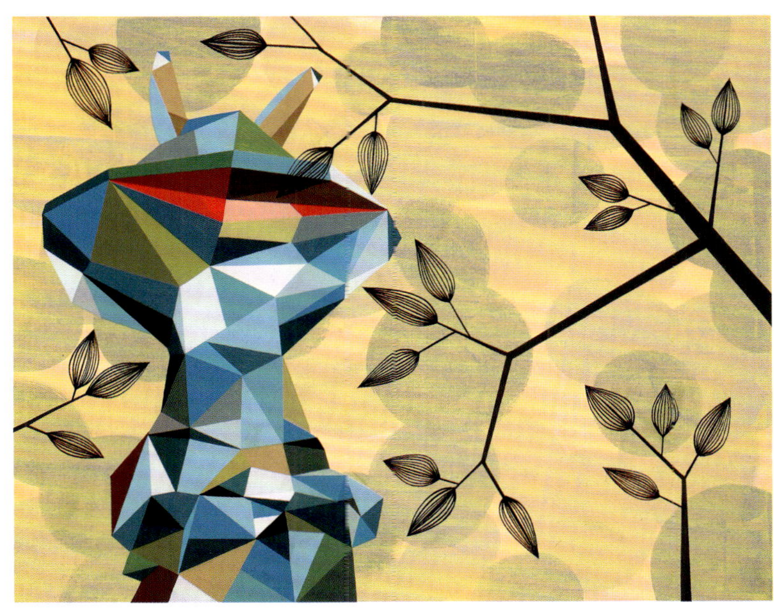

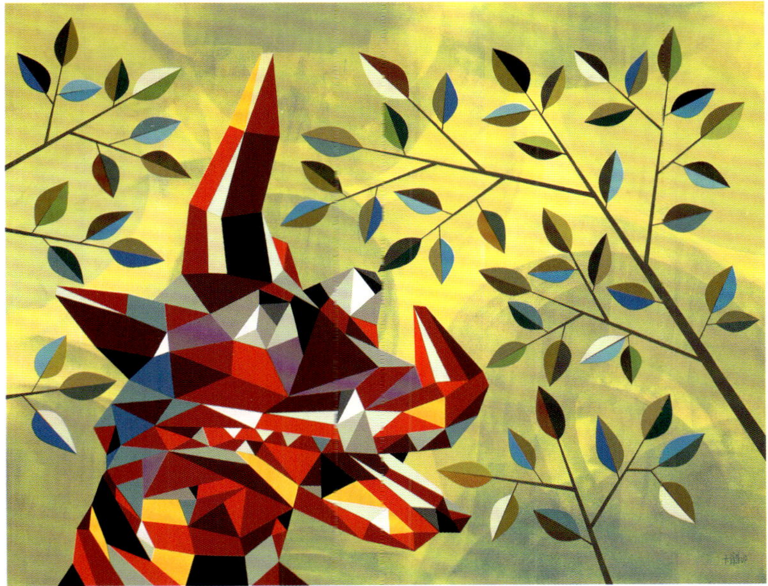

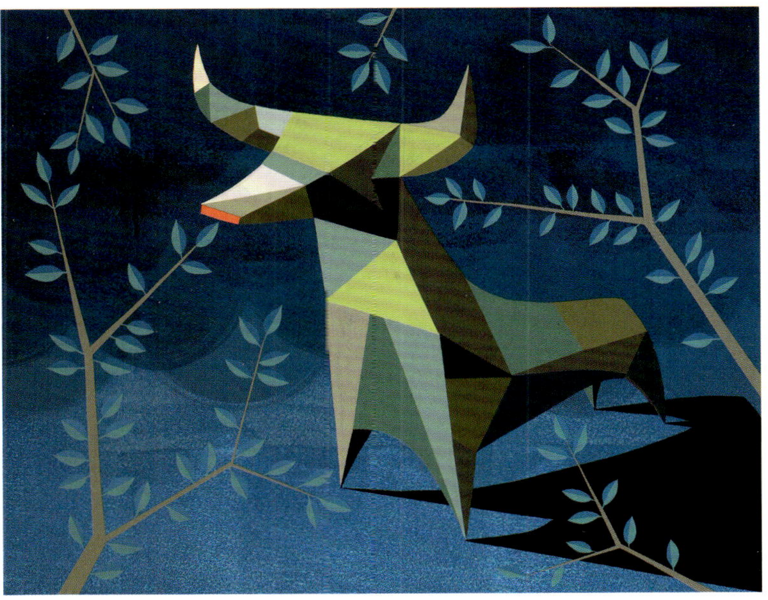

Painting from System No 8
2008. Acrylic on Panel. 9.5" x 12"

Immortal Diary
2008. Acrylic on Panel. 24" x 18"

Painting from System No 4
2008. Acrylic on Panel. 9.5" x 12"

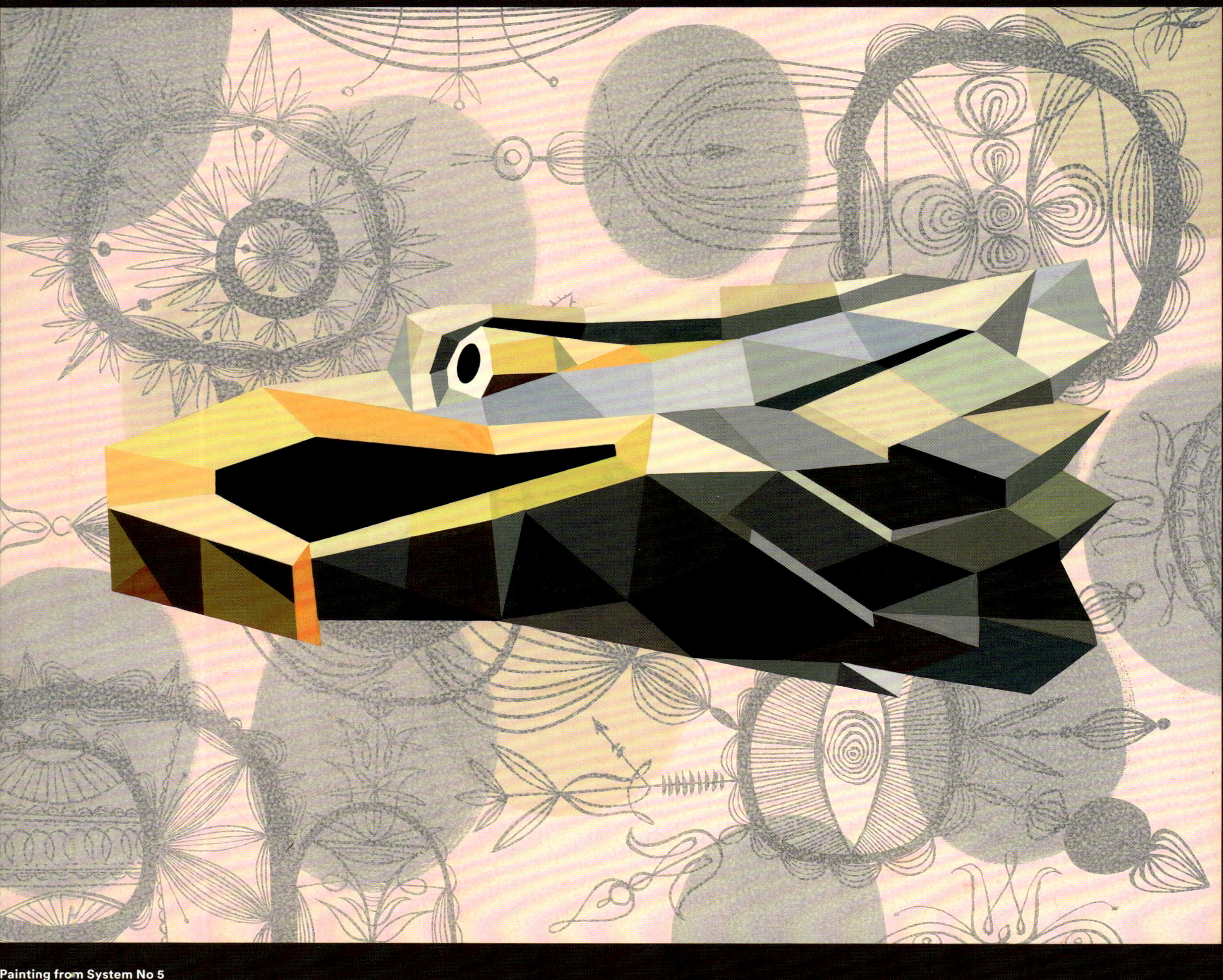

Painting from System No 5
2008. Acrylic on Panel. 9.5" x 12"

Painting from System No 1
2008. Acrylic on Panel. 9.5" x 12"

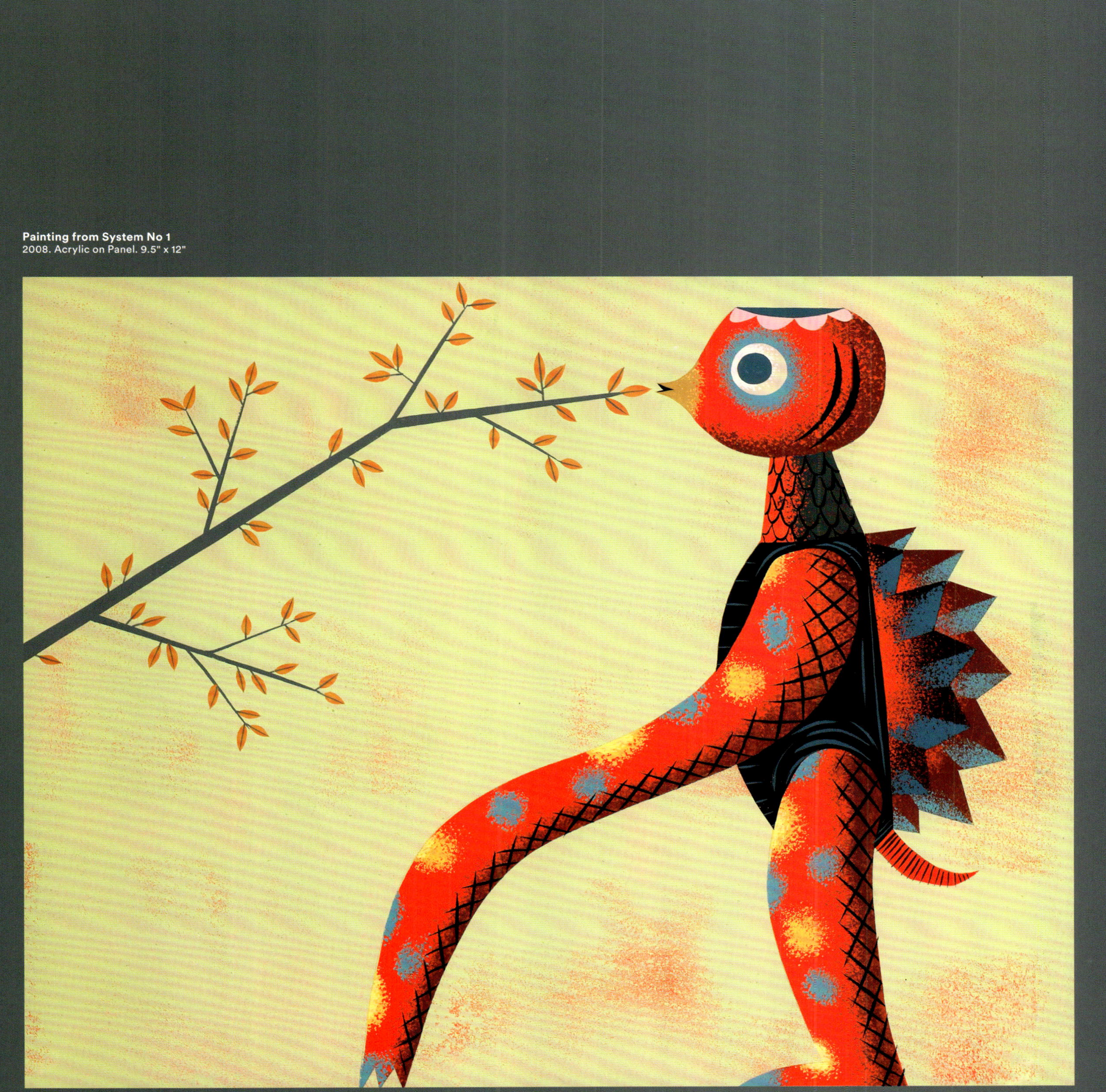

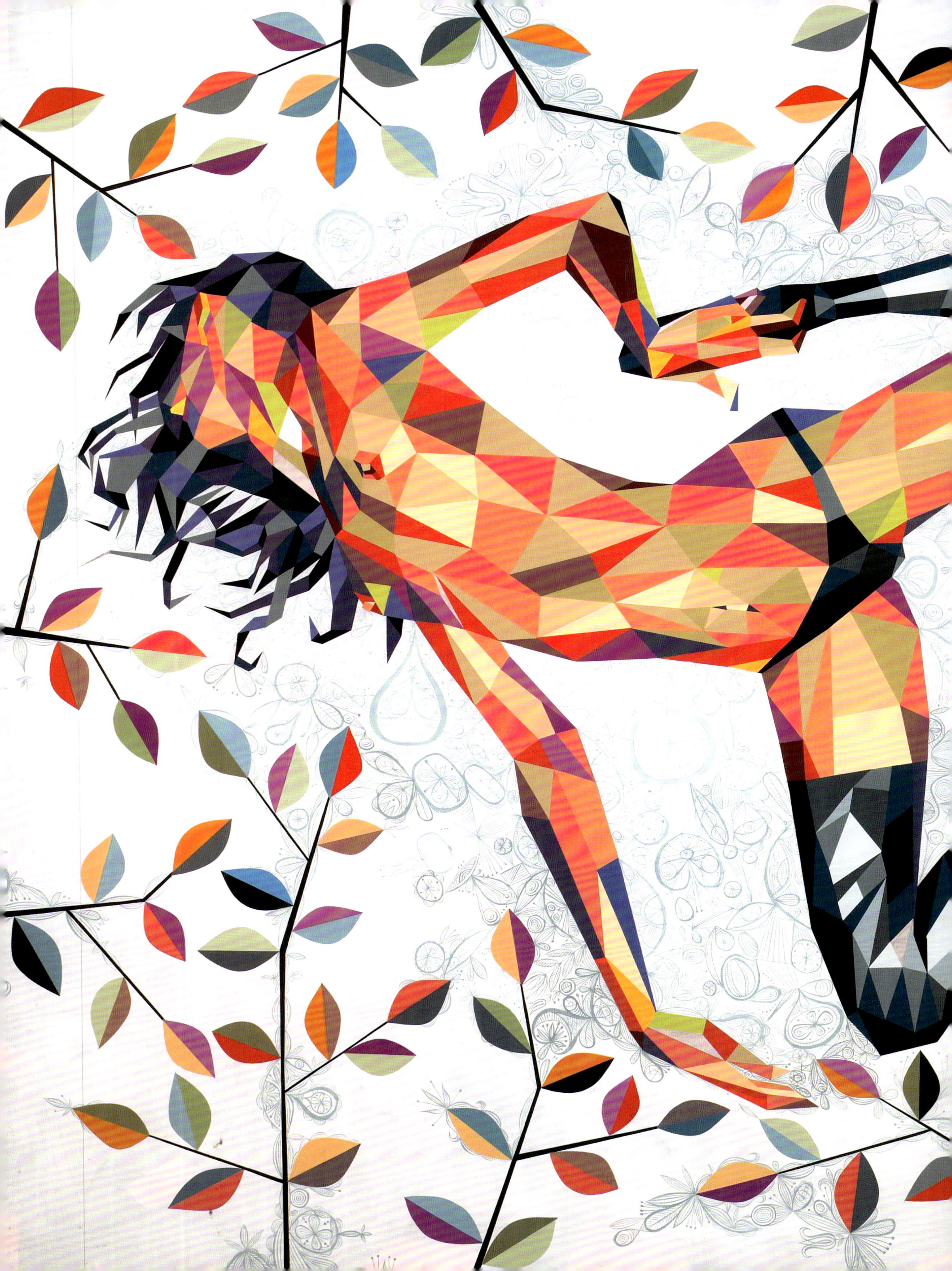

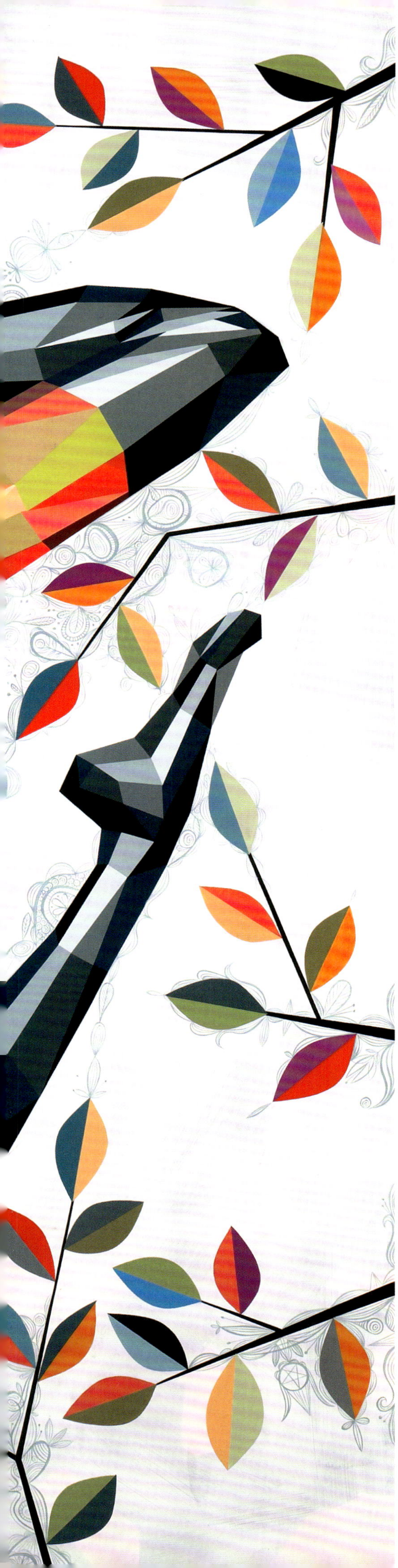

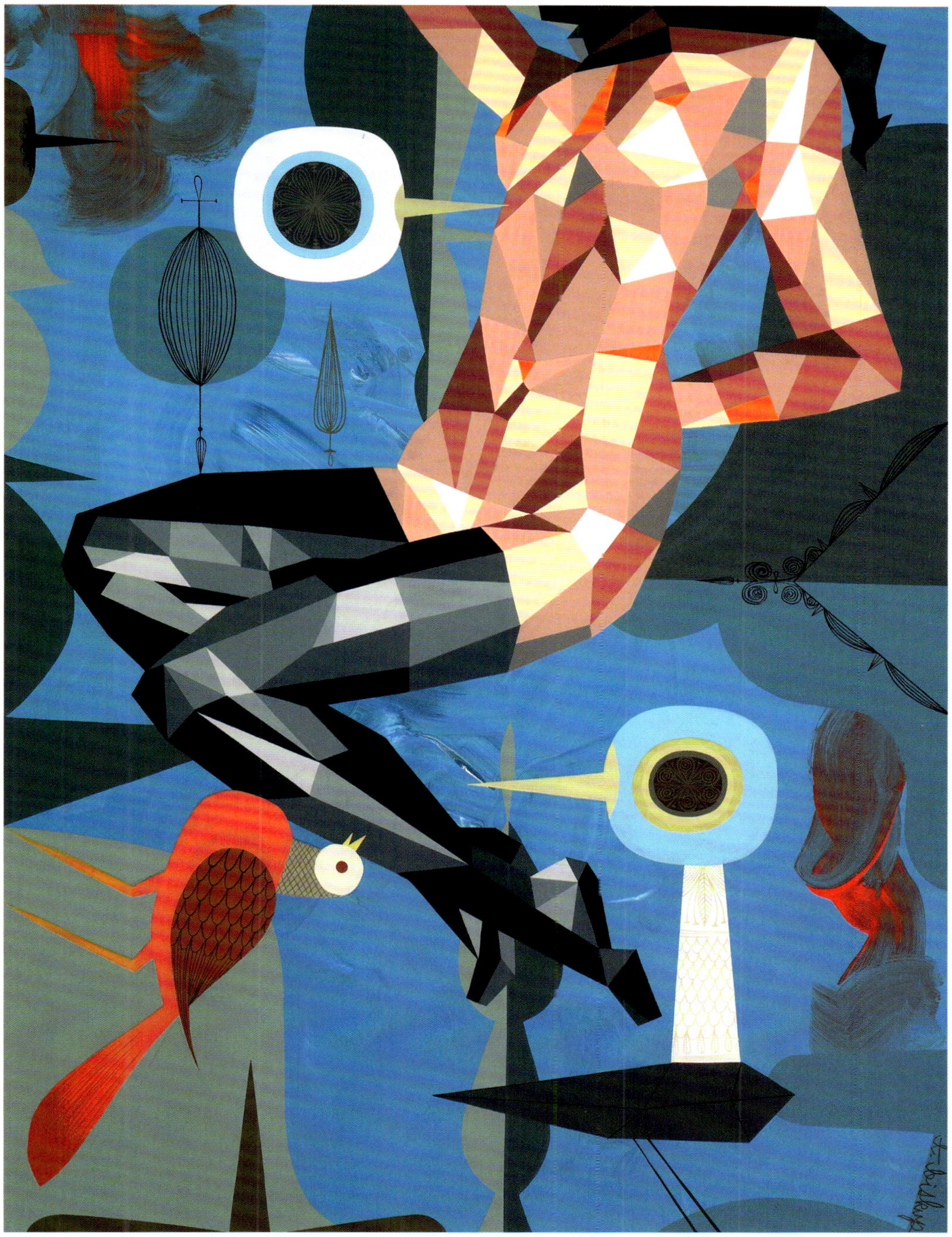

Valentine
2009. Acrylic on Panel. 48" x 48"

The Golden Chord of Time
2009. Acrylic on Panel. 24" x 18"

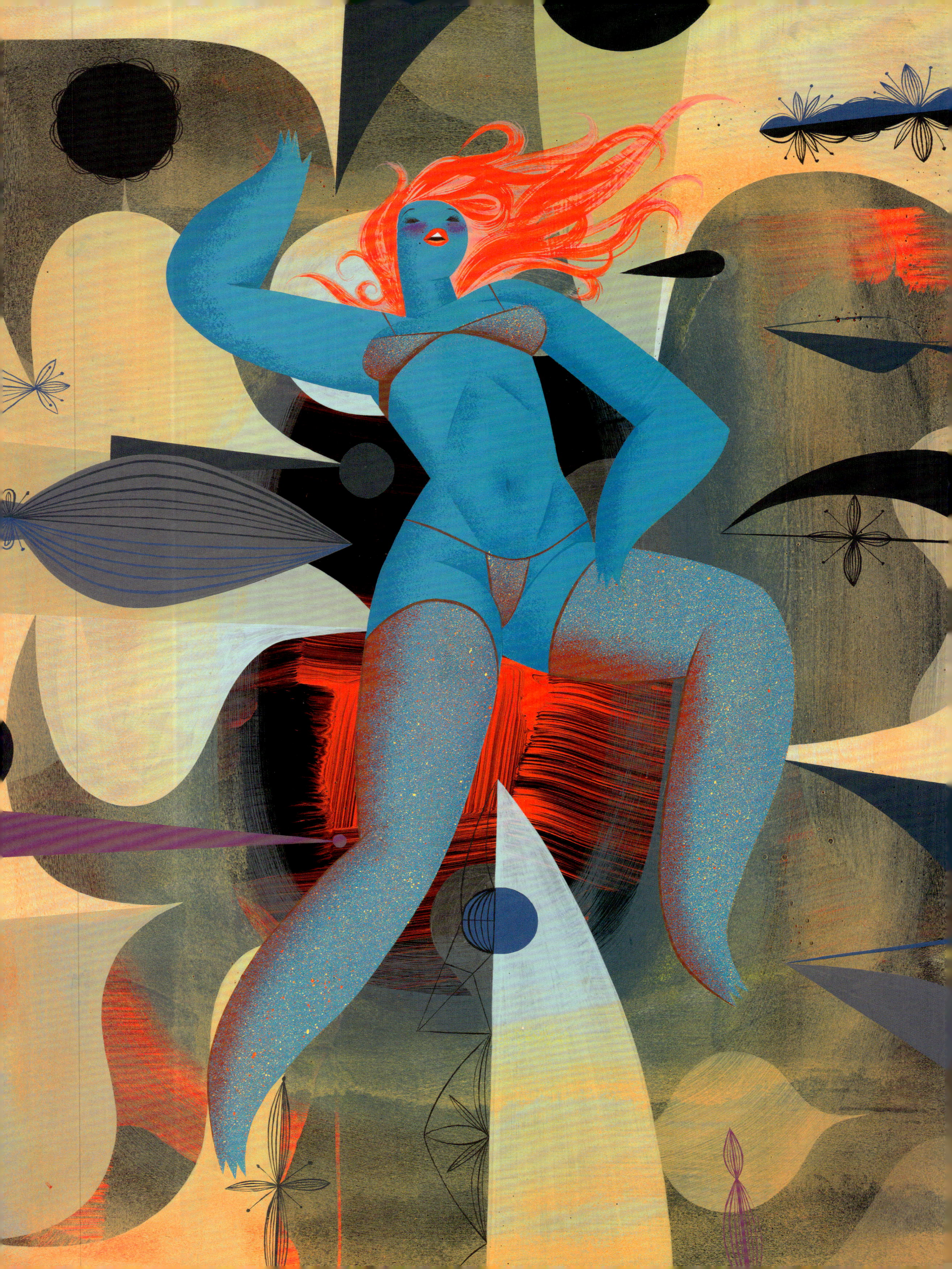

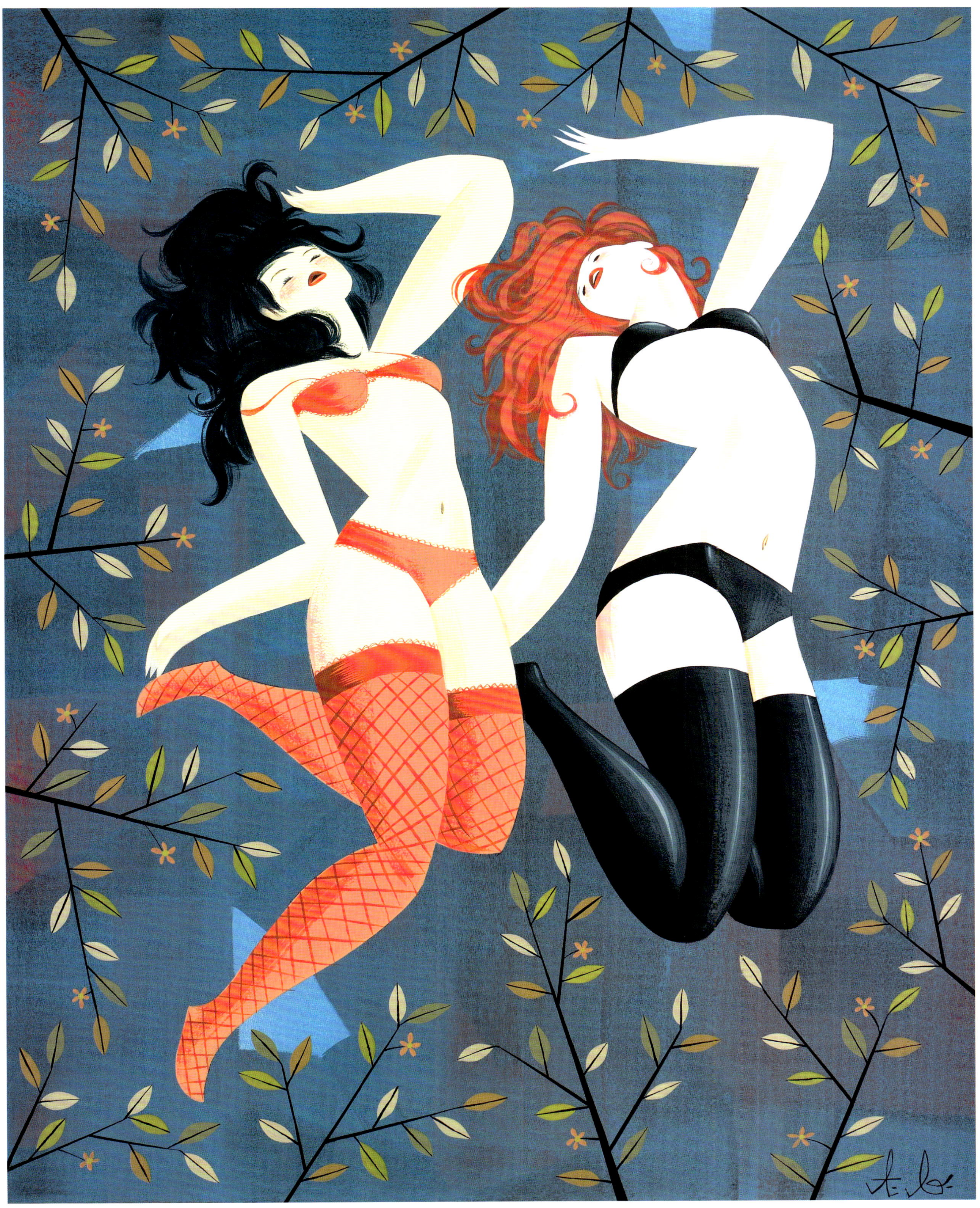

Flag of Order
2009. Acrylic on Panel. 24" x 18"

The Better Angels of Our Nature
2009. Acrylic on Panel. 20" x 16"

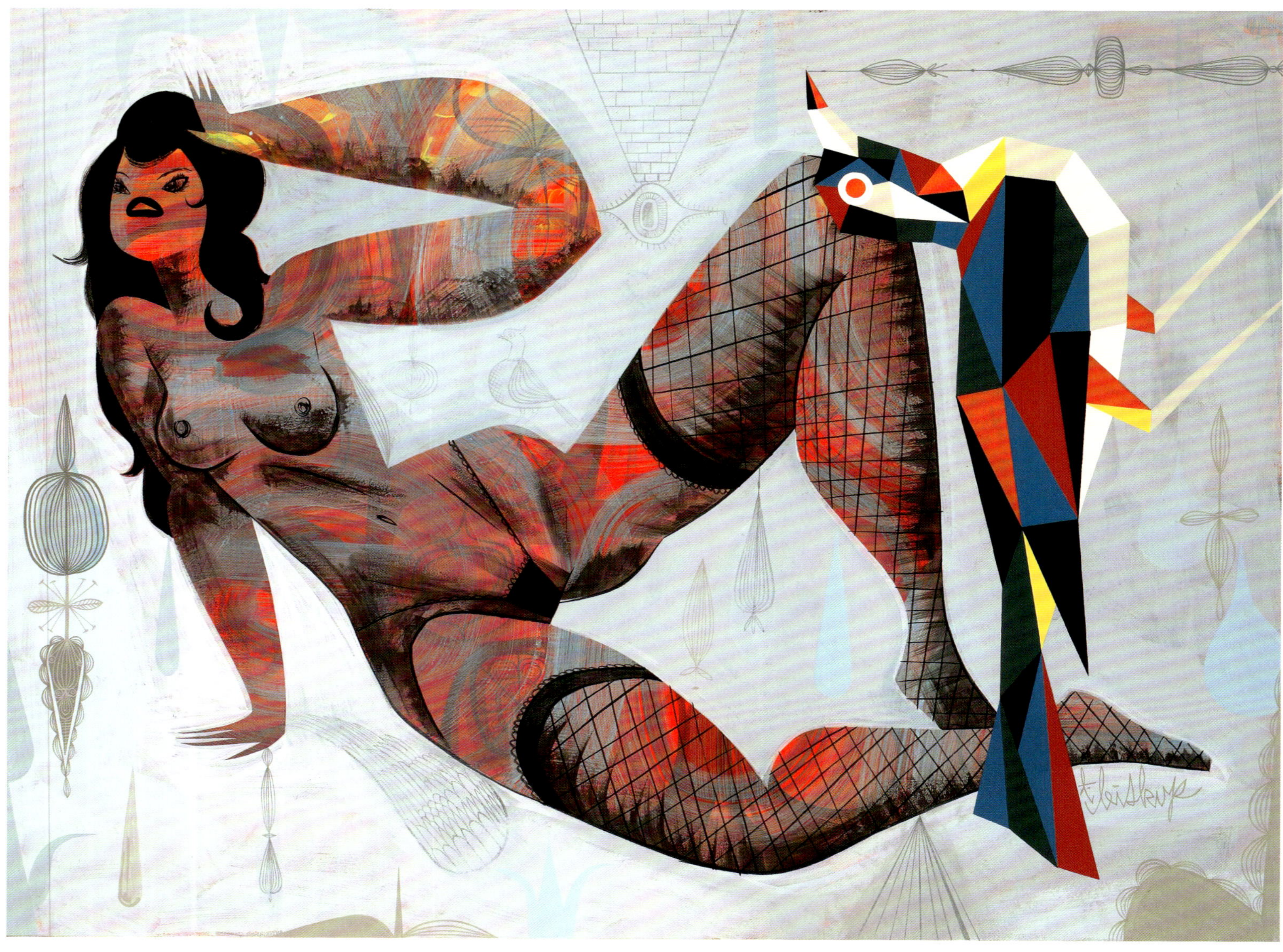

Union Chorus
2009. Acrylic on Panel. 18" x 24"

Deliverance
2008. Acrylic on Panel. 36" x 24"

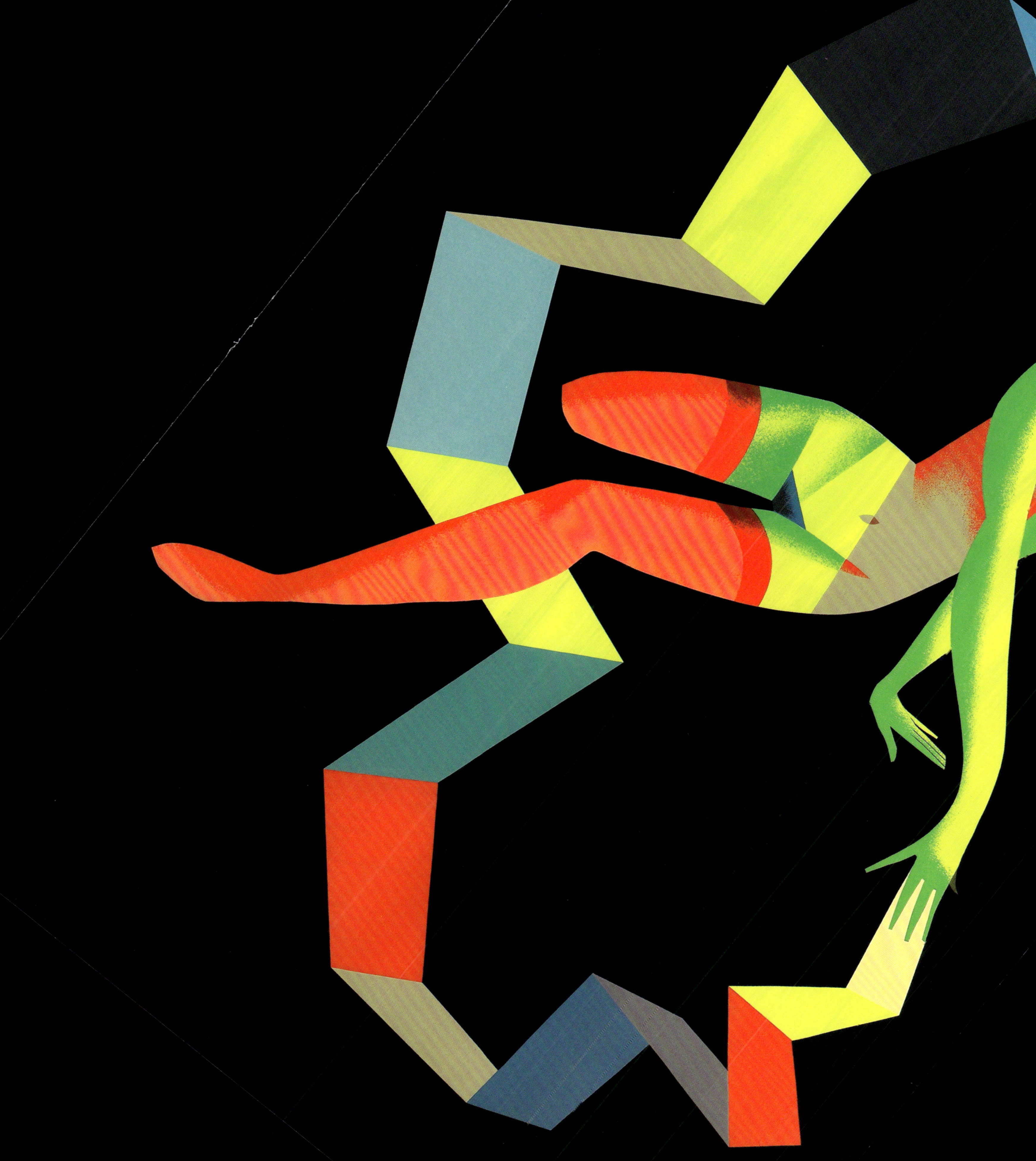

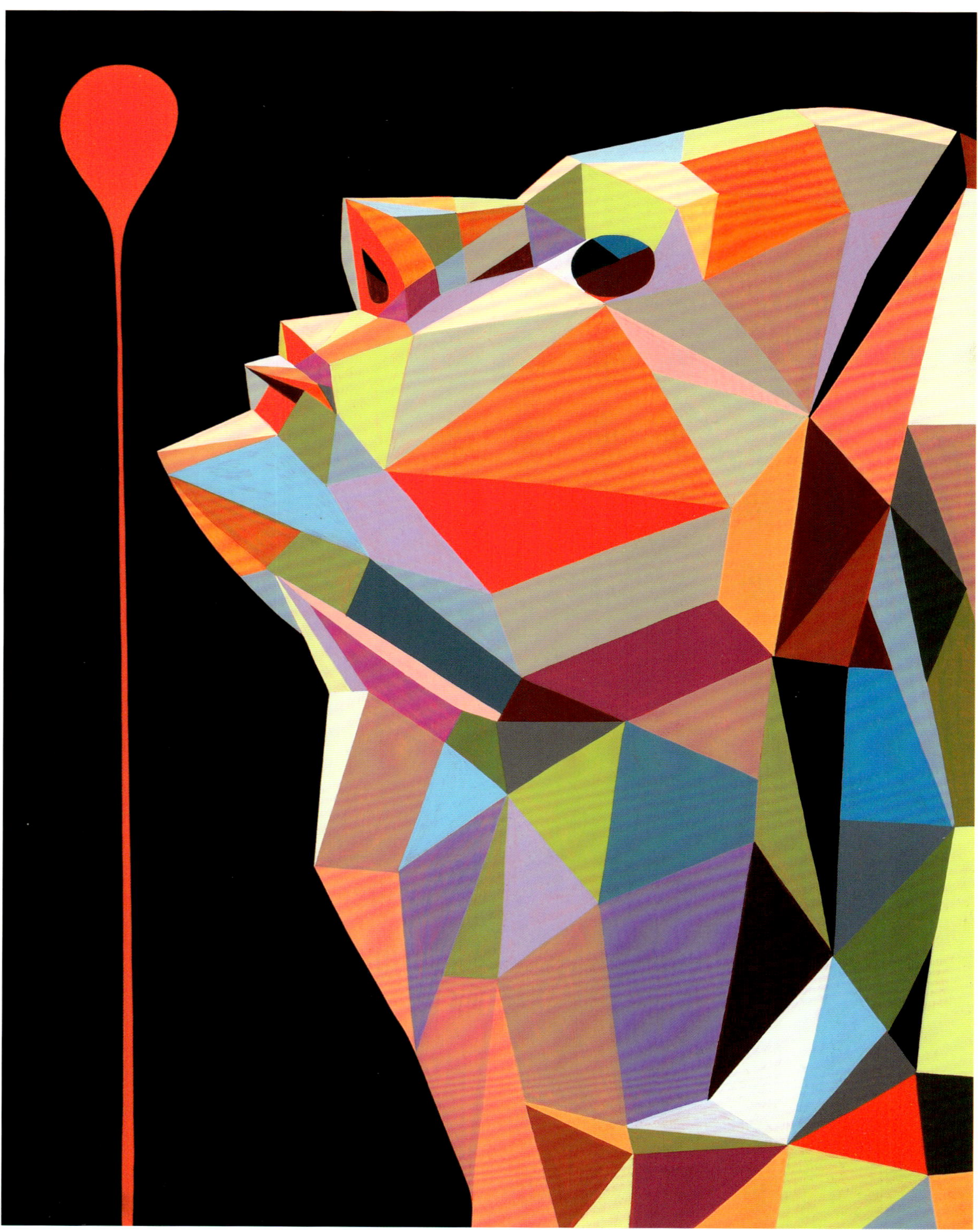

Growth Chart No 3
2008. Acrylic on Panel. 14" x 11"

Growth Chart No 2
2008. Acrylic on Panel. 14" x 11"

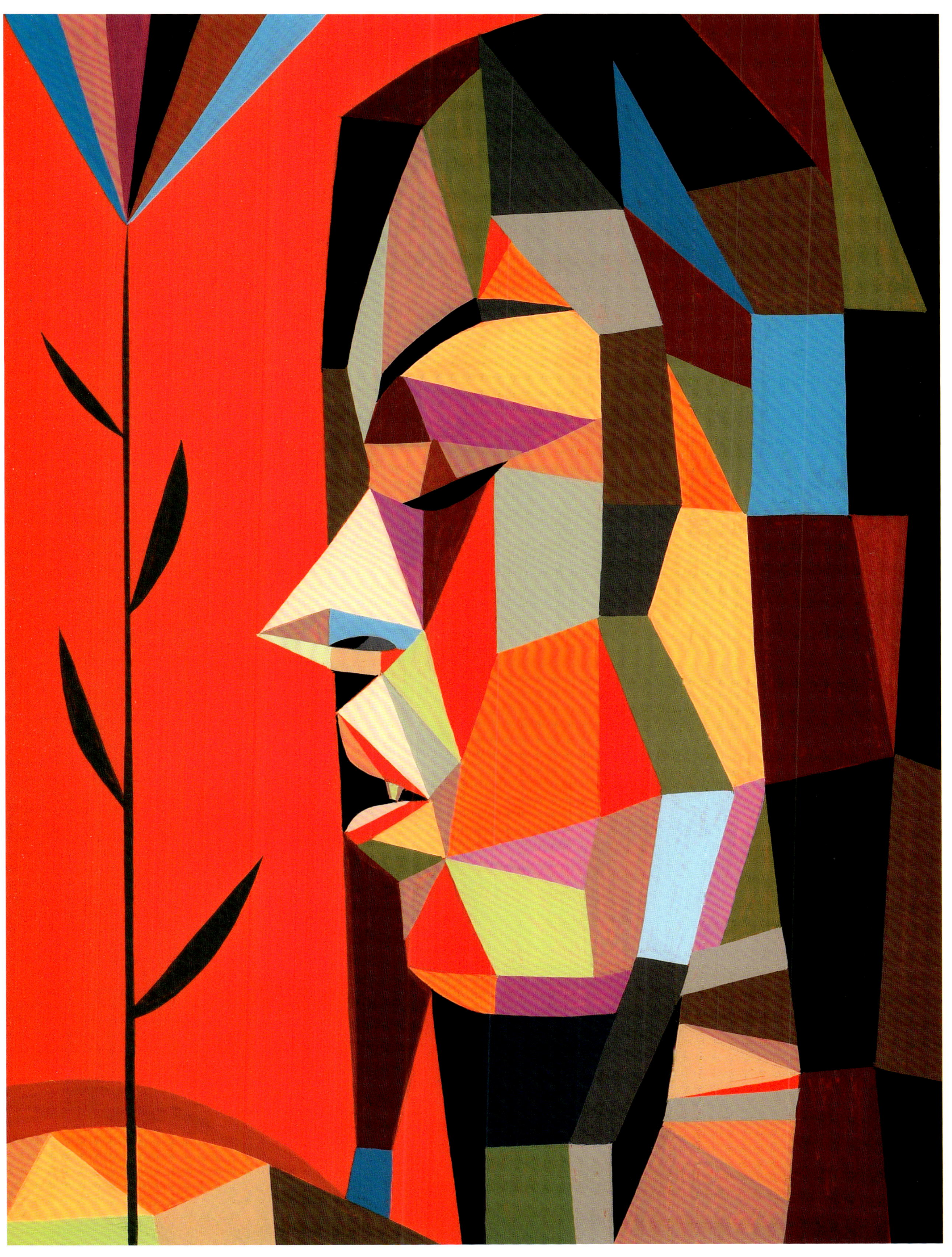

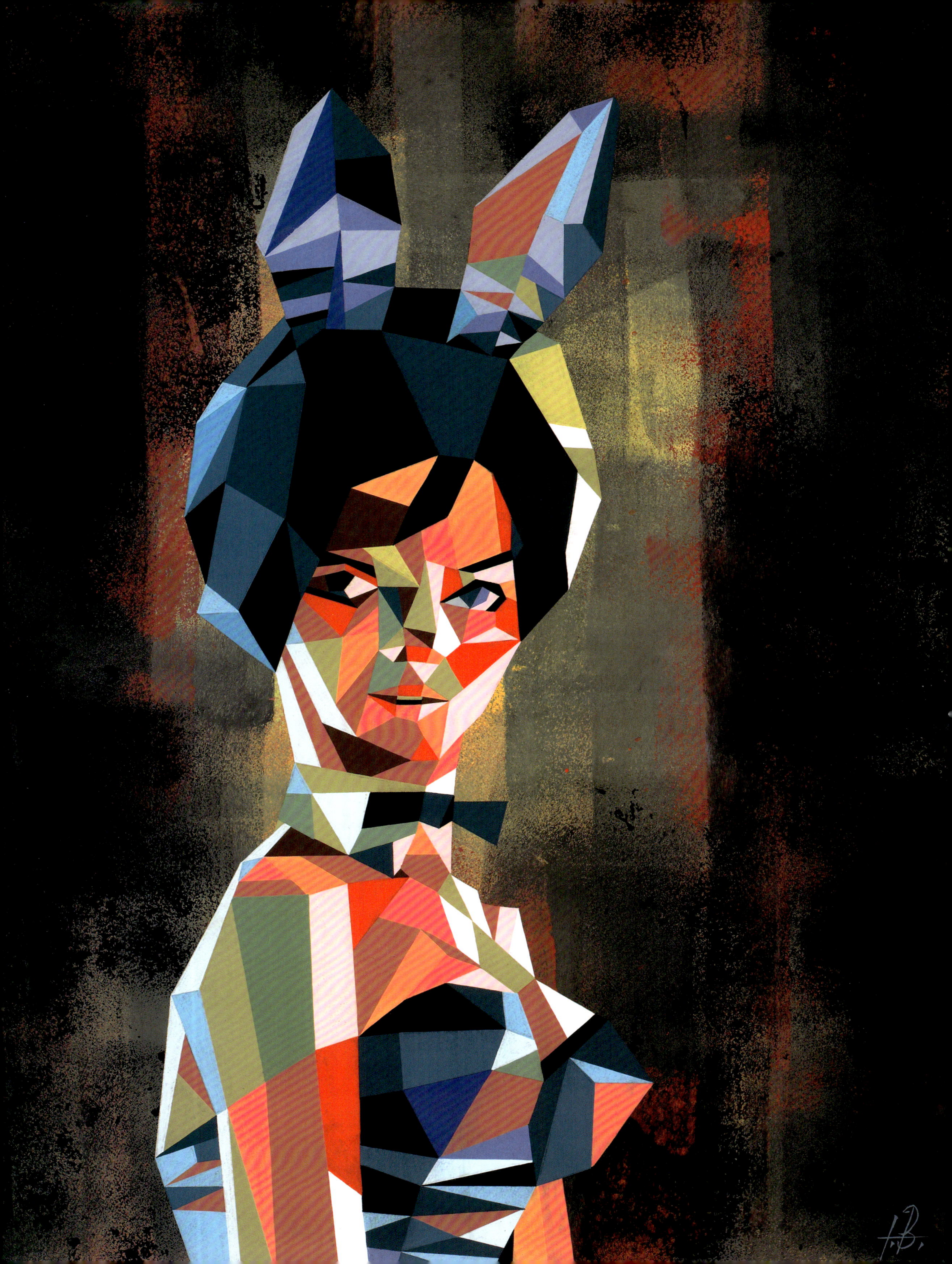

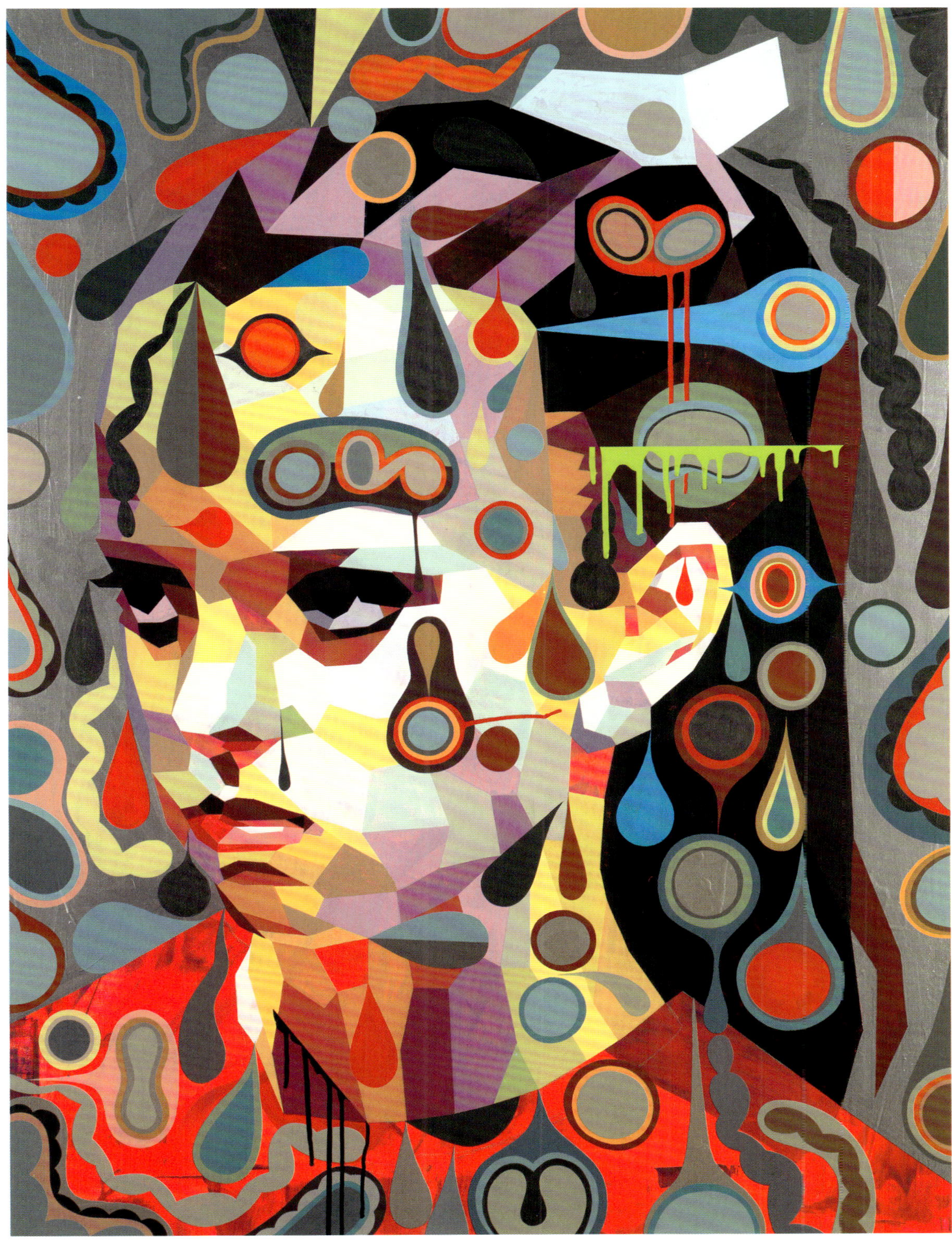

Gorgon
2010. Acrylic on Paper. 24" x 18"

The Litanies of Payton
2012. Acrylic on Canvas. 48" x 36"

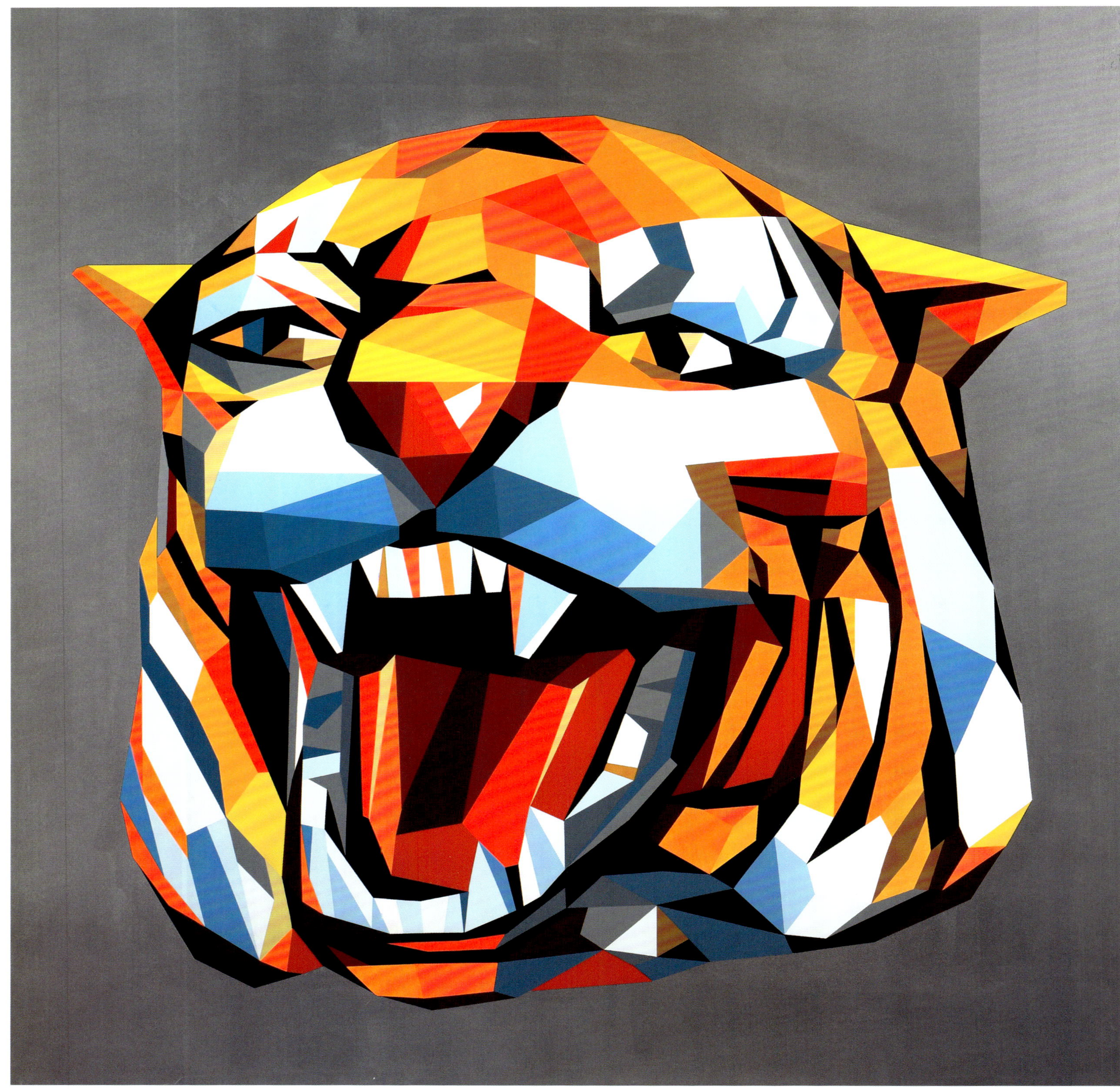

Gomorrah
2011. Acrylic on Panel. 48" x 48"

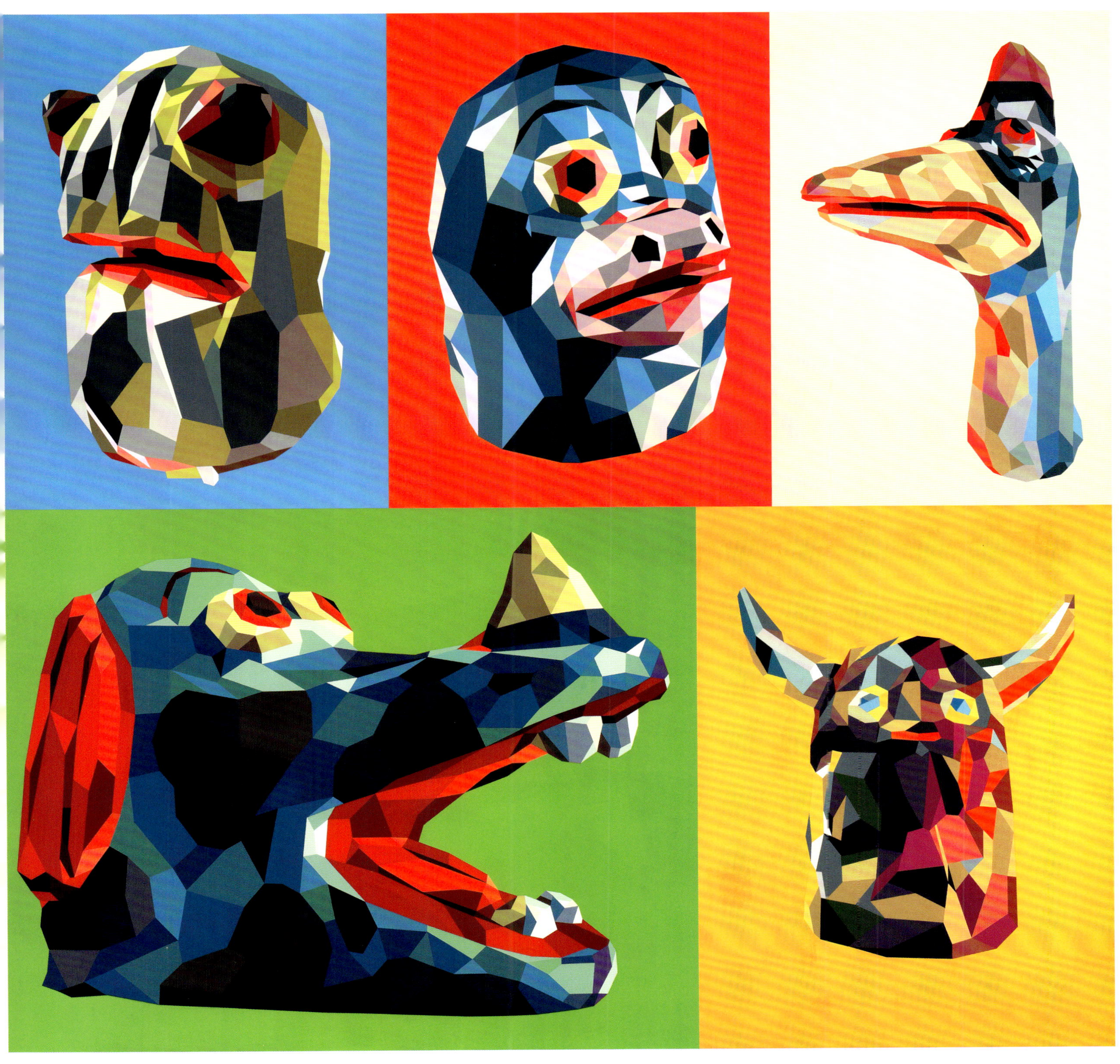

Marshmallow
2011. Acrylic on Canvas. 40" x 30"

Monkey
2011. Acrylic on Canvas. 40" x 30"

Bird
2011. Acrylic on Panel. 72" x 48"

Dragon Dog
2011. Acrylic on Panel. 36" x 48"

Horns
2011. Acrylic on Canvas. 40" x 30"

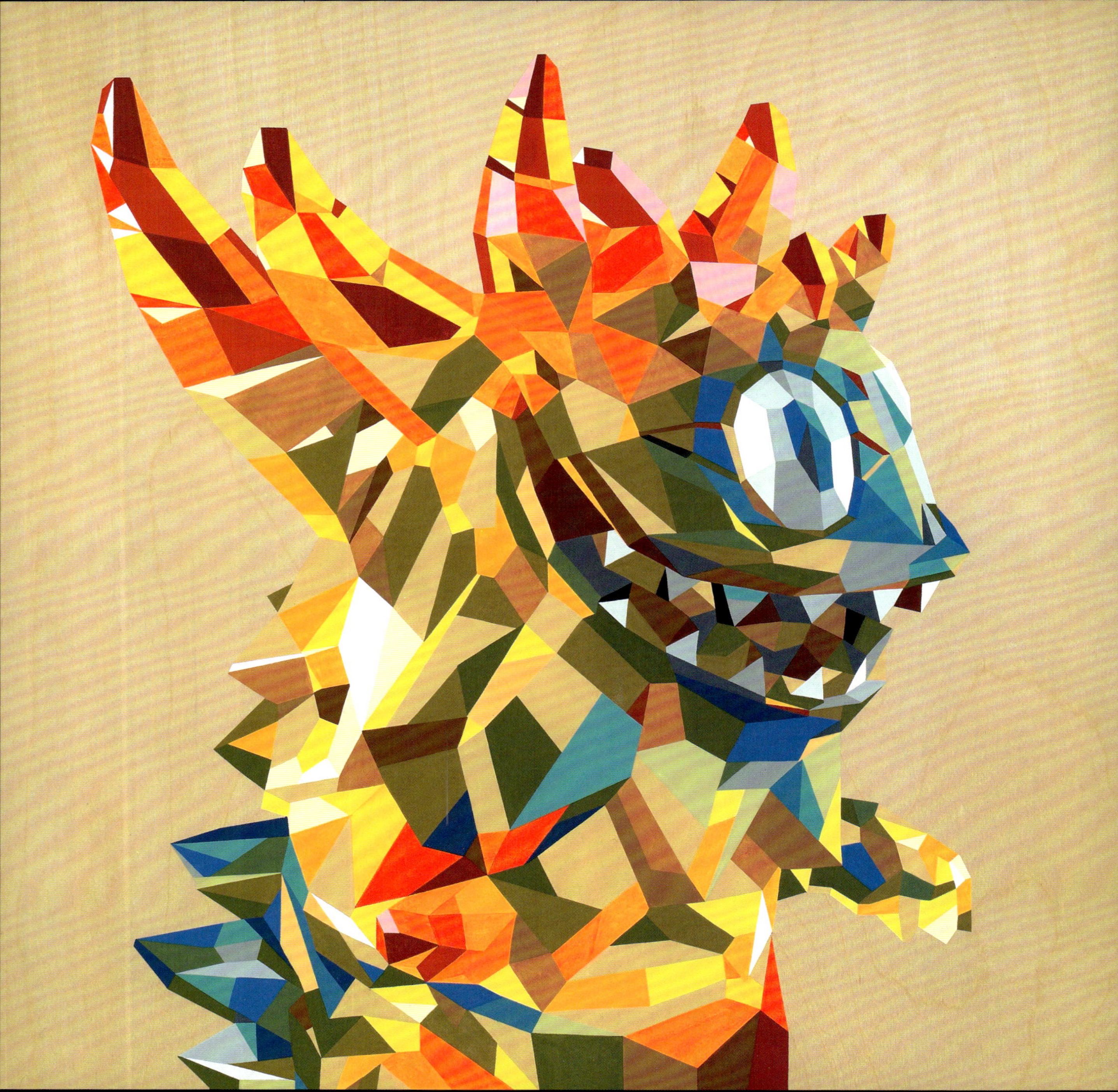

Rangeas No 1 (After T9G)
2009. Acrylic on Panel. 24" x 24"

Rangeas (After T9G)
2009. Vinyl. 8" tall

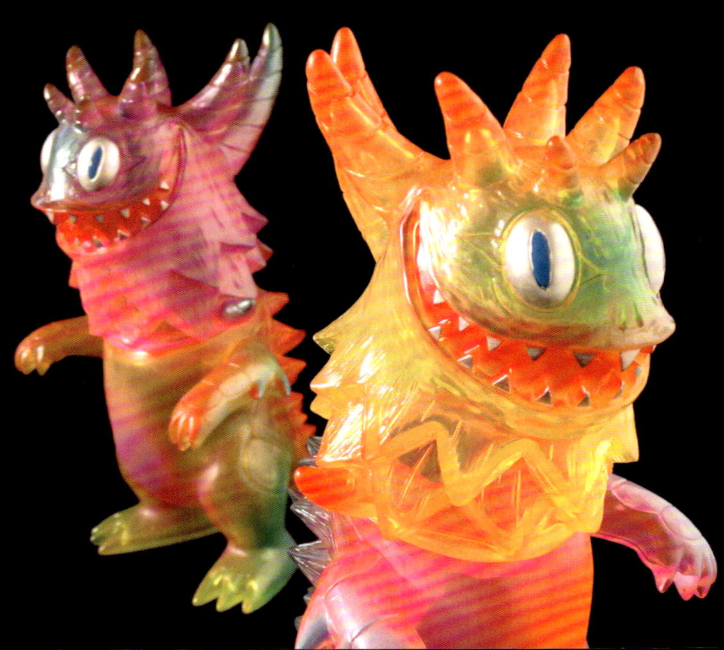

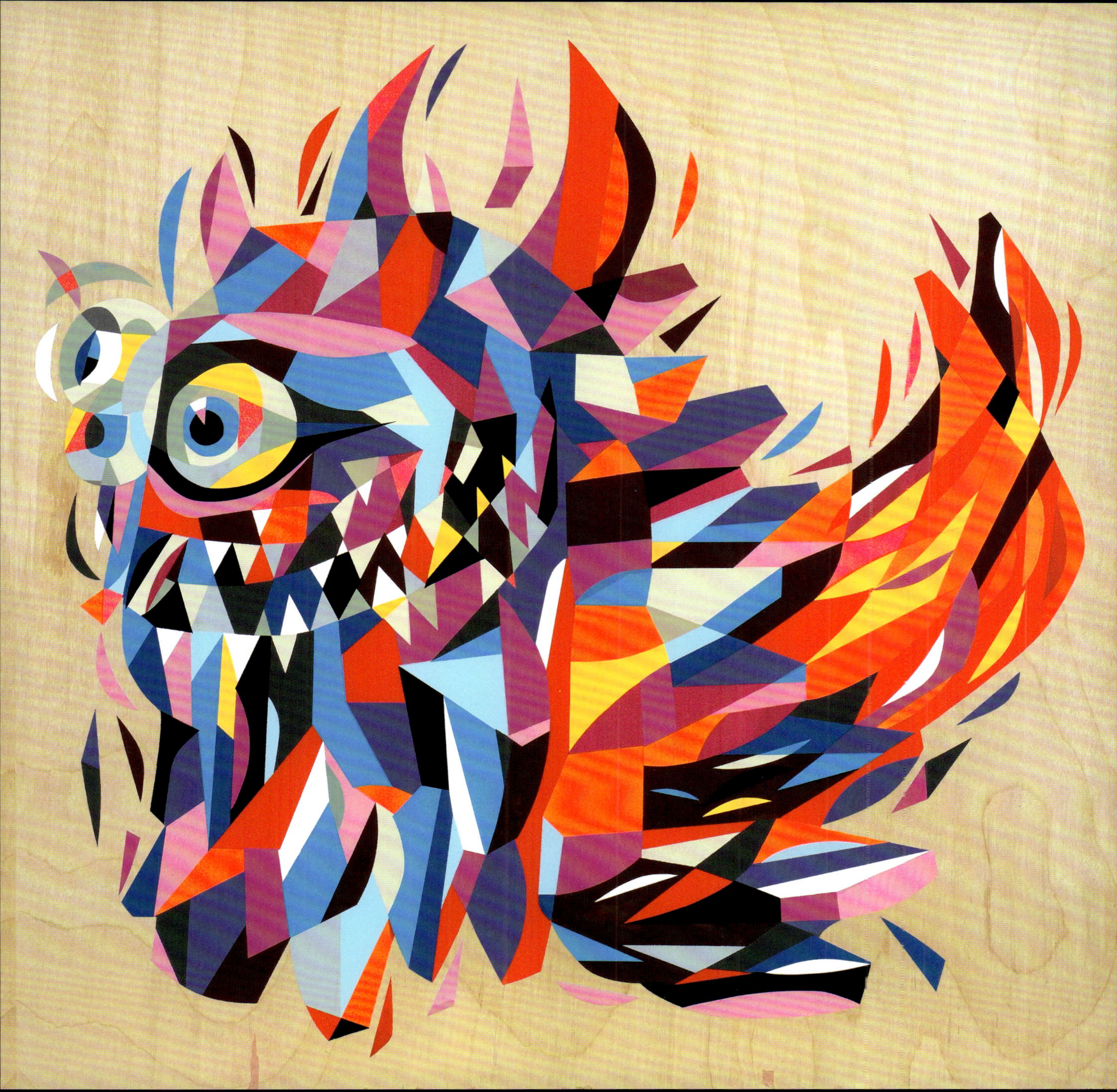

Rangeas No 2 (After T9G)
2009. Acrylic on Panel. 24" x 24"

Rangeas (After T9G)
2009. Vinyl. 8" tall

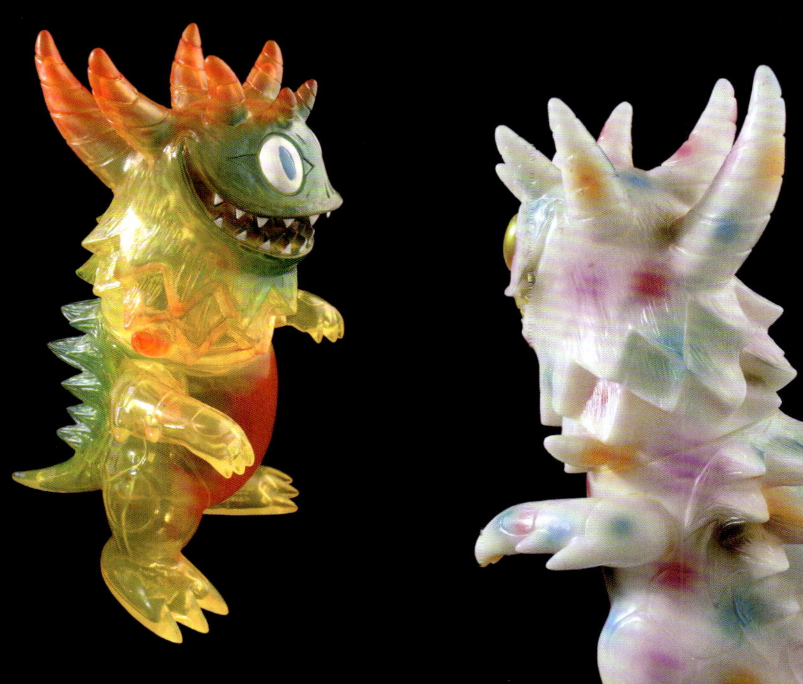

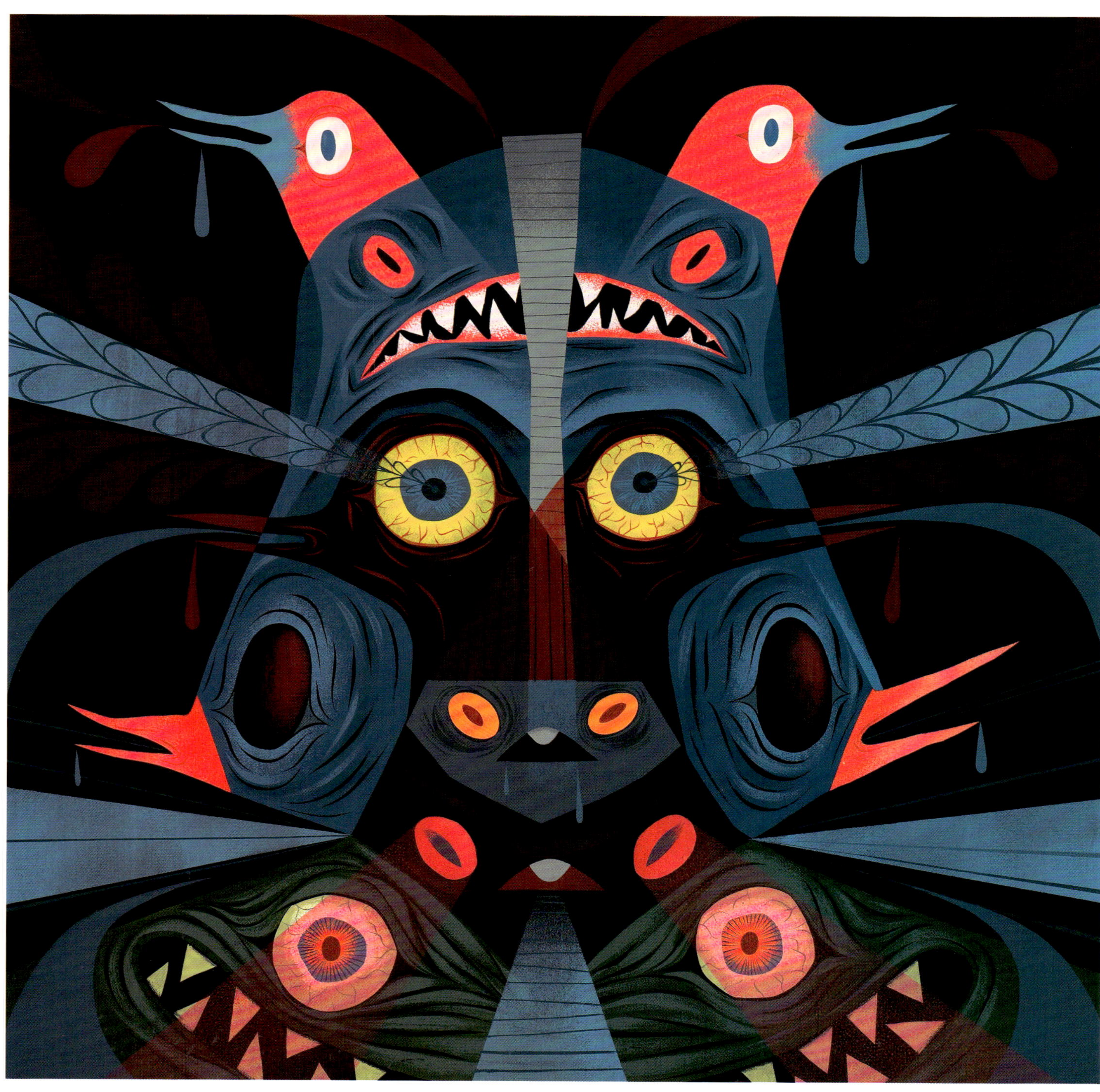

Darth Vader No 2
2010. Acrylic on Panel. 24" x 24"

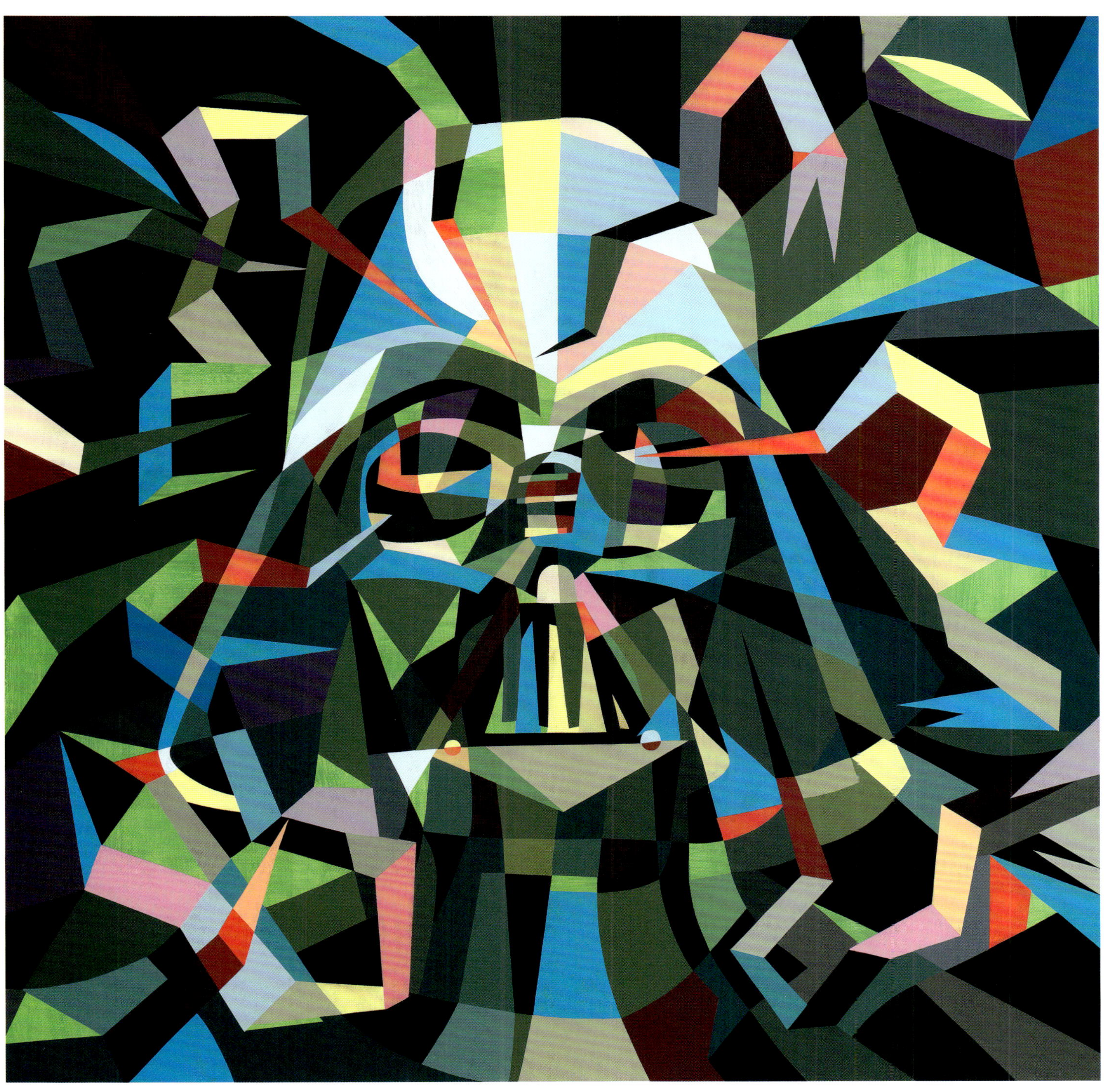

Darth Vader No 1
2008. Acrylic on Panel. 24" x 24"

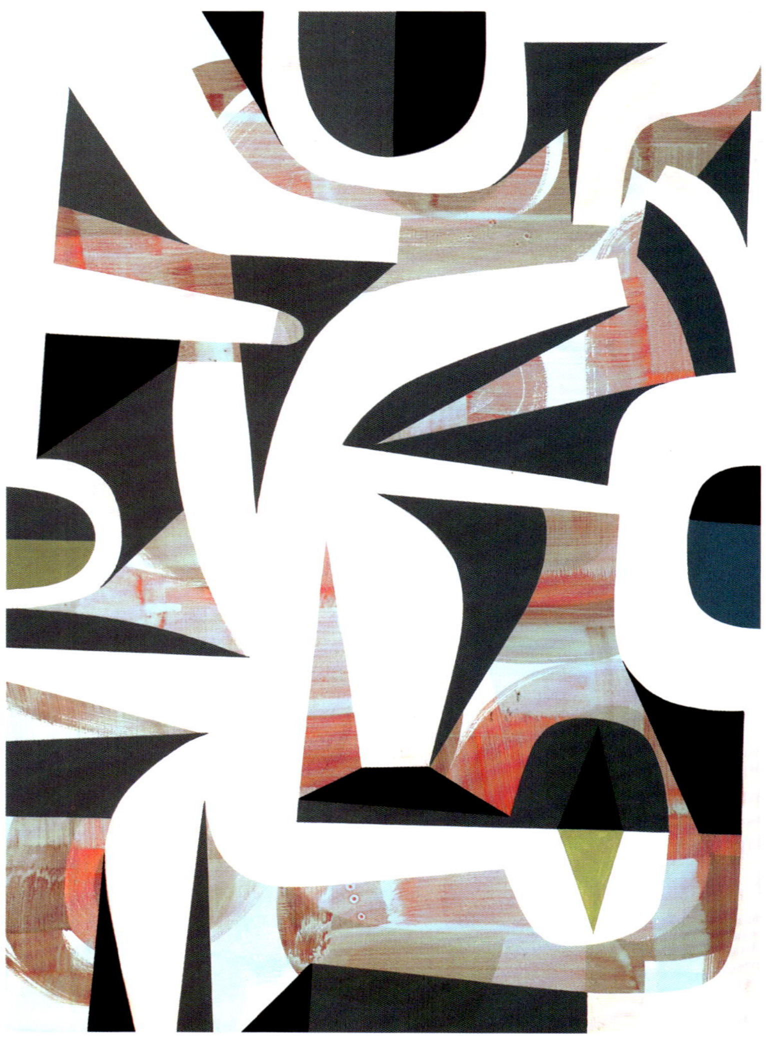

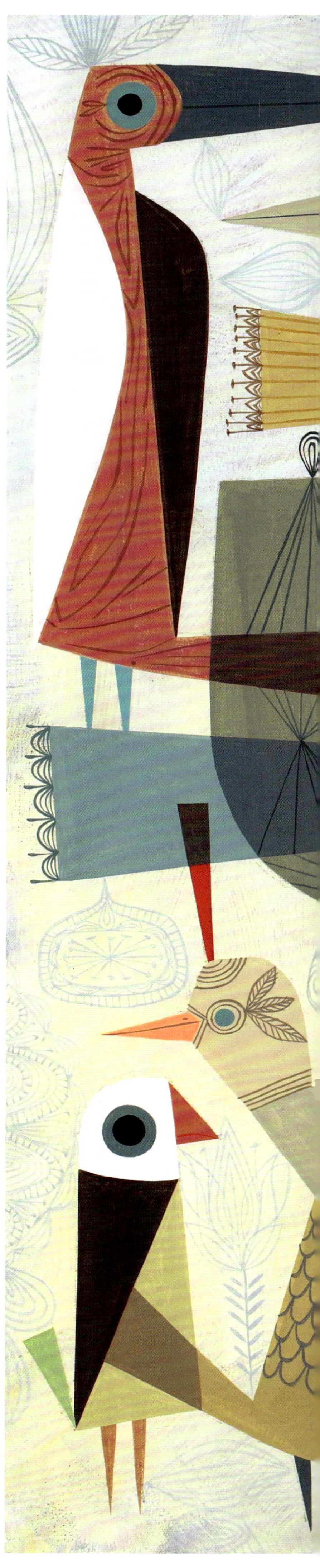

Cement Lift
2011. Acrylic on Panel. 16" x 11"

Volery of Birds
2009. Acrylic on Panel. 18" x 18"

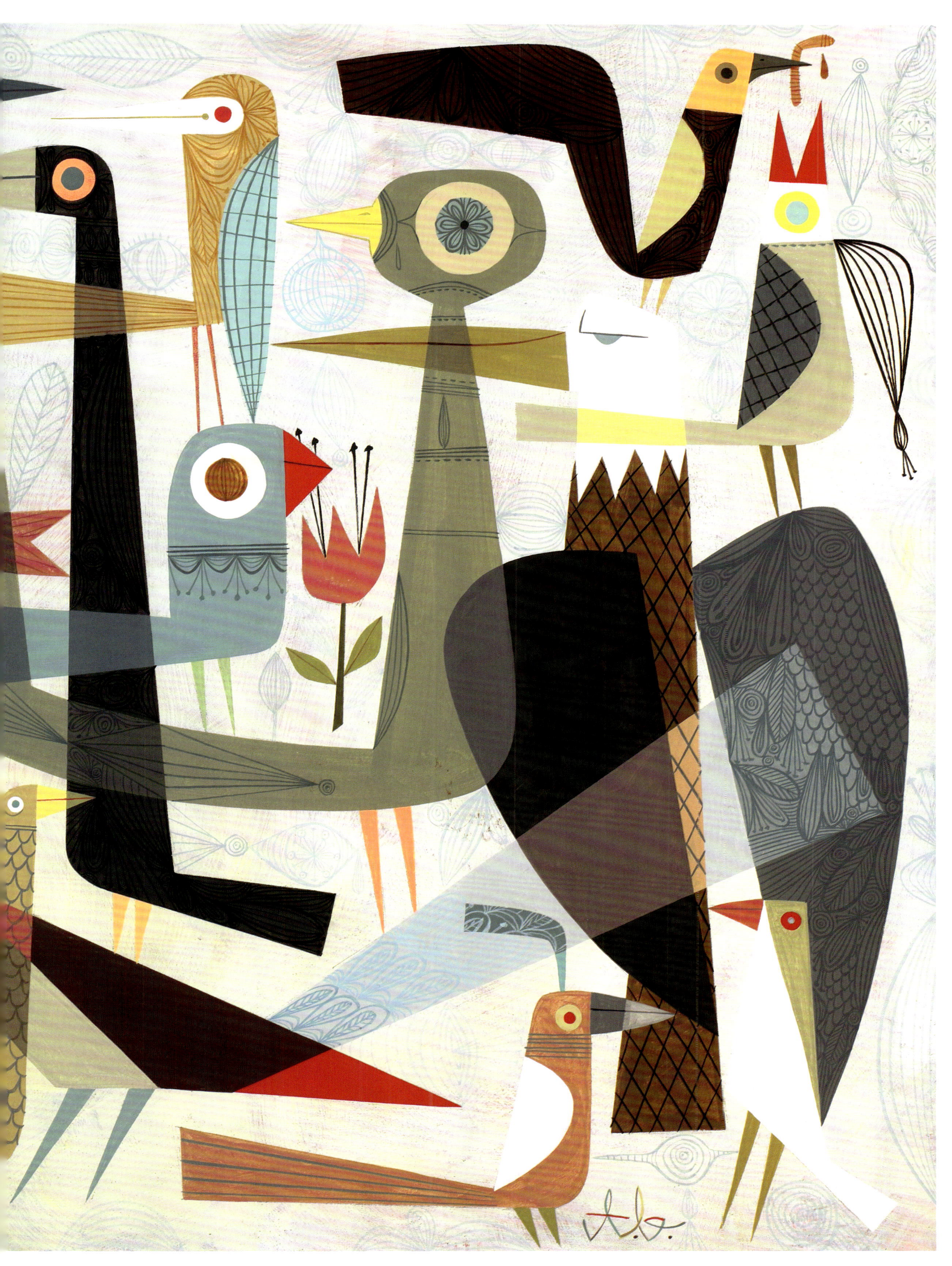

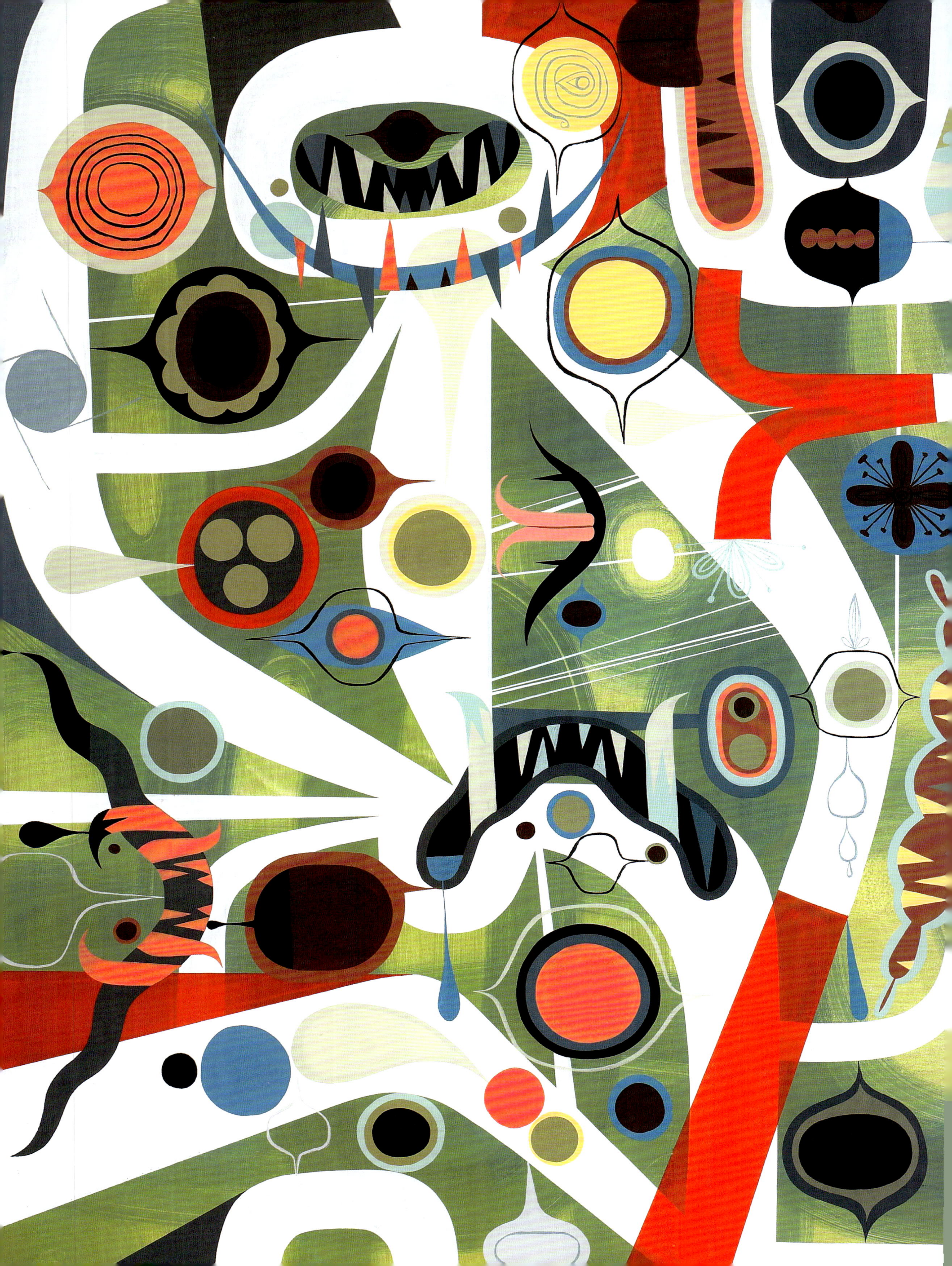

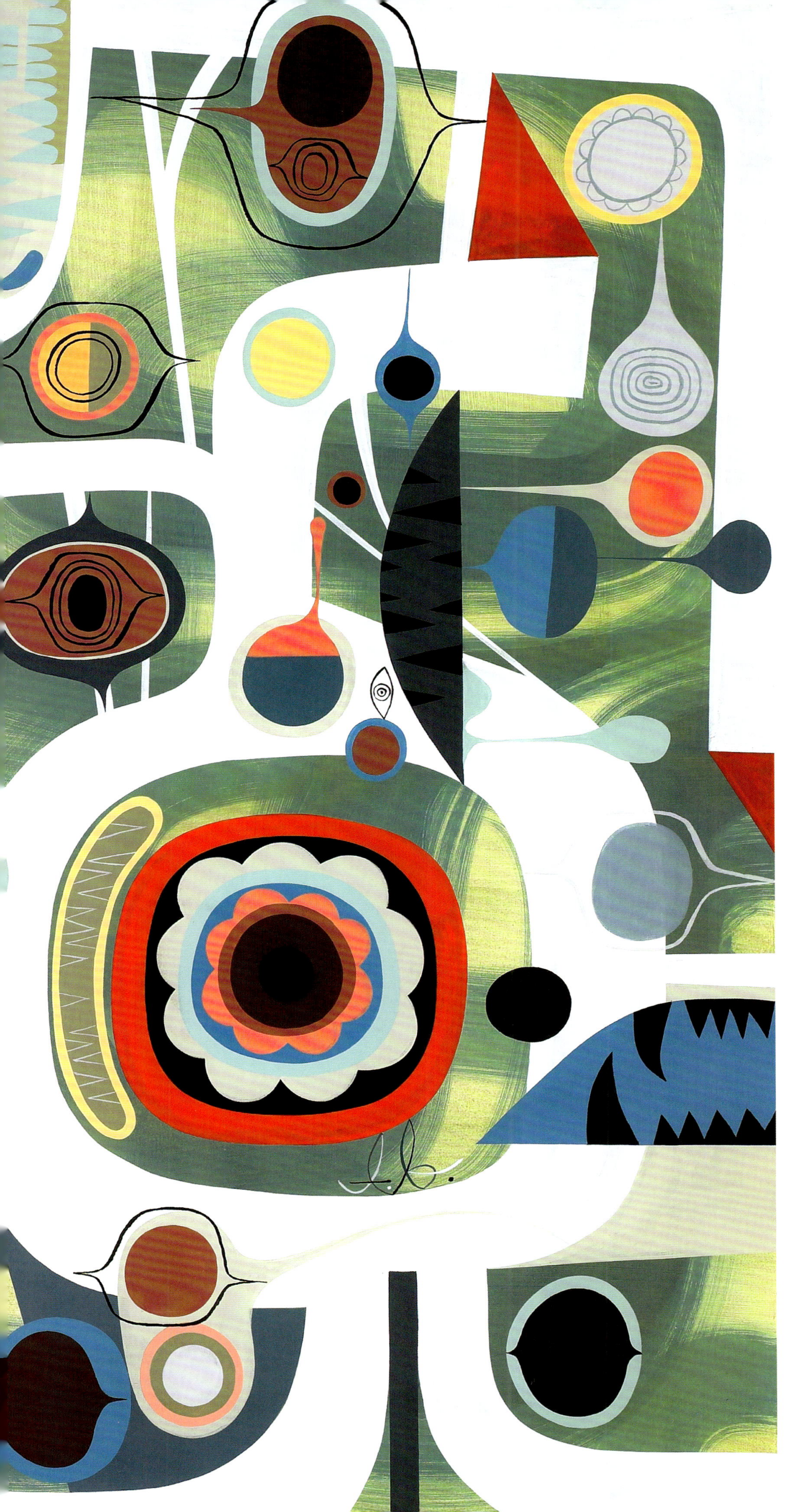

The Deep
2C10. Acrylic on Panel. 24" x 30"

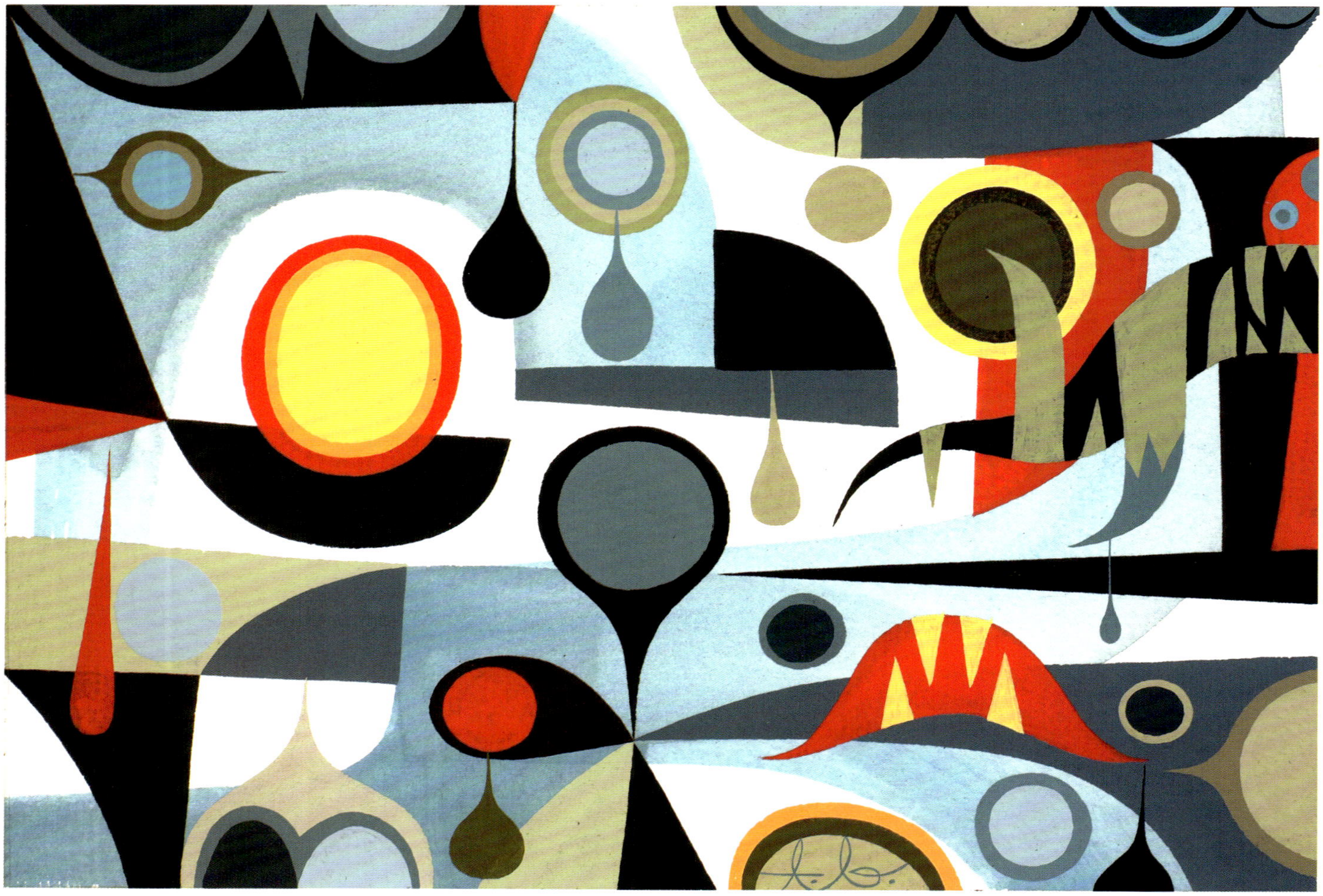

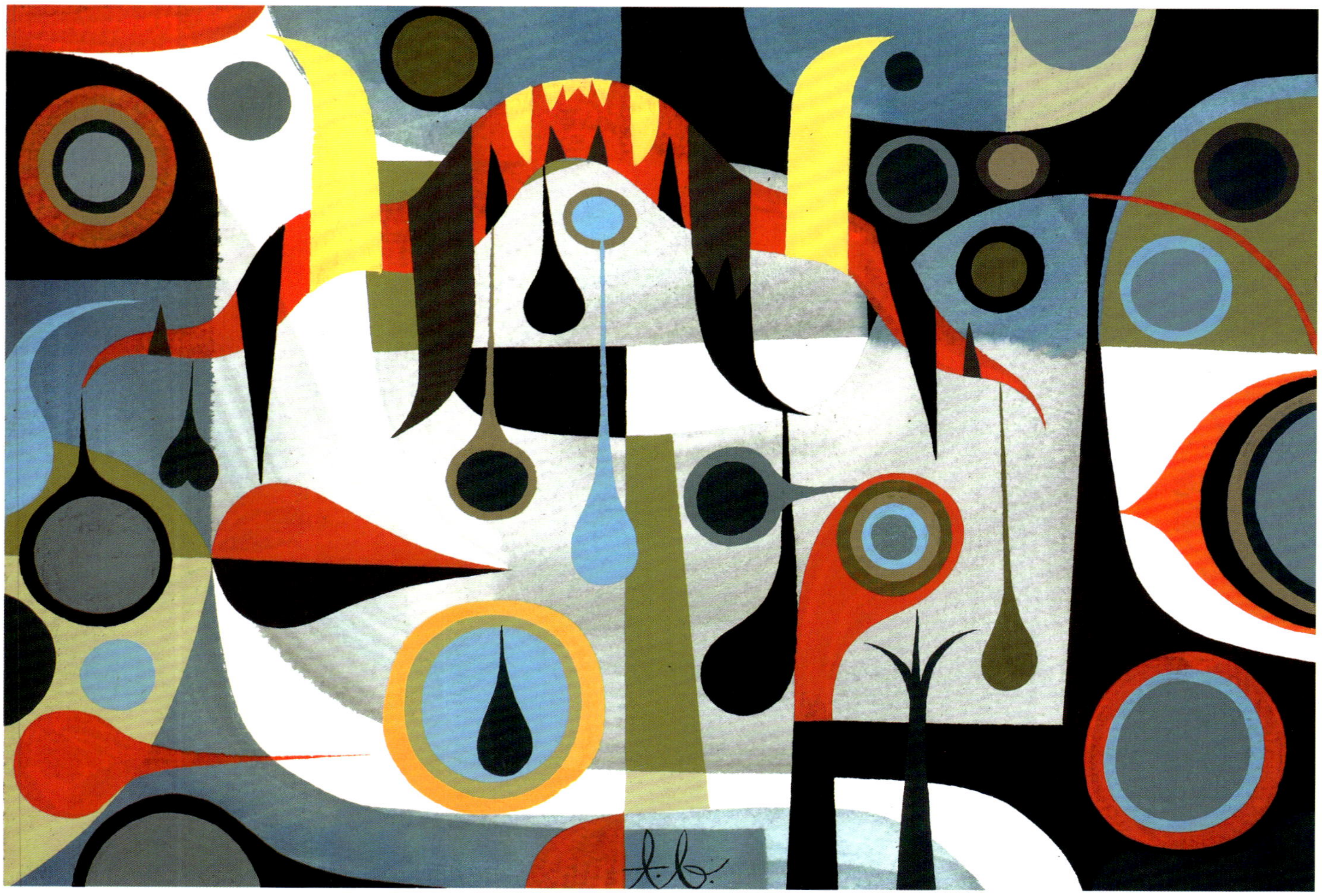

Death Yacht No 1
2011. Acrylic on Paper. 8" x 10"

Death Yacht No 2
2011. Acrylic on Paper. 8" x 10"

Poison Shallows
2011. Acrylic on Panel. 20" x 16"

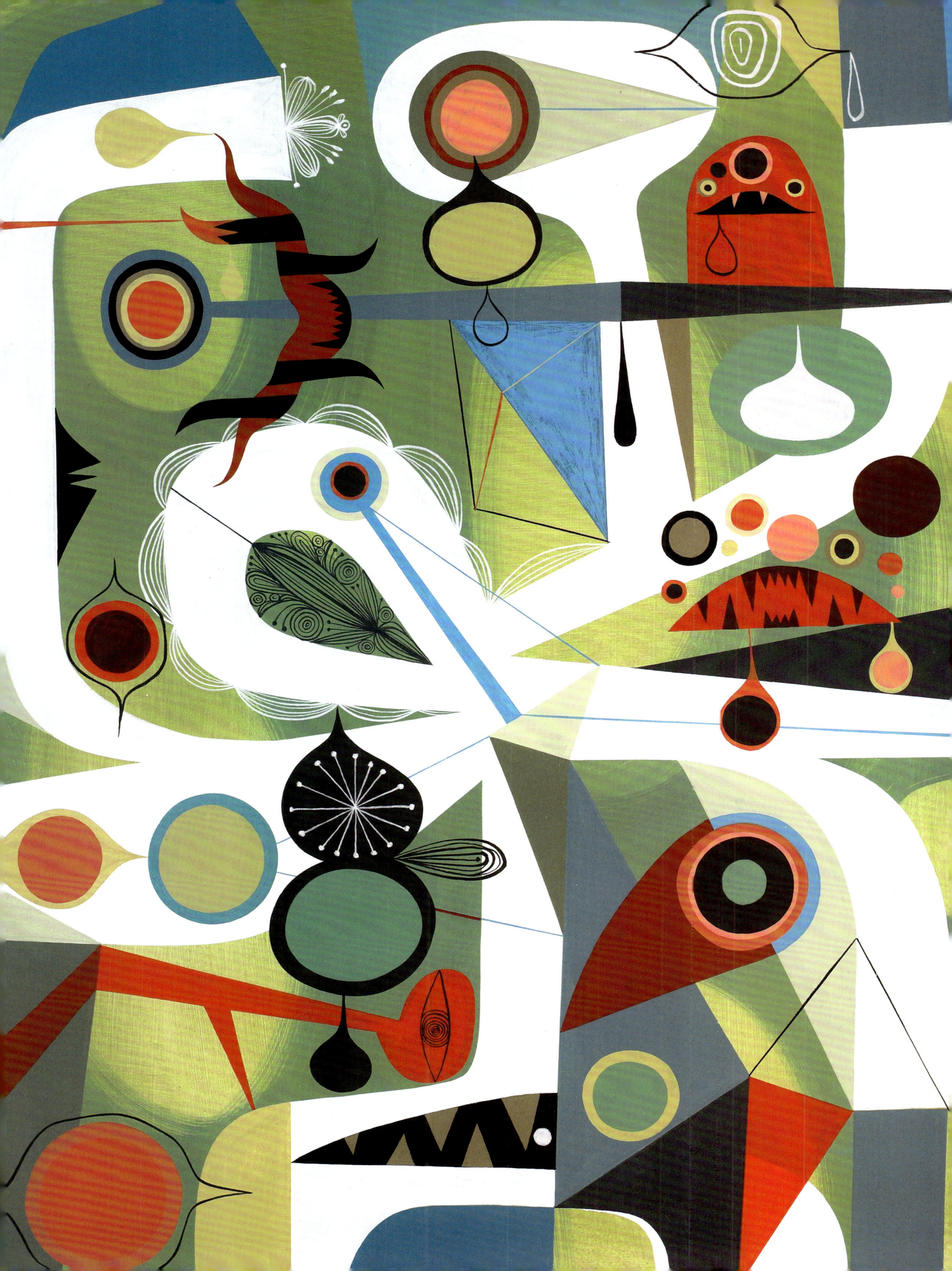

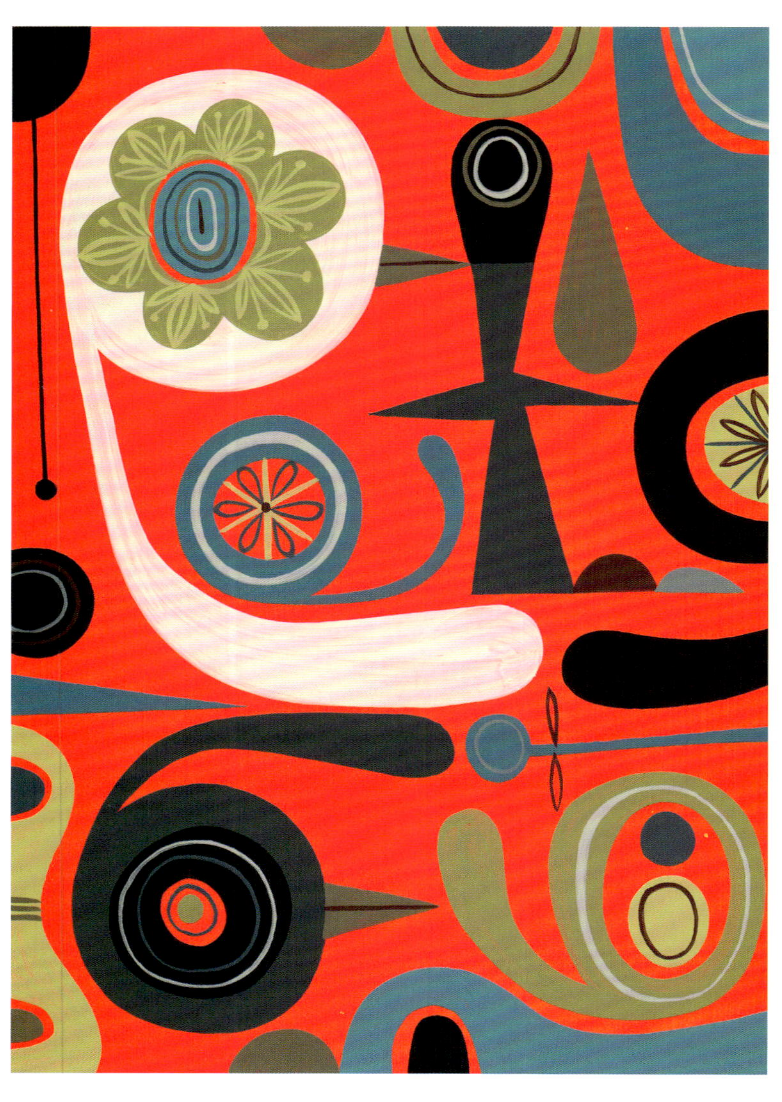

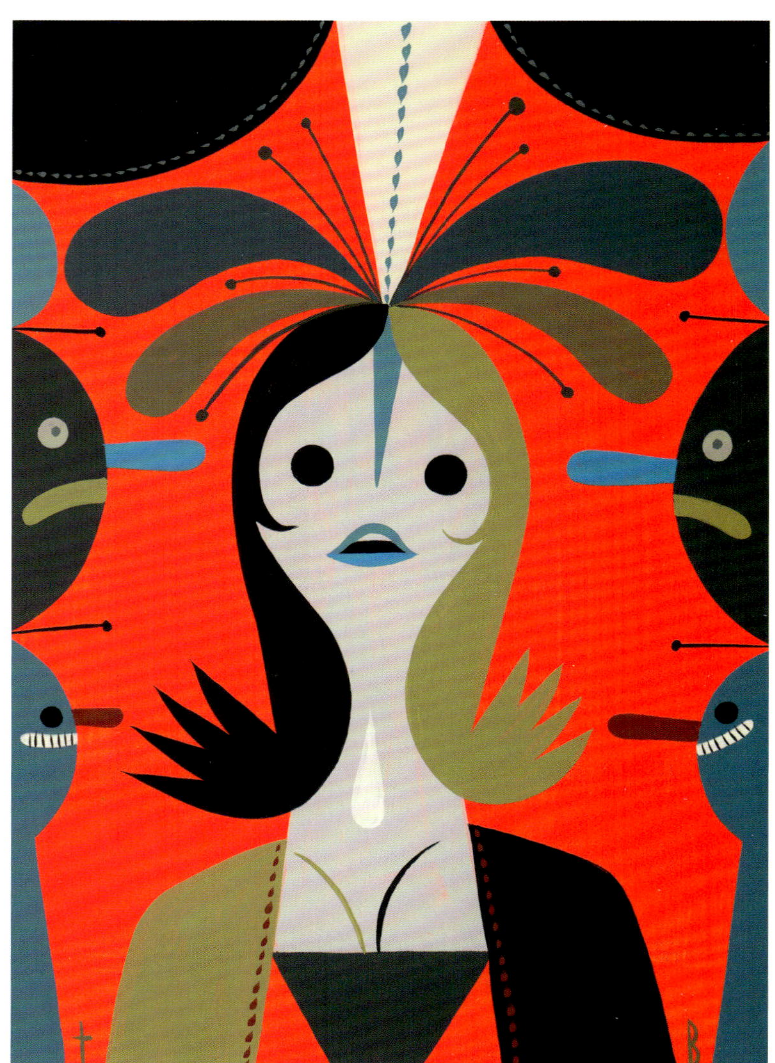

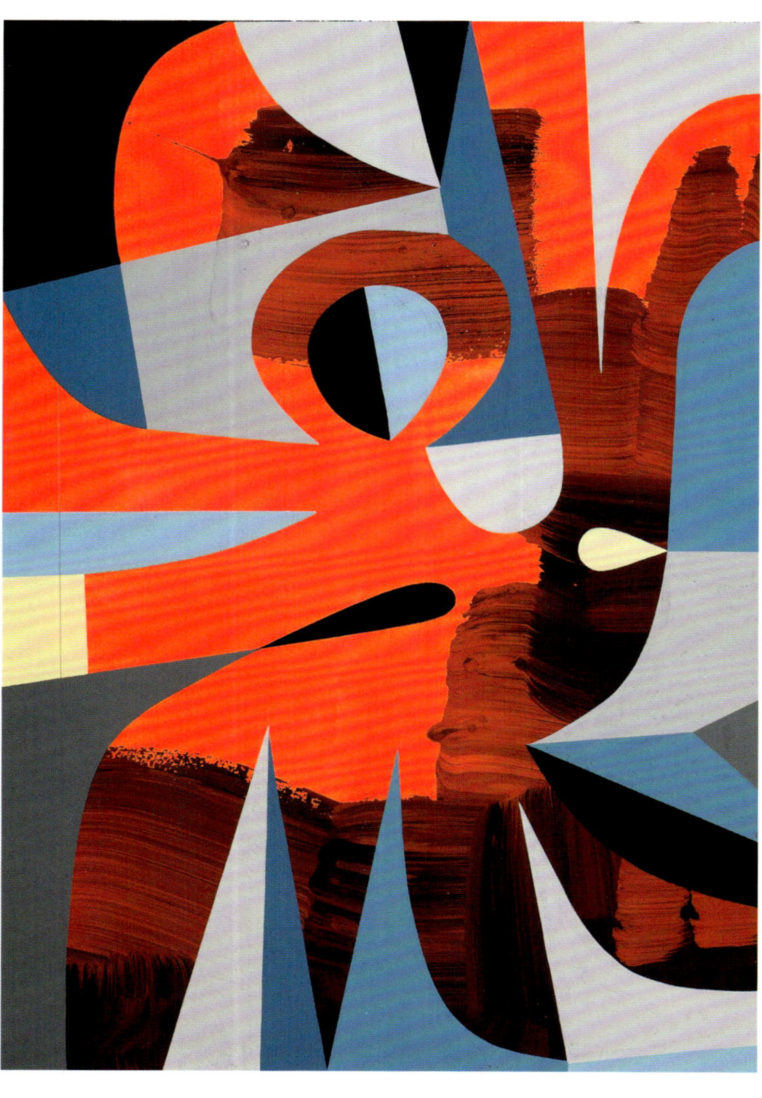

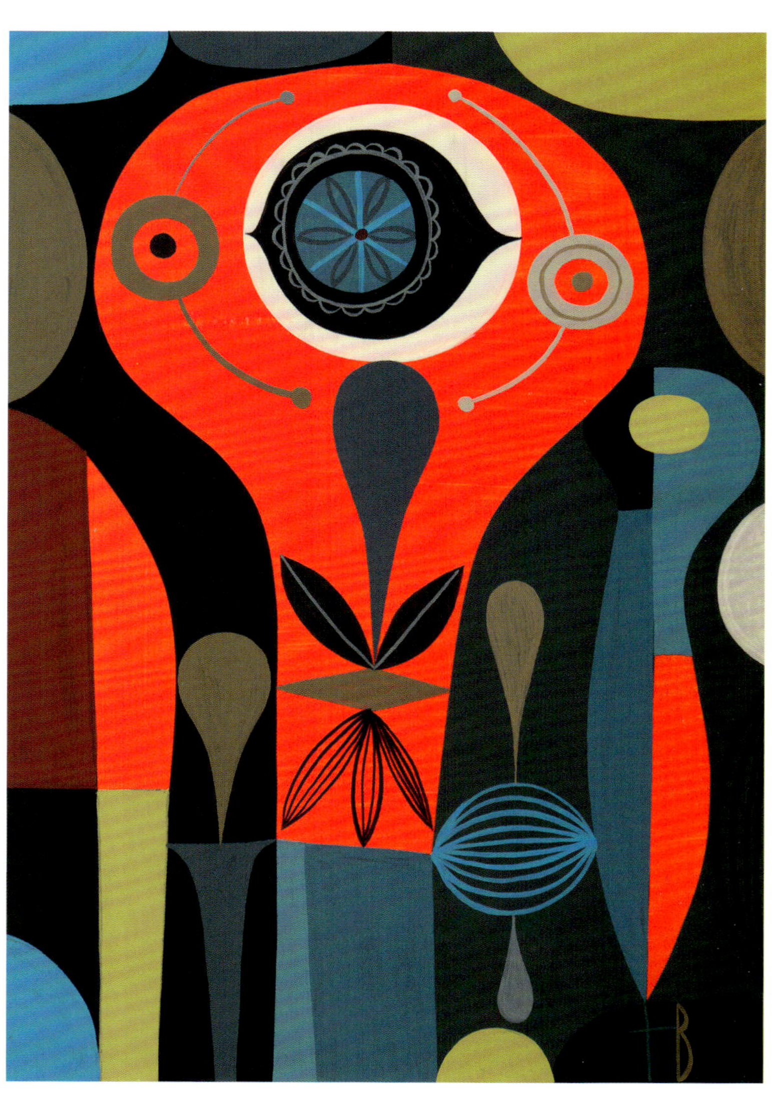

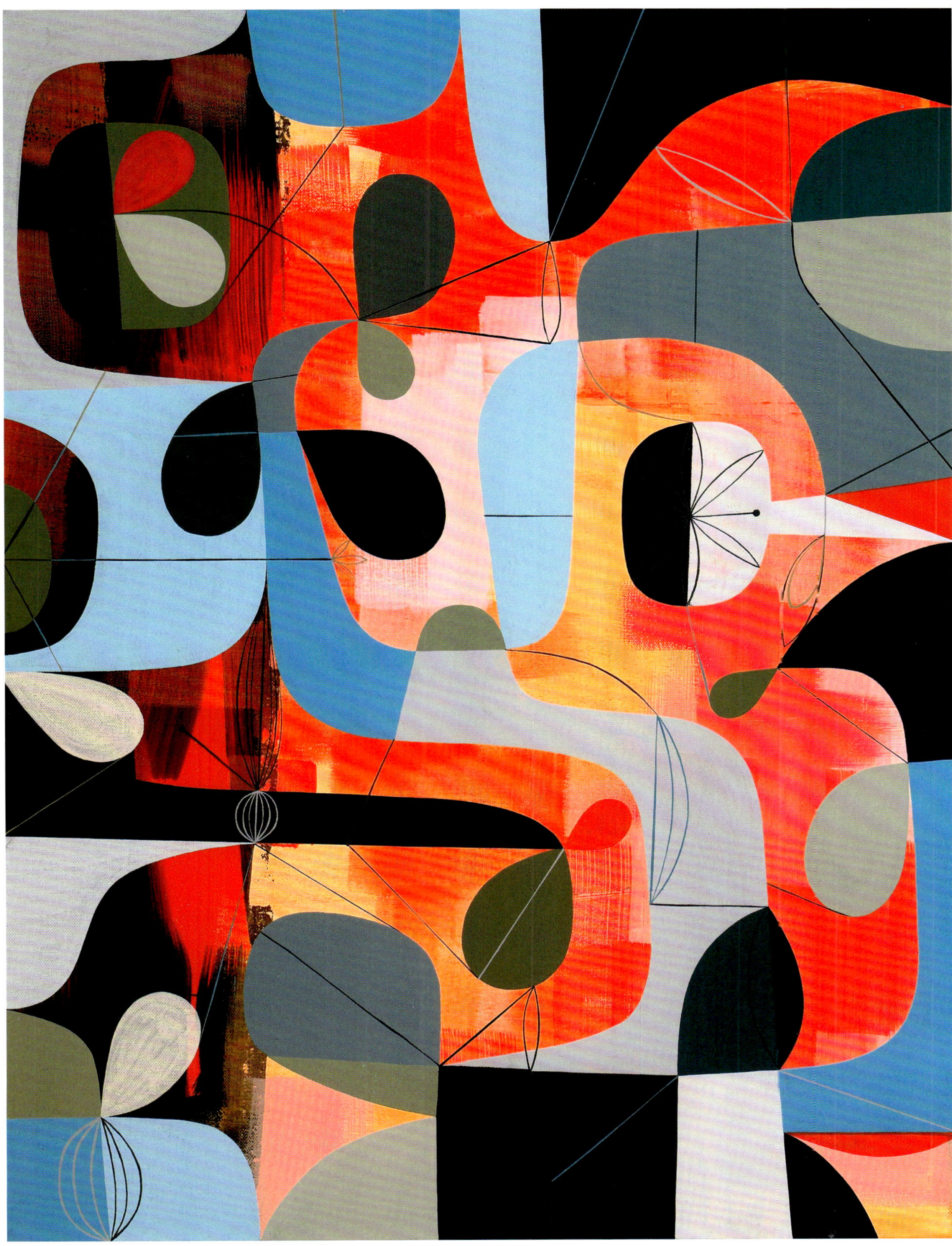

Untitled
2007. Acrylic on Panel. 7" x 5"

Crippling Faith No 2
2012. Acrylic on Paper. 24" x 18"

Untitled
2007. Acrylic on Panel. 7" x 5"

Untitled
2007. Acrylic on Panel. 7" x 5"

Crippling Faith No 1
2008. Acrylic on Canvas. 20" x 16"

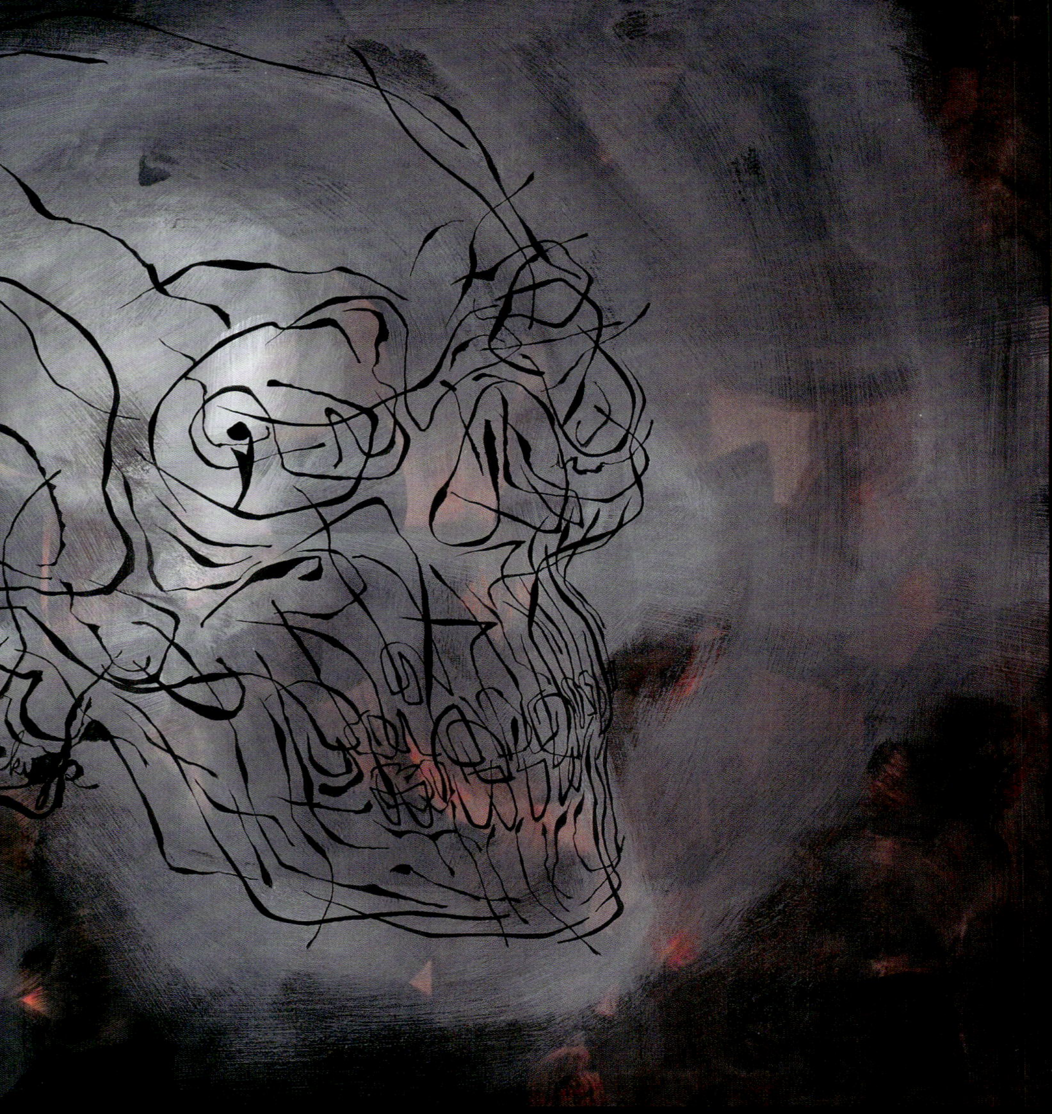

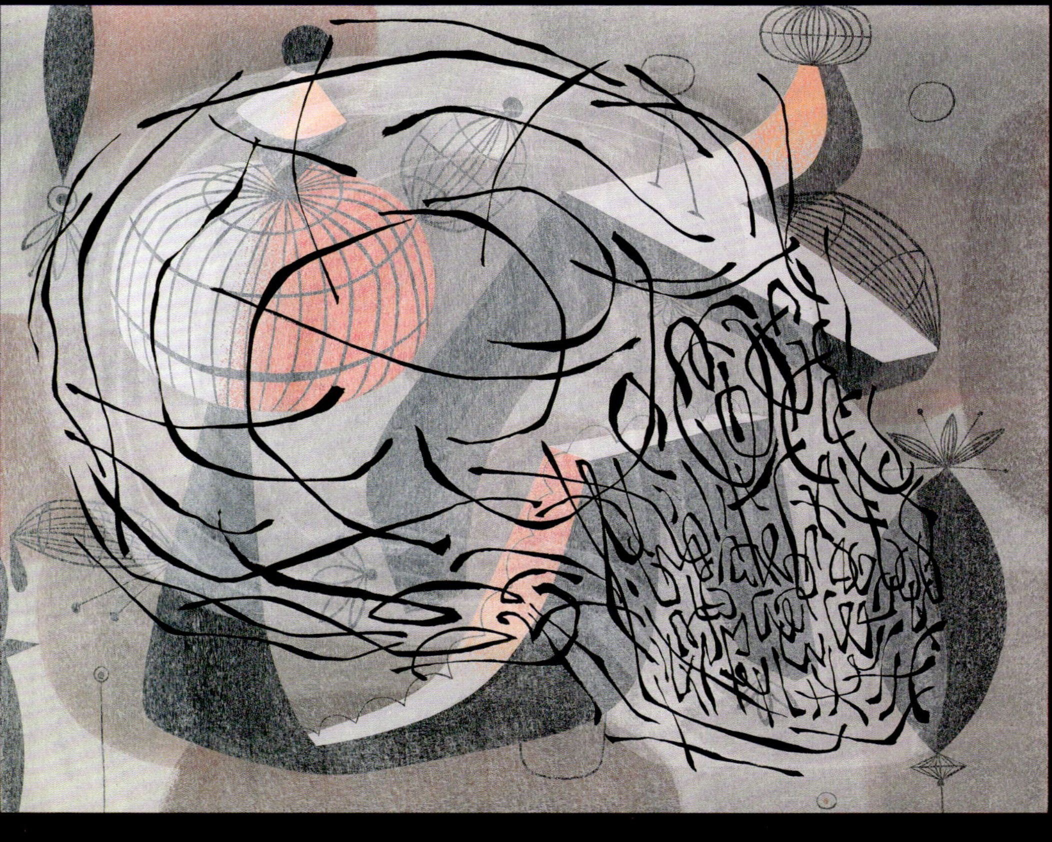

Doom Loop No 13
2009. Acrylic on Panel. 20" x 30"

Painting from System No 3
2008. Acrylic on Panel. 9.5" x 12"

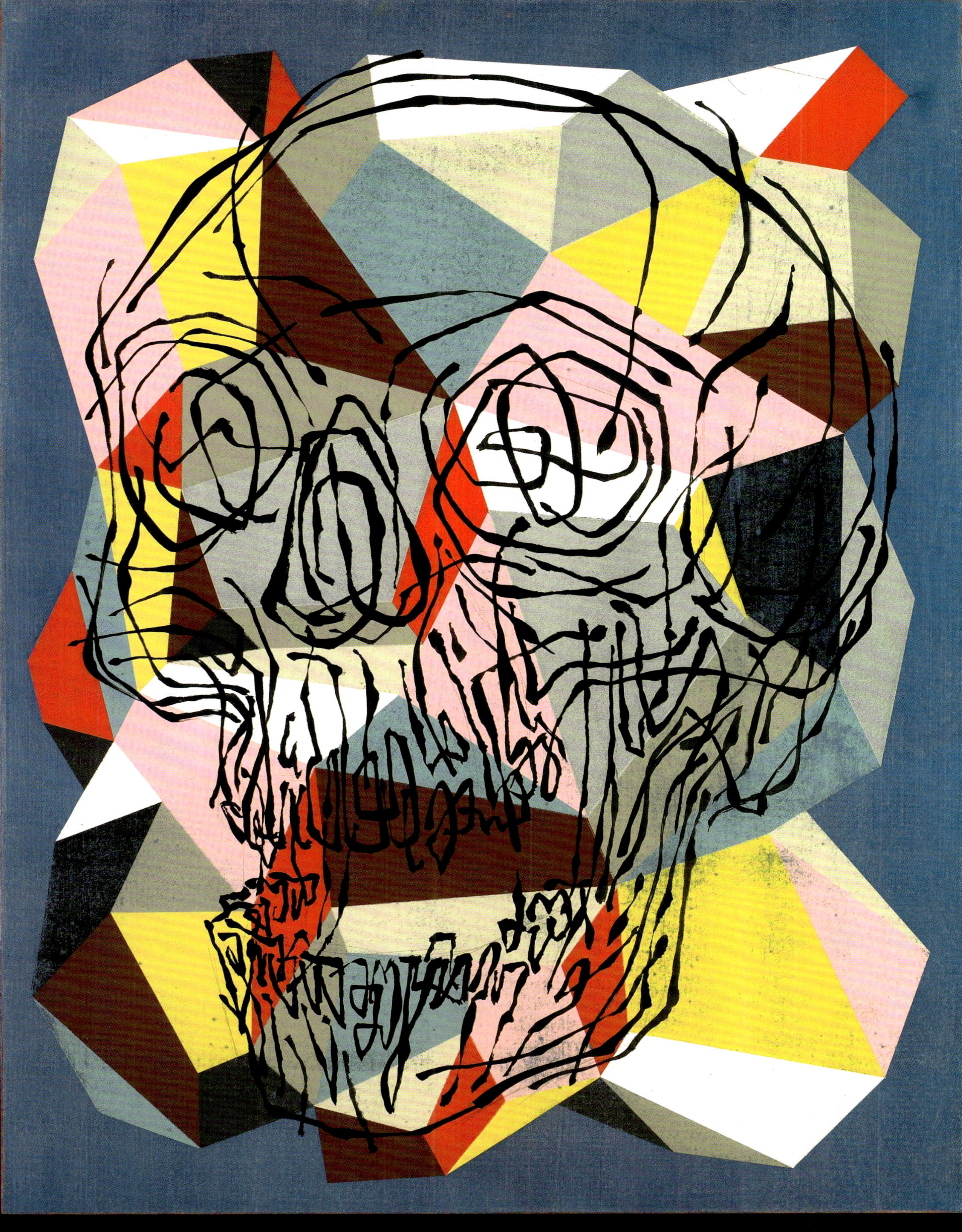

Meteor
2011. Acrylic on Panel. 24" x 18"

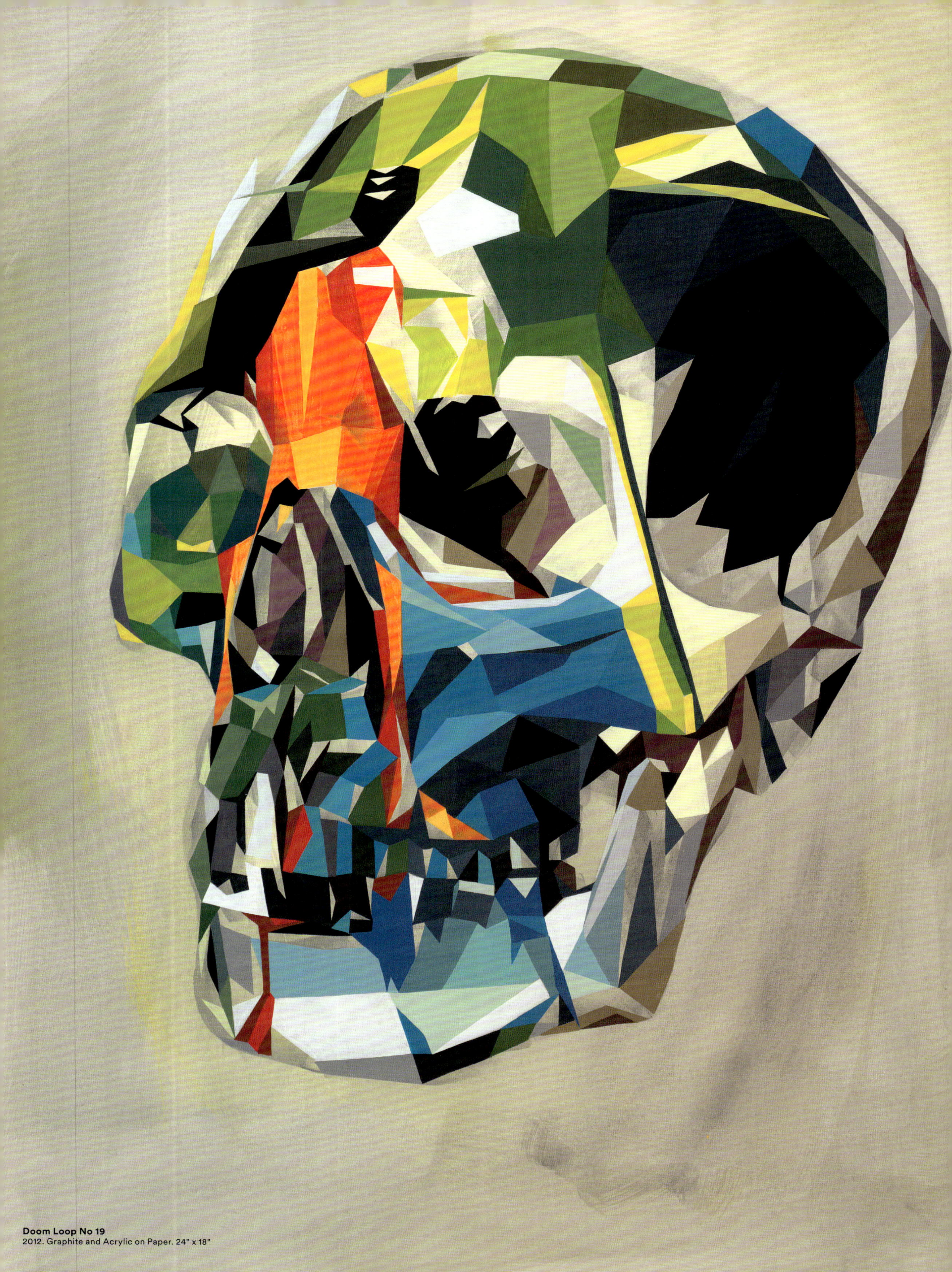

Doom Loop No 19
2012. Graphite and Acrylic on Paper. 24" x 18"

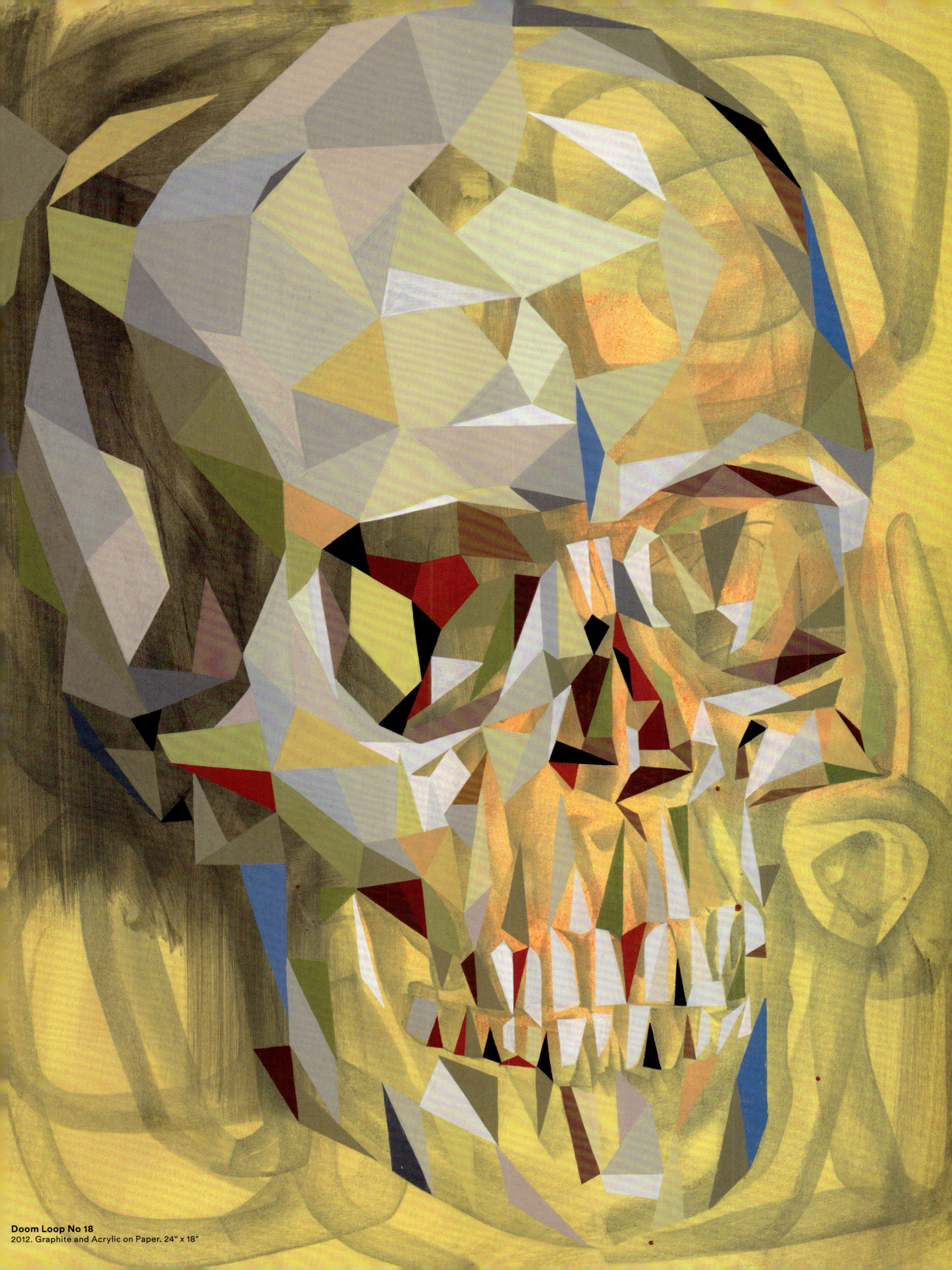

Doom Loop No 18
2012. Graphite and Acrylic on Paper. 24" x 18"

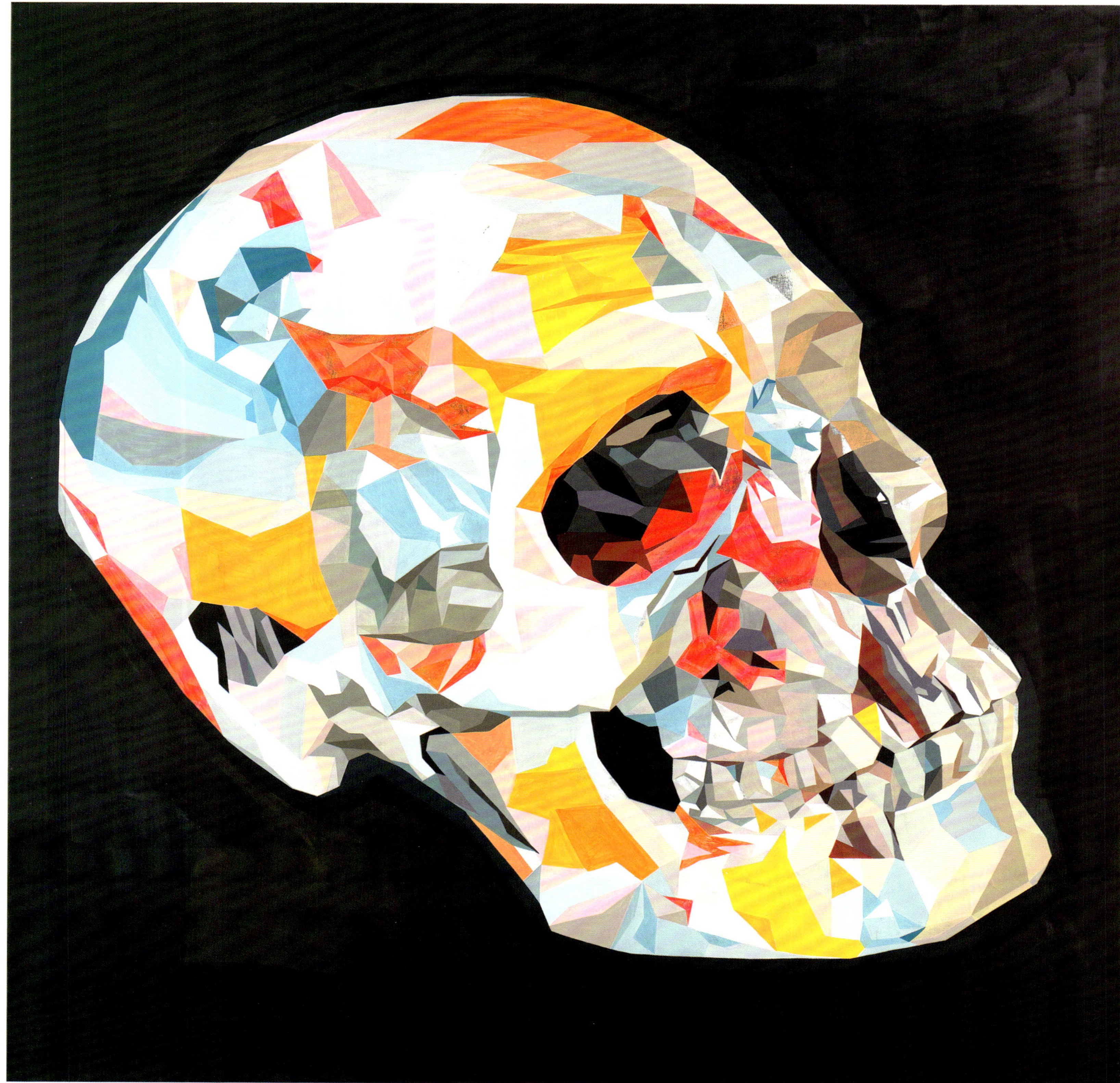

Doom Loop No 22
2012. Graphite and Acrylic on Canvas. 48" x 48"

Doom Loop No 23
2012. Graphite and Acrylic on Canvas. 48" x 48"

Doom Loop No 21
2012. Graphite and Acrylic on Canvas. 36" x 36"

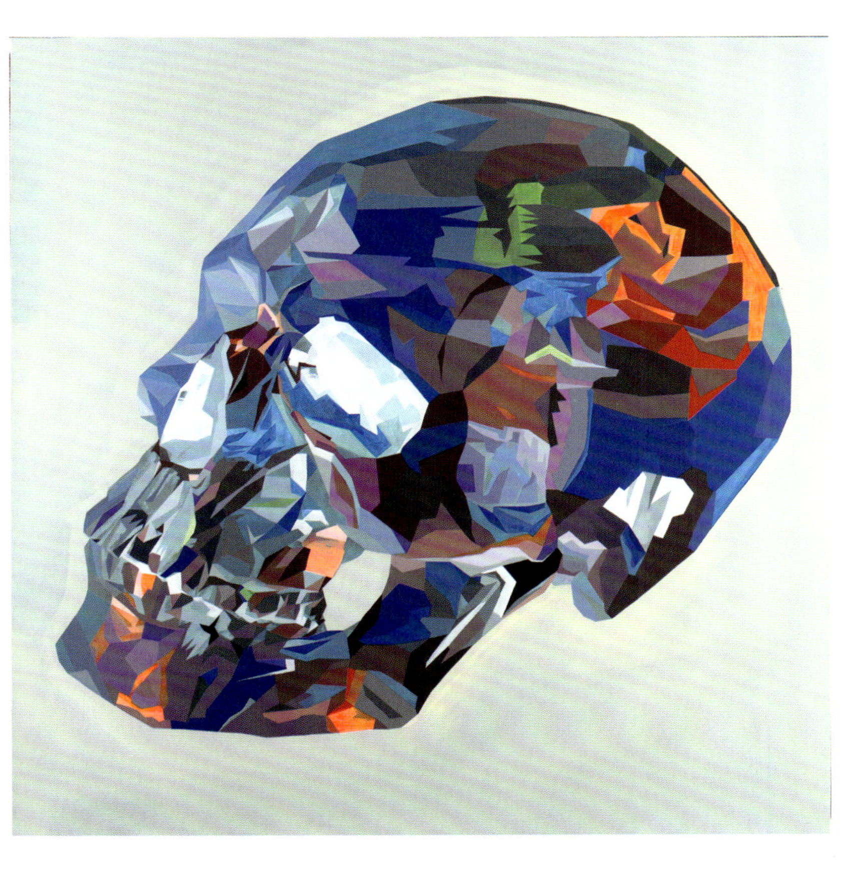

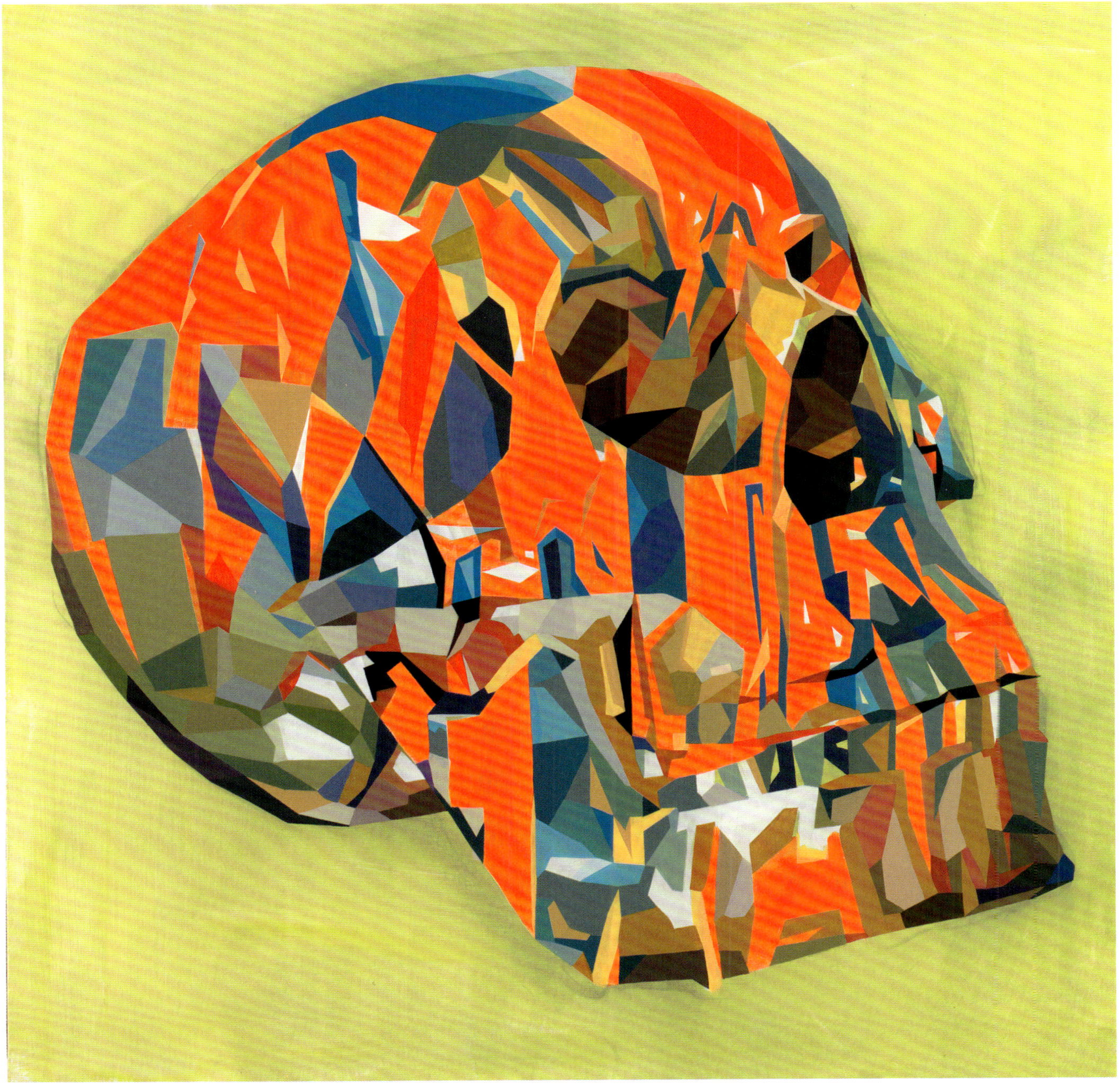

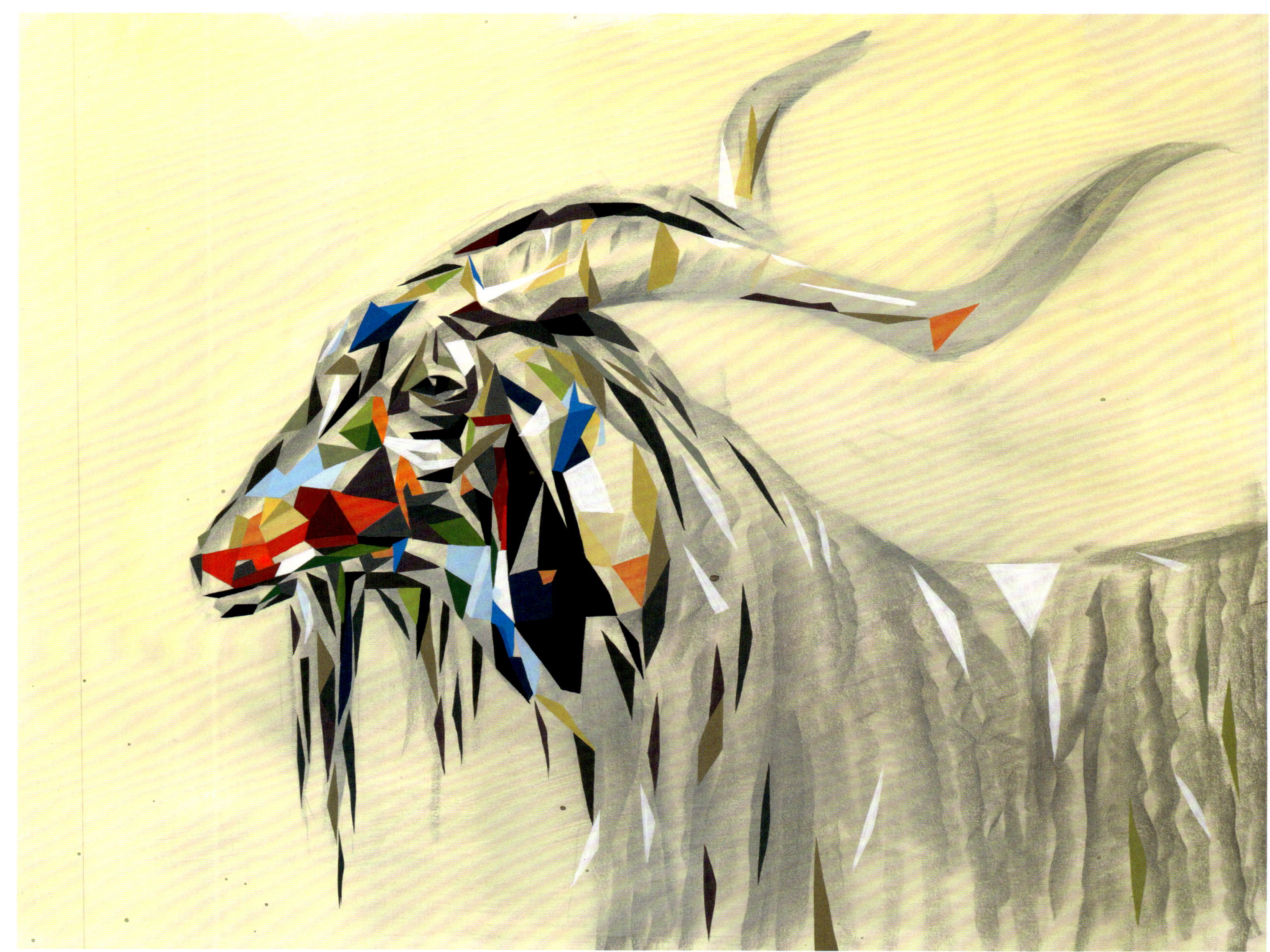

Goat
2012. Graphite and Acrylic on Paper. 18" x 24"

Walk With Bob
2010. Acrylic on Canvas. 72" x 48"

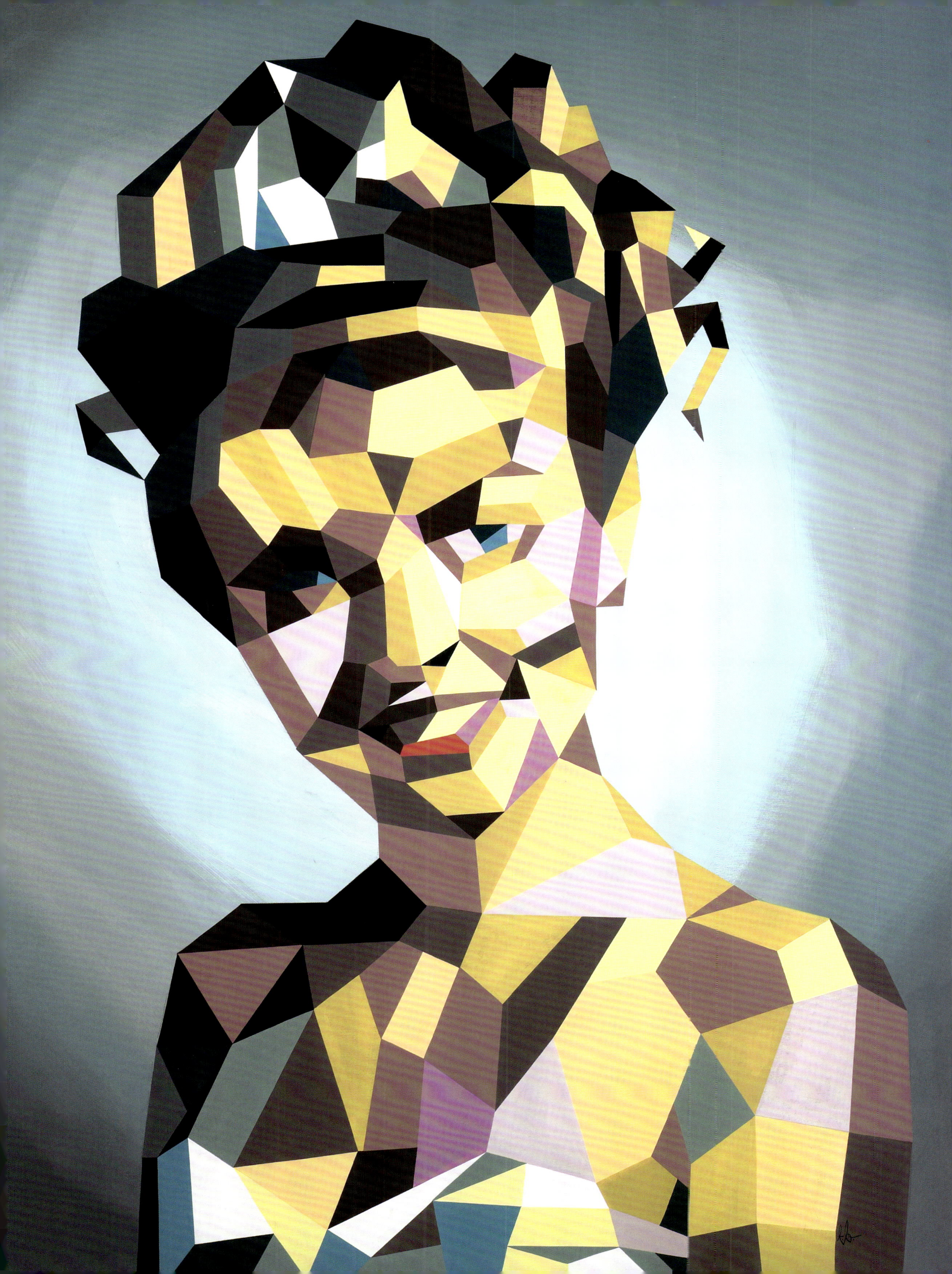

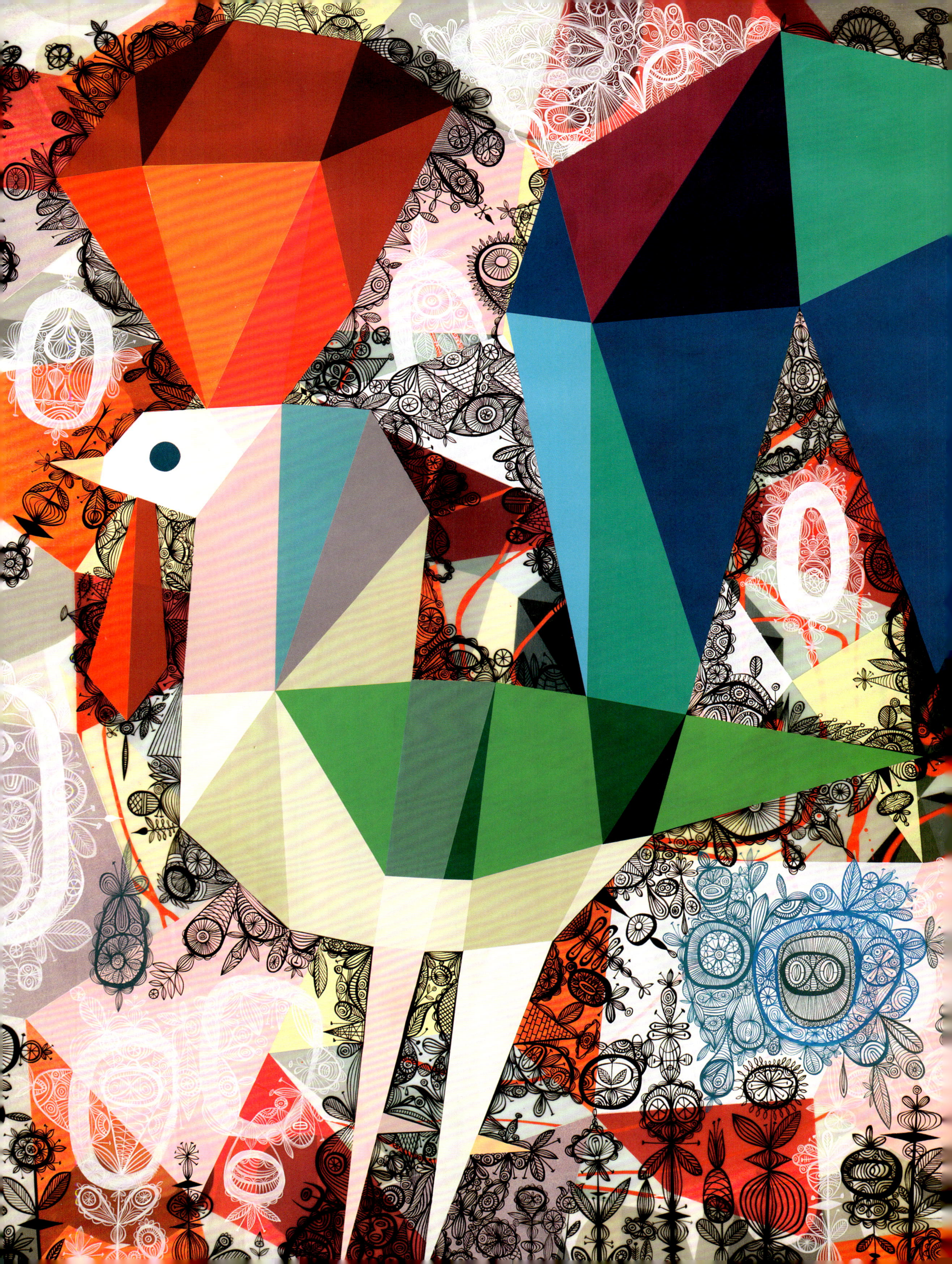

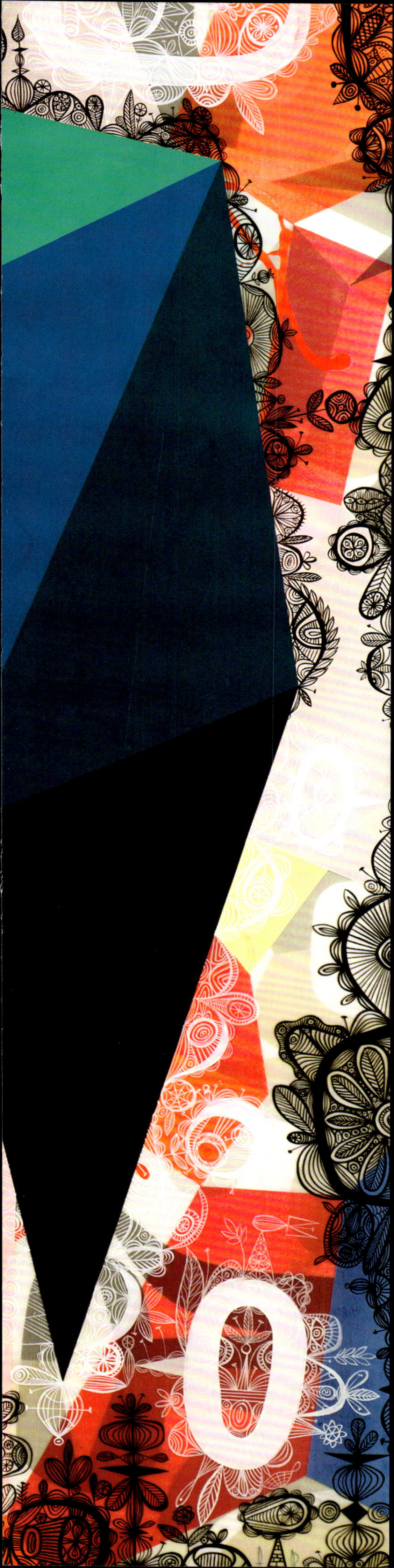

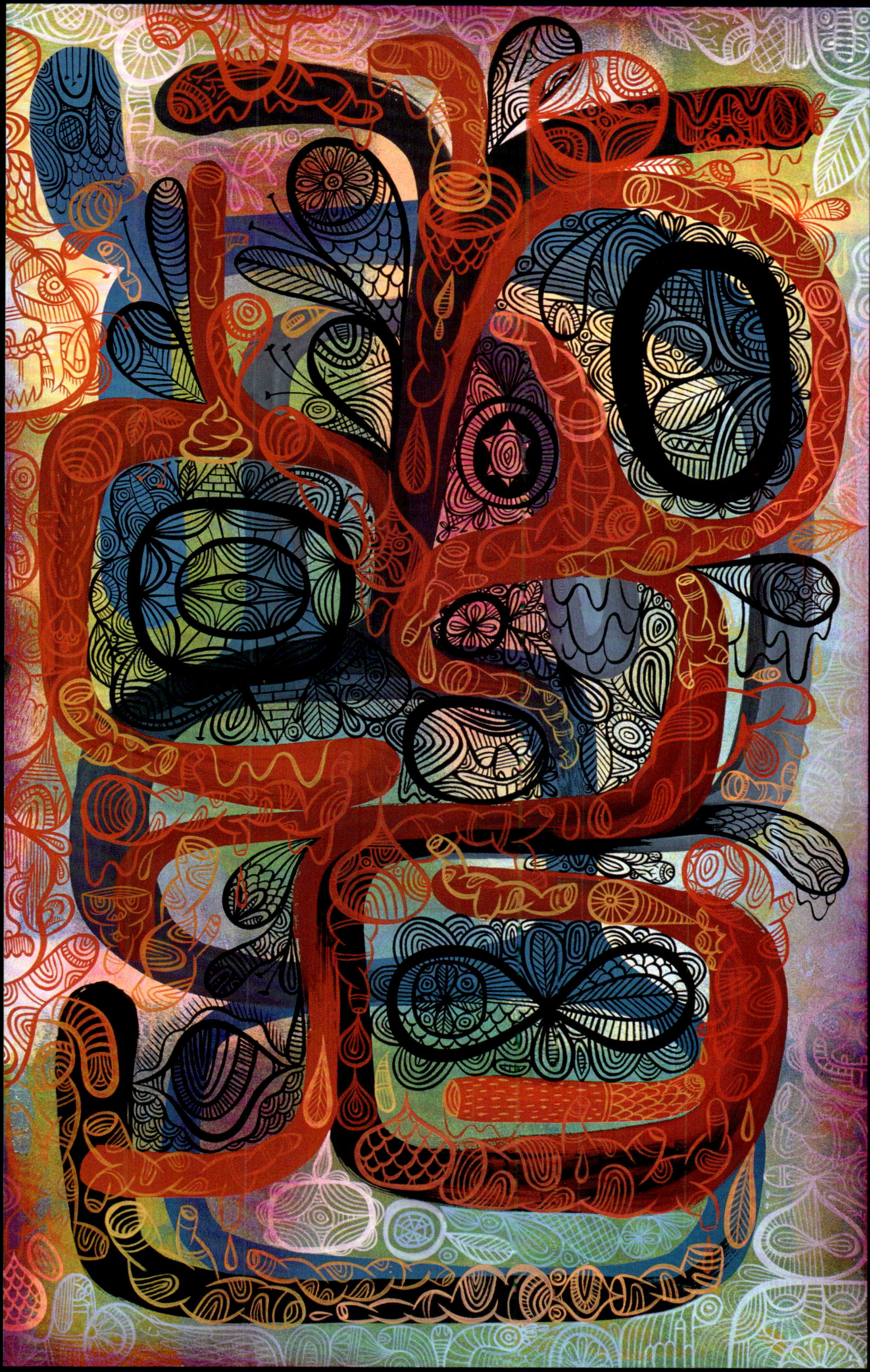

Dawn
2012. Acrylic and Epoxy Resin on Panel. 48" x 48"

This Painting is Thinking About You
2013. Acrylic on Panel. 24" x 15"

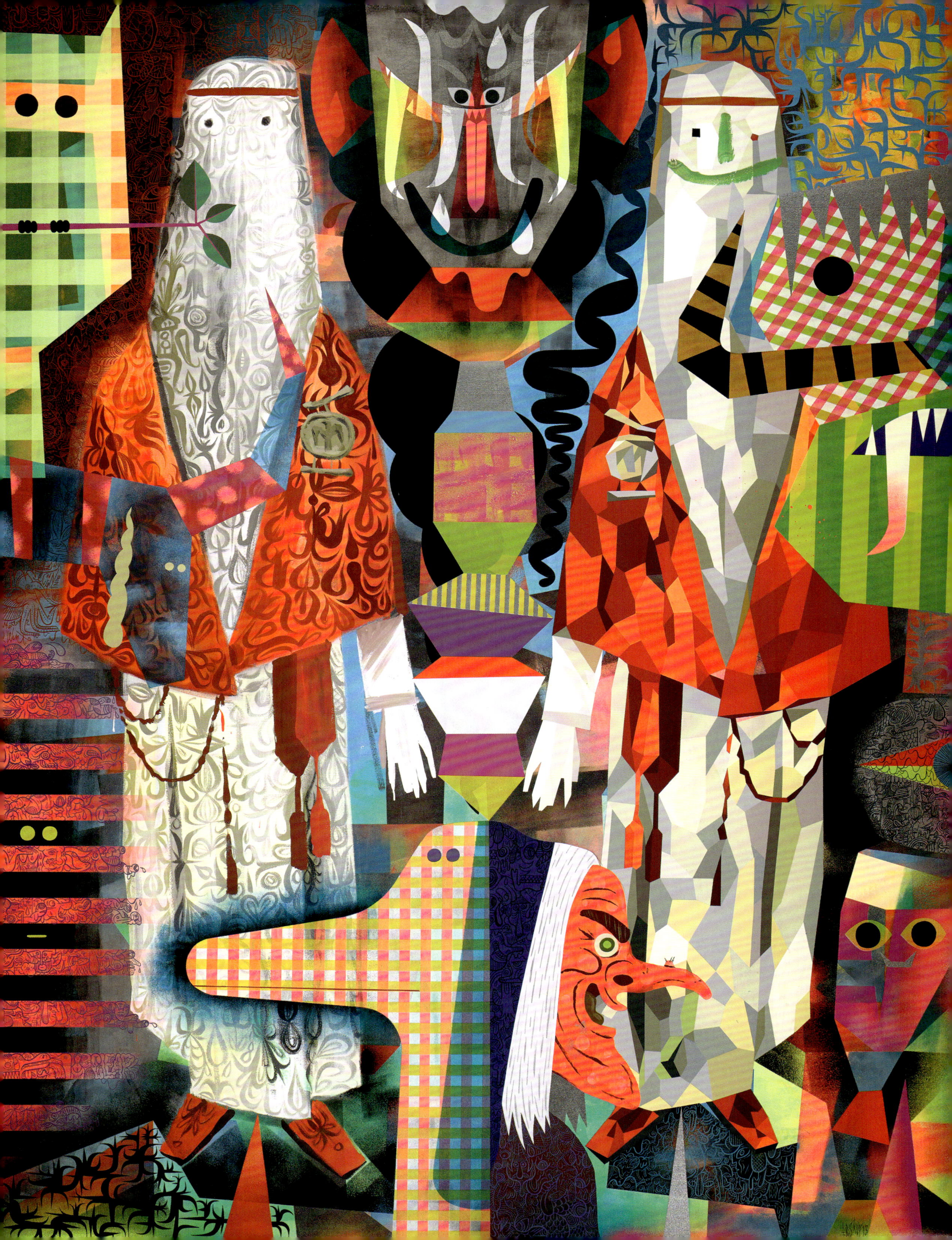

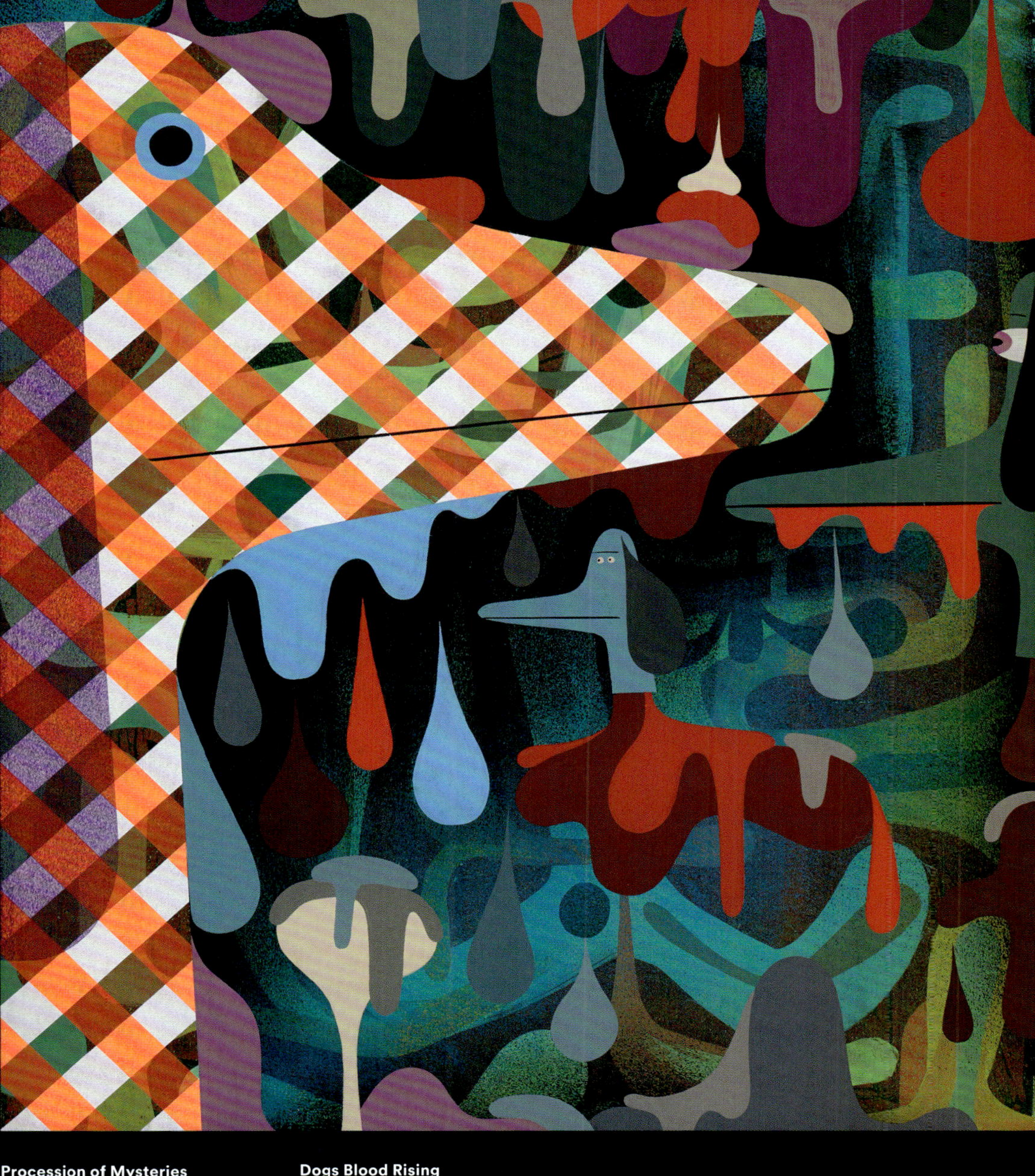

Procession of Mysteries
2014. Acrylic on Canvas. 96" x 72"

Dogs Blood Rising
2013. Acrylic on Panel. 20" x 18"

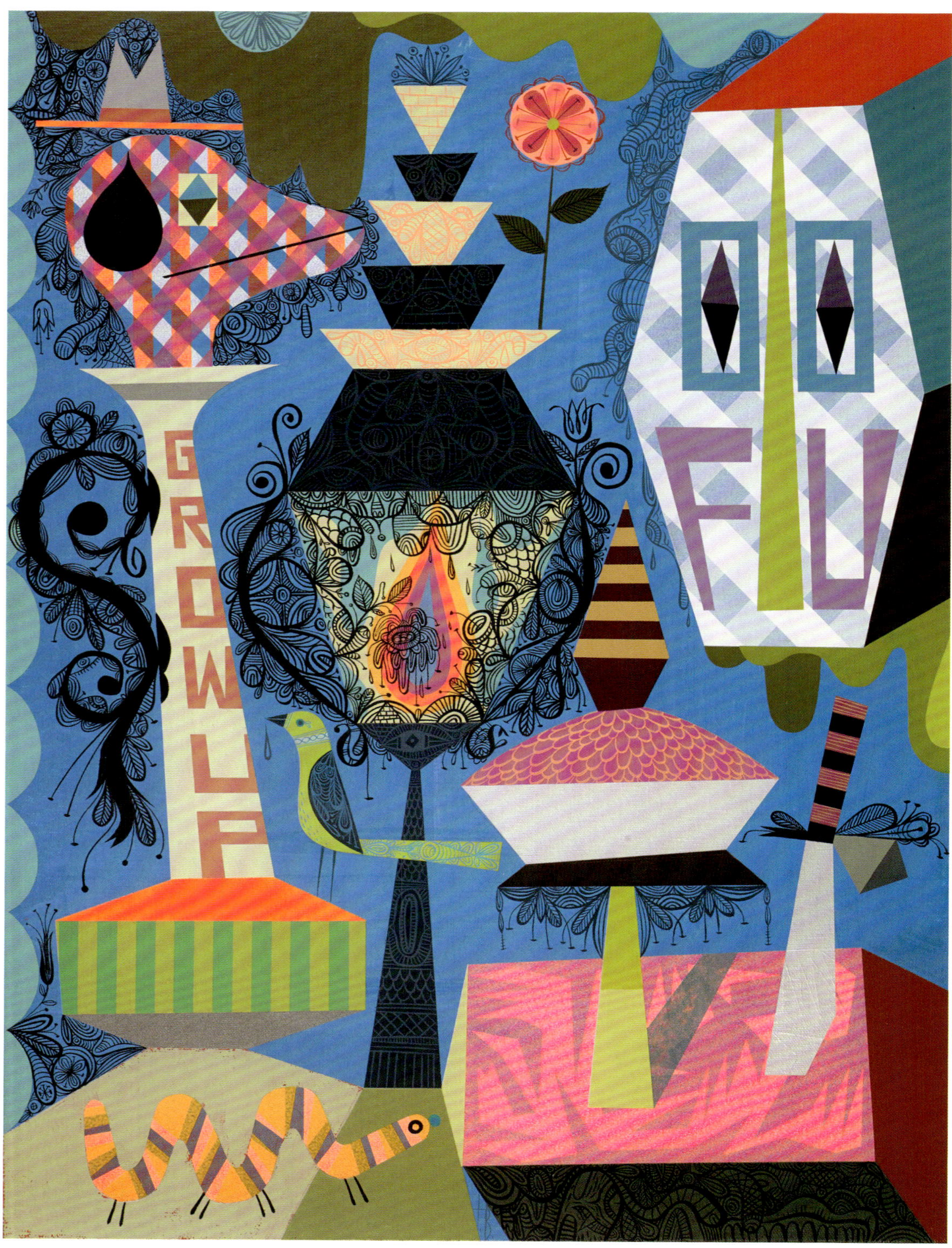

The Dismantling of an Outmoded Paradigm
2013. Acrylic on Canvas. 24" x 18"

The Presumed End of Function
2013. Acrylic on Canvas. 36" x 24"

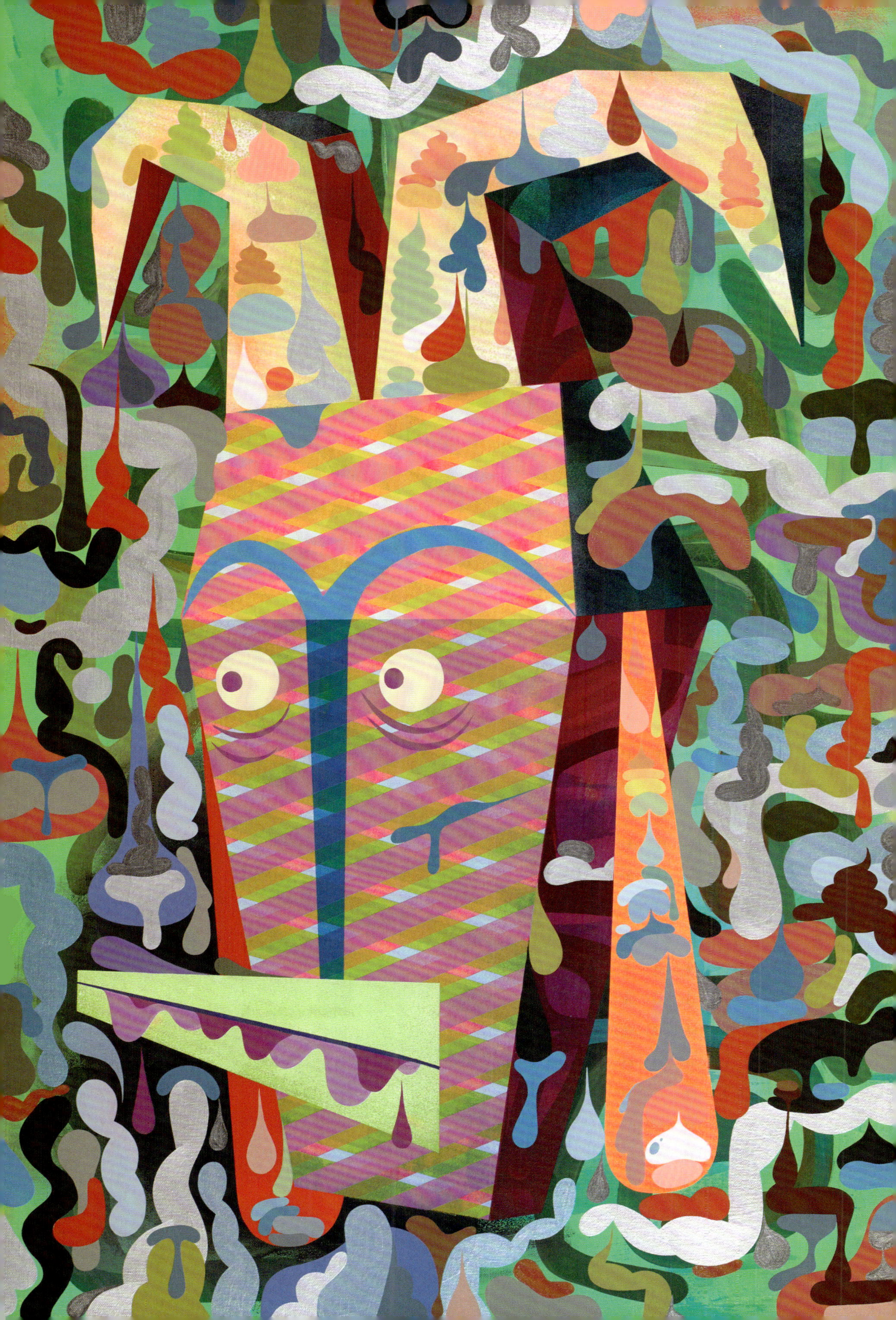

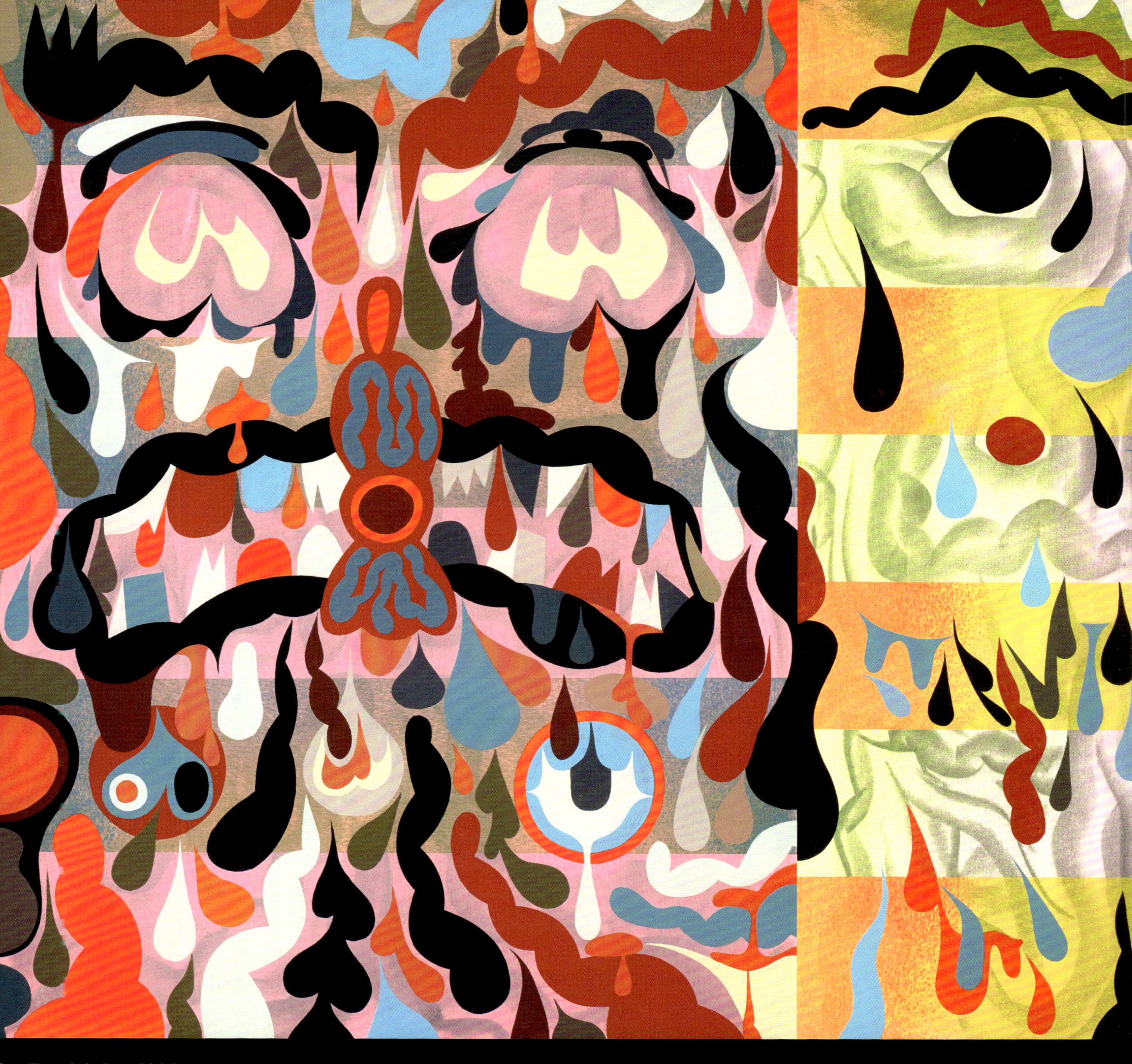

Seen Through the Eyes of Grief
2013. Graphite and Acrylic on Paper. 12" x 9"

Seen Through the Face of Joy
2013. Graphite and Acrylic on Paper. 14" x 10"

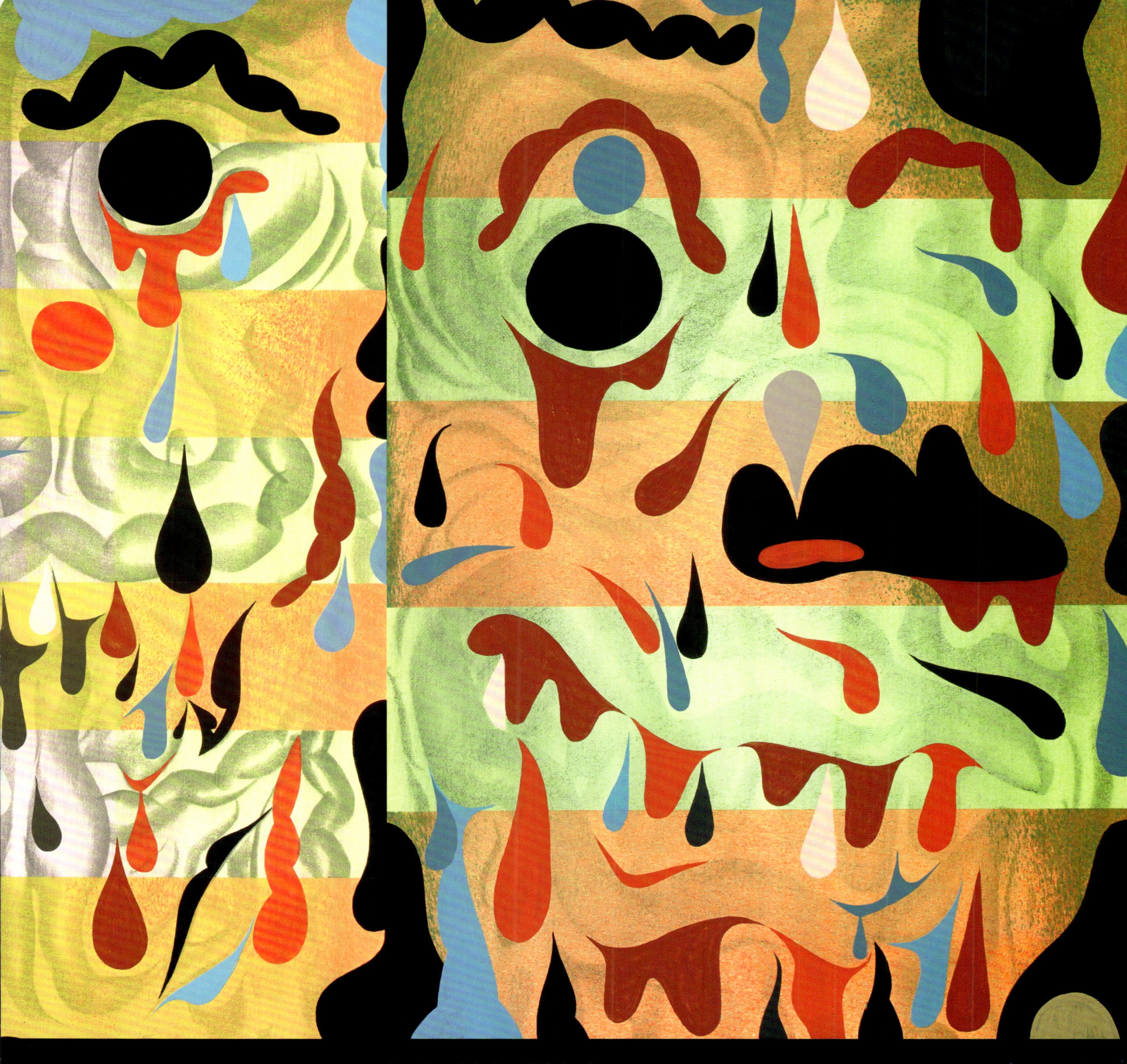

Seen Through the Eyes of Witchcraft
2013. Graphite and Acrylic on Paper. 9" x 7"

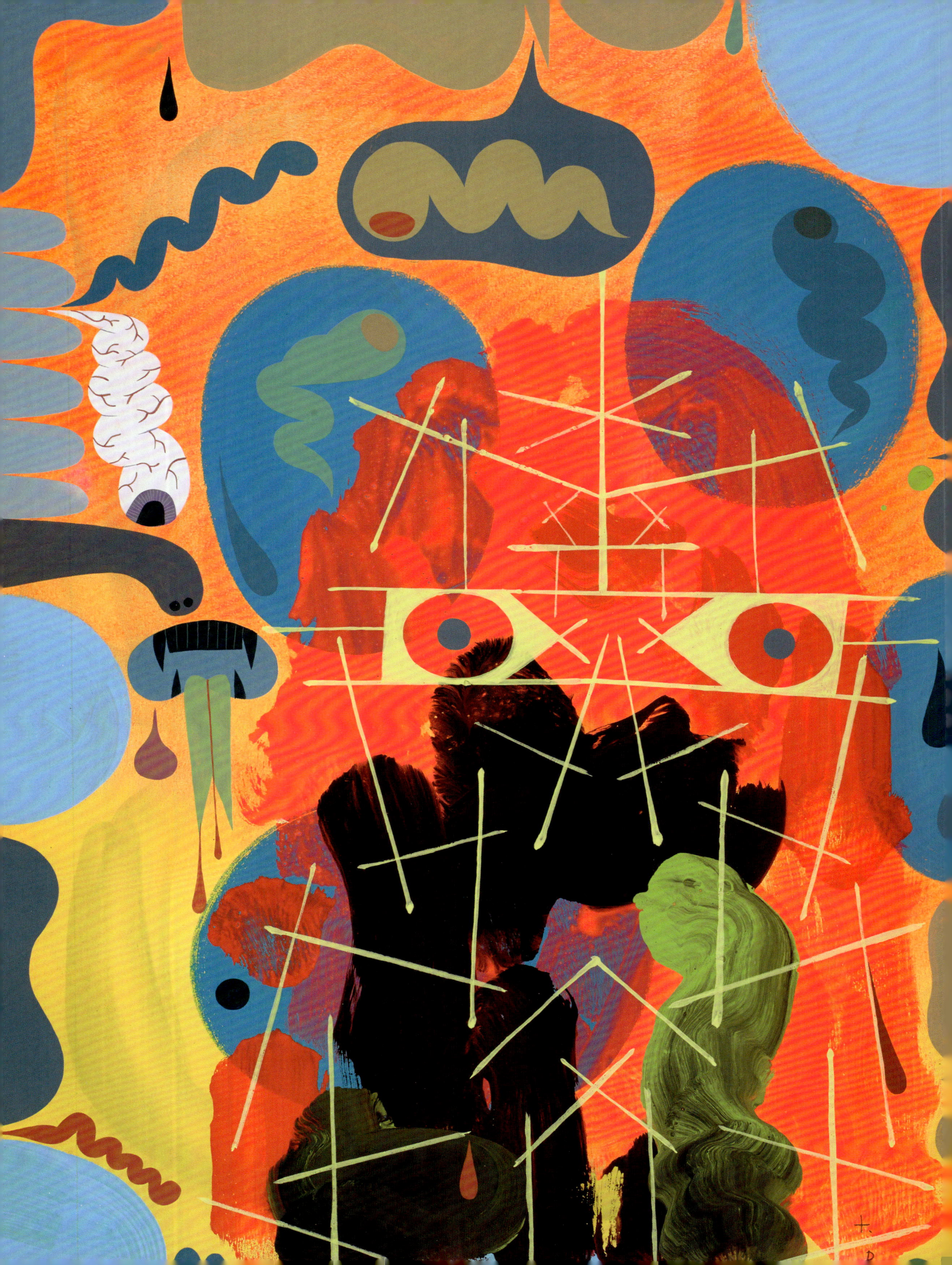

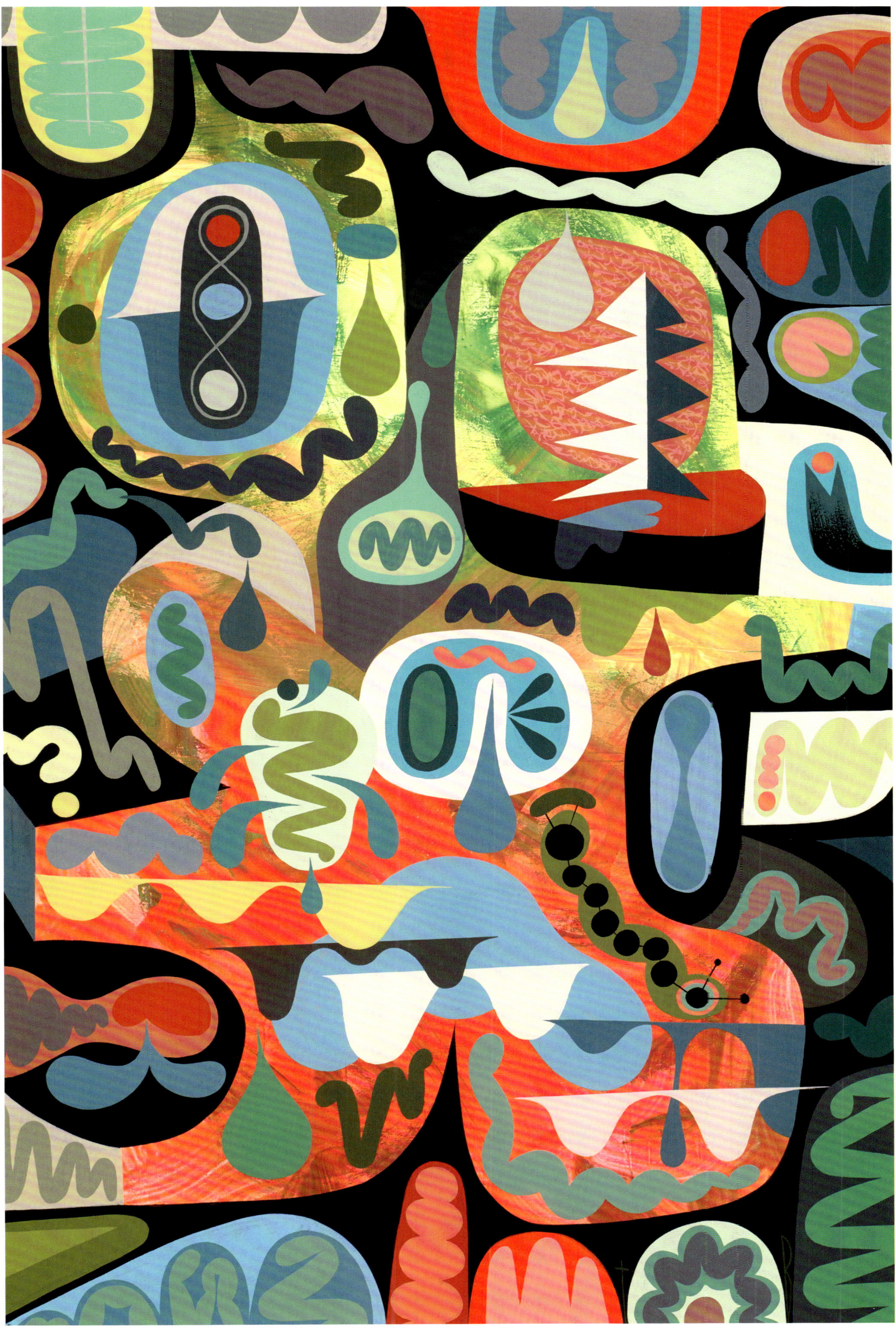

Seen Through the Eyes of Weakness
2013. Graphite and Acrylic on Paper. 16" x 12"

Acid in the Eyes of Science
2013. Acrylic on Panel. 20" x 13"

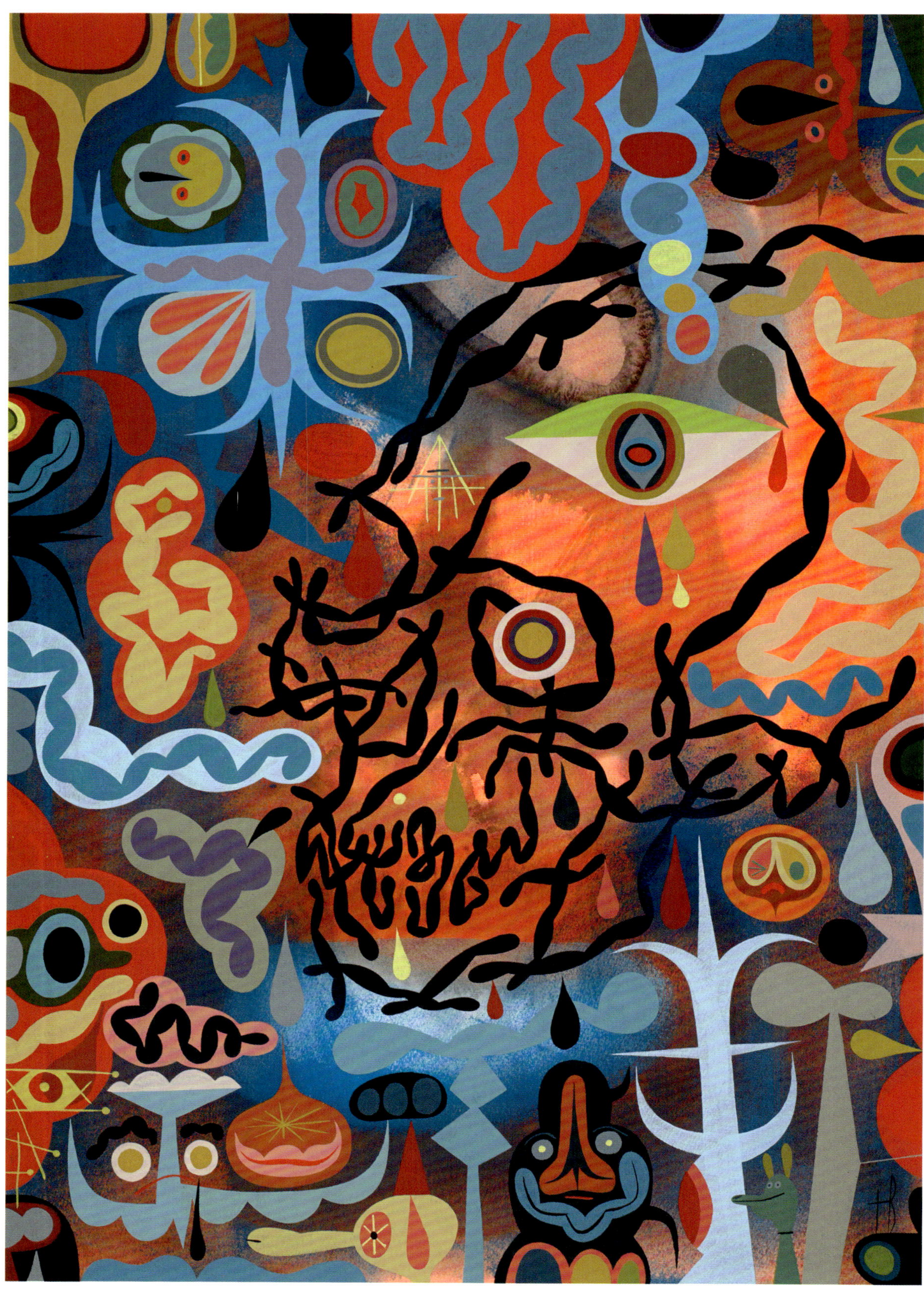

The Brutal End of Foreplay
2013. Acrylic on Paper. 20" x 14"

Cassowary as Invader
2013. Graphite and Acrylic on Paper. 24" x 18"

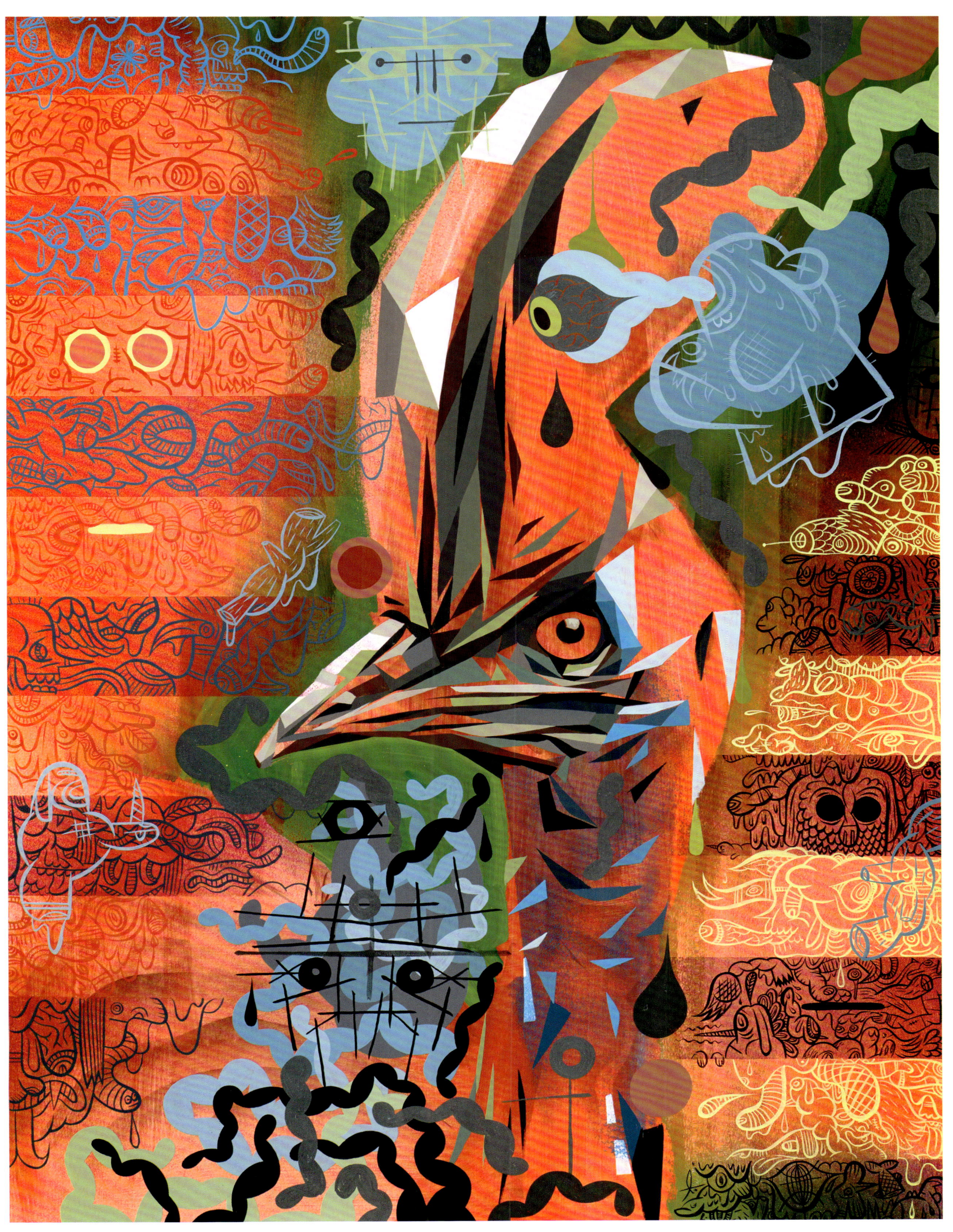

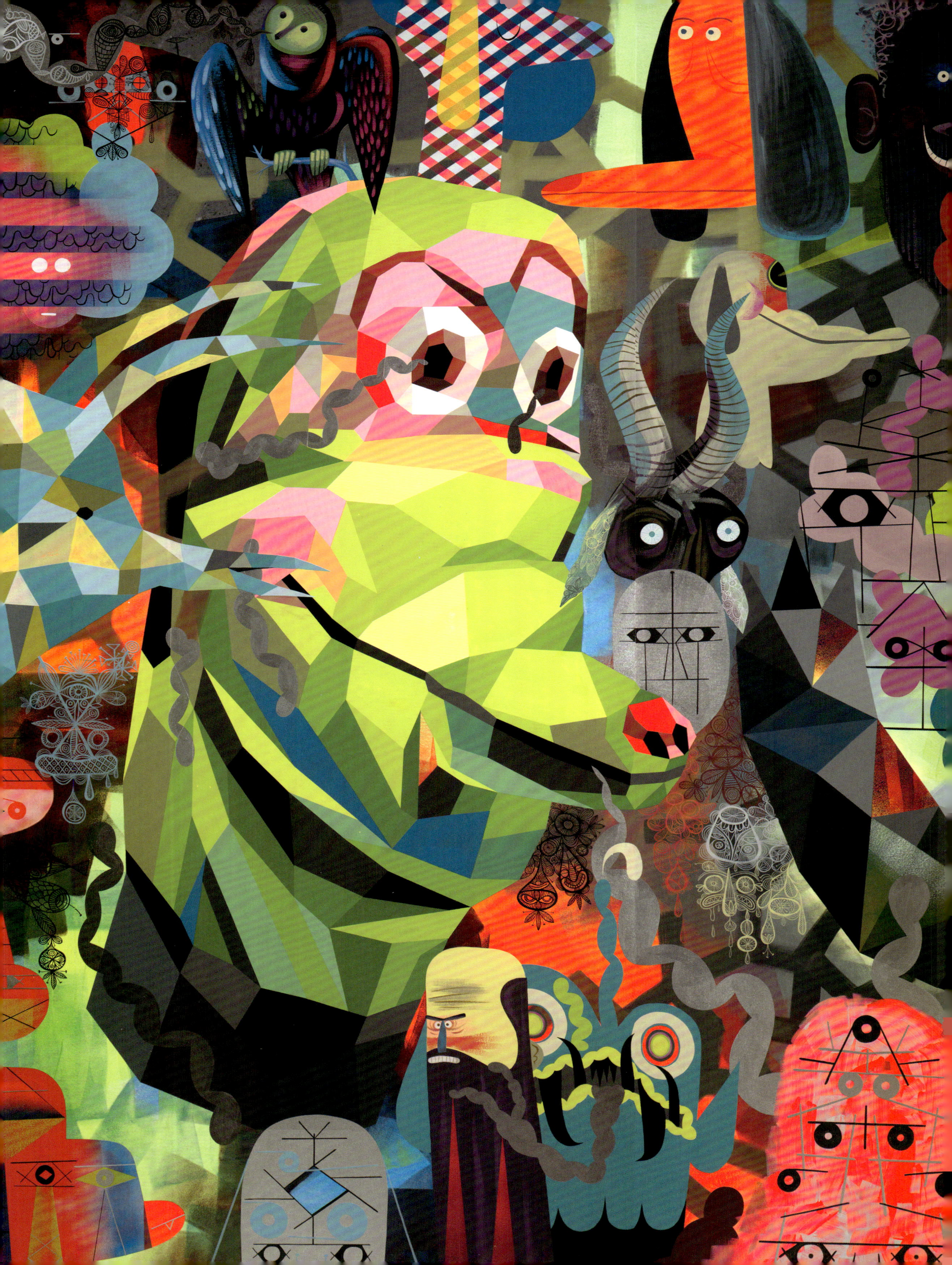

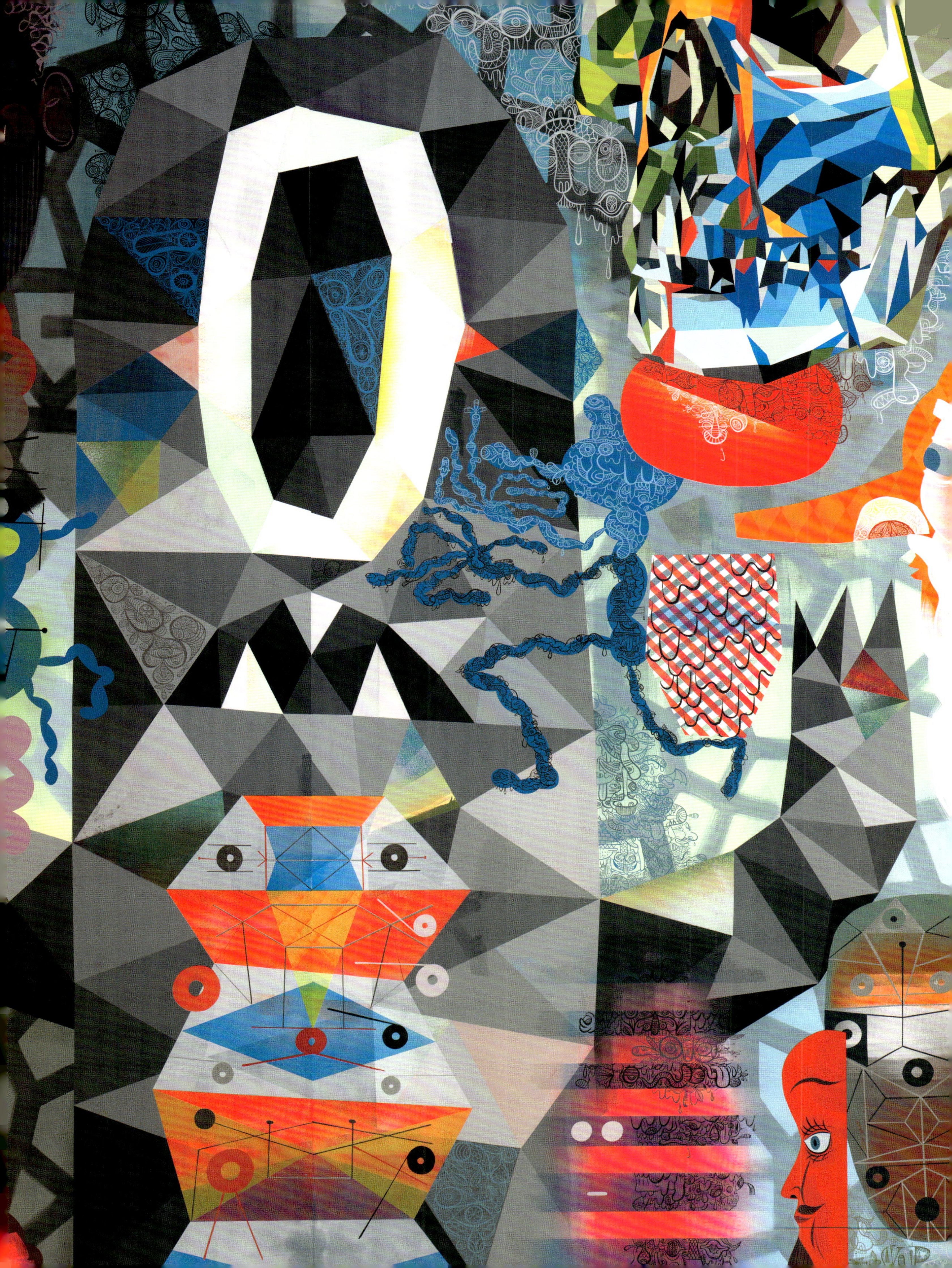

Previous page:

A Subtle Advertisement for Mind-Numbing Pain
2013. Acrylic on Canvas. 96" x 144"

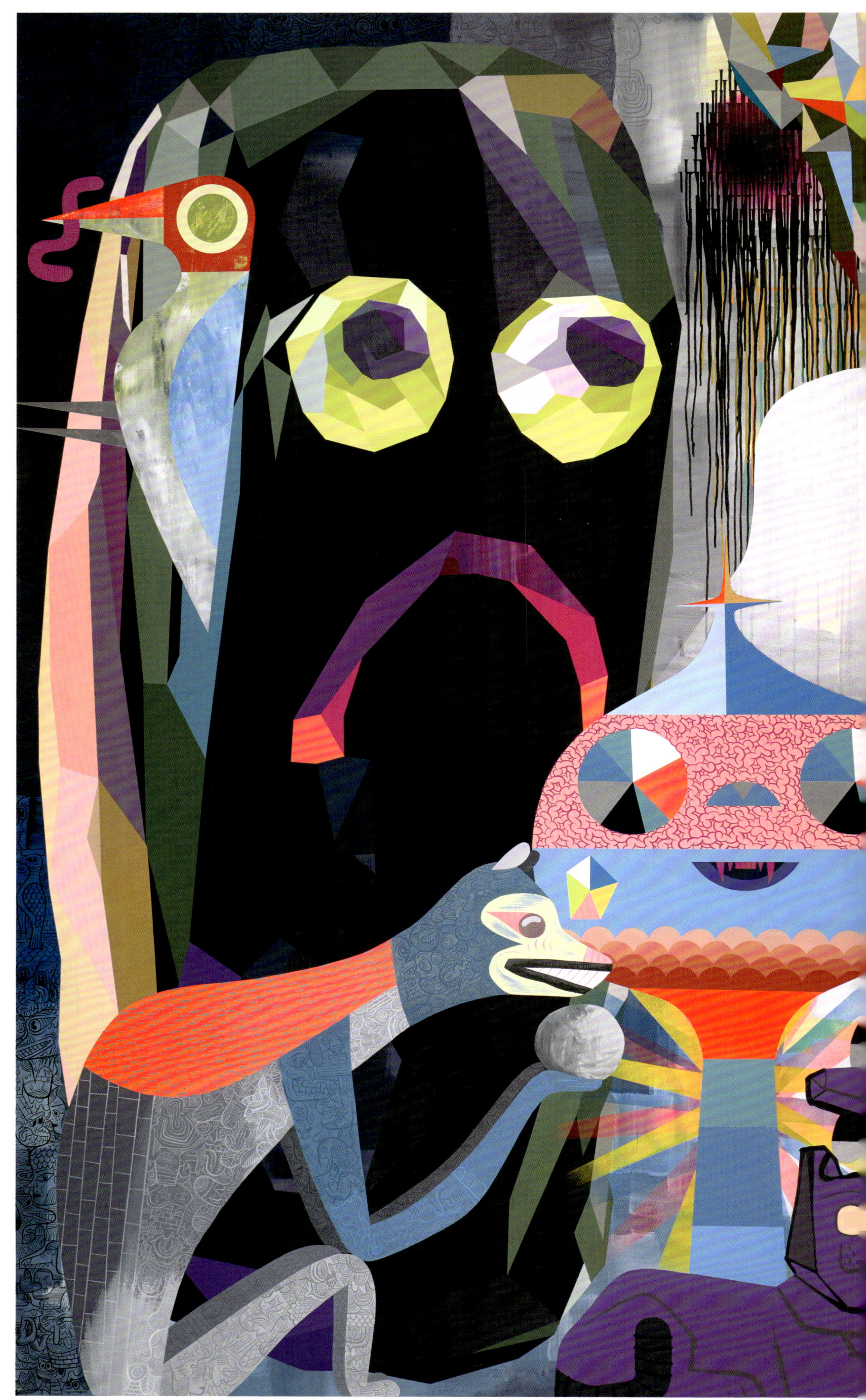

Open Focus Memory
2014. Acrylic on Canvas. 87" x 118"

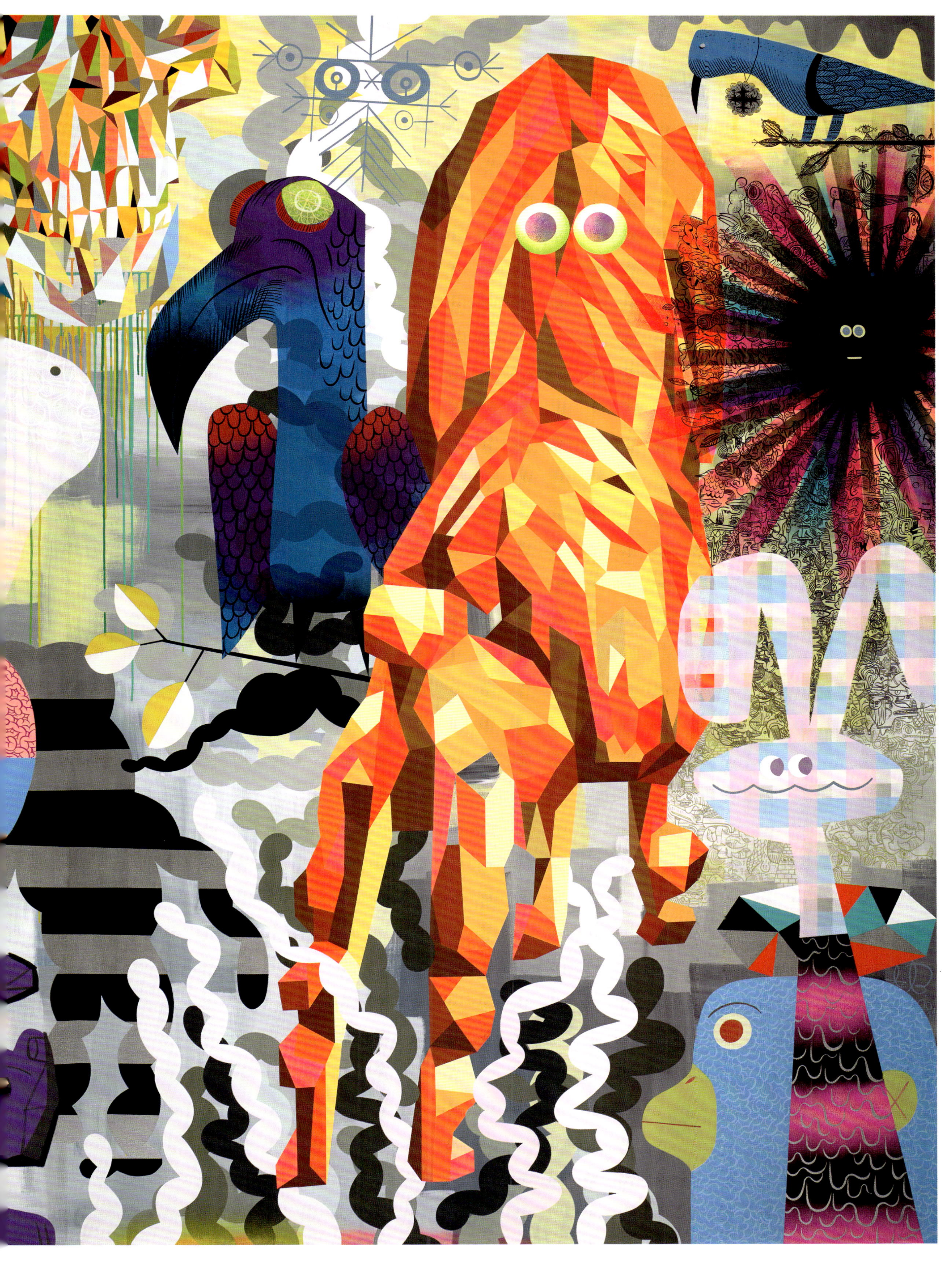

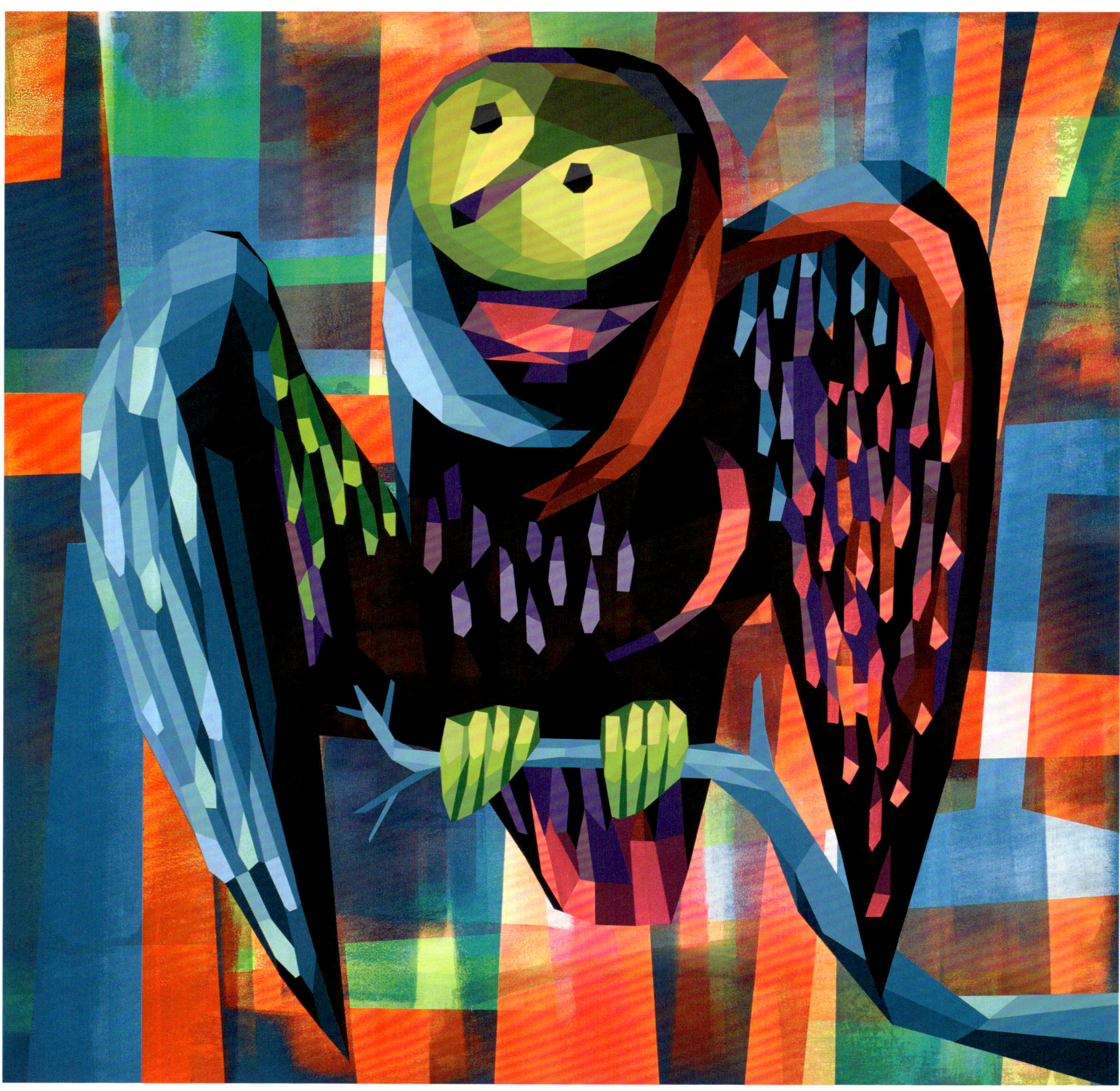

The Sticking Shadow of Truth
2013. Acrylic on Linen. 48" x 48"

Three Brothers
2013. Graphite and Acrylic on Canvas. 48" x 72"

Head in the Hole
2014. Acrylic on Shaped Panel. 84" x 198"

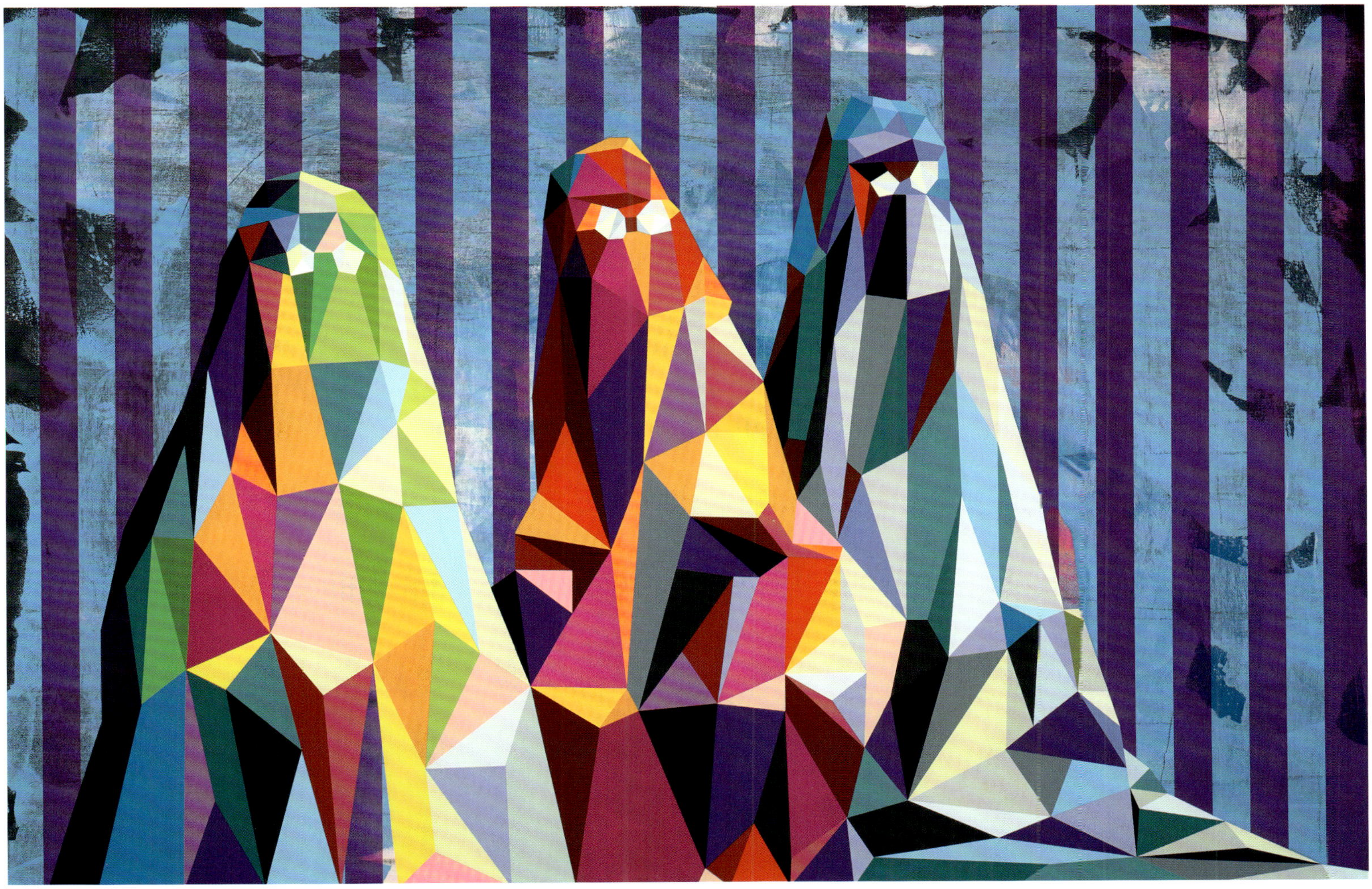

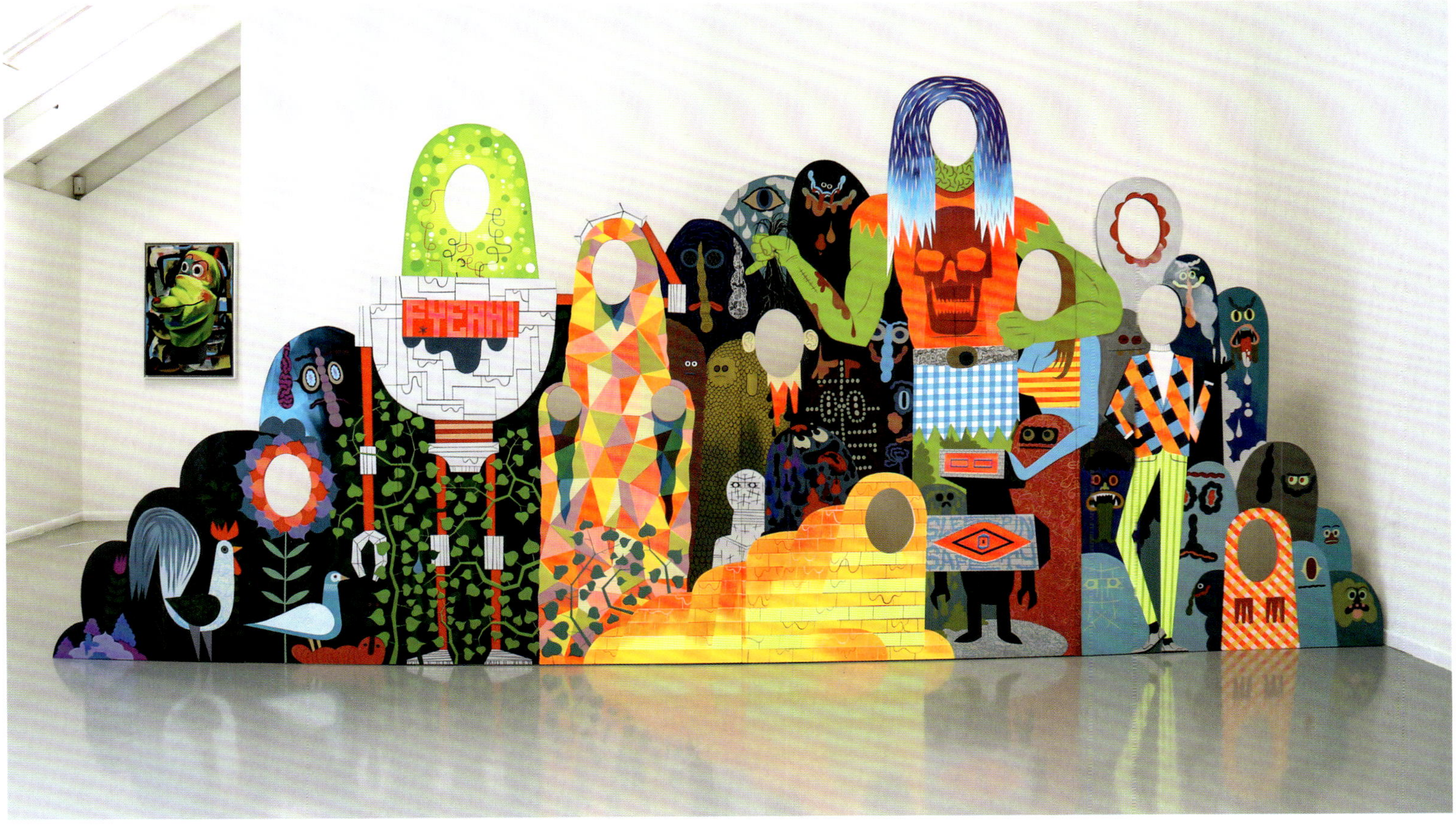

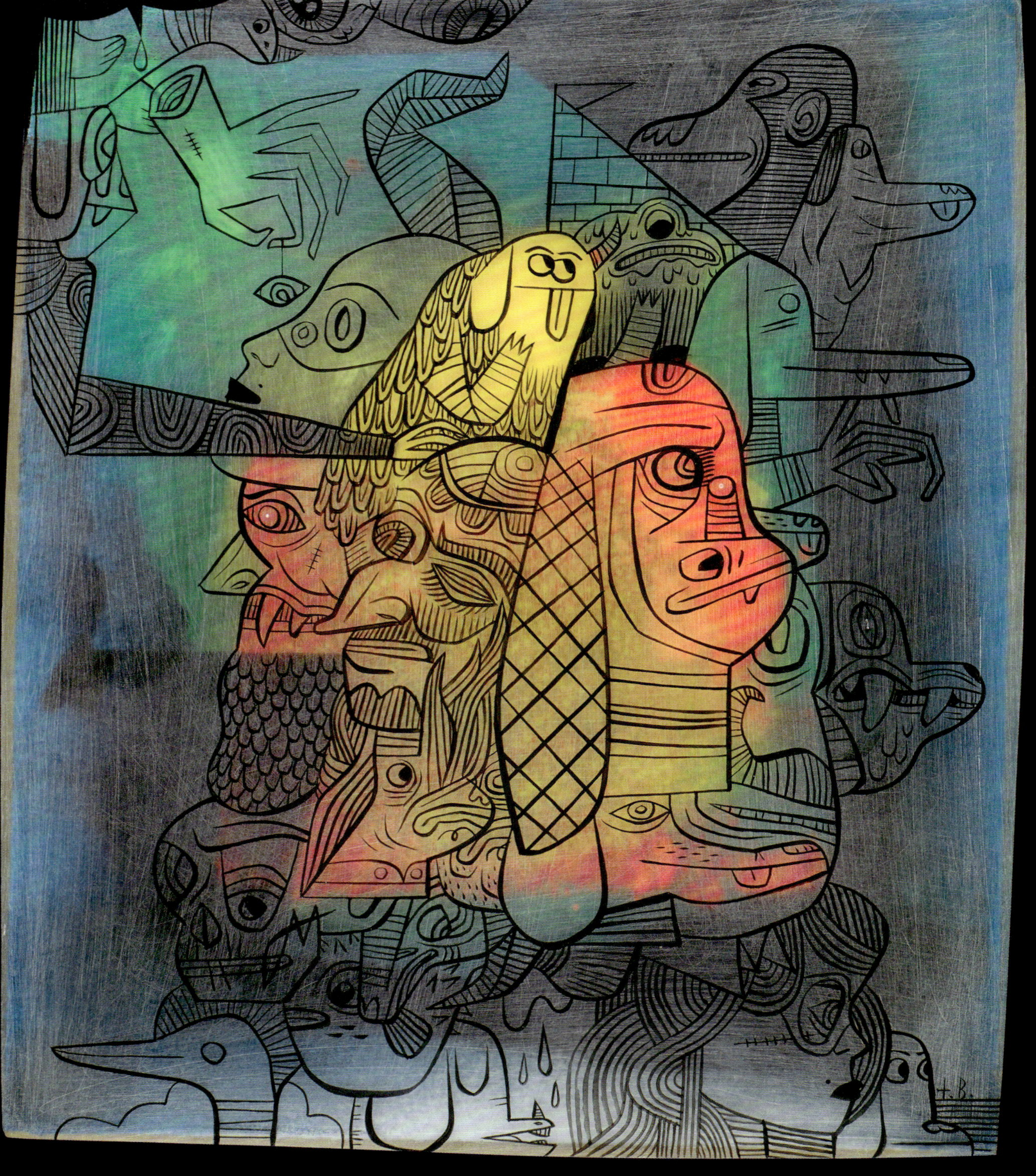

Step 1
2015. Acrylic and Epoxy Resin on Panel. 12" x 9"

Step 8
2014. Acrylic on Paper. 20" x 16"

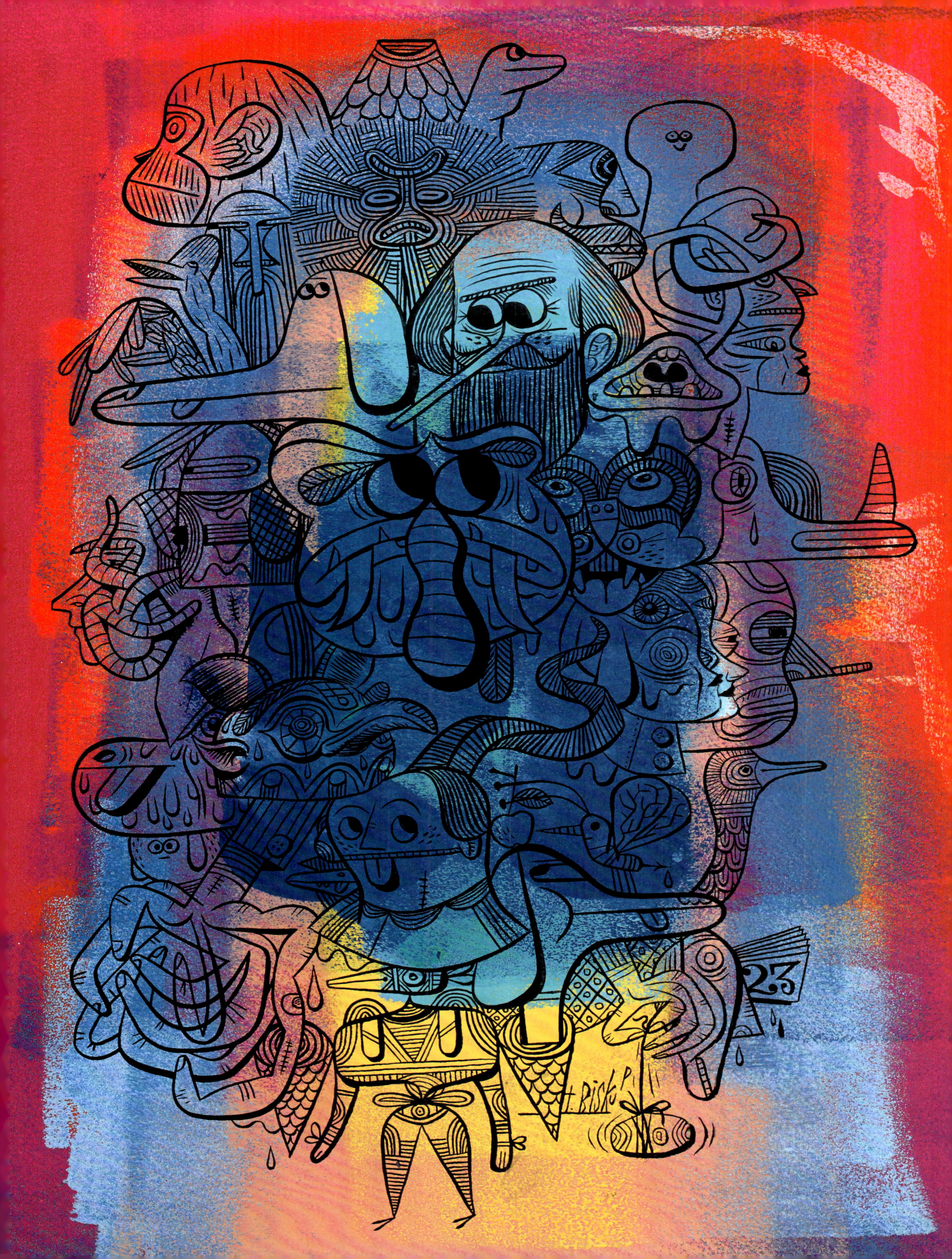
23

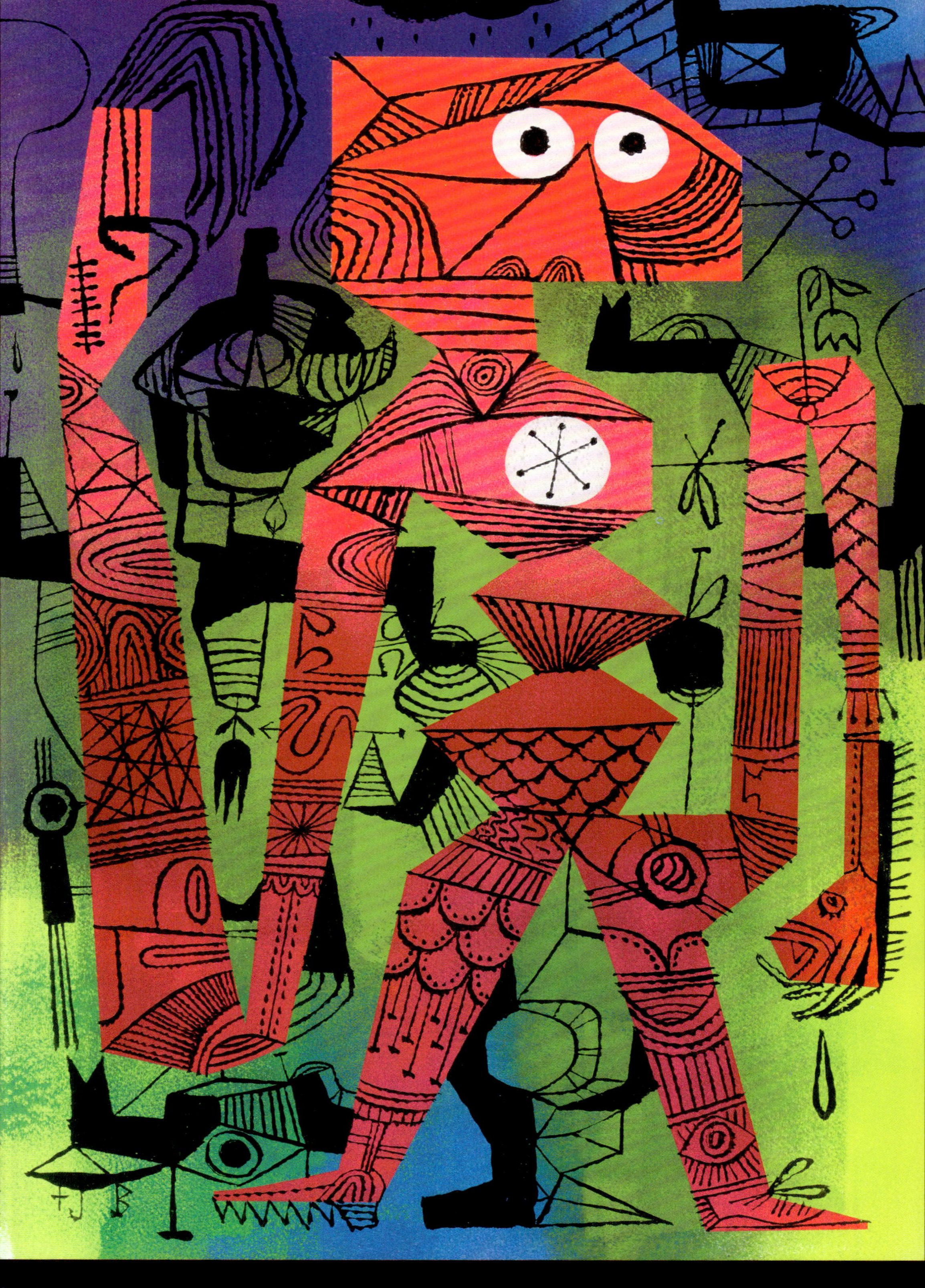

Step 26
2015. Acrylic on Paper. 20" x 16"

Step 14
2014. Acrylic on Panel. 15" x 7"

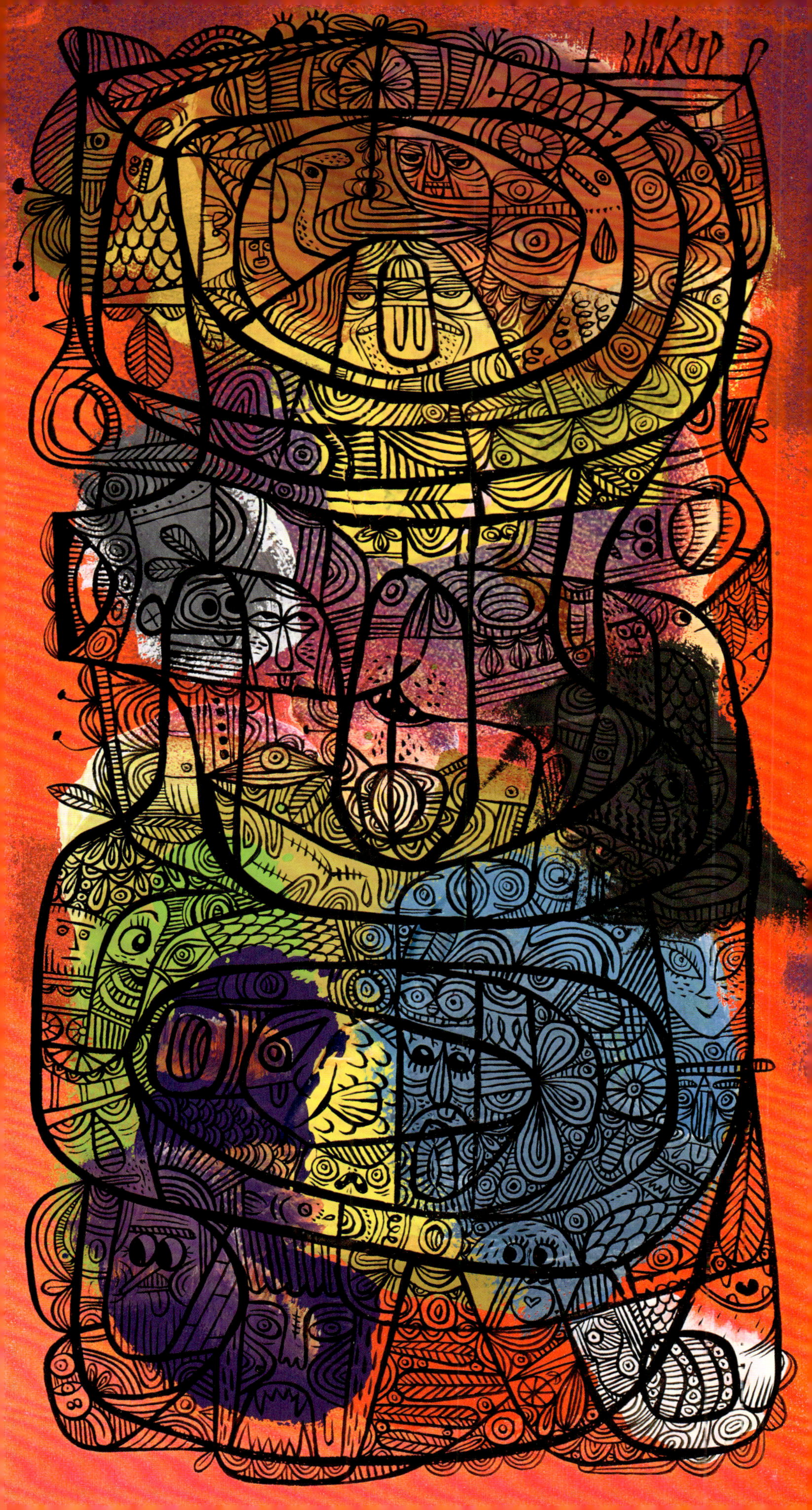
BISKUP

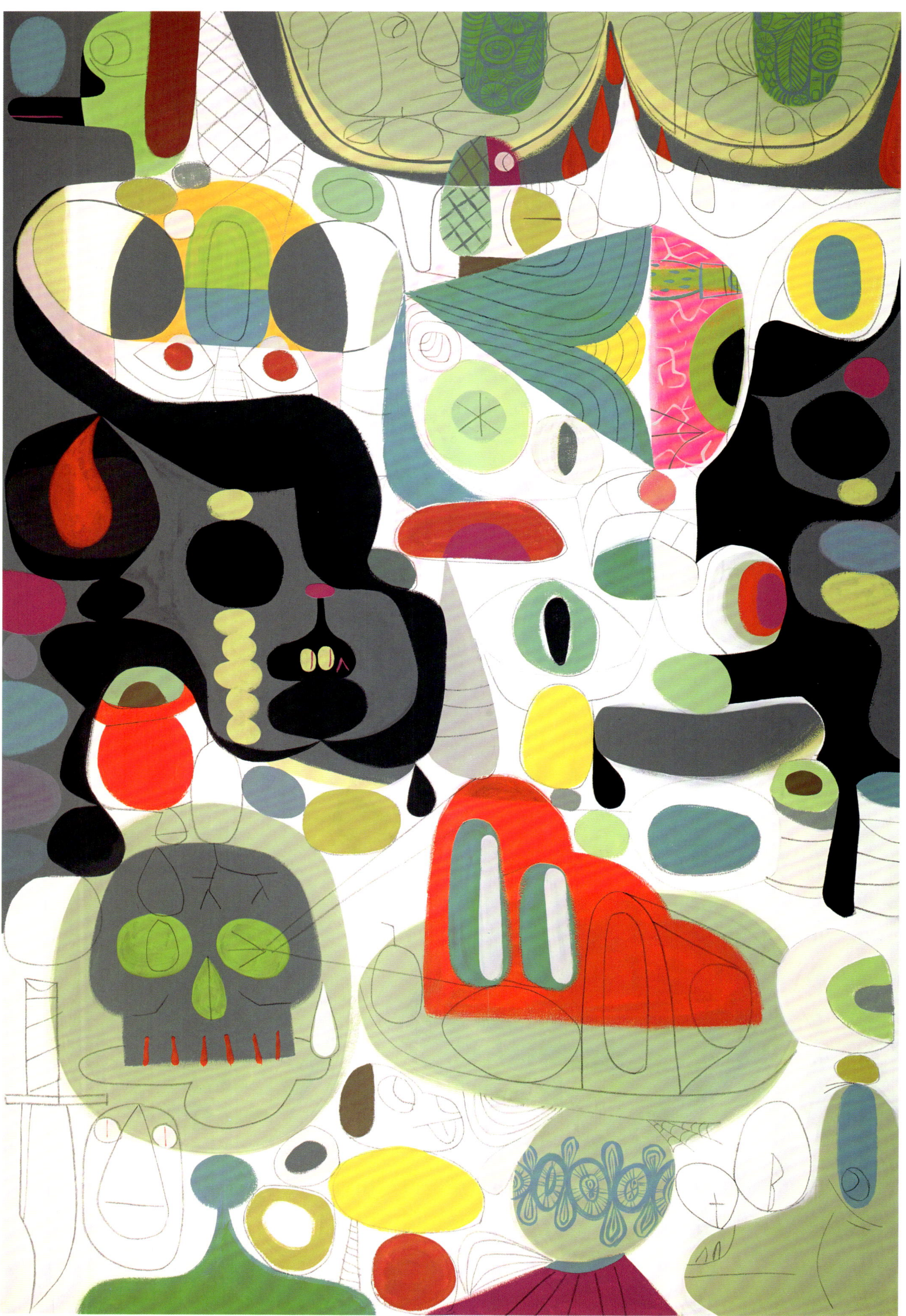

Step 27
2015. Graphite and Acrylic on Canvas. 72" x 48"

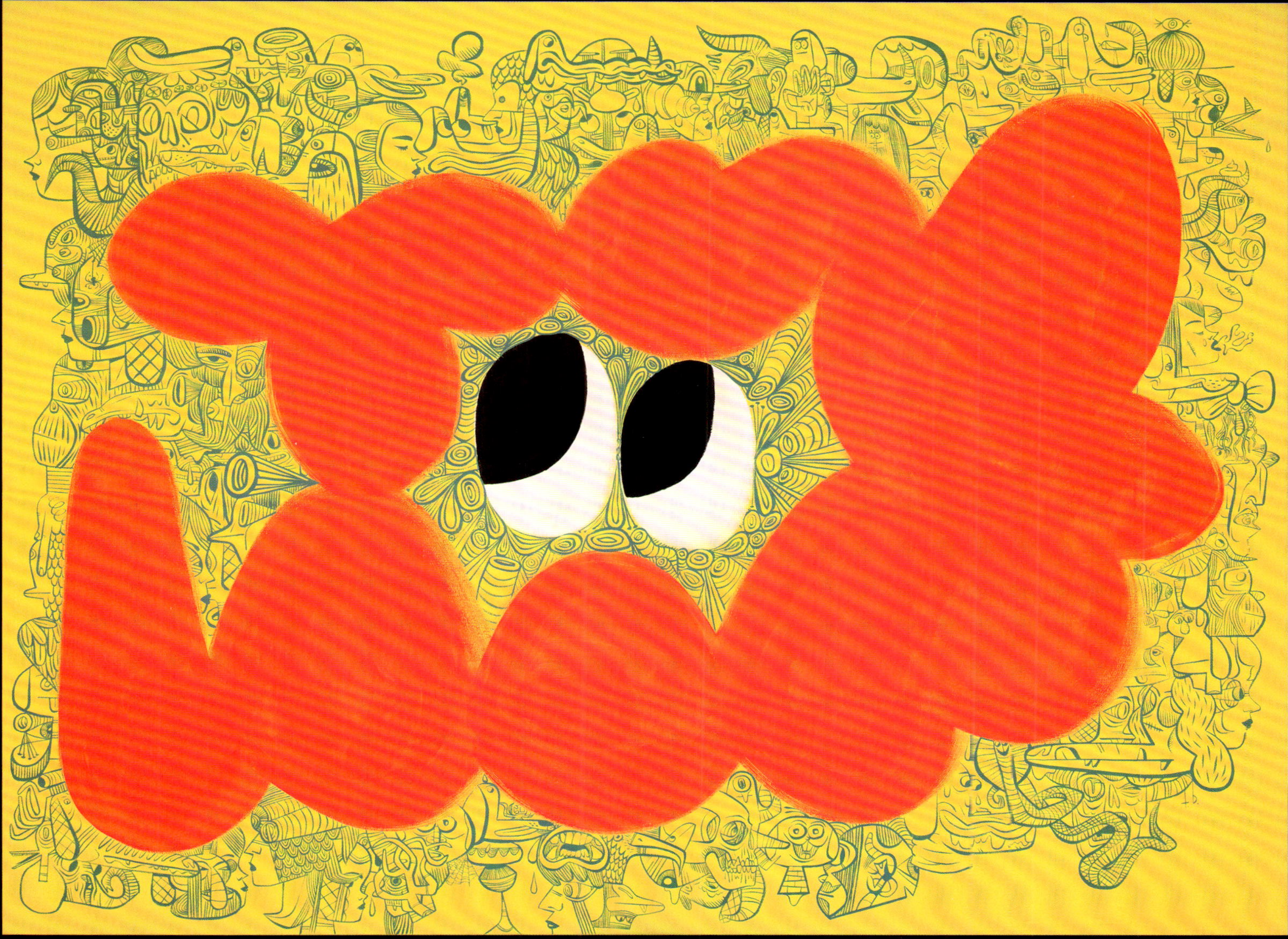

Step 25
2015. Acrylic on Canvas. 36" x 48"

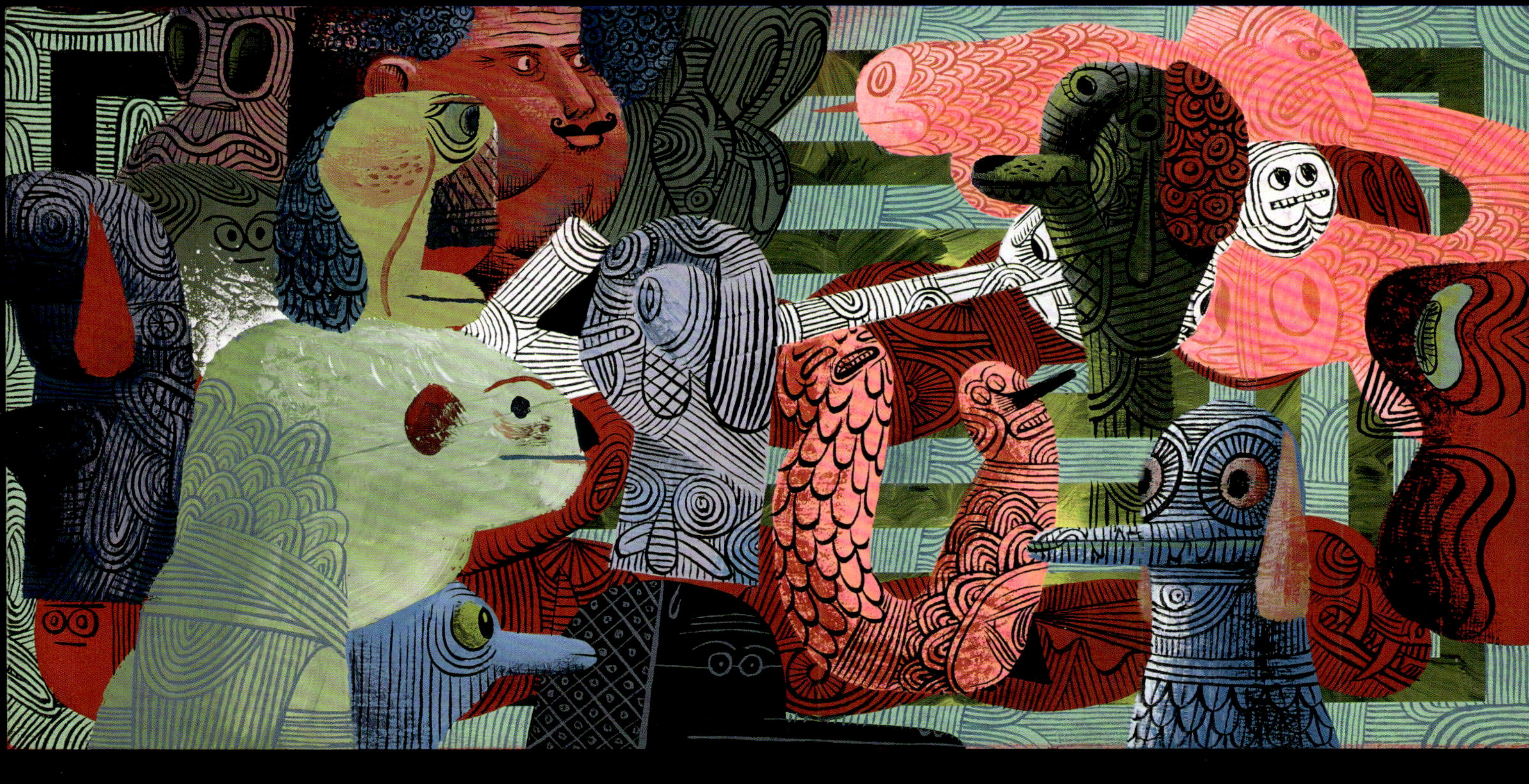

Step 21
2014. Acrylic on Panel. 7" x 14"

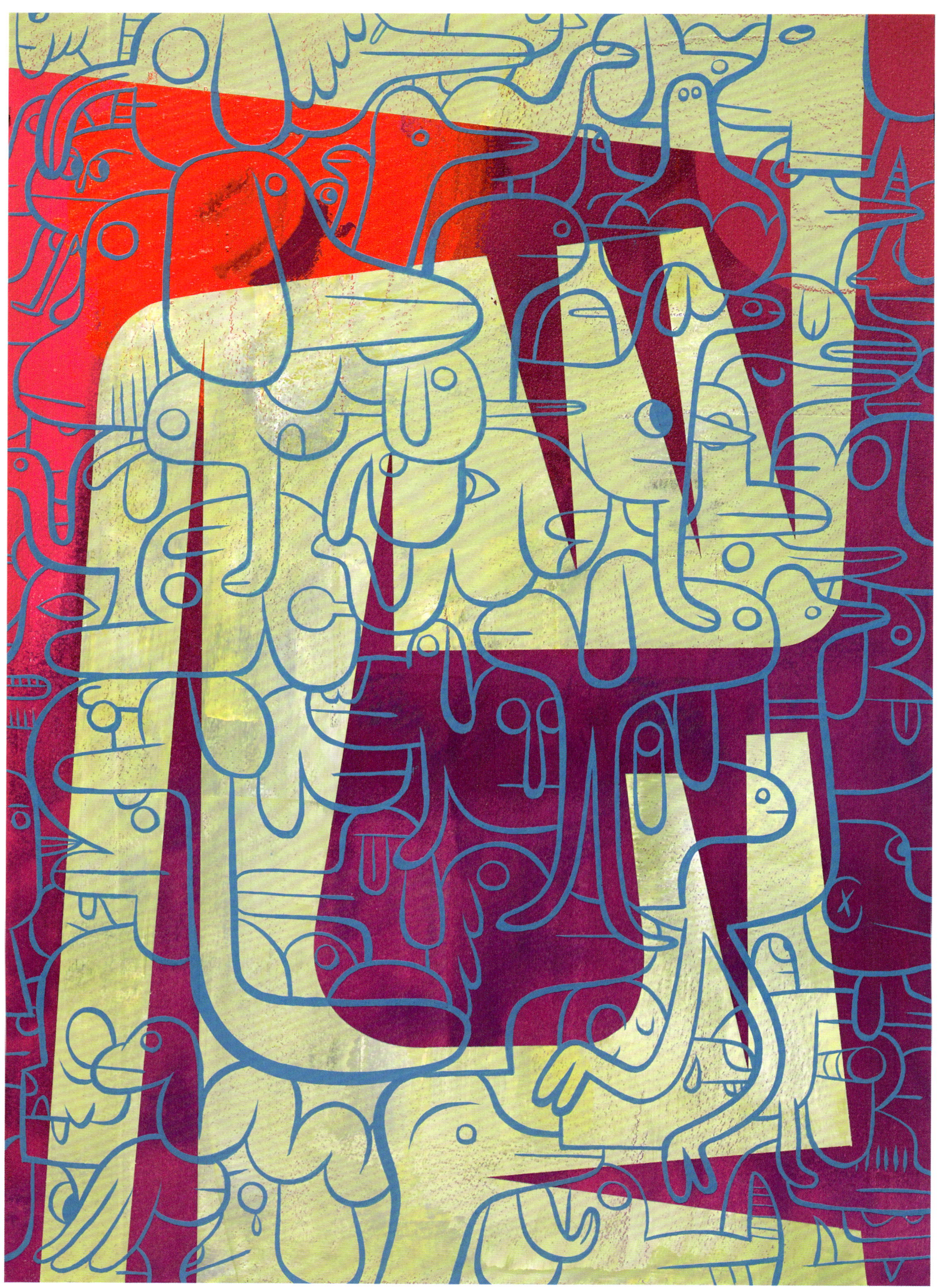

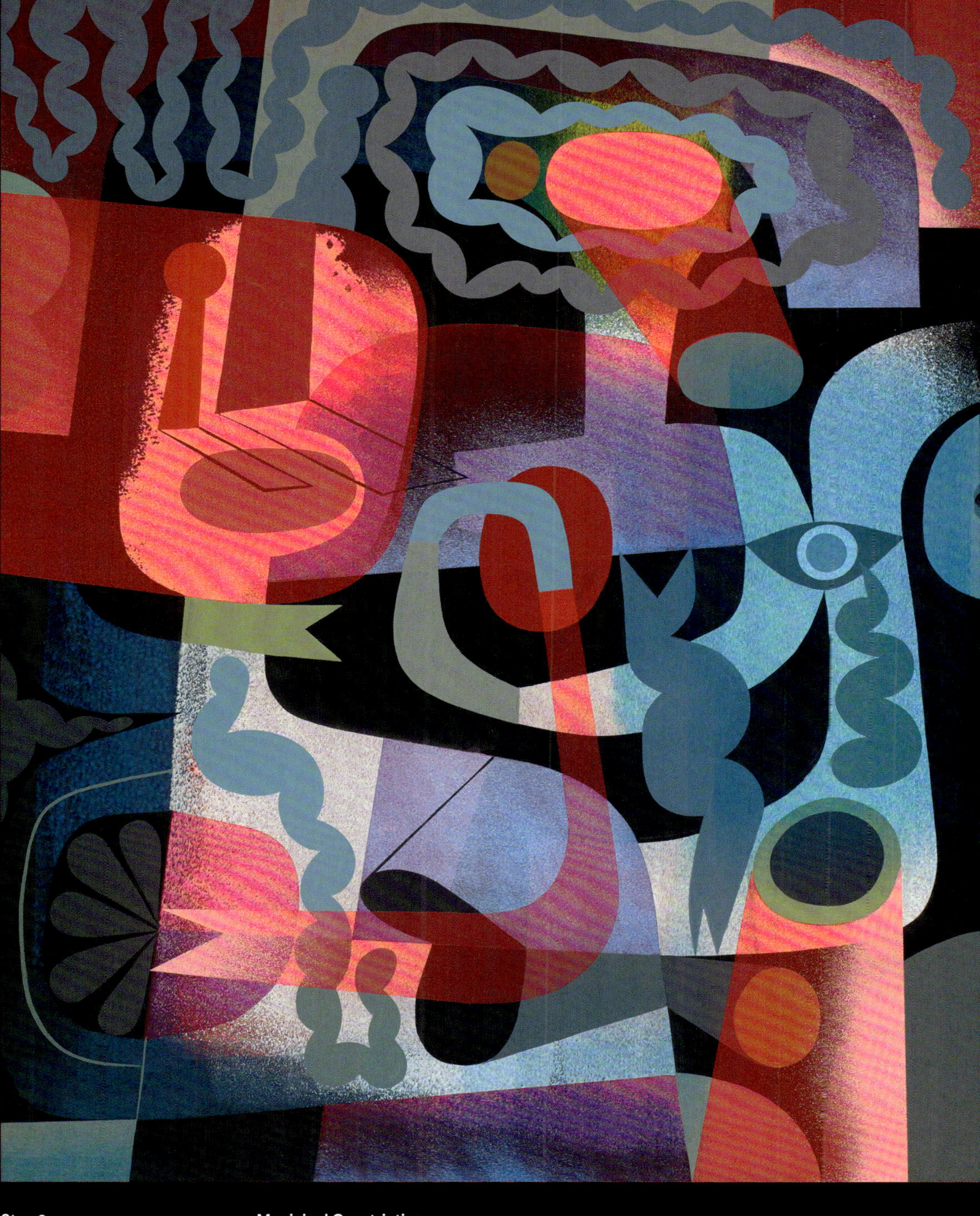

Step 9
2014. Acrylic on Paper. 20" x 16"

Municipal Constriction
2015. Acrylic on Panel. 20" x 18"

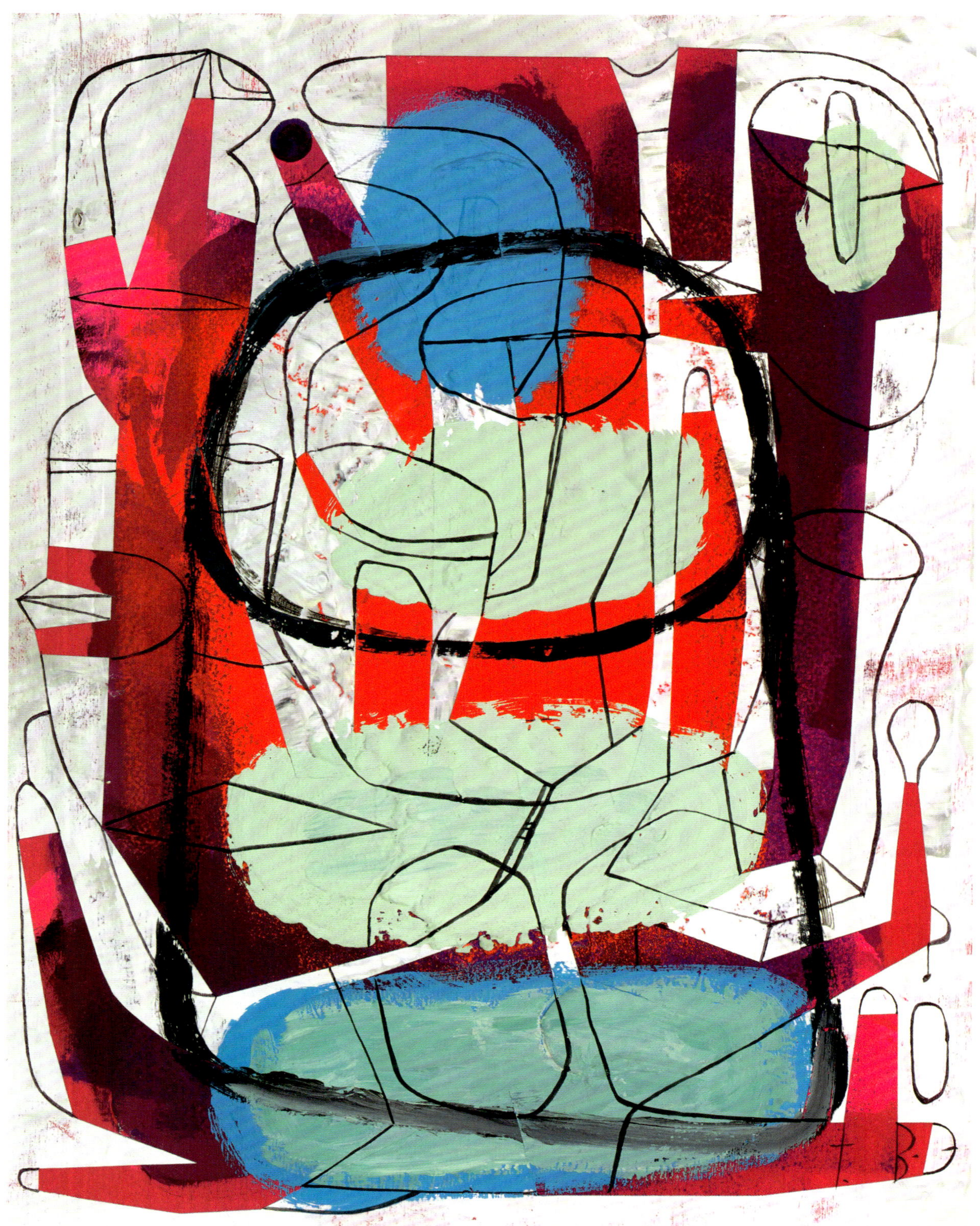

Step 20
2014. Acrylic on Panel. 14" x 11"

Step 4
2015. Graphite and Acrylic on Paper. 16" x 12"

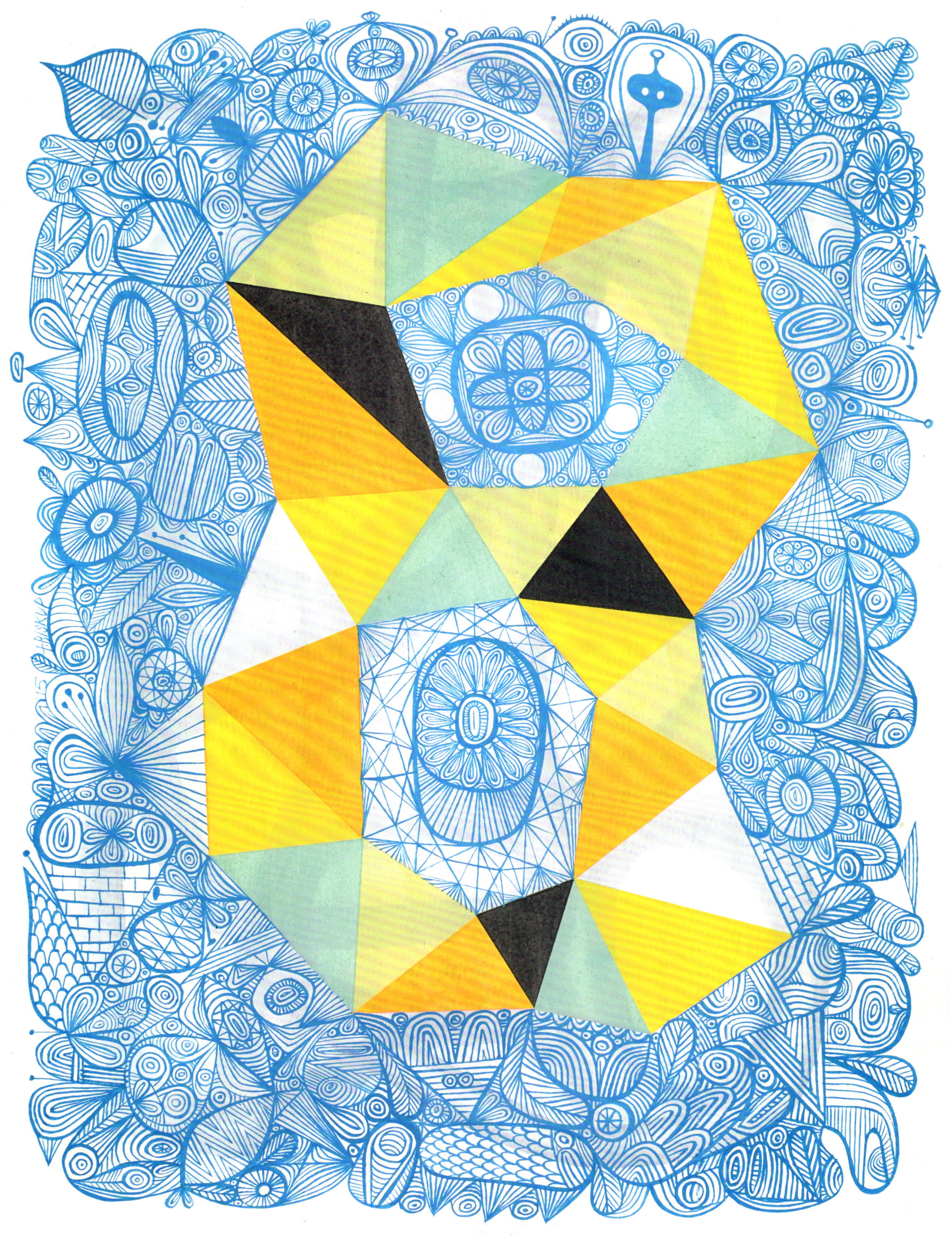

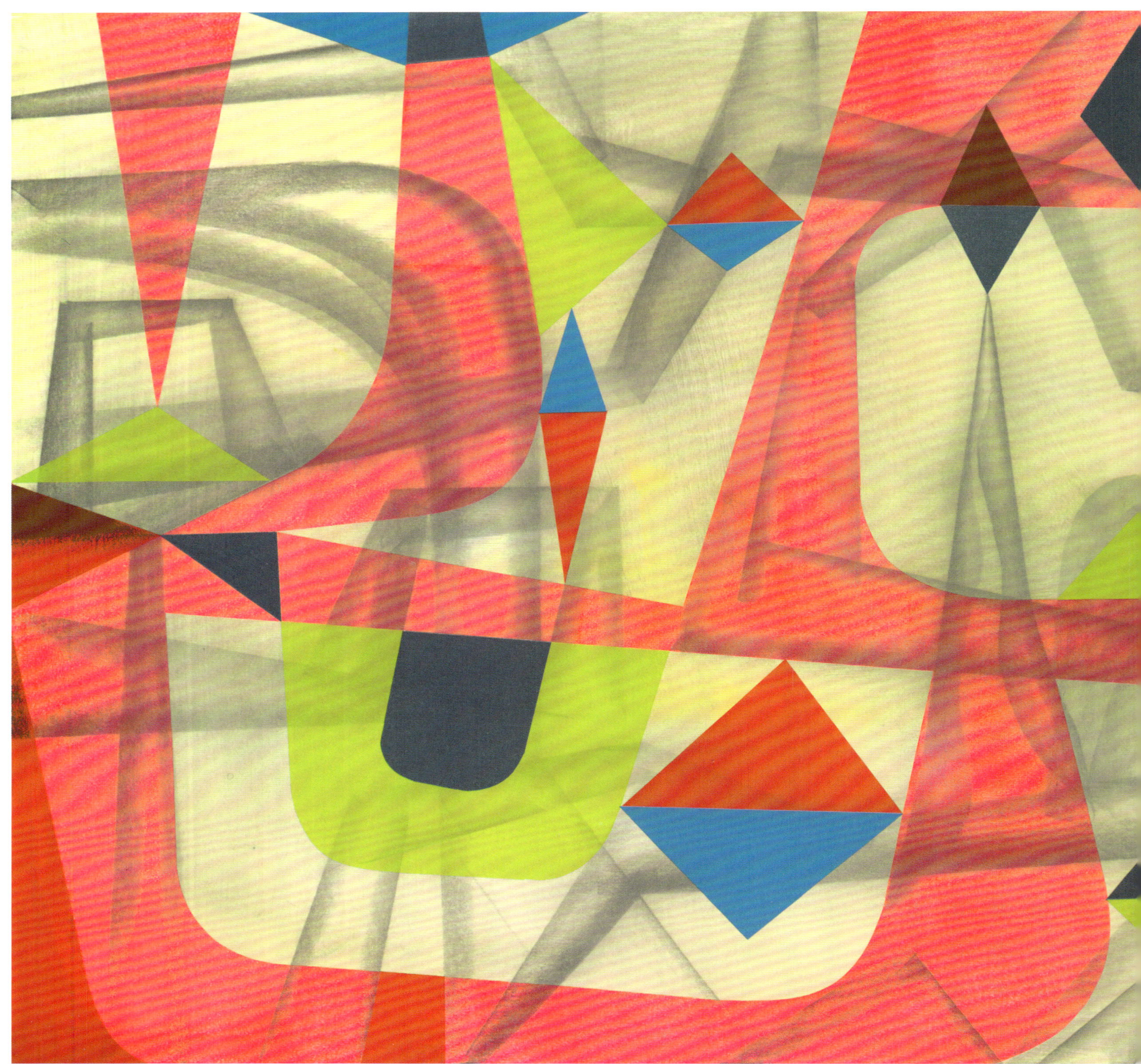

Brainsled No 11
2012. Graphite and Acrylic on Paper. 18" x 24"

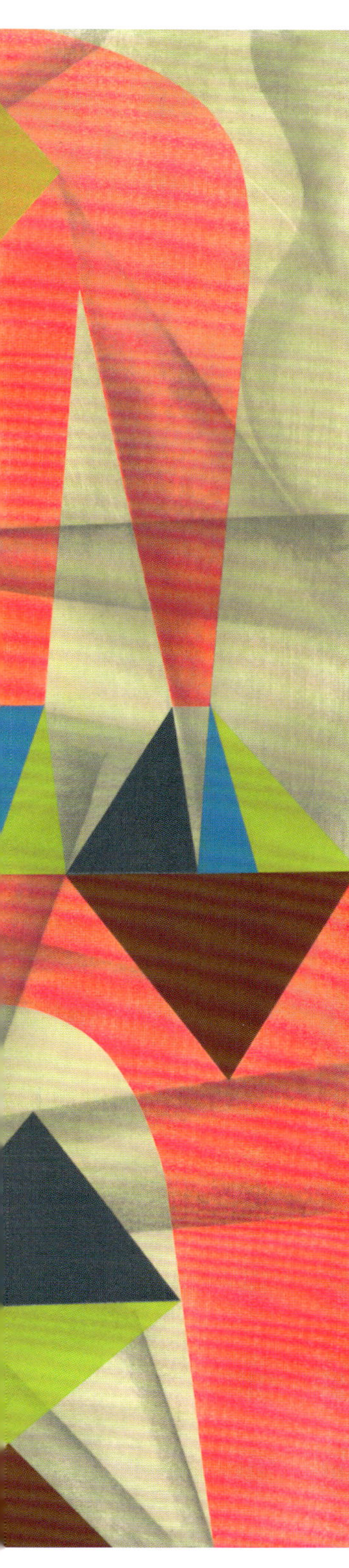

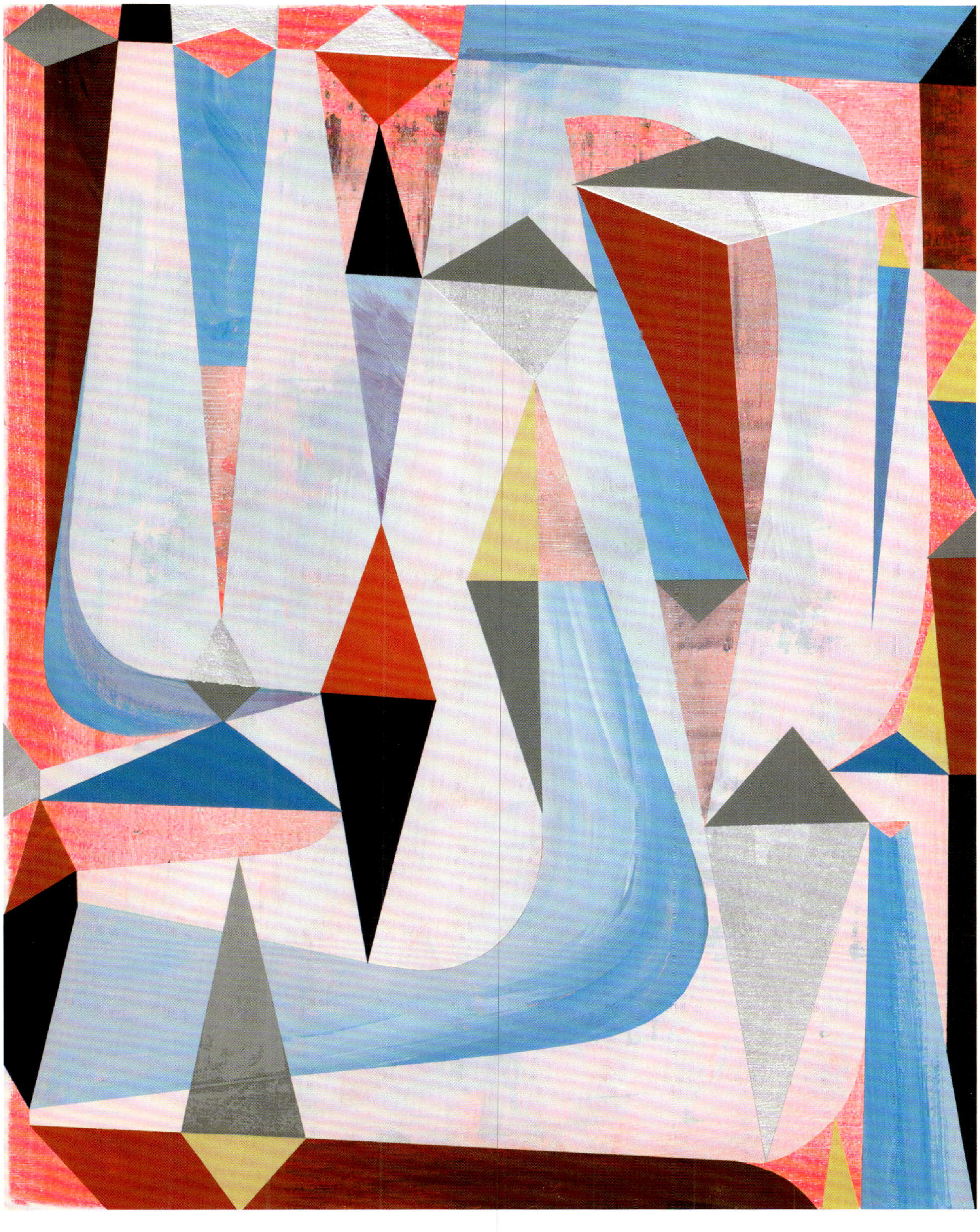

Fellow Stamper
2012. Graphite and Acrylic on Panel. 14" x 11"

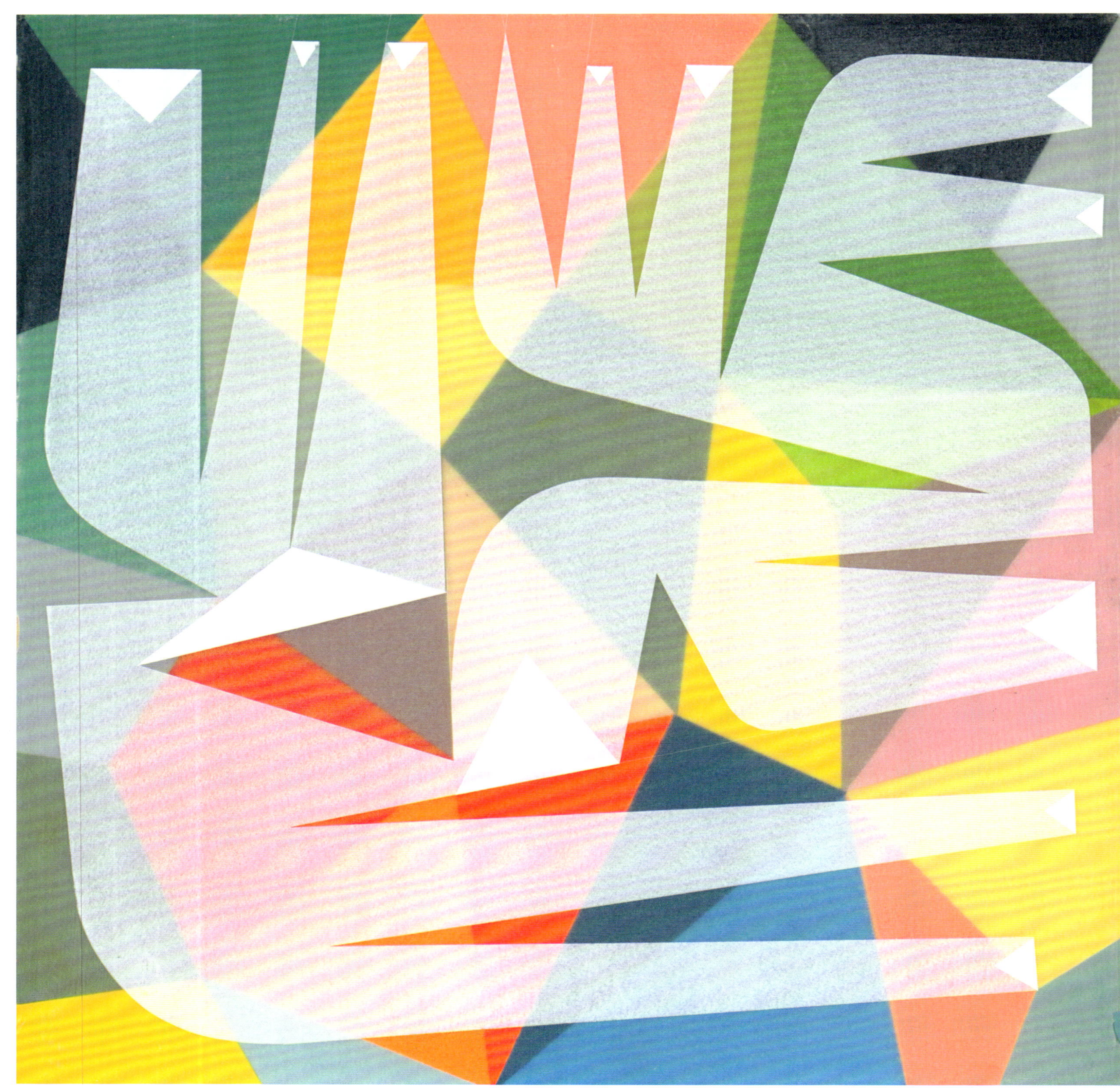

The Shepherd's Whip No 1
2013. Acrylic and Epoxy Resin on Panel. 12" x 12"

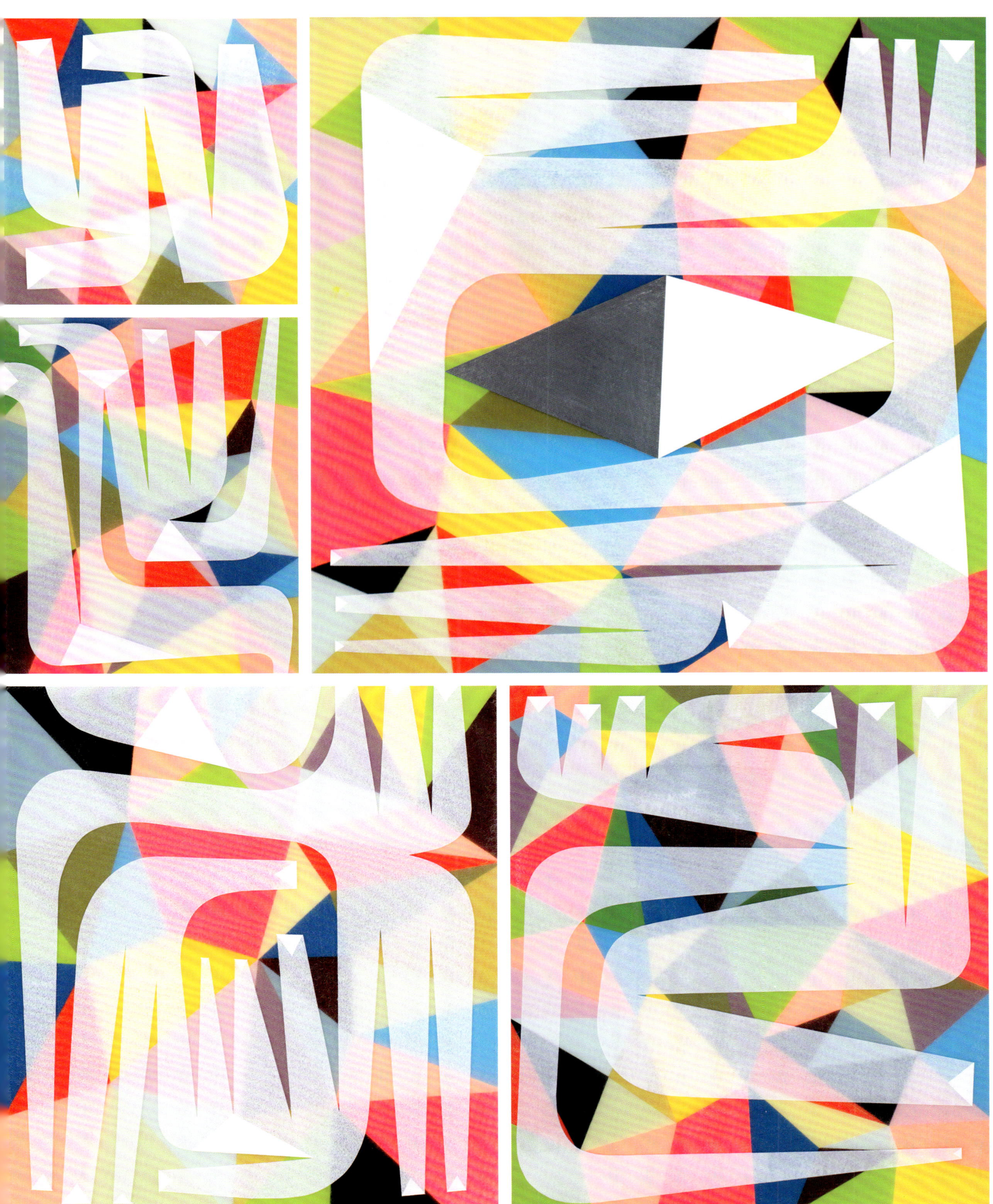

The Shepherd's Whip No 2-6
2013. Acrylic and Epoxy Resin on Panel. Dimensions Vary

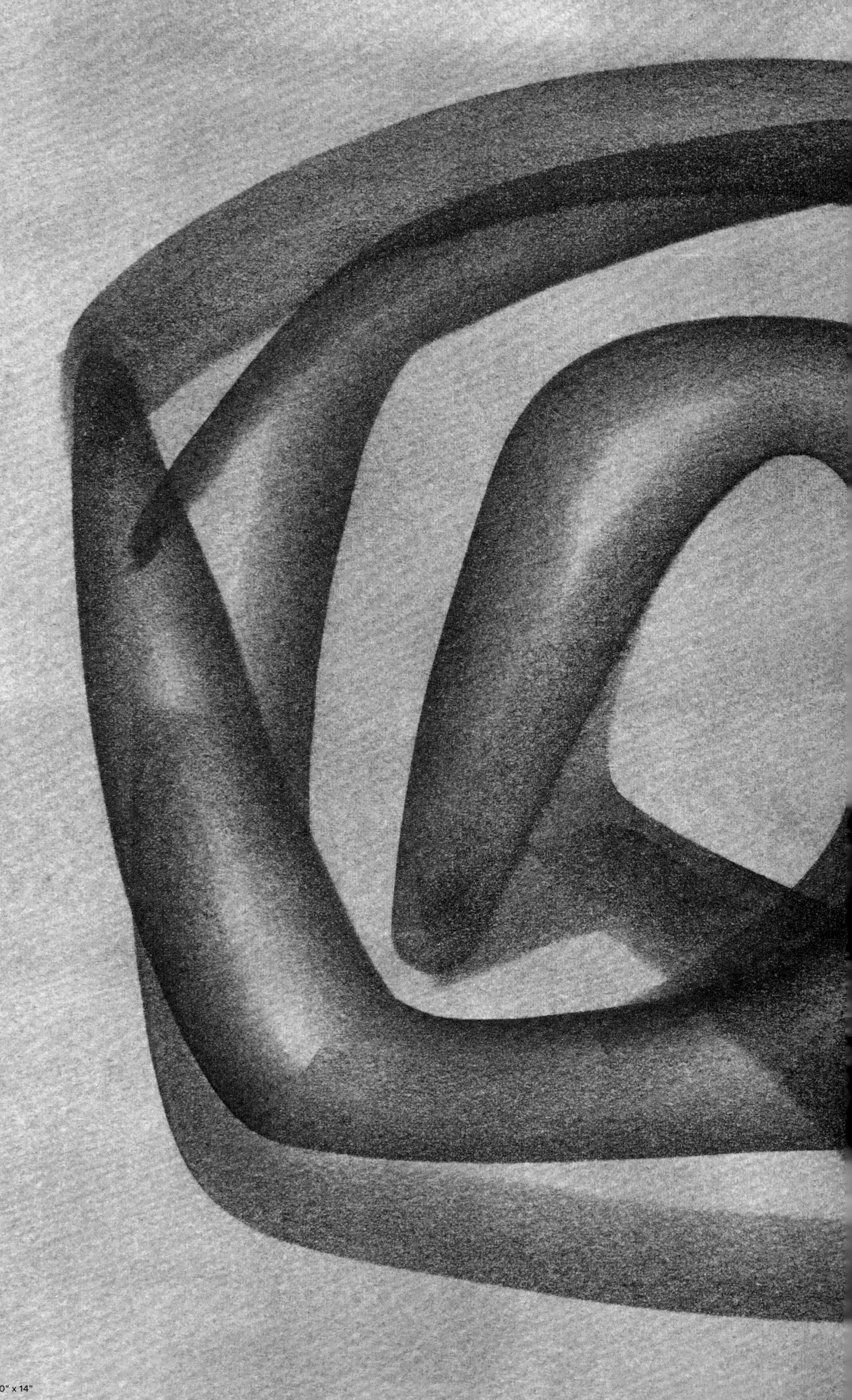

Untitled Graphite Memory
2015. Graphite and Clear Gesso on Paper. 10" x 14"

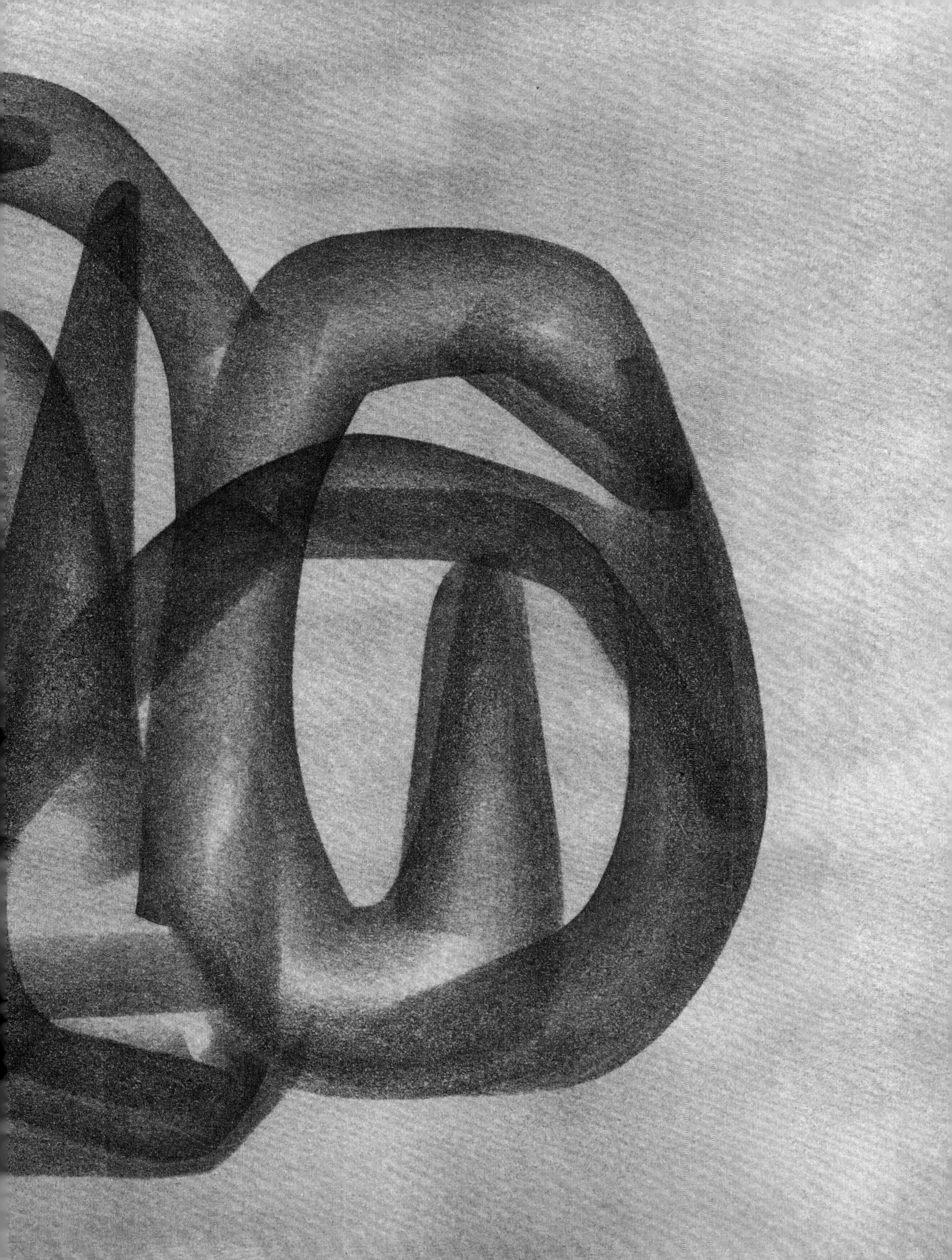

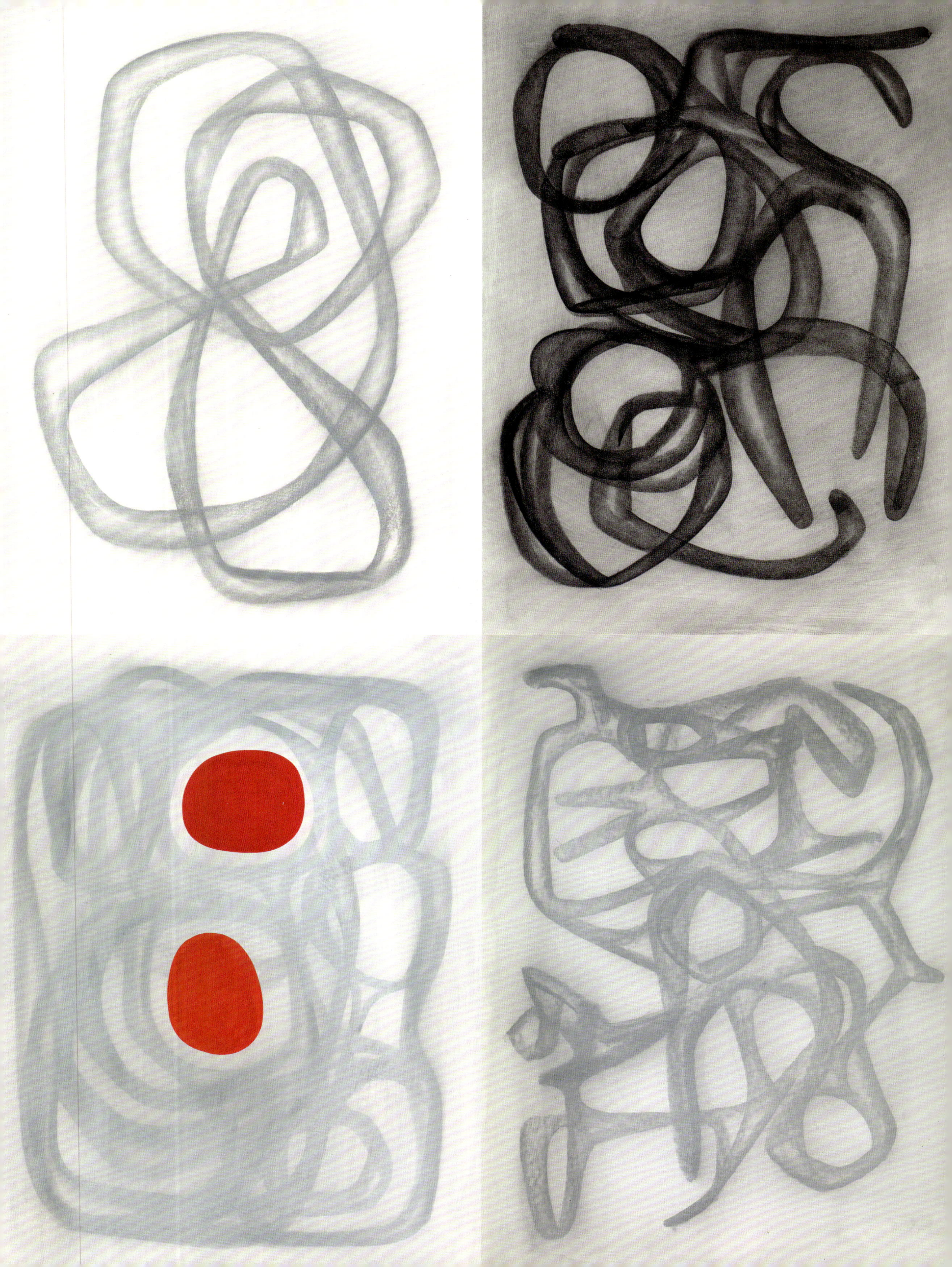

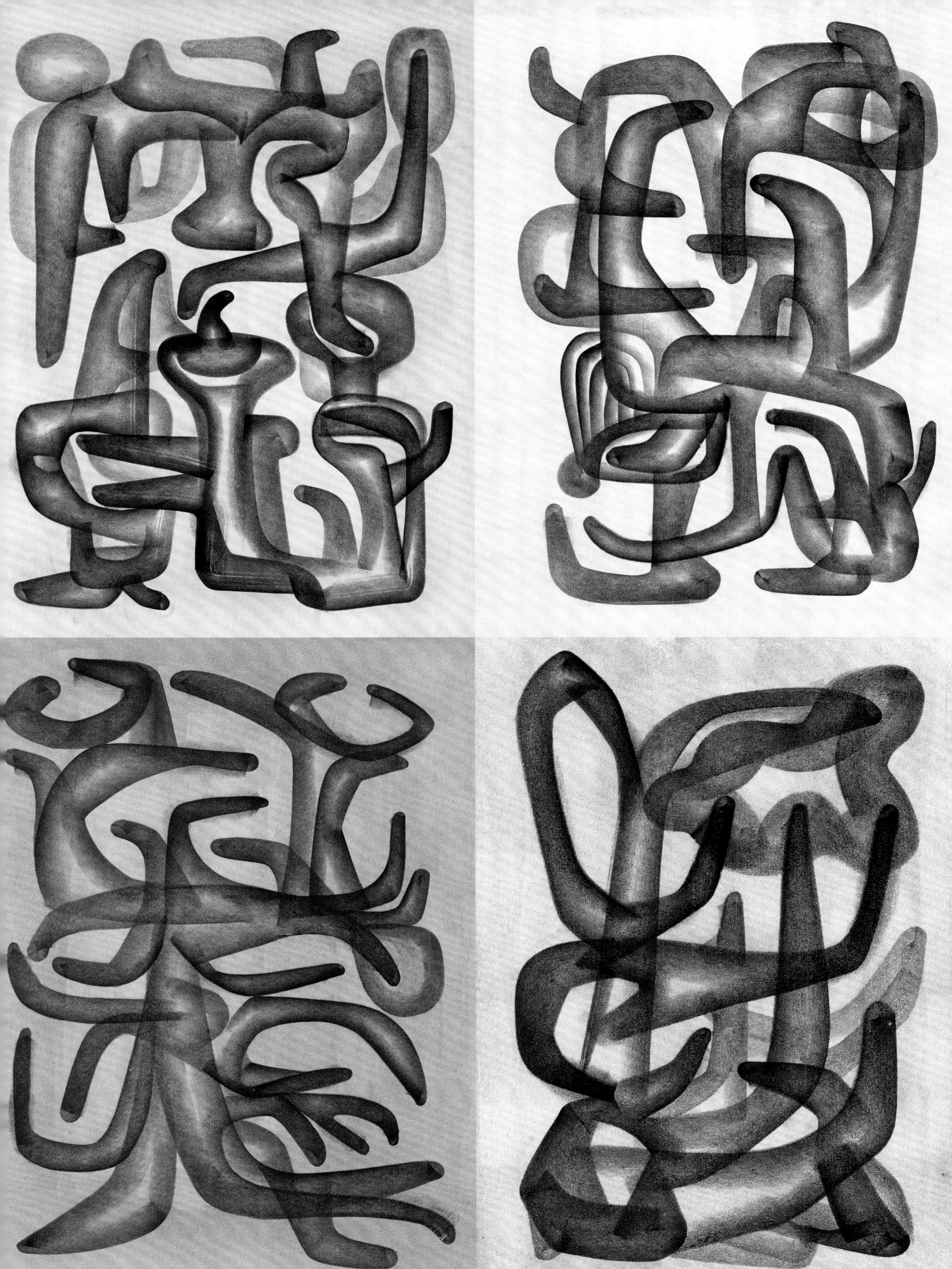

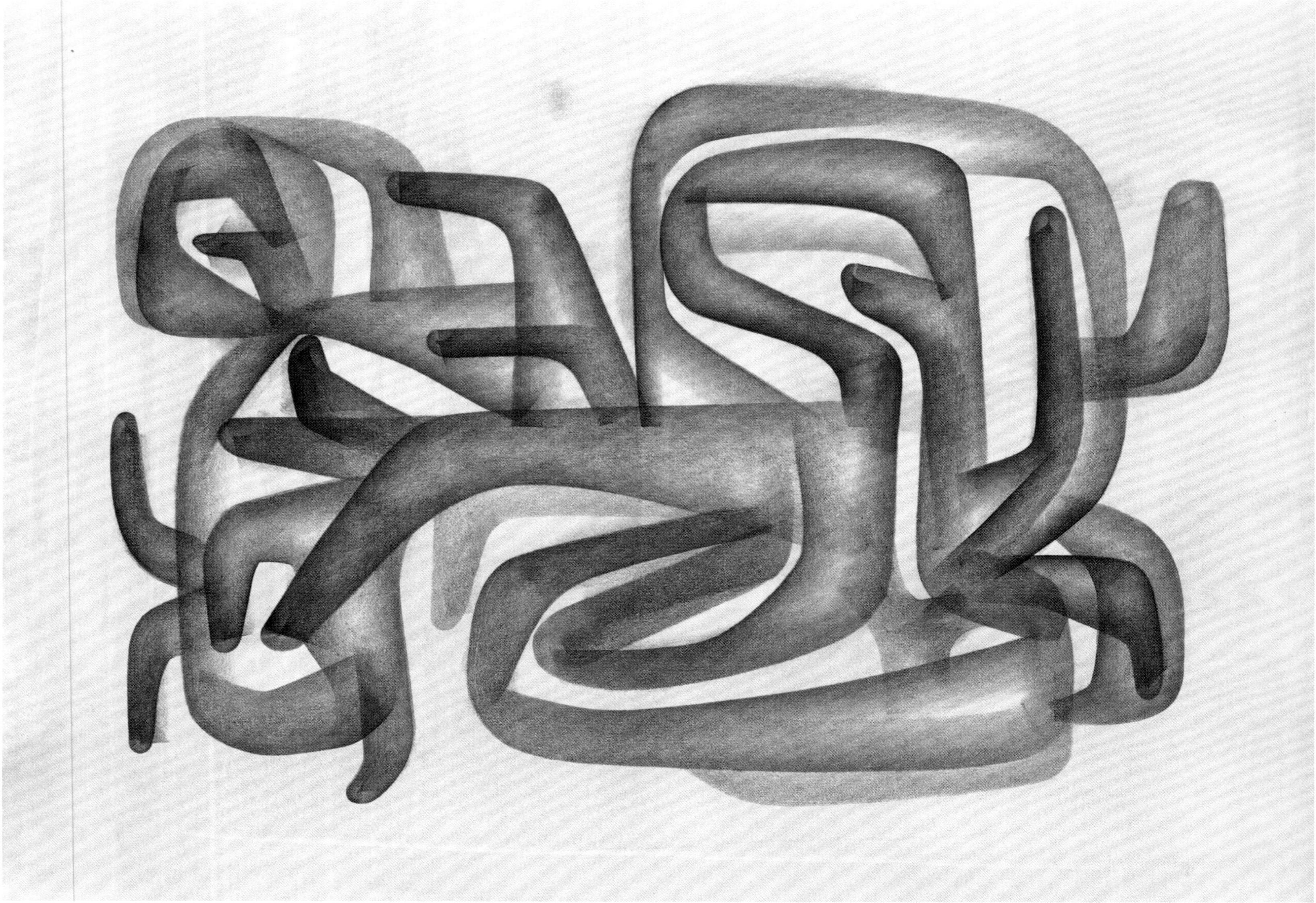

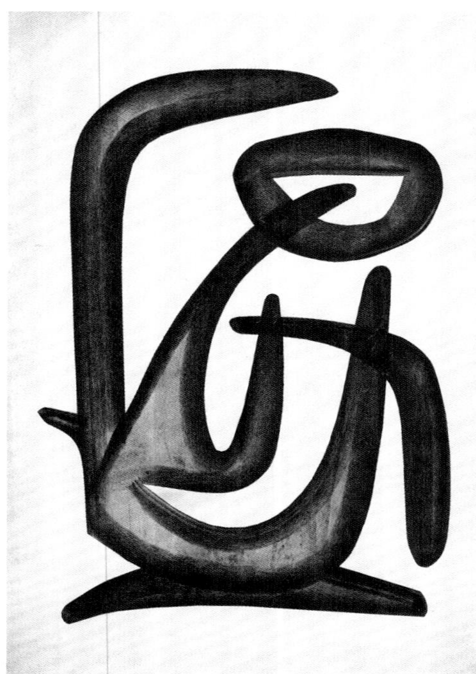

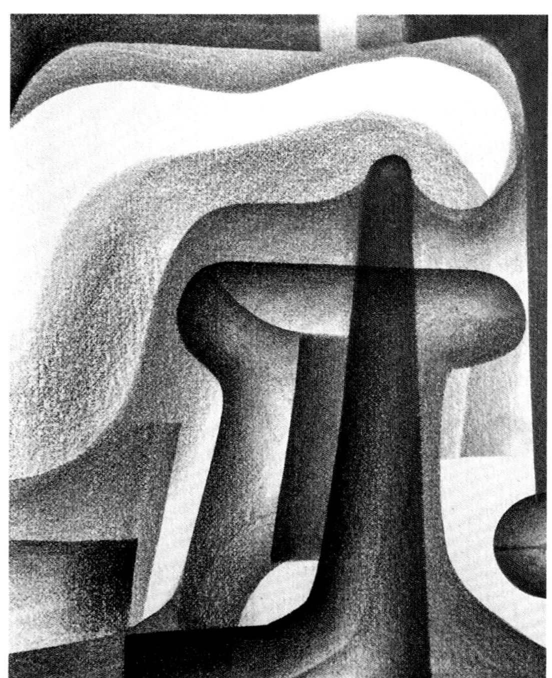

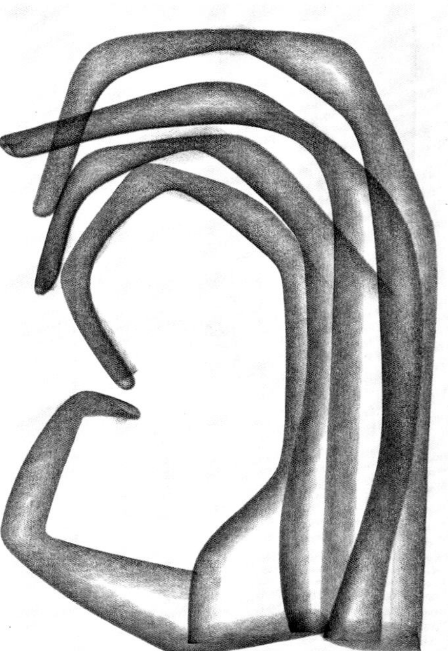

Untitled Graphite Memories
2012-2017. Graphite, Acrylic and Clear Gesso on Paper. Dimensions Vary

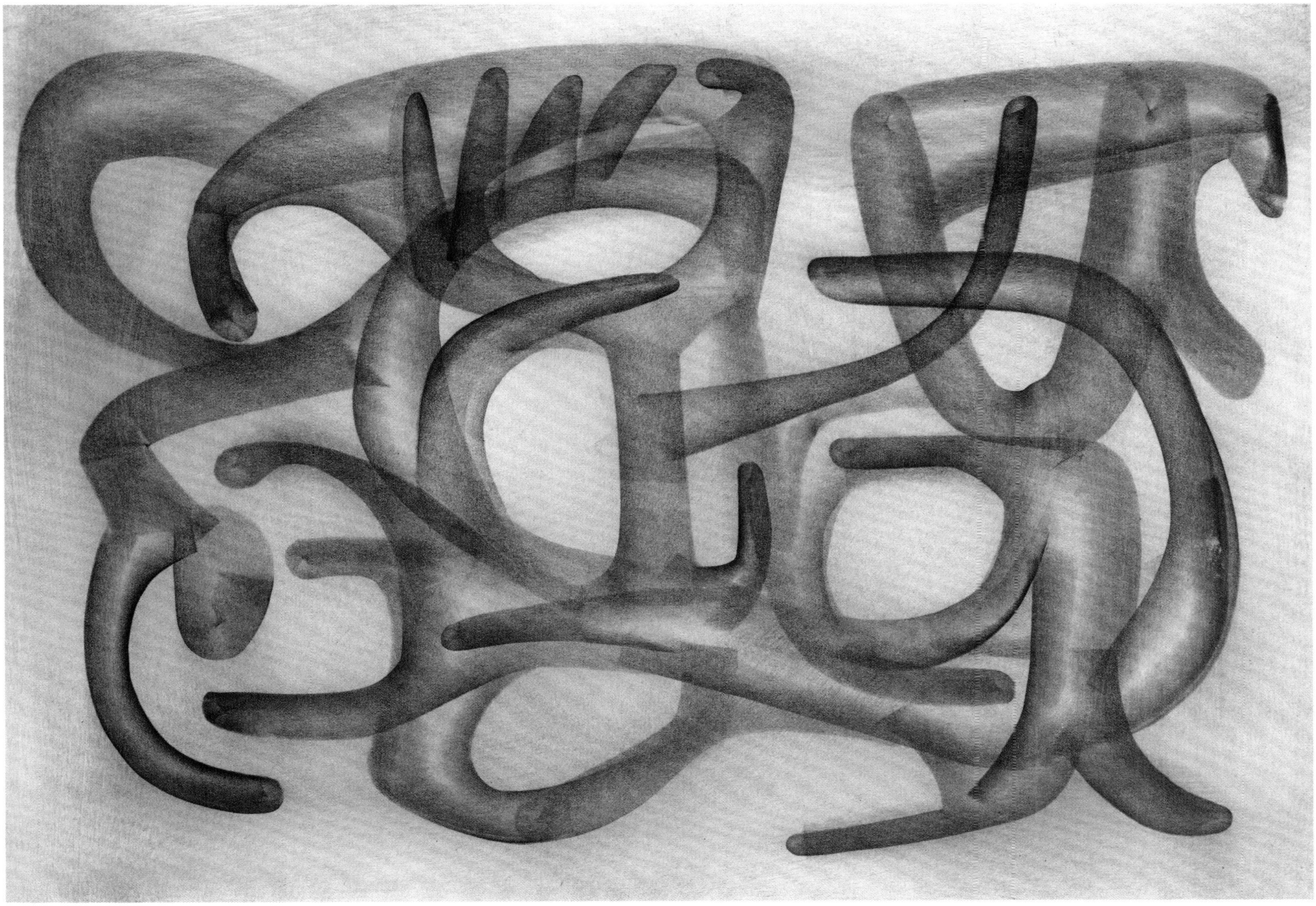

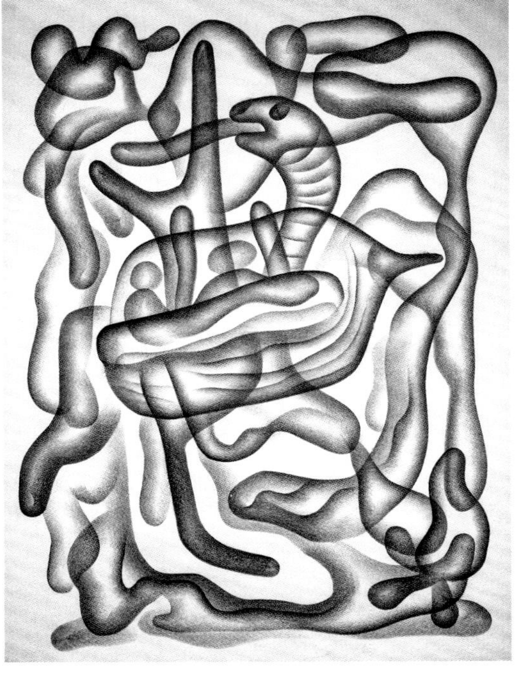

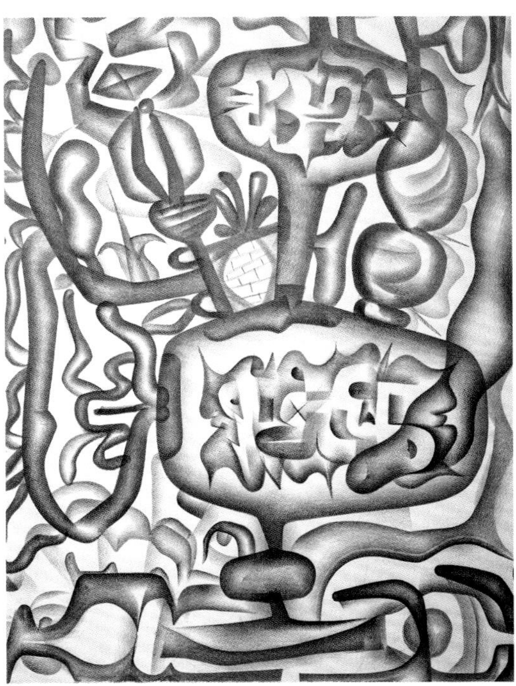

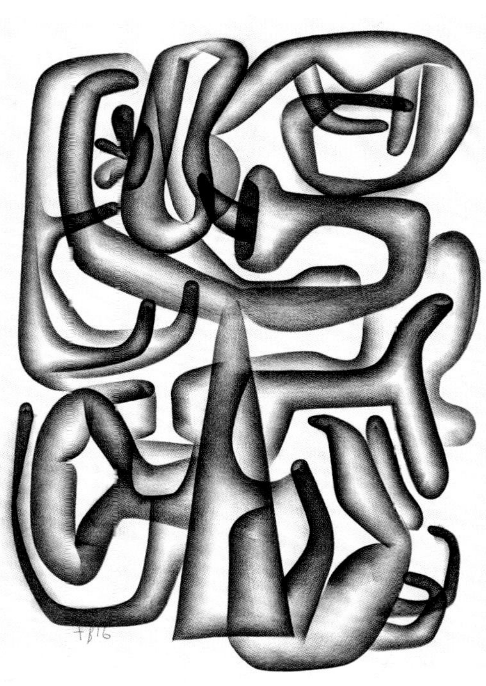

Following pages:

Untitled Graphite Memories
2012-2017. Graphite, Acrylic and Clear Gesso on Paper. Dimensions Vary

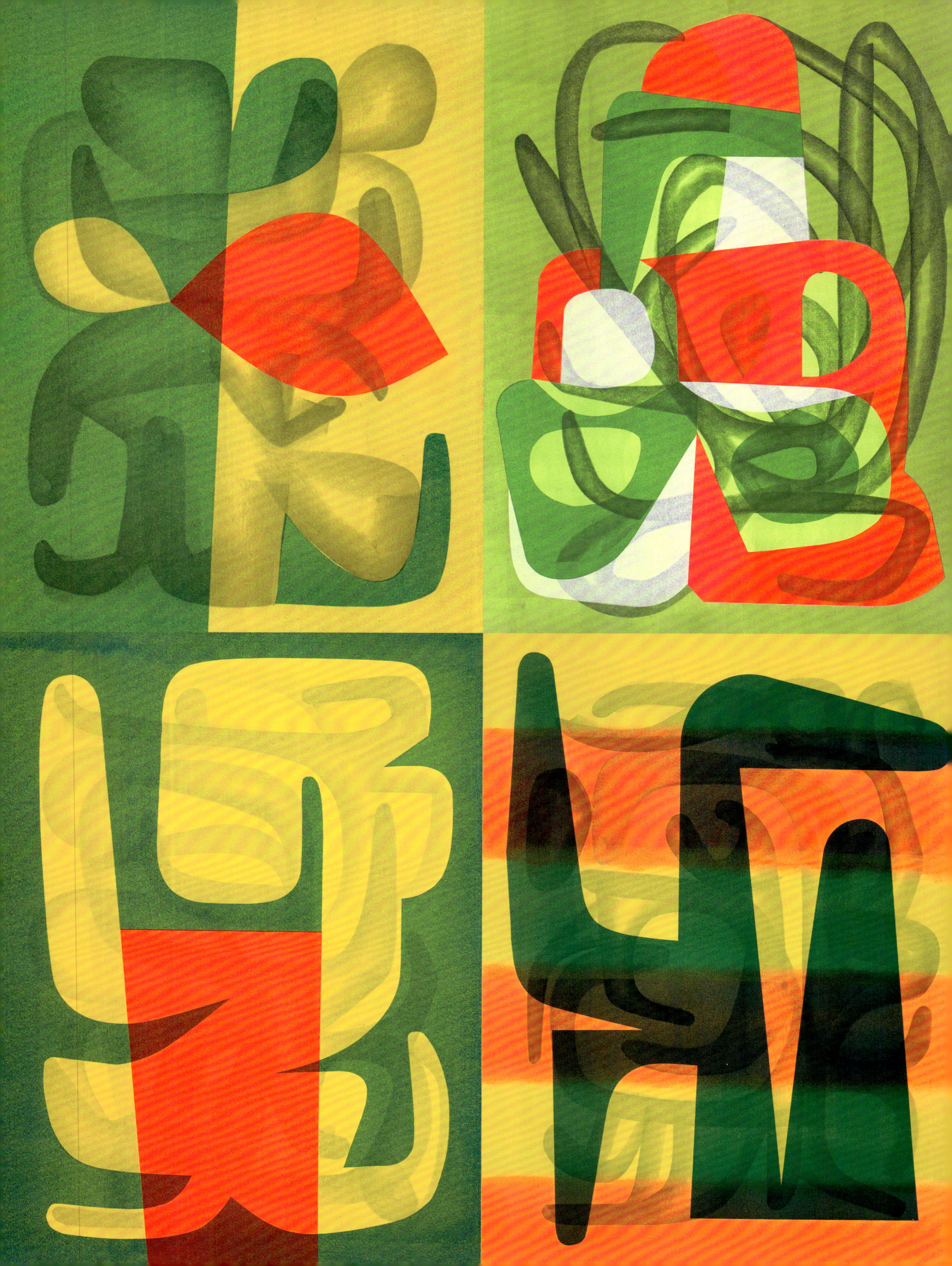

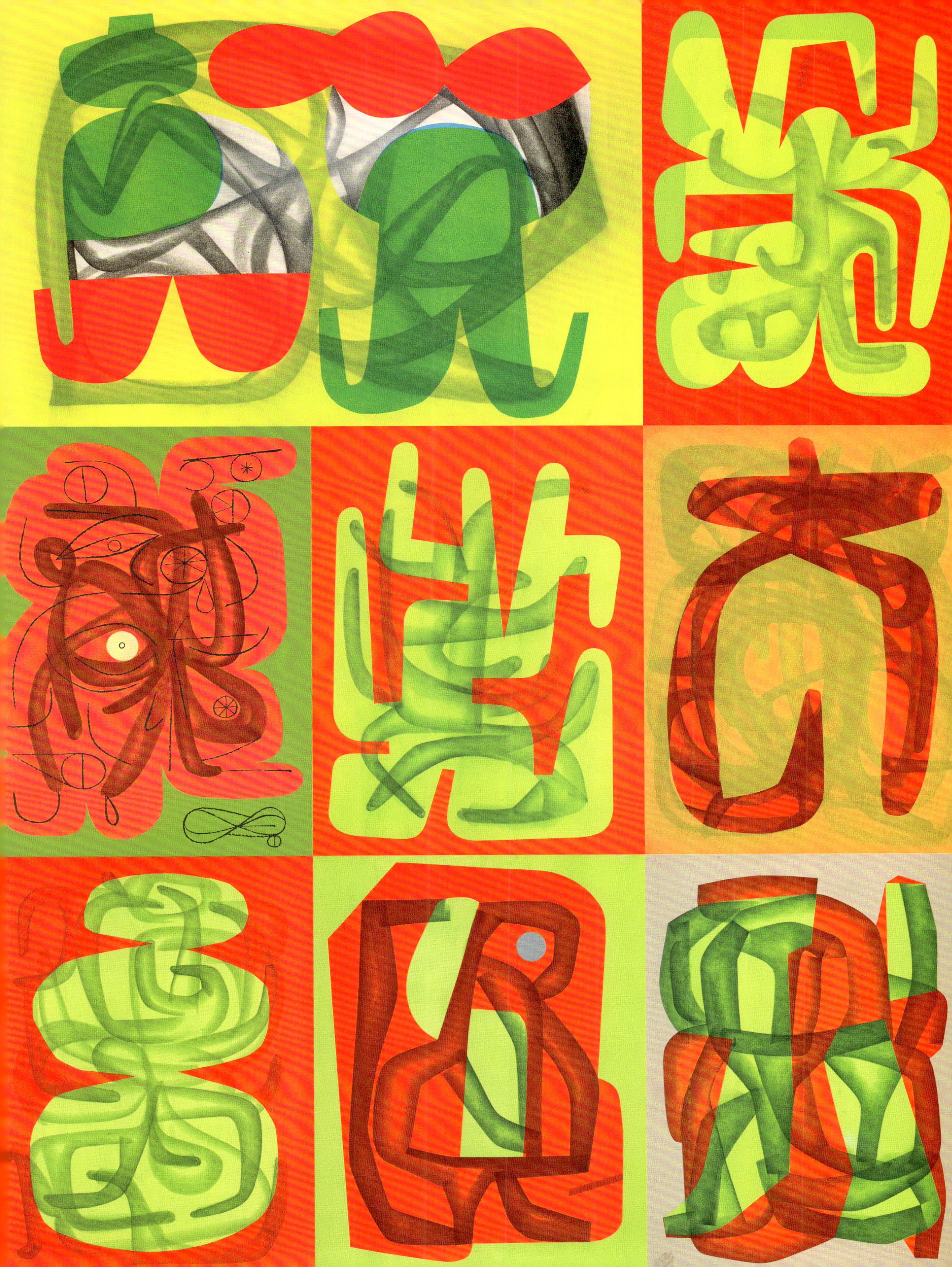

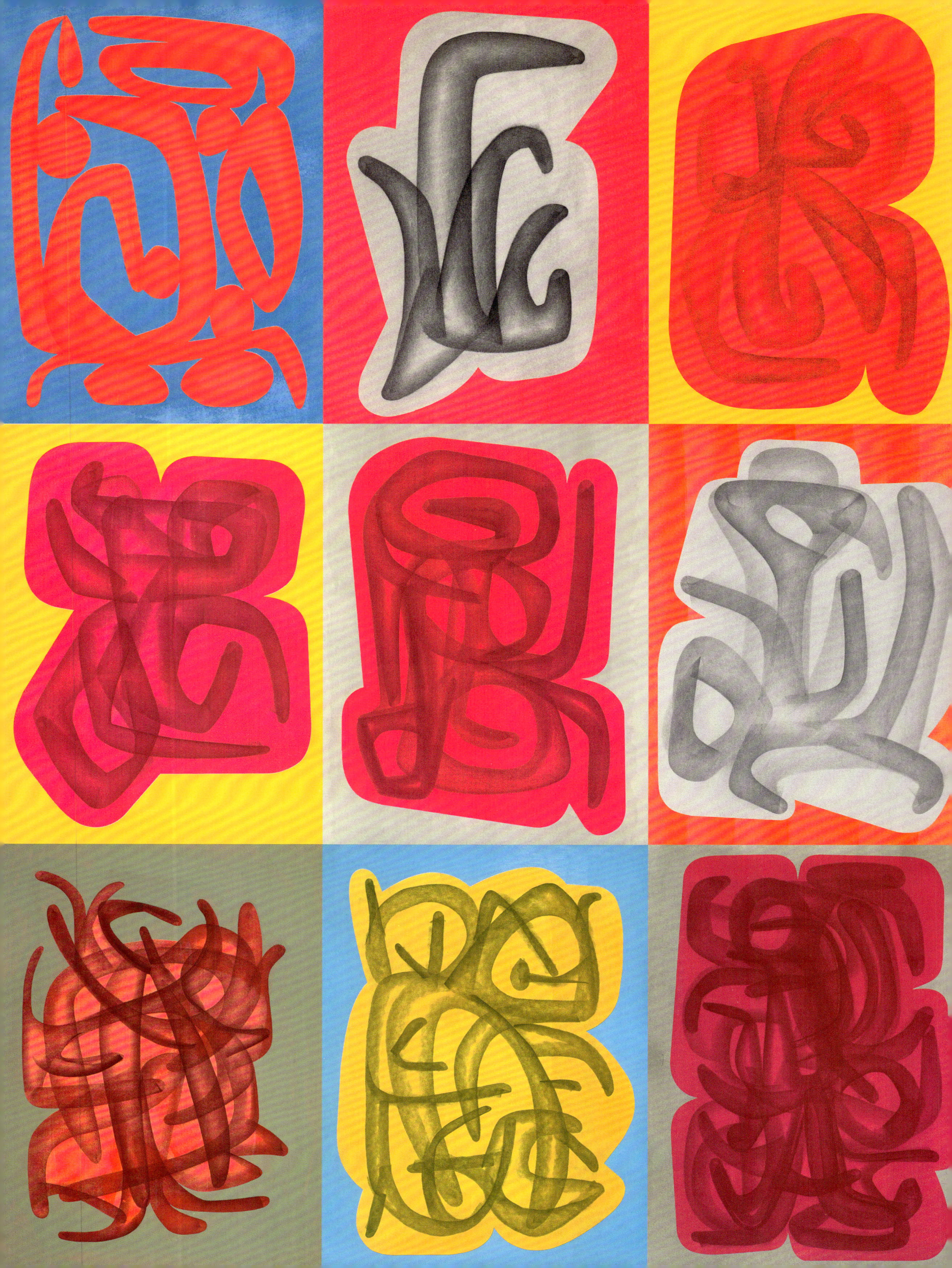

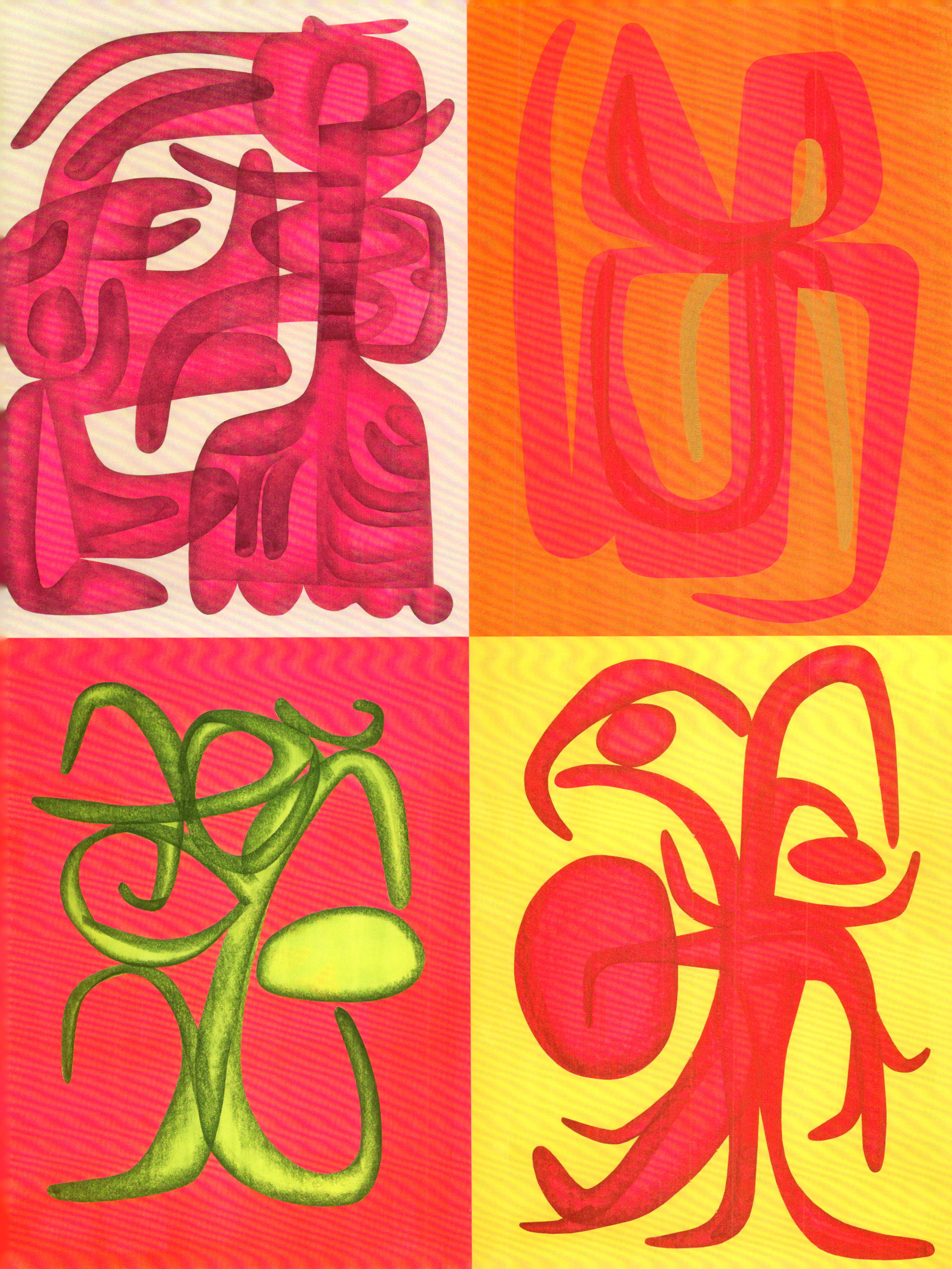

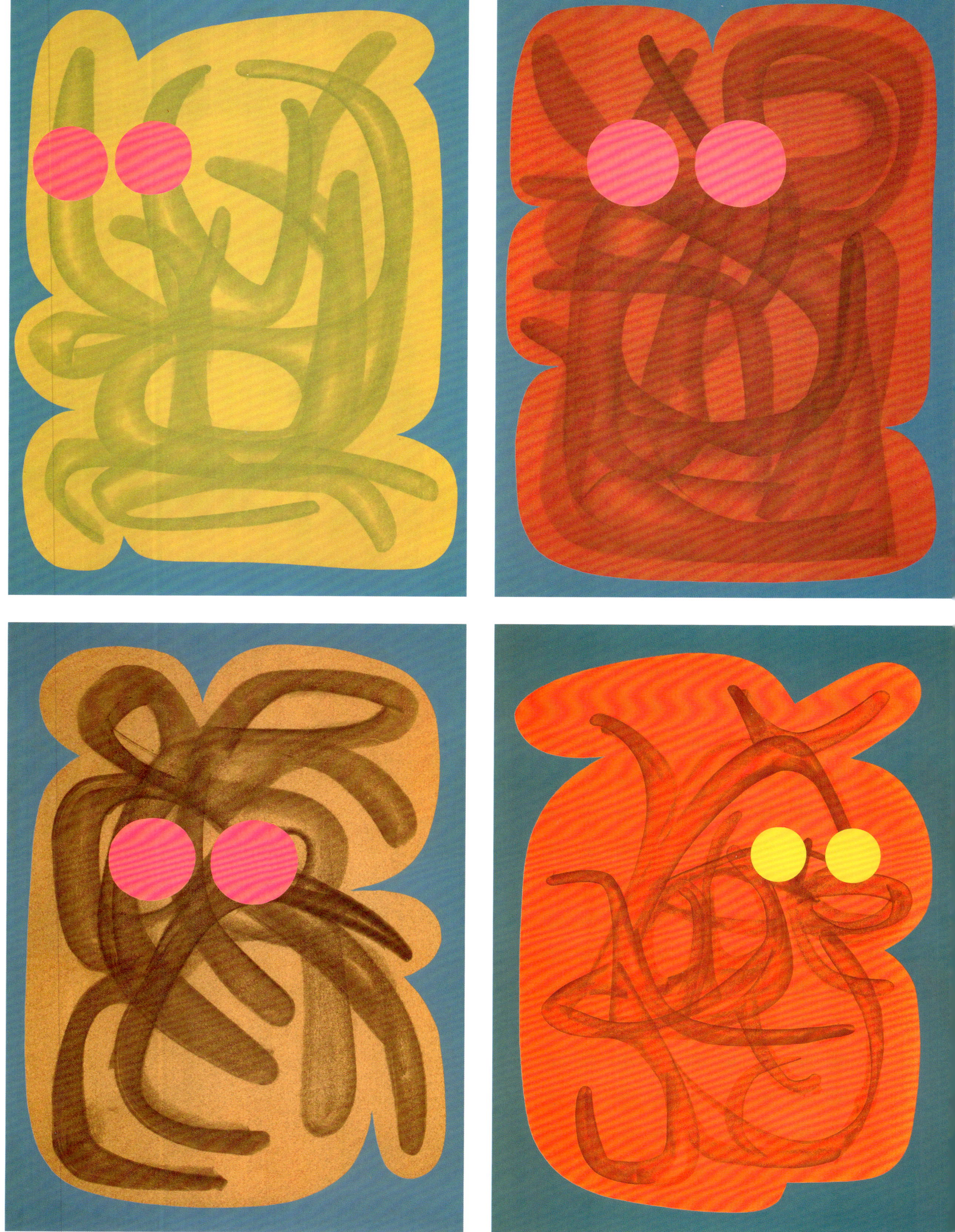

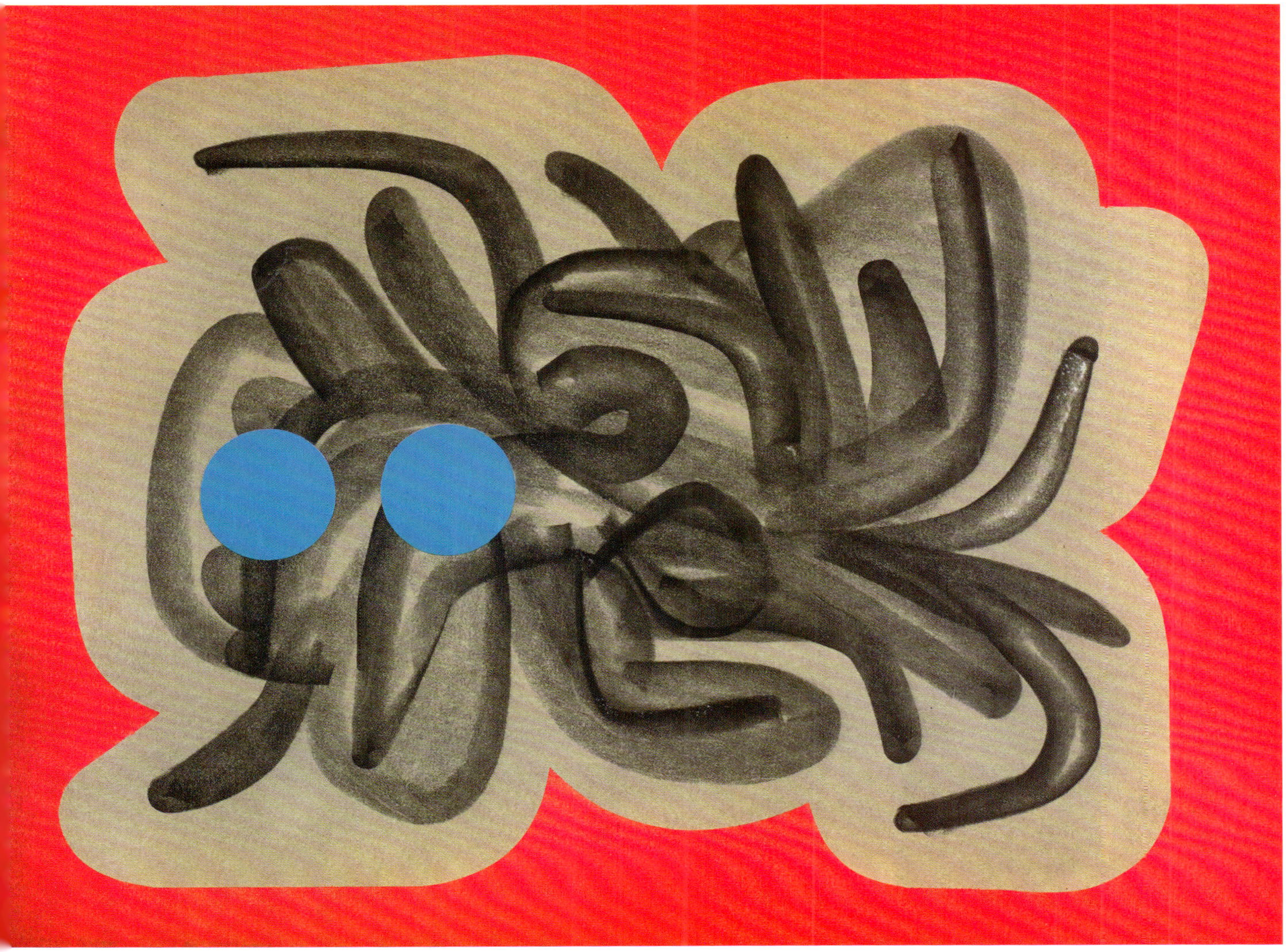

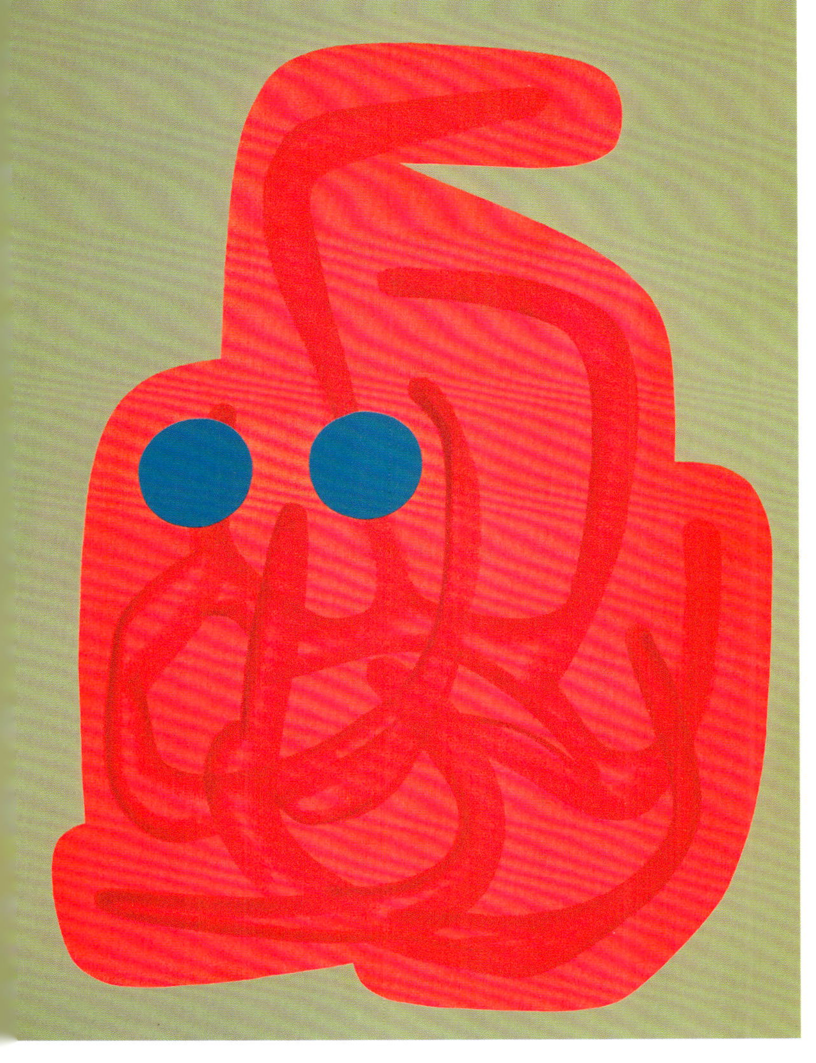
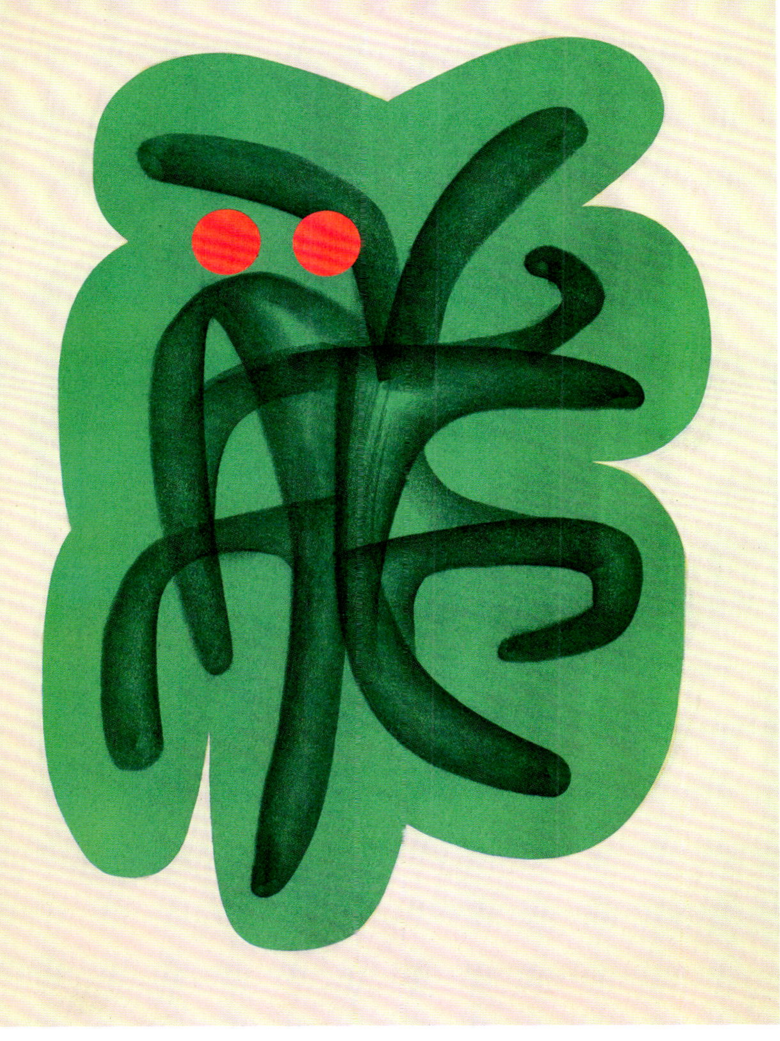

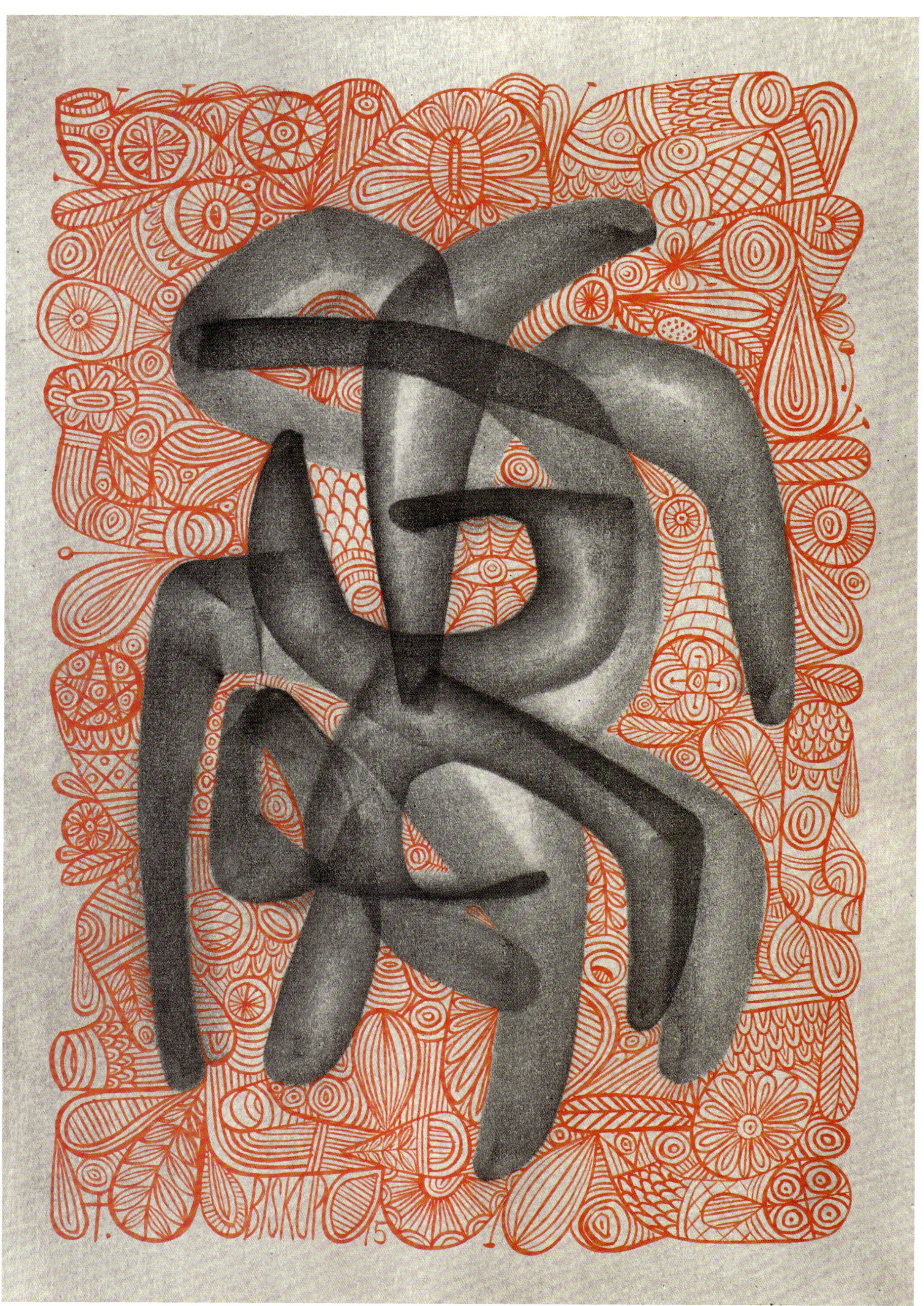

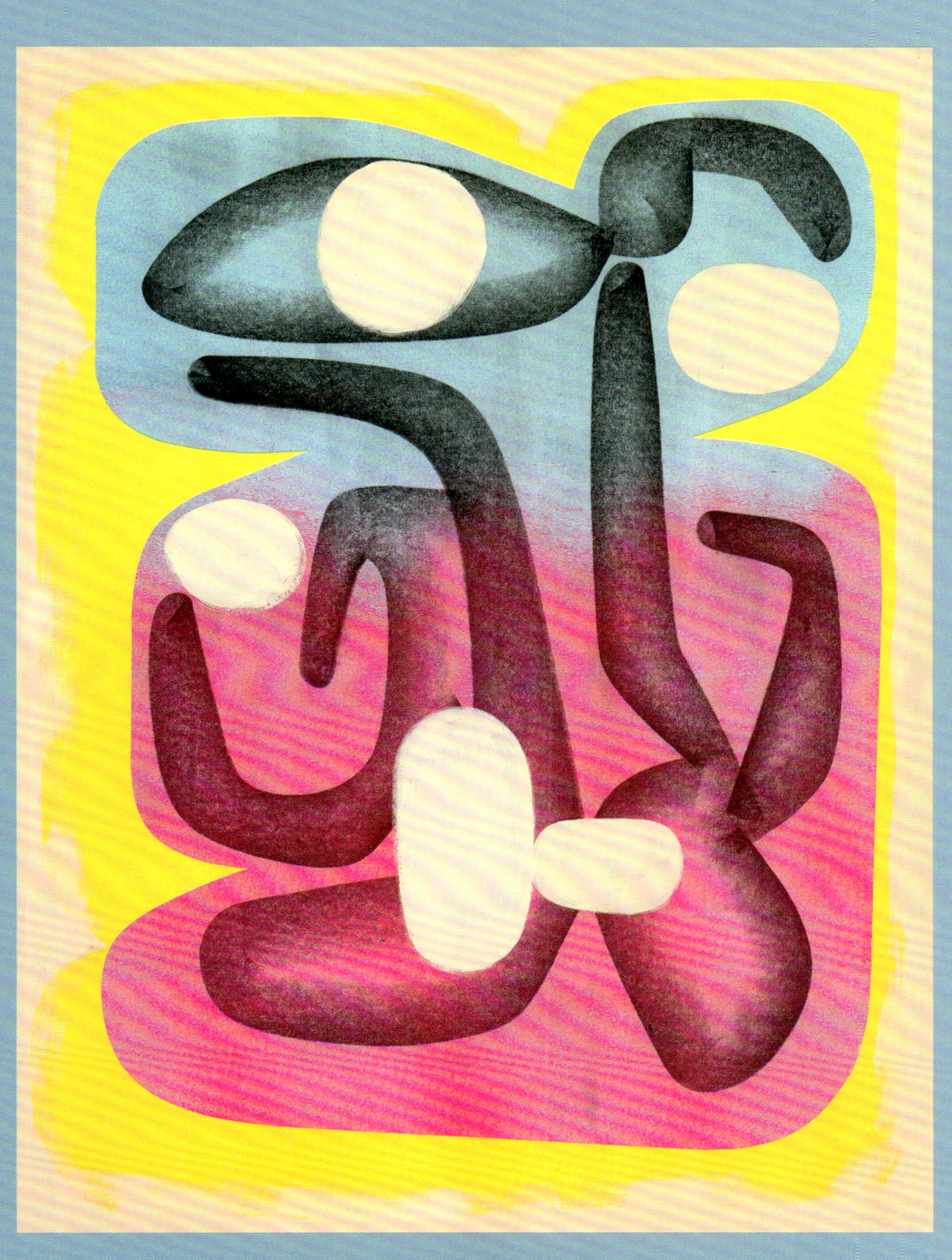

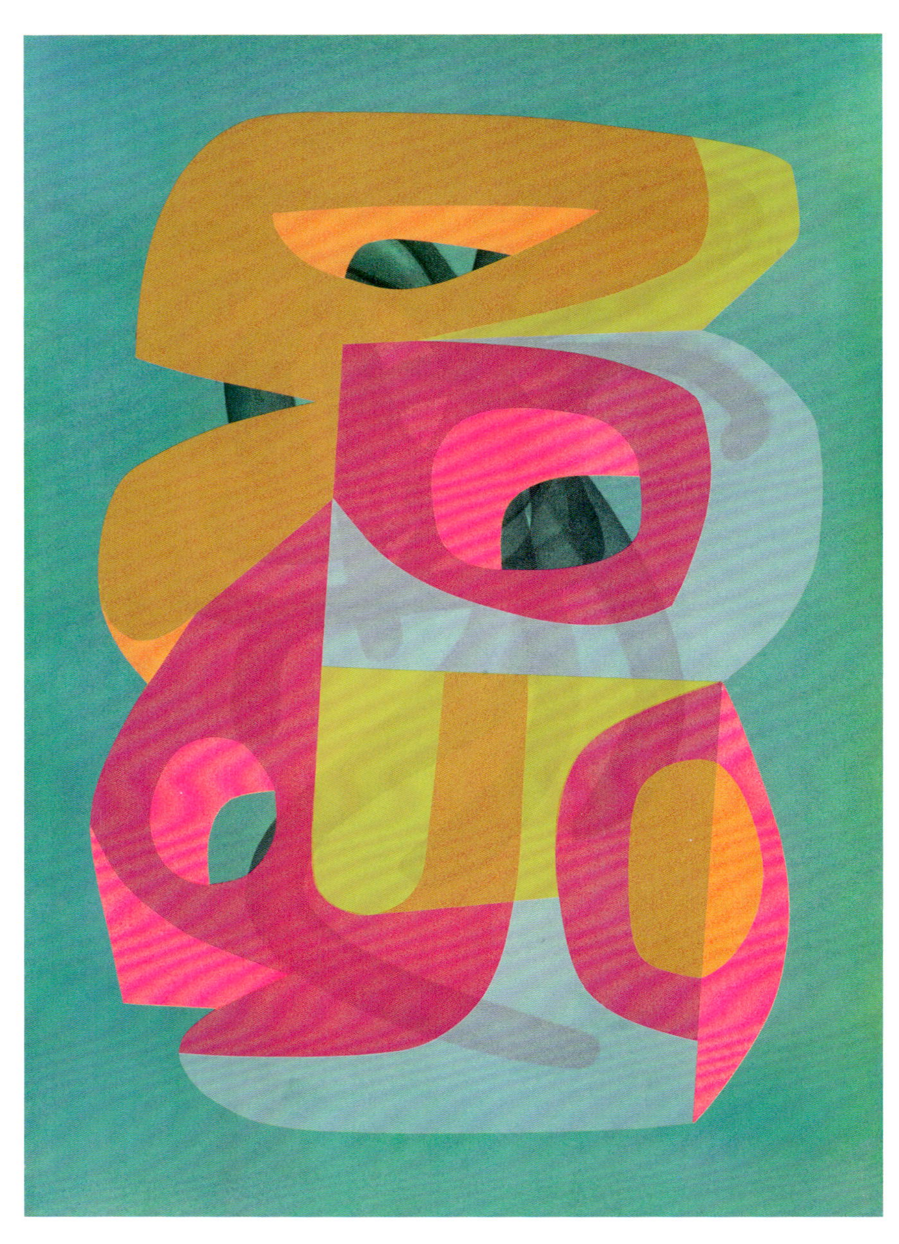

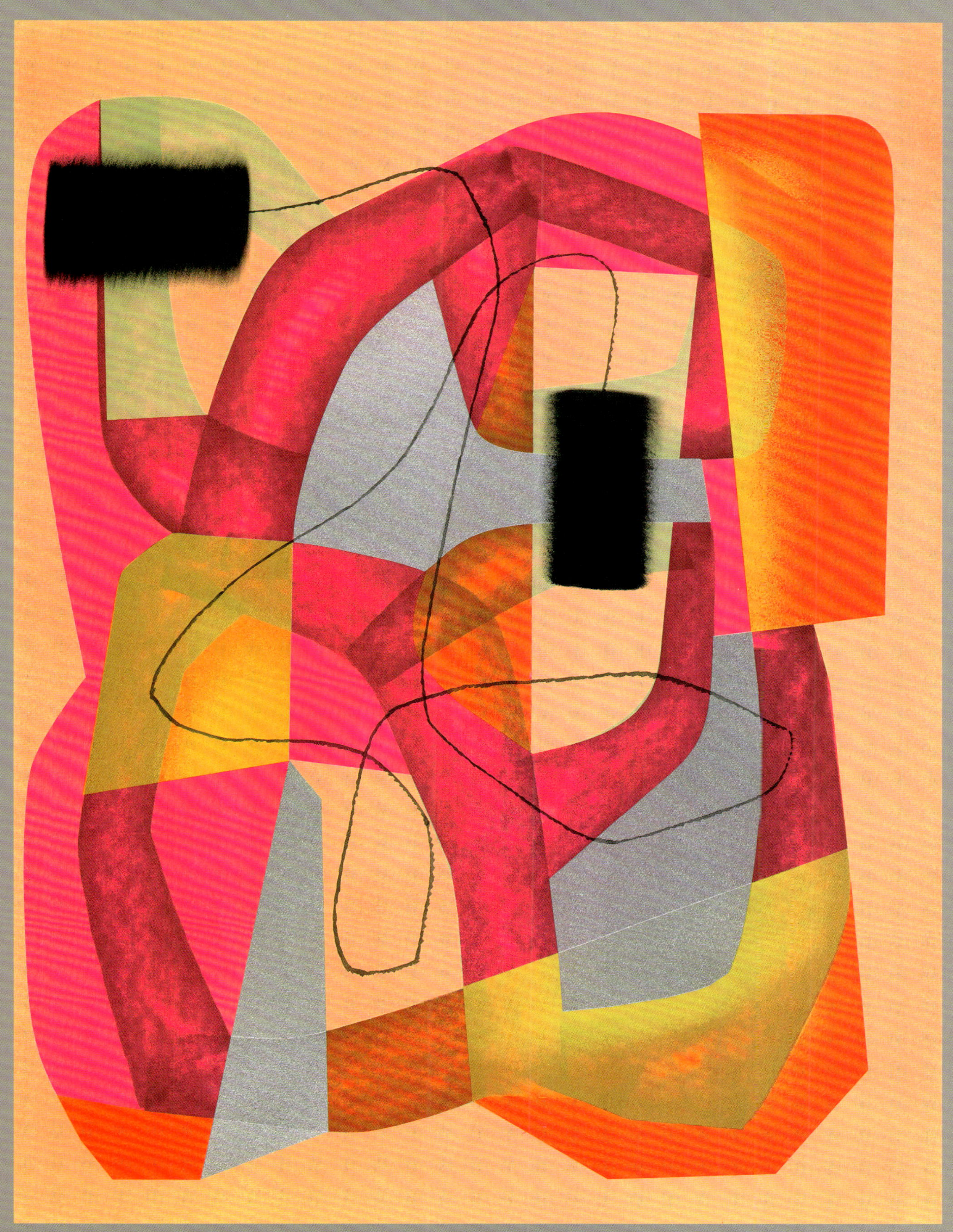

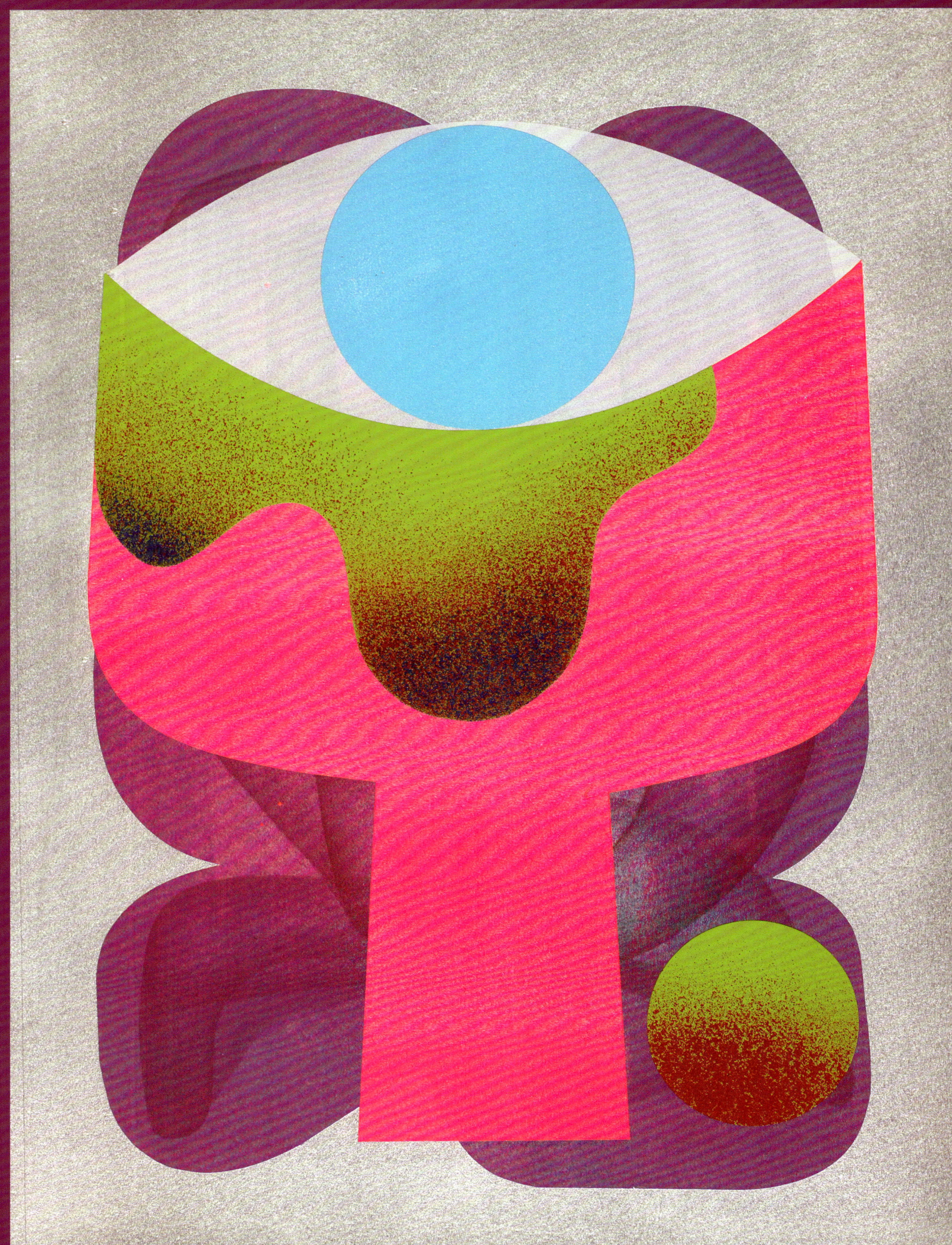

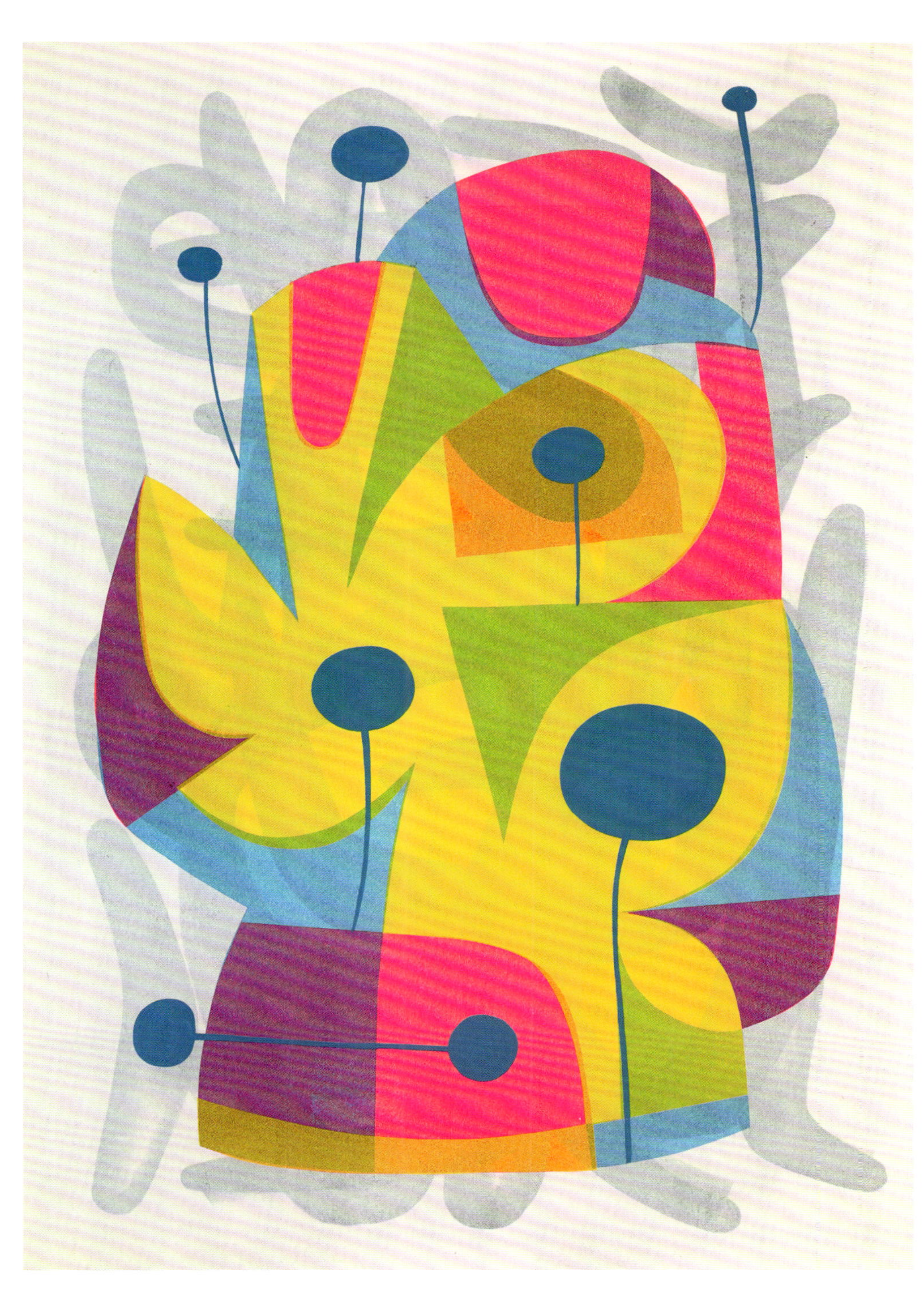

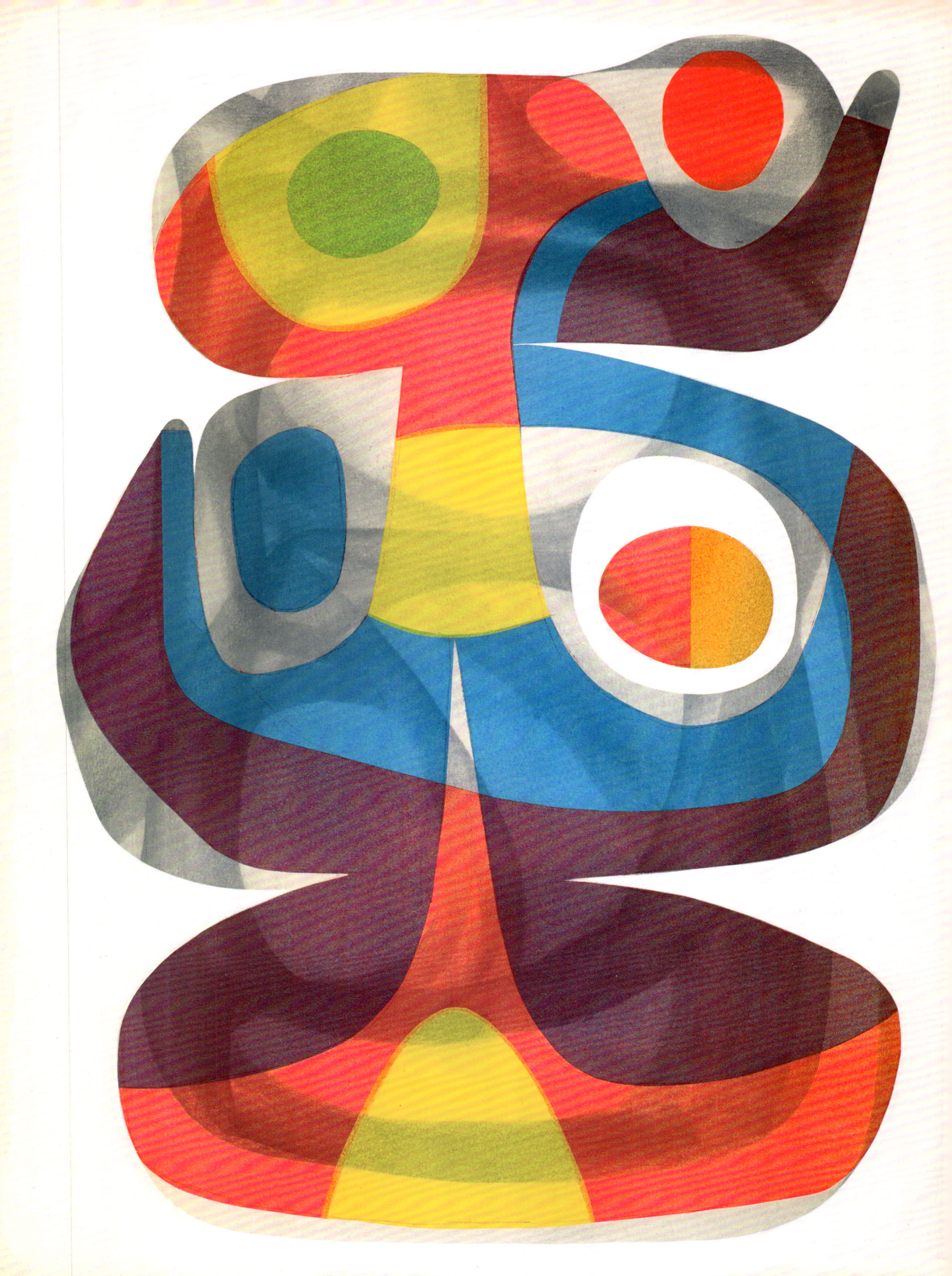

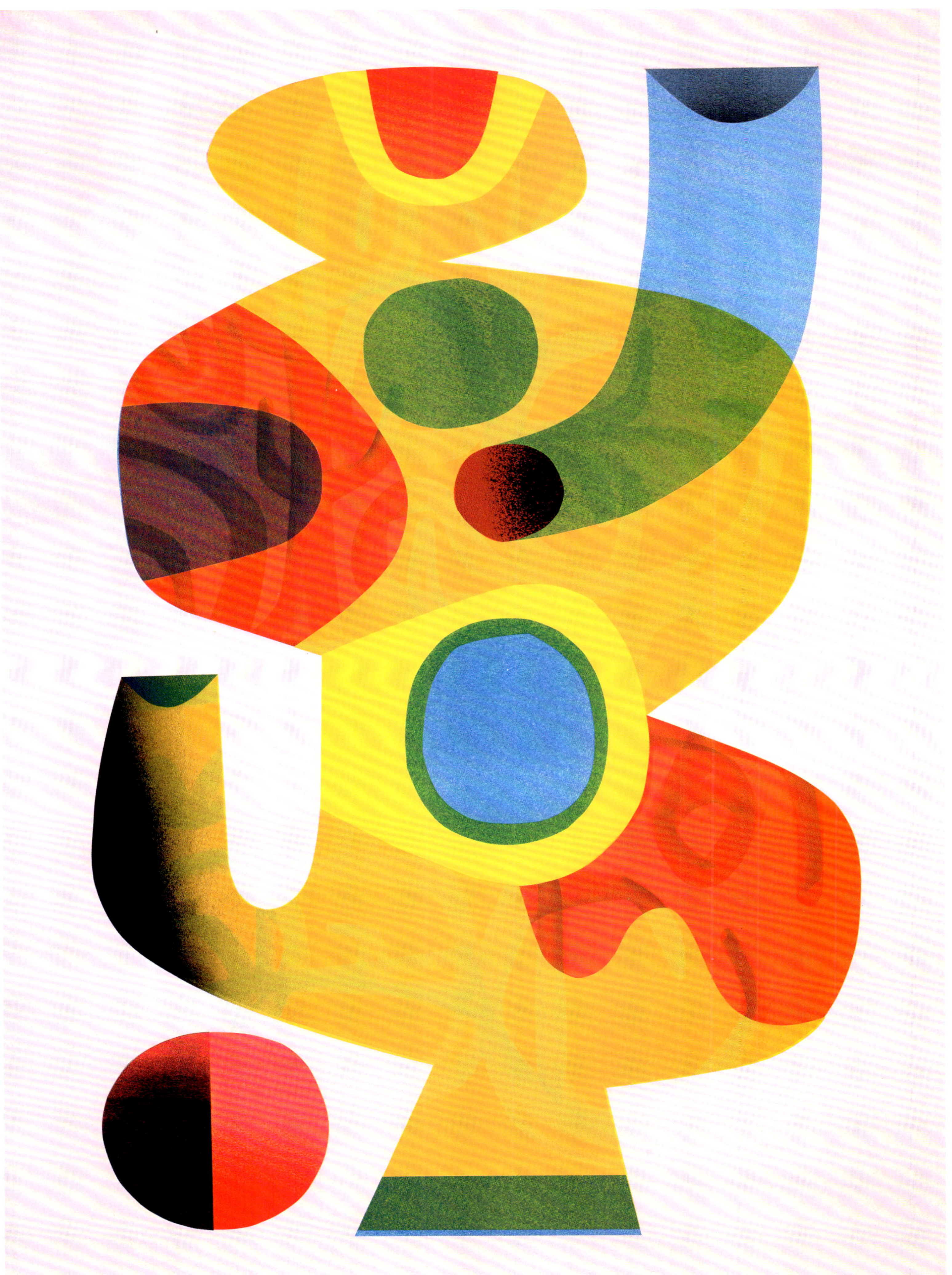

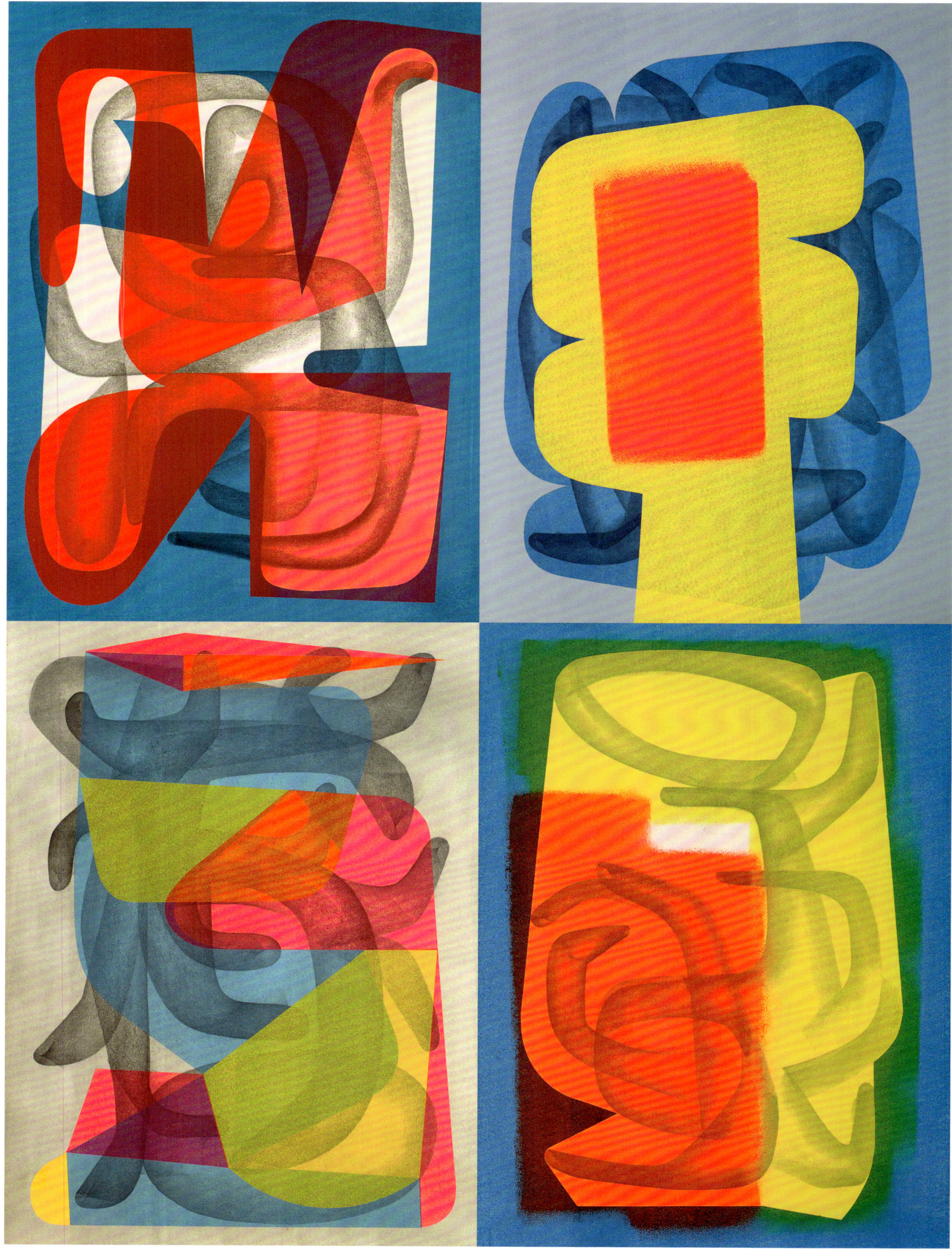

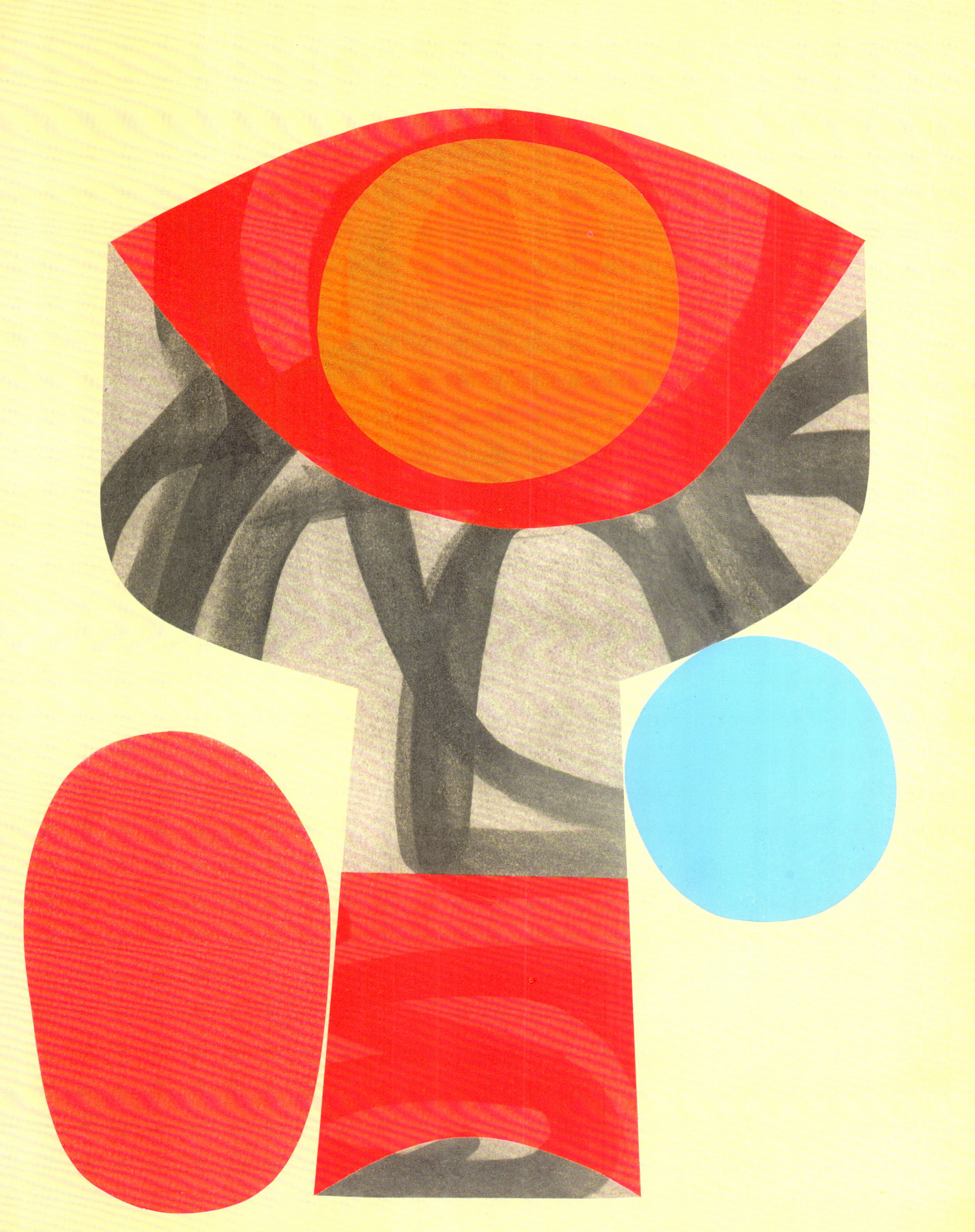

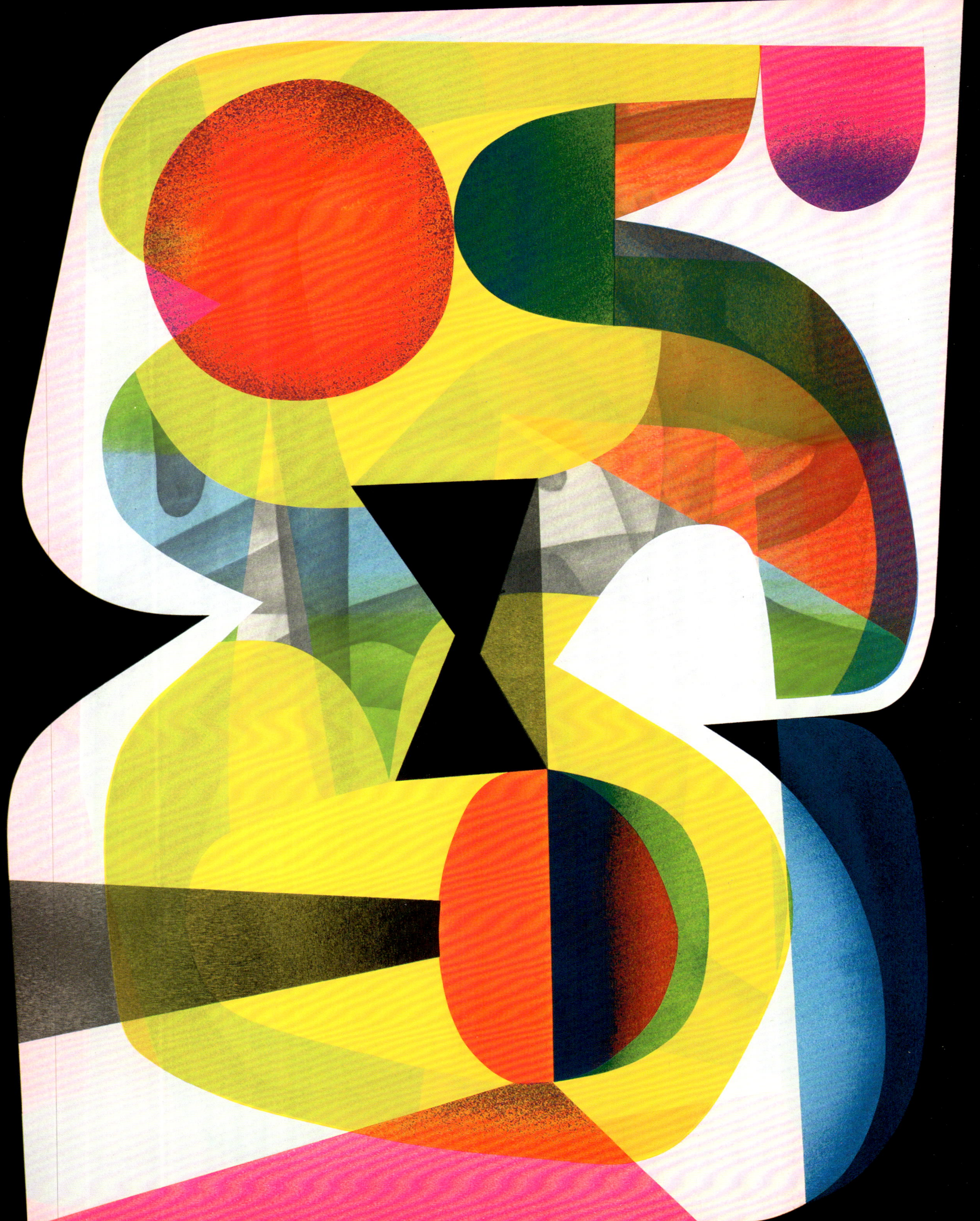

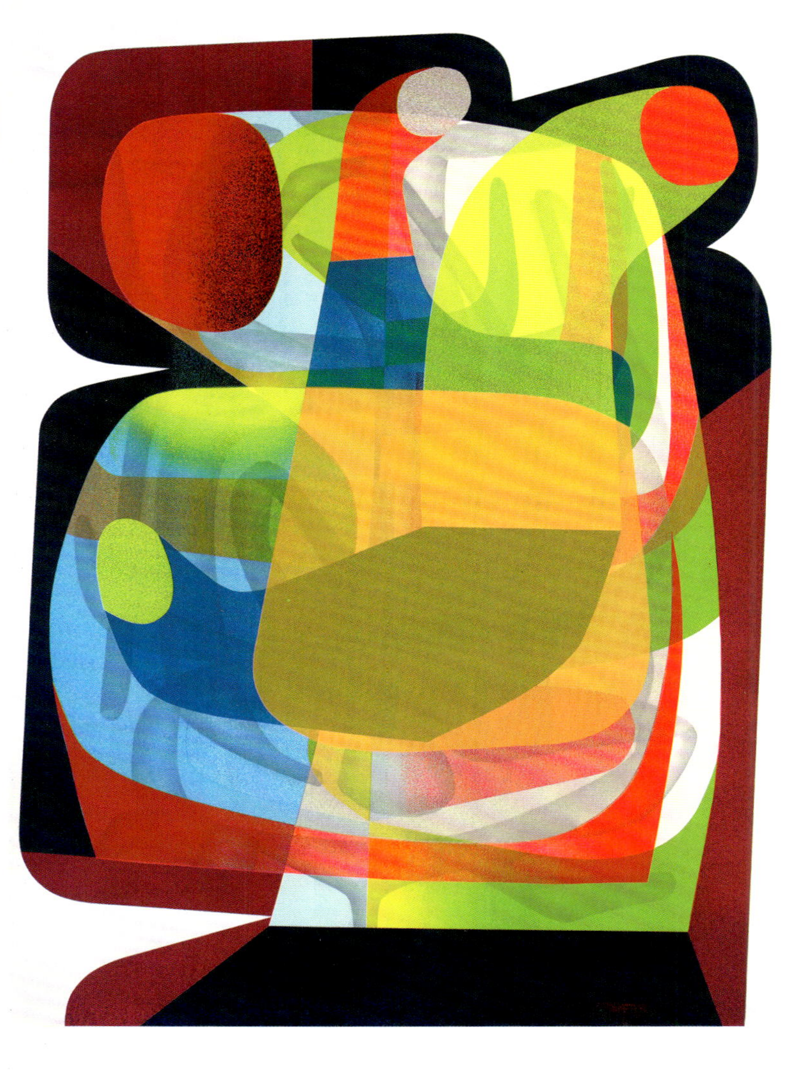

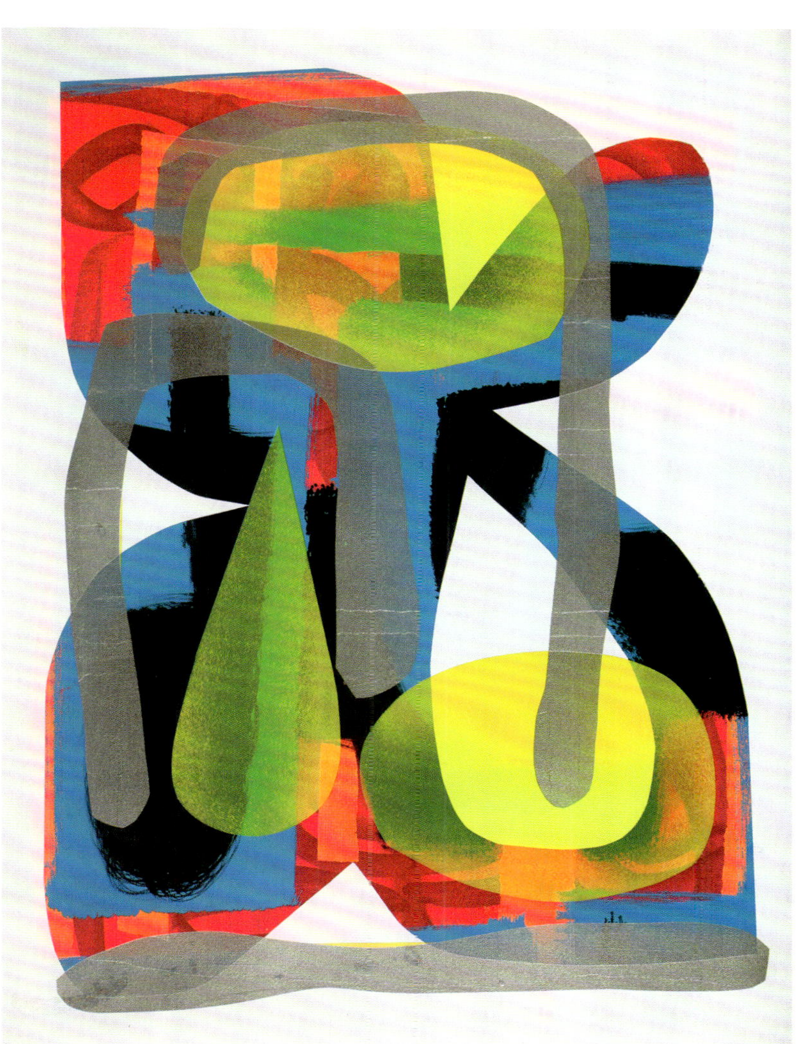

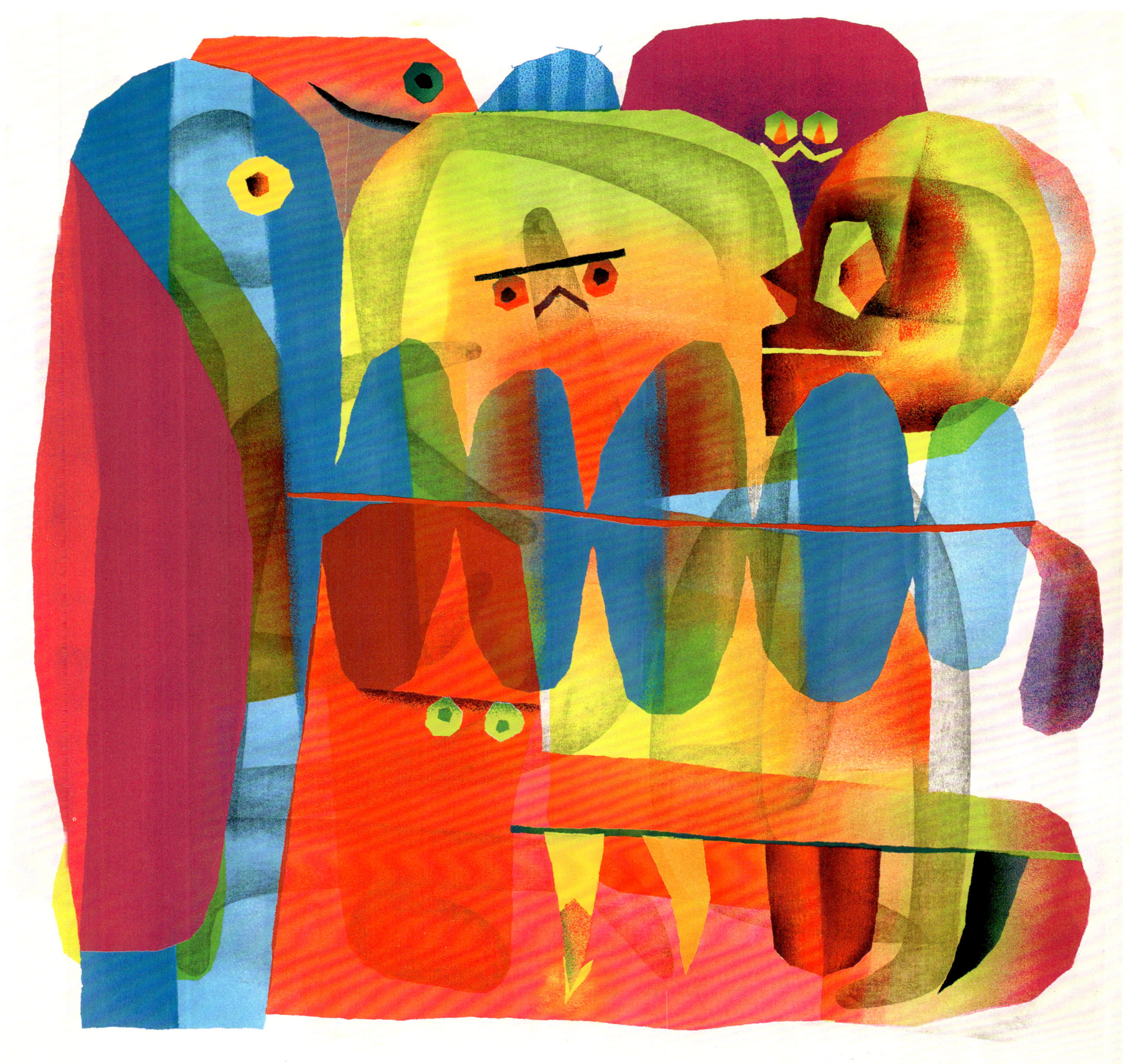

Space Madness No 2
2015. Graphite, Acrylic, Gesso and Clear Gesso on Canvas. 36" x 36"

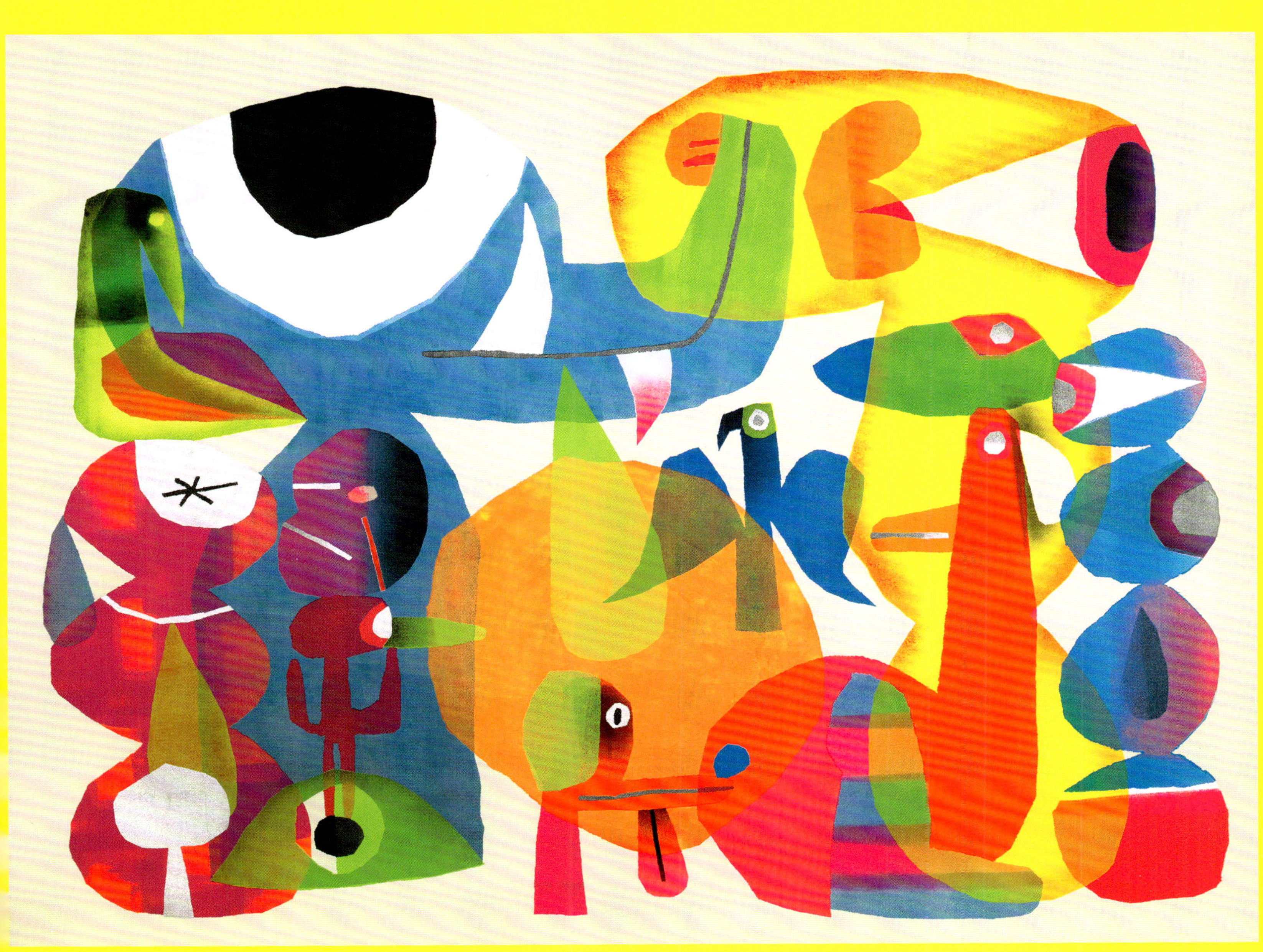

Flat Agency
2016. Acrylic and Gesso on Canvas. 54" x 72"

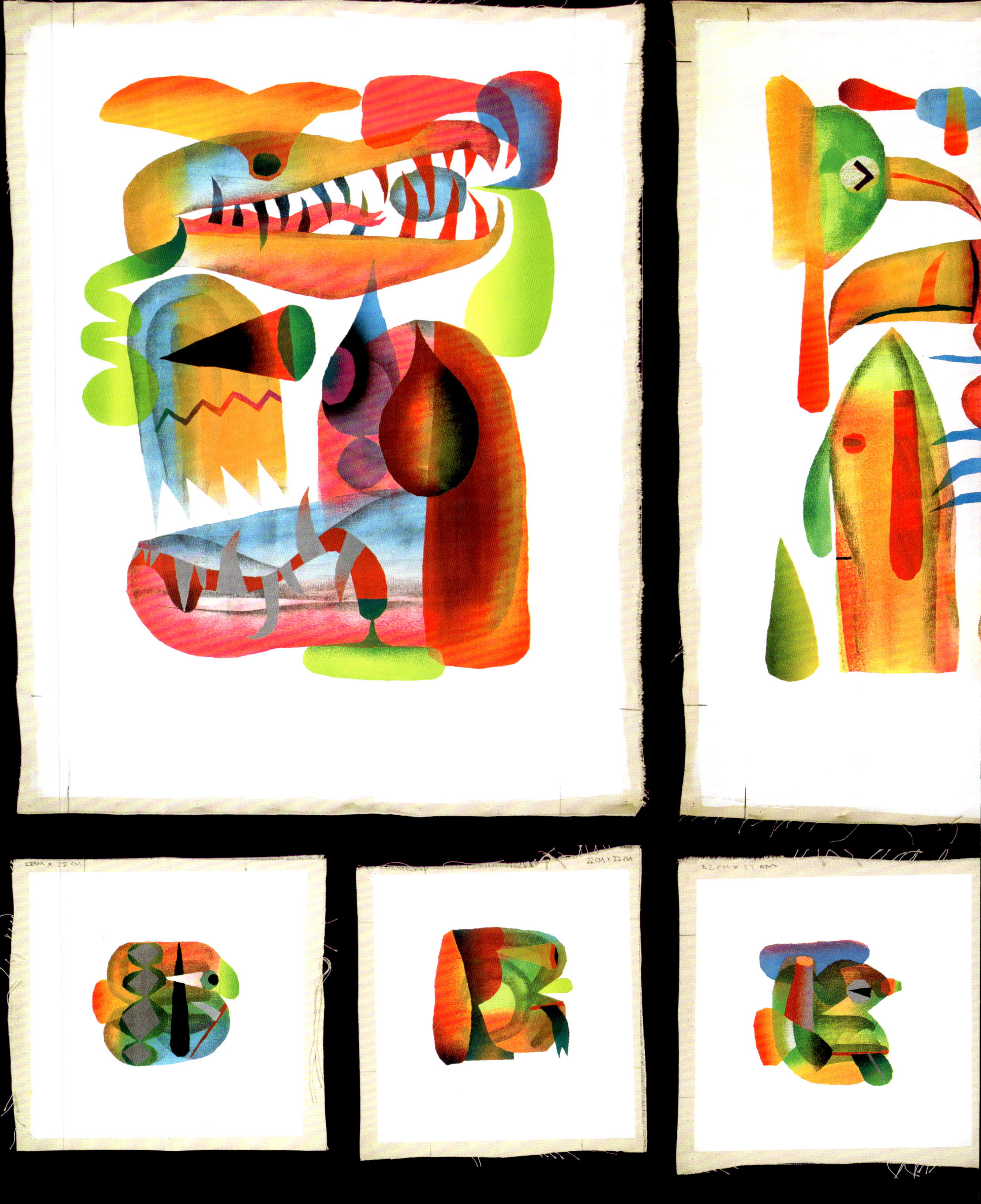

Space Madness No 6 - 8
2015. Graphite, Acrylic, Gesso and Clear Gesso on Canvas. 32" x 24"

Space Madness No 12-17
2015. Graphite, Acrylic, Gesso and Clear Gesso on Canvas. 9" x 9"

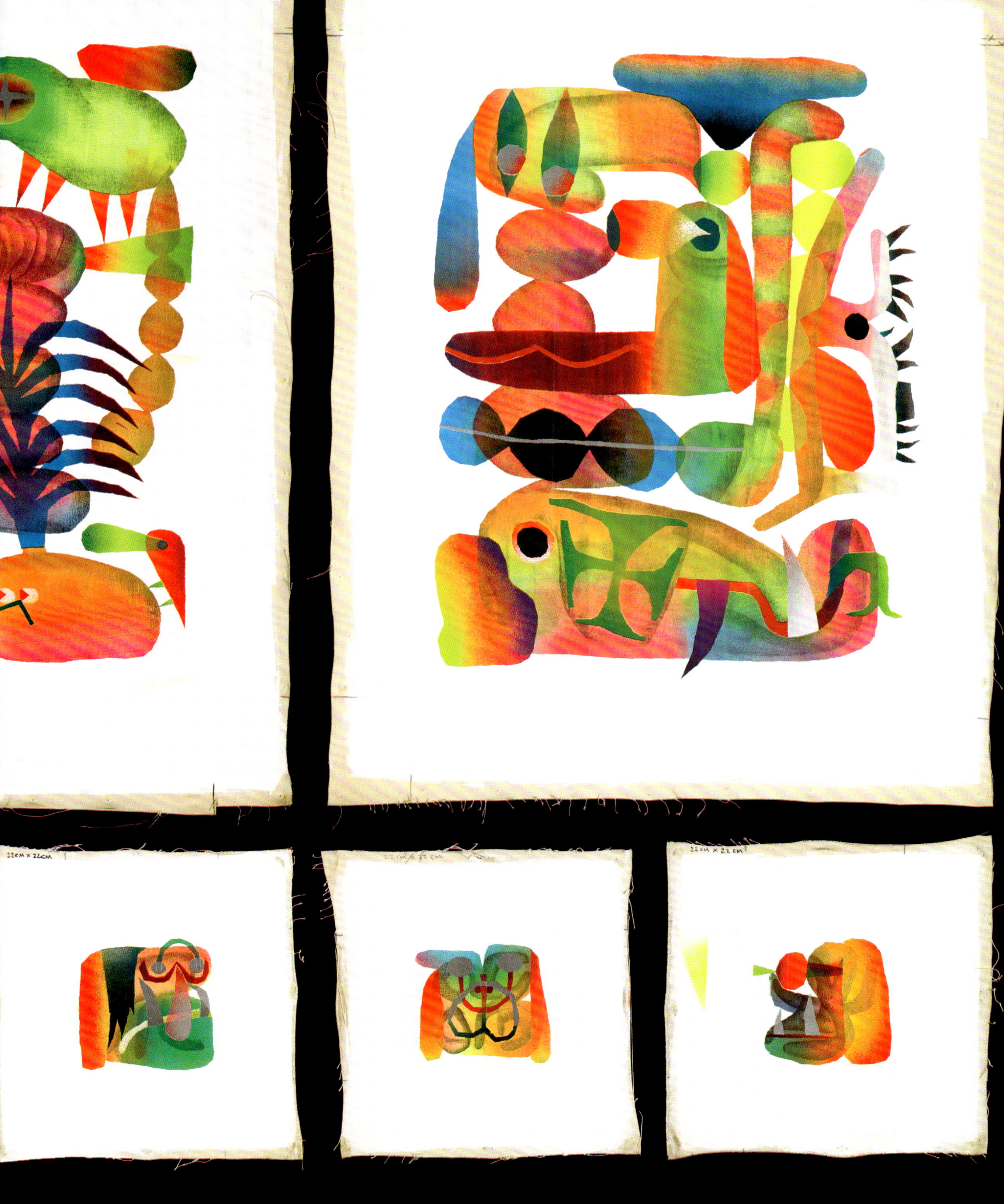
22cm x 22cm
22 cm x 22 cm

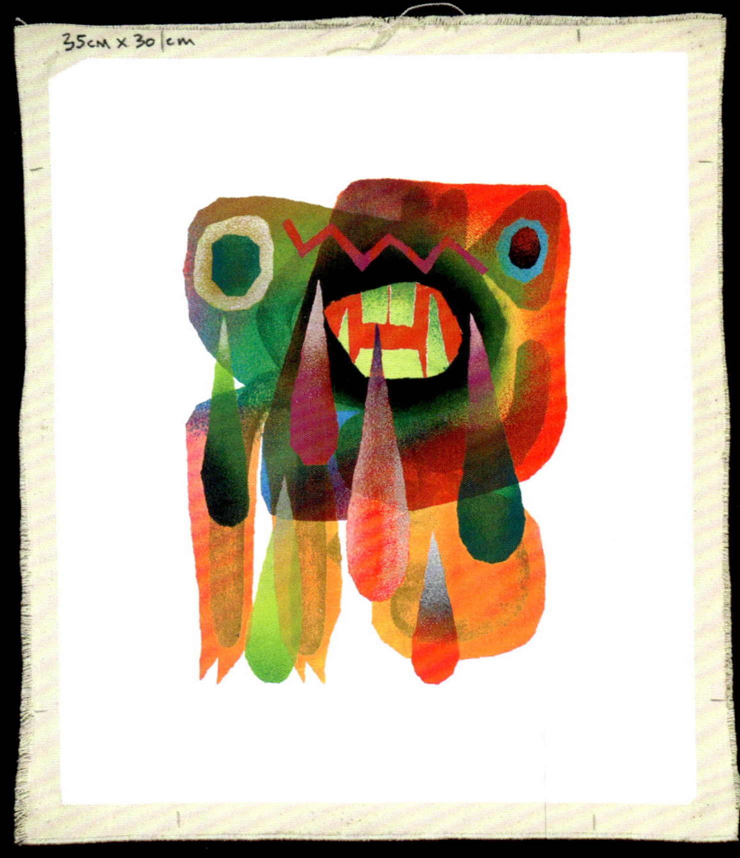

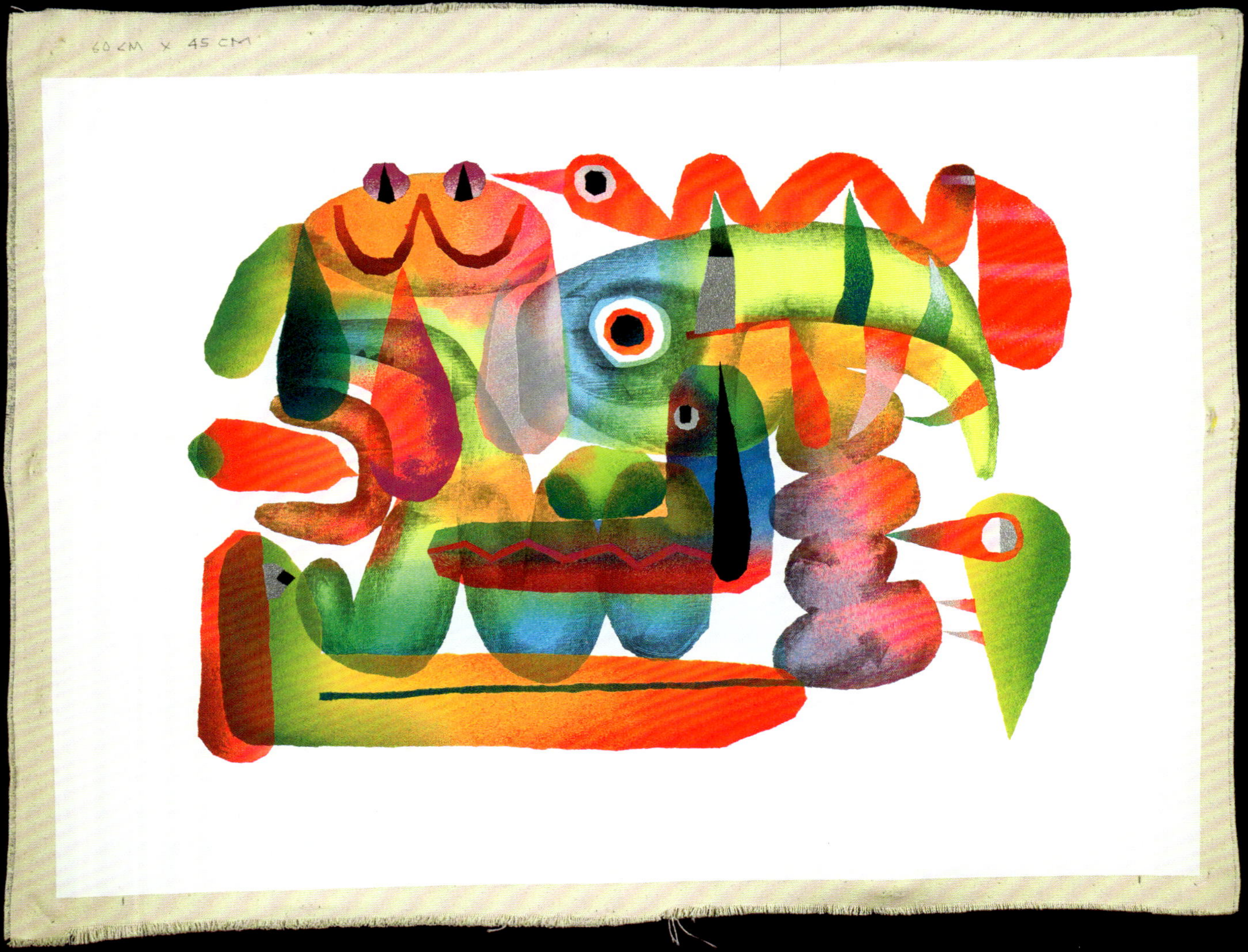

Space Madness No 11
2015. Graphite, Acrylic, Gesso and Clear Gesso on Canvas. 14" x 11"

Space Madness No 9
2015. Graphite, Acrylic, Gesso and Clear Gesso on Canvas. 18" x 24"

Space Madness No 5
2015. Graphite, Acrylic, Gesso and Clear Gesso on Canvas. 40" x 30"

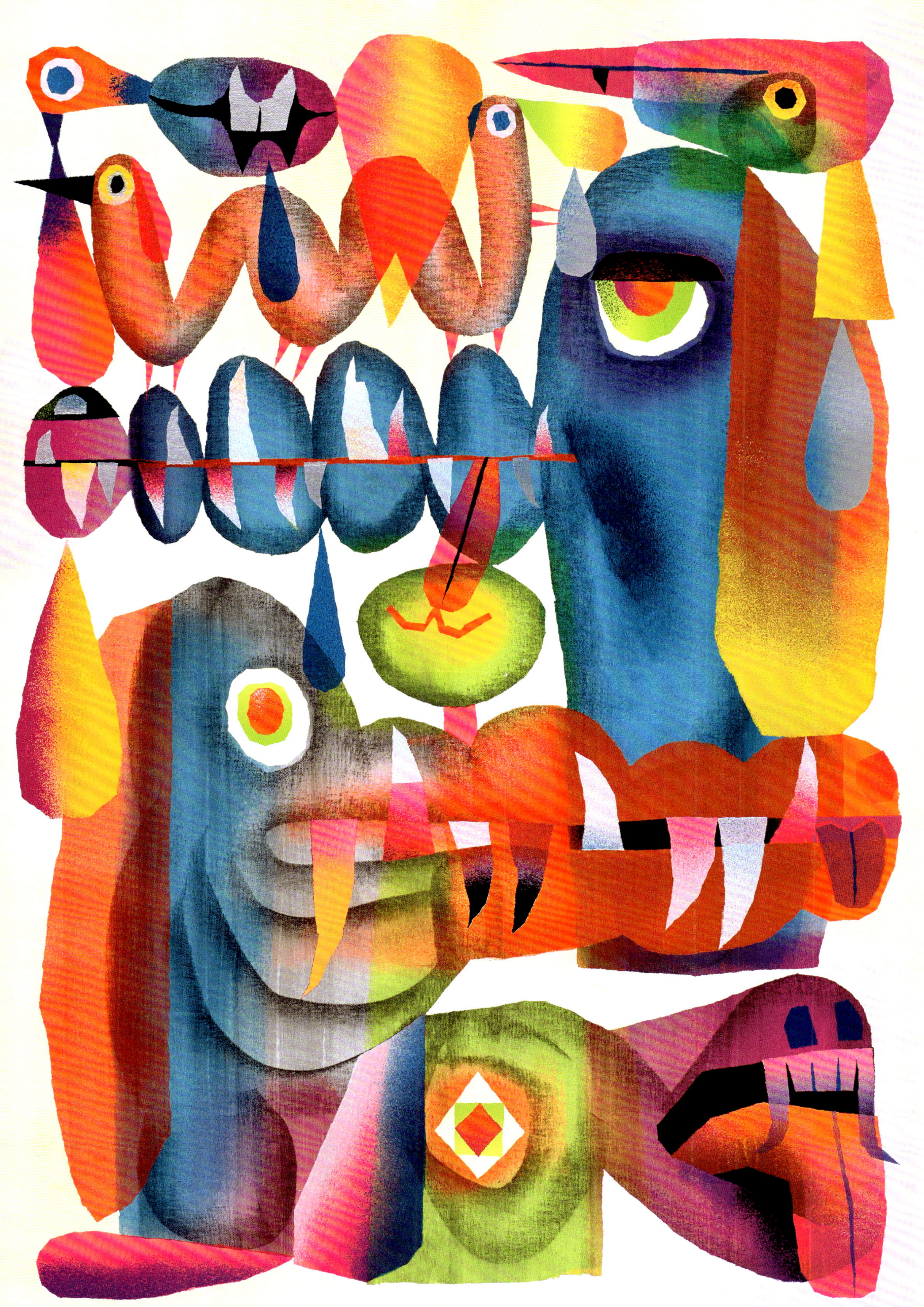

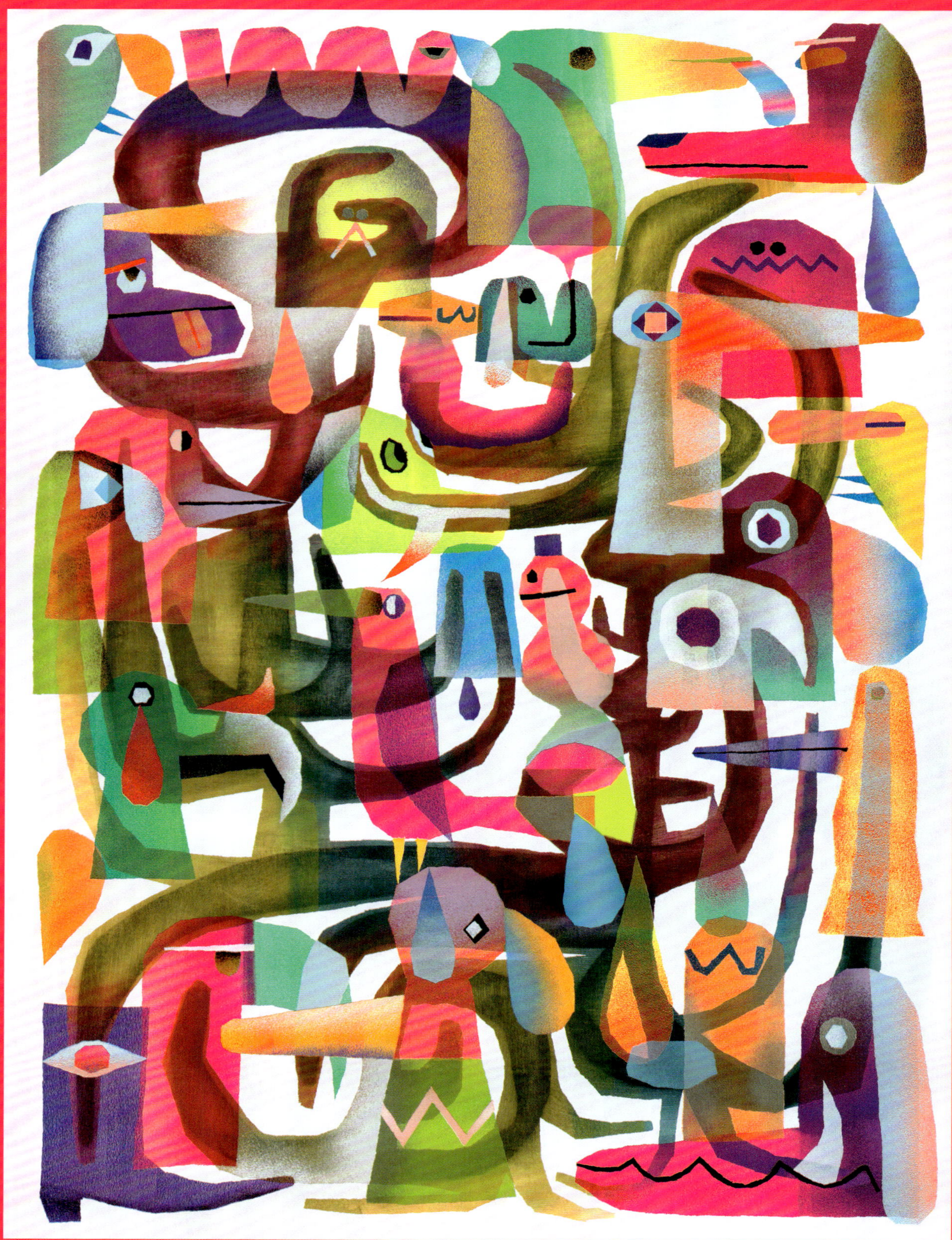

Space Madness No 3
2015. Graphite, Acrylic, Gesso and Clear Gesso on Canvas. 48" x 36"

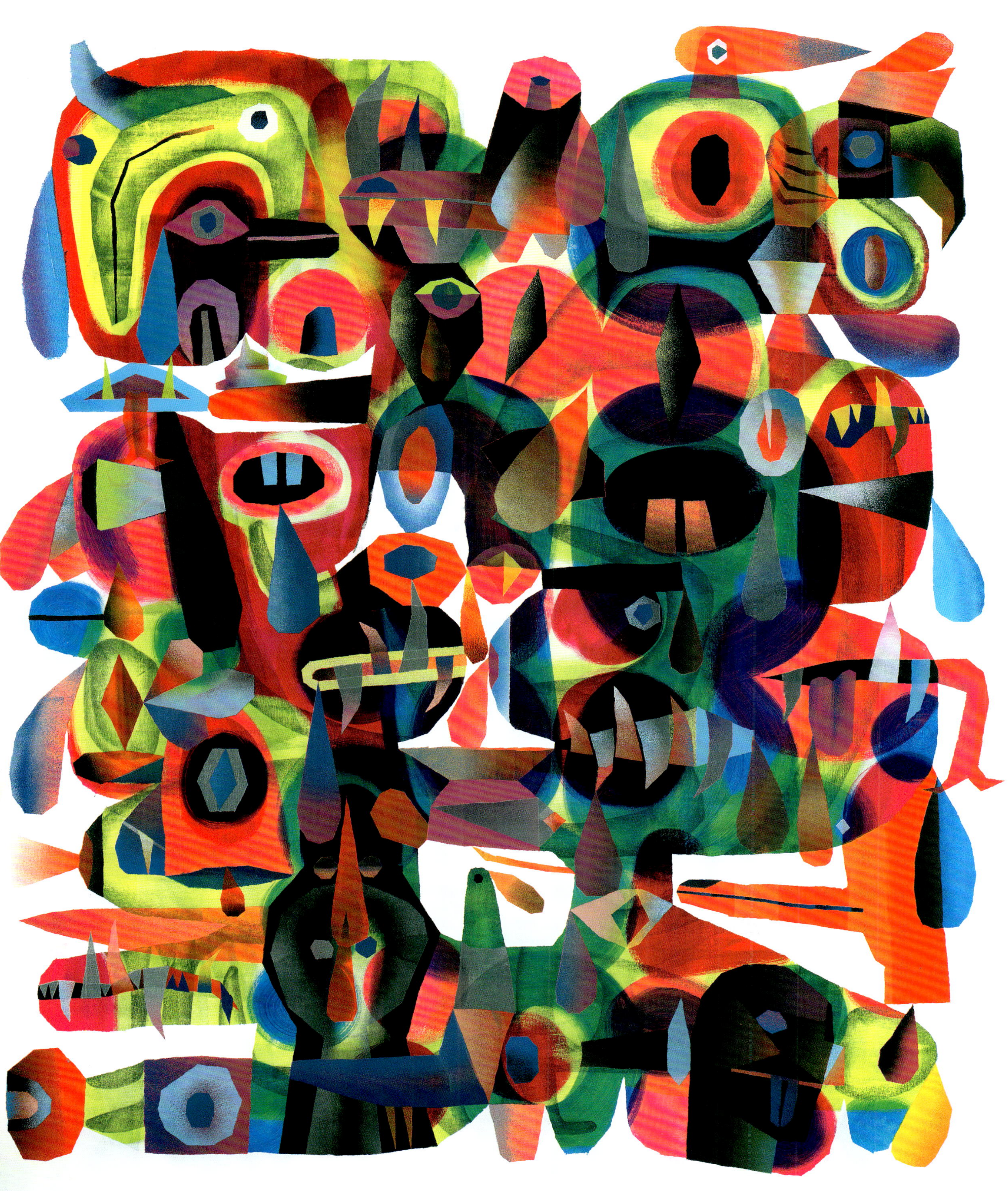

Space Madness No 1
2015. Graphite, Acrylic, Gesso and Clear Gesso on Canvas. 75" x 63"

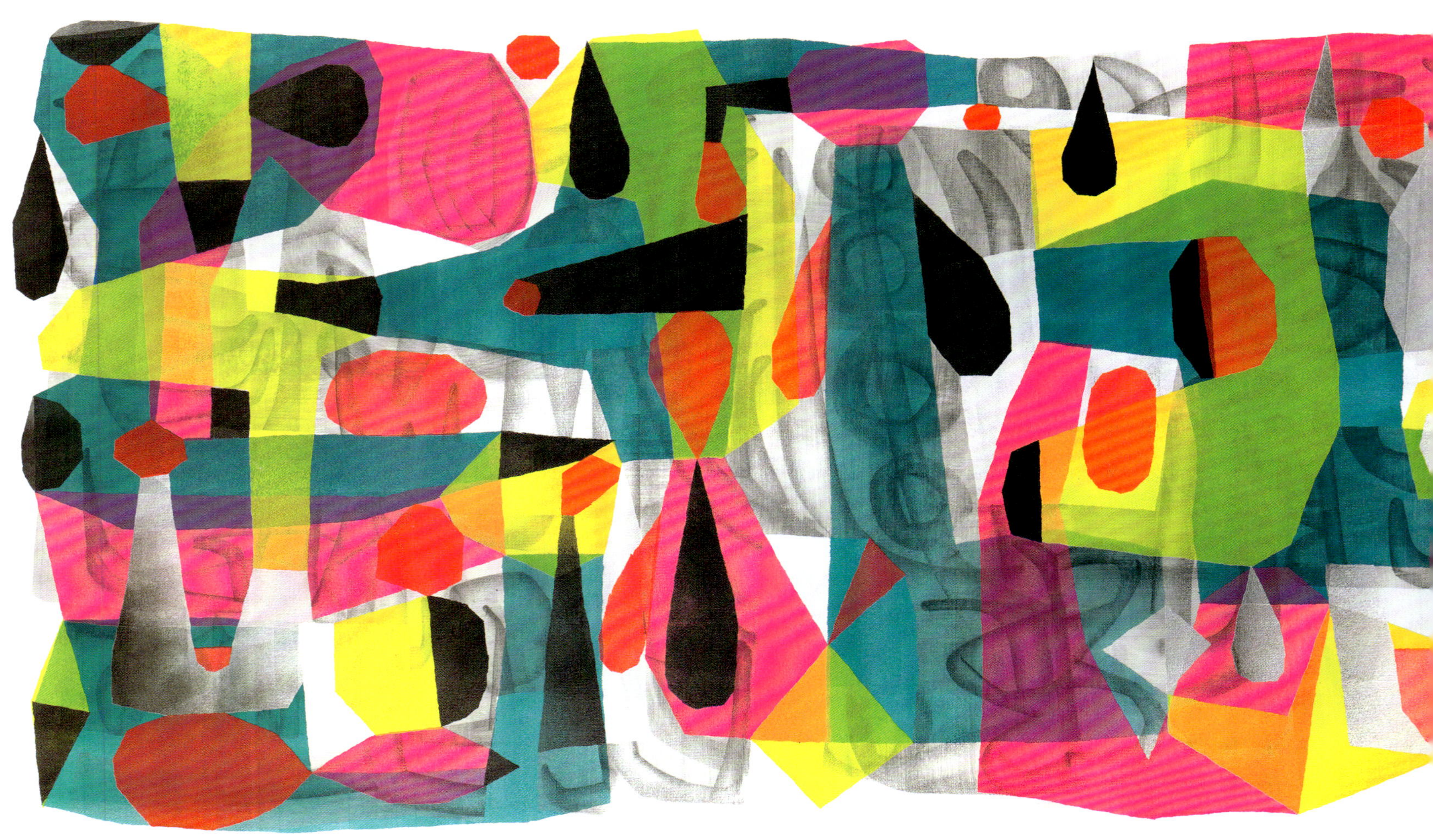

Smoke Juggler
2016. Graphite, Acrylic, Gesso and Clear Gesso on Canvas. 33" x 111"

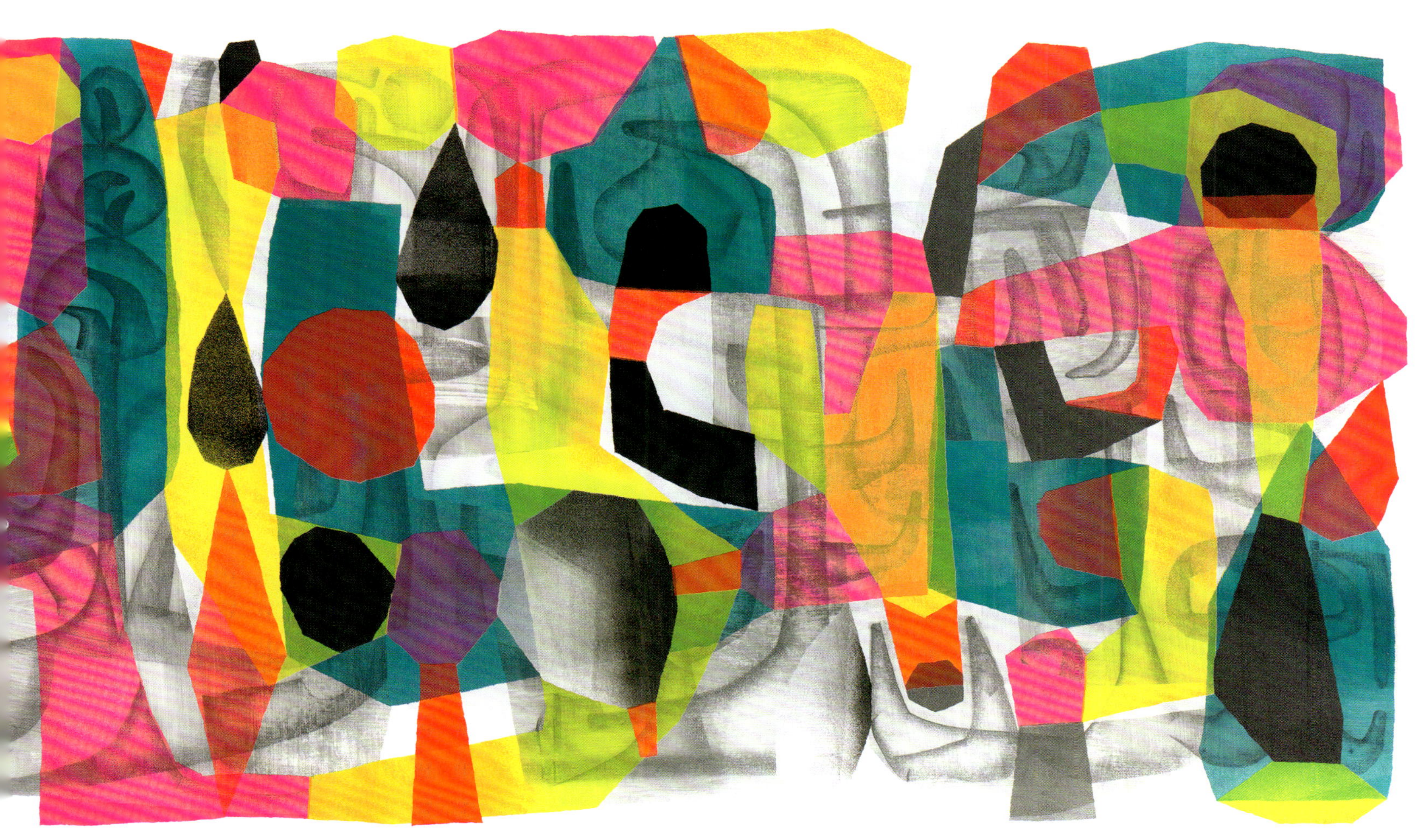

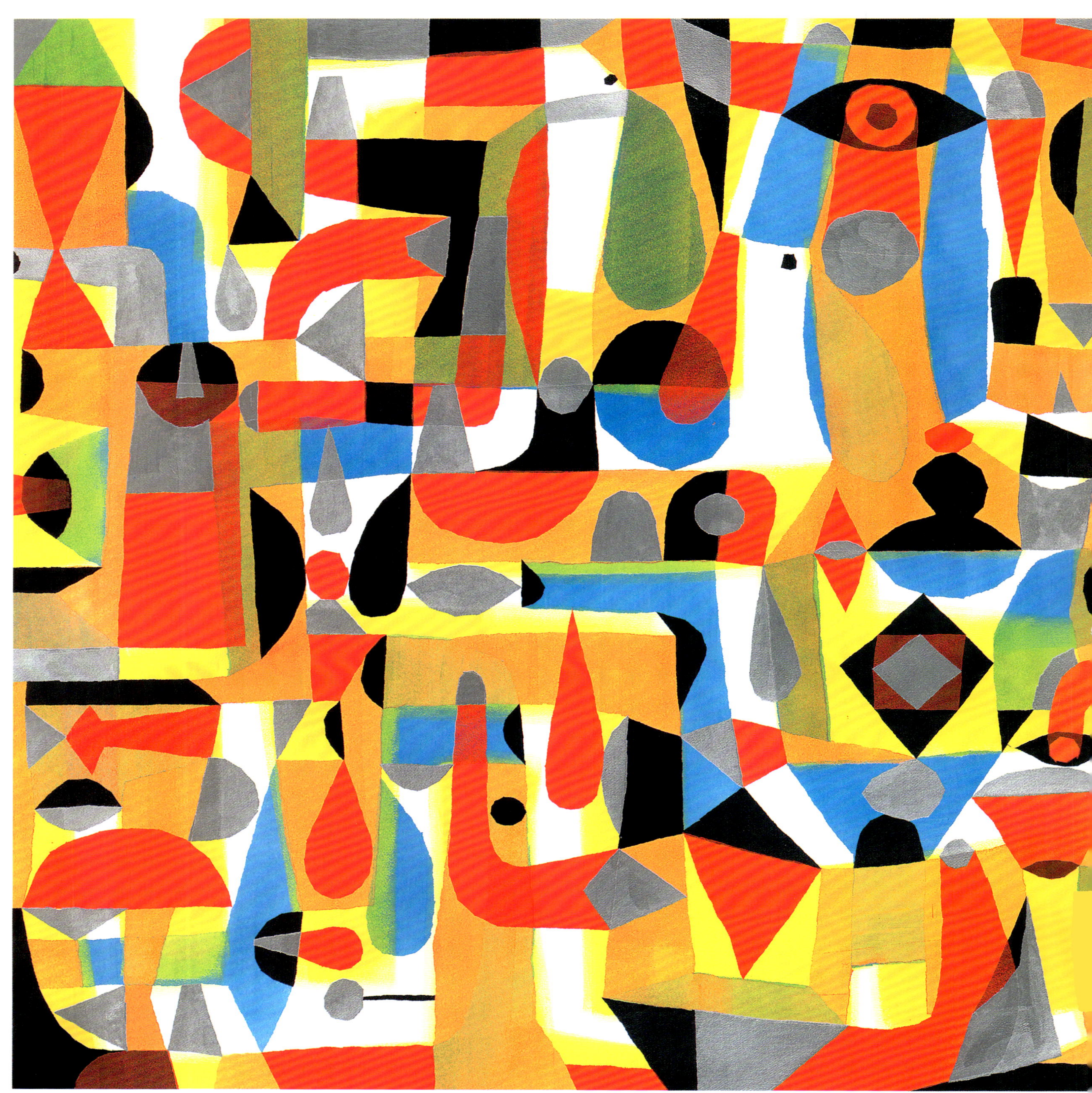

Fictional Mohair Dragon
2015. Acrylic on Paper. 45" x 88"

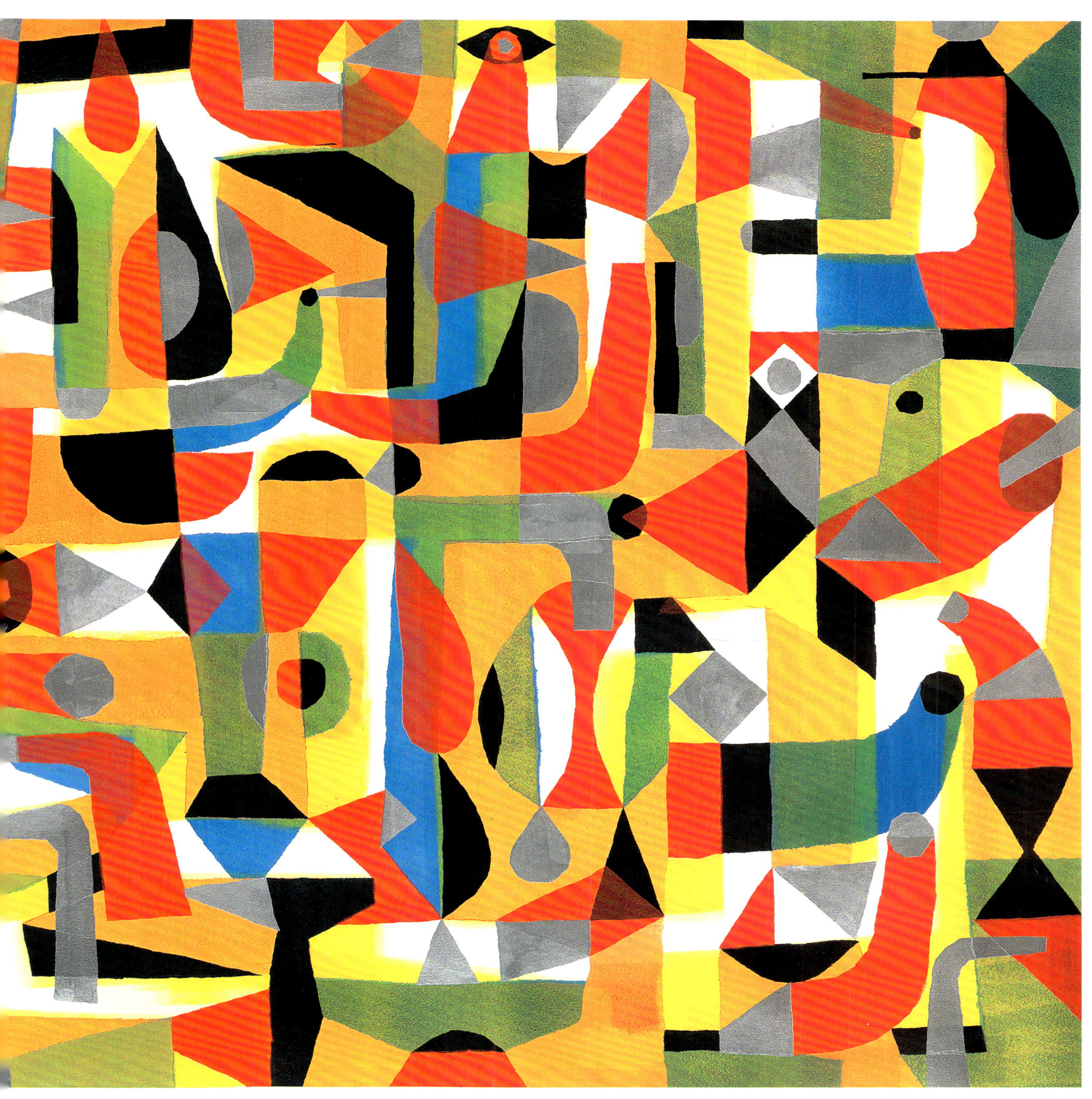

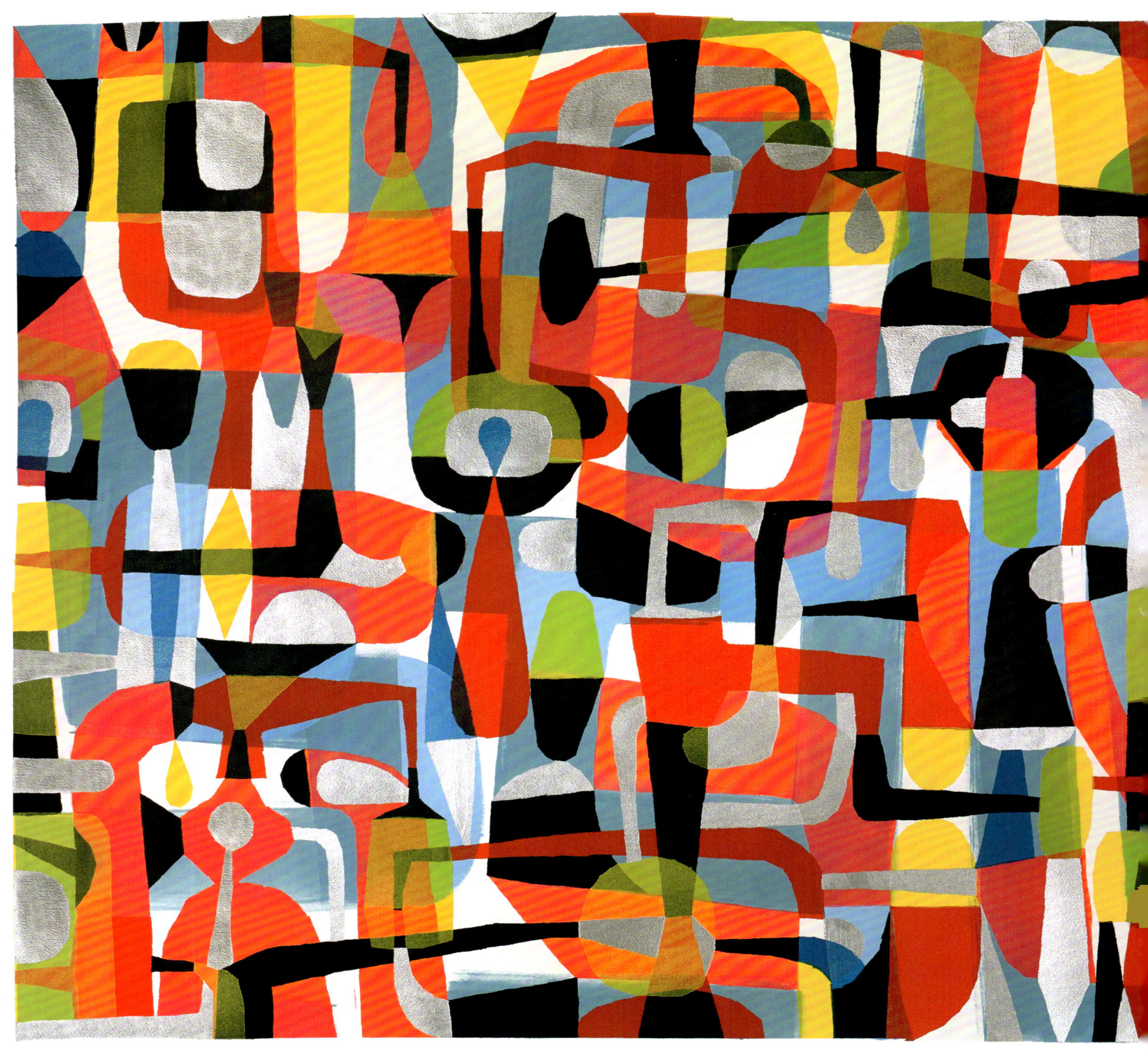

ABDC
2015. Acrylic on Paper. 45" x 96"

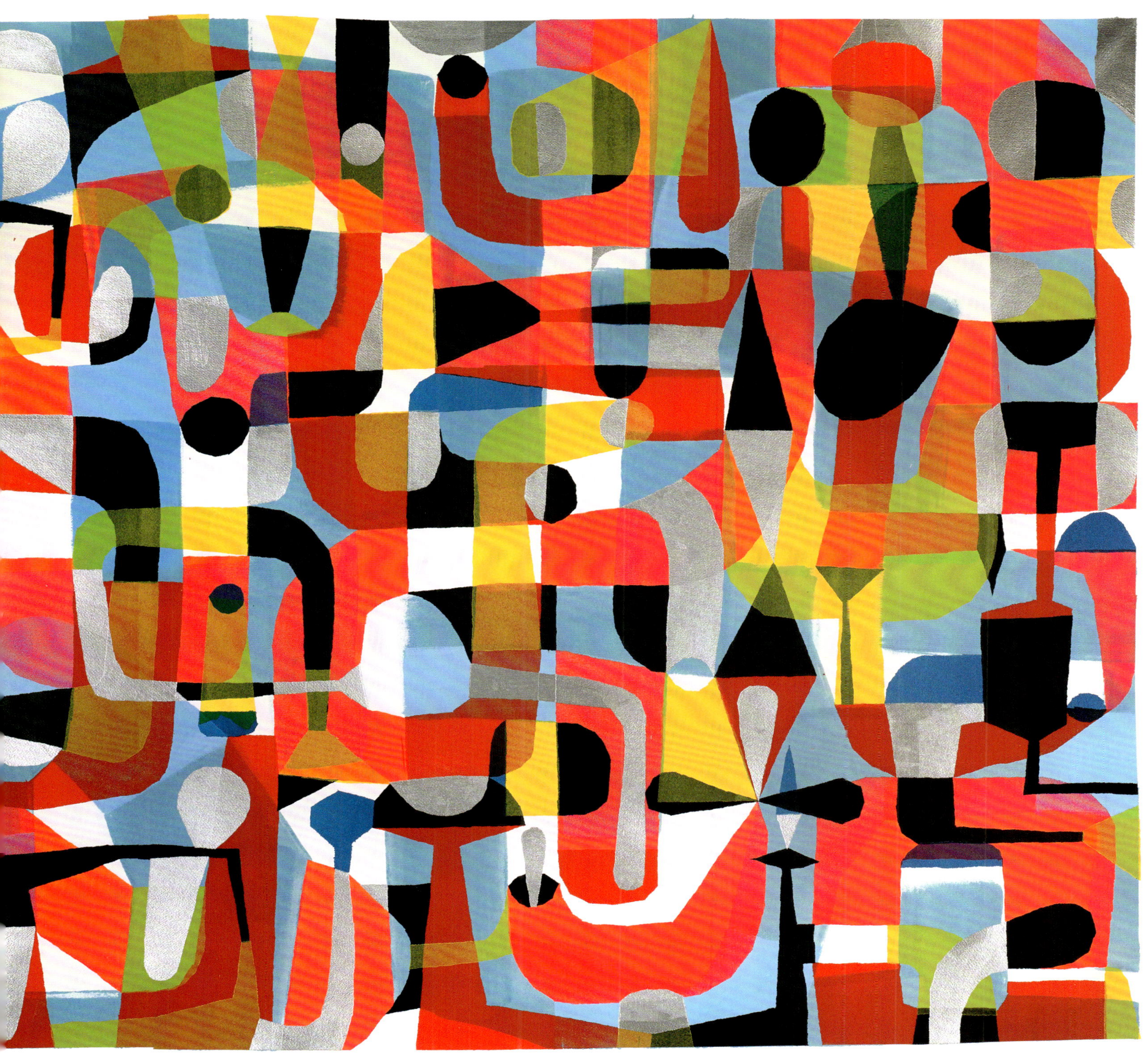

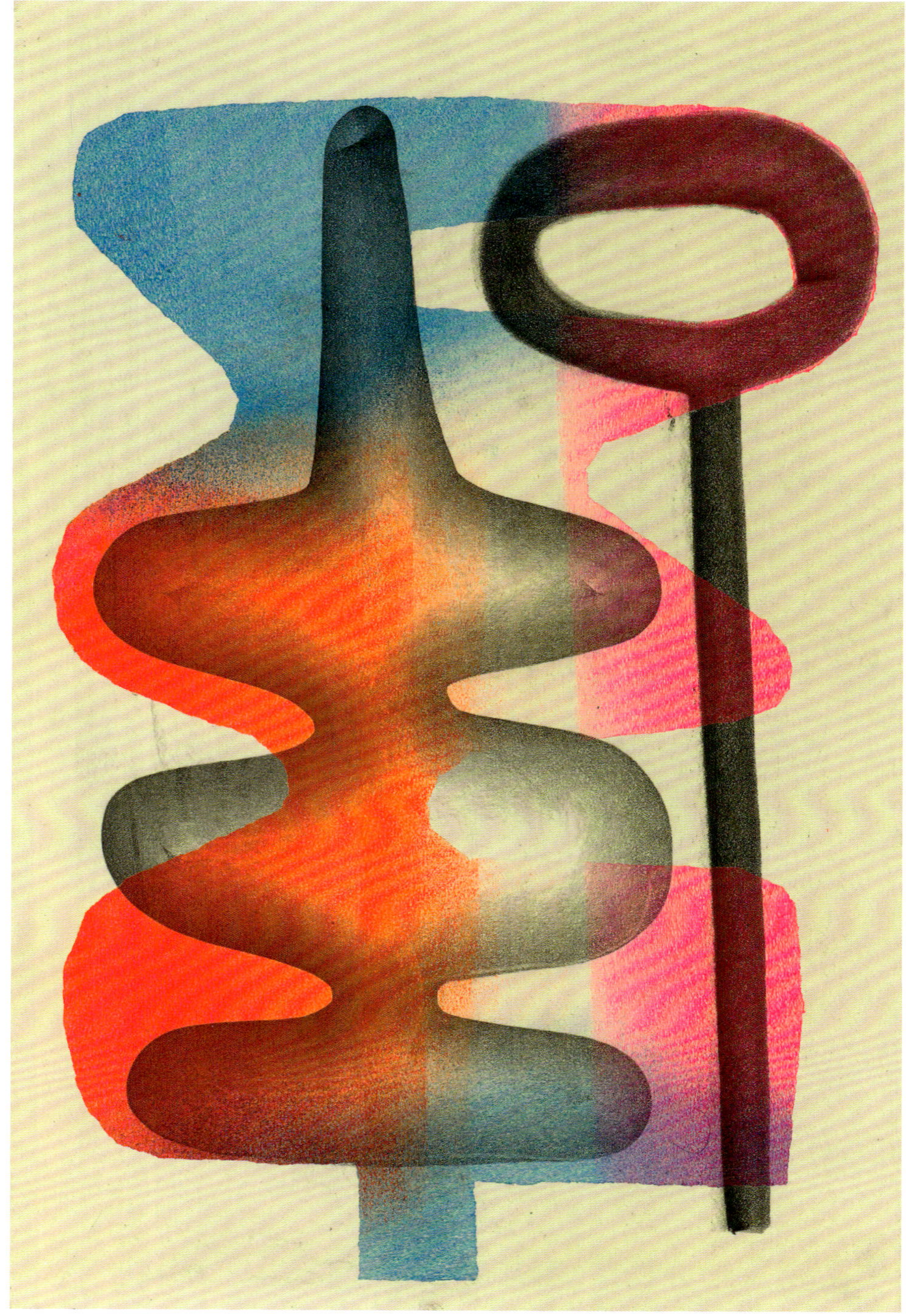

The Dog No 45
2016. Graphite and Acrylic on Paper Mounted to Plywood. 18" x 12"

The Dog No 9
2016. Graphite on Paper Mounted to Plywood. 48" x 36"

Following pages:
Collage of works from The Dog
2016. Graphite and Acrylic on Paper Mounted to Plywood. Dimensions Vary

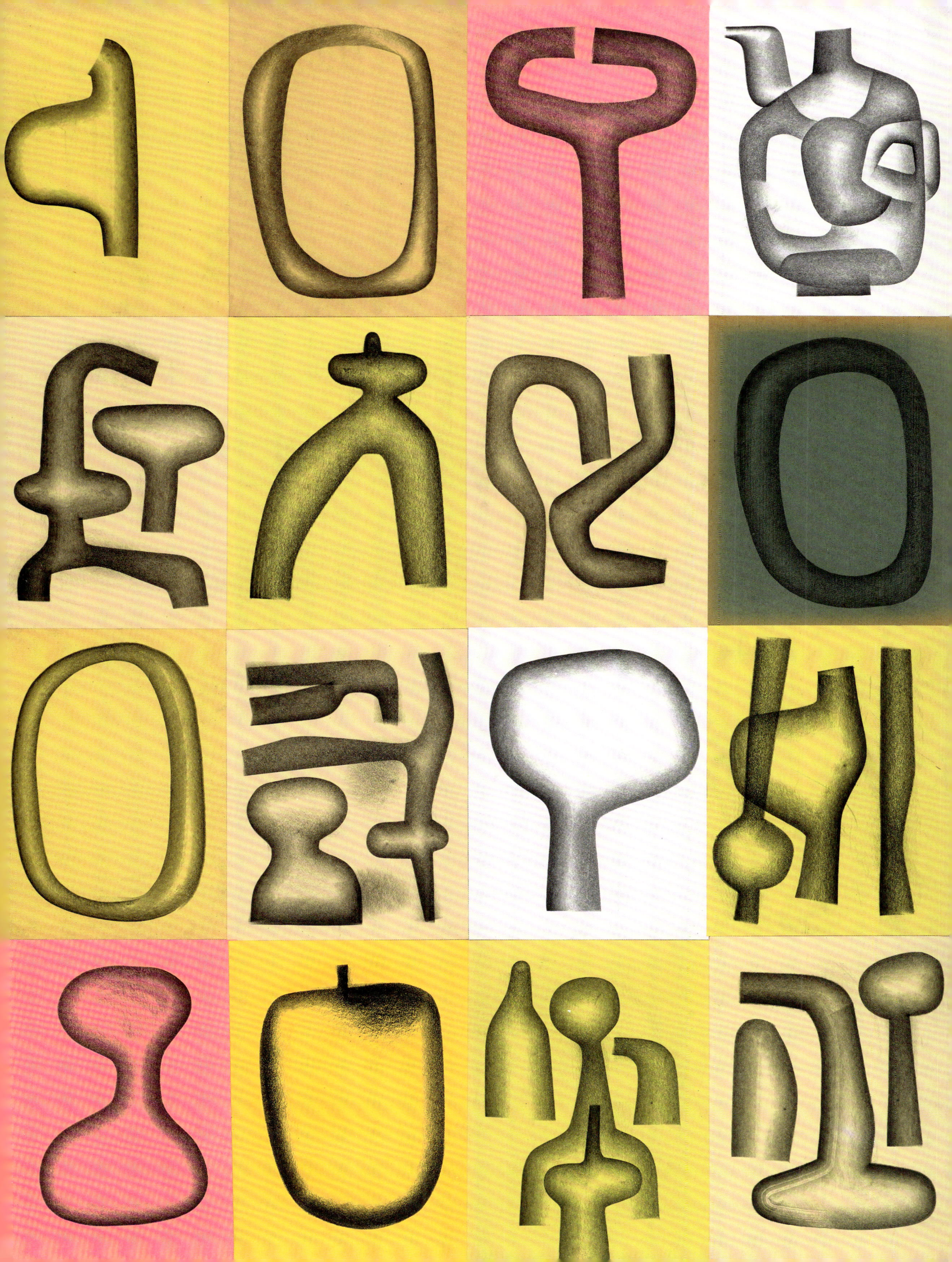

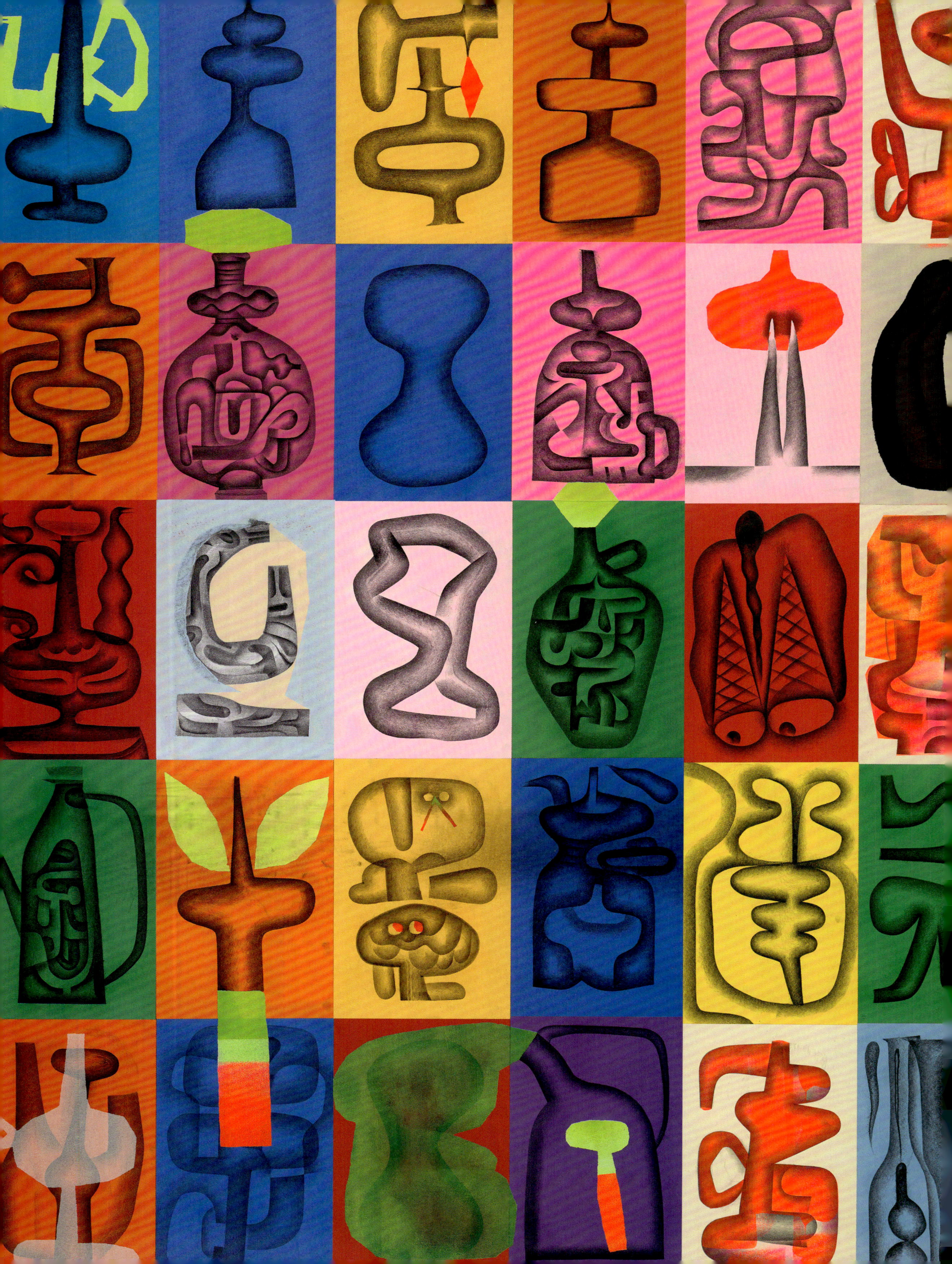

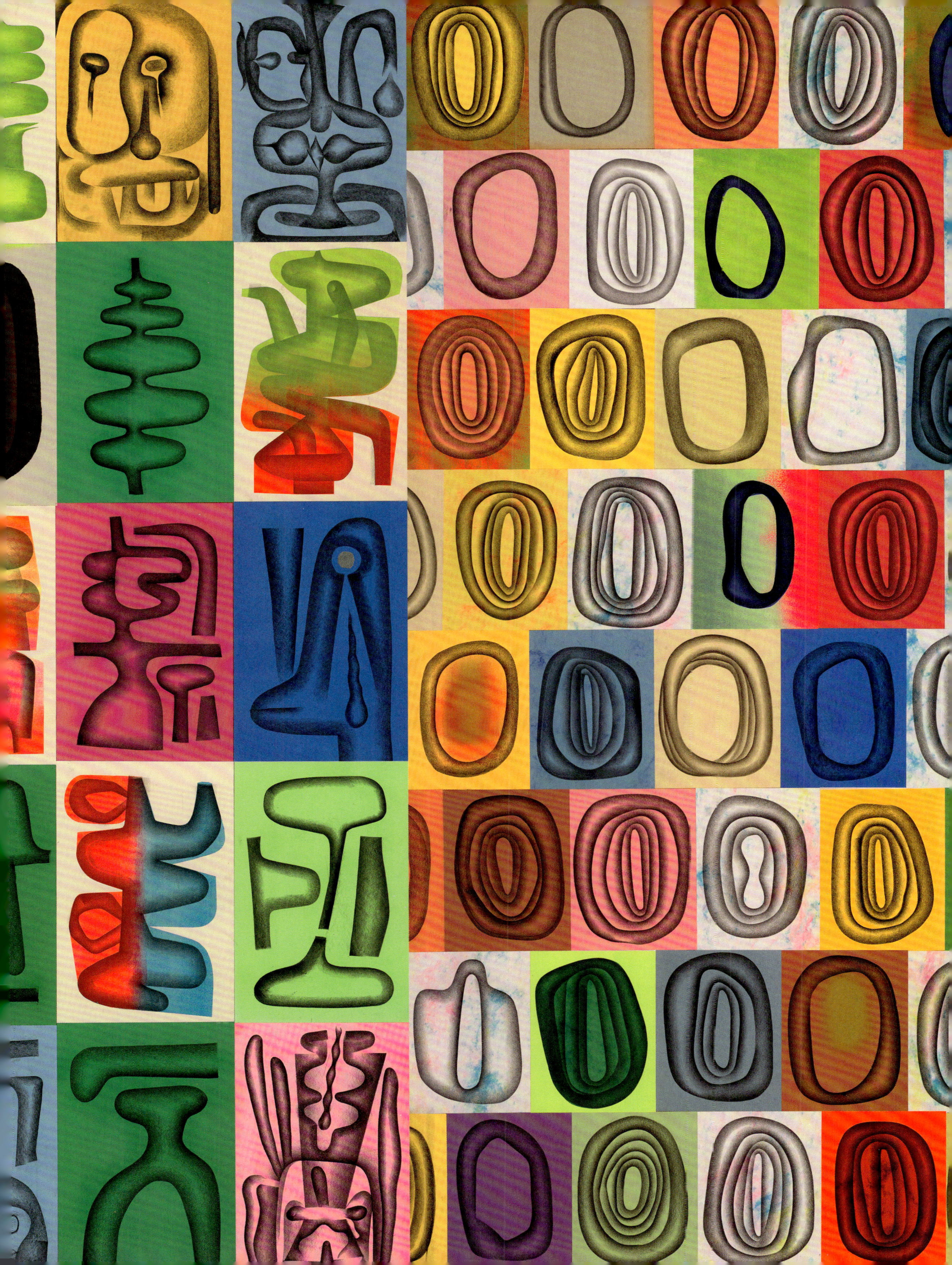

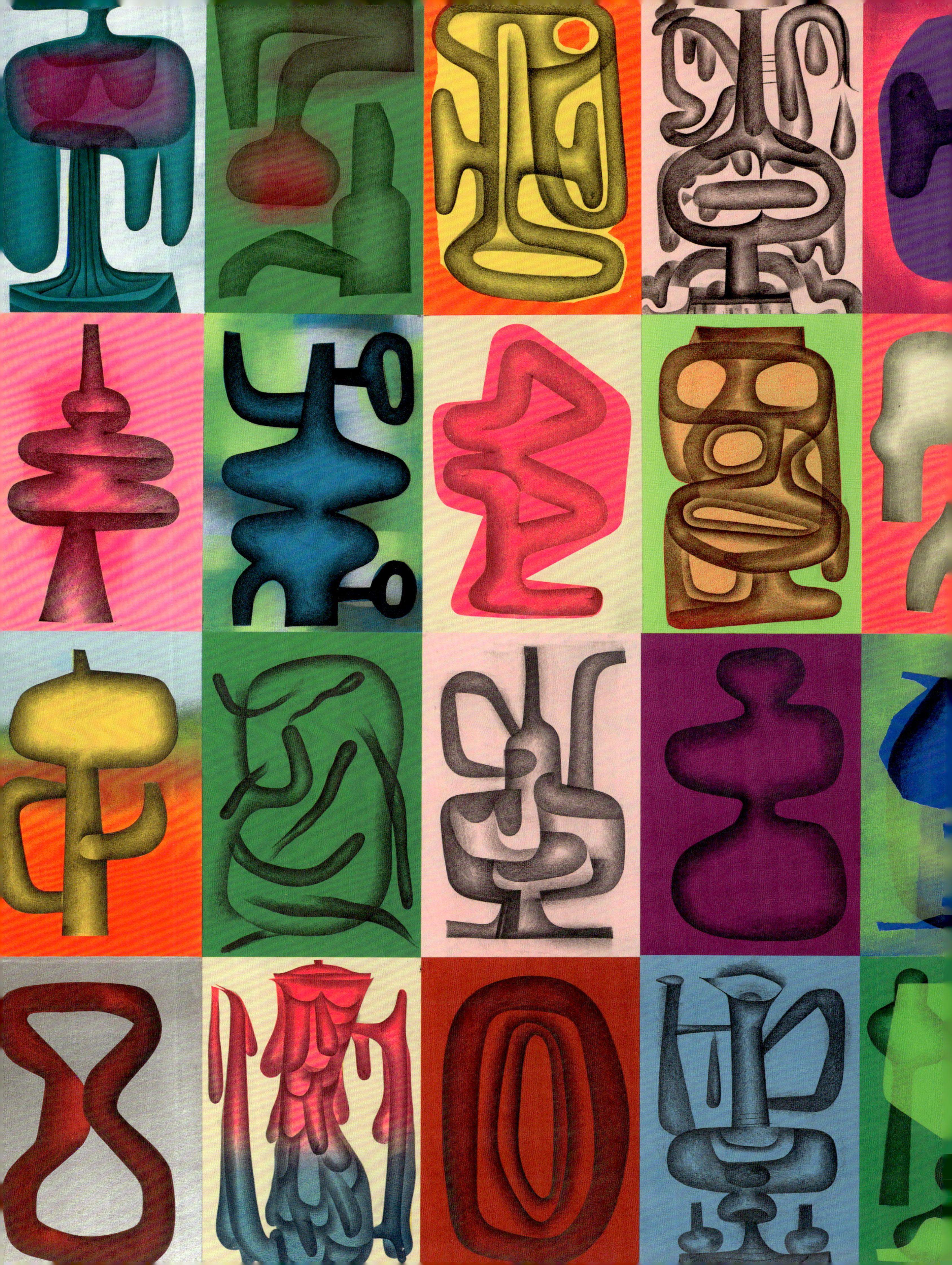

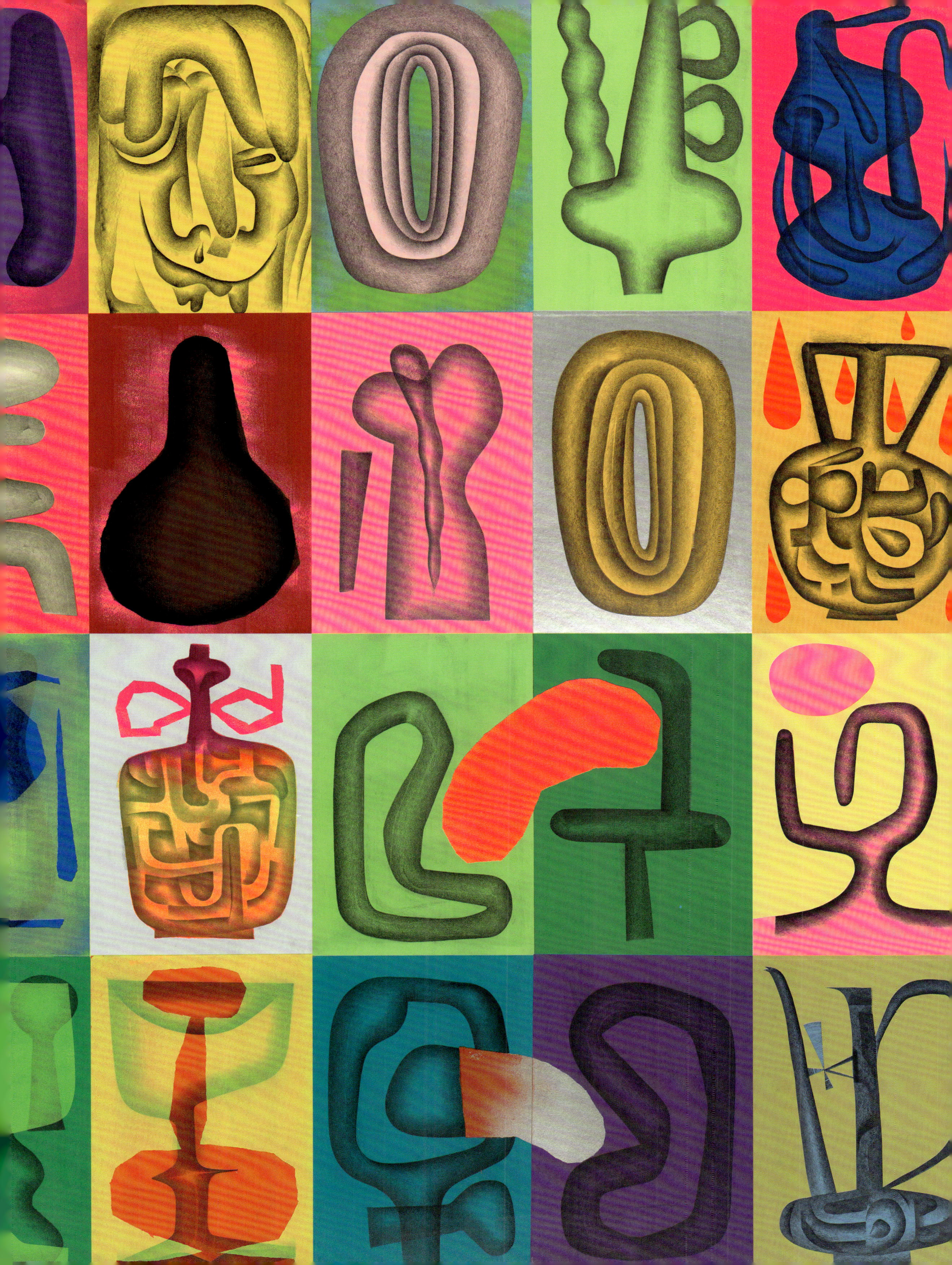

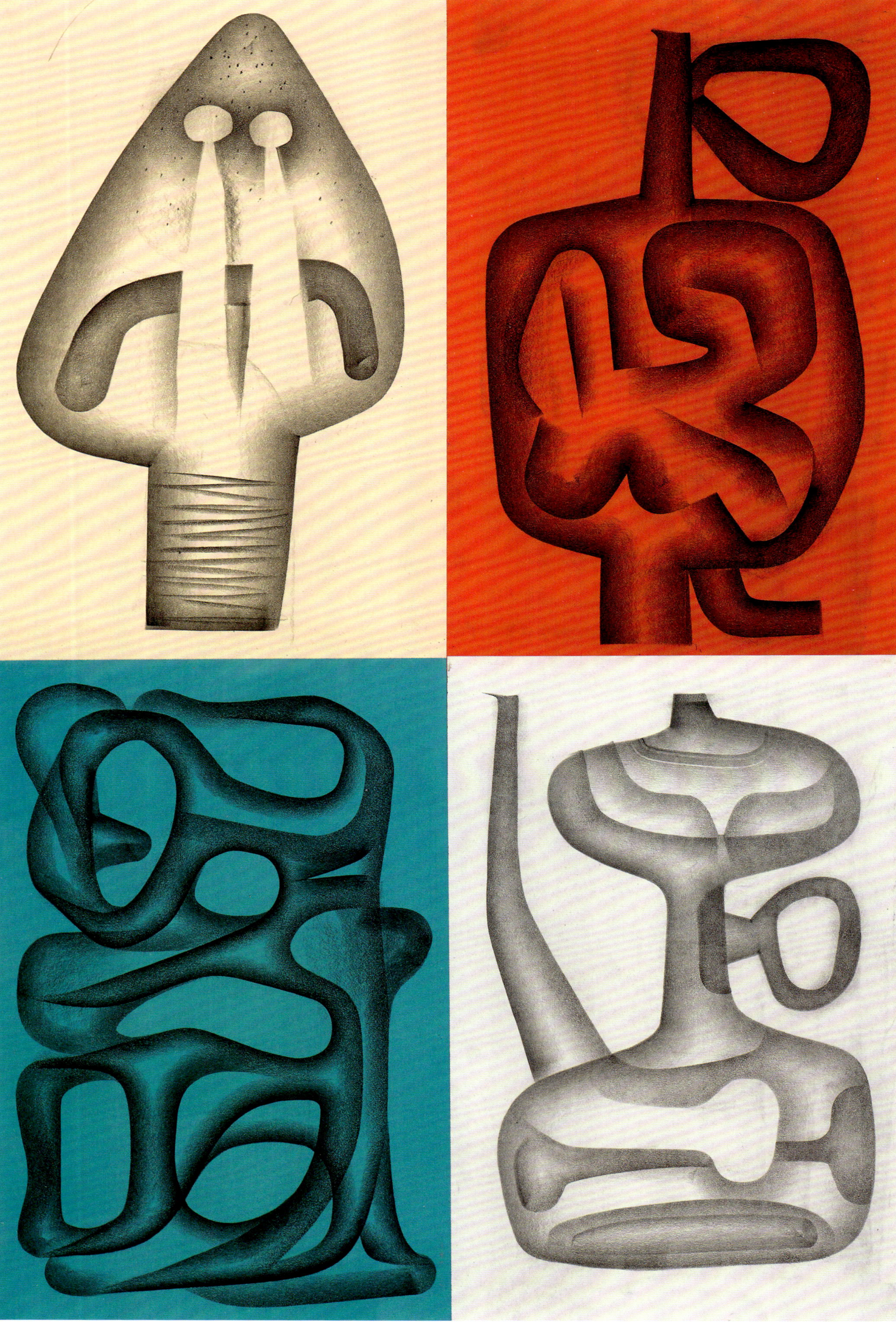

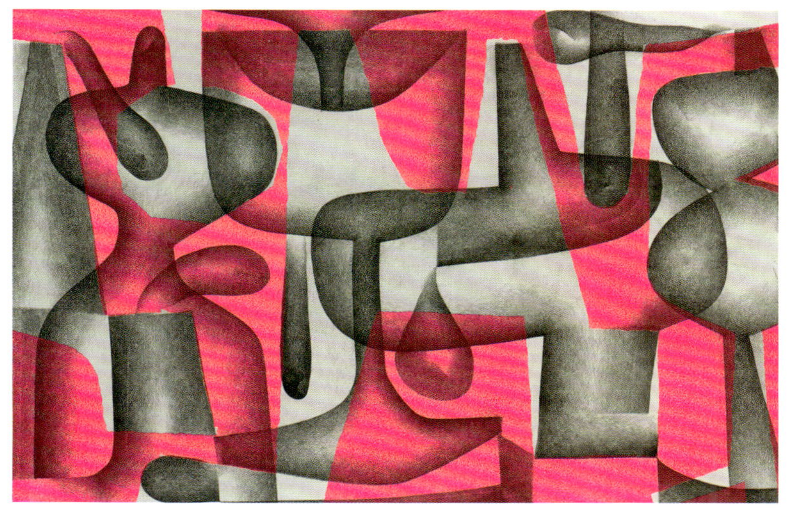

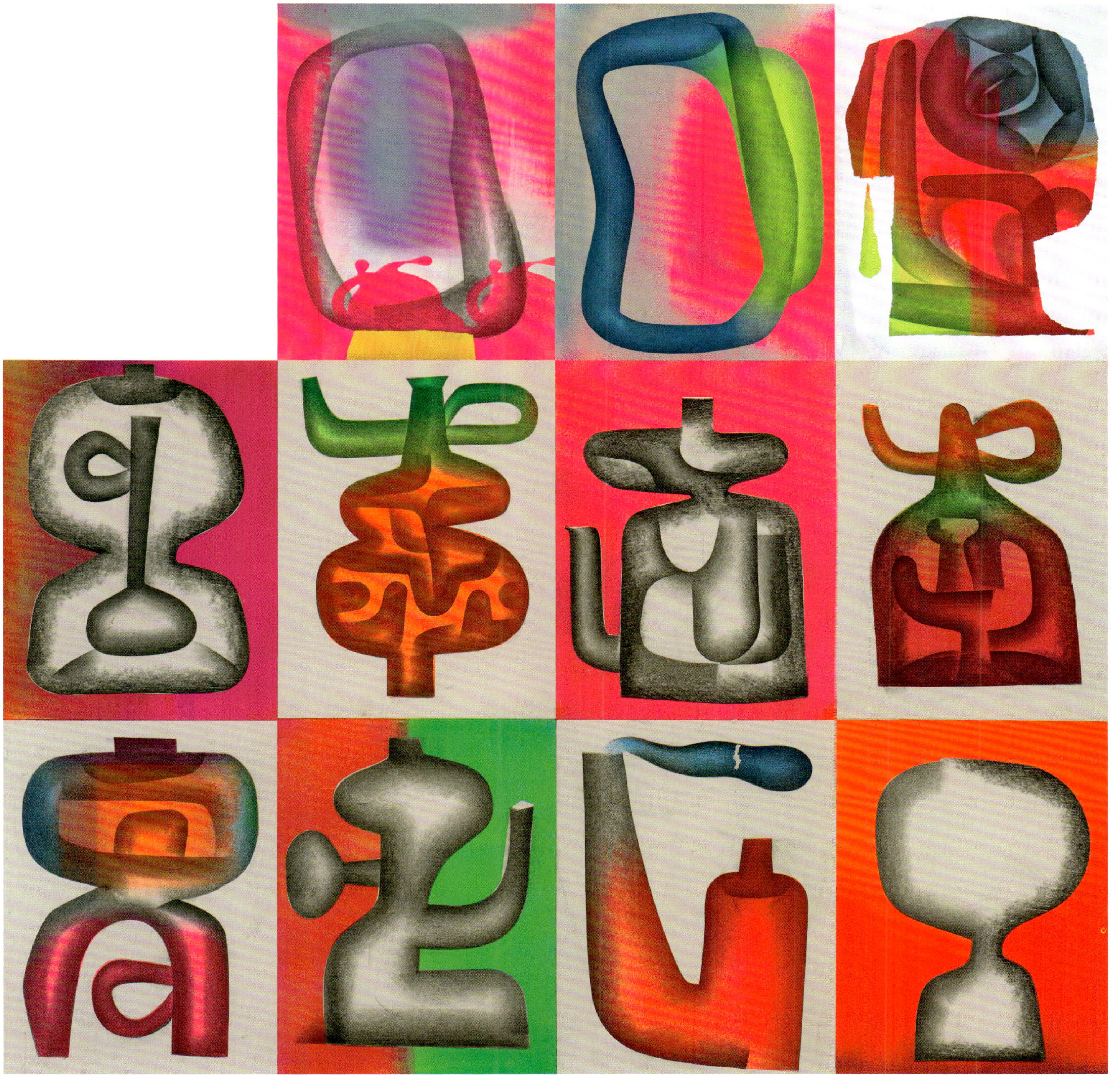

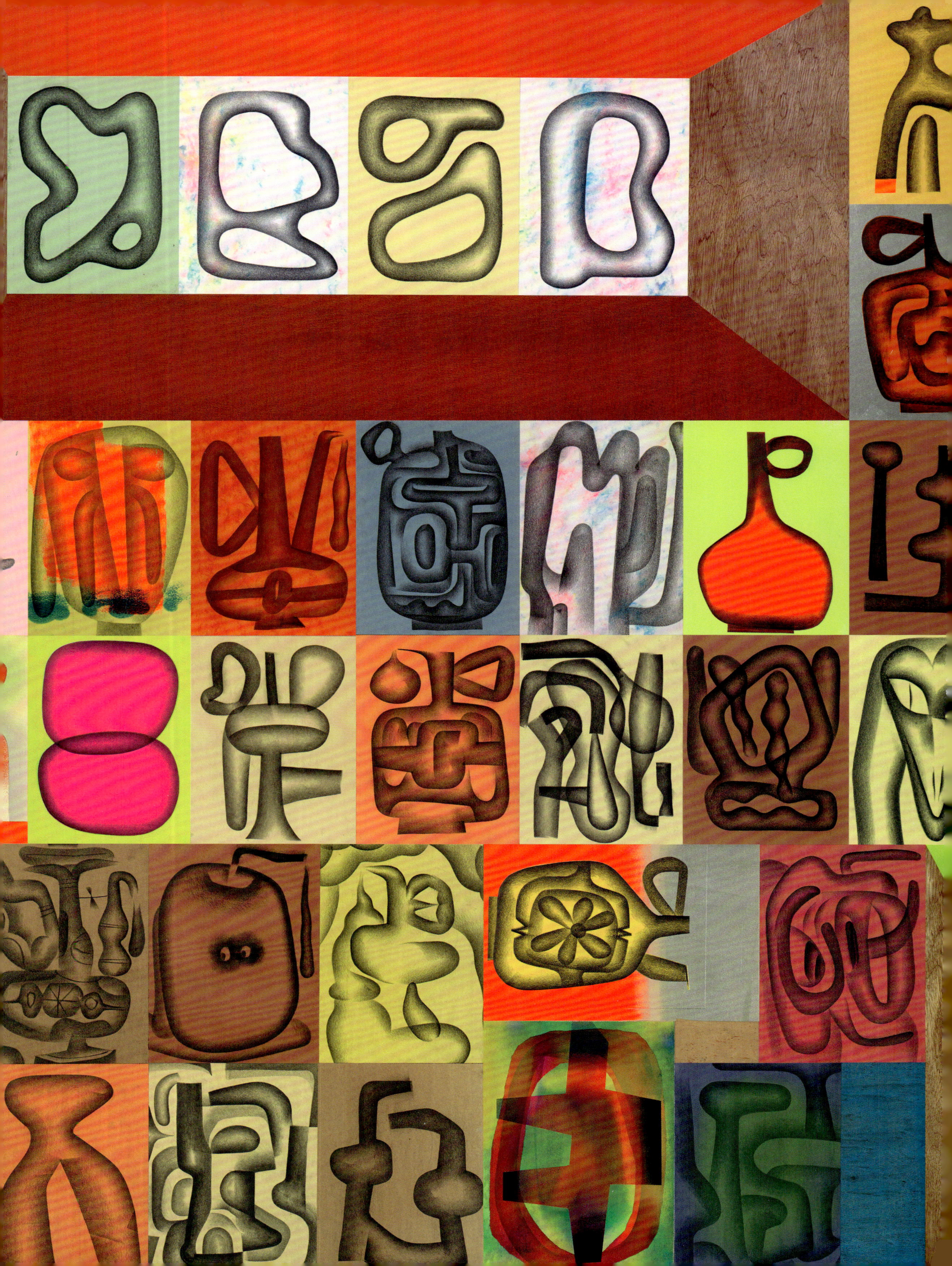

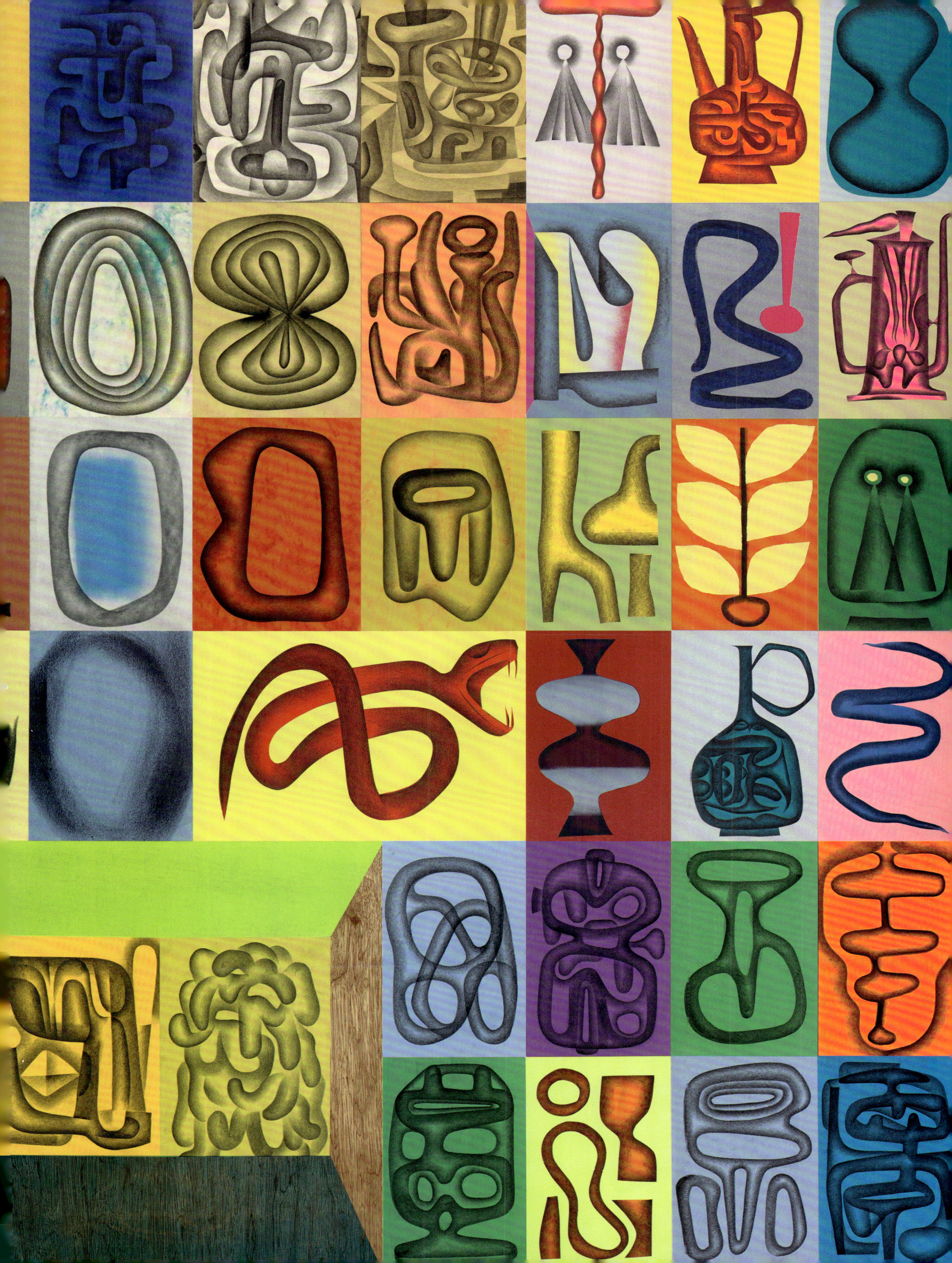

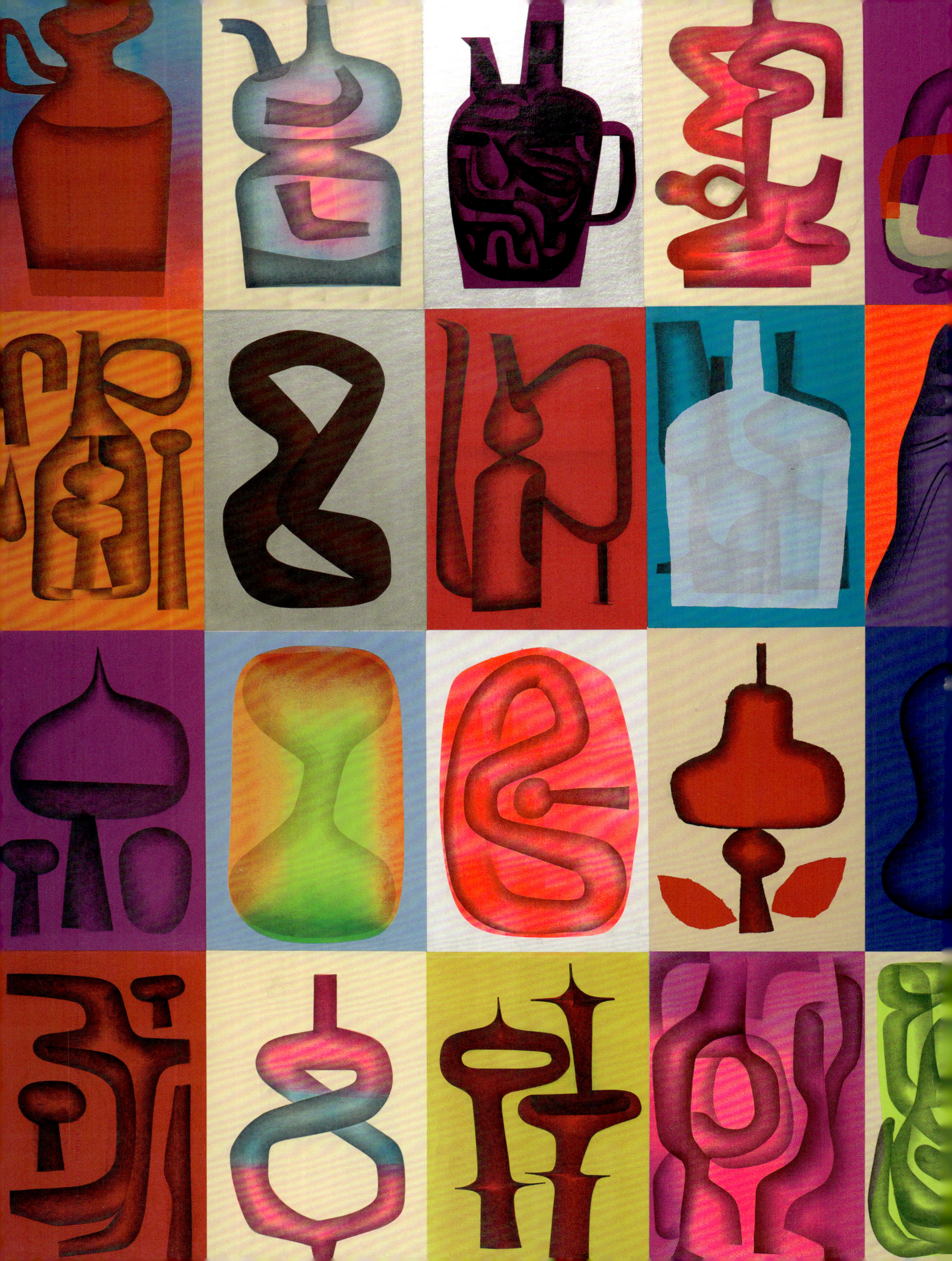

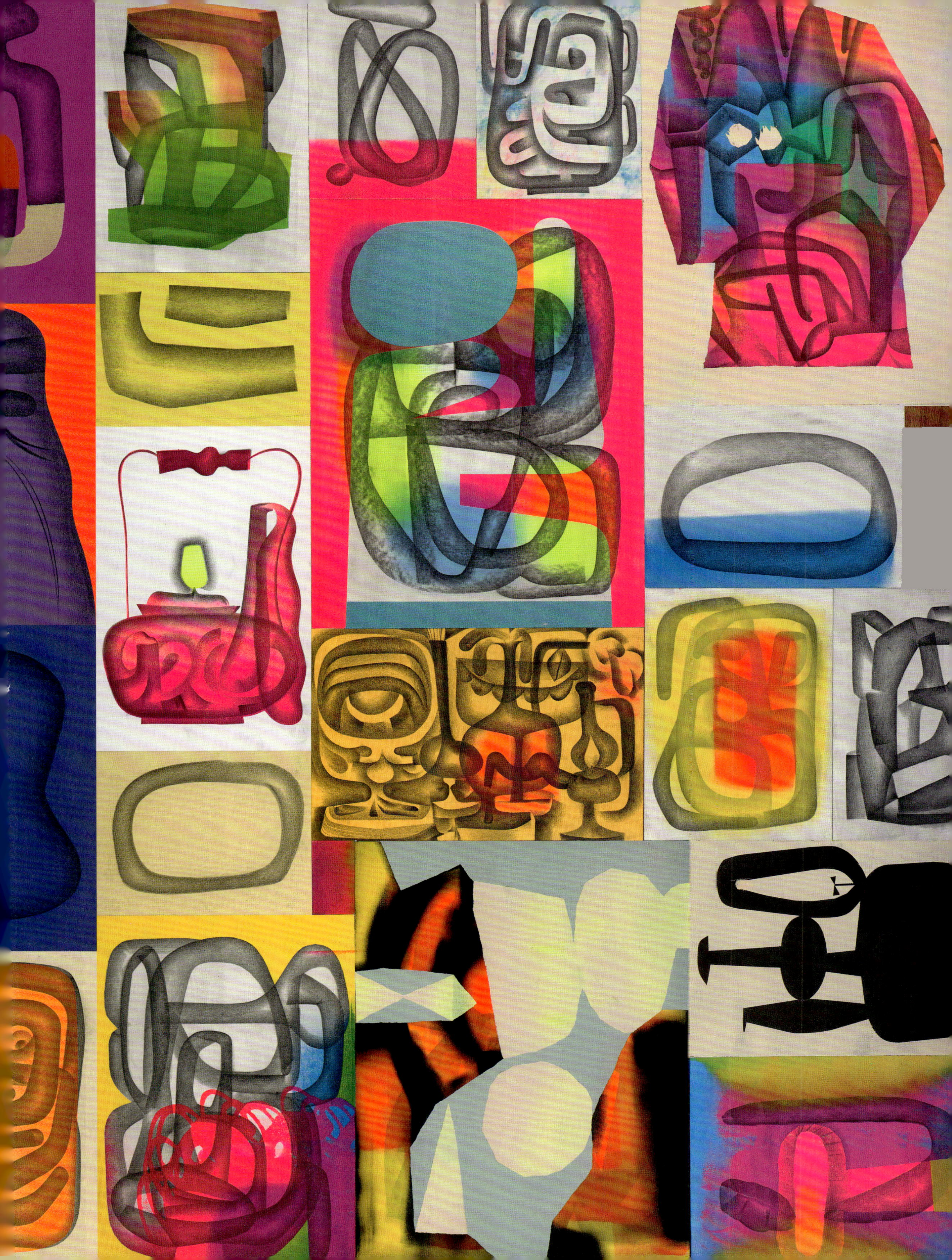

Being an artist is difficult,

I'm a pretty good artist. That's hard for me to say, because most of my life I've felt like there was something wrong with me. I struggled in school, barely able to stay awake much of the time. I just wanted to stare off into space and think up stories, or play with blocks, or draw, rather than try to translate the ideas swimming around inside my head into words and numbers, which were abstractions that didn't really mean anything to me. I caused a lot of problems. I forgot my shoes when my family went camping. I lost things and got lost myself. I was off in my own world. Over time I realized that when I found things I liked doing, I was totally focused and capable. I'm exactly the kind of person that should make art. I'm strange, creative, and sensitive. Those seemed like terrible things to be when I was growing up, but in real life they are valuable skills. I just had to learn how to use them. Being an artist is not about what I do; it's about how my mind works. And being a good artist means first accepting that I am not going to do things the same way that most people do them. When I get beyond that, I can stop trying to fit in and I can figure out what works for me.

My mind is like a roller coaster, full of mixed feelings about myself. Nearly every time I sit down to make art I feel disappointment. Usually, with the first tentative mark, I feel sure that I have lost my ability to draw and that I should just give up. I have learned though that if I keep going, I will warm up and something good will happen. When it does happen I feel like a genius. I become convinced that soon I'll be on the cover of every magazine and will be busy talking to museum curators and talk show hosts. Then I make a line that is all wrong and proves that I am a total failure and I should just give up. It goes on and on like that—always heading upward into glory or down into the abyss. It can, at times, be crippling, but I've learned to look past the spinning ego wheel and relax. When I get to that place, I can laugh at it and cry with it and let it play around with reality while I continue to work. The failure and the genius do battle and I make the art.

I'm the middle child of three boys and that came with a whole other set of challenges. I struggled for space and attention (and here I am writing a book about myself). All three brothers became artists even though my mom used to tell us the story of a distant uncle, a poet and painter, who had lost his mind and would run around in the woods naked, drinking wine with questionable ladies. The message

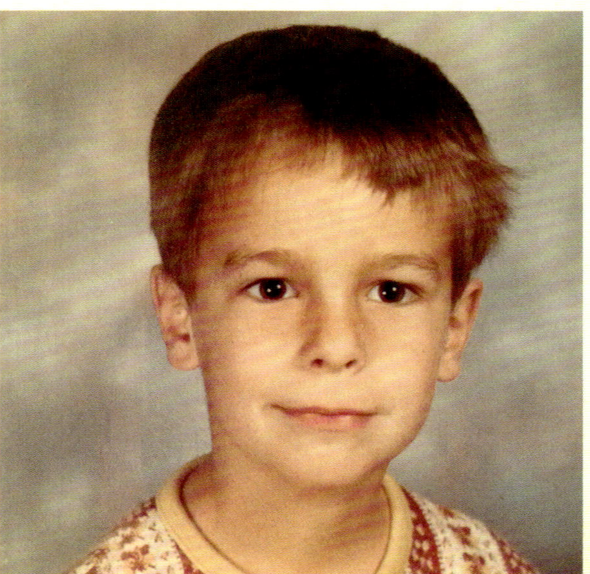

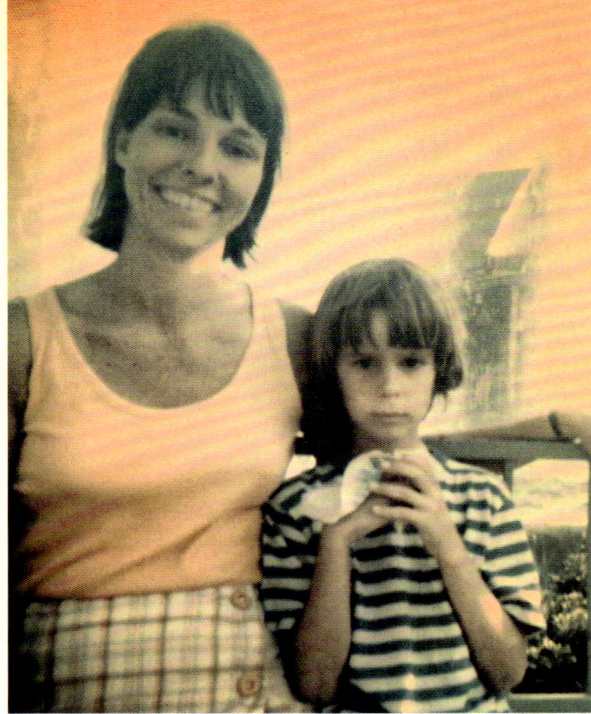

but it's worth it.

was that being an artist was foolish and crazy, but it may not have been received in the way she had intended. My parents were square. They were nice, had normal jobs, and took us to church. The wildest thing in their record collection was The Mamas and the Papas. I had an aunt and uncle that were everything my parents weren't. Their house was a perfect balance of clutter, design, and danger. Costumes, fireworks, skulls, beads, and weapons from their many travels were meticulously placed on endless shelves. I didn't understand how they could have all of those wild things and we just had knickknacks. They took on a sort of mythical role in my life and sparked magical ideas that have never gone away.

When I was born, in 1967, we lived in Woodland Hills, California, a suburb of Los Angeles, in a quaint yellow house surrounded by orange trees and nice neighbors. We were walking distance from school and the main drag, and we had lots of friends that lived nearby. We went to Disneyland, Magic Mountain, and Busch Gardens. My mom's parents lived on the beach in Malibu so we spent lots of time there. Life in Los Angeles was full of potential futures. There was a skateboard park and I had friends that were getting into acting and music. We would occasionally visit movie sets and see famous actors and musicians on the beach. Then, early one morning, a car flew across our lawn while we were eating breakfast and crashed into the side of the house. Nobody was hurt, but that was the end of our idyllic Southern California lifestyle. Mom always wanted to live in the country and the city had finally proven itself to be unsafe.

From around eight years old I lived in the middle of nowhere. Clovis, California, is a small town north of Fresno. We lived five miles outside of Clovis. I hated it. I had felt strange compared to people in Los Angeles. In Clovis, I was an absolute weirdo. I tried to fit in a little but was usually more comfortable in my own world. I got into skateboarding and riding motorcycles and actually got pretty good at skiing. My brothers and I were generally inseparable when we were little. When we got into high school, the elder was much bigger and more popular and had a bit of a mean streak, but he dragged me along to some parties and helped me meet girls. The younger one was funny and strange and we loved him for it. He once made a T-shirt covered in plastic forks and wore it to school, which was a pretty cool move. I had friends but not a lot of them. High school was horrible even though I spent a good part of the year in Lake Tahoe at a private ski racing school that I begged my parents to send me to.

At sixteen, I went to my first punk rock show and finally found people I could really relate to. That was my first real step outside of school or my family. I loved the noise and chaos and smashing into people. Punk rock seemed like it was all about being an outsider. People did strange things that didn't make sense to the general public. They made things happen themselves because they had to. It wasn't long before I started making my own things happen. I drew on blank T-shirts with a marker and sold them at shows. I did one with a big skull and the name of a local hardcore band, Capital Punishment, that caught the eye of their guitarist. He asked me if he could use it for an official band T-shirt. That was my first real art gig. The do-it-yourself ethic of punk rock became the basis for how I think about art and work.

At the same time that I was discovering punk, I fell in love with a charming and hilarious girl that I met at school. We started dating and stayed together even as I went back to Lake Tahoe for most of the school year. Around the end of my final senior semester, life took a horrifying turn. As a child I was always trying to overcome a feeling that life is dangerous. I was afraid of the dark, earthquakes, lightening, monsters, deep water, ghosts, and wild animals. Some scary things happened that justified some of my fears, but I felt pretty stable by the time I was sixteen. I did not see this coming. The cruelty and depravity of other human beings was not something that I worried about. We were out in the countryside together late at night and were ambushed by a pair of men with a knife. It's the single most devastating event of my life and what it did to her was certainly worse. The guilt that I felt for not being able to protect her was overwhelming and the weight of this tragedy drove us apart and sent me into a deep depression.

The only thing I really cared about at that point was music. I joined a death rock band called Vicious Bunnyz with a notorious front man who weighed in at about 350 pounds and sported a pink Mohawk and dark eyeliner. At one show we all dressed as priests and he sliced his wrist and sprayed the audience (and us) with blood. He and the synth player were a huge influence on me, turning me on to the dark side of punk as well as experimental, industrial, and modern classical music. In 1986, we drove to San Francisco to see Einstürzende Neubauten play at a giant event where Survival Research Laboratories performed and Keith Haring showed a series of huge paintings. I was floored by the scale and complexity of the show. The mayhem of SRL's robotic machines and Haring's wild fluorescent squiggles were absolutely intoxicating. My ideas about art were expanding and matching my internal mood.

I barely graduated from high school, but I did it because I wanted to study art in college. I wanted to be empowered to make something out of all that I was feeling. A few months before arriving in Los Angeles to start school, I had seen an otherworldly painting by Roberto Matta at the Centre Georges Pompidou in Paris. The dimensional shift that happened when I looked into it turned my love of surrealism and cartoons into a deeper sense of my own potential. I could finally see some of where I wanted to go. At art school, as I feebly played with those visual languages, I met resistance from some of my teachers. That kind of work was really not in vogue in the mid-eighties. I was told bluntly that I'd never be taken seriously if I made work like that. I was mortified. Art school was not going to expand my ideas about art. It was going to contain them.

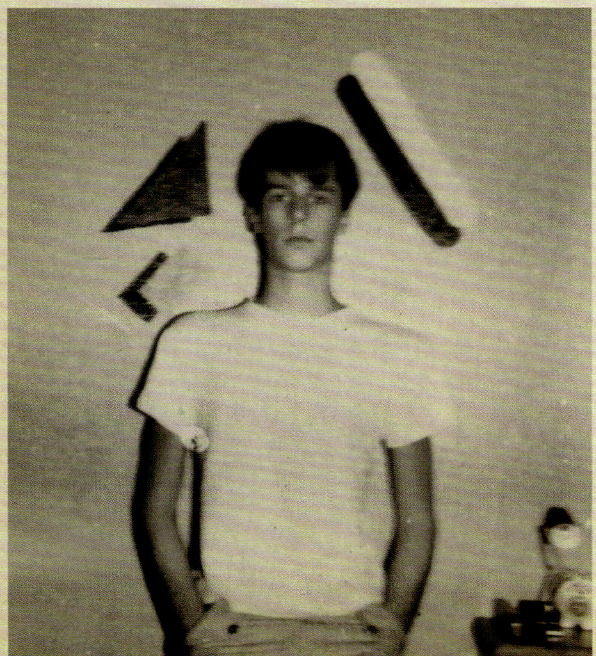

While I was at school I continued to explore music, putting on performances in campus stairwells, hallways, and even the dormitory kitchen. Making music was a way for me to work outside the realm of art that I felt constrained by. One of my teachers asked me to work on a recording project, which made me feel like a legitimate musician. Taking music seriously was the perfect excuse to leave art school. While I felt a sense of loss at giving up my aspirations of being a painter, it felt hopeless to fight what I saw as impossible odds that I would ever be able to make a life out of it. I dropped out at the end of my second year. My final project was not a painting, but a vinyl record by Big Butter, a band that I had started with my younger brother. I moved back up north to Fresno to start a record label and leave the art world behind. I found a day job at a record store making signs and displays. The Big Butter record got picked up for distribution by Ralph Records, a label owned by The Residents. It was a dream come true and inspired me to do more. I released a catalog of strange music as limited edition records and cassettes, opened a store, and booked shows. I became a fixture in the Fresno music scene where I played in several bands and ended up drumming for Capital Punishment. I had continued to make art for them since that T-shirt back in 1985. I was cruising along in the nineties as a music professional.

As much as I enjoyed the work I was doing, everything in my life at this time was tinted with a feeling of unease. I couldn't shake the unresolved feelings from the assault that ended my relationship with my high school girlfriend. I tried to fix things by reuniting with her, but after a brief attempt at a relationship she left me, and I had to face the feelings head-on. She convinced me to see a therapist, and after a long period of resistance I had a major breakthrough. I began to understand how I used our relationship to contain my fear, anger, sadness, and guilt—feelings that had been festering inside me for my entire life. I had developed a vast fantasy based on Disney films and stories from my childhood where love solved every problem forever. Underneath all my illusions about love I found a neglected version of myself that needed to be heard and taken care of. The process took many years of intense individual and group therapy, but I emerged feeling like I was capable of anything. There is no possible way that I would be an artist today without the insight that I got from that work.

All this time I had been creating art. I made record covers, flyers, T-shirts, and so on, but with my newfound clarity I was able to see that I was enjoying the art more than the music. I began to consider shifting my focus back to visual art. I had been looking at Juxtapoz magazine and getting excited about what people were doing. Then I saw Ren & Stimpy. Animation was getting really interesting, as well. I decided to try to follow that path to being an artist. I drove down to Hollywood to look for a job. A veteran animator looked at my work and leveled with me. I had no idea what I was doing. I didn't know the basics of good drawing. I was going to need to work really hard for many years to even scratch the surface. He suggested some books and techniques and sent me back to Fresno to do some soul-searching. I realized that I had been resisting the urge to take art seriously because I knew how far I had to go. It made me rethink my years in art school. Maybe I was actually just lazy! After several years of drawing for about five hours every day and working as an illustrator, I drove south to try again. I landed an entry-level gig in a studio color department cleaning up files. I worked my way through the industry, and within a year I was head of my own color department on another show, and soon after that I was a background painter working for nearly every major studio in Los Angeles.

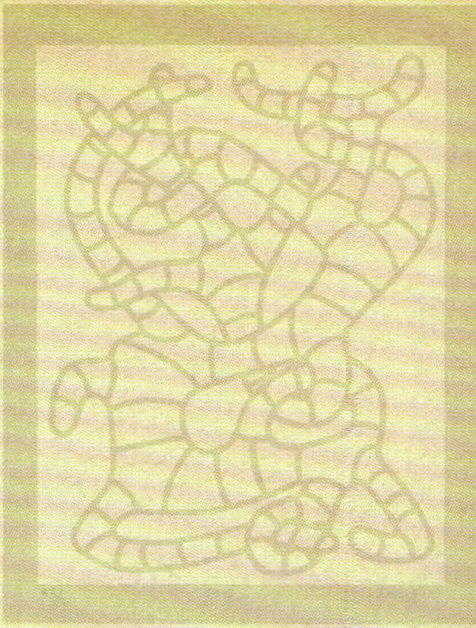

White Worm
1992. Serigraph on Paper. 30" x 20"

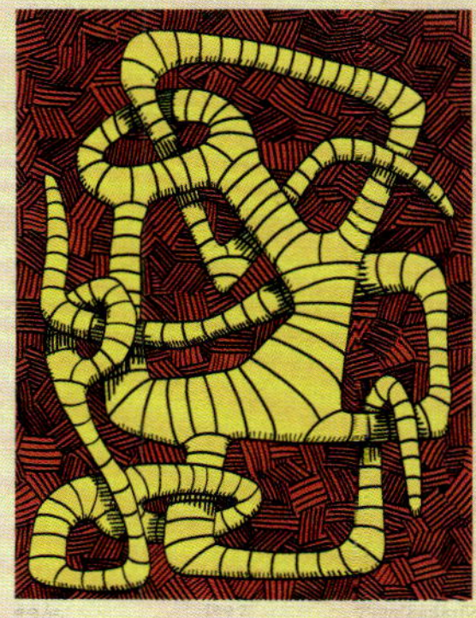

Red/Yellow Worm
1992. Serigraph on Paper. 30" x 20"

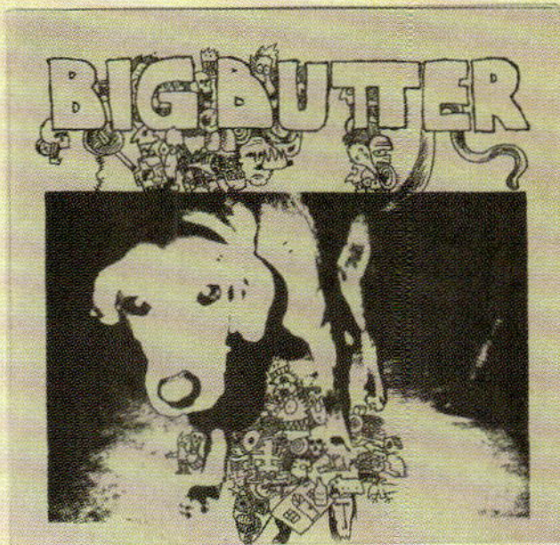

First Big Butter Record, 1988, 7" Vinyl

The doorknob of the universe

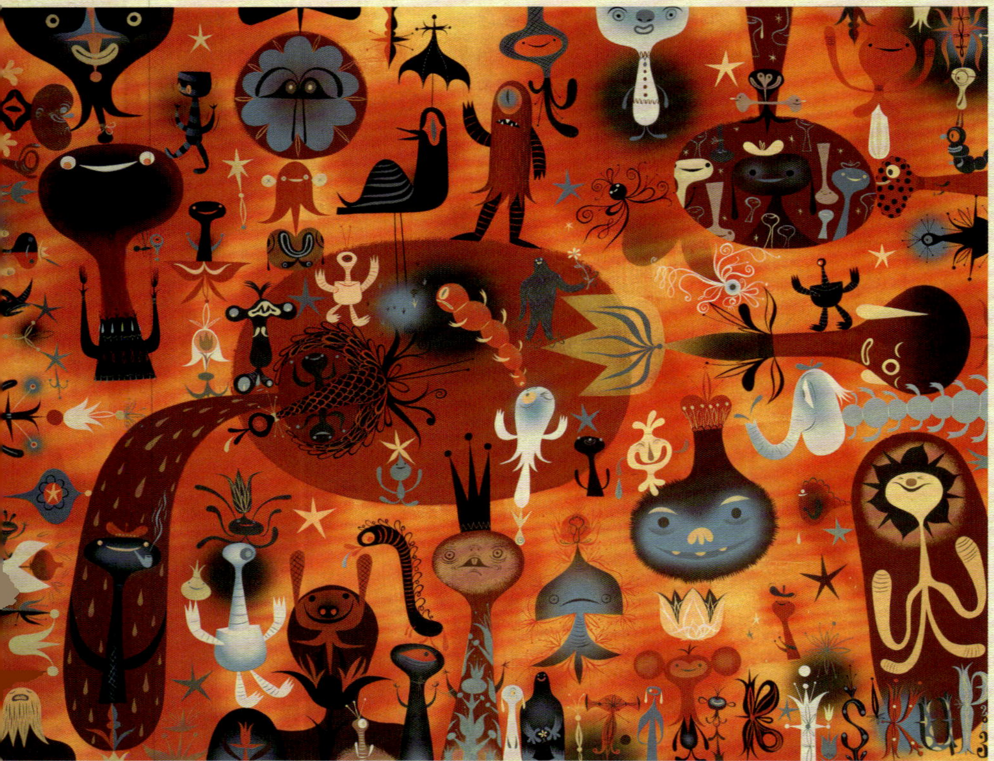

The Doorknob of the Universe
2003. Gouache on Panel. 36" x 48"

Animation is where I got my real technical training in art-making. That education wasn't weighted with the prejudices of 1980s art school. I worked with amazing artists and we drew pictures constantly. Practically every time I got up from my desk, there was an unflattering caricature waiting for me when I got back, hilarious and beautifully drawn, by one of my co-workers. It was not just an attack on my face or the way I walk or what kind of toys I collect. It was a challenge to respond. This created a constant playful trigger to draw that went beyond our daily duties. That simple state of inspired competition was a key for me to learn to be a true professional.

I was glad to be back in Los Angeles, the city that I had been so fond of as a kid. When I was there for art school it felt inhospitable and sketchy. Now I had a well-paying job and could afford to live comfortably in a beautiful mid-century house in Beachwood Canyon right underneath the Hollywood sign. I started dating an artist who I met through a musician friend. She was sweet and engaging and we hit it off immediately. I was so happy to be with someone that could relate to my calling in life. We worked together and traveled and enjoyed life. After a few years we got married and moved to Pasadena where we could spread out and make a life for ourselves.

As a background painter, I painted all the time—wrestling with the volatile properties of gouache and learning to paint straight lines on the endless bits of architecture in animation layouts. I always had scraps of illustration board and watercolor paper lying around to figure out color combinations, lighting, and staging for the work I was doing. I would also use those scraps to make little paintings from my head. I showed them to my co-workers who encouraged me to make bigger pieces, so I snuck in some time at work and set up a little studio at home. I put together a portfolio and showed it to a gallerist. He took a look at what I was doing and told me it was too derivative. I was miffed, but he had a point. I was looking at the same inspiration as a lot of other artists and it showed. I had to work on finding a more personal visual language, but his response also got me questioning how I wanted to sell my art and led me away from the idea of showing my work in galleries.

I built myself a website and I wrote a manifesto called "Why I Hate Art Galleries." It was an angry rant, but it was fun to write. I saw galleries as part of the same crusty old establishment as art school but I was mostly just upset at being rejected by the one gallerist I had shown my work to. I started selling paintings online. It was so simple and beautiful to go directly to buyers, but I missed the sense of community that a gallery can bring. I found that community feeling when I was invited to bring a painting to a party organized by some animation friends. They hosted an art auction where everything was made by the attendees. The garage was a makeshift gallery and the top of the stairs was the podium. Bids stared at fifty cents and chaos ensued. I remember seeing things go for less than the price of their frame and others for over a thousand dollars. I walked away with a few hundred bucks, some original artwork, and an inspiring thought. This could be the solution to my dilemma with art galleries. Before I left that night, I asked the organizers for their blessing to put together my own event. I got the green light and the Burning Brush was born.

The first Burning Brush Art Auction (1999) was a huge success and a great time. It was the first moment that I felt the influence of my grandfather in my life. He was a very successful businessman, and, based on my lack of financial success in the music business, I had figured that that part of the family chemistry just didn't make it to me. The Burning Brush was a whole other way of thinking about business. It didn't fit the traditional model because it didn't really make any money. The value in it was that it was fun and it drew attention to my personal art and the work of these artists that I loved and respected. We showed and sold paintings and some of us even launched careers through the events. Gallerists showed up and bought paintings and made deals with artists to exhibit their work. Even the guy that called me "derivative" took another look at my paintings and offered to put a piece of mine in his next group show. He also convinced me to take the anti-gallery manifesto off my website. After all, I was becoming part of the business now.

I was soon juggling my time between working in animation, making art for gallery shows, and running art auctions. I had a recurring dream that my house was a portal to another dimension. I would wake from the dream with a feeling of responsibility to the creatures that lived on the other side. I made a painting called The Doorknob of the Universe for my first solo show (Alphabeast, 2003). Later, after I had left animation work and stopped doing auctions, a friend pointed out the metaphor that I hadn't seen. The creatures represented my art and I was neglecting them. I believe the painting itself was a way of fulfilling the requirements of the dream. Leaving animation and auctioneering behind gave me the freedom to explore myself and play with my art in a way that I had always dreamed.

By this time my first daughter had been born and my perspective had shifted. I spent more time sitting on the floor playing with blocks, laughing, and taking long walks than I had since I was a child myself. Having a kid around was a constant reminder to be present and alive in my life and my job.

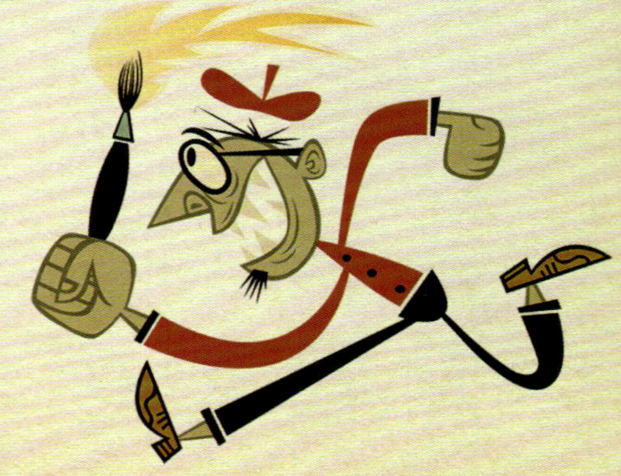

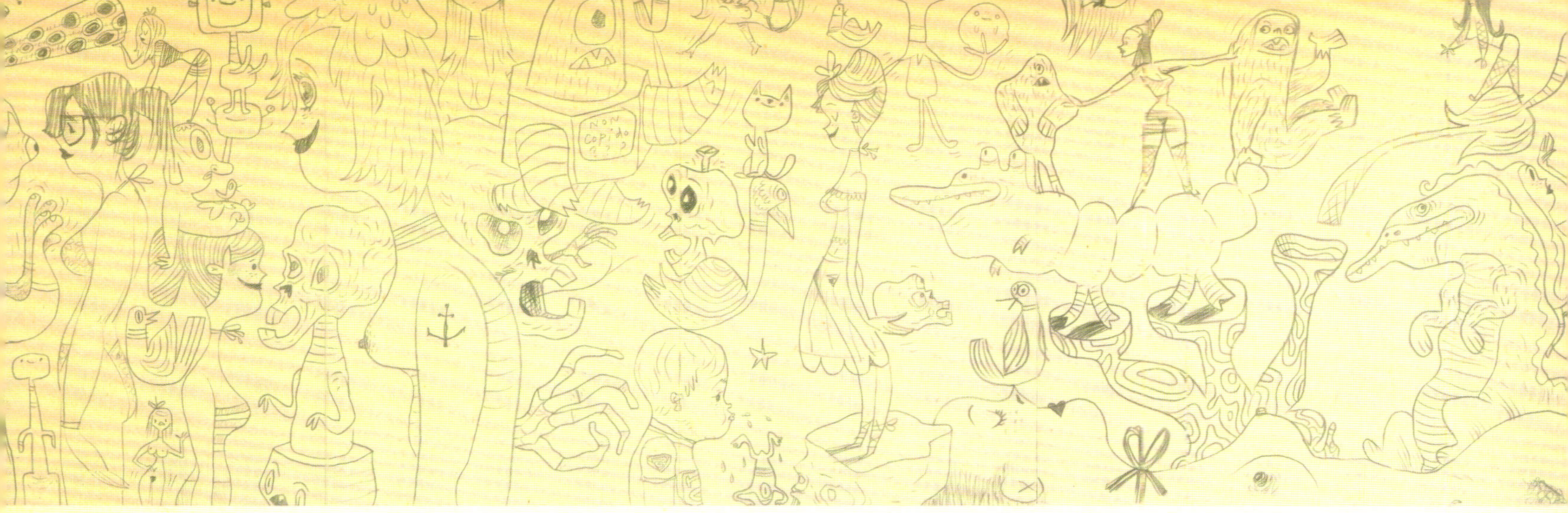

The Phantom Thread

Later that same year, while traveling in Europe, I had a nightmare. In the dream I was watching a story on the news. A lake in the mountains had been suddenly filled with hundreds of dead bodies. The words "Blood Flood" were ringing in my ears. I had been working on a Japanese style sketchbook that was made out of a single nine-foot-long piece of paper. I sat in my hotel room and drew out what the dream made me think. Women falling from the sky surrounded by giant flaming skeletons. Creatures from other dimensions riding in a train that burned bones as fuel. In real life, the second Gulf War was beginning. I kept seeing anti-American graffiti. I had taken the little "Made in America" flag off my jacket sleeve. I was guilty about being an American, but I was also proud and loved the country where I grew up. So I worked with that discomfort and the mysterious symbolism of my dreams for my next show, The Phantom Thread (2003). I wanted to bring that darkness and fear into my work more and more—to change my relationship to my art. It was called The Phantom Thread, because I could not see what the connections were between all these images—the lake of blood, the destroyers from other dimensions, the replacement of men with skeletons, the sexual desperation and portrayal of women as beautiful but in control of this world—but I knew it was there. I'm still confused by it, and maybe that is the point. I was very confused and didn't know what to do.

The Golden Pill

The Golden Pill (2004) was full of more mystery and confusion: scrambled words that could not be decoded, motifs that related to my childhood floating around in the compositions. The exuberant joy of earlier paintings was giving way to imbalance in my psyche and in my relationships. I wrote an artist's statement for the show that compared selling art to being a drug dealer. I didn't use it because it was so clearly not the point. I didn't know what the point was. I just knew that I was seeing cracks in my perfect life of being an artist. The largest piece in the show, The Golden Plague, was a commission that drew on this conflict. It featured gold leaf painted over with acrylic details—the first time that I played with the high/low relationship of materials, something I would come back to over and over. Juxtapoz did an article. Lots of people came to the opening and asked me to decode the words for them and asked me how long it took to make this or that. The show sold out and the gallerist handed me a drink and told me the total of what we had just made. The figure was just abstract to me in that moment. Throughout the night I kept wanting the content of the work to be the conversation and it was almost always not.

The Push-over

I began to question my sanity at this point. I was obsessed with apocalyptic ideas and imagery. I was convinced that I needed to be open about my state of mind and that somehow this would lead to me being appreciated for who I was and not just what I make. The work from The Push-Over (2005) put my inner turmoil on display. I started to tell stories about myself in these paintings. The Executioner is me struggling with the requirements of parenting—trying to figure out how to be in charge when I was not at all sure what I was doing. Armored figures are me grappling with my internal conflicts and trying to be taken seriously. The apocalypse was personal.

My first New York City solo show, Virtue (2005), celebrated the decorative aspects of my work in a city where artistic tastes leaned decidedly away from decoration. The mostly abstract works on paper were presented in traditional frames that highlighted my simple motive of making beautiful paintings. It was satisfying to make that statement but I don't think it came across as particularly revolutionary. I just felt more misunderstood.

"Blood Flood" Sketchbook
2003. Graphite on Paper. 5.5" x 108"

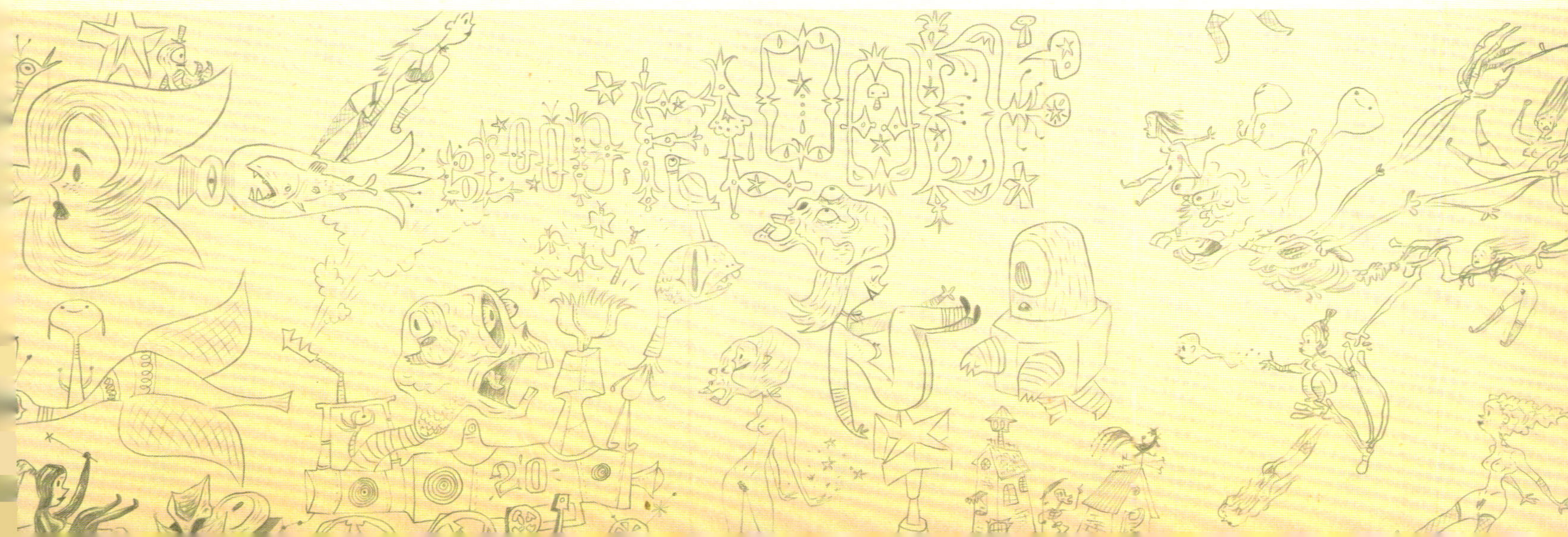

Giving way

The realm of dreams and abstract ideas were the inspiration for most of my work up until this point. I enjoyed the open-ended freedom, but I felt a need to make a concrete statement with my first international solo show. The gallery was in Barcelona, so I decided to study the historical connections between the United States and Spain. I had never done research for a show before. My experience with school had been so unpleasant that it was hard to see how it could be useful, but now that I didn't have a teacher looking over my shoulder asking me to explain what I was learning, I was free to respond in a way that came naturally to me. I could easily convert my feelings about what I was reading into paintings and sculptures. The intertwined histories of the two countries are full of inspiring material, but I found a deep connection with certain aspects of early American history. American Cyclops (2006) centered on Freemasonry and Iroquois law in the formation of our political system as a way to understand my own struggles with personal freedom and integrity. The idealistic optimism of the birth of our country and the way that corruption upended the system began to connect to my life in an unsettling way. I felt guilty about my own capitalist nature, and worries about internal corruption were weighing on me. I had always said that my Cyclops character, Helper, represented something evil, but I started to understand what I was using him for. He was a representation of a man that has lost his ability to see clearly. He is committed to his delusion of knowing everything, including the will of God. He is the embodiment of manifest destiny, a phallic symbol riding into battle and trampling nature to death. My art was sending me painful messages. This work was reconnecting me to my deepest and most difficult feelings. It was a dark time, but what came next was even darker.

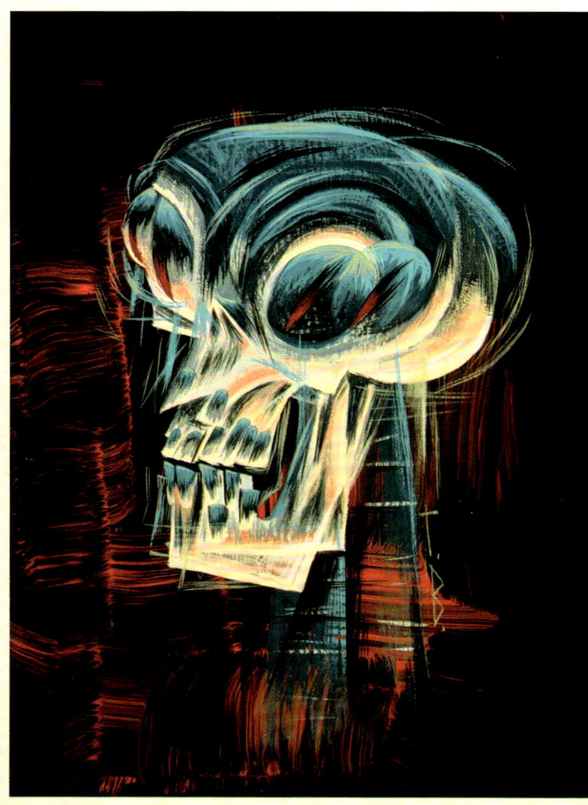

Scatterbrain
2006. Acrylic on Panel. 12" x 9"

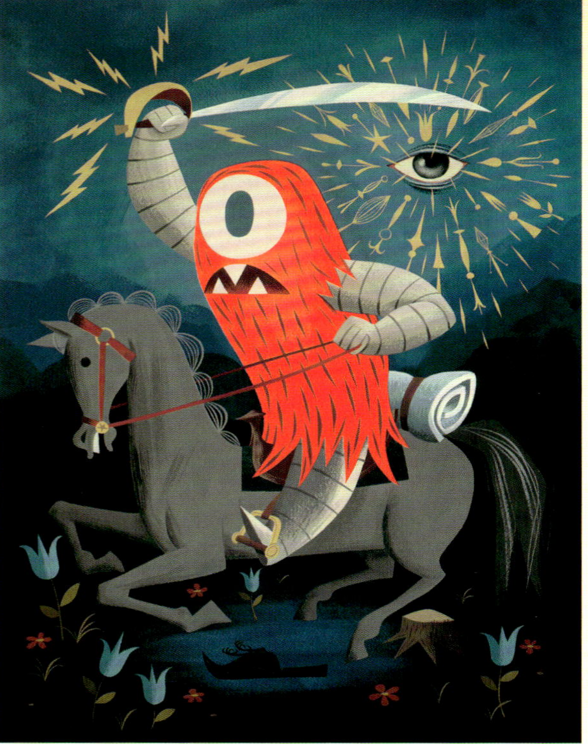

Helper Manifest
2006. Gouache on Paper. 24" x 18"

Whenever my work scares me, I know I am onto something important. Vapor (2006) was a bloodbath. I changed my technique so that I could get into the deeper parts of my mind. The colors and brushwork were creating more space, volume, and emotion. Scatterbrain set the tone for the whole show. It was a gruesome, fractured skull that also felt like a self-portrait. The paintings looked the way that I felt: crazy, disjointed, and frantic. The words "Something is Wrong" kept coming up in my mind and appeared in some of the works. It wasn't just about me. I felt like the world was off balance. The problems in my relationship with my wife were making us both miserable. We had been together for eight years. Our daughter was a few years old. We were good at being parents and solving everyday problems but we were not getting along. I had gone deeper and deeper into my own world, which drove us apart even more. As I was finishing these paintings, our relationship was coming to an end. A few days after the opening, I was scheduled to speak at a conference in Berlin. I couldn't sleep and feared that I would just walk on stage and start crying. What happened next was totally unexpected. Just after the host announced me and I walked out on stage I saw a butterfly flying toward me from just above the audience. It fluttered up and onto the podium where it spread its wings and showed me two big beautiful eyes. Then it flew away. I took it as a sign that I was going to be okay and that whatever happened here was part of something bigger. I started talking and kept myself together. I was open and honest in speaking about my paintings and why they had gotten so dark. Opening up about my fears, depression, and anxiety was an important step in transforming myself and my work. As I finished, I could hear people in the audience crying and I knew I had made a connection. I had changed the conversation.

The floodgates were open, but I still had more to deal with. The work for my next show, Ether (2007), was a continuation of me venting my inner turmoil. The thirteen-foot-tall dragon in the middle of the gallery was a metaphor for how I felt. It had been stabbed through with several knives and swords, and in response it was screaming to the heavens and firing a machine gun into the air. The paintings were filled with anger, conflict, sadness, and sexuality. The demons, and other fantastical creatures surrounded by beautiful women, masonic phrases, and symbols were my way of expressing the loss of power that I felt in my life. I had made so many decisions based on a desire to please others, and in the process I had lost myself. This work was me trying to take my power back. In the end I felt ready to move on from the rage that I felt toward myself and my circumstances and redirect my attention to another source of anger: the art world.

The artist in you

Twenty years after leaving art school, I could still hear my painting teacher telling me that I'd never be taken seriously. It hit me so hard. I felt like she was telling me that this force that was trying to emerge from deep within me was invalid. I struggled with the feeling that she could be right. As much as I felt like I was making serious work, I wasn't sure other people felt the same way. While I had been making paintings for Ether, I made a piece called Asylum that perfectly inflamed my internal debate about my validity as an artist. Among all these confrontational images of ferocious vixens and monsters, I created this portrait of a beautiful placid woman who looked away from the viewer, allowing herself to be admired. She was docile and sweet. The colors were bright and sunny. She had flowers in her hair and delicate jewelry. It was pretty and I couldn't handle it. When people came into the studio they were drawn to this painting. I wanted them to look at my gut-wrenching problems and they were being serenaded by this beautiful piece of folly. I finally decided to sell it just to end the distraction. The decision haunted me. Why was I so irritated by something so sweet and lovely? Why did I want to get away from it? It was because it wasn't difficult. It wasn't challenging. It was passive and enjoyable and I didn't think it would be taken seriously by the people that I was trying so hard to impress. My art school ghosts were still alive and controlling my life. I decided to open up the subject and attack it head-on. I had a show planned at a gallery in New York City. What better place to wage the eternal war between art and expectation?

I hadn't published anything that I wrote about art since my rant against art galleries on my first website. I was overwhelmed by the thought of it. I was an art school dropout. What did I know? The decision to write a book that would be published along with the show was just the right kind of terrifying for me at that point in my life. The discomfort that the gallerist expressed about the prospect only encouraged me. He tried to talk me out of it but I persisted. I began to talk with friends about what it was that bothered me so much. I read everything I could find on the subject of artists' relationship to their audience, curators, and peers. It was daunting to approach these heavy, intellectual books and articles. There is nothing in this world that annoys me quite as much as art-speak. So often, the goal seems to be nothing more than to make the author sound smart. But I was trying to overcome my bias enough to find the messages buried within the byzantine foliage of words. When I picked up a book called The New Administration of Aesthetics, it was not because of the title alone, but because the very design of the book seemed so intentionally awkward and confrontational with its colored paper and angular cut-out interior corner. It turned out to be exactly what I was looking for. There was an article inside that became the basis of my understanding of how intellectual thinking is used to confuse and distract emotional and intuitive thinkers from determining their own destiny within the confines of the established art world. What it said in a nutshell is that most conversations about art end up in the territory of the brain rather than the heart, so all of us sensitive artists who would rather paint than talk about painting don't end up being a part of the conversation. Perhaps that is old news to those of you who finished art school, but for someone like me who doesn't have the patience to study art theory, it was shocking the realize that someone actually understands the problem that I was having and was talking about it.

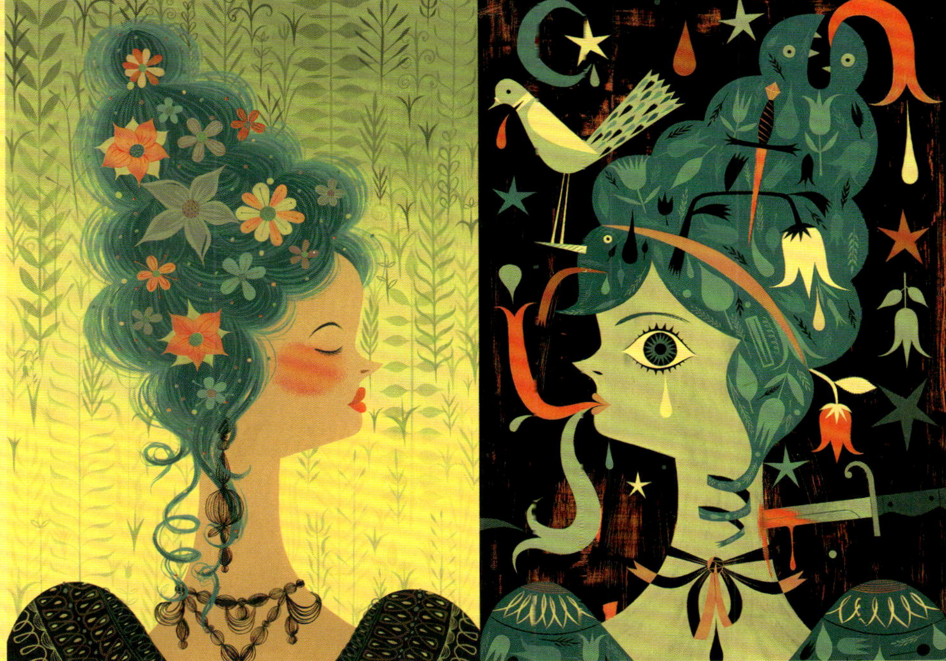

Asylum
2008. Acrylic on Panel. 36" x 24"

Asylum No 5
2008. Acrylic on Panel. 36" x 24"

The book that I wrote was an assault on everything that I hated about the art world, but it was also a conceptual art project that was helping me understand my personal hang-ups while intentionally trying not to prove how smart I am. I was willing to make myself the butt of the joke. The title was The Artist in You (2008), which was meant to sound foolish. The fact that the book had a white dust jacket with simple text wrapped around a full-color illustrated cover was an attempt to illustrate my own feelings about the project. I felt like an imposter and I wanted to talk about how awkward I felt. I begged the gallerist to set up conversations between myself and some art writers and critics. I wanted to see how my raw emotions would fare in relation to other strong opinions about the nature of art, but I think the gallerist was concerned that I would be criticized and appear silly if pressed to defend my writing, so that part of the project never happened. The response to the show and the book was generally that nobody seemed to care. Certainly not the people that I was writing about. A few people called me brave for writing about these taboo subjects. The whole thing made my skin crawl and felt like a complete success because of that.

The paintings were attempts to illustrate what I was talking about in the book, and because the book was so confusing and frustrating, the paintings were as well. The fractured and angular style matched my disjointed thoughts. The reworking of that beautiful portrait that gave me so much grief was a curious exercise that led me to more confusion. I walked away from the show feeling like I had unveiled my crippled ego to an audience that wanted something else. The nagging feeling that I had was that I was trying really hard to prove that I am a real artist by being honest about how fucked up I am.

I didn't feel better. If anything I felt worse. I needed to keep dealing with these feelings, but I didn't want to keep writing. I came up with an idea that summed up the general irritation that I felt about working with galleries. I devised a sculpture that worked as a combination display stand and shipping container for each painting in my next show, O/S (Operating System) (2008). They were heavy and distracting, which was the whole point. Everyone asked the same question: "Can I buy the painting without the sculpture?" Or they suggested that the sculpture was unnecessary. I agreed that it was unfortunate that they had to have the sculpture and then explained that it was a representation of the infrastructure of the art world, and the fact that it distracted and annoyed them made my point. The show opened in Paris in September of 2008, a few days after Lehman Brothers failed. Nothing sold, and eventually I had to pay the gallery to ship my work home. The financial crisis that followed crippled the market for artists like me. My complaints about the art world suddenly seemed to matter less than my concerns about the future.

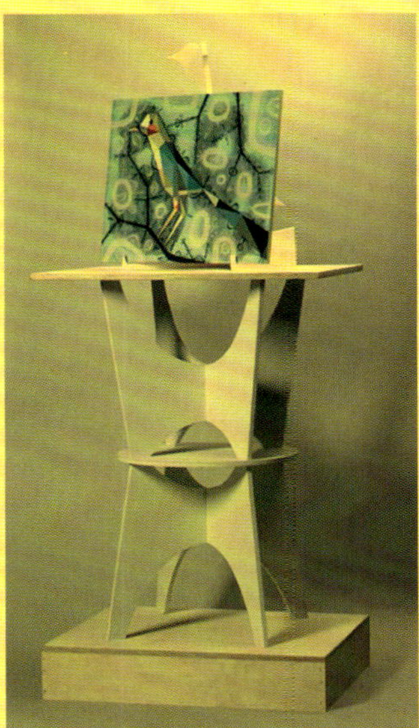

System #10
2008. Acrylic, Gesso, Mailing Label and Postage on Shaped Plywood, Nails and Glue. 68" x 30" x 22"

"After the destruction of the object, the invalidation of sentiment and the passing of art into a post conceptual anti-world what is there to argue about? It is hard to refute the death of art. I'm sad to see it go. I could claim that I believe that art will be re-born, but I am not up to the task of making that argument. If it comes back let me know. In the meantime, I will be in my studio making luxury items."

Excerpt from "The Art of Destroying Art" 2008

The Mystic Chords of Memory

I had another meaningful dream around this time that I tried to jump over a huge chasm. I couldn't see the other side. I hung in the air, arms and legs reeling slowly. Like the dream, my life was in limbo. I wasn't broke exactly, but times were tight. I was doing everything I could to hold onto my home. Spending half my time with my kid and half my time deejaying, working on commercial art gigs, and painting. My daughter was a constant source of encouragement and a reason to slow down and let go of the stress of money problems. I would tell her my troubles in kid-size terms and she would hug me and draw something totally inspiring. We would sit on the floor and play and laugh.

I had been single for four years and was finally feeling ready to take a relationship seriously again. As soon as I had that realization, I met a woman that made my head spin. She was breathtakingly beautiful, funny, and smart, but the real clincher for me was her willingness to say exactly what she thought at all times. I was not used to that kind of directness and was taken aback when she unflinchingly challenged my authenticity and honesty, but that rawness was exactly what I needed. Being with her has been a revelation about what it means to love someone and has helped me understand myself more deeply than I ever thought possible.

The presence of love in my world made me feel hopeful about everything. My work began to bloom with life, and soon after we met I showed a series of paintings in Barcelona called The Mystic Chords of Memory (2009). The title of the show and the title of each painting were taken from Abraham Lincoln's Gettysburg Address. I had always loved the ethereal words of encouragement and how he dealt with the tragedy that had led our country to that place in history. Barack Obama's run for president was looking promising and I was feeling hopeful about the future. For the first time in years, my work was full of optimism.

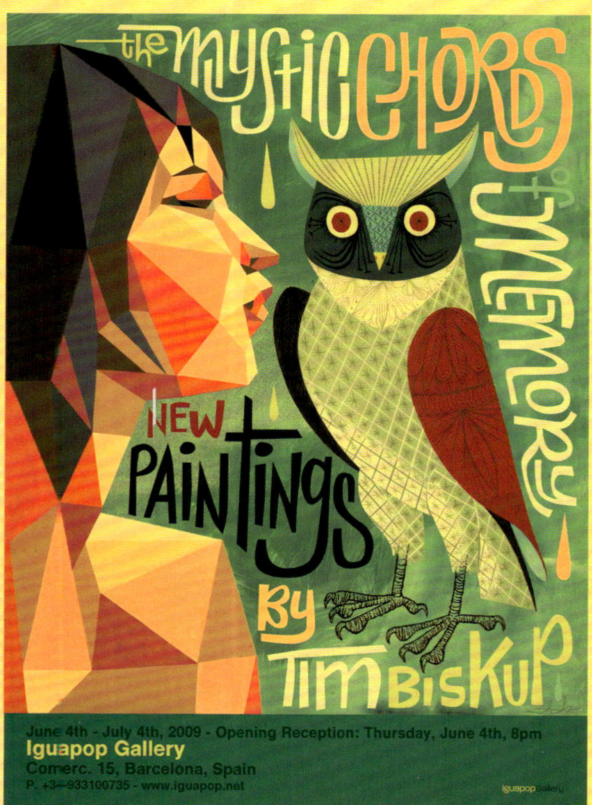

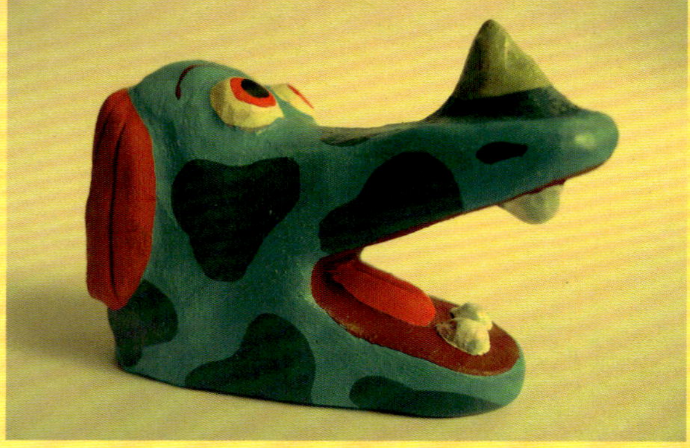

Dog Dragon
2011. Acrylic on Polymer Clay. 2" x 3" x 1.5"

Former State

I started making vinyl toys in 2002; it felt like a perfect way to expand what was happening in my paintings. I put aside the practice around 2006, because it had become a whole other culture and I didn't like where it was taking me. Former State (2011) was a rebirth of my original intention with toys. I wanted them to be seen as archetypes that remained playable and abstract and not as character development. I had been making little sculptures for myself for years and they littered the studio. The idea of making big paintings of these tiny things seemed like an interesting way to keep them in the realm of object and maximize their aesthetic virtues. I had refined my use of painted polygons to build shapes and I loved working with them. The paintings were pure pop fantasies, and placing the sculptures on pedestals next to them gave them context. It was a nicely contained idea and the first time that I made a show that turned out exactly the way I expected it to look and feel.

Another difference with this show was that I was working with a new gallery run by people who were much younger than me. The way that they thought about art was refreshing and open. They had a background in PR and made videos and promoted the show on multiple social media formats. It was a wake-up call for me to engage with younger people. I came to realize that while I was struggling to relate to people from my own and earlier generations, millennials were taking over the world and didn't have the same hang-ups that had been plaguing me for so long. I began to think differently about myself and felt hopeful that I was free of all that art school dogma. My work could be playful and fun without being disregarded as kitsch.

In that same year I put together a wild project with a fellow artist that pushed both of our boundaries of what we were supposed to be doing as creative people. We made a short film with two of our favorite filmmakers in which we played on themes of fandom and critical judgment. In the film the two TV stars that we were celebrating with our paintings turned on us, mocking us, spraying us with paint, and destroying our work over a hilarious and chaotic six minutes. The film was shown at a music festival in upstate New York on a continuous loop in a small gallery space surrounded by our prop paintings. For me it was another step toward freeing myself from expectations by mocking the feelings that had haunted me and by thoroughly enjoying myself in the process.

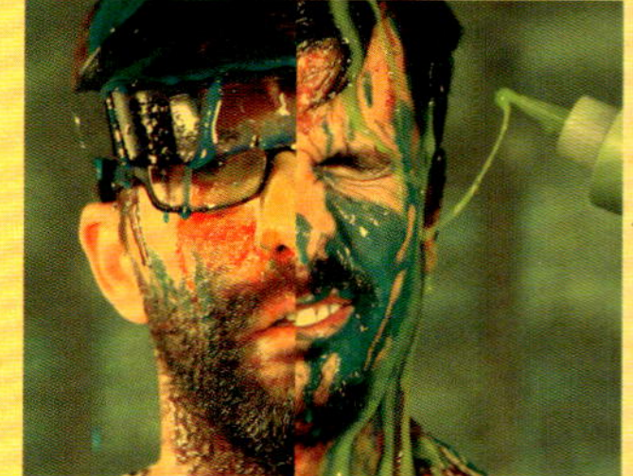

Promotional Image from "Critique" by Eric White and Tim Biskup
2011. Video. 6 Min.

Memento

The title Excavation (2012) was taken from the Willem de Kooning painting of the same name. I had seen his retrospective at MoMA New York and was excited by the ferocity with which he approached his work. I found myself in an unusually calm state of mind and the idea of exploring painting without all the weight of my conflicted thoughts was thrilling. I was so happy to go into the studio and paint every day. The subjects were often skulls, mostly because I've always gravitated to the image as a way of facing (quite literally) my inner self. I was also drawing more. I would make piles of drawings before I picked up a brush, so I was warmed up and relaxed. I used bigger pieces of paper; it forced me to draw with my whole arm rather than just my wrist. At some point I remembered a technique that I had experimented with in art school where I turned a graphite block on its side and swept it across the paper to make a gradation. Kneeling on the carpet in my living room I quickly made a pile of abstract drawings that felt so personal and honest that they brought me to tears. It was a beautiful moment and the beginning of a new era in my work. I didn't understand the physicality of what I was doing until a friend shot a video of me drawing with graphite and posted it online. I hadn't realized that I was grabbing the paper and turning it while a drew, and I didn't know that what I was doing looked a bit like sleight-of-hand. What I did know is that I found the process deeply relaxing and inspiring. It put me into a state of attention that felt like meditation.

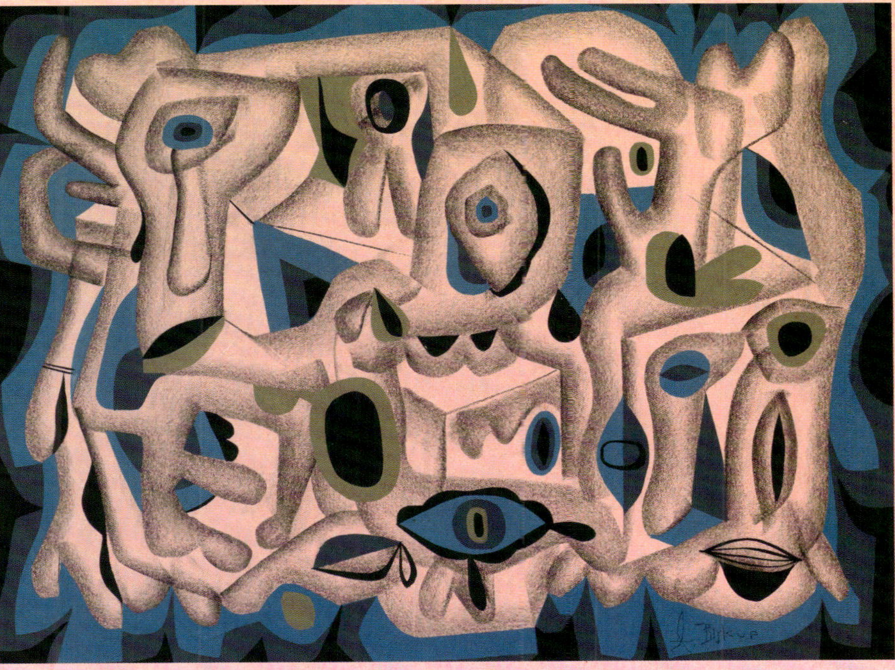

Balkan Window
2012. Graphite and Acrylic on Paper. 11" x 14"

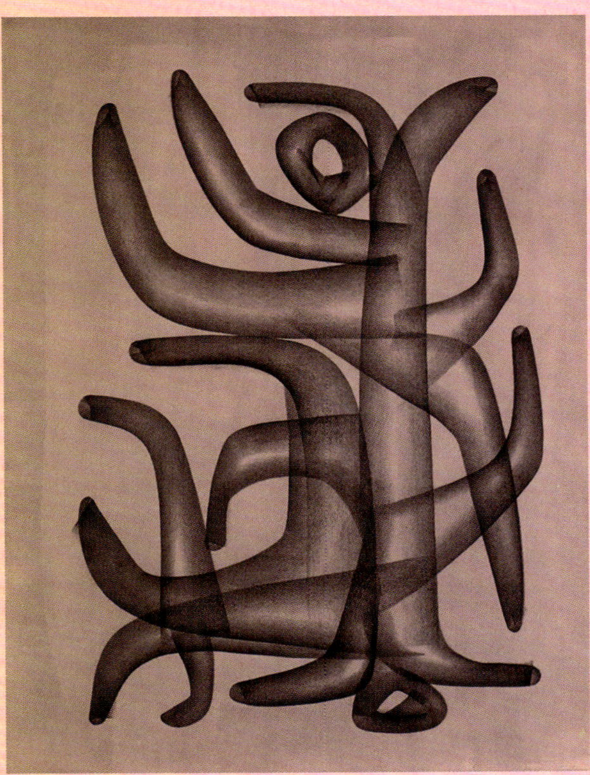

Untitled Graphite Memory
2015. Graphite and Clear Gesso on Paper. 24" x 18"

Mori

My whole body moved when I made these airy voluminous structures that seemed to float above the surface. I breathed along with the flow of the work—exhaling as I started a new shape. The path of each line started before the graphite touched the paper, like an airplane approaching the runway and landing softly but with committed force. The pain in my hand building over the hours of drawing showing me just how much weight I was investing as I leaned into the surface. Like yoga, it's painful but the pain is worth the burst of energy that envelops you. The drawings happen so fast. That's why I call them Graphite Memories. Because I spend so little time thinking about them, they exist almost entirely in the past. I can experiment more because, if I don't like a piece, I just throw it on the floor and start another. The work that comes out feels so natural and organic. It reminds me of the Roberto Matta painting I had seen in Paris all those years ago. I turned a corner in the museum and felt like I fell into another world. He was showing me an abstraction of his spirit and I connected with it. I feel like he awoke my artistic soul in that moment when I was eighteen and just about to go off to art school, showing me what was possible so that when I got there, I was able to know how pointless it was to follow the rules. There was something deeper that I needed to find. As these drawings started to pour out of me I understood that Matta had been manifesting his own universe and now I was doing the same thing—attempting to show something that binds us all. I've seen it in dreams and visions. It can't really be drawn or painted. I can only be in awe and try to express it. It is the energy that flows through everything. It is magic and life and love, death, loss, pain, consciousness, truth, reality, and non-reality. It's the distance that I put between myself and what is expected of me. The call away from the fire and into the darkness. When I have been truly lost at some moments of my life and have found my way back to joy, that place between dissolution and recovery is where I have learned the most. So, that's what's happening in this work. I'm manifesting physical objects that attempt to express the inexpressible. This may be as close as I ever get to succeeding.

A Subtle Advertisement for Mind-Numbing Pain

In 2011 I was asked to contribute a painting to a museum show in Spain. I felt ready to tackle a really big piece after playing with larger formats for a while. I asked for a whole wall and told them I would make something special. What I made was a nine-by-twelve-foot painting called A Subtle Advertisement for Mind-Numbing Pain. I called it that because it looked like a peek into my mind. At times I'm overwhelmed by this stream of images and ideas that overlap and intertwine. There is beauty and joy in it, but the overall feeling that I have come away with is that it is painful to be alive. It's brutal to be overwhelmed. This painting felt like a movie trailer for my life. The images had meaning to me, but I didn't always know what their meaning was. I just kept thinking, "This thing that I'm painting is the next thing that needs to be there." I worked on it for four months but never saw the whole image until it was finished. It's painted on three mounted canvas panels and I couldn't put them all up next to each other in my studio. There was not enough room. When I finally took them out to the porch and lined them up it all made sense. It looked beautiful. It's one of my favorite paintings. It's the one that I show people when they ask what I do.

After the museum show the painting was returned, but it had not been shown in the United States, and I decided to make it the centerpiece of Charge (2013), an exhibition that I felt was going to be a breakthrough for my career. I was working with a gallerist that had connections to the art world that I had been skewering for so long, but she seemed very open-minded and willing to commit herself to introducing my work to an audience that I felt ready to meet on my own terms. As the work for the show came together, there were hints that she was not as confident of my work as she had claimed, and by the time the show was open, it became clear that her interest was mainly financial. I had sold my huge painting and was commissioned to do another one of similar scale. Through a series of behavioral shifts on her part, I understood the nature of her interests, and when the show closed I severed our relationship and we parted ways.

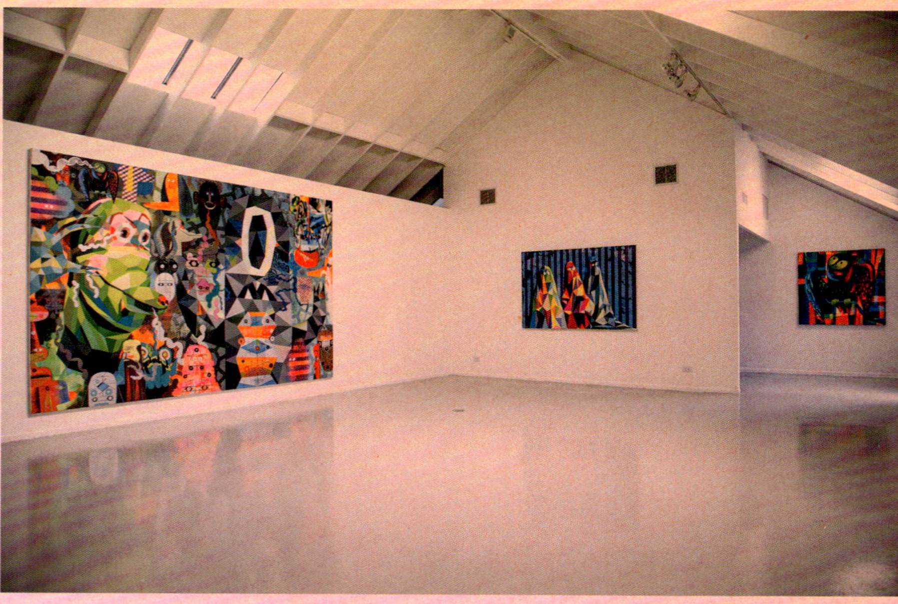

"Charge" Exhibition View, 2013

Somewhere in the middle of all of this I developed chronic back pain that kept getting worse. I tried everything: chiropractic treatments, acupuncture, pills, and booze. It was relentless and it felt like it was going to kill me. The pain was not coming from an injury or illness though. I came to realize that the problem was not physical, but emotional. I could feel the tension radiating out of my mind and into my body, constructing my nerves and torturing me with mind-numbing pain. All of those years of wrestling with my problems had not set me free like I had thought. I was still full of unresolved conflict that I had abandoned because I wanted so badly to stop feeling sorry for myself and wallowing in fear and sadness. Now I saw a way out of my pain. I had to go back into myself and find the places that were haunted and kill the ghosts. I was terrified of what I might find, but with the help of a therapist I dug deep into my past. I felt the knee in my back from a childhood bully, the horrible teacher dragging me through a classroom calling me stupid, and the knife at my throat while I heard the muffled cries of my girlfriend. I was drenched in tears and sweat as I felt the waves of anger and sadness unwinding from my body. I visualized the perpetrators of these assaults against me being attacked by wolves and faced with their own guilt so I could be released from mine. The years of self-hatred that I had turned all of this into had become a part of me, but now the tentacles began to retreat. By the end of a single session I was practically free of pain. This miraculous event helped me understand how to use my gifts of sensitivity and creativity for their greatest purpose. The raw nerves that I have been navigating my whole life have made me feel defenseless against fear, pain, and sadness. They've sent me into despair and seclusion. Now I was using this place where my art comes from to truly set myself free.

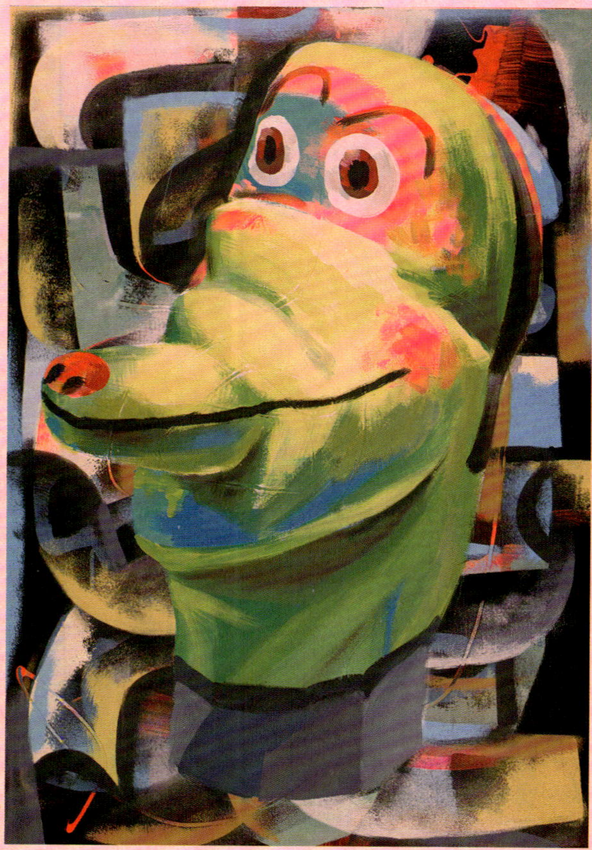

The Stare of Unwitting Love
2013. Acrylic on Canvas. 36" x 24"

A Step felt in Full

My younger brother, who had been painting his whole life, finally decided to quit his day job and take an art career seriously, and while I was working through the disappointing relationship with my highbrow gallerist, he was developing his own ideas about how to be an artist. Doing a show together was a perfect way to move on from the past and ignite new ideas. We had been working on music together off and on since our previous record had come out in 1991 and had enough material for at least one new album. With the encouragement of a new, young group of gallerists and the support of an enthusiastic sponsor, we launched into a combination gallery show / live event / album release that guaranteed us both a good time and a change of focus. A Step Felt in Full (2015) was inspiring and well received. It encouraged me to let go of my past and see my career as an open-ended opportunity to find myself through my art. The most successful projects that I had worked on were always the ones that came from a desire to enjoy myself. Every time I tried to think too strategically, I ended up disappointed. I decided to relax a little and let my next opportunity find me.

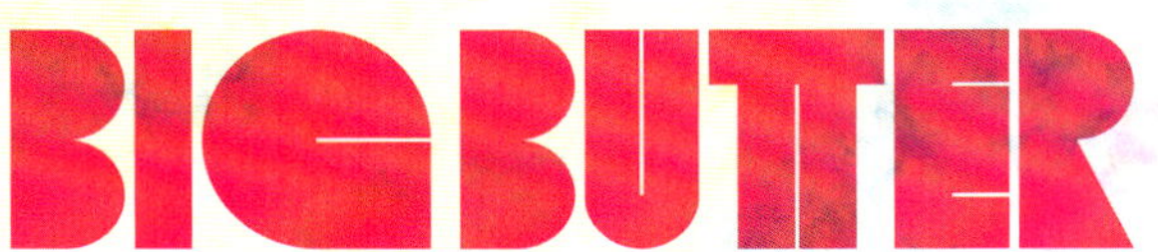

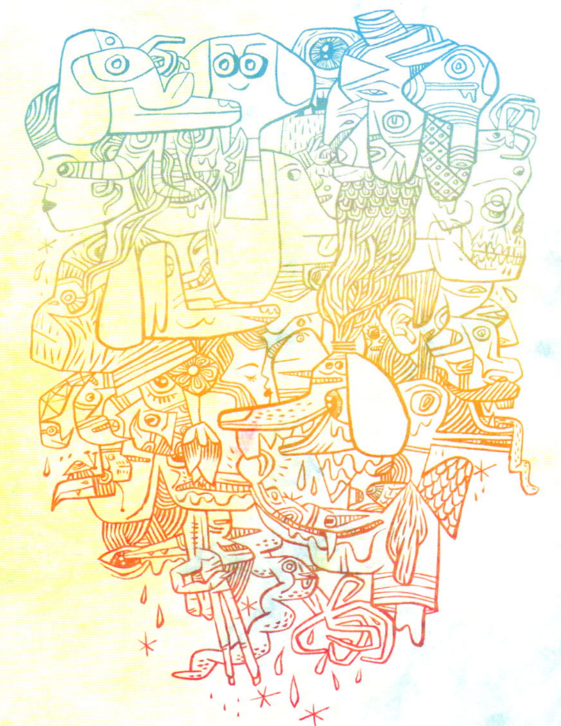

"Big Butter: A Step Felt in Full"
Promotional Material. 2014

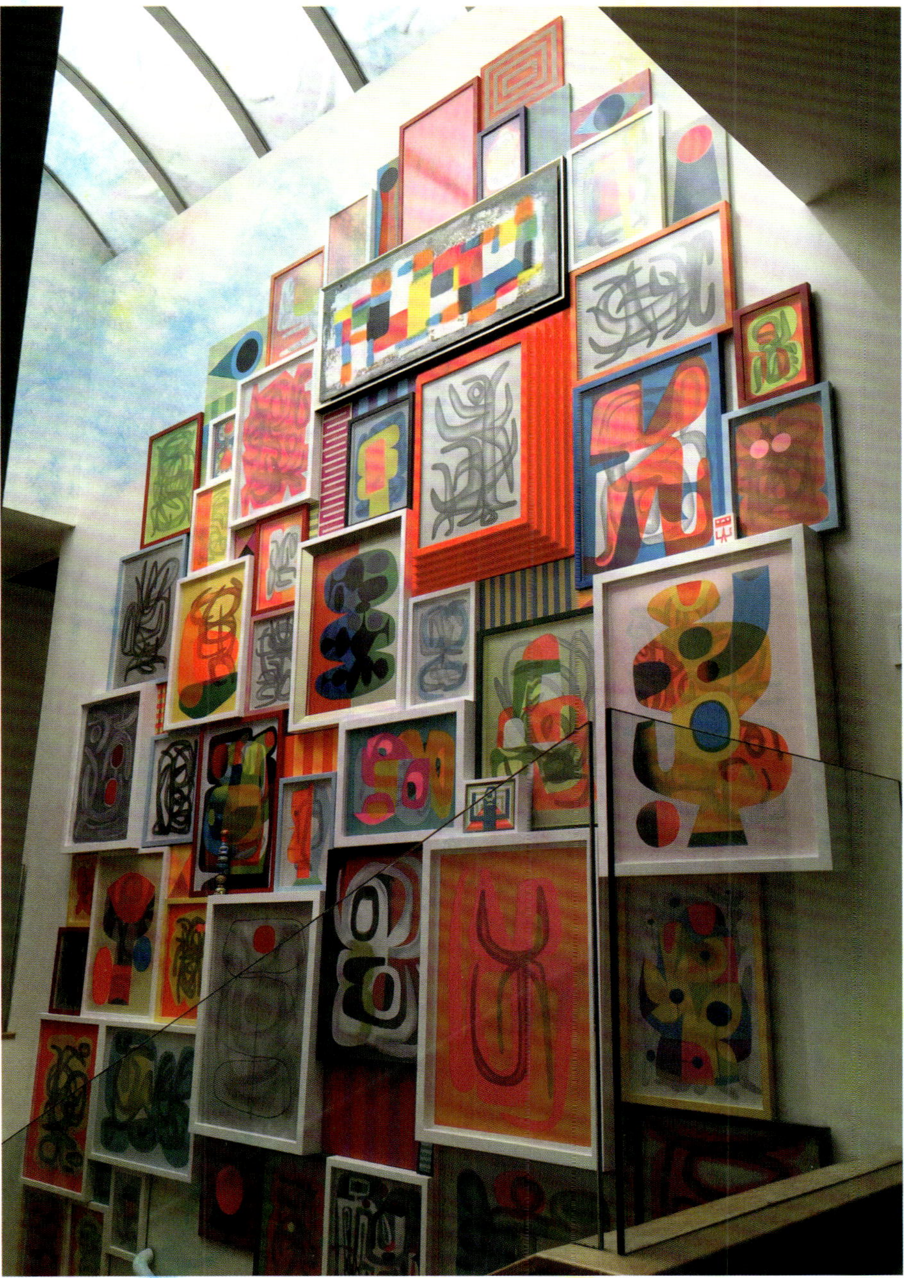

Memory Staircase (Detail). 2015

Memory staircase

Up until this point I had always been making work for a specific purpose. Now I wanted to see what it was like to make whatever I wanted with no particular idea of what it was for or where it was headed. I made piles of graphite drawings and added layers of translucent color to them, painted large abstract pieces on rolls of paper and canvas and continued to experiment with sculpture. I was reluctant to plan another gallery show and vowed to wait until an opportunity came along that sounded like fun. I invited collectors over to look at work. One of those collectors pulled out several paintings that he liked. We laid them out on the floor in the living room like a patchwork quilt. He couldn't decide which ones he wanted, so I suggested that I could create an installation of framed paintings that would fill a wall like a mosaic—salon style but tighter and with more variety in depth and color of frames. He said he had the perfect wall: a seventeen-by-twelve-foot expanse of stairway in the center of his house. It was an incredible opportunity for me to place that much work together and know that it was all going to stay there. I developed Memory Staircase (2015) over many months, seeing it come together, making adjustments, and editing along with the patron. It stands as the largest collection of my work in a single place. Nearly eighty individual paintings combined into a permanent gallery on a single wall.

Space Mad ness

My work is constantly changing but nothing ever really goes away. I'm obsessed with working out new ideas and I think of my past work as a box of art supplies that I can go back and use whenever I see fit. The explosion of color and form in my recent work had felt like an expansion into new land. When I decided to add characters into the mix, they came straight out of my past, but now I was more free with my lines and shapes. The creatures were more wild and disjointed. I called the series of paintings Space Madness (2015), after a favorite episode of Ren & Stimpy. An artist friend had offered me his gallery in Hong Kong, so I mounted the show and turned it into a working vacation. The sense of ease that surrounded this well-received project left me with a new understanding of how to approach exhibitions. I could feel my lighter attitude lifting me to a happier life.

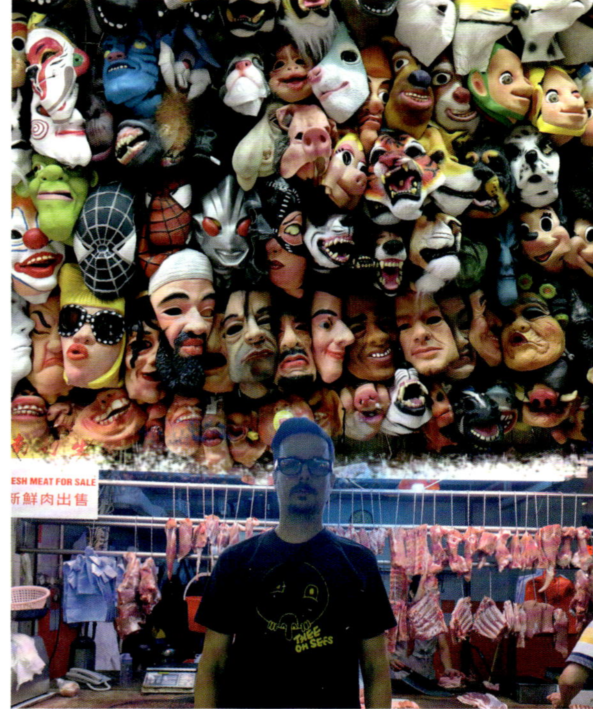

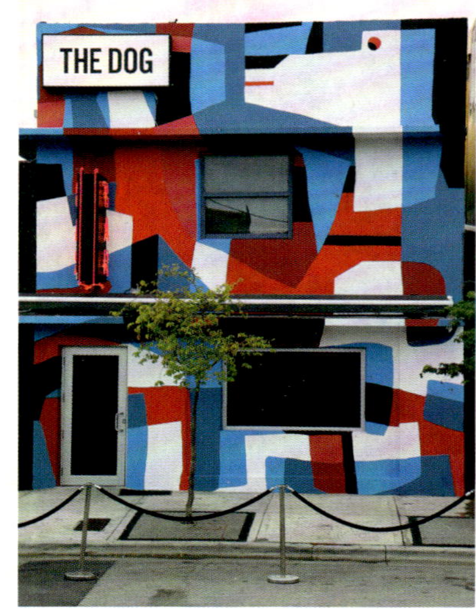

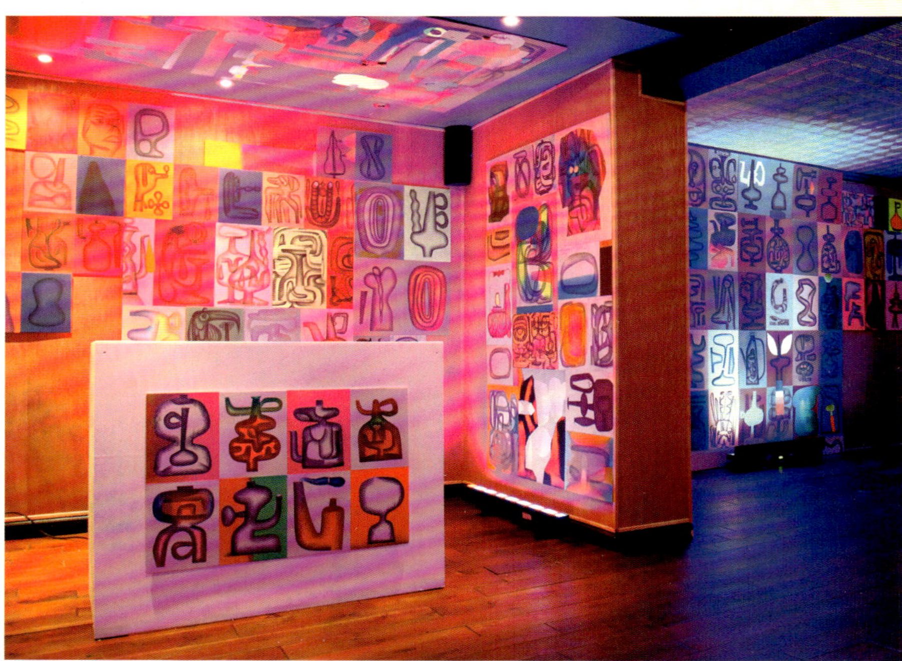

The DOG

After so many years of seeing my work as individual pieces, I was inspired by Memory Staircase to think more about their relationship to each other. I showed pictures of the installation to a musician friend who suggested that we take over a small bar in Miami during the 2016 art fair season. A few months later, I had turned a pile of graphite drawings into colorful mosaics mounted on wooden panels. The process of working on my salon style installation had been distilled down to simple materials that I could work with quickly. We gutted the bar of all furniture and decorative elements and then paneled it with plywood. The chairs and tables were replaced with large wooden blocks. It became a paired down abstraction of a bar. I covered the walls, inside and out, with my art and set up a drawing table in the middle of the space where I could make more work while the party happened around me. The Dog (2016) was constantly active and packed with people until late every night for its four-day life span. I returned home feeling like whatever I did next had to have the same feeling of open-ended creativity. I wanted to live like that. To be free.

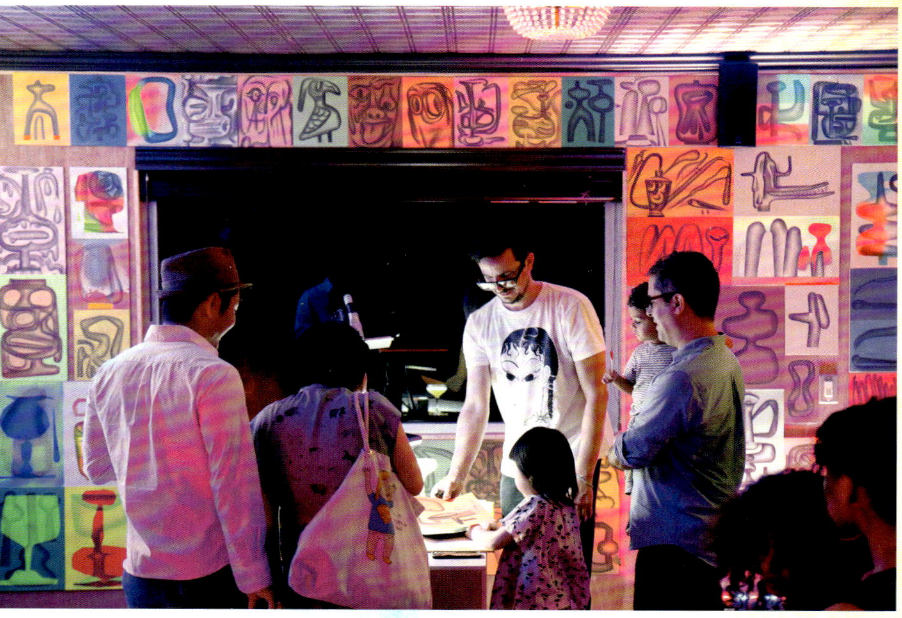

Face Guts

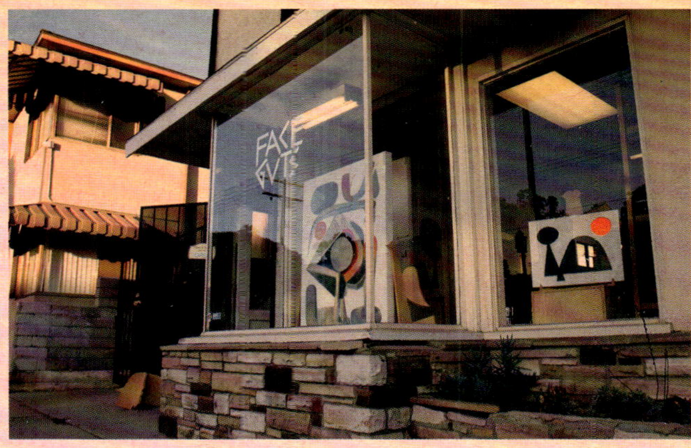

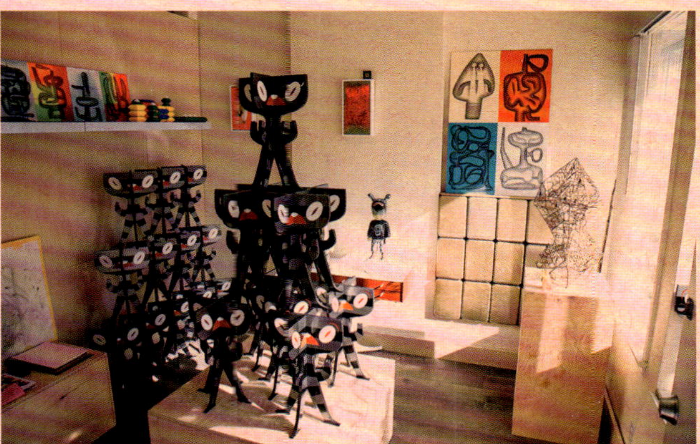

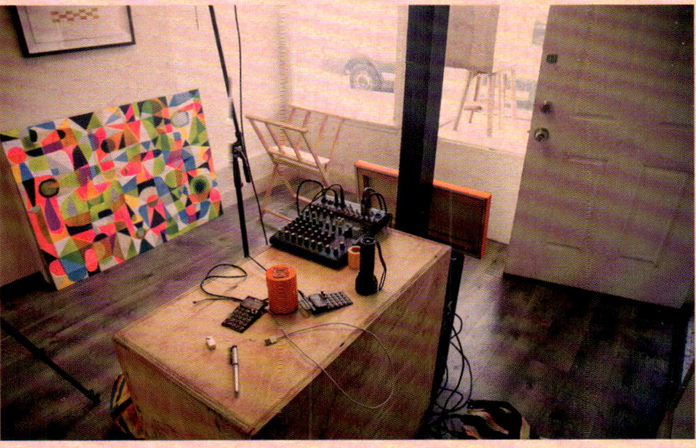

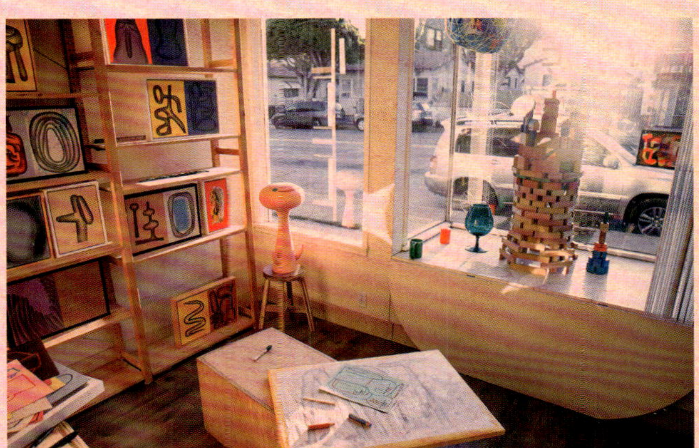

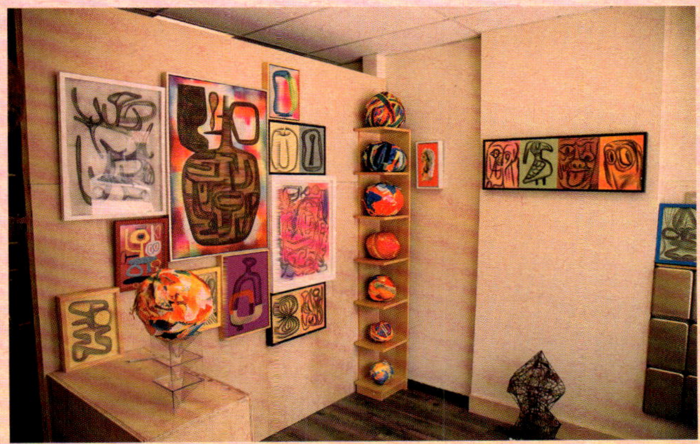

I loved working on The Dog because I got to think about every aspect of the experience. I didn't want to run a bar, but I liked having a space to work with. For years I had been renting an office with a storefront that had some potential. I would display interesting objects in the front window for people walking by and kept thinking I'd figure out an interesting use for the space someday. One night, the inspiration for a project entered my mind. I would create a place where I could experiment with my ideas for installations—a low-key art space where I could do whatever I wanted. The next day I was in there moving things around and brimming with motivation. The place was packed full with my collection and archives. I had been making things steadily since my hand-drawn punk rock shirts thirty years before. Records, books, vinyl toys, prints, and original artwork needed to be carefully organized so I could move around and know what I was dealing with. Months went by, and as the space was transformed I felt myself relaxing, enjoying the process, and understanding what I was going to do in there. I built a tiny gallery area and used metallic tape to put a logo onto the front window. In February of 2017, I opened Face Guts, and it began to slowly redefine my understanding of my purpose in life.

I love making my art and it's what I do most of the time, but the connection that my work creates between myself and other people is what gives it meaning. When I talk to someone about it, we get to know each other in ways that go far beyond casual conversation because my work opens me up, and when I open up other people do the same. It's not uncommon for me to have revelations about myself or what motivated a specific piece during conversations at Face Guts. As I understand myself more clearly, It changes my art and how I live. I feel more in tune to my nature and a willingness to try new things. The opportunity is always there to expand my practice: To draw, play with blocks, make music, and write. To rearrange things and plan for the future. The constant change keeps it alive and gloriously chaotic. Face Guts is a business, but I'm always carefully considering the entire experience to make it more vibrant and meaningful. When someone buys something, the exchange is more than just financial. It's personal.

About a year after I opened Face Guts, I celebrated my fiftieth birthday there, surrounded by my family and friends. The gravity of the event made me stop and appreciate the life that I have been given and what I've done with it. I'm still the same person that grew up struggling to find balance, but I've changed the way that I deal with those thoughts. I've learned to pay close attention to my intuition, to remain open to the infinite possibilities that life has to offer, and to direct my energy toward positivity and happiness. I feel more free than ever.

Thank you:

Nicki, Tiger and Xixi, My Parents, My brothers, Steve and Mike, Steve Crist, Gloria Fowler, Steve Alexander, Maggie, Richie & Calvin, Dee & John, Tessa & Kent, Eric Ayzenberg, Mike Lazzo, Mark Ryden, Marion Peck, Gary Baseman, Eric White, Patricia Arquette, Rob Reger, Bwana Spoons, Todd James, James Marshal, JJ Abrams, Mark Parker, Fritz Costa, Jennifer Powell, Nedra Gallegos, Todd Oldham, Xavier & Lauren, Jaime Hayon, Iñigo Martinez, Fer & Fer Frances, Shepard & Amanda, Money Mark, Seonna & Paul, Mark, Esther & Lili Todd, Rob & Frieda, Antonio Columbo, Billy Shire, Sean Kelly, Jonathan LeVine, Kirsten Anderson, Christian Clayton, Josh Agle, Craig & Jolene Myers, Jane & Phillip Straley, Simon Birch, Rich Jacobs, Sam & Tury, Brian Donnelly, Eric Nakamura, Jeff & Stacey Mann, Andrew Brandou, Slow Culture, Max, Steve and Fred, Wendy Bryan, Gargamel, Oka, Mama Luli, Ben Butcher, Jamie O'Shea, Dave Choe, David Cantolla, Ana Gervas, Coleccion Solo, Raymond Lemstra, Carlos & Timony, Bill Fold, James Jean, Devin Corbit, Miles Nielsen, Brann Dailor, Jen Stark, Brian Bell, Trent (Trout), Everlast, R. Brandt Daniels, Claire Darrow, Ramsey Dau, Sky Dayton, Scott Denton-Cardew, Kristopher, Keenen, Dita Eyewear, Joel Knoernschild, Dan Ruth, Jillionaire, Conor Libby, Matt Kennedy, Stanley Donwood, John, Theo & Leah, Ginger Gonzaga, Tristan Eaton, Mick & Caskey, Chris & Greg, Barry & Deborah, Fred Eric, Wayne White, Greg Escalante, Espai Tactel, Aaron Farley, Mark Murphy, Jay & Mi-Shell Nailor, Eric Nakamura, Day 19, Gary Felton, Linda Lose, Russel & Gerry, Ann Field, Carole Caroompas, Renee Petropoulos, Christopher Williams, Chas Smith, Joe Sorren, Jeff Soto, Morgan Spurlock, Louisa St Pierre, Robert Standish, Dale & Joceylin, Sonja Teri, Emilie Trice, Homer & Hardy, Tom Timony, Erik Foss, Kristen Schiele, Catherine Sutton, Framing House, Debbie Frank, Paul Cruikshank, Paul Frank, Mark Mothersbaugh, Boing-Boing, Alvaro Ilizarbe, Aimee Friberg, Matt Furie, Albert Reyes, Miguel Garcia Larios, Gary Garay, Mong Skillman, Miyoko Baensch Nather, Lilian Garcia, Roger Gastman, Tyler Gibney, Mat Gleason, Marsea Goldberg, Matt & Junna, Bobby Green, Julie Machado, Judd Katz, Christian Parkes, Koji Harmon, Steve Harrington, Justin Krietemeyer, Naomi Harris, Tom Hazelmyer, Eric Wareheim, Jim Hodgeson, Cody Hudson, Matt Abergel, Lin Lin, Jason Jagel, Josh Jefferson, Jones Fu, Nathan Jurevicius, T9G, Merry Karnowsky, Joshua Katz, Eric Yahnker, Brad Keech, Dov Kelemer, Phil & Lulu, Heather & Josh, Doug Lussenhop, Kevin Lyons, Evan Mack, Dimitri Martin, Martin Ontiveros, Carlo McCormick, Mendy Medina, Long Gone John, Susan Michaels, Ben Mohapi, Cedd Moses, Kyle Ng, David O'Reilly, Mike Parisi, Jose Parla, Darren Romanelli, Scott Patt, Mike Patton, Cleon Peterson, Izzy & Arielle, Doug & Gayle, Rita and her people, Evan Pricco, Pushead, Ragnar, Brian Ray Turcotte, Bert Rodriguez, Camille Rose Garcia, Michael Rytz, Dale Zine, Souther Salazar, Ben Sanders, Devin Sarno, Kenny Scharf, Jiro Schneider, Andrew Schoultz, Allison & Eric, Skullphone, Colin & Ron Turner, Michelle & Amanda, Justin Vanhoy, Mark Dean Veca, Jeff Vespa, Adam Wallacavage, Ang Wilson, Rob Wilson, Clint Woodside, Karen Knecht, Willy Grier, Mark Growden, Das, Martin Macintosh, Al Moran and Darrel Crow. I'm sure I've forgotten someone and I feel terrible about it.

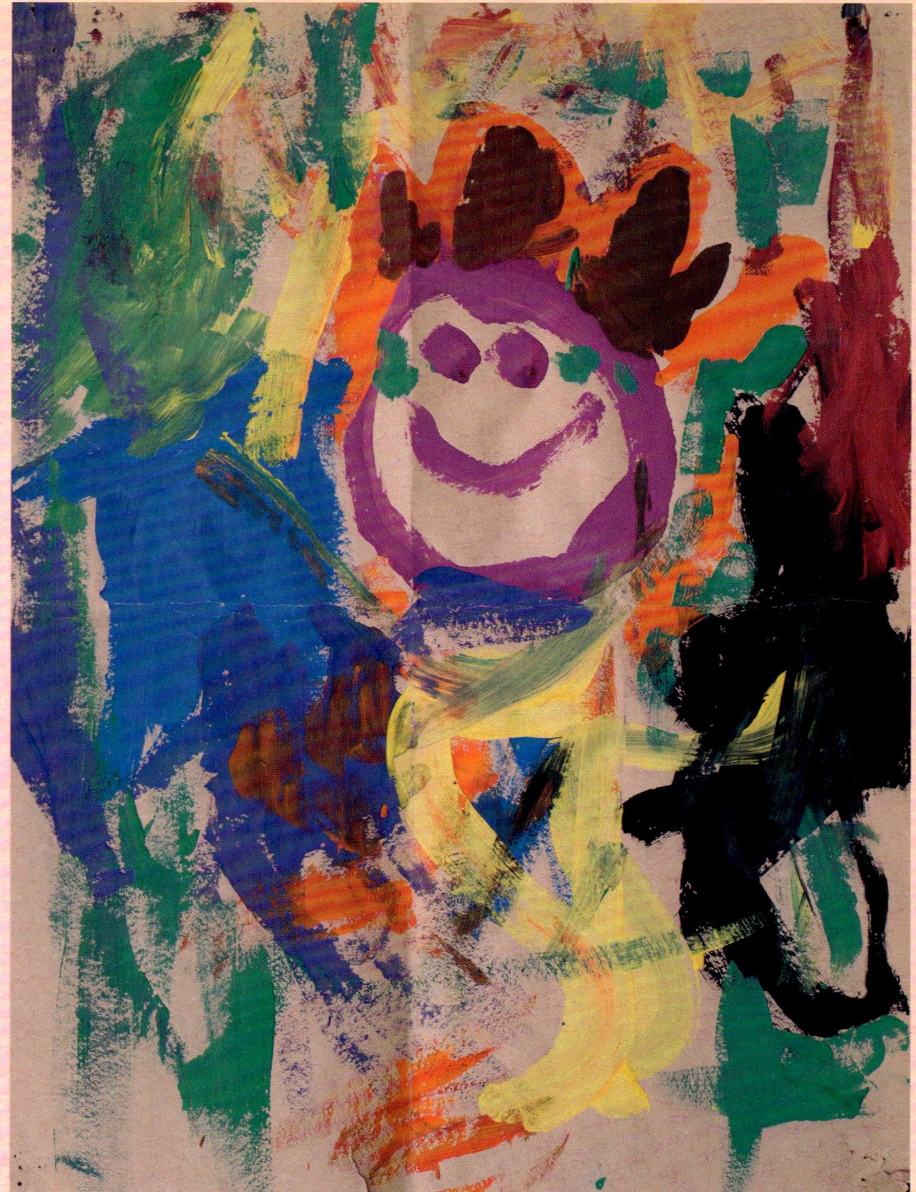

I painted this when I was 4

Tree of Life
by Tim Biskup

Introduction by Tim Biskup

Design by Steve Alexander

ISBN: 978-1-4521-8208-7
Library of Congress Cataloging-in-Publication Data available.

Manufactured in China

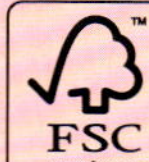

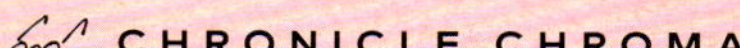

Chronicle Chroma is an imprint of Chronicle Books
Los Angeles, California

chroniclechroma.com